WHERE HAVE ALL THE PROPHETS GONE?

WHERE HAVE ALL THE PROPHETS GONE?

SCOTT R. PETERSEN

CFI
SPRINGVILLE, UTAH

ISBN: 1-55517-847-2
v.1

Published by CFI,
an imprint of Cedar Fort, Inc.
925 N. Main Springville, Utah, 84663
www.cedarfort.com

Distributed by:

Cover design by Nicole Williams
Cover design © 2005 by Lyle Mortimer

Printed in Hong Kong
10 9 8 7 6 5 4 3 2 1

Printed on acid-free paper

DEDICATION

To my father, who inspired my interest in history and writing.
To my wife, Marilyn, who supported my continuous fourteen-hour days.
And to Marion Say, who believed in my project and
gave me the courage to finish what I started.

CONTENTS

PREFACE

My objective in writing this work is not to compose an exhaustive, thoroughly balanced view of the development of Christianity, including its roots beginning with Adam and Eve. Doing so would require significant language skills in both Greek and Latin and would create a work so large it would reach beyond the interest of most individuals. Clearly, my goal is to write to the masses, not just the scholarly few. Thus, I will not attempt to detail all of the existing philosophies that have ever been written on various doctrinal subjects; rather I will explore one seemingly incontrovertible theme of religious history—that of apostasy from God's original teachings to Adam after the Fall. Catholic and Protestant scholars have long agreed with this thesis, including the fact that God's true Church cannot be divided up, its doctrines cannot be discarded because they become unfashionable, and God's truth will never be achieved through compromise, negotiation, or political pressure. Unfortunately, agreement ends with that realization, and solutions to Christian unity seem far away. My desire is to present a condensed but accurate view of the evolution of Christianity and apostasy from pure, revealed religion, from the days of Adam to the modern world, and to rightly pose the question, "Where have all the prophets gone?"

ACKNOWLEDGMENTS

This book would not have been possible without the generous help of first-rate scholars John A. Tvedtnes, Jim Faulconer, Eric Durotellar, and Carl Griffin.

I am also indebted to the late Hugh Nibley for his pioneering work in early Christian studies, particularly the period following Christ's resurrection known today as the "forty-day teachings." I have followed and expanded his ideas of this brief but critical time.

I also express gratitude to Don Deshler, Victoria Williams, Ronald Petersen, Roger Petersen, Dan Schaper, John W. Welch, Dan McKinley, Noel Reynolds, and the late Steven Adams for reading and assisting with portions of this work at various stages.

I am grateful for the significant contribution of my editors, Dan Hogan and Marion Say, for making the book more readable; and for Don Norton and Heather Seferovich, who helped proofread the text and endnotes.

Finally, I wish to express appreciation to Lee Nelson, Lyle Mortimer, and the dedicated editors and employees of Cedar Fort Publishing for their belief in and contribution to my book.

INTRODUCTION

"In the beginning," states the Holy Bible, "God created the heaven and the earth." Shortly after came plants, animals, and eventually man and woman. These latter were God's pride and joy, for they were His children, and He began to teach them how He would like them to live. But mankind rebelled, and thus began the cyclical pattern of revelation and apostasy that would mark and mar God's dealings with His children throughout recorded history.

At the center of it all is the question of how one receives God's word. Although the Holy Bible contains God's revealed religion, His covenant and plan for man's redemption, and His commandments and instructions to humanity throughout the ages, convincing evidence suggests that other writings were also reliable sources. But living oracles (prophets), not writings, were the most valuable source of divine inspiration. For example, the early Christian bishop Papias wrote in approximately A.D. 140:

"If ever someone who had accompanied the presbyters should come, I examined carefully the words of the presbyters, [to learn] what Andrew, Peter, Philip, Thomas, John, Matthew, or any other of the disciples of the Lord said and what things Aristion and the presbyter John, disciples of the Lord, are saying. *For I did not suppose the contents of books would profit me so much as the words and living voice*" (quoted by Eusebius, *Ecclesiastical History* 3.39.1, 3–4; emphasis added).

Using the Bible, selected Pseudepigrapha and Apocrypha, the Dead Sea Scrolls, and the earliest Christian writings, *Where Have All the Prophets Gone?* is a study of man's response to prophecy in each dispensation. We witness that the righteous, typified by Abel, ultimately reject God, typified by the followers of Cain. We observe righteous Enoch gathering followers, leaving the wicked to be destroyed by the Flood when they reject Noah's final warning from God. The righteous seed of Noah eventually succumb to evil, build the Tower of Babel, and are scattered. The venerable line of Abraham through Ephraim is finally severed because of apostasy; Israel's consequent worship of Egypt's false gods results in its enslavement. Following Moses, Israel on numerous occasions turned its back on God, rejected Him and His covenant, and was eventually conquered and scattered. Christ's fulfillment of the law of Moses, the reestablishment of His Church on earth, and the apostolic ministry that followed were also rejected in time by succeeding Christian leaders and the membership at large, causing again the repetition of apostasy, as in each preceding dispensation.

The Reformation attempted to correct heretical teachings and end centuries of corruption; however, disunity and lack of authority prevented a full restoration of primitive Christianity. After the Age of Reason and the Great Awakening, the establishment of America and freedom of religion inspired another awakening

1

and doctrinal reformation, including a proliferation of new Christian denominations and nineteenth-century restorationist movements. One plausible claim of restoration is more fully examined as a possible answer to the promised gathering of Israel and the return of Jesus Christ to the earth.

Where Have All the Prophets Gone? documents in depth just what the early Christians really believed about salvation and other core doctrines and then compares those findings with the teachings given through Old Testament patriarchs and with those purported to be restored through an American religion that claims ancient roots.

CHAPTER ONE

THE EARLY CHRISTIAN FATHERS AND NONBIBLICAL WRITINGS

He who seeks will not rest until he finds.
And he who has found shall marvel.
And he who has marveled shall reign.
And he who has reigned shall rest.

—"The Sayings of Jesus," in Charlesworth, *Authentic Apocrypha*

When Pilate asked Jesus, "What is truth?" Pilate likely was unaware that he would be quoted frequently two thousand years later. However, he may have been very aware that this is one of the most complex and controversial issues of all time. Part of the reason it remains so alive lies in how we perceive truth.

Too often we confuse *man's perception* of truth with *God's truth*, that is, *revealed truth*. For example, when Old Testament prophets said, *"Thus saith the Lord,"* we can be quite certain that God was speaking *His* will or *His* truth to man, and we can thus rely on those words for divine direction. Similarly, the Bible records that God revealed Himself in vision to such well-known

prophets as Noah, Abraham, Moses, and Isaiah. Judeo-Christian groups rarely question that these revelations originated from God and that He was speaking His will through His chosen servants. Religious history also shows that many revelations from God were not specific to doctrine or His plan for man's redemption (critical as they were) but rather provided inspired guidance regarding everyday decisions, such as who should be anointed as Israel's king, whether Israel should go into battle, or encouragement to accomplish the divine will.

God is an accepted source of truth among believers. Conversely, truth espoused by early religious *philosophers* relies on a combination of revealed truth *and* secular ideas. For example,

Augustine often blended the words of scripture with Greek philosophy (known as Neoplatonism). The result was that when certain biblical doctrines—such as the nature of God—seemed confusing by an appeal to the Bible alone, intellectual concepts were applied to formulate a more precise, though usually not more accurate, theology. It seems almost inevitable that man will insert his own thinking in an attempt to apply revealed truth to secular circumstance. Nonetheless, belief in a higher power almost demands that God's truth, though perhaps not always clear, must not be confused or mixed with man's truth.

At the heart of this book lies a pursuit of God's truth. This pursuit was born of the desire to learn what happened to the original laws and commandments as God revealed them to Adam and Eve after the Fall. Interestingly, one theme that emerged from this pursuit that led through several decades and countless libraries was *recurring apostasy*. Thus, as we search for truth in this book, our journey may very well take us in directions that confront some concepts of traditional Christian history; that is, it will likely challenge beliefs that some have always simply accepted without close examination. As the Lord so clearly taught, "For my mouth shall speak truth" (Proverbs 8:7); thus God's truth comes to us through His prophets and from the inspired records that these holy men leave behind.

Genuine freedom from sin, as revealed by Jesus (John 8:31–32), comes from hearing, accepting, and living the *whole* truth of God's plan for our happiness. Unfortunately, historical accounts suggest that the "fullness" of His laws and commandments has not always been available, and apostasy has prevented many from hearing pure truth during various periods of the earth's history. How, then, would individuals subjected to such apostasy receive salvation? Was John Calvin, the sixteenth-century Reformer, correct when he asserted that God's elect are saved and the rest are damned? Or does God's plan include free will (agency), which allows, even requires, that *we* choose for ourselves whether we will accept and follow Jesus when we learn of His glorious atonement and are moved upon by the Holy Spirit? If we are free agents, God's plan must somehow create an avenue of fairness for those who never hear the gospel plan or of those whose opportunities and environments have been limited.

To consider the matter of religious truth, we must adopt certain standards by which we judge evidence. For this book, I have chosen standards that are regarded as authoritative by informed parties who profess to believe in the God of ancient Israel. First, the Holy Bible must serve as the foundation for our study. Next in line would be certain ancient religious writings known generally as apocryphal and pseudepigraphal works. Finally, secular history and other early Christian writings have certain value as we search for truth concerning the history of God's teaching through the centuries. The earliest such sources referred to by historic Christianity are known as the Apostolic Fathers, the Apologists, and the Polemicists. While much of the later theology taught by Church Fathers of the mid-second century still appeared to be closely aligned with New Testament Christianity, other doctrines had already been notably altered. This changing of doctrine over time, as recorded in early Christian literature, is instructive and helps to tell the important story of Christianity.

Let us examine each of these categories of standards.

The Holy Bible

The Holy Bible is an inspired record containing God's revelations to His prophets and apostles. This book is accepted by Christians, who receive it in its entirety; Jews, who revere the Old Testament; and Muslims, who acknowledge several biblical prophets mentioned in the Qur'an, including Jesus. Although the Bible provides a common link between these major world religions, achieving united scriptural views has proven difficult.

The process known as the canonization of the Bible required several centuries, beginning no earlier than the late second century and not achieving its finished form until late in the fourth century. In fact, whatever beliefs or discussion may have taken place between individual leaders in earlier centuries regarding which books were genuine and authoritative, it is now clear that the real debates and "lists" were *all* generated in the fourth century.[1] In fact, the term *canon* is not found in any early writings until it was used by Eusebius in connection with the four Gospels.[2] The Bible is not a collection of all the inspired books ever written as they came from the pens of the prophets; rather, it is a consensus of opinion rendered by *late fourth-century* Church leaders as to which writings they believed were fully inspired, in contrast with those whose authorship could not be verified or whose theology stood in opposition to *current* orthodoxy, which by this period had been notably altered from the original doctrines of apostolic Christianity. The earliest Christians accepted many more books as genuine revelation from God than are contained in today's Bible.

No surviving documents exist to suggest that first- and early second-century Church leaders made any effort to record official interpretations of doctrine or theology; however, Christianity in the fourth and fifth centuries sought to apply rigid scholarship to doctrinal subjects. While most theologians of that day chose to say and write a great deal, little about many of the doctrines they discussed had actually been covered in the scriptural accounts; the result was much speculation. I say speculation because the revised Christian doctrines the theologians created depended on sources other than the Bible and other prophetic writings (God's truth) for their formulation. The ideas of the Greek philosophers that were taking the Mediterranean world by storm were often merged with Christian doctrines, and the resultant hybrid replaced the more reliable historical and literal interpretations of the holy scriptures. However, the influence of Greek philosophy was not new. Judaism in Alexandria, Egypt, through Philo Judaeus (20 B.C.–A.D. 50) underwent significant change early in the first century due to its admixture with Hellenistic ideas. The Apostles John and Paul also used Greek philosophy (nominally) to *defend* Christianity, but it is not clear at what point Hellenism actually infiltrated the Church's doctrine.

Although today's Bible does not contain all the books that were considered inspired by the earliest Christians, and although it is known to have been corrupted (intentionally and unintentionally—(see pages 176–79) to some extent by transcribers and copyists, *it is the word of God* and stands as revelation to the human family on how man can be reconciled to God.

New Testament Apocrypha and the Pseudepigrapha (Old Testament Apocrypha)

The Hebrew Bible was the only source of scripture fully accepted by the early apostolic Church.[3] By the middle of the first century, however, the *Sayings of Jesus* appears to have carried equal authority among Christians. By the end of the first century, some *apostolic writings* were being granted equal status. Soon a wide range of divergent views began to surface, clouding what original Christianity may have been. It is important to note that the New Testament Church in Jerusalem *was* in fact unified for a short period, its members being "of one heart and of one soul" (Acts 4:32). Unfortunately, various groups—such as converted Jews still clinging to the law of Moses (see page 75), Christian Docetists (see page 128), Gnostic Christians (see pages 127–30), and Christians influenced by Platonism and Neo-Platonism (see pages 130–31)—generated significant turmoil within the Church that Jesus had organized and sought to unify. What was the cause of such an upheaval so soon after the death of the apostles? Bible scholar Bart Erhman explains:

> Diversity soon became a problem for Christian leaders intent on the unity of the religion, who saw Christianity as *one* thing rather than lots of *different things*. . . . The diversity of the movement came to be especially evident around the middle of the second century. . . . Forceful and charismatic Christians came forward, advocating beliefs and practices that were seen by others as totally unacceptable. Battle lines were drawn, with each side claiming to represent the authentic Christian tradition passed down from Jesus himself to the disciples. In the debates that ensued, nothing proved more important than the Christian literature that had been produced earlier.[4]

What Ehrman argues in his highly regarded treatise is that Christianity had spread over a wide geographic area. Communication was primitive, and without the

apostles to officially define doctrine, conflicting ideas began to emerge wherever Christianity had been preached, even in such basic concepts as the nature of God and correct performance of the sacraments. Christian leaders argued, and sometimes fought, over the precise definitions of basic doctrines; in the end, the only tools available to resolve such disputes were letters and other writings left behind by the apostles. Even with these authorities to rely on, however, contention arose because the writings were interpreted differently by various groups. Following the death of the apostles, there was simply *no universally recognized body or living authority* to distinguish truth from error.

The body that considered itself *orthodox*, meaning "correct, or sound," in doctrine eventually prevailed; it was later named the Catholic, or Universal, Church. That this particular group (composed of both the eastern and the western Church until the eleventh century), or any group, for that matter, was able to retain the purity of original Christian doctrine is not only unclear but improbable. Evidence of this can be determined by comparing certain well-known and relatively well-defined theological tenets of the earliest Christians—such as the purpose and mode of baptism—with parallel doctrines of later Christianity, which by that period had been altered (see pages 182–90). For various reasons, Christianity was straying from key, simple teachings as they had been laid out by Jesus. Furthermore, speculative changes to Christian doctrine were made by such later theologians as Tertullian, Origen, and Augustine. In time, even Christians who considered themselves orthodox gradually became contaminated by Greek philosophy, retention of portions of Jewish law, and the influence of pagan ritual. The library of Christianity was stretched and pulled, added to and taken from; in spiritual terms, it became at least in part an indistinguishable blend of truth mixed with some error.

The tragedy of these early stages was that well-meaning Christians, without the guidance of the apostles, were forced to choose which of the sacred writings were authentic and which were forgeries or alterations made by defectors from true Christianity. Unfortunately, some of the manuscripts held sacred by the earliest Christians were rejected by the leaders of the orthodox movement that followed, notwithstanding the fact that their value was comparable to that of many books eventually accepted into the official canon. Buttressing this conclusion, James H. Charlesworth has written: "Far too often scholars jettison the early Christian apocryphal compositions from the study of Christian origins. New Testament experts ignore them because they are not in the canon. This is an unsophisticated approach, since the decision to include only twenty-seven writings within a category called "New Testament" postdates the origins of Christianity by centuries."[5]

According to Charlesworth, many non-biblical writings are "authentic" because the earliest Church Fathers thought they were genuine. Such documents, he said, must be distinguished from "false apocrypha," or rather, known forgeries.[6]

Discussing the value of the Pseudepigrapha to modern Christians, Charlesworth more recently added:

> In the past two decades scholars have come closer to a consensus of when and how the canon took shape. The [Old Testament] canon was not closed before 70 C.E. . . . I am also convinced that the group of Jews behind the Temple Scroll, which is surely pre-Qumranic, would have judged it to be quintessential Torah—that is, equal to, and perhaps better than, Deuteron-

omy. It is now clear that the so-called Pseudepigrapha must not be treated as if they were produced on the fringes of a monolithic Judaism; . . . we should perceive the Pseudepigrapha as they were apparently judged to be: God's revelation to humans.[7]

Bible scholar Peter Stuhlmacher is another strong advocate of the Pseudepigrapha. In a well-regarded essay, he judges that the "so-called Septuagintal Apocrypha" thus belongs inseparably to the holy scripture of early Christianity.[8] Although others—including myself—are less willing to take such a strong position, they acknowledge that some New Testament scriptures are probably dependent on the Pseudepigrapha.[9] While there is limited concrete evidence for *New Testament usage* of these early writings, substantial evidence documents their widespread acceptance among the *early Christian writers.* Included in this growing list of advocates, Daniel Harrington draws this precise conclusion,[10] going so far as to recommend that the inclusion of these works may improve Christian unity: "There are, of course, more obvious and difficult obstacles to Christian unity than the extent of the Old Testament canon. In any truly ecumenical council that might involve Roman Catholic, Protestant, and Orthodox Christians, it would probably not be high on the agenda. But to prepare for that blessed event, it might be beneficial if all Christians (and Jews) began to take these books more seriously in their own right."[11]

One objective of this book is to establish that the opinions of the earliest known Christian leaders, or Fathers, ought to be considered when determining the value of Christian writings. In order to provide a more thorough treatment of some of the historical aspects of the patriarchal and apostolic dispensations, it is necessary to include some of the ancient writings from the Old Testament Pseudepigrapha, the New Testament Apocrypha, and the Dead Sea Scrolls. Included in the Dead Sea Scrolls are several copies of the oldest surviving *complete* manuscripts (absent Esther) of the Old Testament. Additionally, the scrolls contain other writings that the earliest Christians deemed to be not only authentic but authoritative.[12]

Although many Christians will not (and perhaps should not) place the same value on noncanonical Old Testament writings included with the Dead Sea Scrolls as they will on the books of the Bible, such writings can be helpful in adding detail to the historical and theological patterns introduced in the Old Testament and preserved in the New Testament.

Canonized scripture includes the thirty-nine books of the Old Testament and the twenty-seven books of the New Testament. A number of additional writings considered both authentic *and* authoritative by the early Church and by some Christian scholars today were not admitted into the original canon. These include such Old Testament-era writings—known as Pseudepigrapha—as the "Life of Adam and Eve," the "Conflict of Adam and Eve with Satan," the Testament of Adam, the Apocalypse of Adam, the Treatise of Shem, Enoch 1 and 2, the Apocalypse of Abraham, the Testaments of the Twelve Patriarchs, the Testament of Moses, the Testament of Job, Odes of Solomon, the Fourth Book of Ezra, Jubilees, and the Apocryphon of Ezekiel.

New Testament-era Apocrypha includes such surviving documents as the traditional Catholic and Orthodox (septuigintel) Apocrypha, the Gospel of Peter, the Apocalypse of Peter, the Apocryphon of James, the First and Second Apocalypses of James, the Apocryphon of John, the Gospel of the Twelve Apostles, and Epistle of the Apostles.[13]

While some authentic apocryphal and pseudepigraphal writings are of limited value, many of those quoted in this book were treasured by the earliest Christians and acknowledged by modern scholars as important to early theology. Although in many cases questions arise as to who the actual authors were, the theology itself was judged by the primitive Church as orthodox. And while many of these books were probably altered by scribes, it is also well documented that New Testament writings were subjected to the same kind of abuse (see page 177). Because significant turmoil continues today over the nature of original Christianity, we will examine in some detail the writings of those immediately following the apostles in order to understand what they believed. By seeking the common threads found repeatedly in both the canon and nonbiblical writings, it is possible to filter through much error and to achieve considerable accuracy in discerning what the earliest Christians esteemed as true.

Other Early Christian Writings

The Apostolic Fathers

The term *Apostolic Fathers* in this book refers to those Church leaders who immediately succeeded the apostles. Three of these men were some of the earliest bishops of the Church and wrote authoritative letters that still survive. Clement (A.D. 30–100), bishop of Rome from A.D. 90–100, wrote 1 Clement. Another writing, 2 Clement, is named after this early bishop but was almost certainly written by a different author, though its theology is also considered orthodox. Ignatius (A.D. 30–108), bishop of Antioch sometime between the 80s and 108, wrote seven surviving letters—preserved by the later Church historian Eusebius of Caesarea—to the

Ephesians, Magnesians, Trallians, Romans, Philadelphians, Smyrnaeans, and Polycarp, the bishop of Smyrna. Polycarp (ca. A.D. 69–155), bishop from about 100 to 155, wrote one surviving letter to the Philippians (see page 146). Other writings attributed to early leaders under the title of Apostolic Fathers include the Shepherd of Hermas (ca. A.D. 100), the Epistle of Barnabas (ca. A.D. 120), the Epistle of Methetes to Diognetus (ca. A.D. 130), and the Martyrdom of Polycarp (ca. A.D. 155) The Didache, or the Teaching of the Twelve Apostles (ca. A.D. 70–110),[14] is also claimed by many scholars to have been of early date.[15]

The Apologists

The Apologists were heroic defenders of early Christianity against such external influences as political rulers or adversarial Jewish or pagan religious leaders. Justin Martyr, a lay theologian (ca. A.D. 100–165), wrote the lost book of Against All Heresies, the letters First Apology and Second Apology to Antoninus Pius, Dialogue with Trypho the Jew, and Fragments on the Resurrection (see page 147). Tatian (ca. A.D. 110–ca. 180), a pupil of Justin Martyr, penned Address to the Greeks and compiled the earliest known harmony of the Gospels entitled the Diatessaron. Two other Apologists, Athenagoras and Theophilus of Antioch, composed Supplication for the Christians and Apology to Autolycus, respectively. The leading Apologist of the western Church, Tertullian of Carthage (ca. A.D. 150–225), also wrote extensively in an attempt to explain Church doctrines (see page 148).[16]

The Polemicists

While the Apologists wrote to defend the Church against external influences, the Polemicists were intellectuals who wrote for the purpose of shielding the Church against internal heresies, which they felt threatened the purity of Christianity. St. Irenaeus of Lyons (ca. 140–ca. 202), the foremost early Polemicist, composed his well-known five books titled *On the Detection and Refutation of the Knowledge Falsely So Called*, more commonly known as "Against Heresies" (see pages 147–48). Hippolytus (ca. A.D. 165–ca. 235), the most influential theologian of the Roman Church in the third century, wrote several surviving commentaries, the *Refutation of All Heresies*, Against the Heresy of One Noetus, Treatise on Christ and Antichrist, the Apostolic Tradition, and a number of other homilies (see pages 148–49). In the East, Clement of Alexandria (ca. A.D. 155–ca. 220), and Origen (ca. 185–254) were two of the early leaders of the Alexandrian School of theology in Egypt. Influenced by Greek philosophy, these theologians wrote a great number of books refuting Gnosticism and other Christian factions which they considered heretical (see pages 149–51).[17]

These men—the Apostolic Fathers, the Apologists, and the Polemicists—principally formulated early Christian theology as it is commonly taught and accepted today. Although it is very difficult to guarantee without clear evidence, it seems likely that the earliest known Church Fathers, such as Ignatius, Clement of Rome, and Hermas, provided a more reliable picture of Christianity's original doctrines than could later Churchmen such as Tertullian, Origen, or Augustine. Clement and Ignatius almost certainly had direct interface with one or more of the apostles, or at the least were well acquainted with other leaders who did. Whether these Apostolic Fathers wrote all they knew makes no difference—according to their own testimonies, *they understood the mysteries of the kingdom,* while the latter authorities listed above made no such claim. Just before his death, Ignatius told the Trallian saints that although he could explain the mysteries to them, he would not, because *they would be strangled by them*":

"The angelic orders, . . . the diversity between thrones and authorities, the mightiness of the Aeons, and the pre-eminence of the cherubim and the seraphim, the sublimity of the spirit, and above all, *the incomparable majesty of Almighty God, . . .* I am acquainted with these things."[18]

Unlike Clement and Ignatius, Church leaders who followed them began to speculate about the doctrines of Jesus—expounding where the Bible did not—without the authority of the apostles and without claim to specific revelations that would clarify disputed doctrines.

For example, even though Clement and Ignatius served as bishops of major cities nearest to the early apostolic ministry, one acclaimed Christian historian implied that these men were "often naive," that they did not understand the "problem of the relation of the Three to each other" (speaking of the Trinity), and thus charged Clement with being "oblivious" to this doctrinal dilemma.[19] Making such a statement is tantamount to saying that Paul and Peter were naive for not explaining the Godhead more precisely in the Bible. That Clement and Ignatius elected not to spend time writing postapostolic letters about what they plainly understood cannot be confused with naivety or oblivion; rather, their lack of discussion should more justly be judged as either being content with what the Lord had revealed or as prudently discreet: "It is given unto you to know the mysteries of the kingdom of heaven, but to them it is not given" (Matthew 13:11).

Much of the infighting that began in the second century was over which of the ancient manuscripts should be accepted as genuine scripture. Many modern Christians consider the process of canonization inspired and hold that these sacred texts are pure and undefiled, perfect in every way. Although the Bible, including many inspired noncanonical books, as originally written was undisturbed, careless transcribers, ignorant translators, and biased early Christian groups caused many corruptions in the text. These factions altered manuscripts or rejected writings that failed to support their particular interpretations of various doctrines; the result was a loss of truths vital to a complete understanding of God's laws and commandments.[20]

The standard canon used by most Christians today was not officially compiled until late in the fourth century after Christianity had undergone numerous revisions in theology.[21] Various versions of the canon *included* books not in the present Bible and *excluded* some that are. For example, the Codex Sinaiticus (early fourth century) included the Epistle of Barnabas and the Shepherd of Hermas.[22] The Codex Alexandrinus (early fifth century) included 1 and 2 Clement. The Codex Claromontanus (early sixth century) omitted Hebrews but included the Shepherd of Hermas, the Epistle of Barnabas, the Acts of Paul, and the Apocalypse of Peter. Moreover, various Church Fathers rejected the canonicity of such books as Hebrews, James, 1 and 2 Peter, 2 and 3 John, Jude, and Revelation.[23] In fact, the most current scholarship asserts that "there are no known catalogues of the Christian canon until the fourth century, when there is a sudden and widespread appearance of fifteen undisputed lists and four complete codices."[24]

The most popular book of the early Church was arguably the Shepherd of Hermas, from which I quote extensively. The Shepherd's translator, the Reverend F.

Crombie, writes, "The Pastor of Hermas was one of the most popular books, if not *the* most popular book, in the Christian Church during the second, third, and fourth centuries." Its author was most widely believed to be the Hermas mentioned in Paul's epistle to the Romans (Romans 16:14), this opinion being shared by Origen, Eusebius, and Jerome. Irenaeus quotes it as scripture, Clement of Alexandria said its statements were "divinely" made, and Origen referred to it as "divinely inspired." A second opinion, obtained from a spurious fragment (published by Muratori) of unknown authorship and containing disputed language, said, "The Pastor was written very lately in our times, in the city of Rome, by Hermas, while Bishop Pius, his brother, sat in the chair of the Church in the city of Rome" (A.D. 142–54).[25] More recent scholarship provides convincing evidence that while perhaps neither of these views is accurate, the dating of the document must be the "turn of the first century." According to Geoffrey Hahneman,

> Internal evidence for dating the *Shepherd* all suggests a date around the turn of the first century, 40–50 years before the beginning of Pius' episcopacy. . . . For instance, there is no mention or influence of the later prominent teachers at Rome [neither orthodox nor heretical]. . . . Nor does there appear mention of any of the early documents to or from Rome. . . . A date at the turn of the first century agrees with the *Shepherd's* mention of Clement of Rome, the death of the Apostles, and a persecution under Domitian or Trajan, as well as the lack of a monarchial episcopacy.[26]

Moreover, Hahneman, citing Bruce Metzger, documents that paleographers have dated a surviving fragment of the Shepherd to the early second century.[27] Inasmuch as the "oldest extant testimony"—one with significant impact—comes from Irenaeus in about A.D. 180, "Well said the Scripture,"[28] there can be little doubt concerning the Shepherd's complete acceptance and influence among the earliest Church leaders. All of this evidence, in concert with both *its message and unique theology* suggest a dating of ca. A.D. 100.

Another influential volume of scripture in the primitive Church not admitted to the canon was the "lost" books of Enoch. Early Christian writers, including writers of books now in the New Testament and Apocrypha, were well acquainted with this ancient work, including St. Jude, who quotes the Enoch text, and the author of the Epistle of Barnabas, who also cites the book of Enoch as scripture. Charlesworth states that it was used by the authors of the Jubilees, the Testaments of the Twelve Patriarchs, the Assumption of Moses, 2 Baruch, and 4 Ezra (highly regarded pseudepigraphal writings); and its themes are found in various New Testament books, including the Gospels, Jude, and Revelation. Charlesworth also insists that the book of Enoch played a "significant role" in the early Church, being used by the authors of the Epistle of Barnabas, the Apocalypse of Peter, and a number of Apologetic works. Church Fathers Justin Martyr, Irenaeus, Origen, and Clement of Alexandria either knew 1 Enoch or were inspired by it. Tertullian wrote, "The true worth of Enoch and other books like it should be measured by their proclamation of Christ. . . . And we read: 'all scripture is inspired by God which is useful for teaching'" (2 Timothy 3:16).[29] Charlesworth concludes, "I have no doubt that the Enoch groups deemed the Books of Enoch as fully inspired as any 'biblical' book."[30]

R. H. Charles, translator and author of *The Book of Enoch* in 1913, maintains that "some of its authors . . . belong to the true succession of the prophets, . . . exhibiting on occasions the inspiration of the O. T. prophets."[31] Although certain of Charles's specific claims have been disputed by more recent scholarship, his assertion that the influence of Enoch literature is found in numerous New Testament scriptures remains unchallenged;[32] moreover, he insists that the early Church Fathers and Apologists accorded it equal canonical weight. He further declares that 1 Enoch has had "more influence on the New Testament than all of the apocryphal and pseudepigraphical books taken together."[33] Charles lists more than thirty passages that influenced early orthodox Jewish and Christian writings in which the book of Enoch is specifically mentioned.[34] Unfortunately, these inspired manuscripts were systematically removed from Church use by those who misunderstood them at a time when the Church Jesus organized exhibited all the characteristics of apostasy.

Charlesworth records that "beginning in the fourth century, the book of Enoch came to be regarded with disfavor and received negative reviews from Hilary, Jerome, and Augustine," gradually passing out of circulation and becoming lost to the knowledge of western Christendom.[35] C. C. Torey concludes that Enoch "fell into early disuse" because it had no strong appeal to later Christians and was "too bulky to copy and handle."[36] Likewise, Augustine also proffered a weak explanation for his opinion, writing, "We cannot deny that Enoch, the seventh from Adam, left some divine writings, for this is asserted by the Apostle Jude in his canonical epistle."[37] Augustine's decision to exclude Enoch from the canon was based largely on its status with contemporary Jewish leaders—an argument that Tertullian and earlier Christians rejected.[38] One scholar wrote that 1 Enoch was "official rabbinic-pharisaic Judaism" that was "systematically suppressed and removed, ostensibly on the grounds of [its] apocalyptic

content."[39] A seventh-century Syriac bishop, Jacob of Edessa, claimed that Anthanasius unfairly condemned the book of Enoch, whose authenticity was confirmed by Jude. Although one should exercise discernment when evaluating pseudepigraphal works, he wrote, the fact that God had taken such care to preserve them was evidence of their usefulness.[40] Unfortunately, because the book of Enoch was of ancient date and some of its doctrine unfamiliar, later Christianity simply discarded this inspired treasure.

Conclusion

The importance of my argument that the Bible is not the only standard of truth for Christians seeking to understand God's plan cannot be overstated. The late first-century bishop, Ignatius, once testified to the members of the Church in Philadelphia: "For when I was among you, I cried, I spoke with a great voice, . . . God's [voice]. . . . But if ye suspect that I spake thus, as having learned beforehand the division caused by some among you, He is my witness, . . . that I learned nothing of it from the mouth of any man. But the Spirit made an announcement to me."[41]

The Church has always enjoyed the benefit of revelation—continuing revelation. There should never have been any such thing as a closed canon of scripture. Lee McDonald has written recently that there are "in fact many examples of noncanonical authors who either claimed, or were acknowledged by others, to have been filled or inspired by the Spirit in their speaking or writing."[42] Unfortunately, "inspiration," he concludes, "played no discernible role in the later discussion of the formation of the biblical canon."[43] McDonald affirms that Everett Kalan's exhaustive study "could find no evidence that the early church confined inspiration to an already past apostolic age, or even a collection of writings."[44]

The Shepherd of Hermas, book of Enoch, and many other noncanonical writings contain significant theology that was considered genuine and revered by those closest to the ministry of Jesus. Some of these books will be cited in this volume, including the Dead Sea Scrolls, to fill important historical and theological gaps. By so doing, and by placing them in harmony with the Old and New Testaments, we will set off on our search for truth concerning Christian doctrine and its history throughout all ages of the world.

Notes

1. Outside of the Muratorian "list" of accepted books, now believed by many scholars to be of eastern (not Roman) origin and dated to the fourth (not late second century) as earlier thought, all fifteen extant lists are dated in the fourth century. See Geoffrey Mark Hahneman, "The Murtatorian Fragment and the Origins of the New Testament Canon," in *The Canon Debate*, ed. Lee Martin McDonald and James A. Sanders (Peabody, Mass.: Hendrickson Publishers, 2002), 412. The term *canon* is used to define the twenty-seven books of the New Testament and the thirty-nine books of the Old Testament bound together in the modern Bible.

2. Hahneman, "Murtatorian Fragment," 406.

3. The Hebrew Bible was compiled perhaps in the third century B.C. and is thus the only accepted scripture of the early apostolic Church.

4. Bart D. Erhman, *The New Testament and Other Early Christian Writings* (New York: Oxford University Press, 1998), 3.

5. James H. Charlesworth, *Authentic Apocrypha* (Richland Hills, Texas: Bible Press, D. and F. Scott Publishing, 1998), ix. Charlesworth is recognized by many scholars to be the foremost authority and translator in the world of pseudepigraphical and ancient material. Charlesworth is the George L. Collard Professor of New Testament Language and Literature at Princeton

Theological Seminary in Princeton, New Jersey.

6. Charlesworth, *Authentic Apocrypha*, ix.

7. James H. Charlesworth, *The Old Testament Pseudepigrapha and the New Testament* (Harrisburg, Pa.: Trinity Press International, 1998), xxii.

8. Peter Stulmacher in Meuer, *The Apocrypha in Ecumenical Perspective*, 12, in Daniel J. Harrington, "The Old Testament Apocrypha in the Early Church and Today," in McDonald and Sanders, *Canon Debate*, 201.

9. Harrington, "Old Testament Apocrypha in the Early Church and Today," in McDonald and Sanders, *Canon Debate*, 200–201.

10. Harrington, "Old Testament Apocrypha," in McDonald and Sanders, *Canon Debate*, 202.

11. Harrington, "Old Testament Apocrypha," in McDonald and Sanders, *Canon Debate*, 202.

12. Most of the extrabiblical quotations used in this work are taken from recent publications and translated and compiled by the world's most recognized Christian scholars. See Charlesworth, *Old Testament Pseudepigrapha*, 2 vols. (New York: Doubleday, 1983); Wilhelm Schneemelcher, ed., *New Testament Apocrypha*, 2 vols. (Louisville, Ky.: Westminster/John Knox Press, 1990); Florentino Garcia Martinez, *The Dead Sea Scrolls Translated* (Grand Rapids, Mich.: William B. Eerdmans, 1996); Rutherford Hayes Platt, *The Lost Books of the Bible and the Forgotten Books of Eden* (Cleveland, Ohio: World Bible Publishers, 1926–27).

13. See books referenced in note 6 to obtain additional information.

14. Henry Chadwick assigns this early dating to the Didache but suspects that it has undergone some later revisions. *The Early Church*, rev. ed. (London: Penguin Books, 1993), 47.

15. One of the most accessible publications of these early works can be found in *The Apostolic Fathers*, 2 vols., trans. Kirsopp Lake (Cambridge, Mass.: Harvard University Press, 1960).

16. The most complete source of these early writings is found in Alexander Roberts and James Donaldson, ed. *The Ante-Nicene Fathers*, 10 vols. (1885; reprint, Peabody, Mass.: Hendrickson Publishers, 1999). See vols. 1 and 2.

17. See Roberts and Donaldson, *Ante-Nicene Fathers*, vols. 1–4.

18. Ignatius, Epistle to the Trallians, in Roberts and Donaldson, *Ante-Nicene Fathers*, 1:68.

19. J. N. D. Kelly, *Early Christian Doctrines*, 5th rev. ed. (London: A. C. Black, 1977) 90–91.

20. See Bart D. Ehrman, *The Orthodox Corruption of Scripture* (New York: Oxford University Press, 1993); Bruce M. Metzger, *The Text of the New Testament* (New York: Oxford University Press, 1992); see also ch. 6 herein, "The Doctrine of Biblical Inerrancy."

21. Athanasius, Thirty-Ninth Festal Epistle (A.D. 367), in Alexander Roberts and James Donaldson, ed., *The Nicene and Post-Nicene Fathers*, Second Series, 14 vols. (1885; reprint, Peabody, Mass.: Hendrickson Publishers, 1999), 4:505. "The year 367 marks, thus, the first time that the scope of the New Testament canon is declared to be exactly the twenty-seven books accepted today as canonical." Bruce M. Metzger, *The Canon of the New Testament* (New York: Oxford University Press, 1987), 212. The canon of Athanasius was not universally accepted by the Catholic Church for several more centuries.

22. Metzger, *Canon of the New Testament*, 207.

23. Metzger, *Canon of the New Testament*, 230, 305–15.

24. See ch. 1, note 1.

25. Rev. F. Crombie, "Introductory Note to the Pastor of Hermas," in *Ante-Nicene Fathers*, 2:6–7. Origen's opinion of the Pastor's authorship is stated in his Commentary on Romans 16:14, lib. x. 31; Eusebius, *Ecclesiastical History*, 5 vols. (Cambridge, Mass.: Harvard University Press, 1984), 3:83–84; Jerome's comments are contained in De Viris Illustribus, c. x.; Irenaeus's quote, "Against Heresies" 4.20.2, in *Ante-Nicene Fathers*, 1:488.

26. Hahneman, "Murtatorian Fragment," in McDonald and Sanders, *Canon Debate*, 410.

27. Hahneman, "Murtatorian Fragment," 410.

28. Hahneman points out this thought and then quotes Irenaeus, "Against Heresies" 4.20.2, in Hahneman, "Murtatorian Fragment," 410.

29. Tertullian, Cult. Fem. 3 (SC 173; ed. M. Turcan; Paris: Cerf, 1971). See William Adler, "The Pseudepigrapha in the Early Church," in McDonald and Sanders, *Canon Debate*, 224.

30. Charlesworth, *Old Testament Pseudepigrapha*, xxii.

31. R. H. Charles, *The Book of Enoch* (London: Oxford University Press, 1913), ix, note 1. Compare his *Apocrypha and Pseudepigrapha of the Old Testament*, 2 vols. (Oxford: Clarendon Press, 1912) 2:163, in Nibley, *Enoch the Prophet*, ed. Stephen D. Ricks (Salt Lake City: Deseret Book; Provo, Utah: Foundation for Ancient Research and Mormon Studies, 1986), 95.

32. Charles, *Book of Enoch*, xcv–ciii, indicates that many "passages of the New Testament . . . either in phraseology or idea directly depend on or are illustrative of passages of 1 Enoch." "In the New Testament," according to the *Encyclopedia Britannica* (24 vols. [Chicago: Encyclopedia Brittanica, 1973], 8:604), "Enoch himself is mentioned in Luke iii:37; Hebrews xi:5; and Jude 14, while there is reference to him in Jude 4–15, Matthew 19:28, 26:24, Luke 16:9, John 5:22, 1 Thessalonians 5:3, 1 Peter 3:19ff., and Revelation." Nibley, *Enoch the Prophet*, 95.

33. Charles, *Book of Enoch*, xcv, 96.

34. Charles, *Book of Enoch*, xii–xiii, 97.

35. Charlesworth, *Old Testament Pseudepigrapha*, 1:8.

36. C. C. Torrey, *The Apocryphal Literature* (New Haven, Conn.: Yale University Press, 1945), 27; cf. Nibley, *Enoch the Prophet*, 97.

37. Augustine, City of God 15.23, in *Nicene and Post-Nicene Fathers*, 1:2:305. Augustine's defense is fatally flawed. Says he, "But it is not without reason that these writings have no place in that canon of Scripture which was preserved in the temple of the Hebrew people by the diligence of successive priests; for their antiquity brought them under suspicion." Unfortunately for Augustine, the Old Testament is yet a living witness—particularly during that period following David—that Israel, including its priests, was in perpetual apostasy. For example, with the exception of the generations ruled by Hezekiah and Josiah (and a small handful of other kings), over hundreds of years, Israel and Judah were in complete violation of their covenant with God. Therefore, the "diligence of successive priests" as judges of inspired scripture is unfounded.

Jude (a New Testament apostle) and the earliest Christian leaders are far more competent judges than was Augustine to appraise the value of this wonderful revelation. Notwithstanding his pure motives, extensive evidence regarding the state of the Church during which he served as a bishop (A.D. 395–430) renders his opinion—in contrast with the apostolic Church—less reliable.

38. Tertullian, Cult. Fem. 3 (SC 173; ed. M. Turcan; Paris: Cerf, 1971), in William Adler, "The Pseudepigrapha in the Early Church," in McDonald and Sanders, *Canon Debate,* 224.

39. Hans-Friedrich Weiss, *Untersuchungen zur Kosmologie des hellenistischen und palästinischen Judentums* (Berlin: Akadamie-Verlag, 1966), 119, in Nibley, *Enoch the Prophet,* 97.

40. Jacob of Edessa, Epistle 13.15, in W. Wright, "Two Epistles of Mar Jacob, Bishop of Edessa," *Journal of Sacred Literature and Biblical Record,* n.s. 10 (1867): 430ff, in Adler, "The Pseudepigrapha in the Early Church," in McDonald and Sanders, *Canon Debate,* 228.

41. Ignatius, Epistle to the Philadelphians 7, in *Ante-Nicene Fathers,* 1:83.

42. Lee Martin McDonald, "Identifying Scripture and Canon in the Early Church: The Criteria Question," in McDonald and Sanders, *Canon Debate,* 436.

43. *Ante-Nicene Fathers,* 1:438.

44. *Ante-Nicene Fathers,* 1:439. See Everett R. Kalin, "The Inspired Community: A Glance at Canon History," *CTM: A Theological Journal of the Lutheran Church—Missouri Synod* 42 (1971): 541–49; see also Albert C. Sundberg, "The Bible Canon and the Christian Doctrine of Inspiration," *Int* 29 (October 1975): 4:365ff.

CHAPTER TWO

THE DISPENSATIONS OF THE GREAT PATRIARCHS

Because thou hast done this thing, and hast not withheld thine only son, . . .
I will multiply thy seed as the stars of heaven, and as the sand which is upon
the seashore. . . . And in thy seed shall all the nations of the earth be blessed;
because thou hast obeyed my voice.

—Genesis 22:15–18

After the fall of Adam and Eve from the Garden of Eden, God did not leave them alone to make their way through life without direction. To the contrary, He taught them of His one and only plan for mankind's redemption. He was, after all, God and had no need to develop multiple plans. It was perfect in every way—simple enough to apply across the variety of cultures that would mark mankind throughout the coming millennia, thorough enough to ensure that no individual would be left out, ever. Although the details of God's covenant with Adam are not recorded in the book of Genesis, they are more plainly communicated in the "Life of Adam and Eve," the "Conflict of Adam and Eve with Satan," the Testament of Adam, the Apocalypse of Adam, 1 Enoch, and other early documents. Not surprisingly, the ancient traditions and doctrines presented in these manuscripts match those found in the Old Testament and in primitive Christianity. There has only ever been one God, one Savior, one faith, one way (Ephesians 4:5).

Despite this simple principle, both in the ancient world and in modern times, a vast number of religions, many that pursue God in a clearly distinctive manner, have emerged. Collectively, they employ a variety of ways to serve and please Him. People worldwide of sincere belief, from every race and culture, strive genuinely to follow the dictates of conscience in worshipping God.

Even within Christianity, the options of

worship are amazingly abundant. Where would the modern-day Adam turn for assistance in regaining God's favor and eventual divine presence? While certain doctrines would sound familiar to his ears, others have been altered significantly. Modern Christianity quarrels over such issues as baptism, salvation, celibacy, homosexuality, predestination, grace, and works. And yet the eternal principle of free agency—or the ability to choose our own way, be accountable, and suffer consequences—almost demands that our path be uncertain at times, that we learn to use both mortal judgment and divine guidance to make our way. This gift, however, provides ample opportunity for man's judgment to be clouded, and clouded judgment leads to the errors that lie at the heart of this chapter.

Gospel Dispensations: A Divine Reordering

Practically speaking, a dispensation occurs whenever God reveals Himself to man through prophets and sets in order that which man has altered. The Greek word in the New Testament that is translated as *dispensation* is connected with the idea of a household stewardship; that is, God establishes His household on the earth and gives the stewardship for running that household to particular individuals—His prophets. This notion of stewardship for God's household can help us better understand the role of prophets and their relationship to God.

The first dispensation on this earth occurred with the first mortal man and his posterity. God established through Adam the laws and commandments that he, Eve, and their children would need to follow to overcome the Fall and return to His presence. In other words, He established His household on the earth in such a way that it would pre-

pare His children to return to His heavenly home. An important part of His teaching was the establishment of instructive rites or ordinances, such as the Old Testament law of animal sacrifice.

The law of animal sacrifice is introduced early in Genesis, first to Abel (Genesis 4:4), later to Noah (Genesis 8:20), and then explained in greater detail to Abraham; the pseudepigraphal writings describe it just as plainly beginning with Adam. As Christians, we know that animal sacrifice was performed in ancient times *to keep men pointed toward Christ,* looking forward to the ultimate sacrifice of God's only begotten Son. Unfortunately, man has always believed that he is more ingenious than his Maker and thus far too frequently attempts to enhance or embellish the simple truths revealed by God. As man was influenced by his fallen environment and by Satan, man began to alter the sacred rites and pure knowledge revealed by God. The first such recorded occurrence involved Cain: "And in process of time it came to pass, that Cain brought of the fruit of the ground an offering unto the Lord. And Abel, he also brought of the firstlings of his flock and of the fat thereof. And the Lord had respect unto Abel and to his offering: but unto Cain and to his offering he had not respect. And Cain was very wroth, and his countenance fell" (Genesis 4:3–5).

Cain disobediently offered fruit from his field rather than the prescribed "firstlings" from the flock. The rite of animal sacrifice was very specific about how the ordinance should be performed, given its intent. Jesus Christ was the Lamb of God, not the Gourd or Bushel Basket. Because of his hardened heart, under the influence of Satan, Cain was the first to attempt to alter the sacred rites revealed by God. When Cain attempted to worship God insincerely in a variant form, he was severely chastened. In his anger, Cain killed his brother Abel, and when wickedness became widespread among Adam's descendants, the Lord established a pattern He would follow throughout history: He called another prophet to whom He revealed His gospel plan anew and through whom He could set His house in order.

Religious history as recorded in the Old Testament (which includes the Torah), Pseudepigrapha, and Qur'an indicates that five significant dispensations occurred, begun by Adam and followed by Enoch, Noah, Abraham, and Moses. I will demonstrate that each received a special appointment and covenant from God, and each was considered the head of a divinely established order or age. In a general sense, people had strayed from the truth each time, and these prophets were called by God to bring about significant course corrections.

We will explore these first five major dispensations previous to the Apostolic Dispensation, thus confirming not only God's love and mercy but also the scriptural, apocryphal, pseudepigraphal, and historical evidence that *apostasy from truth has been a pattern since the beginning.*

Apostasy: A Departure from Original, Pure, and Undefiled Religion

Man's insistence on setting out his own path separate from God's revealed truth, as characterized by Cain, is known throughout history as apostasy, defined as a departure from *original, pure, and undefiled religion* as it was first introduced to Adam and Eve after they were expelled from the Garden of Eden.

The Greek word *apostasia* was rendered by the King James Version translators as "falling away" (2 Thessalonians 2:3; see also vv. 1–2). *Thayer's Greek-English Lexicon* also describes it as "a falling away" or "defection from true religion."[1] *Strong's Exhaustive Concordance* translates it as "turning away, rebellion, abandonment, or falling away."[2] The precise roots are *apo* and *stasis*. *Stasis* means "to stand firm," while *apo* can mean either "away from" or "against"; thus, *apostasia* means quite literally *standing against* in rebellion (firmly), or possibly revolution, or mutiny.[3] Perhaps even more accurately, apostasy could be described as a particular group turning its back on God or rejecting the covenant relationship offered *through* His household (2 Chronicles 29:6; Jeremiah 2:27). Accordingly, apostasy is not necessarily a *desertion* from religion itself but rather *a perversion* of, or a rebellion against, *true* religion.[4] Thus, apostasy does not require *total departure* from one's faith but rather *a rejection of God's laws* and *His prophets* or *divinely appointed leadership.*[5]

Biblical and historical evidence suggest that general apostasy is *not* necessary for God to introduce a new dispensation, although it sometimes happens that way. Just as apostasy can be seen as a deviation from the true course, so can a new dispensation be seen as a course correction. Put another way, sometimes *divine reordering* is necessary to correct both the orientation and the operation of the household of God.

Characteristic Effects of Apostasy

As illustrated by the Old Testament and supported by the Pseudepigrapha, extended periods of apostasy usually include four major characteristics:

1. The *rejection of living prophets* called by God to teach and guide His people, often resulting in their temporary withdrawal. As

seen with the dispensations of Adam, Enoch, Noah, Abraham, and Moses, prophets are essential to God's work since the Fall. They are, after all, the ones who have the stewardship from God to run His operations on the earth. Before the Fall, God taught Adam and Eve directly, face to face in the Garden of Eden. However, after mankind was cut off from the direct presence of God because of Adam's fall, God called prophets to represent Him in teaching the plan of redemption to His children.

Direct revelation from God to these prophets, as recorded in both the Bible and noncanonical writings, kept God's chosen people in line—as long as they committed to obey divine counsel. Imagine, for example, the children of Israel without a Moses, or the apostolic Church without Peter and the apostles. Chaos, confusion, and total apostasy would have prevented the redemption of *any* of God's children. No wonder the Lord declared: "Surely the Lord God will do nothing, but he revealeth his secret unto his servants the prophets" (Amos 3:7). God's saving work can *only* be orchestrated through prophets whom *He* has called and to whom *He* has given the stewardship to run his household. The rejection of living prophets clearly constitutes apostasy from the divine Church.

2. The loss of God's divine *authority and power*. Throughout much of our Judaeo-Christian religious history, the authority to act in God's name and to lead His people was typically passed on from one generation to the next along patriarchal lines, from father to son, as evidenced by the birthright passing from Abraham to Isaac to Jacob to Joseph and Levi and to Ephraim (Genesis 48:17–19). When wickedness became widespread, the rightful heirs (the sons of the Patriarchs) no longer sought God's blessings and power, and God's recognized authority

on earth was effectually withdrawn temporarily. Obviously, God's approved Church or "household" relationship with His covenant people was also withdrawn. In the opening of a new dispensation, *God's direct revelations* to a chosen and prepared son, such as Abraham or Moses, enabled a rebirth of true religious devotion for both individuals and entire communities, even nations (Genesis 12:1–3; Exodus 3:4–8).

3. The loss of *pure and undefiled doctrines* communicated by God. God will not communicate to or through unholy servants (1 Samuel 28:6) or support an unholy people.[6] As a result, during times of apostasy, revelations from the heavens come to a virtual stop, at least in terms of *His household* at large. (He will always answer the sincere prayers of the humble individual, regardless of the spiritual condition of the larger community.) The Bible includes obvious historical gaps when His power and presence are withheld. For example, no record has survived revealing God's interactions with man between Joseph/Ephraim and Moses;[7] and prior to Samuel, we are told, "There was no open vision" (1 Samuel 3:1). During the seasons of wickedness that followed, pure and undefiled doctrines were perverted and had to be restored through God's chosen servants.[8] Apostasy was so pronounced between Malachi and John the Baptist that no religious records exist, excepting the apocryphal books of the Maccabeans. The loss of revelation that accompanied apostasy during much of the Mosaic dispensation (finally resulting in a splintering of the Jewish religion) allowed polluted doctrines to spread unrestrained, and God was able to put a temporary end to such pollution only by establishing a new dispensation—that of Jesus Christ and the apostles.

Just as patriarchal leadership passed from father to son, apostasy in some cases followed specific bloodlines, such as Cain, the son of Adam, and Ham, the son of Noah. These apostate family organizations often became the cradle for pagan religions which in many ways copied, then corrupted, such authorized rites as animal sacrifice and baptism. Without righteousness and revelation, animal sacrifice occasionally became human sacrifice (2 Kings 16:3; 21:6; Jeremiah 7:31); and baptism, anticipating the atonement of the Son of God,[9] was eventually transformed into the pagan rite of baptism in a bull's blood. Because of apostasy, even the seed of Abraham often embraced defiled doctrines, as characterized by the worship of false gods, which ultimately led to Israel's captivity and destruction.[10]

4. The loss of *authority to perform sacraments or rites*, such as baptism. The earliest Christians believed that baptism and other sacred ordinances were essential to salvation. Let us examine just one of those rites: baptism. During times of apostasy, the loss of God's authority meant that there were no authorized servants of the Lord to perform important sacraments, such as baptism. Evidence documents that the early Christians believed water baptism was probably practiced anciently. This should not be surprising; the prophets have testified that God loves *all* His children (Acts 10:34; 1 Timothy 2:4) and that He is consistent (Hebrews 13:8–9). Because the Christian religion is a system of worship communicated by God to living prophets, I would also argue that baptism was not borrowed from pagan religions as some scholars have supposed. But since the act of baptism itself was being performed in many belief systems before Christ, where did this rite come from? Early writings suggest that pagans replaced the pure ordinance of baptism, as it was revealed to Adam, with a defiled version. Ironically, the corrupted rite of baptism performed by pagans actually made it easier for

Gentiles to accept this ordinance generations later when it was restored by John the Baptist and Jesus, because people were already somewhat familiar with its form and substance, if not with the God-sanctioned authority to perform it properly.

Let us now review the major dispensations to look both at events that preceded their establishment and events that may have led to their downfall.

The Dispensation of Adam— God's Laws for the Redemption of Man Revealed

To understand apostasy, let us return to the beginning of religious history. Here we learn that Adam, the first man, and Eve, the first woman, were united by God in the Garden of Eden (Genesis 2:23–24). The Lord revealed Himself to Adam and Eve, and He walked and talked with them (Genesis 2:16–17; 3:9–19). In time, however, our first parents succumbed to the temptations of Satan and partook of the forbidden fruit, thereby introducing sin into the world. After they were cast out of the garden, God sent holy angels to teach them of His plan for redemption.[11] This plan for their salvation and happiness was made clear to them, and they in turn taught their children, who "call[ed] upon the name of the Lord" (Genesis 4:26; Psalm 78:5–7). The plan included a covenant between God and man that required the future sacrifice of Jesus Christ, the unblemished Lamb of God, who would atone for the sins of mankind. This covenant acknowledged man's dependence on God for redemption and included the development of faith in the future advent and sacrifice of His Son and the process of repenting of individual sins (with the knowledge that Jesus Christ would atone for Adam's transgression).

The New Testament acknowledged the grace and blessings associated with this covenant when Paul instructed the saints at Corinth: "For since by man [Adam] *came* death, by man [Jesus] *came* also the resurrection of the dead. For as in Adam['s transgression] all die, even so in Christ['s atonement] shall *all* be made alive" (1 Corinthians 15:21–22; emphasis added).

Adam's fall brought spiritual death into the world, separating man from God because of sin. But Adam's transgression also introduced physical death into the world. These two deaths are distinct from one another. Physical death is overcome solely by the mercy and grace of Jesus Christ, regardless of individual merit. In other words, the resurrection and immortality of every person is guaranteed by the atonement of Jesus Christ, whether or not any single individual accepts or follows Him (John 5:28–29). The second, or spiritual, death (separation from God) is conquered on an individual basis only by a combination of a person's choosing good over evil (faith, Revelation 2:7) and the Savior's atonement (gift of grace, John 3:16). Although the resurrection of the physical body was guaranteed by the Savior when He *broke the bands of death,* eternal reward was conditional upon man's *choosing* to abide by the terms of His covenant and by the Atonement, without which no amount of good works could hope to overcome even the most insignificant flaws of fallen man.

Through *no fault* of his posterity, Adam transgressed and brought about the Fall. The good news of the gospel was that *no merit* or act of human agency was required to save mankind from the *physical effects* of the Fall through the atonement and resurrection of Jesus Christ, the Son of God. Accordingly, man was placed in a position to "*work out [his] own salvation* with fear and trembling" (Philippians 2:12; emphasis added), mean-

ing, "Because God is at work in you, you can know what you need to do and you should do it with *awe and reverence.*" Through the exercise of agency (Deuteronomy 30:19), man could elect to develop faith in Jesus Christ and repent of individual sin.

Early Christians believed that baptism was instituted from the beginning as a witness of God's covenant with fallen man.[12] The covenant was that the Savior's future sacrifice would enable mankind not only eventually to escape temporal death but also ultimately to return to live in God's presence, becoming "heirs of God, and joint-heirs with Christ; if so be that we suffer with him" (Romans 8:17) by accepting the grace of Jesus Christ and obeying God's commandments. So John testified in his Apocalypse: "And the dead were judged out of those things which were written in the books, *according to their works*" (Revelation 20:12–13; emphasis added). The Bible warrants that although salvation is a free gift from Jesus Christ, man's ultimate eternal reward depends on how obedient he is to the laws and ordinances of the gospel, e.g., faith, repentance, baptism, and working toward sanctification and perfection through the Savior (Hebrews 6:1–2).

Although the book of Genesis is silent on many of these subjects, independent historical evidence supplies detail that is consistent with what *is* known from the Bible and rehearses what the early Christians believed. For example, Ethiopian and Arabic manuscripts titled the "Conflict of Adam and Eve with Satan" reveal much of what probably transpired after the Fall. Speaking to Adam, God said:

"Oh Adam, I have made My covenant with thee, and I will not turn from it. . . . I have made thee a promise; when that promise is fulfilled, I will bring thee back into the garden, thee and thy righteous seed. And

God [The Father] ceased to commune with Adam."[13] Although comforted by God's promise of eventual salvation, Adam and Eve were frightened by their new environment outside the garden. God sent His Word, His Firstborn, to console them and to teach them:

All this misery that thou hast been made to take upon thee because of thy transgression, will not free thee from the hand of Satan, and will not save thee. But I will. When I shall come down from heaven, and shall become flesh of thy seed, and take upon Me the infirmity from which thou sufferest, then the darkness that came upon thee in this cave shall come upon Me in the grave, when I am in the flesh of thy seed. And I, who am without years, shall be subject to the reckoning of years, of times, of months, and of days, and I shall be reckoned as one of the sons of men, in order to save thee. . . . I shall shed My blood upon thy head in the land of Golgotha. "For My blood shall be the Water of Life unto thee, at that time, and not unto thee alone, but unto all thy seed who shall believe in Me."[14]

Then, teaching Adam and Eve about the Resurrection, the Word of God (Jesus) foretold: "Satan will raise the Jews to put Me to death; and they will lay Me in a rock, and seal a large stone upon Me, and I shall remain within that rock three days and three nights. But on the third day I shall rise again, and it shall be salvation to thee, O Adam, and to thy seed."[15]

As an additional witness, the Testament of Adam also prophetically declares the ministry of Christ and explains that righteous individuals belonging to the family of Adam will be saved by the Atonement:

Adam said to Seth, his son, "you have heard, my son, that God is going to come into the world after a long time, (he will be) conceived of a virgin and put on a body, be born like a human being, and grow up as a child. He will perform signs and wonders on earth, will walk on the waves of the sea. He will rebuke the winds and they will be silenced. He will motion to the waves and they will stand still. He will open the eyes of the blind and cleanse the lepers. He will cause the deaf to hear, and the mute to speak. . . . [The Messiah said to me] For your sake I will be born of the Virgin Mary. For your sake I will taste death and enter into the house of the dead. For your sake I will make a new heaven, and I will be established over your posterity. And after three days, while I am in the tomb, I will raise up the body I received from you. And I will set you at the right hand of my divinity."[16]

Adam and Eve truly repented of their transgressions. In addition to offering sacrifices to the Lord, they prayed all night long for forgiveness.[17] From this time forward, Adam and his posterity were commanded to offer sacrifices in similitude of the future atonement of Jesus:

And God sent a bright fire upon the offering of Adam and Eve, and filled it with brightness, grace, and light; and the Holy Ghost came down upon that oblation. . . . And the souls of Adam and Eve were brightened, and their hearts were filled with joy and gladness and with the praises of God. And God said to Adam, "This shall be unto you a custom, to do so, when affliction and sorrow come upon you." Adam continued to offer this oblation . . . and had begun to pray, with his hands spread unto God. Then Satan hastened with the sharp iron-stone he had with him, and with it pierced Adam on the right side, when flowed blood and water, then Adam fell upon the altar. . . . [God] then sent His Word, and raised him up and said unto him, "Fulfil thy offering. . . . Thus will it happen to Me on earth, when I shall be pierced and blood shall flow . . . and water from my side [shall] run over my body, which is the true offering; and which shall be offered on the altar as a perfect offering." Then God commanded Adam to finish his offering. . . . And God healed Adam.[18]

Further evidence that God revealed detailed instructions to the ancient Patriarchs regarding what His plan entailed, including those actions required to overcome spiritual and physical death, is furnished in the Secrets of Enoch. Enoch testified to his posterity: "And now my children, lay thought upon your hearts, mark well the words of your father, which are all come to you from the Lord's lips. Take these books of your father's handwriting and read them. For the books are many, and in them you will learn all the Lord's works, all that has been from the beginning of creation, and will be till the end of time. And if you will observe my handwriting, you will not sin against the Lord."[19]

While Genesis records little about God's instructions to Adam, writings contained in the Pseudepigrapha, such as those we have just discussed, make it clear that he was taught the laws and doctrines pertaining to the Atonement *after the Fall*. Although developing faith in Jesus Christ has been a primary teaching in every dispensation, God has also revealed other requirements necessary for man's salvation. Genesis, in combination with other early texts, is clear that Abraham and others of the patriarchal prophets were taught about animal sacrifice; beginning with Adam, they *looked forward to the ultimate sacrifice of the Lamb of God.*

As God revealed His laws and commandments to Adam and his posterity, He clearly taught that the doctrine of free will was the overarching principle encompassing the entire plan of redemption. Speaking of the agency of man, J. P. Migne describes how Adam's posterity divided themselves according to the desires of their own hearts: "The Cainites dedicated to following Satan . . . lived in a fertile country but very far distant from Eden, . . . [and] devoted themselves to all the pleasures of the flesh and all manner of immorality," and the Sethites who "dwelt in the mountains near the Garden, were faithful to the divine law and bore the name of the Sons of God."[20]

The Slavonic Enoch texts also reveal that Adam and his descendants were "free agents"; in this sense they fully agree with the Bible, noncanonical writings, and the early Christian Fathers,[21] for all four sources declare that agency is a crucial element in our Heavenly Father's plan to redeem mankind: "And I [God] assigned him to be a King, to reign on the earth, and to have my wisdom, . . . and called his name Adam. And I gave him his free will; and I pointed out to him the two ways—light and darkness. And I said to him, 'This is good for you, but that is bad,' so that I might know whether he has love toward me or abhorrence, and so that it might be plain who among his race loves me."[22] In a fascinating passage in the apocryphal book Epistle to the Apostles, Jesus Himself used the account of Adam to teach the apostles the importance of agency:

> Adam was given the power that he might choose what he wanted of the two; and he chose the light and stretched out his hand and took (it) and left darkness and withdrew from it. Likewise every man is given the ability to believe in the light; this is the life of the Father who

sent me. And whosoever has believed in me will live, if he has done the work of light.[23]

Apocryphal writings agree with pseudepigraphal and biblical teachings that free agency plays a critical role in the salvation process. God does not force or compel mankind to be obedient. Through prophets, beginning with Adam, God has revealed the eternal laws and conditions that would be required to rescue fallen man, leaving mortals to choose for themselves whether or not they would follow Him.

Finally, as to the role of baptism in the redemption process, a scroll entitled the Apocalypse of Adam is alleged to be a book handed down from Adam himself; it encompasses the laws pertaining to man's salvation, including water baptism: "These are the revelations which Adam made known to Seth his son, and his son taught his seed about them. This is the secret knowledge of Adam which he imparted to Seth, which is the holy baptism of those who know the eternal knowledge through the ones born of the word [the living water]."[24]

Further supporting the belief held by early Christians that baptism was practiced before the ministry of either John the Baptist or Christ, Justin Martyr explained his understanding of this ordinance during the Old Testament era as follows:

And it is said through Isaiah the prophet, as we wrote before, in what manner those who have sinned and repent shall escape their sins. He thus spoke: "*Wash, become clean,* put away the evil doings of your souls, learn to do good, judge the orphan and plead for the widow, and come and let us reason together, says the Lord. And though your sins be as scarlet, I will make them wool."[25]

Note that while quoting Isaiah, Justin Martyr emphasizes the Christian salvation process of repentance and "washing" in order to become clean. Also mirroring the teachings of Jesus, Isaiah underscored the importance of eliminating sin from our lives and taking care of the orphans and widows. From this passage, Justin seems to advocate the principle of repentance, followed by baptism or "washing," and then living a life of obedience, righteousness, and service. In explaining this pattern, Justin confirms Isaiah's teaching that one's sins shall be white as wool and thus receive complete forgiveness. Hippolytus also attested to Justin Martyr's interpretation. Quoting the same passage from Isaiah he wrote:

Do you see, beloved, how the prophet [Isaiah] spake beforetime of the purifying power of baptism? For he who comes down in faith to the laver of regeneration, and . . . joins himself to Christ; . . . and puts on the adoption,— he comes up from the baptism brilliant as the sun, flashing forth the beams of righteousness, and . . . he returns a son of God and joint heir with Christ.[26]

Many scholars also believe that the Jewish community at Qumran also practiced baptism by immersion. Before his death, Professor Yigael Yadin of Hebrew University, a leading archaeologist involved with the Dead Sea Scrolls, wrote:

We know that the Essenes practiced baptism not only from their literature but also from the baptismal installations found at Qumran. These baptismal installations are quite different from the ritual baths . . . in the Jericho area, and in Jerusalem. . . . At Qumran . . . there is only a single pool (with steps) in which the people could be baptized. Baptism as we know it in early Christianity may have been adopted under

Essene influence through John the Baptist.[27]

The loss of the ancient ordinance of baptism appears to be nothing more than the fruit of apostasy. As we have shown, evidence exists that the rite of baptism was likely revealed to Adam. Certainly, the early Church held to this belief, for we have the testimony of Justin Martyr and Hippolytus that baptism was practiced in the Old Testament during the time of Isaiah. We have also documented the practice of baptism at Qumran. Thus, apocryphal writings, the Dead Sea Scrolls, and some early Christian authors furnish evidence that baptism may have been practiced anciently.[28]

The Doctrine of *Original Sin* Reconsidered

The term *original sin* is not mentioned in the Old Testament and is never used in the New Testament. Augustine (A.D. 354–430), the famed bishop of Hippo (north Africa), developed a speculative doctrine that man is born inherently evil and that his entire nature is depraved until, by the grace and will of God (not his own election), man comes unto Christ and is born again. In support of his doctrine, Augustine apparently offered a single *primary* passage in Romans, which he misconstrued: "Wherefore, as by one man sin entered into the world, and death by sin; and so death passed upon all men, *for that all* have sinned" (Romans 5:12; emphasis added).

Augustine believed that this isolated phrase "in whom" meant that all men are born depraved because of Adam's sin.[29] The Bible translation used by Augustine came from the Latin Vulgate Bible, a translation composed by Jerome, an influential priest and scholar in the mid-fourth century. This translation has revealed itself as somewhat inferior to modern versions. The King James Version (KJV), translated in A.D. 1611, interprets the same phrase from the Greek as "*for that*" all have sinned, rather than "*in whom*" all have sinned. This rendering makes clear that all humans sin but that we are not *born* corrupt because of Adam's transgression. In spite of Jerome's poor translation of this particular passage, his own Bible commentary suggests that the fourth-century Church actually understood the phrase to mean *because* all have sinned.[30] Modern scholars, both Catholic and Protestant, as attested by its use in the popular New International Version Bible, agree that *because* is the best translation. Rendered thus, Paul's intended meaning would be: Men are not *born* depraved, they *become* sinful by choice, although considerably influenced by a *fallen world* and the enticements of Satan.

The mistranslation and thus the distorted interpretation of Romans 5:12 led to the mistaken belief that Adam's guilt was passed on to the entire human race. Such a doctrine, aside from this one faulty translation, is unknown in all of our remaining scripture. Augustine's error further led to an assumption that unbaptized children were doomed to eternal damnation, for even newborns were apparently tainted from birth by Adam's sin. Although man inherited a fallen environment when Adam sinned, responsibility for the sin of Adam or of any other person cannot be passed to another. This doctrine is plainly taught in the Old Testament: "The soul that sinneth, it shall die. The son shall not bear the iniquity of the father, neither shall the father bear the iniquity of the son: the righteousness of the righteous [man] shall be upon him, and the wickedness of the wicked shall be upon him. . . . Therefore I will judge you, O house of Israel, every one according to his ways" (Ezekiel 18:20–30; see also 2 Kings 14:6; Deuteronomy 1:39).

The number of early Christian writings testifying of the purity and innocence of children and of their standing before the Lord is considerable. These records stand as a witness that the primitive Church taught no such doctrine as original sin as interpreted by Augustine.

One of the earliest apocryphal narratives shedding light on the sanctity of children and those with limited mental capacity is found in the Apocalypse of Paul. Although the authorship of this writing is questionable, its doctrine is consistent with that of the early Church and is quoted as scripture by Origen. This revelation describes Paul's experience from 2 Corinthians 12, wherein he describes being caught up to the third heaven:

> Again he led me where the river of milk was; and I saw in that place all the infants whom king Herod had slain for the name of Christ, and they greeted me. And the angel said to me: All who preserve their chastity and purity . . . are brought to the children and they greet them saying, "You are our brothers and friends and (fellow) members." Among them they will inherit the promises of God.
> And I turned and saw . . . thrones set in another rank which appeared to be of greater glory. . . . These are the thrones of those who had goodness and understanding of heart and (yet) made themselves fools for the Lord God's sake in that they neither knew the Scriptures nor many Psalms but paid heed to . . . the commandments of God and hearing them acted with great carefulness in conformity to these (commandments). . . . The saints . . . discuss with one another and say: Wait and see these unlearned men who understand nothing more, how they merited such a great and beautiful robe and such glory because of their innocence.[31]

This account, cited as a teaching of Paul, describes the fate of those who die in infancy, regardless whether or not they were baptized, and of those who have mental limitations. According to Paul's vision, they will receive the "promises of God" and "great glory."

Echoing this sentiment, the Shepherd of Hermas recorded: "They are as infant children, in whose hearts no evil originates; nor did they know what wickedness is, but remained as children. Such accordingly, without doubt, dwell in the kingdom of God, because they defiled in nothing the commandments of God; . . . for all infants are honorable before God."[32]

St. Irenaeus recorded in the late second century that even Adam and Eve were not cursed because of their sin: "Therefore at the beginning of Adam's transgression, as the scripture tells, God did not curse Adam himself but the earth that he worked. As one of the ancients says, 'God transferred the curse to the earth so that it would not continue in man.' . . . For God hated the one who seduced man while he felt pity for the one seduced."[33]

Clement of Alexandria, also a late second-century Christian theologian, opposed the Gnostic belief in *original guilt*[34] (popularized later by Augustine) when he wrote: "It is for them to tell us how the newly born child could commit fornication or in what way the child who has never done anything at all has fallen under Adam's curse. The only thing left for them to say and still be consistent, I suppose, is that birth is evil not just for the body but for the soul for which the body exists."[35] Clement thus agrees with his contemporary, Irenaeus, that a newborn is neither born in sin nor can it commit sin. Significantly, Clement recognized that although the mortal state that man inherited from Adam is fallen, the spirit that comes from God to inhabit that mortal body is pure and without sin.

Such early Christian views are important because as they clearly oppose the later teaching, that man is born depraved, promoted by Augustine (early fifth century) and John Calvin, the Reformer (mid-sixteenth century). Because Hermas, Irenaeus, and Clement (orthodox leaders) lived so much closer to the time of the original teachings and doctrine of Christ, one would assume that their views would hold closer to the founding intent.

Similarly, Cyril of Jerusalem, in the mid-fourth century was still preaching the innocence of little children: "And learn this also, that the soul, before it came into the world, had committed no sin, but having come in sinless, *we now sin of our free will.*"[36]

Finally, from J. N. D. Kelly, quoting Bishop Ambrose of Milan (A.D. 340–97), we learn: "The point is that . . . as for Ambrose, we are not punished for Adam's sin, but only for our own sins. As he says, 'You perceive that men are not made guilty by the fact of their birth, but by their evil behaviour.' Baptism is therefore necessary, not as abolishing inherited guilt, but as delivering us from death and opening the gates of the Kingdom of heaven."[37] The leading Churchmen following the time of the apostles held that children were not responsible for Adam's sin. Infants, they taught, came into this world innocent and clean. No wonder the earliest Christians believed in the purity of children—the Savior Himself declared, "Suffer little children to come unto me, and forbid them not: for of such is the kingdom of God" (Luke 18:16).

Nevertheless *Adam did fall,* mankind became subject to the wicked influence of Satan, and a change occurred in the earth itself, as attested to by Irenaeus, and thus also in man's environment. The fall of Adam punctuates the need for man to be *born again* and to receive the Holy Spirit (Psalm 51:11)

in order to overcome the tendencies of the *natural man* (1 Corinthians 2:14). However, the assumption that Adam's descendants are somehow still responsible for Adam's guilt, or that man has inherited it—and thus is totally depraved—is contrary to accepted scripture. Children are innocent until they arrive at an accountable age to *elect* to follow an unrighteous path when opposing choices are placed before them. Consequently, we are commanded to be *born again,* that is, changed from our carnal and fallen state to one of righteousness through the grace of Jesus Christ. This was the doctrine taught by Jesus and His early followers.

God revealed to Adam certain conditions associated with man's redemption. Originating with Adam, the same essential elements of salvation detailed in the New Testament are also recorded in the Old Testament and the extrabiblical records, namely the atonement of Jesus; justice, mercy, and God's grace; free agency and personal responsibility; the purity of children; repentance and baptism for those accountable and capable of sin; divine judgment and eternal reward or punishment based on that judgment.

Pertaining to salvation and eternal reward, a just God holds all His children equally accountable to the same basic laws and principles (see pages 93–96)—to the extent of course that all His children have the opportunity to know of and live according to those principles. But man's general rejection and perversion of God's laws resulted in the withdrawal of His Spirit and pure covenant from the majority of those living during the dispensation of Adam. Because so many people departed from the truth, forsook God's covenant, and consciously chose to disobey during this period, they fell into apostasy. They effectively prevented God's children from hearing the gospel plan and deliberately brought chaos and confusion to the household of God on earth.

All was not lost, of course. The Bible and Pseudepigrapha confirm that at various intervals God called other prophets to reveal anew His plan for man's redemption and reestablish His household.

The Dispensation of Enoch

According to the Apocryphon of John, the pervasive wickedness during Enoch's day was characterized initially by immorality and later by more deceptive methods of perversion: "At first they [Satan's followers] did not succeed. When they had no success, they gathered together again and they made a plan. . . . They created a counterfeit spirit," a clever imitation of the true order of things: "They brought gold and silver and a gift and copper and iron and metal. . . . And they steered the people who followed them into great troubles, by leading them astray with many deceptions. . . . And they closed their hearts, and they hardened themselves . . . through the counterfeit spirit."[38] In Enoch's time, the hearts of the people were so depraved that they sought to imitate the heavenly ordinances of salvation revealed to Adam: "You are full of works that are not the truth, . . . having defiled the water of life [baptism]."[39] "Woe unto you who alter the words of truth and pervert the eternal law! [covenant]," and "reckon [yourselves] not guilty of sin."[40] Thus we see that these acts were not blatantly rebellious; they were a cunning manipulation of God's name. They did not abandon religion—they defiled it!

Consequently, God called upon Enoch to preach repentance to His people. Enoch records, "And the Lord called me with his own mouth and said to me, 'Come near to me, Enoch.'"[41] Regarded as very young, Enoch wondered why he had been chosen: "I heard my brothers say when I was small how wicked the world is; how then can I all alone achieve anything?"[42] Trusting God, Enoch went forth to accomplish what he had been commanded. Enoch's glorified presence and the power of his preaching were such that many listened and followed his admonitions:

> And all the people gathered together to Enoch . . . to hear this thing; and Enoch taught the children of men the way of God. . . . And the spirit was upon Enoch, and he taught all his people the wisdom of God and his ways. . . . And all the people were astonished and awed by his wisdom and knowledge, and bowed down to the earth before him. And all the people gathered together unto Enoch. . . . and Enoch taught all the people again to keep the ways of the Lord and gave them all his peace.[43]

The pseudepigraphal account of 1 Enoch records several visions received by Enoch spanning the history of mankind. He views the wickedness of the present world and foresees the Flood, which is about to come upon the earth.[44] He beholds the throne of God and the brilliance and glory of His heavenly abode.[45] The Lord calls Enoch a "righteous man" and with His own voice commands Enoch to preach repentance to the wicked.[46] Enoch sees the "Elect One" and the place where the spirits of man resided with "the Lord of the Spirits" prior to coming to earth:

> And I gazed at that place . . . and I blessed and praised, saying, 'blessed is he, and may he be blessed, from the beginning and evermore. There is no such thing as non-existence before him. (Even) before the world was created, he knows what is forever and what will be from generation to generation. . . . They shall bless, praise and extol (you), saying, Holy, Holy, Holy, Lord

of the Spirits; the spirits fill the earth. . . . And my face was changed on account of the fact that I could not withstand the sight.' And after that, I saw . . . ten million times ten million, an innumerable and uncountable (multitude) who stand before the glory of the Lord of the Spirits.[47]

Continuing the account, Enoch is blessed to comprehend a series of cosmic secrets such as the origin of lightning and thunder, the mysteries of how the winds are dispersed over the earth, the formulas of clouds and dew, the operations of the sun and moon—all of these abiding the laws and commandments of the *Lord of the Spirits*.[48] He observes the stars of the firmament, the angel referring to each of these by name. The Lord reveals to Enoch the balance of the universe and the eternal purposes of all God's works.[49] He sees in vision the future of the earth, including the Flood,[50] Israel's clashes with its enemies,[51] the first advent of the Son of Man,[52] and, finally, an event in the distant future known as the "day of tribulation," followed by the Resurrection and the Day of Judgment.[53] Clearly, the Enoch visions are among the most remarkable that God has ever given to man, comparable to the Apostle John's apocalyptic revelation or Daniel's and Ezekiel's prophecies regarding the end of the world. No wonder the early Church held the books of Enoch in such high regard, to the extent that the Apostolic Fathers understood their full meaning and import.

Enoch became one of the Lord's great prophets, inspiring an entire people to live together in harmony and righteousness. In due time, Enoch and his people were taken from the earth into heaven: "Therefore I now took away Zion, to visit the world in its own time more speedily."[54] The wicked who remained behind did not repent of their sins,

nor did they refrain from perverting the true gospel.

The Enoch documents reveal that the genealogical records and sacred histories of God's covenant people were passed down from the righteous Patriarchs and were transferred with a divine trust to those so charged with this responsibility (see also Numbers 33:2; Malachi 3:16). Enoch records in his writings that total annihilation, as would transpire under Noah, required the *utter depravity* of a people who would "deliberately and systematically corrupt heavenly things to justify wickedness."[55] The intentional perversion of baptism and animal sacrifice were only some of the corrupt practices of this unrepentant generation. The early third-century Christian theologian Hippolytus cautioned that the Antichrist impersonates Christ in every detail by copying "the seal" (water baptism), imitating worship patterns, performing miracles, organizing his own church, and ordaining his own priesthood. According to Hippolytus, this is the manner in which "the deceiver seeks to liken himself in all things to the Son of God," beguiling his followers. Appropriately have the prophets warned us of his foul antics.[56]

Enoch rebuked the people in his day: "Woe unto you who deliberately go astray, who promote yourselves to honor and glory by deceitful practices . . . ; who misapply and misinterpret straightforward statements, who have given a new twist to the everlasting covenant, and then produce arguments to prove that you are without guilt!"[57] The "everlasting covenant" (the gospel) was upon the earth during portions of previous dispensations but was lost at other times due to sin and corruption. The Enoch texts state that "God gave them [those who were wicked] a respite all the time that the righteous men Jared, Methuselah, and Enoch were alive; but when they departed from the world, God let punishment descend . . . , 'and they were blotted out from the earth.'"[58]

Enoch was chosen by God to be His prophet in a day of utter depravity. God had two distinct purposes in preparing and calling such a prophet: (1) to gather the elect who would hear the voice of God and repent of their wicked practices; and (2) to raise the warning voice of prophecy, thereby leaving the wicked without excuse. The writings of Enoch contained in the Dead Sea Scrolls substantiate the theme of recurring apostasy:

[Then I, Enoch, replied saying:] Surely [the Lord] will [restore his law upon the earth, according to what I saw and related to you, my son.] In the days of Yared [Jared], my father, they infringed [the word of Lord; . . . they si]nned and infri[nged; . . . they changed in order to go] with women and sin with them; . . . There will be [great anger and flood over the ear]th [and there will be great devastation for a year. But this boy] born to you [and his three sons] will be sa[ved when those that are above] the earth [die. Then will the earth rest], and it will be cleansed from the great corruption. [Now say to Lamech: He is your son] truly [and . . . this] boy [who was born.] He is to be called [Noah, for he will be your repose when you repose in him;] [and he will be your deliverance, for] he [and his sons] will be delivered [from the depravity of the earth—caused by the actions of all sinners] [and by the wicked of the earth—which] will occur in his days. Subsequently there will be even worse wickedness [than this which will have taken place] in their days. For I know the mysteries [of the Lord which] the Holy Ones have told me and have shown me [and which] I read in [the tablets] of heaven. In them I saw written that generation after generation will perpetuate evil in this way.[59]

In this passage, Enoch testifies that "the Lord will restore his law upon the earth." He implies that because of sin in the days of his father, Jared, he was called to preach repentance. Most of the people refused to listen. Enoch then states that Noah and his sons will be saved, while the rest of the earth will be flooded, and that Noah will deliver mankind from the wicked in Enoch's and Noah's day. Enoch then confides that "subsequently [after the Flood] there will be even worse wickedness." He reveals the source of his revelations when he asserts that he knows "the mysteries of the Lord" which he received from "the Holy Ones" and from the "tablets of heaven" they permitted him to read. Finally, Enoch discovers from the heavenly writings that apostasy will be a continuing problem upon the earth. Accordingly, when Enoch was translated and taken into heaven, God called Noah to serve as a final witness before His irrevocable judgments would descend.

Because the books of Enoch fell out of favor through the influence of Augustine and others of his era, Christians of the modern age have not been exposed to this wonderful prophet of God. When Enoch was called as a prophet, the world was in a state of utter apostasy. As he preached with great power and authority, those who had "ears to hear" followed Enoch and built the great city of Zion. Because gross wickedness continued unrestrained, Zion, "the city of Enoch," was taken into heaven, and Noah was called as a final warning voice preceding the Flood. In the days of Enoch, while one dispensation was concluding because of general apostasy, another, through Noah, was being announced, paving the way for Noah's descendants to hear the gospel plan.

The Dispensation of Noah

Like the righteous Patriarchs before him, Noah was "a just man and perfect in his generations" (Genesis 6:9). God revealed to Noah that the "end of all flesh is come before me; for the earth is filled with violence through them; and, behold, I will destroy them" (Genesis 6:13). Noah was instructed to build an ark and to gather his family members and two of every animal species, male and female, both fowl and mammal, in order to preserve humanity and living creatures. First Enoch testifies that Noah may have had help in building the ark:

"In those days, the word of God came to me, and said unto me, "Noah, your lot has come before me—a lot without blame, a lot of true love. At this time the angels are working with wood (making an ark) and when it is completed, I shall place my hands upon it and protect it, and the seed of life shall arise from it; and a substitute (generation) will come so that the earth will not remain empty (without inhabitants)."[60] In fulfillment of prophecy, the rains descended and were sustained for forty days and nights, thus destroying all flesh upon the face of the earth except those souls and animals residing in the ark. Following the Flood, the Lord *reestablished* His covenant with Noah (Genesis 6:18, 9:1–9) and established the rainbow as a token of His oath (Genesis 9:13–17).

Unfortunately, and frankly quite amazingly, the descendants of Noah learned nothing from the watery grave that claimed nearly all of the previous generation: they too rejected the truth. As they should have predicted, when their apostasy became widespread, God's judgments descended on them as dramatically as those that had occurred at the end of Adam's and Enoch's dispensations. Even as the wicked were attempting to build a tower to reach the heavens, God said:

Let us go down, and there confound their language, that they may not understand one another's speech. . . . Therefore is the name of it called Babel; because the Lord did there confound the language of all the earth: and from thence did the Lord scatter them abroad upon the face of all the earth. (Genesis 11:7–9)

In this passage, we observe the repeating pattern of apostasy: truth is revealed and established through God's prophet, but over a period of time the gospel is rejected or altered. In the case of those building the great tower, God judged his children anew by separating them and confounding their language. We learn from each of these dispensations that God is merciful and just. In spite of gross wickedness, He continues to reveal His gospel plan, grant opportunities for His children to repent—complete with free agency to choose their own path—and then righteously judge them according to their responses.

The Dispensation of Melchizedek and Abraham

The priesthood and the household of God (His chosen people) continued through Melchizedek and Abraham.[61] Melchizedek was the "King of Salem" and the "priest of the most high God" to whom Abraham paid the "tenth part of all." So great was Melchizedek that the higher order of priesthood was named after him (Hebrews 7:1, 2; 5:6). Paul praises Melchizedek when he asserts, "Now consider how great this man was, unto whom even the patriarch Abraham gave the tenth of the spoils" (Hebrews 7:4). Corroborating the Genesis and Pauline narratives, the Genesis Apocryphon from the Dead Sea Scrolls records the meeting of Abram and Melchizedek (compare Genesis 14:18–20):

He went to Salem, which is Jerusalem. Abram was encamped in the valley of Shaveh, which is the Valley of the King. . . . Melchizedek, king of Salem, brought out food and drink for Abram and for all the men that were with him. He was a priest of the Most High God. He blessed Abram and said: Blessed be Abram by the Most High God, Lord of heaven and earth and blessed be the Most High God, who has delivered your enemies into your hands. And (Abram) gave him a tithe of all the flocks of the king of Elam and his allies.[62]

Paul's choice of the word *spoils* in the New Testament is interesting and may imply that he had more information about this tithe than is contained in the modern Genesis account. The Genesis apocryphal record informs us of an eventful battle waged by Abraham and 318 strong men chosen from among his servants to make war against their enemies. With the help of the Lord, Abraham was victorious in defeating the king of Elam, who with his allies had held captive Sodom and Gomorrah and other confederate kingdoms for more than twelve years. Abraham not only recovered the possessions which had been confiscated from their own lands but also captured "spoils" (meaning the "top of the heap," or by analogy, "best of the booty") from their oppressors, to whom his neighbors had been paying tribute for many years while in bondage. These events led to the momentous meeting between Abraham and Melchizedek, after which Abraham returned those flocks and herds belonging to his neighbors.[63] Abraham did not give him just a tenth; he gave him the very best tenth.

Paul tells us about a higher priesthood held by Melchizedek but later withheld from the children of Israel because of sin; this priesthood was renewed in Jesus Christ: "If therefore perfection were by the Levitical priesthood, (for under it the people received

the law,) what further need was there that another priest should rise after the order of Melchisedec. . . ? For the priesthood being changed, there is made of necessity a change also of the law" (Hebrews 7:11–12). Paul reveals that had God's first covenant been faultless, there would have been no need of the second; the New Covenant was indeed necessary because they "continued not" in His covenant under Moses (Hebrews 8:9). Melchizedek had received God's covenant, and it was preserved under Abraham and those of his righteous seed who followed. It was then lost when Israel rejected the covenant God initially offered under Moses. Melchizedek was a celebrated high priest, the king of Salem, and an important spiritual ruler over the people after the order of the great Patriarchs.

Abraham embraced the righteous desires characteristic of the ancient Patriarchs. Rejecting his father Terah's idolatrous lifestyle, Abraham sought the God who created the heavens and earth.[64] He relates that as he pondered eternal things the "voice of the Mighty One came down from the heavens . . . calling, 'Abraham, Abraham!'" Responding, Abraham said, "Here I am." God replied, "You are seeking for the God of gods, the Creator, in the understanding of your heart. I am he. Go out from Terah, your father, and go out of the house, that you may not be slain in the sins of your father's house."[65] God then declared to Abraham, "I will announce to you guarded things and you will see great things which you have not seen, because you desired to search for me, and I called you my beloved."[66] As instructed, Abraham continued pleading with the Lord, saying, "Accept my prayer and delight in it. . . . Receive me favorably, teach me, show me, and make known to your servant what you have promised me."[67] God then showed unto Abraham the expanse

33

of the firmament and opened up a glorious vision. Though not recorded in as much detail as Enoch's revelation, his vision must certainly have been comparable: "Look from on high at the stars . . . and count them for me and tell me their number!"[68] When Abraham insisted that he was only a man and could not, God replied, "As the number of the stars and their power so shall I place for your seed the nations and men."[69]

Expanding on this promise, God instructed Michael the archangel to say to Abraham: "Thus says the Lord your God, who led you into the promised land, who blessed you *more than the sand of the sea and the stars of heaven,* who opened the womb of the barren Sarah and graciously granted to you Isaac, the fruit of the womb in old age. Truly I say to you that *blessing I will bless you and multiplying I will multiply your seed.* And I will give to you whatever you ask of me; for I am the Lord your God and besides me there is no other."[70] After Abraham inquires about a "handsome temple" he views in this vision, the Lord answers, "Hear, Abraham! This temple which you have seen, the altar and the works of art, this is my idea of the priesthood of my glory, where every petition of man will enter and dwell."[71]

Supporting the account of Old Testament pseudepigraphal writings, the Bible likewise testifies that Abraham's exceeding faith and desire to be obedient was evidenced by his willingness to sacrifice the *only son* of Sarah, his covenant wife. This remarkable demonstration of faith is the reason God entered into a singular covenant with Abraham that his seed, through Isaac, would be blessed thereafter, the token of which was signified by the introduction of the law of circumcision (Genesis 17:17–27; 22:15–18).

Abraham's call to be a prophet of God and the sacrificial experience with his son Isaac established a type or a foreshadowing of the eventual sacrifice of the Son of God. Abraham's appointment ushered in a new dispensation that established a line of patriarchal prophets for many generations. Following the apostasy of the wicked after Noah, the laws and commandments pertaining to redemption were reestablished among men through the God-fearing seed of Abraham.

The Dispensation of Moses

Righteousness and God's covenant passed from Abraham to Isaac to Jacob, who was later called Israel, then through Joseph and Ephraim (Genesis 48:17–19). The Genesis account indicates that not long after Joseph died, his name was forgotten by the Egyptians, and the children of Israel were placed in captivity in the land of Goshen. Although the Bible is silent on this subject, apostasy is the probable cause of Israel's enslavement, the result of their worship of Egypt's false gods (Joshua 24:14). Nevertheless, God remembered His promise to Abraham, and when Israel's vassalage had extended some 210 years, Moses was called as a prophet of God to lead the Lord's chosen people out of physical and spiritual bondage.[72] After securing Israel's freedom, Moses guided the Israelites from Egypt to Sinai, but notwithstanding many extraordinary miracles—such as the devastating plagues exercised against the Egyptians, parting the Red Sea, and raining manna from heaven—the children of Israel, still weak in faith, complained of their burdens and disobeyed important commandments.

Israel's decline during this period reached its lowest point when the Israelites fashioned and then worshiped a golden calf. Because they rejected the pure teachings of God by embracing worldly practices, including idolatry and immorality, Moses destroyed the original tablets containing the laws of the *Melchizedek,* or greater, Priesthood and replaced them with a lesser law known as the *Levitical Priesthood* or the *Priesthood of Aaron* (Exodus 40:15). This is implied by the highly regarded early second-century Epistle of Barnabas:

> So it is. But let us see whether the covenant which he sware to the fathers to give to the people—whether he has given it. *He has given it.* But they were not worthy to receive it because of their sins. For the prophet says, "And Moses was fasting on Mount Sinai, to receive the covenant of the Lord for the people, forty days and forty nights. And Moses received from the Lord the two tables, written by the finger of the hand of Lord in the Spirit"; And Moses took them, and carried them down to give them to the people. And the Lord said to Moses, "Moses, Moses, go down quickly, for thy people whom thou didst bring out of the land of Egypt have broken the law. And Moses perceived that they had made themselves again molten images, and he cast them out of his hands, and the tables of the covenant of the Lord were broken." *Moses received it,* but *they* were not *worthy.* But learn how *we* received it. Moses received it when he was a servant, but the Lord himself gave it to us, as the people of the inheritance.[73]

This passage suggests that Moses himself received a higher law from God but *was prevented from revealing it to the Israelites* because of their idolatry and rejection of God's covenant. Note the words "*Moses received it, but they* [the Israelites] *were not worthy.*" Moving from the Mosaic period to the apostolic era, the author of the Epistle of Barnabas adds, "*But learn how we received it.*" The followers of Jesus received a higher law than the Israelites,

which law they (the Israelites) never received. In place of the higher law, Israel was given the law of Moses as a schoolmaster until the actual coming of Christ (Galatians 3:24), as alluded to by the author of Barnabas's epistle. From that time until the Savior's ministry, Israel was in varying degrees of apostasy and apparently did not practice ordinances or rites associated with the higher law, as may have been received from time to time in prior dispensations and revealed anew during the apostolic dispensation.

Israel's rebellion was not unexpected. Just as Enoch had prophesied repeating patterns of apostasy, Moses foretold that God's chosen people would reject His covenant: "For I know thy rebellion, and thy stiff neck. . . . I know that after my death ye will utterly corrupt yourselves, and turn aside from the way which I have commanded you" (Deuteronomy 31:27–29).

The Israelites had a short memory. Because they lacked faith in God's power, when Moses sent spies into Canaan, God kept them wandering in the wilderness for forty years. He refused to allow His people entry into the promised land when they had witnessed so many miracles and yet turned their backs on Him to worship false gods. When Joshua led Israel across the Jordan, they witnessed its parting, as with the Red Sea, and observed the hand of the Lord in conquering all the nations occupying lands promised to the seed of Abraham. Just before he died, Joshua warned Israel *again,* reminding them of all that God had done for them:

> I have given you a land for which ye did not labour, and cities which ye built not, and ye dwell in them: of the vineyards and oliveyards which ye planted not do ye eat. Now therefore fear the Lord, and serve him in sincerity and in truth: and put away the gods which

your fathers served on the other side of the flood, and in Egypt . . . or the gods of the Amorites, in whose land ye dwell: but as for me and my house, we will serve the Lord. . . . If ye forsake the Lord, and serve strange gods, then he will turn and do you hurt. (Joshua 24:13–20; emphasis added)

Unfortunately, the rising generation, as in earlier dispensations, forgot the Lord: "And there arose another generation after them, which knew not the Lord, nor yet the works which he had done for Israel. And the children of Israel did evil in the sight of the Lord, and served Baalim: and they forsook the Lord God of their fathers, which brought them out of the land of Egypt, and followed other gods, . . . and provoked the Lord to anger" (Judges 2:10–12).

The account of Jeroboam in the Old Testament provides additional evidence of how Satan introduces a counterfeit gospel to lead God's children away from Him:

The king took counsel, and made two calves of gold. . . . And he set the one in Beth-el, and the other put he in Dan. And this thing became a sin: for the people went to worship before the one, even unto Dan. And he made an house of high places, and made priests of the lowest of the people, which were not of the sons of Levi. And Jeroboam ordained a feast in the eighth month, on the fifteenth day of the month, like unto the feast that is in Judah, and he offered upon the altar. So did he in Beth-el, sacrificing unto the calves that he had made. (1 Kings 12:28–32; see also 2 Kings 16:1–4, 10–17)

Thus, Jeroboam fabricated his own gods, made his own temple, ordained his own priests, established his own feasts, and sacrificed his own offerings to his false gods.

The wickedness of Israel in turning its back on God by rejecting Samuel's inspired counsel *not to choose a king* over them (1 Samuel 8:19) at that time (in fulfillment of prophecy) resulted in the division between the tribes faithful to the house of David (Rehoboam) and those whose allegiance remained with the ten tribes, or Ephraimites (Jeroboam), which occurred in approximately 975 B.C. and ultimately led to the destruction and captivity of Israel.

In about 722 B.C. (2 Kings 17:6), Assyria conquered those distinguished as the ten tribes and removed them to Assyrian lands. Thereafter, they became so thoroughly dispersed as to be known as the lost tribes. The kingdom of Judah remained a sovereign nation until about 586 B.C., when they were defeated by King Nebuchadnezzer (2 Kings 25:21). Judah's defeat was followed by the Babylonian captivity predicted by Isaiah and Jeremiah, which came because of wickedness and rejection of the prophetic teachings of the Lord's anointed (Isaiah 48:18–22; Jeremiah 16:10–15). Judah remained in captivity until Cyrus of Persia defeated Babylon in 539 B.C., overthrowing the Chaldean dynasty and granting Judah's freedom to return to Judea and rebuild the temple at Jerusalem in 537 B.C. (Ezra 1:2–3).

While Israel's dispersion, when viewed over a long period, is somewhat complicated, history records that a portion of the Jews returned with Ezra the prophet to Jerusalem, while most remained in Babylon, where they could gain certain economic and agricultural benefits. Between 400 B.C. and 200 B.C., Israel dispersed itself, establishing colonies throughout most of the known world. Judah's subjugation in Palestine persisted intermittently through the final centuries preceding the birth of Christ, being assailed by Greece, Egypt, and Syria prior to the revolt of the

Maccabees in 164 B.C., and some years later becoming a tributary nation to the Roman Empire, in which state it remained throughout the Savior's ministry.[74]

The prophecies of Isaiah and Jeremiah had thus been vindicated. Israel had suffered greatly because of rebellion, yet the Lord's promise to Abraham was not forgotten. These prophets also foretold the future recovery of apostate Israel: "And it shall come to pass in that day, that . . . ye shall be gathered one by one, O ye children of Israel" (Isaiah 27:12). Jeremiah added, "Behold, I will send for many fishers, saith the Lord, and they shall fish them; and after will I send for many hunters, and they shall hunt them from every mountain, and from every hill, and out of the holes in the rocks" (Jeremiah 16:16).

Reliable evidence of widespread apostasy within the tribe of Judah is manifest throughout the Old Testament, culminating with an approximately four-hundred-year gap in Jewish history (between Malachi and John the Baptist) when no prophecy is recorded and when the Lord gave stewardship to no recognized prophets upon the earth. Substantiating this claim, we find that at the time of the rededication of the temple by Judas Maccabeus in the early second century B.C., there was a question about what to do with the altar that had been polluted by the sacrifice of swine's flesh. The decision was made to build a new altar. We read that they "laid up the stones in the mountain of the temple in a convenient place, until there should come a prophet to show what should be done with them" (1 Maccabees 4:46).[75]

Without living prophets, *even though they had the prior written law,* they did not have the revealed knowledge of what to do with the defiled altar. Israel had never encountered the problem of a polluted sacrifice, and there was nothing in the law directing them what the Lord would have them do. This passage furnishes poignant evidence of the need for living prophets *in addition* to the written word of God.

In reaction to events immediately following the death of Judas Maccabaeus, we read: "So was there a great affliction in Israel, the like whereof was not since the time that a prophet was not seen among them" (1 Maccabees 9:27).[76] Consistent with this picture is the fracturing of the Jewish religion, in which, without prophets to guide the Jews as in the past, they drifted toward rabbinical philosophizing, human interpretations, and doctrinal speculation rather than reliance on Israel's prophets. While it is difficult to imagine significant differences between Israel under its righteous kings versus its wicked ones, nonetheless, when prophets were present, Israel remained a single religion; without them, they split into several belief systems, all varying in their theological views, worship patterns, and lifestyle practices.[77] As it entered into the meridian of time, Israel was in general apostasy.

Early Witnesses Linking Patriarchal Dispensations with the Mission of Christ

Early Christianity understood the various dispensations and recognized that the gospel itself was not new. The Apostolic Father Ignatius, bishop of Antioch, testified in approximately A.D. 108: "For the divine prophets [referring to the ancient Patriarchs and prophets of old] lived according to Jesus Christ. Therefore they were also persecuted, being inspired by his grace, to convince the disobedient that there is one God, who manifested himself through Jesus Christ his son."[78]

Justin Martyr is also a dependable

witness regarding God continuing His covenant through Christianity's dispensations: "For the prophetical gifts remain with us, even to the present time. And hence *you ought to understand that [the gifts] formerly among your nation* [ancient Israel] *have been transferred to us.*"[79] Justin understood the apostasy of the Jews and used the loss of living prophets to reason that the prophetic gifts had been transferred to those who followed Christ in fulfillment of Jewish prophecy. From Justin's exposition Dialogue with Trypho the Jew, we learn a great deal about the relationship between the patriarchal dispensations and the apostolic dispensation. From Justin's knowledge and perspective, Israel's prophets taught of Christ, knew of Christ, and looked forward to His coming. Justin believed that because of disobedience, prophets were withdrawn from among the people; thus the Jews became limited in the knowledge of Christ, misunderstanding or not recognizing *even those revelations previously granted them.*

Irenaeus testified of four principal dispensations: first, the dispensation under Adam; second, the dispensation under Noah; third, the dispensation under Moses; and fourth, the dispensation under Jesus Christ and the apostles. Why Abraham was excluded from Irenaeus's list, given the explicit scriptural documentation in Genesis, is unclear. However, that Enoch was overlooked is more understandable, inasmuch as Irenaeus was a contemporary of the philosophers of the Alexandrian (Eygpt) School in the late second century who weakened the value of the Enoch texts to future Christianity. Nevertheless, Irenaeus's witness lends crucial support to Justin Martyr's position that God's covenant has always been present since the fall of Adam.[80] Specifically, Irenaeus taught:

But if Christ did then [only] begin to have existence when He came [into the

world] as man, and [if] the Father did remember [only] in the times of Tiberius Caesar to provide for [the wants of] men, and His Word was shown to have not always coexisted with His creatures; [it may be remarked that] neither then was it necessary that another God should be proclaimed.[81] For it was not merely for those who believed on Him in the time of Tiberius Caesar that Christ came, nor did the Father exercise His providence for the men only who are now alive, but for all men altogether, who from the beginning, according to their capacity, in their generation have both feared and loved God, and practiced justice and piety towards their neighbors, and have earnestly desired to see Christ, and to hear His voice.[82]

As Justin and Irenaeus testify, Jesus came not to introduce a new gospel but to restore the gospel *in its purity as it had previously existed* and to fulfill the law of Moses.

Eusebius, the widely regarded early fourth-century Church historian and bishop wrote:

Should any one, beginning from Abraham, and going back to the first man, pronounce those who have had the testimony of righteousness, Christians in fact, though not in name, he would not be far from the truth. . . . They obviously knew the Christ of God, as he appeared to Abraham, communed with Isaac, spoke to Jacob; and that he communed with Moses and the prophets after him. . . . Whence it is evident that the religion delivered to us in the doctrine of Christ is not a new nor a strange doctrine; but if the truth must be spoken, *it is the first and only true religion.*[83]

Eusebius's testimony is particularly powerful because he summarizes in unambiguous language that Christianity, or "the religion delivered to us in the doctrine of Christ," was neither new nor unfamiliar. Christianity was the first (beginning with Adam) and only true religion.

We also have the compelling witness of Athanasias, the venerated fourth-century bishop who is credited by some scholars with closing the New Testament canon. He testified that the tradition of the *perennial gospel* was known to the early Church and explained that the gospel was not new but had been preached by and known to Adam, Abel, Enoch, Noah, Abraham, and Moses, *before the time of Christ*.[84] Pico della Mirandola, when translating an apocryphal manuscript of Ezra, related with astonishment, "I see in it (as God is my witness) the religion not so much of Moses as of Christ!"[85]

The witness of the prophets of old, the witness of the New Testament, the witness of the early Church Fathers, and the growing evidence furnished by recent, reliable manuscript discoveries testify that Christianity existed anciently from the days of Adam and Eve.

Unfortunately, although God has continued to reveal Himself to man throughout the ages, apostasy has also accompanied every dispensation. Irenaeus, when writing about the Apocalypse of the book of Revelation, attempts to explain the number of the beast, 666, and draws on various passages of scripture to explain how this number came about. He refers to the 600 years of Noah's life until the time of the Flood, then the 60 cubits height of Nebuchadnezzar's statue and its 6 cubits breadth, which Daniel's friends Hananiah, Azariah, and Mishael (better known as Shadrach, Meshach, and Abed-nego) refused to worship. He then writes:

> Thus, then, the six hundred years of Noah, in whose time the deluge occurred *because of the apostasy*, and the number of the cubits of the image for which these just men were sent into the fiery furnace, do indicate the number of the name of that man in whom is concentrated *the whole apostasy of six thousand years*, and unrighteousness, and wickedness, and false prophecy, and deception; for which things' sake a cataclysm of fire shall also come [upon the earth].[86]

Continuing, Irenaeus explains in the very next chapter that the number 666, "indicates *the recapitulations of that apostasy*, taken in its full extent, which occurred at the beginning, during the intermediate periods, and which shall take place at the end."[87] Irenaeus believed the Flood occurred because of apostasy and that "the recapitulations of that apostasy" occurred periodically thereafter and will again at the end. In other words, Irenaeus supports the claim of recurring apostasy throughout the patriarchal dispensations and the idea that it would take place again.

Conclusion

Like any loving parent, God the Father communicated with His son Adam and daughter Eve after they disobeyed Him and ate the forbidden fruit. Although the Bible is not specific on God's detailed communication, many other authentic writings, *which we do have*, furnish evidence that God revealed to Adam and Eve the laws and conditions pertaining to man's future redemption. The fall of man effected a physical separation from God's direct presence and, although the Bible gives us little to work from, many other inspired writings testify that He established an "everlasting covenant" with Adam. In addition to certain laws designed to make men happy and to become clean and pure again, Adam and Eve also received a commandment to perform animal sacrifice, foreshadowing the holy offering of God's Son to atone for the sins of mankind. Adam and his posterity were given agency to accept or reject God's counsel, either to choose eternal life and liberty through obedience, or death and captivity by Satan.

As Adam's offspring rejected the covenants and commandments God gave them, Old Testament scripture affirms the renewal of priesthood authority and the subsequent reestablishment of His covenant through other righteous sons (Enoch, Noah, and Abraham). Because they received revelation, these men were known as prophets, and God endowed them with power and authority to act in His name. After the Flood, those in total apostasy were responsible for the rise of pagan religions, completely perverting the rites and ordinances belonging to salvation and the pure doctrines taught by God. Even the chosen lineage of Israel developed serious problems when they rejected God's covenant and the teachings of the prophets; to the extent that it repudiated God's counsel, the people suffered both temporally and spiritually. When considering the subject of *apostasy*, it is evident that some righteous individuals continue to exist side by side with the majority of the wicked, and the just are saved by God's grace, according to their righteous desires, including a comprehensive plan that takes into consideration such environmental circumstances. History indicates that apostasy results in God withdrawing His power, authority, and prophets when mankind turns his back on Deity and alters or counterfeits His ordinances and teachings.

Notes

1. Carl Ludwig Wilibald Grimm, *Thayer's Greek-English Lexicon of the New Testament*, trans. Joseph H. Thayer (Milford, Mich.: Mott Media, 1982), ref. no. 646, 67.

2. James Strong, *The Strongest Strong's Exhaustive Concordance of the Bible*, ed. John R. Kohlenberger III and James A. Swanson (Grand Rapids, Mich.: Zondervan, 2001), ref. no. 646, 584.

3. *Apo*, ref. no. 575, and *stasis*, ref. no. 2476, in Strong, *Strongest Strong's Exhaustive Concordance*, 1481, 1505.

4. Although examples of apostasy are replete throughout the Old Testament period, the following noteworthy episodes (during the Mosaic dispensation), in the form of Israel rejecting God's covenant, are particularly striking: after Joshua (Judges 2:11–12, 20); Jeroboam (1 Kings 12:28–33); Ahab and Jezebel (1 Kings 19:14). Finally, the wickedness of Ahaz was so complete that he sacrificed his own son, constructed a new altar, destroyed the brasen sea, and changed the order of the sacrifice. Accordingly, God chose this moment to scatter Israel and subject it to the rule of heathen nations (2 Kings 16:1–4, 10–17).

5. The Old Testament, as described in note 4 above, is replete with evidence that the major element in apostasy was rejecting God's prophet and His counsel that came through prophets. In the New Testament, the same pattern is seen in the rejection of the counsel and authority of the apostles, specifically as witnessed with Paul, Peter, Jude, and John in Revelation. Another precise example is the sedition of the Corinthian church in A.D. 96 (see page 121).

6. See Judges 3:8; 10:7; 13:1; 1 Kings 11:6–11; 14:15; 2 Kings 15:37; 17:23; 24:1–2.

7. From the first commandment, "Thou shalt have no other gods before me" (Exodus 20:3), we can deduce that Israel fell into the worship of Egypt's gods while they lived in Goshen, "put away the gods which your fathers served . . . in Egypt" (Joshua 24:14), just as they did later at Sinai and after the Lord established them in Caanan (Judges 2:11–12).

8. See ch. 2, note 4, to review the extensive evidence of Israel counterfeiting sacred rites. When Josiah reigned in righteousness, a book of

the law was found by the priest Hilkiah, which, in concert with revelation (see v. 21), was used to restore temple worship and sacrifice (2 Chronicles 34:14, 19, 21).

9. Attesting to the early Christian belief in baptism prior to John the Baptist: Apocalypse of Adam 8:17 in Charlesworth, *Old Testament Pseudepigrapha,* 1:719; Life of Adam and Eve 37:3–6, in Charlesworth, *Old Testament Pseudepigrapha,* 2:287–89. For evidence of early perversions of doctrines and rites: Charlesworth, *Old Testament Pseudepigrapha,* 1:718; Enoch 99:2 in Charlesworth, *Old Testament Pseudepigrapha,* 1:79; Secrets of Enoch 22, in Andre Vaillant, ed., *Le livre des secrets d'Henoch* (Paris: Institut d'études Slaves, 1952), 72; see also Joshua 24:14: "Put away the gods which your fathers served on the other side of the flood." That the ordinance of baptism would later degenerate even further than "a baptism of filthy water" to baptism in a bull's blood is indicated by independent historical accounts. Satan is not the great inventor but rather the great copier, the great imitator, and the great deceiver. As the early Christian writings Pseudepigrapha and Dead Sea Scrolls indicate, baptism probably did exist at various times during the patriarchal dispensations. Satan inspired those who followed him to replace genuine rites with corrupt counterfeits.

10. See ch. 2, note 2; cf. 1 Kings 18. Elijah destroys the prophets of Baal; Jeremiah 7.

11. Although the Bible does not state this fact explicitly, it is implicit because God now no longer spoke directly to Adam but still needed to communicate His desires for Adam and Eve and their posterity. Although the Bible is not definitive in this matter, the Pseudepigrapha is. The "Conflict of Adam and Eve with Satan" clearly describes how the word of God and angels revealed God's plan for the redemption of Adam's seed. See Rutherford Platt, ed., *The Forgotten Books of Eden* (New York: Alpha House, 1927).

12. Apocalypse of Adam 8.9–11, 17 in Charlesworth, *Old Testament Pseudepigrapha,* 1:718–19.

13. "Conflict of Adam and Eve with Satan" 7, 10, in Platt, *Forgotten Books of Eden,* 8, 10.

14. "Conflict of Adam and Eve with Satan" 14, 42, in Platt, *Forgotten Books of Eden,* 13, 28.

15. "Conflict of Adam and Eve with Satan" 49, in Platt, *Forgotten Books of Eden,* 33.

16. Testament of Adam 3.1–4, in Charlesworth, *Old Testament Pseudepigrapha,* 1:994. The interpretation of "the Messiah" comes from the translation furnished by Stephen E. Robinson, *The Testament of Adam,* SBL Dissertation Series 52 (Chico, Calif.: Scholars Press, 1982), 75.

17. "Conflict of Adam and Eve with Satan" 26:18–19, in *Forgotten Books of Eden,* 18.

18. "Conflict of Adam and Eve with Satan" 68–69, in Platt, *Forgotten Books of Eden,* 47–49; see also 23; 25:8.

19. Secrets of Enoch 47, in Platt, *Forgotten Books of Eden,* 97–98.

20. Nibley, *Enoch the Prophet,* 178.

21. Justin Martyr (A.D. 155), Irenaeus (A.D. 180), Clement of Alexandria (A.D. 185) and many other early Christian authors have written on the subject of free will, which I cite in ch. 6, under "The Foreordination of Jesus Christ, the Prophets, and All Mankind," and in ch. 7, under "Speculative Doctrines of Augustine."

22. 2 Enoch 30:12–15, in Charlesworth, *Old Testament Pseudepigrapha,* 1:152.

23. Epistle of the Apostles 39, in Schneemelcher, *New Testament Apocrypha,* 1:271; parentheses in original.

24. Apocalypse of Adam 8:17, in Charlesworth, *Old Testament Pseudepigrapha,* 1:719; brackets in original.

25. Justin Martyr, First Apology, in *Ancient Christian Writers,* trans. Leslie William Barnard (Mahwah, N. J.: Paulist Press, 1997), 66; emphasis added.

26. Hippolytus, Discourse on the Holy Theophany 10, in *Ante-Nicene Fathers,* 5:237.

27. Hershel Shanks, ed., *Understanding the Dead Sea Scrolls* (New York: Random House, 1992), 107.

28. From the documentation presented in the "Conflict of Adam and Eve with Satan," animal sacrifice was introduced with Adam and Eve. The Bible itself is clear that animal sacrifice was practiced by Noah (Genesis 8:20) and was common in Abraham's day (Genesis 22:13) with the offering of animals such as sheep, goats, and

rams performed in similitude of the future sacrifice of the unblemished Lamb of God (Jesus)
who would atone for the sins of the world. Adam
and his descendants practiced this law looking forward to the future sacrifice of Jesus; they
knew of Jesus' coming atonement and the plan
of redemption. The pagan forms of baptism were
surely borrowed from and perverted by those who
apostatized from the original truths communicated to Adam. Although the law of Moses had
unique requirements due to Israel's rebellion, the
basic plan of redemption, together with each of
its conditions, has been the same from the beginning. Moreover, the writings recovered from the
break-off Essene movement at Qumran attest pre-
Christian baptism and may have been revealed to
the "teacher of righteousness" who founded this
sect. Apostasy, as recorded during the Mosaic dispensation, has been the cause of the loss of, or the
perversion of, sacred writings since the beginning
as confirmed by Justin Martyr's documentation
of the Jews altering the manuscripts of the Old
Testament. This is the manner in which the loss
of pure doctrines and ordinances such as baptism
occurred. See Dialogue with Trypho 72–73; cf.
Ehrman, *Orthodox Corruption of Scripture,* 3–47.

29. Augustine, Against Palagiens 7, in *Nicene
and Post-Nicene Fathers,* 2:5:419; cf. Augustine,
On the Merits and Forgiveness of Sins, and on
the Baptism of Infants 3.19.

30. Fillion, La Sainte Bible, Comment'ee,
8:46.

31. Apocalypse of Paul 29, 30, in Schneemelcher, *New Testament Apocrypha,* 2:728–29.

32. Although the use of the term "original
guilt" in connection with Gnostic groups is an
oversimplification (the Gnostics believing that all
materiality is evil and thus that birth is a result of
Adam's having been created by the demiurge, or
evil god), nonetheless, the Gnostic idea of physical
matter being evil, in tandem with similar beliefs
held by the Greek philosophers, clearly influenced
Christian doctrine.

33. Pastor of Hermas, sim. 9, 29, in *Ante-
Nicene Fathers,* 2:53.

34. Irenaeus, "Against Heresies" 3.23.3–23.5,
in *Ante-Nicene Fathers,* 1:456–57.

35. Clement of Alexandria, Stromateis 3.16,

trans. J. Ferguson (Washington, D.C.: Catholic
University of America Press, 1991), FC 85:319.

36. Cyril of Jerusalem, Catechetical Lectures
4.19, in *Nicene and Post-Nicene Fathers,* 2:7:23;
emphasis added.

37. Kelly, *Early Christian Doctrines,* 355–56.

38. Apocryphon of John 29:22–35; 30:1–12,
in James M. Robinson, ed., *The Nag Hammadi
Library in English* (Leiden: E. J. Brill, 1988),
121–22.

39. Apocalypse of Adam 8.10–11, in Charlesworth, *Old Testament Pseudepigrapha,* 1:718.

40. 1 Enoch 99:2; cf. Odes of Solomon 38:9–
15, in Charlesworth, *Old Testament Pseudepigrapha,* 2:767; Nibley, *Enoch the Prophet,* 72; see also
note 2.

41. 1 Enoch 14:24, in Charlesworth, *Old Testament Pseudepigrapha,* 1:21.

42. Book of Adam 1:165, in *Dictionaire des
Apocryphes,* 2 vols. (Paris, 1856).

43. *Bet ha-Midrash* 4:129–31, 6 vols. (Jerusalem: Wahrmann Books, 1967), in Nibley, *Enoch
the Prophet,* 251.

44. 1 Enoch 6–9 chronicles wickedness; ch.
10 discusses the Flood, in Charlesworth, *Old Testament Pseudepigrapha,* 1:15–17.

45. 1 Enoch 14, in Charlesworth, *Old Testament Pseudepigrapha,* 1:21.

46. 1 Enoch 15, in Charlesworth, *Old Testament Pseudepigrapha,* 1:21.

47. 1 Enoch 39:12–14; 40:1, in Charlesworth,
Old Testament Pseudepigrapha, 1:31–32.

48. 1 Enoch 41, in Charlesworth, *Old Testament Pseudepigrapha,* 1:32.

49. 1 Enoch 43; 59; 72–80, in Charlesworth,
Old Testament Pseudepigrapha, 1:33, 40, 50–59.

50. 1 Enoch 54:7–10, 65–66, in Charlesworth,
Old Testament Pseudepigrapha, 1:38, 45–46.

51. 1 Enoch 56:5–8; 57, in Charlesworth, *Old
Testament Pseudepigrapha,* 1:39.

52. 1 Enoch 46; 48; 90, in Charlesworth, *Old
Testament Pseudepigrapha,* 1:34, 35, 69–72.

53. 1 Enoch 51; 55–56, 100, in Charlesworth,
Old Testament Pseudepigrapha, 1:36–37; 38–39;
81–82.

54. 2 Baruch 20:1–3, in Charlesworth, *Old
Testament Pseudepigrapha,* 1:627; cf. 1 Enoch 70,
in Charlesworth, *Old Testament Pseudepigrapha,*

1:49; Genesis 5:24; Hebrews 11:5.

55. Nibley, Enoch the Prophet, 180.

56. Hippolytus, Treatise on Christ and Antichrist, in *Ante-Nicene Fathers*, 5:6:206. See Ethiopic Apocalypse of Peter, in Schneemelcher, *New Testament Apocrypha*, 2:626, which states that Enoch and Elias would be sent to warn of such deceit in the last days.

57. Mathew Black, *Apocalyptus Henochi Graece* (Leiden: E. J. Brill, 1970), 23–24, in Nibley, *Enoch the Prophet*, 181; emphasis added.

58. "Life of Enoch," in *Bet ha-Midrash* 4:130; *The Zohar,* Bereshith 56b, in Nibley, *Enoch the Prophet*, 266; cf. Genesis 7:23.

59. Books of Enoch, Frag. 5, col. 11 (= 1 Enoch 106:13–107:2), vv. 16–27, in Florentino Martinez, *The Dead Sea Scrolls Translated* (Leiden: E. J. Brill, 1996), 254. All brackets and text reproduced as printed in the translation, excepting [Jared], Enoch's father.

60. 1 Enoch 67, in Charlesworth, *Old Testament Pseudepigrapha*, 1:46; parentheses in original.

61. Genesis 12:1–2, 14:18–20; Hebrews 7.

62. Genesis Apocryphon, Col. 22, vv. 13–17, in Martinez, *Dead Sea Scrolls Translated*, 236; parentheses in original.

63. Genesis Aprocryphon, Cols. 21–22, in Martinez, *Dead Sea Scrolls Translated*, 235–36.

64. Apocalypse of Abraham 7:11, in Charlesworth, *Old Testament Pseudepigrapha*, 1:692.

65. Apocalypse of Abraham 8:1–4, in Charlesworth, *Old Testament Pseudepigrapha*, 1:693; emphasis added.

66. Apocalypse of Abraham 9:6–7, in Charlesworth, *Old Testament Pseudepigrapha*, 1:693.

67. Apocalypse of Abraham 17:20–21, in Charlesworth, *Old Testament Pseudepigrapha*, 1:696.

68. Apocalypse of Abraham 20:1–4, in Charlesworth, *Old Testament Pseudepigrapha*, 1:699.

69. Apocalypse of Abraham 20:5, in Charlesworth, *Old Testament Pseudepigrapha*, 1:699.

70. Testament of Abraham 8:5–8, in Charlesworth, *Old Testament Pseudepigrapha*, 1:886; emphasis added.

71. Apocalypse of Abraham 25:4, in Charlesworth, *Old Testament Pseudepigrapha*, 1:702.

72. Exodus 3:1–10 details Moses' prophetic call; Exodus 12:40–41 places Israel's "sojourn" in Egypt at 430 years; and Acts 7:6 states Israel's "bondage" was 400 years. Early Jewish tradition supported by some external evidence indicates actual captivity at about 210 years. See Pirqe de Rabbi Eliezer 48; Midrash Rabbah Exodus 18:11; Jasher 81:3–4. The 400–year figure probably dates back to Abraham.

73. Epistle of Barnabas 14, in *Apostolic Fathers*, 1:391; emphasis added.

74. John Bright, *A History of Israel*, 3d ed. (Philadelphia: Westminster Press, 1981), 465–73.

75. *The Apocrypha KJV* (Iowa Falls, Iowa: World Bible Publishers), 147.

76. *Apocrypha KJV,* 156.

77. Bright, *History of Israel*, 460–63, discusses the splintering of Jewish theology and the emergence of sectarian offshoots.

78. Ignatius to the Magnesians 8, in Bright, *History of Israel*, 205; brackets added.

79. Justin Martyr, Dialogue with Trypho 82, in *Ante-Nicene Fathers*, 1:240; emphasis and second bracket added.

80. Irenaeus, "Against Heresies" 3.11.8, in Robert M. Grant, *Irenaeus of Lyons* (New York: Routledge, 1997), 132.

81. Irenaeus, "Against Heresies" 4.6.2, in *Ante-Nicene Fathers*, 1:468; brackets in original.

82. Irenaeus, "Against Heresies" 4.22.2, *Ante-Nicene Fathers*, 1:494.

83. Eusebius, *Ecclesiastical History* (Grand Rapids, Mich.: Baker Books, 1995), 1:26–28; emphasis added.

84. Athanasius, De Decretis Nicaena Synodi 5, in J. P. Migne, *Petrologiae Graecae* 25:424, (Paris, 1857), discussing 1 John 2:7.

85. Schmidt, *Book of Enoch*, 46–47, in Nibley, *Enoch the Prophet*, 153.

86. Irenaeus, "Against Heresies" 29.2, in *Ante-Nicene Fathers*, 1:558.

87. Irenaeus, "Against Heresies" 30.1, in *Ante-Nicene Fathers*, 1:558.

CHAPTER THREE

THE APOSTOLIC DISPENSATION

Thou art Peter, and upon this rock I shall build my church; and the gates
of hell shall not prevail against it. And I will give unto thee the keys of the
kingdom of heaven: and whatsoever thou shalt bind on earth
shall be bound in heaven: and whatsoever thou shalt loose
on earth shall be loosed in heaven.

—Matthew 16:18–19

The fifth dispensation, headed by the prophet Moses, was unique for at least one reason: the Lord extended to Moses and the children of Israel the full authority and organization of His "household" on earth but then withdrew a portion of both. As a result, the rites and teachings of the law of Moses were intended to be not only a preparation for the coming of Jesus Christ but also for the return of the full authority and Church structure that would accompany His coming.

To some extent the reduction worked. Certain elements of the Mosaic law were still firmly embedded in Jewish culture and religious practice when the Son of God was born in Bethlehem. Animal sacrifice was practiced at the temple, many citizens of the culture believed in God and in a coming Messiah, and religious leaders appeared to teach the word of God as contained in their written scriptures, at least as they understood those scriptures.

There were, however, two significant problems: (1) there had been no prophets in the Old Testament world for approximately four hundred years before Jesus Christ's birth, and (2) the doctrines had become so muddled that when the Messiah came as prophesied, few recognized the signs, the Prophesied One Himself, or the significance of the event.

The prophets of each dispensation leading up to the apostolic period had looked forward to the coming of Christ. They had built altars to the Lord and had given thanks by offering unblemished sacrificial lambs (Deuteronomy 15:19–21). They understood the fall of Adam and the need for the Son of God to redeem mankind. Certain Old Testament prophets, such as Job, Isaiah, Ezekiel, Daniel, and Zechariah, had prophesied of the Messiah and His coming ministry in the meridian of time.[1] Thus, centuries later in fulfilment of those early prophecies, the Apostle Paul was able to testify that "when the fulness of the time was come, God sent forth his Son" (Galatians 4:4).

The opening of the sixth major dispensation of the gospel, the apostolic dispensation, was an event of incredible importance, the moment to which all of the previous dispensations had looked and of which the Old Testament prophets had spoken. The household of God was to be reestablished by none other than God's Only Begotten Son. But to establish that household, Jesus Christ would have to also fulfill and thus complete the need for the Mosaic law. This establishment took place through three world-changing events:

1. *The Atonement:* By this act, principally accomplished in the Garden of Gethsemane where "his sweat was as it were great drops of blood falling down to the ground" (Luke 22:44) so intense was his suffering, Jesus enabled all mankind to repent of their sins, thus allowing the laws of divine justice and mercy to coexist. It also empowered the earthly kingdom to truly act as a preparation ground or precursor to life in the Father's heavenly kingdom, through the grace of Jesus Christ and the faith of individual followers, for without the Atonement no one could hope to become clean enough to regain the presence of God and His angels in the heavens above.

2. *The fulfillment of the Mosaic law through the voluntary sacrifice of the Savior's life for all humanity:* Jesus' divine commission granted Him the higher authority that had been removed from the children of Israel, which authority He passed on to His apostles. His teachings restored the higher doctrine that had been written on the first set of stone tablets, which Moses had destroyed in anger. And now, with this final, supernal sacrificial rite of offering Himself, He fulfilled the need for animal sacrifice, which had been instituted for the sole purpose of reminding God's people of the coming sacrifice of the perfect Lamb of God. The purpose of the Mosaic law was thus fulfilled to every whit and could now be put completely to rest in favor of the wholly restored gospel plan.

3. *The Resurrection:* When Jesus Christ was resurrected in all His divine glory, He became the "firstfruits of them that slept" (1 Corinthians 15:20), thus effecting the holy resurrection for *all,* both the wicked and the righteous. Again, because physical death, and thus the grave, would no longer be the eternal resting place of all mankind, the earthly kingdom—with all its doctrine, rites, and living prophets—could truly act as a preparation for the Father's heavenly kingdom. Mortality had a purpose and a way out.

In addition to being a record of Christ's redeeming work, the New Testament provides us with a framework of tasks He accomplished before He would utter the words "It is finished" (John 19:30). This framework can be seen as paralleling the framework of the formal structure of the Church of God. At the age of about thirty, Christ began His mortal mission by being baptized (Matthew 3:15), undertaking a forty-day fast during which He received His official commission to begin his ministry (Matthew 4:2), and then developing a Church organization to assist Him in His saving work and to usher in the new dispensation. He called the Twelve Apostles and ordained them (John 15:16) to the work of the ministry, as well as other disciples who would assist in conducting the operations of the Church and carrying the gospel to the world (Luke 10:1). The Twelve Apostles were given special "keys," or authority (Matthew 18:18), that empowered them to administer the affairs of the Church and to carry on the work of the ministry when the Savior's mission was complete. In addition to bestowing the "keys of the kingdom" upon the apostles, Jesus prepared them by His example, His miracles, and His teaching the doctrines of salvation, including specific instructions to take the gospel to all the world. Jesus then promised the apostles He would send the Holy Spirit to be their comforter and guide (Acts 1:8).

As Jesus set about establishing His Church and its organization, the diversity of religious cultures existing at the time certainly influenced how receptive individuals and communities were to His message. God's chosen people, the Jews, were in a state of apostasy. Indeed, several Jewish factions had evolved over centuries of rejecting the prophets and replacing God's counsel with human wisdom. They were surrounded by a whole host of pagan religions, including some whose roots were buried deep in Greek intellectualism. Some of these pagan religions were supported by the Roman Empire that controlled regional politics. Fortunately, though somewhat ironically, given that ultimately the Savior's mortal life was brought to an end at the hands of Roman soldiers, His ministry occurred during what is known as the Pax Romana (Roman Peace), a two-hundred-year period beginning with Octavian (27 B.C.), when the Roman Empire was relatively free of internal strife and conflict, allowing the Savior to complete His mortal mission largely unrestrained by Roman interference.

Religions in the Meridian of Time

As mentioned, the Mediterranean world of this period included a strange mixture of cults coexisting quite peacefully among themselves. Various Jewish factions and other religious entities or communities had a significant impact on how Christian theology was accepted and interpreted as the gospel spread under the direction of Jesus' apostles. Understanding the religions of the time implies that we also understand something about the politics and government of the day, for religions often spread or died out as political boundaries changed and powerful rulers came and went.

The Roman Empire at this time extended from the Atlantic Ocean in the west to the Euphrates River in the east. It controlled the Greek cultural world around the Mediterranean, most of the Near East, present-day Italy, the recently conquered societies of western Europe, and also the Balkan states. Some of the more ancient religions worshiped gods who ruled the elements, nature, and fertility. Interspersed were the classic Greek gods and goddesses and their Roman counterparts, including Zeus (Jupiter), Hera (Juno), Poseidon (Neptune), and others. Greek philosophy, Stoicism, and astrology were also becoming increasingly popular among the ruling class, aristocrats, and intellectuals.[2]

Just before the birth of Christ, the old religions were in various stages of decay from long neglect. Local cultures whose gods had been unable to prevent Roman conquest questioned the effectiveness of their gods and began to look to the seemingly more powerful pagan gods of the conquering Romans. Greek intellectualism and philosophy also played a role in destroying some of these ancient religions by arguing against their "irrational" beliefs in multiple gods. In an effort to reinforce religion and the associated values and national benefits, Augustus (63 B.C.–A.D. 14) enshrined the old gods, made them symbols of the Empire, and revitalized temple worship, pagan priesthood, and religious ceremonies. Unfortunately, this increased attention included rites that not only made the emperor equal to God but actually assumed that the emperor was indeed a god, requiring the adoration and loyalty of his subjects.[3]

Other forms of worship also became prominent, filling the void created by the religious apathy previously mentioned. People wanted religion, and they reached out to whatever seemed both effective and practical. The worship of Isis and Serapis from Egypt, and also of Cybele, the great earth-mother goddess of Asia Minor, had reached Rome within the past two centuries. The latter had a strong following that persisted in some areas until the late fourth century. Mithraism from ancient Persia and India, characterized by a strong sense of self-denial, gained distinction among Roman army officers.

Interestingly, each of these religious orders included some form of belief in a savior-god or goddess. Baptism (usually in a bull's blood) and other ceremonies or rites that were required to achieve eternal life were also fairly typical.[4] Ironically for gentile converts, such forms of worship seem to have made acceptance of such rites as the genuine and legitimate sacrifice of Jesus Christ, baptism, and the sacrament of the Lord's supper easier to understand and accept (Hebrews 9:13–14).

Nestled among these divergent sects and philosophies existed a religion that the Romans poorly understood. By the time Augustus came to power, Jewish colonies were rooted in nearly every major city of importance within the realm. Given the empire's propensity to adopt religions that worshiped many gods, Roman leaders were challenged to comprehend a people who believed in what they felt was the one true God. Jews on the whole were peaceful, hardworking contributors to the stability of the Republic; however, because of their refusal to integrate into Roman society, the Jews residing in Palestine were viewed as fanatical and contentious. They were kept in check for many years by Herod the Great. Ten years after Herod's death in 4 B.C., the emperor placed Judea, Samaria, and Idumea directly under Roman rule, leaving the rest of Palestine to be governed by some of Herod's sons.

While the Jews in many places throughout the Roman Empire were well respected, the Jews of Palestine were resented by their neighbors because of their open disregard for Graeco-Roman customs and the peculiar practice of circumcision. Accordingly, Palestinian Jews looked upon other nations with contempt. Notwithstanding, the Jews were anything but united among themselves. The primary Jewish parties or sects included the Pharisees, Sadducees, Zealots, and Essenes. Other Jewish communities included the Nazarites, the Herodians, and the Galileans, each known for specific traditions and practices.

The most prominent Jewish sects were the Pharisees and Sadducees. The Pharisees believed in the premortal existence of spirits, life after death with reward or punishment, individual self-denial, the immortality of the soul, and the Resurrection. They sought to preserve the theocratic character and strict religious traditions of the Jews, including ceremonial purity and scribal customs of interpreting the law; and they resisted Hellenistic influences and Roman interference. The Sadducees, who were mainly priests, held firm roots in aristocratic families, were marked by their sharp denial of the Resurrection and, according to the early Church Fathers (Tertullian, Hippolytus, Origen, and Jerome), claimed all prophetic writings that addressed the subject were written long after Moses' time and thus lacked genuine authority; accordingly, they were well known for adherence only to the written law of Moses. The Jewish party known as the Zealots was a radical movement among the Pharisees that determined to resist Roman or foreign authority in Palestine.[5]

Modern historians believe that the Essenes were a relatively small group that formed communities who lived away from the main Jewish settlements and cities. The prevailing view usually places the Essenes in settlements along the western shores of the Dead Sea, although they certainly were not restricted to that small area. Josephus refers to Judas the Essene teaching in the temple at the time of Aristobulos (115–104 B.C.), Menahem who labored in the court of Herod the Great (37–4 B.C.), Simon the Essene, who prophesied at the close of Archaelaus's reign (4 B.C.–A.D. 6), and John the Essene, the governor of Zama during the war against Rome.[6]

For some time following their discovery, the Dead Sea Scrolls were thought to have been written specifically for the Essenes residing at Qumran. However, more recent scholarship indicates that the inhabitants of Qumran may not have been Essenes in the strict sense but were actually *a break off* of the Essene sect. A leading expert on the Dead Sea Scrolls, Florentino Martinez, asserts that a rift occurred among the Essenes over interpretations of temple ceremonies and that a minority of believers followed the "Teacher of Righteousness" into the desert, where they established a settlement at Qumran. Many now believe that the Dead Sea Scrolls were taken from existing libraries at Jerusalem and hidden together with papyri containing the

"rule of faith" and other documents written specifically for the Qumran covenanters just before they were all killed by the Romans in approximately A.D. 68.[7]

Characterized by their close-knit society, the Qumran Jews resembled the early Christians at Jerusalem in that they shared community property according to need and used their resources wisely. Although a recognized hierarchal order existed, they believed in the equality of man, rejecting slavery as being in conflict with principles taught by God. The Qumran Jews also participated in regular ceremonial washings associated with the wearing of white clothing and followed by a sacred meal in which only worthy members of the community could participate. This meal was similar to early Christianity's Eucharist:

> And when they shall prepare the table to dine or the new wine for drinking, the priest shall stretch out his hand as the first to bless the first fruits of the bread and of the new wine. . . . If one is found among them who has lied [or broken other rules of the community] he shall be excluded from the pure food.[8]

Although much is still unknown regarding the Essenes, they seem to have been devoted to strict obedience to the law of Moses before the Savior's sacrifice on the cross. Other practices are less certain. For example, from excavations unearthing only men's remains, early studies reported that full membership required celibacy. Recent findings, however, have established that men were simply buried separate from women and children. And nowhere does the "rule of faith" mention that celibacy was a requirement. Plainly, we have much yet to learn regarding the Essenes and the Qumran Jews.

In addition to groups of Jews with particular sets of beliefs, there were also other groups with distinctive customs that had little to do with religious principle or practice. For example, the Nazarites were Jews of any sect bound by a vow of abstinence from grape products, as well as abstinence from cutting hair during the term of the oath (Numbers 6). The Herodians were politically active, supporting the designs of Herod Antipas with hopes to maintain the status of the Jews, while the Galileans were characterized by the rabbis as "people of the land," an unflattering term used to denote non-Jews living in the land of Canaan. The Samaritans, neither Jew nor Gentile, were a separate society consisting of Israelites who had intermarried with Cuthaeans imported by the Assyrians.

Distinctions of the Apostolic Dispensation

The years leading up to the apostolic dispensation, ushered in by the Savior's birth, were similar to the beginnings of previous dispensations in that God's chosen people had distorted the truth; priesthood authority in general was confined to the Levitical order at best, thus rendering priestly authorities incapable of performing all ordinances necessary for salvation; and sin and error prevailed. The fruits of Judah's apostasy were manifest in the following ways: (1) Judah's scholarly scribes were more highly esteemed than the priesthood itself; (2) rabbinical oral teachings were valued as equal to written scripture; (3) ecclesiastical authority was mixed with secular authority insofar as Roman law allowed; (4) the temple ceremonies, although but slightly altered in form, had lost their sacred emphasis; and (5) Judah had lost the spirit of simple worship and of maintaining a close personal relationship with God. Such conditions were fulfillment of prophecies uttered long before that the time had come for Israel's Messiah

to fulfill His earthly mission. And we cannot forget that even though Judah was divided and in myopic apostasy, the people in general attempted to serve God.

The apostolic dispensation was unique among dispensations because, although the circumstances characterizing apostasy were basically the same, the meridian of time was unquestionably reserved for the Son of God to reveal His gospel plan anew in the flesh. The Dead Sea Scrolls, coupled with the Old Testament and recorded Jewish history, indicate varying views of messianic prophecy. Some Jews expected a Messiah who would suffer and die. Most Jews in Palestine envisioned a warrior-type Savior who would free them from the shackles of imperial control. This preconceived notion blinded them from comprehending Christ's simple message of salvation from sin and death and the re-establishment of His Church. They failed to understand that the "great and dreadful day of the Lord," the warrior personality whom they anticipated, was reserved to come near the end of the world.[9] Israel had apostatized from truth, having "gone away from the ordinances" and "killed the prophets,"[10] and having failed to perceive that the long-awaited Messiah had actually come.

Jesus Christ came to fulfill the law of Moses. Under the old law, animal sacrifice was performed with an eye looking toward the ultimate sacrifice of the Son of God. During Passover, the lambs used in such sacrifices were always the unblemished first-born (Deuteronomy 15:19–21), just as Jesus was the firstborn of the Father, both in spirit (Colossians 1:15) and in body (Luke 1:35), and His unblemished life qualified Him for the infinite atonement He would make for mankind.

Despite compelling witnesses and remarkable miracles, Israel rebelled against

God during the Mosaic dispensation, as manifested by its worship of the golden calf. Accordingly, the higher order of priesthood—*the Priesthood after the order of Melchizedek*—was withheld from Israel. In its place, they were left with the *lesser law,* or *Levitical order,* through the tribe of Levi. Without the presence of the Melchizedek Priesthood, men could not partake of the fullness of the gospel as they had in previous dispensations. In addition to Christ's redemptive work, part of the Savior's mission included restoring this authority and establishing His Church. The purpose of the Church organization was to provide the structure necessary to (1) perform the ordinances and rites essential for salvation, (2) teach the doctrines of the kingdom and the principles of the gospel by which His followers were to conduct their lives, and (3) strengthen and sanctify the saints so they might bless one another and help each other endure to the end.

The Savior's Authority, or "Keys," and System of Church Government

The concept of "keys," or God's authority to act in His name, is probably as old as Adam. In the Old Testament, Isaiah prophesied messianically: "And the key of the house of David will I lay upon his shoulder; so he shall open, and none shall shut; and he shall shut, and none shall open" (Isaiah 22:22; cf. Matthew 16:19). The Old Testament established a pattern of patriarchal succession and God's authority to act in His name, including the prophetic office that passed from Adam to Noah and Abraham to Ephraim. Similarly, when Moses completed his earthly mission, Joshua was called to replace him. In Deuteronomy we read:

"And Joshua the son of Nun was full of the spirit of wisdom; for Moses had *laid his hands upon him:* and the children of Israel hearkened unto him, and did as the Lord commanded Moses" (Deuteronomy 34:9; emphasis added; see also Numbers 27:18–23). The same type of succession can also be seen in the transfer of God's authority from Elijah to Elisha (2 Kings 3:13–15). Just as Isaiah foretold the coming of Christ and the "keys" of Christ's power to "open and shut," Peter was appointed to lead the Church after Christ's ascension, as evidenced by (1) the Savior's promising to give Peter the "*keys of the kingdom*" near Mount Hermon at Caesarea Philippi, (2) Peter's participation with Jesus at the Mount of Transfiguration, and (3) Peter's taking charge of the Church during his sermon at the Day of Pentecost and thereafter until his martyrdom.

The New Testament details the calling of the Twelve Apostles to administer the operations of the Church, to perform priesthood ordinances such as baptism, and to preach the gospel to the world; it also records the calling of others to assume specific responsibilities of service within the Church. The scriptures are clear that conferral of priesthood authority preceded actual ecclesiastical service. Such authority was given by one who already possessed the priesthood, and the ordination was performed according to the methods established by the Savior Himself. Such calls to serve were divinely inspired: for example, Jesus sought guidance from His Father and then taught His apostles that *He* had chosen them (John 15:16). Notice that it was not a matter of the apostles seeking the authority of Christ. The New Testament also emphasizes the importance of a higher priesthood, the priesthood *after the order of Melchizedek,* the same held by Jesus and later transferred to the apostles (Hebrews 7:11). Finally, the pattern established in the Old Testament and

(Philippians 2:10–11) and until all are unified in one faith in Jesus Christ. All will not be unified in Christ nor come to a knowledge of Him until the Savior returns in His glorious second coming. Paul explained why the Church organization and hierarchy was important: "That we henceforth be no more children, tossed to and fro, and carried about with every wind of doctrine, by the sleight of men, and cunning craftiness, whereby they lie in wait to deceive" (Ephesians 4:14).

Paul used an effective image to make his point when he stated that children change their minds from one minute to the next and that many ways exist in which mortal man can be beguiled by the father of lies. These passages explain that *having such offices as the apostles and prophets to identify false doctrine* are necessary to help men judge between truth and error and to keep them on the straight and narrow path that leads to eternal life.

As mentioned, apostles and prophets were not the only offices operating in the Church organized by Christ. We learn of deacons (Philippians 1:1; 1 Timothy 3:8), teachers (Ephesians 4:11; 1 Corinthians 12:28–29), elders (Acts 14:23; 15:6; Titus 1:5; James 5:14), seventies (Luke 10:1), and high priests (Hebrews 3:1; 5:1, 8–10; 8:3). The role of a bishop (1 Timothy 3:1–13; Titus 1:5–9) is also detailed as a divinely appointed priesthood office.[12]

Paul's teachings to the Corinthians established the significance of ranked priesthood offices (a leadership hierarchy), the gifts of the Spirit, and the importance of each member providing service to the Church. He compares the Church with the human body, explaining, "For as the body is one, and hath many members, and all the members of that one body, being many, are one body: so also is Christ. . . . And the eye cannot say unto the hand, I have no need of thee: nor again the head to the feet, I have no need of you. . . . That there should be no schism in the body; but that all members should have the same care one for another. . . . And God hath set some in the church, first apostles, secondarily prophets, thirdly teachers, after that miracles, then gifts of healings."[13] The Savior and His apostles spoke clearly about how such calls to serve in the priesthood were authorized, how the calls were extended, and, finally, how these men were then ordained and empowered to act authoritatively in behalf of Jesus Christ. There was order in the Church and there was unity in its order, and the priesthood offices were designed to bless every follower of Jesus and lead all to Him.

The Necessity of Approved Priesthood Authority

Authority was not a new issue, even to apostate Israel. For example, why else would the chief priests and elders of the people pose to Jesus these questions: "*By what authority* doest thou these things? and *who gave thee this authority?*" (Matthew 21:23; emphasis added). The New Testament states that *Christ Himself* calls and gives such authority. One cannot simply be appointed or ordained to the ministry because one has righteous desires and a love for the Savior. Nor can one merely "*feel*" called to the ministry. Procedures and patterns were established by our Lord to avoid imposters and pretenders. Said Jesus: "Ye have not chosen me, *but I have chosen you, and ordained you*, that ye should go and bring forth fruit, and that your fruit should remain" (John 15:16; emphasis added).

Another New Testament reference confirms how the priesthood is given, by whom it is given, and under what circumstances: "And no man taketh this honour [Christ's high priesthood] unto himself, *but he that is called of God, as was Aaron*" (Hebrews 5:4; emphasis added).

Let us examine this verse more closely. The history of the Levitical Priesthood can be traced to Aaron through the Old Testament. The Levitical Priesthood during the Mosaic dispensation was reserved for those of the tribe of Levi. When Jesus Christ fulfilled the law of Moses, this tribal assignment was done away with, and all duly ordained male followers of Jesus Christ were authorized to act in the name of the Lord *in their respective callings.* For example, a presbyter (elder) had spiritual jurisdiction specific only to his assignment, and a bishop possessed spiritual jurisdiction over only his congregation. On the other hand, the apostles were given the "keys" of the kingdom over the entire Church with authority to bind on earth and have such actions bound in heaven (Matthew 16:19; 18:18).

The Old Testament records that Aaron received his authority in the following manner: "And *take thou unto thee Aaron thy brother,* and his sons with him, from among the children of Israel, *that he may minister unto me in the priest's office,* even Aaron, Nadab and Abihu, Eleazar and Ithamar, Aaron's sons" (Exodus 28:1; emphasis added). Moses received divine revelation from God, witnessing that He, God, was in control, that this was His Church, and that order and structure were part of His Church. Aaron was called by revelation from God to the Lord's recognized prophet, Moses.

The Old Testament also informs us regarding the manner in which God's authority was transferred to those whom He had called:

And thou shalt bring Aaron and his sons unto the door of the tabernacle of the congregation, and wash them with water. And thou shalt put upon Aaron the holy garments, and anoint him, and sanctify him; that he may minister unto me in the priest's office. And thou shalt bring his sons, and clothe them with coats: and thou shalt anoint them, *as thou didst anoint their father,* that they may minister unto me in the priest's office: for their anointing shall surely be *an everlasting priesthood throughout their generations.* Thus did Moses: according to all that the Lord commanded him, so did he. (Exodus 40:12–16; emphasis added)

This passage clarifies that Aaron and his sons were washed, anointed, and empowered to perform their priesthood responsibilities following the specific procedures revealed to Moses and performed at the express direction of the Lord.

The apostles were called by this same procedure. After spending all night in prayer to the Father, Jesus received revelation as to whom He should call as His apostles (Luke 6:12–13). These men were then ordained by Jesus Christ, probably *through the laying on of hands,* observing the Old Testament pattern, and those ordinations performed later in the New Testament were performed likewise. Matthew 10:1 documents that Jesus gave to the apostles authority and power to fulfill their divine callings. John 15:16 declares that the Savior "ordained" the apostles, meaning that he gave them authority to "legislate and set in order" the affairs of the kingdom. Finally, the examples of Stephen and his brethren (Acts 6:6) and Saul and Barnabas (Acts 13:3) demonstrate the method by which ordinations or authority was bestowed.

The apostles, after the Lord's ascension, continued this established pattern. The book of Acts records that the apostles prayed to God for direction and that the Holy Spirit revealed to them the calling of Mathias, who was then sustained by the common consent of the 120 others who were present and "numbered with the eleven apostles."[14] Following established policy, the apostles identified, selected, and ordained other Church officers, including Stephen, Saul, and Barnabas, under the inspiration of the Holy Ghost (Acts 6:6; 13:1–4). None of these men volunteered themselves as candidates or expressed interest in being called. They did not campaign nor jockey for position. The process used by the apostles duplicated the process used by Jesus, and the process used by Jesus was the same process revealed to Moses. This is the process:

1. God's *authorized and recognized* representative seeks revelation from God regarding whom He wants to call to serve.

2. God reveals the identity of the candidate to His *authorized and recognized* representative.

3. By virtue of the "keys" and responsibilities given him, God's authorized representative ordains the newly called servant. For example, Aaron and his sons were properly called and then *duly anointed or authorized by Moses, who held the keys and the authority of the Holy Priesthood* given him by God (Numbers 27:20, 23).

The Old Testament introduces the procedure by which God's servants are appointed; the New Testament reconfirms and validates the process.

Apostles Given Authority to Perpetuate the Savior's Church

The Savior conferred divine authority upon His apostles to administer the affairs of the Church. This authority and the hierarchy of the Church was intended to be *preserved beyond His mortal ministry*. The Savior promised to give the "keys of the kingdom" to Peter at Caesarea Philippi (Matthew 16:19); and in Matthew 17:1–8, Peter, James, and John joined the Savior on the Mount of Transfiguration. There, in one of the most sacred events recorded in holy writ, Moses and Elias [Elijah][15] appeared to Jesus and the three apostles closest to the Savior, implying that these three disciples of Christ were pre-eminent among the Lord's apostles because they were frequently alone with Jesus and were permitted to participate in extraordinary events. They were present when Jesus raised Jairus's daughter from the dead (Mark 5:22–24, 35–43). They witnessed the singular occasion of Jesus' transfiguration. So sacred was this experience that these apostles were forbidden to inform the others of the Twelve of this sublime event until after our Lord's resurrection (Matthew 17:9). Peter, James, and John alone were privileged to observe the central drama of all human history when they were taken to a garden place within Gethsemane and witnessed the agony of the Son of God as He took upon Himself the sins of the world (Mark 14:32–42).

The events at the Mount of Transfiguration occurred one week after the Lord promised to give Peter the keys of the kingdom of heaven; it may have been at that time that Peter, James, and John were given keys, authority, and instructions necessary to carry on the work of the kingdom when Christ's mortal ministry was complete. In Matthew 18:18, all the apostles had been given these keys. Before the Savior's ascension, the apostles were commissioned to preach the gospel to the world. Said Jesus, "Go ye into all the world, and preach the gospel to every creature. He that believeth and is baptized shall be saved" (Mark 16:15–16). The Savior had been systematically preparing the apostles for His departure by providing them with the keys, the authority, the organizational structure, and the guidance necessary for fulfilling the commandment of taking the gospel to the world. Thereafter, they would not be able to rely on Jesus directly, but through inspiration and revelation from the Holy Spirit, they would be expected to conduct the affairs of the Church (John 16:7–8; 20:21–22).

Paul established the prominence of the Twelve when he declared them to be the foundation of the Church, Jesus Christ Himself being the chief cornerstone (Ephesians 2:20; 1 Corinthians 12:28). When Judas betrayed Jesus and was removed from that sacred body, a replacement, as noted in scripture (Acts 1:20; Psalm 109:8), was necessary. The following account recorded in the book of Acts substantiates the importance of apostolic succession as the means of preserving the "foundation" of the Church:

> And in those days Peter stood up in the midst of the disciples, and said, (the number of names together were about an hundred and twenty,) Men and brethren, this scripture must needs have been fulfilled, which the Holy Ghost by the mouth of David spake before concerning Judas, which was guide to them that took Jesus. For he was numbered with us, and had obtained part of this ministry. . . . For it is written in the book of Psalms, Let his habitation be desolate, . . . and his bishoprick let another take. Wherefore of these men which have companied with us all the time that the Lord Jesus went in and out among us, beginning with the baptism of John, unto that same day that he was taken up from us, must one be ordained to be a witness with us of his resurrection. And they appointed two, Joseph called Barsabas, who was surnamed Justus, and Matthias. And they prayed, and said, Thou, Lord, which knowest the hearts of all men, shew whether of these two thou hast chosen, that they may take part of this minis-

try and apostleship by which Judas by transgression fell, that he might go to his own place. And they gave forth their lots; and the lot fell upon Matthias; and he was numbered with the eleven apostles. (Acts 1:16–26)

Some scholars, notably David Smith and G. Campbell Morgan, have questioned whether the calling of Mathias was inspired. They reason that the apostles moved ahead of the Holy Spirit, not receiving this gift until the day of Pentecost, an event that took place after the choosing of Mathias. They assert that Paul should have been chosen instead. Regarding this conjecture, Dr. William McBirnie has written, "We must reject this idea as unrealistic. Paul's conversion did not occur until a very long time after the date of Mathias' election, and Paul's ministry as an apostle was yet further removed in time. Paul had to endure years of obscurity in Tarsus after his conversion."[16] Not only is such a theory unrealistic, but it is also harmful to truth. If we cannot rely on the actions and testimony of the apostles, who just days earlier had concluded nearly six weeks with the risen Lord receiving instruction, how can we possibly depend on the philosophic speculations of modern writers two thousand years removed from this event?

Importantly, the calling of Mathias established a pattern consistent with that of the Old Testament. From Adam through Noah, Abraham through Ephraim, Moses to Joshua, Elijah to Elisha, Jesus to Peter and the apostles, and, finally, from the apostles to Mathias, the process of apostolic succession is documented and credible.

The pattern of God's procedure for apostolic succession gains greater confirmation when we consider how Barnabas and Saul (Paul) were apparently ordained as apostles by revelation and through the laying on of hands by the other apostles (Acts 13:2–3). Before this occasion, they had already been ordained elders, but from this moment on, Luke refers to them as apostles (Acts 14:4, 14). The death of James in approximately A.D. 44 created another vacancy (Acts 12:2), but the New Testament is silent on whether Paul specifically replaced James or if Barnabas or others, such as James the Lord's brother, were called to succeed him and other members of the original Twelve as the latter were killed. Paul told the Galatians that "other of the apostles saw I none, save James, the Lord's brother" (Galatians 1:19), suggesting that James also succeeded one of the original Twelve. Clarifying the meaning contained in the Galatians account, the earliest Church historian, Hegesippus, recorded, "But James the brother of the Lord . . . received the government of the church with the apostles."[17] John, in the book of Revelation, mentions that some pretended to be apostles (Revelation 2:2), thereby implying that others may have been duly called.

By the time of John's writing, all the original apostles were deceased, excepting himself, of course. In light of the Lord's established pattern, the apostleship was designed to be a continuous and indispensable element of the Church's highest leadership. In other words, if one apostle were to die or leave the body of the Twelve because of personal apostasy, the recognized apostolic leadership, by revelation, would appoint another worthy priesthood holder to succeed the deceased or fallen apostle. The Church, by common consent, would vote to sustain or ratify the new apostle (Acts 1:26). The body of the Twelve Apostles, with priesthood authority, would remain intact, having the "keys" of the kingdom and the responsibility to administer the spiritual and temporal affairs of the Church.

Paul provides additional insight into both the significance of the apostleship in one of its signal roles of *setting forth correct doctrinal positions* and the widespread recognition of the apostolic office and stature within the Church. We read in 2 Timothy: "But continue thou in the things which thou hast learned and hast been assured of, *knowing of whom thou hast learned them;* and that from a child thou hast known the holy scriptures, which are able to make thee wise unto salvation through faith which is in Christ Jesus" (vv. 14–15; emphasis added).

Paul exhorts Timothy to be faithful to the truths of the gospel and the plan of salvation, as administered through faith in Jesus Christ. Paul has previously testified to Timothy concerning God's plan for man's salvation, reminding him that it was he (Paul) who had taught him these truths. Paul's position in the Church as an apostle provides Timothy with additional assurance of the veracity of his testimony and the accuracy of his doctrinal teachings. This is perhaps one of the clearest lessons that Paul teaches: the people knew who the apostles were and recognized them as God's duly appointed and inspired leaders. Members of the Church trusted the apostles and knew that they were special witnesses of the Atonement and the Resurrection. Paul further reminds Timothy that he (Timothy) had been taught from the holy scriptures since the days of his childhood, thus giving him two keys in discerning truth from error: (1) the testimony of living apostles or prophets, as implied in verse 14, and (2) the witness of earlier prophets and doctrinal teachings contained in the holy scriptures, as stated in verse 15.

The Twelve Apostles, or disciples, understood the broad nature of their apostolic mission, including the authority they possessed to direct the affairs of the Church. So it was that they called Stephen and six other men of "honest report, full of the Holy Ghost and wisdom" (Acts 6:3). The growth of the Church was such that the apostles were unable to care for all the needs of the saints. Stephen and his associates were called and ordained by the authority and procedure (Acts 6:6) established by Jesus and "appoint[ed] over this business" (Acts 6:3). Using the authority of the priesthood and directing all other offices within the Church allowed the apostles to perform their primary assignment: to travel the known world, proclaiming the everlasting gospel to the earth's inhabitants and establishing the Church and God's priesthood authority wherever they preached.

The Bible Explains the Necessity of the Melchizedek Priesthood

In the Mosaic law, we learn of the Levitical Priesthood, or, as the Jewish historian Josephus termed it, the "Priesthood of Aaron."[18] Aaron was called by the Lord, through Moses, to receive the priesthood, and it was to be "an everlasting priesthood throughout . . . generations" (Exodus 40:15). Aaron and his sons after him officiated under the authority granted them by the Levitical order. They performed functions similar to those of priesthood leaders called in Christ's day. However, the Mosaic law and the Levitical Priesthood were given to the children of Israel for the purpose of preparing people for the coming Christ. Once He came, the preparation was over, and the Levitical authority was insufficient for the rites or sacraments that would be performed in the New Covenant introduced by Jesus Christ.

Accordingly, the Melchizedek, or higher, Priesthood is indispensable in any "divine re-ordering" or restoration of truth *from ages past.* The author of the Epistle of Barnabas testified that Moses "received it, but they [the

Israelites] were not worthy" (see page 35). Priesthood authority was paramount to the gospel introduced by Jesus Christ, and the process by which the priesthood is transferred has been constant throughout religious history. Both scripture and history indicate that the type of priesthood or *authority or keys* one holds determines the type of ordinance or rite one can perform.

An illustration of the necessity of the higher, or Melchizedek, priesthood in the performance of certain ordinances can be found in the Acts of the Apostles. Philip (the evangelist, not the apostle) was preaching the word in Samaria, and it was received with great joy. Even Simon, a recognized sorcerer of some repute, believed. Simon, at least superficially, accepted the gospel because he recognized that his powers, based on evil foundations, could not compare with the power and authority of the true and living God. Those who received the word with gladness were baptized by Philip, but it appears that Philip *may* not have held the Melchizedek Priesthood *at this time,* for they "sent for Peter and John," apostles who were undoubtedly ordained to the higher priesthood:

Now when the apostles which were at Jerusalem heard that Samaria had received the word of God, they sent unto them Peter and John: who when they were come down, prayed for them, that they might receive the Holy Ghost. . . . And when Simon saw that through the laying on of the apostles' hands the Holy Ghost was given, he offered them money, saying, Give me also this power, that on whomsoever I lay hands, he may receive the Holy Ghost. But Peter said unto him, Thy money perish with thee, because thou hast thought that the gift of God may be purchased with money. (Acts 8:14–20)

It would appear that Philip did not at this time have authorization from the apostles to confer the baptism of fire (Luke 3:16). Otherwise, he would not have sent for Peter and John to perform the ordinance of bestowing the gift of the Holy Ghost. Simon was so impressed by the power demonstrated by Peter that he offered money to receive this priesthood authority. However, Peter, calling the priesthood a "gift of God," scolded Simon, stating that the priesthood could not be purchased with money.

A similar passage may be found in Acts 19. In this instance, Paul discovers a group of believers in Ephesus. When he asks them whether they have received the Holy Ghost, he is told that they have not. Paul responds by probing further into the nature of the baptism performed:

> And he said unto them, Unto what then were ye baptized? And they said, Unto John's baptism. Then said Paul, John verily baptized with the baptism of repentance, saying unto the people, that they should believe on him which should come after him, that is, on Christ Jesus. When they heard this, they were baptized in the name of the Lord Jesus. And when Paul had laid his hands upon them, the Holy Ghost came on them; and they spake with tongues, and prophesied. (Acts 19:1–7)

Perhaps Paul baptized the believers at Ephesus again because the first time they had been baptized *by one without authority.* Or perhaps John's disciples were not aware of the baptism of fire (Luke 3:16); thus, as John directed his followers away from himself and toward Jesus and the apostles, upon learning from Paul of the Holy Ghost, John's former disciples desired to receive this gift. When they understood that they "should believe on him [Jesus] which should come after him

[John the Baptist]," John's disciples were immediately "baptized in the name of the Lord Jesus." After learning of the Holy Ghost from Paul, he laid his hands upon them. Regardless of interpretation, this passage seems to recognize the distinction between Aaronic Priesthood rites administered by John the Baptist and Melchizedek Priesthood rites administered under the direction of the apostles. There is an obvious requirement for legitimate priesthood authority when performing the sacraments of the Church, such as baptism and bestowing the gift of the Holy Ghost.

Further confirming the necessity of holding this higher priesthood, Paul counsels Timothy: "Neglect not the gift [of the priesthood] that is in thee, which was given thee by prophecy, with the laying on of the hands of the presbytery [elders]. . . . give thyself wholly to them [your congregation]. . . . Take heed unto thyself, and unto the doctrine; continue in them: for in doing this thou shalt both save thyself, and them that hear thee" (1 Timothy 4:14–16).

As alluded to by Paul and documented by the historian Eusebius, Timothy was a bishop in the Church charged with presiding over and ministering to a congregation of believers. Paul advised Timothy to officiate in his calling tirelessly, reminding him that he had received the priesthood under the hands of the elders of the Church (who held the higher priesthood given them by the apostles). Paul added that if Timothy, in the righteous exercise of his priesthood (gift), would follow the doctrine and keep it pure, he would save himself and those who heard him. That Timothy received the higher priesthood rather than the Levitical Priesthood from the elders of the Church is evident in his calling as a bishop, which office held the "keys" associated with baptism *and* bestowing the gift of the Holy

Ghost in the earliest Christian communities (see page 62).

The law of Moses was a schoolmaster designed to lead the children of Israel to Christ. Further, it recognized that only those of the tribe of Levi were authorized to officiate in the temple. When Jesus fulfilled the law of Moses and introduced the New Covenant, He specifically empowered and authorized the apostles to administer the affairs of the Church, just as God had specifically directed Moses to call Aaron and his sons. The New Testament verifies that no ordinances or rites were performed other than by those specifically known to have been given priesthood authority (by those already in authority). That an orderly system had been established by Jesus Himself, through the apostles, to authorize His servants to serve in the ministry is a firm New Testament theme.

The book of Hebrews substantiates the priesthood after the order of Melchizedek when Paul explains: "Wherefore, holy brethren, partakers of the heavenly calling, consider the Apostle and High Priest of our profession, Christ Jesus; who was faithful to him that appointed him" (Hebrews 3:1–2). In this passage, Paul asserts that *Jesus Himself was an apostle and high priest.* Since the Savior called those whom he chose "apostles," they were likely high priests, after the order of Melchizedek, as was Jesus (Hebrews 5:10).

Under the Mosaic law, the firstborn of Aaron's sons served as the high priest within the Levitical or Aaronic order. The remaining direct descendants were priests who served in the temple and had responsibilities for the sacrifices. Those of the tribe of Levi but not directly of Aaron's lineage helped with other aspects of the temple rites.

When Jesus Christ fulfilled the law of Moses, the priesthood was also changed (Hebrews 7:12). The daily ritualistic sacrifice was replaced by the Savior's atoning sacrifice (Hebrews 7:27). The Savior restored the higher priesthood, which was previously held by Melchizedek, for whom this priesthood was later named. The Epistle of Barnabas implies that Moses also held this higher priesthood (see page 35). When the Apostolic Fathers called the bishops of the early Church "high priests," it is unlikely that they were considered Aaronic high priests, since the law of Moses had been fulfilled, and none of the early writings indicate that the office of Aaronic high priest continued in Christianity after the ministry of Jesus. Ignatius testified, "Honor thou God indeed, as the Author and Lord of all things, but the bishop as the high-priest, who bears the image of God."[19] Clement of Alexandria stated that when a man was inducted into the mysteries of God, he became a "truly kingly man; he is the sacred high priest of God."[20] Similarly, Hippolytus prayed, "Grant unto this Thy servant whom thou hast chosen for the episcopate to feed thy holy flock and serve as Thine high priest."[21] In addition to these Fathers, the Didache also refers to prophets as high priests: "Therefore, take all first fruits of vintage and harvest, of cattle and sheep, and give these first fruits to the prophets; for they are your high priests."[22] Given Christ's introduction of a new law and a new priesthood and these statements by the early Christian Fathers—apostles, bishops, and perhaps other Church leaders may have been considered high priests *after the order of Melchizedek* by the earliest Christians.

The Testimony of the Early Christian Fathers Regarding Priesthood Authority

The early Church Fathers believed in and understood the importance of the "keys" that Christ gave to the apostles to govern the whole

Church, and a bishop was granted spiritual authority or "keys" over his congregation. A highly regarded early Christian work titled *The Apostolic Constitutions* asserts: "Neither do we permit the laity to perform any of the offices belonging to the priesthood; as, for instance, neither the sacrifice, nor baptism, nor the laying on of hands, nor the blessing, whether the smaller or greater: 'for no man taketh this honor unto himself, but he that is called of God.' For such sacred offices are conferred by the laying on of hands of the bishop."[23] The importance of this passage is twofold: first, it affirms the necessity of priesthood authority to perform the rites and sacraments of the Church; second, it establishes the proper interpretation of Hebrews 5:4, as viewed by the early Christian Church, that distinctive requirements did exist for receiving the holy priesthood.

Ignatius discusses the important responsibilities entrusted to the bishop, the presbyters, and the deacons. He admonishes the members to follow the inspired counsel of the bishop and reminds them that the bishop must authorize and oversee baptism, the Eucharist, and the other sacraments of the Church:

> See that ye all follow the bishop, even as Christ Jesus does the Father, and the presbytery as ye would the apostles. Do ye also reverence the deacons, as those that carry out the appointment of God. Let no man do anything connected with the Church without the bishop. Let that be deemed a proper Eucharist, which is [administered] either by the bishop, or by one to whom he has entrusted it. . . . It is not lawful without the bishop either to baptize, or to offer, or to present sacrifice, or to celebrate a love feast. But that which seems good to him, is also well pleasing to God, that everything ye do may be secure and valid.[24]

Ignatius also declared that without genuine priesthood authority, no Church organization existed: "And do ye reverence them [the deacons] as Christ Jesus, of whose place they are the keepers, even as the bishop is the representative of the Father of all things, and the presbyters are the Sanhedrin of God, and assembly of the apostles of Christ. Apart from these there is no elect Church, no congregation of holy ones, no assembly of saints."[25]

Ignatius did not make such strong statements carelessly. He testified with great power that this direction to follow the bishop had come to him from the Lord: "The Spirit made an announcement to me, saying as follows: Do nothing without the bishop."[26]

One should not be surprised by the testimony of the early Church Fathers, for their statements matched precisely those of Paul to the Hebrews: "Obey them that have the rule over you, and submit yourselves: for they watch for your souls, as they that must give account [to God]" (Hebrews 13:17). The apostles, seventy, and bishops presided over the Church and were revered by the early Christians. Only apostasy changed that fact. Thus, in addition to New Testament witnesses, the early Church Fathers also contribute important testimony of the need for properly ordained members to ecclesiastical offices. These men were then authorized to preside over congregations and to perform the sacraments and rites of the Church, such as baptism and bestowing the gift of the Holy Ghost, and to act in the offices to which they had been appointed.

In the early Christian community, a professionally trained priesthood did not exist. An extensive lay priesthood was responsible for governing the affairs of the Church. Following the model established by Jesus, the apostles ordained faithful male members of the Church as deacons, teachers, elders, and bishops. Peter's declaration to the saints of his day fulfilled earlier promises made by the Lord to Moses (Exodus 19:5–6): "But ye are a chosen generation, a royal priesthood, an holy nation, a peculiar people; that ye should shew forth the praises of him who hath called you out of darkness into his marvellous light" (1 Peter 2:9).

This royal priesthood was composed of untrained men who were inspired by the Holy Ghost. Other than instructions and exhortations supplied by the apostles (under inspiration from the Lord), those ordained to the priesthood received no formal training. Instead, obedience to the commandments, humility, and charity qualified them to be directed by the Spirit so that they might perform their callings as God desired. Although the priesthood was a lay priesthood, it was nonetheless a formal priesthood and the foundation upon which the Church of Jesus Christ was founded, being completely integral to its continuation and progress.

Revelation: A Consistent Principle During Times of Righteousness

The one principle that has guided every dispensation is continuing revelation, a doctrine and practice that joins man to God and ensures that God's will is performed over man's desires. Although Christianity in general holds that revelation ceased with the death of the apostles, this presumption cannot be supported by religious history, because it supposes that revelation was no longer necessary. The Old Testament affirms that God revealed His will to man through revelation; the Gospels contain the revelations of the Father to the Son and the apostles; the remainder of the New Testament provides an account of the Church being guided by revelation from

God through direct administration and by the Holy Ghost. Other than the foreboding prophecies of apostasy, nothing in the New Testament foreshadows that the heavens would be silent following the apostolic ministry. To the contrary, the postapostolic vision, the Shepherd of Hermas, was broadly recognized by the early Church as inspired and authentic scripture. The significant confusion, discord, and controversy following the death of the apostles punctuate the need for continuing revelation. Thus, God's silence cannot be attributed to a lack of need or sole reliance on past scripture and revelation; rather, His children disobediently sought their own way, as in prior dispensations.

God has always taught His law and His commandments through prophets. The Old Testament documents that God systematically and periodically revealed Himself to man. However, during notable periods the gospel did not exist in its purity and fullness. These "gaps" in the religious record indicate intervals of apostasy when wickedness prevailed and the heavens were silent. Just before the Lord called Samuel as a prophet, there is this note: "And the child Samuel ministered unto the Lord before Eli. And the word of the Lord was precious in those days; *there was no open vision*" (1 Samuel 3:1; emphasis added).

In another example, when Saul could not receive revelation because of his wickedness, "neither by dreams, nor by Urim, nor by prophets" (1 Samuel 28:6), he resorted to enlisting the help of a woman who, by "familiar spirits," might summon Samuel from the dead. These illustrations demonstrate that disobedience and rebellion are responsible for the Lord withholding revelation from the heavens. Nowhere in Old Testament history is this fact more evident than in the Lamentations of Jeremiah. Recounting the wickedness that caused the downfall of Israel, it laments,

"Her gates are sunk into the ground; he hath destroyed and broken her bars: her king and her princes are among the Gentiles: the law is no more; *her prophets also find no vision from the Lord*" (Lamentations 2:9; emphasis added). Thus, although the Old Testament period is commonly identified as an age of revelation, the nearly four hundred years between Malachi and John the Baptist stand as a monument reminding Israel that God will not provide direction, even to His chosen people, when they reject Him (see also Psalm 74:9).

Maccabees supports this assertion. After rebuilding the altar and not knowing what to do with it, Maccabeens determined to wait until another prophet should be sent among them (1 Maccabees 4:46). Other prophets did not come until John the Baptist and Jesus.

The Apostle Peter recognized the importance of continuing revelation when he wrote to the saints in his day:

> For we have not followed cunningly devised fables, when we made known unto you the power and coming of our Lord Jesus Christ, *but were eyewitnesses of his majesty.* For he received from God the Father honour and glory, when there came such a voice to him from the excellent glory, This is my beloved Son, in whom I am well pleased. *And this voice which came from heaven we heard, when we were with him in the holy mount. We have also* a more sure word of prophecy; *whereunto ye do well that ye take heed . . . :* knowing this first, that no prophecy of the scripture is of any private interpretation. For the *prophecy came not in old time by the will of man: but holy men of God spake as they were moved by the Holy Ghost.* (2 Peter 1:16–21; emphasis added)

In verse 16, Peter declared he was not persuaded by fables as to his testimony of Jesus; rather, he was an actual eyewitness of the Savior's ministry, and he had personally heard the voice of God proclaim His Son. When Peter said, "We have also a more sure word of prophecy," the word *we* implied that all the apostles had received "a more sure word of prophecy." Peter added, "Where unto ye do well that ye take heed." Peter was saying that if his audience would obey the "more sure word of prophecy," they would be blessed. In other words, "We receive revelation which you would do well to obey." These verses may also allude to the importance of personal revelation, so that man may be found doing God's will and not simply his own. If so, when Peter referred to the "more sure word of prophecy; where unto ye do well that ye take heed," he may have been saying that we must seek our own "sure" or *certain* salvation by exhibiting profound faith in God and "tak[ing] heed" to personal revelation *and then submitting* to such, as Jesus Himself exemplified in the Gospel of John (John 8:38–40).

Peter was quick to point out that man is not at liberty to render private interpretations of ancient scripture, implying that this sacred role is reserved for God's apostles and prophets as they are inspired by the Holy Ghost. He teaches us that the prophecy he refers to is not just anecdotal; rather, revelation occurs when holy men speak as directed by the authority and power of the Holy Ghost.

Paul communicated the idea of continuous revelation to the saints at Corinth: "Your faith should not stand in the wisdom of men, but in the power of God. . . . We speak wisdom . . . yet not the wisdom of this world. . . . But we speak the wisdom of God in a mystery, even the hidden wisdom, which God ordained before the world unto our glory: which none of the princes of this world knew. . . . But God hath revealed them unto us by his Spirit: for the Spirit searcheth all things, yea, the deep things of God" (1 Corinthians 2:5–8, 10).

Who was to reveal the "hidden wisdom" after the death of the apostles? That which is hidden cannot be written in a book, or it would no longer be hidden. It cannot be disguised in parable, allegory, or a "type" for the masses; otherwise, who will decipher the hidden parts, absent a recognized living prophet, and give an authoritative interpretation to the faithful? Christianity over the centuries has proven time and again that interpretation of scripture is a very serious problem. John Calvin never rendered a commentary on the book of Revelation because he said he did not understand it.[27] What purpose would revelation from the heavens serve if it were not meant to be understood and used to benefit those who sincerely desire to know and love God? If Christianity is ever to be united, it will happen only when a prophet speaks authoritatively in the name of God, as in ages past. Paul teaches that the "deep things" of God are fully understood only when revealed by the Holy Ghost, not simply by a well-schooled grammarian or theologian.

Scripture itself is not for private interpretation, as *regards the doctrine to be preached to the entire Church*. For example, we don't see a lay Church member of apostolic times declaring doctrine in the Bible—we see Peter, John, and Paul. Significant theological and communication problems would arise if all Christians laid claim on the right to *authoritatively* interpret scripture in behalf of the Church. This problem alone points dramatically to the need for living prophets. No wonder one of the earliest bishops, Papias, wrote:

> If ever someone who had accompanied the presbyters should come, I examined carefully the words of the presbyters, [to learn] what Andrew, Peter, Philip, Thomas, John, Matthew, or any other of the disciples of the Lord said and what things Aristion and the presbyter John, disciples of the Lord, are saying. *For I did not suppose the contents of books would profit me so much as the words and living voice.*[28]

Peter and Paul's witness regarding continuing revelation is vindicated by the Old Testament prophets, by the Savior's ministry, and by the apostolic ministry that followed; there is no indication in any apostolic writings that divine communication (such as with Paul on the road to Damascus, or when he was "caught up to the third heaven") would be *permanently* cut off after the death of the Apostles. Of course, the only scriptural exceptions to this claim are the many prophecies of coming apostasy, a condition that would preclude revelations from the Lord.

If one admits an apostasy after the apostolic age, as many profess, by what inspired method would God set the record straight? Revelation to His prophets, such as with Moses, has been His pattern of the past.

Conclusion

Scripture, pseudepigraphal and apocryphal writings, early Christian literature, and historical documentation support the following:

1. Christ organized His Church.

2. Christ called twelve Apostles and other priesthood officers to preside over the Church.

3. The "keys" of the kingdom and priesthood authority were conferred first on Peter and then on the rest of the Apostles. Other leaders subsequently called to serve—such as the seventy, bishops, and elders—were duly called by priesthood officers *who already possessed* proper authority.

4. Priesthood authority was requisite to official priesthood service, such as presiding (as a bishop or presbyter) and performing the

sacraments and rites of the Church.

5. Men may not call themselves or seek ecclesiastical positions of responsibility. Christ reserved that privilege for Himself, operating through servants whom *He* called and to whom He gave formal authority to act in His name and in His behalf, under the inspiration of the Holy Ghost.

6. The higher priesthood, or *Priesthood after the order of Melchizedek,* was necessary to perform certain types of ordinances.

7. Apostolic succession, mirroring the succession of patriarchal prophets in earlier dispensations, was intended to continue.

8. Continuing revelation, when God's covenant people have been obedient, has been a constant in God's Church from the beginning.

The apostolic office did not survive the first century, and, as in ages past, *a general apostasy of God's people was responsible for this loss.* During their mortal ministry, prophets and Apostles both anciently and during the meridian of time prophesied of this predicament, a condition further examined in chapter 4.

Notes

1. Job 19:25; Isaiah 7:13–14; 9:6–7; Ezekiel 34:23–24; Daniel 9.

2. *World Religions,* ed. Jeffery Parrinder (New York: Facts on File Publications, 1971), 162–76; Nicholas Cheetham, *Keepers of the Keys* (New York: Charles Scribner's Sons, 1983), 1–3.

3. Cheetham, *Keepers of the Keys,* 167–68.

4. Cheetham, *Keepers of the Keys,* 164–76.

5. Bright, *History of Israel,* 460–62; *The Complete Works of Josephus,* trans. William Whiston (Grand Rapids, Mich.: Kregel Publications, 1981), Antiquities of the Jews 18.1; *New International Bible Dictionary,* ed. J. D. Douglas and Merrill C. Tenney (Grand Rapids, Mich.: Zondervan, 1987); Chadwick, *Early Church,* 11.

6. Martinez, *Dead Sea Scrolls Translated,* liii.

7. Martinez, *Dead Sea Scrolls Translated,* lii–liv.

8. Rule of the Community, Cave 1 Copy, IQS 5.15–6.8, col. 6, vv. 4–6, 25, in Martinez, *Dead Sea Scrolls Translated,* 9–10; carets in original; brackets added.

9. See Malachi 3–4.

10. Malachi 4:7, Malachi testifies the Jews had "gone away from the ordinances, . . . and not kept them"; Matthew 23:31, Jesus testifies that the Jews rejected, stoned, and killed the prophets. Elijah also testifies "the children of Israel have forsaken thy covenant, thrown down thine altars, and slain thy prophets with the sword; and I, even I only, am left; and they seek my life, to take it away" (1 Kings 19:14).

11. Eusebius, Ecclesiastical History 24, 108; emphasis added.

12. See also Eusebius, Ecclesiastical History 3.4, 84–85. Most references in Hebrews regarding the office of high priest are specific to Jesus Christ Himself, with the exception of Hebrews 3:1, which states that Jesus, an Apostle, was a high priest, implying that the twelve he called Apostles were also high priests.

13. 1 Corinthians 12:12, 21, 25, 28.

14. Acts 1:22 references the mandate to call another Apostle to replace Judas; vv. 23–25 reveal the process used to select the new Apostle; v. 26 states that the 120 present "cast lots" or voted, or in some fashion ratified the selection; and Acts 6:6 and 13:3 indicate how Mathias was probably ordained.

15. All Bible scholars recognize that Elias in this setting is referring to Elijah the prophet, also referred to in Malachi 4:5–6. The Hebrew name rendered Elijah in the King James Version (KJV) is "Eliyahu." The New Testament reflects the same name with the addition of the masculine singular suffix "s."

16. William Stuart McBirnie, *The Search for the Twelve Apostles,* Living Books ed. (Wheaton, Ill.: Tyndale House Publishers, 1986), 241.

17. Hegesippus, in Eusebius, Ecclesiastical History 2.76.

18. Josephus, Antiquities of the Jews, 8.1.

19. Ignatius, Epistle to the Smyrnaeans 9, in *Ante-Nicene Fathers,* 1:90.

20. Clement of Alexandria, Stromata 7.7, in *Ante-Nicene Fathers,* 2:533.

21. Hippolytus, Apostolic Tradition, 3.4–5.

22. Didache 13.3, in *Ancient Christian Writers* 6:23.

23. Apostolic Constitutions 3.10, in *Ante-Nicene Fathers,* 7:429.

24. Ignatius, Epistle to the Smyrnaeans 8, in *Ante-Nicene Fathers,* 1:89–90.

25. Ignatius, Epistle to the Trallians 3, in *Ante-Nicene Fathers,* 1:67; brackets added.

26. Ignatius, Epistle to the Philadelphians 7, in *Ante-Nicene Fathers,* 1:83.

27. Earle E. Cairns, *Christianity through the Centuries,* rev. and enl. 2d ed. (Grand Rapids, Mich.: Zondervan, 1981), 305. Philip Schaff writes, "The opening and closing chapters [of the book of Revelation] are as clear and dazzling as sunlight, and furnish spiritual nourishment and encouragement to the plainest Christian; but the intervening visions are, to most readers, as dark as midnight." *History of the Christian Church,* 5 vols., 3d ed. (Peabody, Mass.: Hendrickson Publishers, 1996), 1:827, brackets added. Schaff's view seems in conflict with the Savior's testimony to his Apostles, "It is given unto you to know the mysteries of the kingdom of heaven, but to them [the faithless] it is not given" (Matthew 13:11). The mysteries of God, given to the likes of Adam, Enoch, Abraham, Daniel, and the Apostles (including John), must be revealed (to the faithful) through prophets as in all other ages of the earth.

28. Fragments of Papias I, in *Ante-Nicene Fathers,* 1:153. Also quoted by Eusebius, Ecclesiastical History 3.39, 1, 3–4.

and doctrinal reforms within Christianity. People of faith strove to furnish the words of the Bible to the common man so that he might hear and read it in his own language. A number of Christian sects arose, each seeking to follow the Lord according to its own understanding. Additionally, a number of groups of people emerged known as "Restorationists" or "Seekers," many of whom were hoping or waiting for a future day when New Testament Christianity would be restored to the earth. Amos may have been alluding to a time when the Lord's *living* prophets and *the true gospel* could no longer be found upon the earth and may have been foretelling the apostasy of the Church from pure Christianity *after* the death of the Apostles.

New Testament Prophecy of Apostasy: A Falling Away from Truth

In the New Testament, the Apostle Paul warned the elders at Ephesus: "Take heed therefore unto yourselves, and to all the flock, over the which the Holy Ghost hath made you overseers, to feed the church of God, which he hath purchased with his own blood. For I know this, that after my departing shall grievous wolves enter in among you, not sparing the flock. Also of your own selves shall men arise, speaking perverse things, *to draw away disciples after them*" (Acts 20:28–30; emphasis added).

This passage is directed to the presbyters (elders) of the church at Ephesus. "Take heed," Paul exhorts, not only for your own lives but also for those sheep (Church members) for whom you have responsibility (having been made "overseers" by the Holy Ghost; in other words, God had made some of them leaders and expected them to watch over Church members under their supervision). Paul fur-

ther informs them that "after my departing shall grievous wolves enter in among you, not sparing the flock" (Acts 20:29), indicating that after the death of Paul and the other Apostles, apostates waiting in the wings would enter their congregations with the intent to deceive them. Paul advises them that even some "of your own selves" (that is, some of the faithful) may attempt to establish corrupt doctrines, perverting the gospel and attempting to draw disciples after them. Apparently, this tragedy is already occurring, because Paul bemoans the fact that "all they which are in Asia be turned away from me" and identifies some of the men leading Church members into heresy (2 Timothy 1:15; 2:14–18). Paul declares that apostasy would take place *within* the ranks of the Church, and history attests that less than one hundred years later these events had already occurred. Justin Martyr, writing in approximately A.D. 150, declared:

> And just as there were false prophets contemporaneous with your holy prophets, so are there now many false teachers amongst us, of whom our Lord forewarned us to beware; so that in no respect are we deficient, since we know that He foreknew all that would happen to us after His resurrection from the dead and ascension to heaven. For He said we would be put to death, and hated for His name's sake; and that many false prophets and false Christs would appear in His name, and deceive many: and so has it come about. For many have taught godless, blasphemous, and unholy doctrines, forging them in His name.[3]

Paul advises Timothy in his first letter of a "departure from the faith" preceding Christ's second coming: "Now the Spirit speaketh expressly, that in the latter times some shall depart from the faith, *giving heed to seducing spirits, and doctrines of devils; speaking lies in hypocrisy;* having *their conscience seared* with a hot iron; *forbidding to marry,* and *commanding to abstain from meats,* which God hath created to be received with thanksgiving of them which believe and know the truth" (1 Timothy 4:1–3; emphasis added).

These verses emphasize that the prophetic events just mentioned would transpire in the "latter times." A review of John's later writings and the book of Revelation indicates that he believed that the saints were already in the *latter times:* "Little children, it is the last time: and as ye have heard that antichrist shall come, even now are there many antichrists; whereby we know that it is the last time. They went out from us, *but they were not of us*" (1 John 2:18; emphasis added). The last times would continue until the Savior's glorious return. Later conflicts between the Donatists and the orthodox (see pages 199–200); between those supporting Arian theology and those favoring the party led by Athanasius (see pages 157–58); between Cyril and Nestorius (see page 165); and between Pelagius and Augustine (see page 212) are but a few of the controversies that arose because of "seducing spirits and doctrines of devils." History verifies that the Church of the Middle Ages spoke lies in hypocrisy and operated with a seared conscience (1 Timothy 4:2). History also verifies that the Church forbade the clergy to marry, a doctrine unknown in the earliest Christian communities and that the Church ultimately forbade eating meat on Fridays (now changed as of Vatican II—concluded December 8, 1965), an addition to the prescribed rites authorized by the Savior (1 Timothy 4:3).

Paul continues to paint a broad picture of apostasy when he informs Timothy: "This know also, that in the last days perilous times shall come. . . . men shall be lovers of their own selves, . . . without natural affection, . . . incontinent, . . . lovers of pleasures more than lovers of God; having a form of godliness, but denying the power [authority of the priesthood] thereof: from such turn away" (2 Timothy 3:1–7).

In addition to this passage referring to the "last days," these verses describe precisely our day, when men have become preoccupied with selfish desires and are drenched in lust and greed; the gay-lesbian culture has been portrayed as genetic and ordinary, and it need not be controlled, as though other propensities are less genetic (excessive drinking, gambling, unbridled heterosexual relationships; see endnote for further explanation)[4]; there is little restraint or self-control regarding sexual gratification; and the Sabbath day has become a day of recreation rather than a day of worship. When society succumbs to such behavior and that behavior coincides with the time foretold, prophecy is fulfilled.

Paul cautions Timothy that the time he has foreseen will come in a day when world religions *have a form of godliness* but do not possess the authority of the holy priesthood, and he warns, "From such turn away"!

Paul further advises Timothy regarding doctrinal developments associated with apostasy: "For the time will come when *they will not endure sound doctrine;* but after their own lusts shall they heap to themselves *teachers, having itching ears; and they shall turn away their ears from the truth,* and shall be turned unto *fables*" (2 Timothy 4:3–4; emphasis added).

Sound doctrine cannot be established solely through a trifold approach of grammatical interpretation of scripture, historical precedence, and the prayer of faith, albeit sincere. Inasmuch as prophetic authors never recorded a complete contextual exposition of the settings being described, without the Holy Spirit and *living prophets,* full understanding is improbable. In the foregoing verses,

Paul introduces groups of people surrounding themselves with teachers who will teach them what they want to hear. He asserts that popular opinion will sway the pure doctrines of Christ, and people will actually turn away from the truth because the truth is not what they desire to embrace. Paul attests that the result will be people believing in fables.

When teaching the Thessalonian saints, Paul counsels them not to be deceived into thinking that Christ's second coming is imminent. He discusses with certainty a "falling away" from truth prior to the Savior's much-anticipated second advent:

Now we beseech you, brethren, by the coming of our Lord Jesus Christ, and by our gathering together unto him, that ye be not soon shaken in mind, or be troubled, neither by spirit, nor by word, nor by letter as from us, *as that the day of Christ is at hand* [Christ's second coming]. Let no man deceive you by any means: for *that day shall not come* except there come *a falling away first*, and that *man of sin be revealed, the son of perdition.* (2 Thessalonians 2:1–3; emphasis added)

As previously stated, the definition of the Greek word *apostasia*, used by Paul to explain a "falling away," means rebellion or "standing against."[5] Paul advised the saints that there would be such a rebellion, and once these defectors achieved their spurious objectives, they would replace legitimate priesthood leaders with those whom Christ called "wolves in sheep's clothing."[6] The New Testament actually names some of these imposters: Diotrephes (3 John 1:9–10); Alexander the coppersmith (2 Timothy 4:14–16); Hymanaeus and Philetus (2 Timothy 2:17–18); and the infamous Simon Magus (Acts 8:18–23). Men such as these attempted to usurp the authority of the Apostles and other local leaders.

Peter, like Paul, testified that false prophets had lived in the past and false professors would live in the future, defiling the purity of the precepts taught by Jesus: "But there were false prophets also among the people, *even as there shall be false teachers among you*, who privily shall *bring in damnable heresies*, even *denying the Lord that bought them*, and bring upon themselves swift destruction. And many shall follow their pernicious ways; *by reason of whom the way of truth shall be spoken evil of.* And through covetousness shall they *with feigned words make merchandise of you*" (2 Peter 2:1–3; emphasis added).

Peter was writing of events that immediately followed the death of the Apostles. The writings of those who followed—Clement and Ignatius, the late first-century bishops of Rome and Antioch; Hegesippus, one of the earliest Church historians; and Eusebius, an early fourth-century historian—all wrote and testified of the heresies abounding in the Church at the close of the first century. Peter may have alluded to the false doctrine of indulgences—that is, buying forgiveness for sins (see pages 223–24; 246–47)—when he used the language "*with feigned words* [they will] *make merchandise of you.*"

Even Jude speaks of apostasy when he prophesies: "But, beloved, remember ye the words *which were spoken before of the apostles* of our Lord Jesus Christ; *how that they told you there should be mockers in the last time*, who should walk after their own ungodly lusts. *These be they who separate themselves* [apostatize, or turn their back on God], sensual, having not the Spirit" (Jude 1:17–19; emphasis added). When speaking of apostasy, Jude specifies "in the last time." Again, John taught the saints that they were even then *in the last times* and would be until the millennial reign of Jesus Christ.

Apostasy Begins While Apostles Are Still Alive

The New Testament contains evidence of apostasy while the Apostles were yet alive. As a faithful watchman on the tower, the Apostle Paul captured every opportunity to admonish the saints and warn them of those who would fabricate false truths. Paul observed splinter groups and early forms of apostasy at Corinth when he said: "When ye come together in the church, *I hear that there be divisions among you; and I partly believe it. For there must be also heresies among you,* that they which are approved may be manifest among you" (1 Corinthians 11:18; emphasis added).

Paul recognized that the saints at Galatia were also in a state of apostasy: "I marvel that ye are *so soon removed from him* that called you into the grace of Christ *unto another gospel: which is not another;* but there be some that trouble you, *and would pervert the gospel of Christ*" (Galatians 1:6–7; emphasis added).

Apostasy was apparently widespread among the Galatian saints, who combined portions of the law of Moses with Christianity. These saints failed to give up many of the old rites and rigid rules associated with their former beliefs. Paul constantly reminded the early saints that justification through faith in Christ alone was the only means of redemption (not the works of the law of Moses); that faith was the key to redemption did not imply, however, that obeying the commandments of Jesus was unnecessary for salvation or unrecognized by our Eternal Judge. The inability of many early Jewish Christians to separate the law of Moses from Christianity—because they were unwilling to live the higher law despite the pleadings of the Apostles—was one of the factors that contributed to apostasy from the Church of Christ.

After Paul had already testified to the Thessalonians that Christ would not come until after the Church fell away, he wrote: "For the mystery of iniquity doth already work: only he who now letteth will let, until he be taken out of the way. And then shall that Wicked be revealed" (2 Thessalonians 2:7–8). According to Paul, "the mystery of iniquity" was already at work. The phrase "he who now letteth will let" means "he who is now *restraining*" (perhaps John or other remaining Apostles). Subsequently, when "he" who restrains is taken out of the way, the "Wicked" one will be fully revealed. Righteous leaders—after the Apostles—recognized the apostasy and its effect upon the Church (see John Wesley's testimony, pages 125–26).

Furthermore, the several existing sects of Judaism at the time of Jesus' birth (Pharisees, Sadducees, and Essenes) were the result of apostasy. Just as the early Jewish Christians endeavored to preserve the old law by integrating it with the New Covenant, so the children of Israel had had difficulty separating the life they led in the land of Goshen and the life they were commanded to live by God through Moses. Many Jewish Christians deceived themselves, just as the Israelites did when Moses went into the sacred mount. Each group proved unable to separate itself from former habits and customs.

To Adam was revealed the one true plan of redemption through Jesus Christ. The same plan was also revealed to Enoch, Noah, and Abraham. The law of Moses was furnished as a schoolmaster to lead Israel to Christ. Through Jesus Christ, that law was literally fulfilled, *according to prophecy,* in the meridian of time. The Savior not only reestablished the *everlasting covenant* conferred upon the ancient Patriarchs but also was Himself the original giver of the law of Moses as well as the person of its fulfillment.[7] Paul's

75

warning to the Galatians supplies evidence of the importance of the apostolic office. Were it not for Paul, the Church in Galatia would have continued in apostasy. When the Apostles did die, no one remained in place to protect the Church against false teachers, and it entered an era of apostasy.

The Apostle John was equally vigilant in exposing apostasy and warning against it. John warned the Ephesian saints: "I know thy works, and thy labour, and thy patience, and how thou canst not bear them which are evil: *and thou hast tried them which say they are apostles, and are not, and hast found them liars. . . .* Nevertheless I have somewhat against thee, *because thou hast left thy first love.* Remember therefore from whence thou art fallen, and *repent, and do the first works; or else I will come unto thee quickly, and will remove thy candlestick out of his place, except thou repent*" (Revelation 2:2–5; emphasis added).

John congratulated the Ephesian saints for recognizing imposters who claimed to be Apostles, and he quickly reproved them for "leaving their first love," the true gospel as taught to them by Jesus and the Apostles. He admonished them to remember the truth and to "repent, and do the first works," following the *original* teachings and commandments of Jesus. John warned the Ephesian saints that if they failed to repent, the Lord would *come quickly* and "remove [their] candlestick," meaning "the Church" (the seven candlesticks refer figuratively to the seven churches, or congregations, addressed) from their midst (see also Hebrews 3:8–11).

Through John, the Lord further warned the saints of Pergamos to be constant. He praised them for holding fast His name and not denying the faith (Revelation 2:13) but then rebuked them for "holding [to] the doctrine of Balaam, who taught Balac to cast a stumblingblock before the children of Israel,

to eat things sacrificed unto idols" (Revelation 2:14). Balaam was an Old Testament prophet turned apostate who introduced Israel to the worship of the false god Baal (Numbers 22:1–25; 31:16). It would appear the Pergamos saints were attempting to mix pagan beliefs with Christianity, one of the common elements of apostasy. The Lord censured them for embracing the doctrines of the Nicolaitans, "which thing I hate" (Revelation 2:15).

These problems, summarized in chapters 2 and 3 of the book of Revelation, issue a clarion call of repentance to the entire Church. From the evidence just presented, one may conclude that while John was imprisoned on the Isle of Patmos, false authorities infiltrated the Church. In John's Apocalypse, the Lord symbolically singled out seven branches of the Church, yet He seemed to be addressing the universal problems they all faced. Each congregation was responsible for stopping the spread of false doctrine and for holding fast to the pure truths taught by Christ. One Bible scholar summarizes these events and establishes the general pattern used by John as follows:

> There is a complimentary opening introduced by the phrase "I know thy works," followed by a rebuke beginning with "I have somewhat against thee," and ending with the promise "to him that overcometh." The exceptions to this format are Smyrna (2:8–11) and Philadelphia (3:7–13), which receive no condemnation, and Sardis (3:1–6) and Laodicea (3:14–22), which receive no compliments.
> The Church's spiritual life foundered in six areas. Two were external: a willingness to compromise with paganism and a denial of Christianity due to Jewish harassment. Four were internal: the acceptance of unauthorized leaders, approval of false doctrine promulgated by pseudo-prophets, halfheartedness

and indifference, and a loss of love for the Church and her Master.[8]

The most significant stumbling block discussed in the book of Revelation is authority—who was authorized to oversee the affairs of the Church and define its doctrines. John taught the saints how to test whether a divine manifestation was from God—because "many false prophets are gone out into the world" (1 John 4:1). He explained that if a spirit testified Jesus Christ was the Son of God, who had "come in the flesh," that spirit was "of God" (1 John 4:2). Further, John revealed how early Christian churches could be certain of those who claimed to be true servants of Christ. Said John, "*We* are of God: he that knoweth God heareth *us;* he that is not of God heareth not us. *Hereby know we the spirit of truth,* and the spirit of error" (1 John 4:6; emphasis added). John's witness confirms the vital nature of the apostolic office. Although Jesus and the Apostles taught that Church members would be given the gift of the Holy Ghost to help them discern truth from error, as certain members of the Church began to apostatize and falsely claim the prophetic gift (as early as the sixth or seventh decade A.D.), such false claims presented a significant challenge to the faithful. John's statement is consistent with Paul's testimony: "But continue thou in the things which thou hast learned and hast been assured of, *knowing of whom [the Apostles] thou hast learned them*" (2 Timothy 3:14). Notwithstanding the persistence of the Apostles, the saints in general were deceived because, like their Judean brethren before them, they failed to heed the warning voice of living prophets.

Conclusion

The Old Testament alludes to apostasy from truth prior to Christ's second coming.

The New Testament furnishes a substantial body of evidence predicting general apostasy from truth following the apostolic age. Scriptural accounts confirm that apostasy was developing while the Apostles were still ministering among men and that the Church was rejecting the pure teachings of Jesus in favor of portions of the old Jewish law, selected pagan practices, and various Greek philosophies. The resulting apostasy, consistent with the patriarchal dispensations, witnessed fading priesthood authority followed by false doctrinal innovations; thus divine permission to perform the rites and sacraments of the Church disappeared. The testimony of prophecy was reliable: a general apostasy from revealed truth would destroy the Church Jesus had organized, leaving behind only a dead form.

Notes

1. *Studies in Scripture,* ed. Kent Jackson and Robert Millet, 8 vols. (Salt Lake City: Deseret Book, 1984–88), 4:118.

2. Leviticus 24:7–8 refers to a specific rite within the law of Moses, not the everlasting covenant; Leviticus 16:34 refers to the annual day of atonement; 2 Samuel 23:5 refers to God's covenant with David, evidently that Jesus would be born through the Davidic line; 2 Chronicles 13:5 and 21:7 refer to this same covenant; 1 Chronicles 16:17 does refer to the "everlasting covenant" made with Abraham and Israel; however, a covenant is a two-way agreement that Israel often broke with God. Clearly, this covenant was already severed at the time of Isaiah's prophecy through the likes of Ahaz and, while later reestablished briefly with a portion of Judah through righteous King Hezekiah, others during his reign "laughed them to scorn, and mocked them" (2 Chronicles 30:10). Gross wickedness quickly returned with Manasseh, Hezekiah's son, ultimately resulting in fulfillment of Isaiah's prophecy that Israel would be scattered and slain.

3. Justin, Dialogue with Trypho 82, in *Ante-Nicene Fathers,* 1:240.

4. Dr. Jeffrey M. Schwartz writes: "Even the adult brain is 'plastic,' able to forge new connections among its neurons and thus rewire itself. Sensory input can change the brain, and the brain remodels itself in response to behavioral demands. . . . The existence, and importance, of brain plasticity are no longer in doubt. The brain is dynamic, and the life we lead leaves its mark in the complex circuitry of the brain—footprints of the experiences we have had, the thoughts we have thought, the actions we have taken. The brain allocates neural real estate depending on what we use most: the thumb of the video gave addict, the index finger of a Braille reader, the analytic ability of a chess player, the language skills of a linguist. . . . But the brain also rewires itself based on something much more ephemeral than what we do: It rewires itself based on what we think." Jeffrey M. Schwartz, M.D., and Sharon Begley, *The Mind and the Brain: Neuroplasticity and the Power of Mental Force* (New York: Harper Collins, Regan Books, 2002). This carefully researched clinical conclusion provides secular evidence to the biblical passage, "For as he thinketh in his heart, so is he" (Proverbs 23:7). Accordingly, man is responsible for his own thoughts, desires, and actions.

God's commandments are clear and mankind exercises his own divinely given agency to accept or reject those commandments.

5. See ch. 2 herein, notes 1–3.

6. Matthew 7:15; see also ch. 5 herein.

7. "For the divine prophets lived according to Jesus Christ. Therefore they were also persecuted, being inspired by his grace." Ignatius to the Magnesians 8, in *Apostolic Fathers,* 1:205. "For I have proved that it was Jesus who appeared to and conversed with Moses, and Abraham, and all the other Patriarchs without exception, ministering to the will of the Father; who also, I say, came to be born man by the Virgin Mary." Justin, Dialogue with Trypho 113; cf. also chs. 56, 59, 61, 75. "They obviously knew the Christ of God, as he appeared to Abraham, communed with Isaac, spoke to Jacob; and that he communed with Moses and the prophets after him." Eusebius, Ecclesiastical History 1.28.

8. Richard D. Draper, *Opening the Seven Seals: The Visions of John the Revelator* (Salt Lake City: Deseret Book, 1991), 37.

CHAPTER FIVE

CHRISTIANITY IN THE FIRST CENTURY

The Church continued until then as a pure and uncorrupt virgin; whilst if there were any at all that attempted to pervert the sound doctrine of the saving Gospel, they were yet skulking in dark retreats; but when the sacred choir of Apostles became extinct, and the generation of those that had been privileged to hear their inspired wisdom had passed away, then also the combinations of impious error arose by the fraud and delusions of the false teachers. These also, as there were none of the Apostles left, henceforth attempted, without shame to preach their false doctrine against the Gospel of truth.

—Hegesippus–Eusebius, *Ecclesiastical History*

The New Testament reveals the somber mood of the Apostles and others who loved the Lord Jesus Christ when He was unjustly condemned by Pilate and the Jewish Sanhedrin. Those who were closest to the Savior must have felt a great emptiness, for they did not fully comprehend the meaning of His atonement and the reality of His resurrection; thus, Luke records that His followers "bewailed and lamented" their Savior's coming sacrifice (Luke 23:27). No wonder those whose associations were more casual failed to discern Christ's saving work; no wonder so many refused a complete break with the established traditions of Judaism, pagan devotion, and Greek intellectualism. Unfortunately, this refusal would sow the seeds of doubt, envy, and disunity.

The Lord's resurrection and subsequent forty-day ministry shed new light on doctrines that He had previously only introduced, and the reception of the Holy Ghost on the day of Pentecost provided the Apostles with greater confidence and steadiness. No longer would they wilt under the heat of persecution or adversity; rather, they would press forward to fulfill their divine calling. The Apostles labored aggressively to organize Christ's Church throughout the Roman Empire until, by the end of the first century, Christianity was established in about fifty locations around the Mediterranean. This success sparked resentment among both Jew and Gentile, introducing a climate of mistrust and persecution. Ultimately, the Apostles became martyrs, sealing their testimonies with their own blood and leaving the flock of Christ without reliable shepherds.

A puzzling hole in Christian history appeared between the fall of Jerusalem and the middle of the second century. The Church that Christ organized was conspicuously different from apostolic Christianity *less than one hundred years* later, a fact that has perplexed scholars for many centuries. The Church's first serious problems seem to have transpired within the *first two or three decades* after the death of most of the Apostles. While John was in exile on the Isle of Patmos sometime during the mid-90s, he received a veiled, apocalyptic, forewarning revelation, during which time the Church was in a state of turmoil, divisiveness, and chaos. The Lord's other Apostles had already perished, and the early Church Fathers—Clement, Ignatius, and Polycarp—were striving to correct heresy. Strangely, they seemed eager to suffer the same fate as the Apostles before them.

The Forty-Day Ministry of Jesus

Just as Jesus prepared for His ministry during a forty-day fast (Matthew 4:1–2), so were the Apostles tutored for forty days before being sent forth to proclaim the gospel to the world. Luke summarizes these events in the book of Acts:

The former treatise have I made . . . of all that Jesus began both to do and teach, until that day in which he was taken up, after that he through the Holy Ghost had given commandments unto the apostles whom he had chosen: to whom also he shewed himself alive after his passion by many infallible proofs, being seen of them forty days, and speaking of the things pertaining to the kingdom of God: and, being

assembled together with them, commanded them that they should not depart from Jerusalem, but wait for the promise of the Father. (Acts 1:1–4)

According to Luke, the Apostles were shown "many infallible proofs," of which we unfortunately have no written record in the Bible canon. Jesus, who compressed a lifetime of activity into three short years, was surely a master of time management. Luke writes that Jesus apparently used this brief period to mentor and train the Apostles by giving them detailed direction, providing evidence of His resurrection, and teaching them sacred things "pertaining to the kingdom of God." Christ's instruction during this time must have been of the highest importance. Up to this point, the Apostles were unpolished men who too often succumbed to the frailties and emotions of the flesh. Furthermore, as demonstrated by the many questions they asked Jesus prior to Gethsemane and Golgotha, they simply did not understand many basic doctrines concerning the Savior's atonement and resurrection. By contrast, after the forty-day ministry and the reception of the gift of the Holy Ghost on the day of Pentecost,[1] the Apostles went forth filled with knowledge, power, and authority.

Despite the lack of information in the Bible about this instruction, we fortunately have access to an incredible treasure: apocryphal records, along with other early Christian writings, greatly illuminate this period, providing important details as to what probably transpired. The general theme recorded in this early literature begins with the Apostles being troubled about the future: where were they to go, and what were they to do? Interestingly, centuries earlier, Joshua had discussed this same crisis with Moses: "Now master, you are going away, and who will sustain this people? . . . Who will be for them a leader. . . . Who will pray for them . . . that I may lead them into the land of their forefathers? . . . Master of leaders, . . . the divine prophet for the whole earth, . . . the perfect teacher in the world. . . . What then will happen to these people, master Moses?"[2]

Similarly, the Apostles now questioned Jesus: "Will you really leave us until your coming? Where will we find a teacher? . . . O Lord, is it possible that you should be both here and there? O Lord, it is possible for you to do what you have told us; but how will we be able to do (it)?"[3]

As Moses was to Joshua and the children of Israel, so had Jesus become to the Apostles. They were on their own, uncertain of the future, and had many unanswered questions. They knew Jesus could perform the mission He had assigned to them, but at this point they had little confidence in themselves.

The Savior had already told the Apostles to expect to be treated as He had been: they would be rejected by all men and suffer violent deaths for the cause of truth.[4] He also told them that false shepherds would shortly surface within the Church and pervert the gospel and that an increasing number of those who were worldly minded would soon bring down those who had endured as faithful saints. Possibly remembering the night that Jesus had told them about Judas, the Apostles probed: "Lord, among the believers who . . . believe in the preaching of your name should there be dissension and dispute and envy and confusion and hatred and distress?"[5]

Responding with a rhetorical question, Jesus asked, "Now why will the judgment take place?" Answering, the Lord taught, "That the wheat may be put in the barn and its chaff thrown into the fire."[6] Subsequently, Jesus described to His Apostles the apostasy that would soon take place: "They will also deliberately say what is not (true), and there will come a conspiracy against those who love

me." The Apostles then asked, "Will such, Lord, happen in our midst? . . . Tell us in what way?" Jesus answered them: "There will come another teaching and a conflict; and in that they seek their own glory and produce worthless teaching an offence of death will come thereby, and they will teach and turn away from my commandments even those who believe in me and bring them out of eternal life."[7]

The Apostles could scarcely believe that enemies would surface from *inside* the Church and seek to destroy it. Understanding their dismay, Jesus told them not to be surprised. After all, He had been rejected by his friends the Jews even after He had extended to them the gift of salvation with open arms. He explained that every person has to make a choice between life and death, and He reminded them of the coming judgment: the wheat, He said, would be put in the barn and the chaff would be burned. Jesus informed them that this wholesale rejection of truth would happen right in front of them. These "false shepherds" would produce counterfeit teachings that would eventually lead even the faithful away from the precepts of the true gospel as revealed by Jesus.

Following a rebellion, as later prophesied by the Apostles, the sheep would turn into wolves[8] and a season of spiritual wintertime[9] would begin. The light of truth as revealed by Jesus would withdraw, and an extended age of darkness would commence under the rule of godless men (Jude 1:4) who would assume the authority of Christ. The Testament of Hezekiah describes this event, beginning with the birth, mission, death, and resurrection of the Savior. It also foretells the calling of the Twelve Apostles, along with the apostolic mission to preach the gospel to every nation. Subsequently, we read:

And afterwards . . . his disciples will

81

abandon the teaching of the twelve apostles, and their faith, and their love, and their purity. And there will be much contention. . . . And in those days (there will be) many who will love office. . . . And there will be many wicked elders and shepherds who wrong the sheep. . . . And many will exchange the glory of the robes of the saints for the robes of those who love money.[10]

The New Testament reveals many accounts of emerging rebellion, most notably the schism at Corinth (1 Corinthians 3:3–5; 11:18–19). The saints at Corinth apparently didn't listen to Paul's initial counsel, for some years later apostasy shows up again in this city. Both Paul and Clement of Rome later wrote about the recurring apostasy at Corinth. In a letter reputed to be Paul's teachings, and quoted from by both Hippolytus and Origen, we read:

Paul, the prisoner of Jesus Christ, to the brethren in Corinth—greeting! Since I am in many tribulations, I do not wonder that the teachings of the evil one are so quickly gaining ground. For [my] Lord Jesus Christ will quickly come, since he is rejected by those who falsify his words. For I delivered to you in the beginning what I received from the apostles who were before me, who at all times were together with the Lord Jesus Christ.[11]

Paul acknowledged his tribulations in this narration. He was aware that false teachings were spreading rapidly throughout the Church and that corrupt doctrines were taking hold among the members. He reminded the saints that he had taught them the pure doctrines of Christ *that he had received directly from the original Twelve* and that they were now rejecting these genuine truths in favor of worldly imitations.

Some thirty years later, Clement of Rome described further Corinthian apostasy when he lamented: "From this arose jealousy and envy, strife and sedition, persecution and disorder, war and captivity. Thus 'the worthless' rose up 'against those who were in honour,' those of no reputation against the renowned. . . . For this cause righteousness and peace are far removed, while each deserts the fear of God and the eye of faith has grown dim, and men walk neither in the ordinances of his commandments nor use their citizenship worthily of Christ, but each goes according to the lusts of his wicked heart."[12]

These statements are all consistent and serve as evidence that what Jesus said would happen did in fact happen: His followers "abandon[ed] the teaching of the twelve apostles." To prepare them for this approaching evil, Jesus instructed the Apostles during the forty-day period, informing them of the coming apostasy and the problems they would encounter as they tried to spread the message of truth. Small wonder that the Apostles had more questions regarding the terrible events that would follow: "O Lord, teach us what will happen after this." Jesus in turn prophesied:

In those years and days there shall be war upon war, . . . and persecution of those who believe in me, and of the elect. Then dissension, conflict, and evil of action against each other. Among them there are some who believe in my name and (yet) follow evil and teach vain teaching. And men will follow them and will submit themselves to their riches, . . . depravity, . . . drinking, . . . and gifts of bribery.[13]

Despite this shadow of approaching destruction, Jesus also gave the Apostles assurances of peace and joy with Him after His triumphant but distant return.[14] However, concerned about the wicked, they asked, "Why will the disobedient be treated so harshly? We are truly troubled on their account."[15] Jesus responded, "You do well, for so are the righteous anxious about the sinners. I will hear the requests of the righteous concerning them."[16] The surviving writings of the Apostolic Fathers indicate that they too were probably aware of the gloomy scene portrayed by Jesus and reported by the Apostles. Despite the danger, they seemed to be inspired by a sense of urgency to warn the enduring faithful while remaining somehow at peace regarding their own impending martyrdom.[17]

The Esoteric or Secret Nature of the Forty-Day Teachings

Most of the instruction and doctrine revealed by Christ during His forty-day ministry was described as secret because He delivered it to only a select group of trusted leaders.[18] An important distinction needs to be made between those who were later labeled as Gnostics and those who were true followers of our Lord, having received "gnosis," or "knowledge," from Christ and the Apostles.

In time, those who claimed orthodoxy tended to identify all writings containing "secret" teachings of Jesus into a single category which they called Gnostic. This was ill-fated, for some Gnostic groups developed false religions founded on false revelation and hid their counterfeit identity in a shroud of secrecy. Unfortunately, inspired writings containing divine instruction separate from Jesus' more public doctrine were also labeled as Gnostic. Unlike the Gnostics of the second century, possessors of this true knowledge had no intent to be mysterious or to engender intrigue—they simply wanted to protect sacred matters from profane ears. In fact, a well-defined policy allowed all faithful disci-

ples to obtain greater knowledge as they were adequately prepared to receive it. In an early Christian writing on the subject of sacred or esoteric teachings, entitled Clementine Recognitions (the author of this significant work being uncertain), the Apostle Peter is purported to have instructed Clement as follows:

"Let such a one then hear this: The teaching of all doctrine has a certain order, and there are some things which must be delivered first, others in the second place, and others in the third, and so all in their order; and if these things be delivered in their order, they become plain; but if they be brought forward out of order, they will seem to be spoken against reason."[19] Accordingly, the Apostles taught that the higher and holier the teaching, the more cautiously it should be protected. The challenging nature of this practice is evident in the teachings of Peter to those whom he called the insincere:

Nothing is more difficult . . . than to reason concerning the truth in the presence of a mixed multitude of people. For that which is may not be spoken to all as it is, on account of those who hear wickedly and treacherously; yet it is not proper to deceive, on account of those who desire to hear the truth sincerely. What, then, shall he do who has to address a mixed multitude? Shall he conceal what is true? How, then, shall he instruct those who are worthy? But if he set forth pure truth to those who do not desire to obtain salvation, he does injury to Him by whom he has been sent, and from whom he has received commandment not to throw the pearls of His words before swine and dogs. . . . Wherefore I also, for the most part, by using a certain circumlocution, endeavour to avoid publishing the chief knowledge concerning the Supreme Divinity to unworthy ears.[20]

According to the author of Clementine Recognitions, Peter reviewed with Clement the Savior's teachings given to the Apostles during His mortal ministry to safeguard sacred truths: "Give not that which is holy unto the dogs, neither cast ye your pearls before swine" (Matthew 7:6). Moreover, Jesus informed the Apostles, "I have yet many things to say unto you, *but ye cannot bear them now*" (John 16:12; emphasis added). Continuing, Jesus said, "These things have I spoken unto you in proverbs: but *the time cometh*, when I shall no more speak unto you in proverbs, but *I shall show you plainly* of the Father" (John 16:25; emphasis added). Similarly, Jesus had earlier taught the Apostles regarding His use of parables:

> And the disciples came, and said unto him, Why speakest thou unto them in parables? He answered and said unto them, Because it is given unto you to know the mysteries of the kingdom of heaven, *but to them it is not given*. For whosoever hath, to him shall be given, and he shall have more abundance: but whosoever hath not, from him shall be taken away even that he hath. Therefore speak I to them in parables: because they seeing see not; and hearing they hear not, neither do they understand. (Matthew 13:10–13; emphasis added)

Jesus wanted the faithful and honest in heart to comprehend His message. The Apostles and others who loved truth and despised evil and contention were given increased understanding; however, the knowledge given to the wicked and those unable to break from the false traditions of their fathers was reduced according to the hardness of their hearts. A poignant example of this principle is provided after the parable of the sower, when the Savior revealed the parable's deeper meaning to the Apostles but not to the mul-

titude at large: "But blessed are your eyes, for they see: and your ears, for they hear. For verily I say unto you, That many prophets and righteous men have desired to see those things which ye see, and have not seen them; and to hear those things which ye hear, and have not heard them. Hear ye therefore the parable of the sower" (Matthew 13:16–18).

The consistent manner in which this biblical theme is explained throughout the New Testament is illustrated by Paul when he taught: "We speak the wisdom of God in a mystery, even the hidden wisdom, which God ordained before the world unto our glory. . . . God hath revealed them unto us by his Spirit: for the Spirit searcheth all things, yea, the deep things of God" (1 Corinthians 2:7–10). Verses 6 through 10 clarify that the mysteries of God are not communicated to the worldly minded (v. 6) and those not of the faith (v. 8); they testify that the "deep things" of God are communicated by the "Spirit" to those who love God (v. 9). Thus, Paul taught: "I have fed you with milk, and not with meat: for hitherto ye were not able to bear it, neither yet now are ye able. For ye are yet carnal: for whereas there is among you envying, and strife, and divisions, are ye not carnal, and walk as men?" (1 Corinthians 3:2–3).

He also explained why the mysteries were not given to new or weak members of the Church: "But strong meat belongeth to them that are of full age, even those who by reason of use have their senses exercised to discern both good and evil" (Hebrews 5:14). Paul's analogy asserting that "strong meat" can only be given to those who have spiritually prepared themselves seems to imply becoming *adults in gospel learning*. The unwritten teachings of the forty days may qualify as this kind of higher learning.

The Apostle Peter, reflecting on the secret tradition of the Church as stated in the

Clementine Homilies, declared: "We remember that our Lord and Teacher, commanding us, said, 'Keep the mysteries for me and the sons of my house.' *Wherefore also He explained to His disciples privately the mysteries of the kingdom of heaven.* But to you who battle with us, and examine into nothing else but our statements, whether they be true or false, it would be impious to state the hidden truths."[21] In his characteristic straightforwardness, Peter was very clear when he declared that those who are contentious and "battle" the Apostles—analogous to the Pharisees attempting to entrap the Savior—will not receive *hidden truths.*

The early Christian Church, after the death of the Apostles, continued to hold fast to this practice. For example, the early Church Father Ignatius testified: *"For might not I write to you things more full of mystery?* But I fear to do so, lest I should inflict injury on you who are but babes [in Christ]. Pardon me in this respect, lest, as *not being able to receive their weighty import, ye should be strangled by them."*[22] Ignatius was familiar with doctrines and teachings not recorded in the Old Testament or other apostolic writings. Only the more faithful and those who have overcome the temptations of the world qualify for the knowledge Ignatius describes as the *mysteries.*

At the beginning of the third century, Hippolytus wrote: "But if there is any other matter which ought to be told, let the bishop impart it secretly to those who are communicated. He shall not tell this to any but the faithful and only after they have first been communicated. This is the white stone of which John said that there is a new name written upon it which no man knows except him who receives."[23] If Hippolytus were alive today, one might ask him, "What was the secret knowledge given to the faithful to

which you referred in your letter? And what did you mean when you spoke of a 'new name . . . which no man knows except him who receives'? What enlightenment did the early saints possess that Church members today no longer have?"

Finally, a pseudepigraphal book entitled 4 Ezra confirms that the practice of withholding sacred teachings from the masses has been God's pattern from Old Testament times: "Ezra open your mouth and drink what I give you to drink. . . . And the Most High gave understanding, . . . which they did not know. They sat forty days, and wrote during the daytime, and . . . during the forty days ninety-four books were written. . . . The Most High spoke to me saying, 'Make public the twenty-four books that you wrote first and let the worthy and the unworthy read them; but keep the seventy that were written last, in order to give them to the wise among your people.' . . . And I did so."[24]

Jesus taught the Apostles truths that He considered sacred but restricted. With the evidence accumulated from the Pseudepigrapha, the teachings of Jesus, the Apostles, and the early Church Fathers, it would appear that certain knowledge was reserved for the faithful. This is a doctrine consistently taught in sacred writings from the beginning. Many references to sacred rites and ordinances have been preserved in the apocryphal writings, the sheer volume of which demonstrate their existence and implies their importance to early Christians.

The teachings conveyed by Jesus to the Apostles during the forty-day period compose a substantial body of doctrinal information that answer questions men and women have pondered for centuries. The scriptures teach us that Heavenly Father loves His children and desires them to have knowledge of Him and His laws. God requires a humble and obedient people with whom He will gladly share such knowledge, as indicated by the Savior to His Apostles. Following is a brief sketch of some of these teachings.

The Doctrine of the Origin and Destiny of Man

The Pseudepigrapha, Apocrypha, and early Christian and Jewish writings answer in greater detail questions regarding man's salvation, and these teachings are consistent with doctrines expressed in the Bible. They provide understanding regarding the state of man's existence before the physical creation, the purpose of man's existence or mission here on earth, and the destination of the spirit after the body is laid to rest in the grave. The early records confirm that man will take part in a glorious resurrection and that the spirit will reunite with the body in order to progress to greater heights and glory. Along with the Bible, they describe Jesus' dual ministry to both the living *and the dead*, showing that God is merciful and just and that His plan provides for the redemption of all men, subject to the exercise of free will and personal responsibility.

Answers to such questions as to where the Savior's spirit went during the time His body lay in the tomb until His resurrection are furnished, describing Jesus' mission to the spirits below, offering salvation not only to the living, but also to those who departed from this life *without the law*, consistent with Isaiah's prophecy (Isaiah 61:1; 42:7) and Peter's epistle (1 Peter 3:18–21; 4:5–6). The New Testament teaches that those who accept the Savior's teachings in mortality must be baptized, receive the Holy Ghost, and endure to the end in order to inherit eternal life. Likewise, apocryphal teachings and early Christian writers explain that those

dying *without the law* who receive and accept the knowledge of the Son of God *after* death and are baptized by a living proxy receive the "seal" of eternal life and follow Jesus out of darkness into the light, where they have the opportunity to climb to higher levels and to obtain greater realms of glory. This ascent is described as the spirit returning to its heavenly home where it resided with God before it came to earth. In heaven, a plan was proposed at the creation of the world whereby the human race, through Adam's fall, would be placed in a position to choose between good and evil and receive eternal reward or punishment according to one's own merit. Satan led a revolt against the plan, refusing to honor Adam as the one chosen to stand at the head of the human family under Christ. He was cast out of heaven to the earth with those who followed him, providing the framework required for a genuine test of choosing light over darkness.

The Premortal Nature of Man

The doctrine of man's premortal state as spirit children of God was broadly defended by Jewish tradition, *specifically through the Pharisees*, and was also widely taught by Origen. If Jewish tradition is the descendant of Adam, the ancient Patriarchs, and Moses, and if such traditions have been accurately handed down, then Christianity—the heir of Jewish tradition—would be responsible for preserving these beliefs as God's original teachings to man. The (Jewish) Talmud itself teaches the premortal existence of the soul:

"In the seventh heaven, Araboth, are stored the spirits and the souls which have still to be created (Chag. 12b), i.e., the unborn souls which have yet to be united to bodies. . . . The Guph [is] the celestial store-house where these souls await their time to inhabit a human body."[25]

Alluding to the preexistent nature of the spirits of all men, God asks Job, "Where wast thou when I laid the foundations of the earth? . . . When the morning stars [those who served God] sang together, and all the sons of God shouted for joy?" (Job 38:4–7).[26] We learn from Jeremiah that God knew him before He formed him in the belly (Jeremiah 1:5). It would appear that God had observed Jeremiah's choices in a previous estate, thus knowingly preselecting him to be a prophet. Further declaring man's origin, intimating that his spirit existed prior to the physical creation, the Old Testament reveals that upon death "the spirit shall return unto God who gave it" (Ecclesiastes 12:7). Taken together, these verses may imply that man was created spiritually before he was created physically and that he resided with God the Eternal Father in the heavens above. Evidence for my conclusion (in concert with scripture) comes from a study of two conflicting Christian theories, predestination and free agency: If man, as early Christianity overwhelmingly taught, is a free agent, the idea of a preexistence justifies the variable conditions on earth in which man is placed; if not a free agent, then predestination is the only reasonable explanation for what appears to man to be an unjust favoritism (see pages 161–64; 211–15).

Several pre-Christian documents favor the doctrine of the preexistence of mankind. The books of Enoch (1, 2, and 3 Enoch) describe certain aspects of man's existence before he came to earth. According to 3 Enoch, the human soul predates the physical body and descends from the heavens to enter the body at birth:

Come and I will show you the souls of the righteous who have already been created and returned, and the souls of the righteous who have not yet been created. . . . Taking me by the hand, he led me to the throne of glory and showed me those souls which have already been created and returned. . . . Then I (R. Ishmael) went and expounded this verse, and found with regard to the text "The spirit shall clothe itself in my presence, and the souls which I have made,"(see Isaiah 57:16) that "The spirit shall clothe itself in my presence," refers to the souls of the righteous which have already been created in the storehouse of beings and have returned to the presence of God; and "the souls which I have made" refers to the souls of the righteous which have not yet been created in the storehouse.[27]

This vision to Rabbi Ishmael by an angel named Metatron, said to be the "translated" Enoch and called the "servant of Yahweh,"[28] explains that the souls of man reside with God before they come to earth. Those who have already been clothed with a physical body and *kept the law* return to God, after death, near the "throne of glory," while those spirits who have not yet received physical bodies remain with God until their time is due. They are called "righteous" because they come from God in purity. Those angels or spirits in the premortal existence who were disobedient to God's will, aligning themselves with Satan, were cast out of heaven; thus, they will never have fleshly bodies. According to 3 Enoch and Revelation 12, the remainder of God's spirit children followed righteousness rather than Satan and reside in the "storehouse" until their time. This concept may account for the diverse personalities we seem to carry with us into birth. In concert with other early Christian literature and the Bible, 3 Enoch offers evidence of the preexistent nature of man.

First Enoch records that Enoch was permitted to see the Father's spiritual creations—even an innumerable host of the spirits of man:

(Even) before the world was created, he knows what is forever and what will be from generation to generation. . . . They shall bless, praise and extol (you), saying, "Holy, Holy, Holy, Lord of the Spirits; the spirits fill the earth." And my face was changed on account of the fact that I could not withstand the sight. . . . And after that, I saw . . . ten million times ten million, an innumerable and uncountable (multitude) who stand before the glory of the Lord of the Spirits.[29]

Thus, the account of 1 Enoch is consistent with the report furnished by Rabbi Ishmael in 3 Enoch.

Further corroborating the doctrine of the preexistence, the *Pastor of Hermas* taught that *the Church itself* was preexistent to the creation of the world, raising the question that if the Church was created before the world, for whose benefit was it created? Wrote the Shepherd in answer:

"Who do you think the ancient lady was from whom you received the little book?" I said, "The Sibyl." "You are wrong," he said, "she is not." "Who is she, then?" I said, "The Church," he said. I said to him, "Why is she so old?" "Because," he said, "she was created the first of all things. For this reason is she old; and for her sake was the world established."[30]

The Church is not a church without people but is God's institution for administering to His children. Mankind, it seems, existed before the physical creation as spirit sons and daughters of God, and the world was created for them. The idea that the Church existed prior to the creation of the world is also recorded in 2 Clement: "Thus, brethren, if we do the will of our Father, God, we shall belong to the first Church, the spiritual one

which was created before the sun and moon. . . . Moreover, the books and the Apostles declare that the Church belongs not to the present, but has existed from the beginning; for she was spiritual as was also our Jesus."[31]

The additional witness of 2 Clement strengthens the doctrine of the preexistence of the spirits of all men. Its author testifies that Jesus was preexistent, that the Church was preexistent, implying that man was preexistent to the earth, necessitating the existence of the Church of God before the earth's creation as well.

Origen, piecing together the early literature, speculated that man existed prior to the physical creation:

In that commencement, then, we are to suppose that God created so great a number of rational or intellectual creatures (or by whatever name they are to be called). . . .[32] The Creator gave, as an indulgence to the understandings created by Him, the power of free and voluntary action, by which the good that was in them might become their own, being preserved by the exertion of their own will; but slothfulness, and a dislike of labour in preserving what is good, and an aversion to and a neglect of better things, furnished the beginning of a departure from goodness. . . . From which it appears that the Creator of all things . . . might create variety and diversity in proportion to the diversity of understandings . . .[33] And certain of them, from the hour of their birth, are reduced to humiliation and subjection, . . . Others . . . are brought up in . . . freedom and reason. . . .[34] He created all whom He made equal and alike, . . . but since those rational creatures themselves, . . . were endowed with the power of free will, this freedom of will incited each one either to progress by imitation of God, or reduced him to failure through negligence.[35]

Origen believed that man was created spiritually before he was created physically. He taught that man was endowed with the gift of free will, and based on that will, chose either to imitate God or to become complacent and thus limit his progress. Accordingly, Origen believed that one's actions before birth contributed to certain experiences and conditions one would face on earth. He further taught that free will continued in man throughout mortality, and according to the parable of the talents, man would reap eternal reward according to his choices.

From the books of Enoch, the Shepherd of Hermas, and the author of 2 Clement, it appears that the early Church may have believed that humankind existed premortally with God (and the Savior) and that we are all God the Father's *offspring*. Origen, writing a century later, also believed in man's premortal existence, although he did not agree that Jesus was of the same created class as man, as is implied in the books of Enoch. These early Christian views of man's origin seem to coincide with certain passages from the Old Testament, as earlier indicated.

A Plan Introduced for Man's Eternal Progress

The early Christian literature explains that God introduced a plan whereby man, whose origin began as a spirit son or daughter of God, could progress and become more like Him. The author of the Clementine Homilies alleges that Clement of Rome, when speaking with Peter, stated this plan was *announced in the presence of all the first angels:*

After this, when you had explained about the creation of the world, you intimated the decree of God, which He, of His own good pleasure, announced in the presence of all the first angels, and which He ordained as an eternal law to

all; and how He established two kingdoms,—I mean that of the present time and that of the future,—and appointed times to each, and decreed that a day of judgment should be expected, which He determined, in which a severance is to be made of things and of souls: so that the wicked indeed shall be consigned to eternal fire for their sins; but those who have lived according to the will of God the Creator, having received a blessing for their good works, effulgent with brightest light, introduced into an eternal abode, and abiding in incorruption, shall receive eternal gifts of ineffable blessings.[36]

First Enoch reveals the important role that Jesus Christ was to play in God's plan for the redemption of His creations:

At that hour, the Son of Man was given a name, in the presence of the Lord of the Spirits, the Beforetime; even before the creation of the sun and the moon, before the creation of the stars. . . . He will become a staff for the righteous ones in order that they may lean on him and not fall. He is the light of the gentiles and he will become the hope of those who are sick in their hearts. All those who dwell on the earth shall fall and worship before him; they shall glorify, bless, and sing the name of the Lord of the Spirits. For this purpose he became the Chosen One. . . . They will be saved in his name and it is his good pleasure that they have life.[37]

These two passages describe in some detail that God introduced a plan whereby His spirit sons and daughters could progress through obedience or be condemned through disobedience. Man would come to earth, receive a physical body, be tested and tried, and prove faithful or unfaithful. The Son of God, even Jesus, became the "Chosen One" who would save God's creations "in His name" through the Atonement and the Resurrection—if man would choose Him over worldly pleasures and fame.

Man's Ultimate Destiny If Proven Faithful

The Bible declares the eventual outcome for those who obey God's plan. Paul testified: "The Spirit itself beareth witness with our spirit, that we are the children of God: and if children, then heirs; heirs of God, and joint-heirs with Christ; if so be that we suffer with him, that we may be also glorified together" (Romans 8:16–17).

Additionally, Paul counseled his readers: "Let this mind be in you, which was also in Christ Jesus: who, being in the form of God, thought it not robbery to be equal with God" (Philippians 2:5–6). Paul clearly taught that we should have the same "mind" or thoughts as Jesus, who knew the eventual outcome of those who obey God's laws: we will become *like* God and His Son, Jesus Christ. The Savior further testified, "All things that the Father hath are mine" (John 16:15). He then promised, "He that overcometh shall inherit all things; and I will be his God, and he shall be my son" (Revelation 21:7); and "to him that overcometh will I grant to sit with me in my throne, even as I also overcame, and am set down with my Father in his throne" (Revelation 3:21).

Centuries earlier, the Psalmist recorded, "I have said, Ye are gods; and all of you are children of the most High" (Psalm 82:6). Referring to this specific verse and clarifying whom God addressed through the Psalmist, Jesus chastised the Jews for not believing He was the Son of God: "The Jews answered him, saying, For a good work we stone thee not; but for blasphemy; and because that thou, being a man, makest thyself God. Jesus answered

them, Is it not written in your law, I said, Ye are gods? If he called them gods, *unto whom the word of God came,* and the scripture cannot be broken; say ye of him, whom the Father hath sanctified, and sent into the world, Thou blasphemest; because I said, I am the Son of God?" (John 10:33–36; emphasis added).

God was addressing those "unto whom the word of God came." According to several early Jewish writers, He was also speaking to Israel's judges: "How long will ye judge unjustly?" (Psalm 82:2). The scriptures provide a consistent answer in regards to the nature of our eternal reward *if* we will choose God over the world, accept His Son, and remain faithful to His commandments.

This promise was set forth from the beginning and has been revealed to every dispensation beginning with Adam. In the Testament of Adam, we read:

> He [the Messiah] spoke to me about this paradise after I picked some of the fruit in which death was hiding: "Adam, Adam do not fear. You wanted to become a god; I will make you a god, but not right now, but after the space of many years. I am consigning you to death, and the maggot and the worm will eat your body." And I answered and said to him, "Why, my Lord?" And he said to me, "Because you listened to the words of the serpent, you and your posterity will be food for the serpent. But after a short time there will be mercy on you because you were created in my image. . . . And I will set you at the right hand of my divinity, and I will make you a god just like you wanted. And I will receive favor from God, and I will restore to you and to your posterity that which is the justice of heaven."[38]

The early Christian Fathers were aware of this promise, also taught by other prophets and Apostles. Each of these men, including the Apostolic Fathers who followed, understood the Psalmist precisely as explained by Jesus in the New Testament. Justin Martyr wrote: "God standeth in the congregation of gods; He judgeth among the gods. . . . I said, 'Ye are gods, and are all children of the Most High'; . . . let the interpretation of the Psalm be held just as you wish, yet thereby it is demonstrated that all men are deemed worthy of becoming 'gods,' and of having power to become sons of the Highest."[39] Approximately thirty years later, Irenaeus explained, "If the Word became a man, it was so men may become gods."[40] He then inquired:

Do we cast blame on him because we were not made gods from the beginning, but were first created merely as men, and then later gods? Although God has adopted this course out of his pure benevolence, that no one may charge him with discrimination or stinginess, he declares, "I have said, ye are gods; and all of you are the sons of the Most High." . . . For it was necessary at first that nature be exhibited, then after that what was mortal would be conquered and swallowed up in immortality.[41]

Hippolytus explained that men were born like Christ and should expect to inherit what the Father has granted unto the Son:

This Logos [Christ] we know to have received a body from a virgin. . . . And we believe the Logos to have passed through every period of this life, in order that he might serve as a law for every age. . . . This Man we know to have been made out of the same compound of our humanity. For if he were not of the same nature with ourselves, in vain does He ordain that we should imitate the Teacher. . . . For if that Man happened to be a different substance from us, why does He lay injunctions

similar to those He has received on myself, who am born weak; and how is this the act of one that is good and just? . . . Now in all these acts He offered up, as the first fruits, His own manhood, in order that thou, when thou art in tribulation, mayest not be disheartened, but, confessing thyself to be a man (of like nature with the Redeemer), mayest dwell in expectation of also receiving what the Father has granted unto this Son.[42]

Hippolytus concluded that the final state of the righteous is to become *like* God and to become *a* god:

And thou shalt become a companion of the Deity, and a co-heir with Christ, no longer enslaved by lusts or passions, and never again wasted by disease. For thou hast become God: . . . thou hast been deified, and begotten to immortality. This constitutes the import of the proverb, 'Know thyself'; i.e., discover God within thyself, for He has formed thee after His own image. . . . And God called man His likeness from the beginning. . . . And provided thou obeyest His solemn injunctions, and become a faithful follower . . . thou shalt resemble Him. . . . For the Deity, (by condescension,) does not diminish aught of the dignity of His divine perfection; having made thee even God unto His glory![43]

Clement of Alexandria also testified that man, if obedient, would progress to become like God: "And now the Word Himself clearly speaks to thee, shaming thy unbelief. Yea, I say, the Word of God became a man so that you might learn from a man how to become a god. . . . [44] If one knows himself, he will know God, and knowing God will become like God. . . . His is beauty, true beauty, for it is God, and that man becomes a god, since

God wills it. So Heraclitus was right when he said, "Men are gods, and gods are men."[45] Providing valuable detail to his understanding of the destiny of faithful humankind, Clement further witnessed:

> It leads us to the endless and perfect end, teaching us beforehand the future life that we shall lead, according to God, and with gods; after we are freed from all punishment and penalty which we undergo, in consequence of our sins, for salutary discipline. After which redemption the reward and the honors are assigned to those who have become perfect; when they have got done with perfection, and ceased from all service, though it be holy service, and among saints. They become pure in heart, and near to the Lord, there awaits their restoration to everlasting contemplation; and they are called by the appellation of gods, being destined to sit on thrones with the other gods that have been first put in their places by the Savior.[46]

Speaking on the subject of deification, Origen wrote: "From Him there began the union of the divine with the human nature, in order that the human, by communion with the divine, might rise to be divine, not in Jesus alone, but in all those who not only believe, but enter upon the life which Jesus taught, and which elevates to friendship with God and communion with Him every one who lives according to the precepts of Jesus."[47] Origen also explained his view of the ultimate relationship that will exist between God the Father, Jesus Christ, and those who become His heirs and joint-heirs with Christ:

> And thus the first-born of all creation, who is the first to be with God, and to attract to Himself divinity, is a being of more exalted rank than the other gods beside Him, of whom God is the

God, as it is written, "The God of gods, the Lord, hath spoken and called the earth." It was by the offices of the first-born that they became gods, for He drew from God in generous measure that they should be made gods, and He communicated it to them according to His own bounty. The true God, then, is "The God," and those who are formed after Him are gods, images, as it were, of Him the prototype. . . . Now it is possible that some may dislike what we have said representing the Father as the one true God, but admitting other beings besides the true God, who have become gods by having a share of God. They may fear that the glory of Him who surpasses all creation may be lowered to the level of those other beings called gods. We drew this distinction between Him and them that we showed God the Word to be to all the other gods the minister of their divinity. . . . As then, there are many gods, but to us there is but one God the Father, and many Lords, but to us there is one Lord, Jesus Christ.[48]

Origen expressed the truth that we will always be subject to God and Jesus, but, as Jesus did, all things that the Father has, we also will inherit (Revelation 21:7).

Late in the fourth century, this doctrine was still being taught by the revered Catholic bishops Athanasius and Augustine. Athanasius recorded: "The Word was made flesh in order that we might be enabled to be made gods. . . . Just as the Lord, putting on the body, became a man, so also we men are both deified through his flesh, and henceforth inherit everlasting life. . . . [49] He became man that we might become divine."[50]

Augustine believed that men are "deified of God's grace" but "not born of His substance." Nevertheless, he admits that we become like God and "fellow heirs" with Christ: "But He that justifieth doth Himself deify, in that by justifying He doth make sons of God. For he has given them power to become 'the sons of God' [John 1:12]. If we have been made sons of God, we have also been made gods."[51]

Augustine's Neoplatonist view prevented him from making the distinction between Paul's statements in Acts and Romans. The book of Acts implies that we are genetically the spirit sons of God by birth. The book of Romans suggests both the genetic *and* adoptive relationship: genetic because we are the children of God; adoptive because although we were cut off from the presence of the Father because of Adam's fall, through the grace of Christ we are restored once again to the family of God, "if it so be that we suffer with Him" (see pages 159–61).

The Bible, Pseudepigrapha, Apocrypha, and the earliest Christian Fathers seem to indicate that we are the literal spirit sons and daughters of God and that we resided with Him prior to the physical creation. Through specific laws established by the Father, these spirits would be sent to earth to be tried and tested in the flesh. Through obedience to the laws and ordinances set forth by the Son of God, man was to have the privilege of becoming like the Father—thus being His heirs and joint heirs with the Son. That the early Christian Fathers taught this doctrine so clearly is of great value to modern Christians who attempt to understand holy writ today. No wonder Paul taught, "Eye hath not seen, nor ear heard, neither have entered into the heart of man, the things which God hath prepared for them that love him" (1 Corinthians 2:9). After all, who could ever imagine such a doctrine as this were it not revealed *repeatedly* from the heavens?

Salvation Doctrine and Rites in Primitive Christianity

Although the primitive Church clearly taught the sublime and divine potential of man, the salvation doctrine, ritual ordinances, and the meaning of faith itself to the early Christians (necessary to obtain these promised blessings), these ancient doctrines differ widely in scope and meaning from those taught in many Christian congregations today. The emphasis that New Testament Christianity placed on baptism, its real purpose and symbolism, and other principles pertaining to salvation drifted into obscurity with the passing of the Apostles. Included in this uncertainty was a clouding of the Church's understanding of anything specific about the nature of eternal reward. Diverse interpretation of important events and of the sacred records left behind (beginning in the second century) ultimately led to a distinctive accent on certain principles while others were materially modified or deemphasized. Accordingly, while the doctrines hereafter presented pertaining to salvation were very familiar and important to early Church members, modern Christians may be unacquainted with these ancient practices and even view them with skepticism. Nonetheless, sufficient evidence exists that these were indeed the beliefs of the early Christians.

The Savior's Ministry of Salvation to Both Living and Dead

In the first verse of Isaiah 61, Isaiah foretold the Savior's ministry of preaching good tidings to the meek and binding up the broken-hearted, or in other words, *His ministry to the living*. He also seemed to speak of the "faithful" during the patriarchal dispensations when he recorded that Jesus would "proclaim liberty to the captives," indicating that the righteous souls living on earth prior to the Atonement and the Resurrection would be set free when Christ completed his earthly mission. The "opening of the prison to them that are bound" may refer to Jesus' ministry to *those who died without hearing the gospel* in the flesh or to those who died in disobedience (1 Peter 3:18–20; 4:6).

The ministry of Jesus to the living, as revealed in the New Testament, is straightforward. We are invited to develop faith in Jesus Christ—His wondrous birth; His perfect life; His Divine ministry of salvation; His atonement, death, and resurrection; His return in glory and subsequent millennial reign; and final judgment at His hands. We have been commanded to repent of our sins and live a life consistent with Jesus' example, relying on His grace and mercy to help us overcome our shortcomings. We are to be baptized for the remission of sins and receive the gift of the Holy Ghost to guide us in our earthly sojourn, being born of the water and the Spirit (John 3:5). Like Paul, we are to endure to the end, to fight a good fight, and to keep the faith (2 Timothy 4:6–8). Each of these conditions is documented by scripture. While various denominations advance opposing ideologies regarding specific requirements, Christianity in general accepts certain basic principles.

Although theology surrounding salvation for the living is substantially evident, Christian doctrine regarding redemption for those who die without the law is much less tidy. There are only a small number of references to such within the standard canon. Whether or not certain passages were purposely removed from the canon in the second century, or particular books not accepted due to less familiar content, or simply withheld from the Christian population at large due to their esoteric nature, is unknown. While the Bible contains few references to such doctrines, the Pseudepigrapha, apocryphal writings, and early Christian writings record many passages dealing with esoteric subjects.

Understanding Jesus' forty-day ministry is important in order to appreciate fully what pure and complete Christianity was under Christ's direct administration. Because the Apostles seemingly grasped only basic doctrines before His resurrection, Jesus educated them further in rites and doctrines reserved for the faithful—precisely as He had promised *before* the Crucifixion (John 16:12, 25). By comparing the comprehensive structure of rites and ordinances in the early Christian community with the fragmented and inconsistent theology produced by the Gnostics who followed, it is obvious that much of Jesus' teaching during the forty days dealt with formal, ceremonial worship among the very faithful. Some of the ordinances described in the apocryphal writings are well known, such as water baptism for the living and the Eucharist. Other rites, according to Clement of Alexandria, required induction into the mysteries.[52] Such ordinances included the seal of baptism, not only for the living but also for those who died without the law, such as those preceding the advent of Christ. There followed rituals of washing, anointing, wearing of a white garment, and what is known as a prayer circle. Particular emphasis was also placed on the sacrament of marriage.

The prominence of many of these rituals or ordinances, although relatively unknown in Christianity today, played a central role in the salvation doctrine of the early Church. The gospel plan in its fullness has never been made known to most of God's children, either because the people have been in a state of apostasy or the culture was simply non-Christian. The most fundamental principles hoped for by mankind is that there is a God, that He is a loving and fair God, and that in the end all His children will be judged by an equitable system of justice and mercy. Many have hoped this judgment will take into consideration all the unjust conditions of our mortal experience, evaluating degree of difficulty and rendering fitting judgments against the wicked, consoling and vindicating the righteous. The early Church believed in such a system, evident by the secret (sacred) traditions handed down to that generation, which included the Apostolic Fathers.

The Preaching of the Gospel to Those Who Die without the Law

The pure gospel plan includes preaching the gospel to those who have died without knowledge of the truth. Souls thus taught could either accept or reject the truth, just as in mortality. Those who accept the gospel then receive the opportunity of baptism, vicariously performed by living persons. Peter taught this truth while he was yet alive:

> For Christ also hath once suffered for sins, the just for the unjust, that he might bring us to God, being put to death in the flesh, but quickened by the Spirit: by which also he went and preached unto the spirits in prison; which sometime were disobedient, when once the longsuffering of God waited in the days of Noah, while the ark was a preparing, wherein few, that is, eight souls were saved by water. (1 Peter 3:18–20)

Peter's testimony marked fulfillment of Old Testament prophecy as recorded by Isaiah: "The Spirit of the Lord God is upon me; because the Lord hath anointed me to preach good tidings unto the meek; he hath sent me to bind up the brokenhearted, to proclaim liberty to the captives, and the opening of the prison to them that are bound" (Isaiah

61:1; see also 42:7).

Some individuals have interpreted this passage to refer only to those living on the earth. However, a careful review of Peter's testimony in concert with apocryphal witnesses reveals otherwise. Christ's atonement not only effected salvation for the living who accept Him but also opened wide the prison gates in the spirit world. How was this accomplished? Peter himself provided the clues: "For this cause was the gospel preached *also to them that are dead, that they might be* judged according to men in the flesh, but live according to God in the spirit" (1 Peter 4:6; emphasis added).

God's plan was complete, and the great gulf separating the wicked from the righteous in the spirit world before Christ's resurrection was bridged by Jesus himself (Luke 16:26). Ignatius testifies of this important truth: "For says the scripture, 'Many bodies of the saints that slept arose,' their graves being opened. He descended, indeed, into Hades alone, but He arose accompanied by a multitude; and rent asunder that means of separation which had existed from the beginning of the world, *and cast down its partition-wall.*"[53] From the New Testament and apocryphal literature, we learn that the Savior accomplished this mission during the three days His body lay in the tomb. Thus, Mary was told, "Touch me not; for I have not yet ascended to my Father" (John 20:17). The Savior's spirit went somewhere during those three days but not to see His Father.

In addition to Ignatius, Irenaeus wrote: "And this is why the Lord went down under the earth (Ephesians 4:9) to proclaim to them His coming, the remission of sins for those who believe in Him, . . . those who set their hope in Him (1:12), . . . and He remitted their sins like ours."[54] Clement of Alexandria also wrote about Christ's mission to the dead. He testified that upon completion of their mortal mission, the Apostles assisted the Savior in preaching the gospel to those in darkness: "And it has been shown also, in the second book of the Stromata, that the Apostles, following the Lord, preached the gospel to those in Hades."[55]

Moreover, the Shepherd of Hermas records:

[Before] a man bears the name of the Son of God he is dead. But when he receives the seal he puts away mortality and receives life. The seal, then, is the water. . . . This seal . . . was preached to them [the dead] also, and they made use of it "to enter into the kingdom of God." These apostles and teachers, who preached the name of the Son of God, having fallen asleep in the power and faith of the Son of God, preached also to those who had fallen asleep before them, and themselves gave to them the seal of the preaching.[56]

Finally, the Odes of Solomon, with an approximate composition date of A.D. 100, also testifies of Christ's mission to the dead: "Sheol [hell] saw me [Jesus] and was shattered. . . . And I made a congregation of living among his dead; and I spoke with them by living lips. . . . And those who had died ran toward me; and they cried out and said, 'Son of God, have pity on us. And deal with us according to your kindness, and bring us out from the chains of darkness. And open for us the door by which we may go forth to you. . . . May we be saved with you, because you are our Savior.' Then I heard their voice, and placed their faith in my heart. And I placed my name upon their head, because they are free and they are mine."[57]

According to the early Church, the Savior's redeeming work provides that every soul who has lived or who will yet live on the earth will hear the gospel in its entirety and either accept it or reject it according to the principle of agency and accountability. This is sometimes known as the doctrine of the Two Ways, one of the most common teachings in the Bible and the early Christian writings. In Deuteronomy we read: "I have set before you life and death, blessing and cursing: therefore choose life, that both thou and thy seed may live" (Deuteronomy 30:19).

John's Apocalypse records: "The Spirit and the bride say, Come. And *let him that heareth* say, Come. And *let him that is athirst* come. And *whosoever will,* let him take the water of life freely" (Revelation 22:17; emphasis added).

The Bible teaches the doctrine of free will, of choosing life or death, and of the invitation that is extended to all men to "take the water of life freely." This doctrine is also taught by the early Christian Fathers. In the Didache, also known as the Teaching of the Twelve Apostles, we read: "Two Ways there are, one of Life and one of Death, and there is a great difference between the Two Ways. . . . The Way of Life is this: first love God who made you; secondly, your neighbor as yourself. . . . The Way of Death is . . . murders, adulteries, lustful desires, fornications, thefts, idolatries, etc."[58]

Ignatius affirmed the Two Ways when he wrote: "Seeing then that there is an end to all, that the choice is between two things, death and life, and each is to go to his own place."[59] Man, whether or not he receives the teachings of Jesus during his mortal life or after death in the spirit, will choose for himself his eternal reward or punishment.

Baptism for the Dead in Early Christianity

Included in the conditions set forth for

man's redemption was an orderly system for every individual to receive the ordinances and rites pertaining to salvation, *whether in the flesh or in the spirit.* God's plan accounted for every condition, whether environmental, genetic, political, or otherwise in order to guarantee a righteous and equitable judgment of all His children. Demonstrating that baptism for the dead was indeed an accepted practice in ancient times, Paul himself posed an interesting question to the Sadducees at Corinth: "Else what shall they do which are baptized for the dead, if the dead rise not at all? why are they then baptized for the dead?" (1 Corinthians 15:29).

Admittedly, the subject of Paul's question is not baptism for the dead but the resurrection in which the Sadducees did not believe. However, Paul's matter-of-fact reference to baptism for the dead and apparent familiarity with it certainly make it clear that it was being done. Paul neither condemns it nor expounds upon its full purpose but refers to it as casually as one might indicate that bread is made in a bakery. After Jesus' forty-day ministry, this rite and other sacred rites and sacraments became well known to the faithful. For example, the Shepherd of Hermas recorded: "These apostles and teachers . . . went down therefore with them into the water and came up again, but the latter went down alive and came up alive, while the former, who had fallen asleep before, went down dead but came up alive. Through them, therefore, they were made alive, and received the knowledge of the Son of God."[60]

Likewise, the Epistle of the Apostles attests the performance of baptism for the dead: "And on that account I [Jesus] have descended and have spoken with Abraham and Isaac and Jacob, to your fathers the prophets, and have brought to them the news that they may come from the rest which is below into heaven, and have given them the right hand of baptism of life and forgiveness and pardon for all wickedness."[61]

In the pseudepigraphal book the Life of Adam and Eve, when Adam died he was carried by a seraph "to the lake of Acheron" where he was washed "three times in the presence of God." He was then taken by Michael "into Paradise, to the third heaven."[62] That this doctrine in its full understanding was not practiced long after the first generation of Apostolic Fathers is evident from the many writings that have been discovered; yet baptism for the dead, *without a complete understanding of its purposes,* was performed and commented on as late as Augustine early in the fifth century.[63]

Eternal Reward and Punishment According to the Early Church Fathers

When Jesus was attempting to convey to the Apostles His love for them and His desire to be with them eternally, He taught important doctrine concerning the life to come. Because the doctrine was sacred, it was written only in very general terms. Thus, the Apostle John recorded Jesus as saying, "Let not your heart be troubled: ye believe in God, believe also in me. In my Father's house are many mansions: if it were not so, I would have told you. I go to prepare a place for you. And if I go and prepare a place for you, I will come again, and receive you unto myself; that where I am, there ye may be also" (John 14:1–3).

Clarifying the meaning of "many mansions," the Apostle Paul revealed important truths about the nature of the resurrection: "But some man will say, How are the dead raised up? and with what body do they come? Thou fool, that which thou sowest is not quickened, except it die: and that which thou sowest, thou sowest not that body that shall be, but bare grain, it may chance of wheat, or of some other grain: but God giveth it a body as it hath pleased him, and to every seed his own body" (1 Corinthians 15:35–38).

Replying to the questions, "How are the dead raised up?" and "With what body do they come?" Paul uses a familiar analogy, reminding his audience that a wheat kernel will not become a stock capable of producing multiple kernels unless it is buried in the ground ("die[s]"). Then Paul intimates that the planted grain will be watered, nurtured, and ultimately "quickened" (or, in other words, a tender sprout will push forth through the soil, the stock will grow, and eventually it will mature for harvest). Finally, Paul asks whether it will be wheat or some other kind of grain. He implies that it will produce wheat kernels, not barley or any other type of grain. Continuing the lesson on the Resurrection and eternal reward, he writes:

All flesh is not the same flesh: but there is one kind of flesh of men, another flesh of beasts, another of fishes, and another of birds. There are also celestial bodies, and bodies terrestrial: but the glory of the celestial is one, and the glory of the terrestrial is another. There is one glory of the sun, and another glory of the moon, and another glory of the stars: for one star differeth from another star in glory. So also is the resurrection of the dead. (1 Corinthians 15:39–42)

Paul explains that living things are not all the same. Using familiar examples, he illustrates that men, beasts, fishes, and birds all have a different type of skin or flesh (v. 39). Next he teaches that in the Resurrection there are "celestial and terrestrial bodies," specifically stating there is one glory of the sun, another of the moon, and another of the stars (vv. 40–41). After making this

comparison, Paul states, "So also is the resurrection of the dead" (v. 42). The subject of this entire passage is that our earthly bodies are corruptible and that through Jesus they shall become incorruptible. These verses clarify that our bodies will be resurrected to differing degrees of glory, depending on our receiving and obeying the laws and ordinances of the gospel. Expounding this interpretation still further, in 2 Corinthians 12:2 Paul writes that he knew a man (himself, as the scriptures imply and as attested by Eusebius) who had been caught up to the third heaven:

"Paul . . . had innumerable mysterious matters that he might have communicated, as he had been taken up to the very paradise of God, and had been honored to hear unutterable words there."[64] If a third heaven exists, so must a first and second, precisely corresponding with Paul's earlier teaching of one glory of the sun, moon, and stars—and in harmony with the teachings of the Pseudepigrapha and early Christian Fathers.

Consistent with the Gospel of John, 2 Enoch explains: "Many shelters have been prepared for people, very good houses [for those deserving] and 'bad houses without number' [for those undeserving]. Happy is he who enters into the blessed dwellings; and indeed in the bad ones is no conversion."[65]

In addition to the authors of the Pseudepigrapha, the early Church Fathers had access to this knowledge. For example, Papias (A.D. 140) and Irenaeus (A.D. 180) explained the doctrine of "gradation and ascent" when they declared:

But that there is a distinction between the habitation of those who produce an hundred-fold, and that of those who produce sixty-fold, and that of those who produce thirty-fold; for the first will be taken up to the heavens, the second class will dwell in Paradise, and the last will inhabit the city; and on this account the Lord said, "In my Father's house are many mansions": for all things belong to God, who supplies all with a suitable dwelling-place, even as His word says, that a share is given to all by the Father, according as each one is or shall be worthy.[66]

And as the presbyters say, Then those who are deemed worthy of an abode in heaven shall go there, others shall enjoy the delights of paradise, and others shall possess the splendor of the city. . . . There is a distinction between those who produce an hundred-fold, and that of those who produce sixty-fold, and that of those who produce thirty-fold, . . . that a share is allotted to all by the Father, according as each person is or shall be worthy. . . . The presbyters, the disciples of the Apostles, affirm that this is the gradation and arrangement of those who are saved, and they advance through steps of this nature; also that they ascend through the Spirit to the Son, and through the Son to the Father.[67]

Clement of Alexandria explains his understanding of the three heavens as follows: "There are various abodes, according to the worth of those who have believed, . . . which are three, [and] indicated by the numbers in the Gospel—the thirty, the sixty, the hundred. And the perfect inheritance belongs to those who attain to the 'perfect man,' according to the image of the Lord."[68] Origen, another early witness, agrees with Papias, Irenaeus, and Clement. He explains the doctrine of gradation when he describes the ascent of the soul through the various heavens, referring to the Greek terminology of "spheres or globes" but "which the holy Scripture has called heavens."[69] The Bible, Pseudepigrapha, and early Church Fathers are of one accord as to the meaning of the Lord's doctrine, "In my

Father's house are many mansions."

If there are "many mansions," there must also be certain qualifications associated with the "stages of ascent." Due to apostasy from Christ's New Testament Church, finding agreement as to what those qualifications may be has not been possible.

Other Exoteric and Esoteric Rites Practiced by the Early Christian Church

The sheer volume of records included in the early Christian literature presents a compelling argument that Christianity lost understanding and therefore abandoned the practices of the sacred, exoteric (meaning advanced), and esoteric teachings and rites revealed by Jesus during the forty-day period. This is consistent with what happened to the Maccabees prior to the coming of Christ. They rebuilt the altar in the temple but then waited upon the Lord to send a prophet inasmuch as they did not understand the nature and purpose of the ordinances performed therein. Likewise, Catholic authority accepts the forty-day teaching but has no explanation for its content nor its removal from current liturgy. The importance of the temple in early Christianity is alluded to in the New Testament: "They, continu[ed] daily with one accord in the temple" (Acts 2:46). Unfortunately, some Gnostic groups also altered genuine and sacred practices of the forty-day teachings, confusing the orthodoxy movement that followed and causing it to reject once-pure Christian practices and teachings.

Washing, Anointing, and the Wearing of White Garments

Faith, repentance, baptism, the gift of the Holy Ghost, and enduring to the end were tenets introduced by Jesus and expounded by the Apostles in the New Testament. The Shepherd of Hermas summarizes these steps that lead back to God and warns the saints of that day urgently to repent:

> The building of a great tower was used to symbolize the formation of the Church of God in that age. Twelve angels, or maidens dressed in white linen garments, were required to carry "square stones" that had "come up through a certain deep place" *through the gate,* leading to the tower; first ten, then twenty, then thirty-five, then forty. Thereafter no stones came from below, but were carried in from the mountains. Initially, the stones were various colors, but when they came through the gate they became white. No stone was to be used unless it had come through the gate. The stones represented the sons and daughters of God. Construction of the building, nearly complete, ceased for a period. The shepherd explained that it could not be finished until it was examined by the Master. Each stone was inspected by the Master Himself and He rejected those unworthy to enter the gate. These were removed and replaced by other magnificent square stones gathered from a nearby plain and carried in through the door by the maidens. Those stones that had been rejected were sent back to the shepherd to judge, either to cleanse through repentance, or discard because of entrenched wickedness.
>
> Twelve beautiful, seductive maidens dressed in black gleefully carried away those who were rejected. The stones that remained became a tower so brilliant and exquisite, they no longer resembled many stones, but rather a single stone carved out of the mountain. The stone or Church of God represented the unity desired by the Master Himself in the intercessory prayer. Those so entering became one in purpose. They were not permitted to enter into the kingdom of heaven except they were clothed in the linen supplied by the maidens who were also dressed in white linen. Those not dressed in the white raiment, or in other words, those not possessing the attributes of purity, could not enter into the Kingdom of God.
>
> The shepherd explained that the rock and the door are the Son of God, and that He "is older than all His creation" and was "counselor of His Creation to the Father." He clarifies that the gate is new, "because [the Son] was manifest in the last days," and that all who are to be saved must "enter through it into the kingdom of God." Those entering the gate, *the only entrance,* must be willing to take upon themselves the name of the Son of God. Then the shepherd reiterated that one must not only "receive the name" but also "receive the clothing from [the maidens]," the white linen garments being a representation of His power and authority. "If you receive the name alone but do not receive the clothing from them, you will benefit nothing."
>
> Some entered in through the gate, through Jesus Christ, and acquired the clothing and attributes of the maidens for a time but were subsequently seduced by the beautiful maidens dressed in black "and put off the clothing and power of the maidens [dressed in white linen]." Those enduring to the end, not being deceived by the beauty of the women dressed in black, remained inside the tower, in the kingdom of God, because they were "not ashamed to bear his name." Even so, said the Shepherd, those who repent and finally reject the seductions of the beautiful maidens dressed in black may reenter the kingdom. The angel, speaking to the saints of that day, testifies that those who do not take this *one last opportunity to repent* will not enter the tower.

The first four maidens, representing the tower's cornerstones, are "Faith, Temperance, Power, and Longsuffering." The other eight are "Simplicity, Guilelessness, Holiness, Joyfulness, Truth, Understanding, Concord, [and] Love." The names of the most powerful wearing black raiment are "Unbelief, Impurity, Disobedience, and Deceit." The remaining eight are "Grief, Wickedness, Licentiousness, Bitterness, Lying, Foolishness, Evil speaking, and Hate." The tower, depicting the Lord's Church, was built upon the rock, Jesus Christ.

The first ten stones and the second tier of twenty stones represented the first generation of righteous men. "The thirty-five are the prophets of God and his servants, and the forty are the prophets and teachers of the preaching of the Son of God." The shepherd explained that the first stones forming the foundation and "com[ing] up from the deep" had to "come up through the water that they might be made alive, for they could not otherwise enter into the kingdom of God." The forty of Christ's ministry went down into the water with those of the pre-Christian era. The forty went down alive and came up alive, but those of the patriarchal dispensations went down dead with them and came up alive through baptism. The shepherd declared that those who entered the tower had received the "seal"—water baptism. He proclaimed that the righteous of the pre-Christian era received the preaching of the gospel from those who had already received the "seal" in life and died true and faithful, possessing the white linen garments supplied by the maidens dressed in white. The righteous of these early dispensations were taught the Gospel and then obtained the "seal" from "those apostles and teachers who preached the name of the son of God." [70]

This vision, received by Hermas at the turn of the first century, was a last call to repentance to members of the early Christian Church of that age. It reveals the basic outline of God's laws and salvation requirements from the beginning of religious history. Consistent with the Bible, it reiterates the conditions of faith, repentance, and baptism, both for the living and the dead, in order to be redeemed from one's sins. The Shepherd lists the qualities one must seek and attain through grace to become like the Master and then expounds upon the symbolism of the "white linen garments."

In addition to baptism and receiving the "gift" of the Holy Ghost, the early Church practiced other rites and sacraments pertaining to salvation. Cyril of Jerusalem called these rites "The Lectures on the Mysteries." Such ordinances included washing and anointing, and the wearing of white garments, as expressed above in the Shepherd of Hermas. The concept of washing and anointing finds its origin in the Old Testament in Aaronic Priesthood rites:

> And Aaron and his sons thou shalt bring unto the door of the tabernacle of the congregation, and shalt wash them with water. And thou shalt take the garments, and put upon Aaron the coat, and the robe of the ephod, and the ephod, and the breastplate, and gird him with the curious girdle of the ephod: and thou shalt put the mitre upon his head, and put the holy crown upon the mitre. Then shalt thou take the anointing oil, and pour it upon his head, and anoint him. And thou shalt bring his sons, and put coats upon them. And thou shalt gird them with girdles, Aaron and his sons, and put the bonnets on them: and the priest's office shall be theirs for a perpetual statute. (Exodus 29:4–9)

The priests of Aaron's day were washed, anointed, and clothed in special garments preparatory for service in the temple. Two of these rituals, the washing and clothing of the priest, occurred each time the high priest entered "the holy place" (Leviticus 16:3). A similar initiation can be observed in the Testament of Levi:

> And I saw seven men in white clothing, who were saying to me, "Arise, put on the vestments of the priesthood, the crown of righteousness, the oracle of understanding, the robe of truth, the breastplate of faith, the miter for the head, and the apron for prophetic power." Each carried one of these and put them on me and said, "From now on be a priest, you and all your posterity." The first anointed me with holy oil and gave me staff. The second washed me with pure water, fed me by hand with bread and holy wine, and put on me a holy and glorious vestment. The third put on me something made of linen, like an ephod. The fourth placed . . . around me a girdle which was like purple. The fifth gave me a branch of rich olive wood. The sixth placed a wreath on my head. The seventh placed the priestly diadem on me and filled my hands with incense, in order that I might serve as priest for the Lord God. And they said unto me, "Levi, your posterity shall be divided into three offices as a sign of the glory of the Lord who is coming."[71]

The Pseudepigrapha also records that Enoch was anointed and received sacred clothing: "And the Lord said to Michael, 'Go, and extract Enoch from his earthly clothing. And anoint him with my delightful oil, and put him into the clothes of my glory.' And so Michael did, just as the Lord had said to him. He anointed me and clothed me. And the appearance of that oil is greater than the

greatest light. . . . And I looked at myself, and I had become like one of his glorious ones."[72]

Similarly, in the community at Qumran we learn from the Temple Scroll that those performing rites also wore sacred clothing: "In the house of the laver, the priests would wash themselves and then put on their holy garments."[73]

The records preserved from the early Christian Church attest that the practice of washing, anointing, and clothing in white garments was general among those who were baptized members of the Church. The historian J. G. Davies confirms these early Christian practices when he states that "references to . . . the putting on of Christ have been understood of the anointing and clothing in white garments that were features of the ceremonial in the second century."[74] These rites, performed by orthodox Christians, were also borrowed by Gnostic groups of the same century. At some point, the exoteric, or advanced rites, reserved for those who were mature in gospel understanding, were incorporated into the ever-increasing complexities of the baptismal service. As they did so, these advanced ordinances, having lost their original meaning, ultimately disappeared from Christianity altogether.

Tertullian attested to the simplicity of baptism in the late second century, stating that no special preparation was required. He recorded that the initiate was merely "dipped in water . . . amid the utterance of a few words."[75] However, in about the middle of the fourth century, Cyril of Jerusalem recorded in great detail the ancient sacraments being performed in his city. Beginning with baptism, he outlined a series of rites each candidate was to undergo. Facing the west, the initiate was taken to the forecourt of the baptistery, and words were spoken renouncing Satan, his works, pomp, and service. Turning to the

102

east, the initiate symbolically reentered the Garden of Eden. After repeating a profession of his faith, he entered the inner chamber where he removed his clothing, was anointed, and then was baptized or "washed."[76]

Following baptism, a second anointing took place: "Ointment is symbolically applied to thy forehead and thy other senses; and while the body is anointed with the visible ointment, thy soul is sanctified by the Holy and life-giving Spirit. . . . Ye were first anointed on the forehead. . . . Then on your ears; . . . that ye . . . are quick to hear the Divine Mysteries. . . . Then on the nostrils. . . . Afterwards on your breast; that having put on the breast-plate of righteousness, ye may stand against the wiles of the devil."[77] Bishop Ambrose of Milan also recorded that during approximately the same time frame, in addition to the head being anointed, their feet are washed.[78] Moreover, Cyril taught that the symbolism itself was insufficient: it must manifest itself in the lifestyle of the individual. Thus, those receiving the white garment after baptism, having put off their "old garments," must continue to develop those attributes "that are truly white and shining and spiritual."[79]

Although the Church embroidered the simple sacrament of baptism with the exoteric practice of washing, anointing, and clothing in white garments, documented in the Old Testament, the Pseudepigrapha, the Dead Sea Scrolls, and the earliest Christian communities, the evidence attesting that such ritual ordinances were practiced by the early Church and were of divine origin is evident. The loss of these sacred ceremonies confirms that the Church of the Middle Ages departed from New Testament Christianity.

The Early Christian Prayer Circle

Another early Christian ceremony abandoned several centuries after Constantine was the Christian prayer circle. After baptism, the washing, anointing, and clothing in a white garment, the initiate received the sacrament, or Eucharist. Cyril explained that this rite began with the deacon providing water to the officiating priest to wash his hands. Surrounding the altar in a circle, the deacon enjoined the participants to "receive ye one another" and "kiss one another" in a form of reconciliation.[80] The priest next offered a prayer in behalf of those in the circle, giving thanks, blessing the Eucharist, and requesting a blessing upon "kings, . . . soldiers, and allies, . . . [and] the sick."[81] The priest also offered up petitions in behalf of those deceased: "We commemorate also those who have fallen asleep before us, first Patriarchs, Apostles, Martyrs. . . . Then on behalf also of the Holy Fathers and Bishops who have fallen asleep before us, . . . believing that it will be a very great benefit to the souls, for whom the supplication is put up."[82]

The origin of this rite also appears to be a forty-day teaching which was later merged into what became the elaborate baptismal ceremonies of the third and fourth centuries. Carl Schmidt, when referencing the book of 2 Jeu, claimed it was the most instructive of all the early Christian manuscripts. The following excerpt provides Schmidt's commentary and translation: "The apostles and their wives all form a circle around the Lord, who says he will lead them through all the secret ordinances that shall give them eternal progression. Then 'all the Apostles, clothed in their garments, . . . placing foot to foot, made a circle facing the four directions of the cosmos,' and Jesus standing at the altar proceeded to instruct them in all the signs and ordinances in which the Sons of Light must be perfect."[83]

Similarly, in an old document that has been credited to Clement of Rome and preserved in a seventh-century Syriac translation titled The Testament of Our Lord Jesus Christ as Delivered Orally by Him to Us the Apostles after His Resurrection Following His Death,[84] the bishop "stands in the middle . . . [the men and women are assigned their places, north, south, east, and west, around him]. Then all give each other the sign of peace. Next when absolute silence is established, the deacon says: 'Let your hearts be to heaven. If anyone has any ill feeling towards his neighbor, let him be reconciled. . . . Grant, therefore, O God, that all those be united with thee who participate in these sacred ordinances. . . . Give us unity of mind in the Holy Ghost, and heal our spirits . . . that we may live in thee throughout eternity!'"[85]

Subsequently, certain ordinances and rites were explained to those in the circle, after which they were told, "It is he who gave Adam . . . a garment and the promise after death he might live again and return to heaven."[86] When comparing the complete baptismal ceremony performed in Cyril's day to this earlier rite, it is likely that elements of the prayer circle were integrated into later Christianity's (i.e., Cyril's) baptismal service.

The initiation rites as recorded by Cyril conclude when, having blessed the sacrament, the priest invited the participants to partake of the Eucharist: First cupping the hands to receive the bread[87] and then taking a sip from the cup, the initiates were given a final anointing: "After thou hast partaken of the Body of Christ, . . . hallow thyself by partaking also of the Blood of Christ. And while the moisture is still upon thy lips, touch it with thy hands, and hallow thine eyes and brow and the other organs of sense."[88]

Unfortunately, the prayer circle followed the path of other sacred rites, and by the seventh century, all such ordinances were removed from the Church through apostasy.

The Mystery of Marriage in New Testament Christianity

Although foreign to modern Christianity, an ancient doctrine making the covenant of marriage eternally binding, rather than ending at death, may have been practiced in many dispensations, beginning with Adam. Genesis records that Adam and Eve were joined together in the Garden of Eden before the Fall (Genesis 2:24–25). Being immortal at the time of their union, their (implied) marriage must necessarily have been eternal. When Jesus gave Peter the "keys of the kingdom," He strangely promised that "whatsoever thou shalt bind on earth shall be bound in heaven: and whatsoever thou shalt loose on earth shall be loosed in heaven" (Matthew 16:19). Historic Christianity has never been able to comment authoritatively on this powerful promise and gift. Interestingly, many couples, notwithstanding the teachings of their church to the contrary or the words pronounced in various rites, such as "until death do us part," believe they will be together in the hereafter.

Some have used Christ's response to the Sadducees that "in the resurrection they neither marry, nor are given in marriage, but are as the angels of God in heaven" (Matthew 22:30) to deny the concept of eternal marriage (see chapter 7, note 91). If a couple has labored together in love for many years, reared children, remained true to each other and selflessly served one another through all the trials, tests, and vicissitudes of life, to say that the potential relationship this couple enjoys in heaven is no different from other relationships they may have in that eternal realm is untenable.

The covenant of marriage was considered by the earliest Christians to be one of the great mysteries (Ephesians 5:31–32). A mystery in the primitive Church was the "meat," or sacred doctrine, referred to by Paul, given only to mature members who were strong in the faith (Hebrews 5:14). Presumably, because *marriage in the Church* was such a sacred teaching, it was passed down through oral tradition and not widely taught; thus, the rite associated with eternal marriage was never included in the New Testament. Little has been preserved or is known about it from the Old Testament or apocryphal writings. However, the scriptures do teach that in the beginning God Himself counseled, "*It is not good that the man should be alone; I will make an help meet for him*" (Genesis 2:18). Moreover, God said, "Therefore shall a man leave his father and his mother, and shall cleave unto his wife: and they shall be one flesh" (Genesis 2:24). Inasmuch as Adam and Eve were joined by God before their expulsion from the garden when they were still immortal, perhaps marriage (in righteousness) was intended to endure. Jesus, answering a very plain question from the Pharisees, responded, "For this cause shall a man leave father and mother, and shall cleave to his wife: and they twain shall be one flesh? Wherefore they are no more twain, but one flesh. What therefore God hath joined together, let not man put asunder" (Matthew 19:5–6). Paul taught that "neither was the man created for the woman; but the woman for the man" and that "neither is the man without the woman, neither the woman without the man, *in the Lord*" (1 Corinthians 11:9; emphasis added).

Origen wrote that some Christians, probably orthodox, believed that marriage endured beyond the Resurrection. He suggested that the scriptural interpretation of this group, relative to the eternal nature of marriage, exhibited Jewish influence, implying that the Jewish view had no merit.[89] However, it was not the Jews who altered Christian theology. In fact, both Jewish and Christian doctrine

became heavily influenced by Greek philosophy, Jewish tradition first through Philo (who had significant influence upon Origen), and then upon Christianity as it began to attempt a thorough exegesis of doctrine long after the death of the Apostles. Origen was right when he stated the doctrine of eternal marriage exhibited an earlier Jewish influence, which tradition was perhaps a result of patriarchal traditions and prophecies handed down through the millennia and reaffirmed through the forty-day teachings during the apostolic ministry.

The apocryphal Gospel of Philip provides the most complete surviving description of marriage enduring beyond the grave in early Christianity:

> There were three buildings as places of offering in Jerusalem: the one which opens to the west was called "the holy"; another which opens to the south was called "the holy of holy"; the third which opens to the east was called the "holy of holies," where only the high priest might enter. Baptism is the "holy" house. The redemption is "holy of the holy." "The holy of the holies" is the bridal chamber. . . . The woman is united to her husband in the bridal chamber. . . . Those who have united in the bridal chamber can no longer be separated. . . . . If the marriage of defilement is so secret, how much more is the undefiled marriage a true mystery! . . . If anyone becomes a son or daughter of the bridal chamber, he will receive the light. If anyone does not receive it while he is in the world, he will not receive it in the other place.[90]

The author of the Gospel of Philip agrees with the account of Jesus to the Pharisees. Marriage, like baptism, is an earthly ordinance that must be performed on the earth in order to have it sealed in heaven. Unfortunately, the Gnostics merged corrupt doctrine with authentic doctrine, and the orthodox Church eventually rejected a true teaching that may have been passed down by the Apostles from the oral teachings of the forty days.[91]

Early Christian Doctrine Regarding the Second Coming of Christ

With respect to the forty-day teachings, the early Christian narratives conclude with the triumphant return of the Lord, known as the Second Coming, or *Parousia*. The early saints did not anticipate a lengthy period between the first and second advents of Christ. Such questions as "Lord, wilt thou at this time restore again the kingdom to Israel?" (Acts 1:6) demonstrate the keen interest and expectations the Apostles held regarding this subject. Peter petitioned the Savior, "Make known unto us what are the signs of thy Parousia and of the end of the world, that we may perceive and mark the time of thy Parousia and instruct those who come after us."[92] The Master replied:

Take heed that men deceive you not. . . . Many will come in my name saying, "I am Christ." Believe them not. . . . [L]ike the lightning . . . shall I come on the clouds of heaven with a great host in my glory, . . . that I may judge the living and the dead and recompense every man according to his work. . . . Receive ye the parable of the fig-tree . . . the fig tree is the house of Israel . . . when its boughs have sprouted at the end, then shall deceiving Christs come, and awaken hope. . . . But this deceiver is not the Christ. . . . And there shall be many martyrs by his hand. Enoch and Elias will be sent to instruct them that this is the deceiver who must come into the world and do signs and wonders in

order to deceive.[93]

Then reaffirming the Parousia, the destruction of the wicked, and the resurrection of the just at His coming, the Savior explained: "All will see how I come upon an eternal shining cloud, and the angels of God who will sit with me on the throne of my glory at the right hand of my heavenly Father. He will set a crown upon my head. As soon as the nations see it, they will weep. . . . And he shall command them to go into the river of fire. . . . God [will] raise up on the day of decision those who believe in him . . . the elect who have done good, they will come to me and will not see death. . . . I will rejoice with them."[94]

The New Testament expectation that Jesus would return shortly began to diminish with time. For example, the early Church interpreted from the Epistle of Barnabas (ca. A.D. 120) that the Savior's return was imminent: "For the day is at hand on which all things shall perish with the evil [one]. *The Lord is near, and His reward.*"[95]

However, by Justin Martyr's day (A.D. 150), doubt and disillusionment were beginning to creep into the Church. While Justin continued to express his faith in the millennial reign of Christ, many other Christians rejected this important teaching. Trypho asks, "Do you really admit that this place, Jerusalem, shall be rebuilt; and do you expect your people to be gathered together, and made joyful with Christ and the patriarchs, and the prophets?"

Justin replies, "I and many others are of this opinion, and [believe] that such will take place, . . . but on the other hand, I signified to you that many who belong to the pure and pious faith, and are true Christians, think otherwise. . . . I and others who are right-minded Christians . . . are assured that there will be a resurrection of the dead."[96]

Not many years later, Ireneaus had worked out a systematical explanation for Christ's return: "In as many days as this world was made, in so many thousand years shall it be concluded. And for this reason the Scripture says: 'Thus the heaven and the earth was finished, and all their adornment. And God brought to a conclusion upon the sixth day the works that He had made; and God rested upon the seventh day from all His works.' . . . For the day of the Lord is as a thousand years; and in six days created things were completed. it is evident, therefore, that they will come to an end at the six thousand year."[97]

Irenaeus explained the plight of the wicked and the reward of the faithful. His language is dependent on the apocryphal book Epistle of the Apostles.[98] "The chaff, indeed, which is the apostasy, [will be] cast away; but the wheat, that is those who bring forth fruit to God in faith, [will be] gathered into the barn."[99]

Irenaeus's view of the millennial reign of Christ was plainly biblical: "And when he had opened the seventh seal [the beginning of the seven thousandth year], there was silence in heaven about the space of half an hour. And I saw the seven angels which stood before God; and to them were given seven trumpets. . . . And I beheld, and heard an angel flying through the midst of heaven, saying with a loud voice, Woe, woe, woe, to the inhabiters of the earth" (Revelation 8:1–13). There have been six thousand years of rejecting the prophets, corruption and perversion; for six thousand years He has extended His holy arm of love and invitation to receive salvation. Soon after the opening of the seventh seal, John prophesied, the reapers of heaven will come to claim recompense, sifting the wheat from the tares.

Apparently, before the Second Coming, according to the early Christians, the Savior will appear to a few "righteous and pure souls and faithful."[100] Although the opening of the seventh seal offers a reference point, doctrinal speculations advanced by early writers and modern Christian scholars are of no account. The scriptures declare that no man knows the day or hour of His coming—not the angels in heaven, perhaps not even the Son Himself: Jesus testified that *only the Father* knows the timing of when He will send His Son again to claim His rightful throne (Matthew 24:36). Gratefully, the scriptures and the early Christian literature testify that we need not be worried if we are like the five wise and faithful virgins described by Jesus in His well-known parable (Matthew 25:1–10).

This view of "the last things" in combination with those doctrines previously discussed in this chapter, constitute the traditions of the early Christians regarding our Heavenly Father's plan to redeem His children.

Opposition to God's Plan from the Beginning

The Bible records that Satan attempted to "exalt [his] throne above the stars of God" (Isaiah 14:13) and that Jesus beheld Satan fall as lightning from heaven (Luke 18:10) because of his rebellion against God; his tail drew one-third of the stars (Gr. = self-condemned spirits) of heaven (Revelation 12:4). According to the Apostle John's revelation: "And there was war in heaven: Michael and his angels fought against the dragon; and the dragon fought and his angels, and prevailed not; neither was their place found any more in heaven. And the great dragon was cast out, that old serpent, called the Devil, and Satan, which deceiveth the whole world: he was cast out into the earth, and his angels were cast out with him" (Revelation 12:7–9).

The epistle of Jude adds, "The angels

which kept not their first estate, but left their own habitation, he hath reserved in everlasting chains under darkness unto the judgment of the great day" (Jude 1:6). Jude, who was the brother of James, was writing specifically to the "sanctified" and those yet "preserved in Jesus Christ, and called" (v. 1). He warned them of ungodly men who had turned the "grace of our God into lasciviousness" and had denied the Lord Jesus Christ (v. 4). Using an example from Israel's history, he reminded the faithful how the people were saved "out of the land Egypt, afterward [God] destroy[ing] them that believed not" (v. 5). Jude next related the strange account of "the angels which kept not their first estate." Who were these angels? Apparently, they were the angels, or spirits, revealed by John who were cast out of heaven with Satan for rebellion against God's plan for the salvation of His spirit sons and daughters. Thus, when John recorded that there was "war in heaven," he presumably was referring to a conflict of ideas (not weapons) between the Father and Satan. Evidently Satan's views were not in alignment with God's plan. Accordingly, Jude warned the remaining faithful early Christians not to follow the example of those who had been disobedient previously such as ancient Israel, Sodom and Gomorrah, and the angels who kept not their first estate.

The pseudepigraphal book the Life of Adam and Eve contains Satan's own account of his expulsion from heaven. In it, he blames Adam for his predicament, stating that because he (Satan) refused to honor Adam as the one chosen by the Father to stand at the head of the human family, he was cast down to the earth:

> And I [Satan] answered [Michael], "I do not worship Adam. . . . I will not worship one inferior and subsequent to me. I am prior to him in creation;

before he was made, I was already made. He ought to worship me." When they heard this, other angels who were under me refused to worship him. And Michael asserted, "Worship the image of God. But if now you will not worship, the Lord God will be wrathful with you." And I said, "If he be wrathful with me, I will set my throne above the stars of heaven and will be like the Most High." And the Lord was angry with me and sent me with my angels out from our glory; and because of you, we were expelled into this world from our dwellings and have been cast onto the earth. And immediately we were made to grieve, since we had been deprived of so great glory. And we were pained to see you in such bliss of delights. So with deceit I assailed your wife and made you to be expelled through her from the joys of your bliss, as I have been expelled from my glory.[101]

Consistent with the Life of Adam and Eve, 2 Enoch records:

> But one from the order of the archangels deviated, together with the division that was under his authority. He thought up the impossible idea, that he might place his throne higher than clouds which are above the earth, and that he might become equal to my power. And I hurled him out from the height, together with his angels. . . . And the devil understood how I [God] wished to create another world, so that everything could be subjected to Adam on the earth, to rule and reign over it. And he will become a demon, because he fled from heaven. . . . In this way he became different from the angels. His nature did not change, (but) his thought did, since his consciousness of righteous and sinful things changed. And he became aware of his condemnation and of the sin which he sinned

previously. And this is why he thought up the scheme against Adam.[102]

The obedient and righteous of the Father's spirit sons and daughters followed Michael the Archangel, while those loyal to Lucifer followed him rather than God. The book of Revelation and the Pseudepigrapha declare that those spirits who chose Lucifer were cast out of heaven with him and are they who tempt us in our mortal probation to embrace wickedness, evil ideas, and man-made religions.

The content of Jesus' forty-day ministry and teachings must have been important not only because the Apostles depended on it but also because faithful saints were granted a more comprehensive understanding of the plan of redemption. I suggest that understanding why these teachings were rejected and lost is crucial. Such an understanding leads directly to an understanding of what caused the apostasy of early Christianity as Jesus had established it. For example, did each of the Apostles experience a violent departure from this life as indicated in the forty-day teachings? Were worldly factions seeking to destroy the Church? Why? Did the sheep turn into wolves and *were the doctrines of early Christianity being altered,* as suggested by the early Christian Fathers? Was there a *wintertime of the just* while the world endured an age of spiritual darkness? Even though they knew that doing so would probably cost them their lives, the Apostles went forth fully prepared to meet any obstacle they might face in testifying to the world and establishing Christ's Church—if only for a season.

Christianity faced an uphill battle from the start. John's prophecy to the seven churches in the book of Revelation centered on apostasy and worldly pleasures. John's vision in chapter 12 seems to alternate from just prior to the dawn of physical life to that period of time when John himself lived. The message seems to be that the war in heaven did not end but simply moved to earth. Satan's rebellion, with those who followed him, did not end with their being cast down to the earth; they continued to war against the saints of God. John appears to be addressing the apostasy of Christ's Church directly when he reveals: "And there appeared a great wonder in heaven; a woman clothed with the sun, and the moon under her feet, and upon her head a crown of twelve stars. and she being with child cried, travailing in birth, and pained to be delivered" (Revelation 12:1–2).

The Greek word *semeion* is translated as "wonder" in the King James Version and, according to some scholars, is better interpreted as "sign," therefore, a great sign appeared in heaven.[103] Scholars have also depicted the "woman" as the Church that Christ established, while the crown of twelve stars represents the Twelve Apostles or the authority of the priesthood.[104] The woman seems to have been clothed with the glory of Christ; however, the light does not belong to her but is *reflected* by her.[105] The child, or "man child," as a later verse explains, appears to be a political kingdom, or the kingdom of God on earth, ultimately to be governed by Jesus Christ.[106]

And there appeared another wonder in heaven; and behold a great red dragon, having seven heads and ten horns, and seven crowns upon his heads. And his tail drew the third part of the stars of heaven, and did cast them to the earth: and the dragon stood before the woman which was to be delivered, for to devour her child as soon as it was born. And she brought forth a man child, who was to rule all nations with a rod of iron: and her child was caught up unto God, and to his throne. And the woman fled into the wilderness, where she hath a place prepared of God, that they should feed her there a thousand two hundred and threescore days. (Revelation 12:3–6)

The great red dragon is Satan. The Greek word *(drakon)* depicts a serpent or sea monster but may best be understood as a representation of *seething chaos.* The seven heads wearing the seven crowns (the number seven used in concert with the Greek word (*diadema*— "crowns" in Revelation 19:12, KJV) signifies a temporary political victory, as contrasted with the "laurels of victory" (*stephanos,* or *permanent victory*) worn by the woman; the ten horns symbolize power.[107] Note that the dragon does not work alone but that his tail "drew the third part of the stars of heaven," or one-third of the spirit sons and daughters of God. These are the disobedient servants who followed Satan.[108] The dragon stands before the woman, ready to devour her man-child the minute he is born; that is, he prepares to destroy the Church the moment it is organized and established by Jesus Christ.

Verse 14 informs us that the woman will mount upon the wings of an eagle and be carried safely *into the wilderness,* where the Church will be nourished and safeguarded until a later time when the earth will be prepared for Jesus to assume His rightful position as King of Kings and Lord of Lords as the spiritual *and* political ruler of this world. Verse 17 reveals that the dragon was angry with the woman and went to make war on the remnant of her seed, which endured in the testimony of Jesus and sought to obey the commandments.

John's revelation, although shrouded in symbolism, tells the story of the Savior's Church: It will be organized and established but will come under the vicious attack of Satan, who will seek to destroy it. The period portrayed is the time frame foretold in which Lucifer will win a temporary political victory;

and the Church of Christ, with its keys and authority, will be received into heaven (vv. 6, 14) until the appointed time for Jesus Christ's glorious return to earth, when He will reestablish his Church and kingdom, cleanse the world of wickedness, and reign as its rightful King.

History vindicates at least part of John's prophecy. As soon as the Church was organized and the Savior's authority was successfully transferred to the Twelve Apostles; as soon as the Atonement and Christ's victory over death through the glorious resurrection was complete; as soon as the gospel had been preached to the known world—when all this had happened, the short season of protection ended and the wrath of Satan was unleashed. The Savior's Church was assaulted from every side; persecution was inflicted by the Jews and the Roman Empire; the Apostles were killed; and as prophesied, the most destructive influence came from ravenous wolves within the Church who sought power and dominion, becoming Satan's puppets and destroying the pure work of God.

Oppression from Jewish Hierarchy

At the time of the Savior's birth, the Jews believed they were the only people on earth to worship the true and living God. Although the Jews were God's chosen people, they were unfortunately in apostasy and no longer followed Him in the pure forms revealed through Moses. They failed to recognize the Messiah when He introduced the New Covenant and explained that the law of Moses was fulfilled in Him. If Christianity were accepted as true by the masses, the Jewish leaders felt it would undermine the very foundations of Judaism, so they fought vigorously to destroy this new sect before it could take root.

Following the example [109] and direction[110] of the Savior, the Apostles, upon first entering any city, attempted to proclaim the gospel to the Jews. Converts soon exceeded five thousand baptized members.[111] Shortly thereafter, "multitudes" of believers followed Christ, both men and women.[112] Church membership also included "a great company of the priests who [were] obedient to the faith."[113] The Jewish hierarchy was understandably envious[114] of the success of the Christian-Jews and began to stir up public disfavor against them.

The scriptures and early Church history verify that enemies of the Church first persecuted the Apostles and others who held positions of leadership within the Church. By silencing the presiding authorities, those seeking power and influence who desired to pervert the gospel were no longer hindered from influencing Church administration and policies. Stephen, James the Just, and other strong leaders of early Christianity were soon martyred, which quickened the pace of the deepening apostasy within the Church. Similar examples include Saul's persecutions prior to his conversion;[115] persecution waged against Paul and Barnabas at Antioch,[116] Iconium,[117] and Lycaonia,[118] and of Paul at Jerusalem.[119] The Jewish historian Josephus provided an objective eyewitness of these abuses,[120] as does Justin Martyr, who described widespread Jewish-led calumnies.[121] Jewish oppression was considerable, becoming the first external force attempting to subvert Christianity.

The Jerusalem Council—The Gospel Is Preached to the Gentiles

Tradition holds that both Peter and Paul resided in Rome. The book of Acts indicates that Paul lived in a "hired" or rented house there in about A.D. 58–59.[122] We may also conclude that although Paul was falsely accused and imprisoned, as indicated in the last chapters of Acts, had those charges been brought before a Roman court they would have been disposed of as groundless because of his status as a Roman citizen. He then would have been free to come and go as he pleased. In fact, it is believed that Paul visited Spain and Provence[123] before his death during Nero's persecutions in approximately A.D. 64.

Although Peter probably also eventually ended up in Rome (scholars believe they have found Peter's tomb there), there are no dependable records of Peter's specific whereabouts prior to the tyranny of Nero. The book of Acts refers to Peter's imprisonment in A.D. 48 under the orders of Herod Agrippa in Jerusalem and his subsequent escape from prison.[124] The New Testament also records that Peter performed missionary labors in Asia and met with the other Apostles in about A.D. 50–51, a meeting often referred to by historians as "The Jerusalem Council." At this conference or meeting, Peter answered a controversial question concerning the circumcision of converted Gentiles and also formalized the Church's doctrine regarding Christ's fulfillment of the law of Moses.

Peter had already received a revelation correcting his own errant view that the Gentiles were unclean: "What God hath cleansed, that call not thou common" (Acts 10:15), the Lord said to His prophet. In other words, *all* who repent and whose hearts are changed by the Holy Spirit and are then baptized become clean, whether Jew or Gentile. Unfortunately, the complete picture of how Jew and Gentile were to become one was not yet fully revealed. Thus, when "certain men" were sent to Antioch by the Apostles from Judea, they erroneously taught new gentile converts that circumcision was still a ritual ordinance required for salvation (Acts 15:1, 24). Paul and Barnabas disputed the false doctrine and determined to go to Jerusalem to take up the matter with the Apostles and other leaders of the Church. This general conference established the Church's precedent for solving unfamiliar problems and answering untested doctrinal questions *in the Lord's way*. The book of Acts records this event as follows:

> And the apostles and elders came together for to consider of this matter. And when there had been much disputing, Peter rose up, and said unto them, Men and brethren, ye know how that a good while ago God made choice among us, that the Gentiles by my mouth should hear the word of the gospel, and believe. And God, which knoweth the hearts, bare them witness, giving them the Holy Ghost, even as he did unto us. . . . Then all the multitude kept silence, and gave audience to Barnabas and Paul, declaring what miracles and wonders God had wrought. (Acts 15:6–12)

After Barnabas and Paul had spoken, James responded, saying: "Hearken unto me. . . . Wherefore my sentence is, that we trouble not them [Gentile converts] . . . : but that we write unto them, that they abstain from [sin]. . . . Then pleased it the apostles and elders, with the whole church, to send chosen men of their own company to Antioch with Paul and Barnabas . . . : and they wrote letters by them" (Acts 15:13–23).

These verses reveal that the Apostles and elders were considering issues where no clear policy had been previously established by the Lord. They also reveal that the Apostles recognized the breadth of the authority conferred upon them by Jesus. These were intelligent, capable men, and the Lord expected them to reason through such issues, based on previously clarified doctrine, and then comprehend by the Spirit the appropriate direction. A process was emerging by which inspired decisions could move the Church forward.

Based on his revelation (dream) in Acts 10, Peter taught inspired doctrine, counseling his brethren, "Why tempt ye God, to put a yoke upon the neck of the disciples, which neither our fathers nor we were able to bear? But we believe that through the grace of the Lord Jesus Christ we shall be saved, even as they" (Acts 15:10–11). This idea was echoed by Paul and Barnabas, whereupon James, the presiding local authority, submitted a proposal to his brethren as to the implementation of Peter's inspired doctrine. The Apostles then moved to accept James's recommendation, and authoritative letters were written by them and sent by way of "greeting unto the brethren" informing them of the new policy. In summation, the process went as follows:

1. One or more of the Church leaders identified a question, problem, or dispute.

2. The Apostles and other Church leaders gathered to consider the dispute.

3. After sufficient discussion and debate, the recognized leader of the Church (Peter, in this case) taught inspired doctrine, based on personal revelation from God rather than on scholarship or philosophy.

4. Others of the Apostles voiced their agreement, offering support for Peter's counsel.

5. The Apostles and elders ironed out a specific policy, written in the form of an authoritative letter, which was accepted by all present.

6. This policy was then communicated as the newly established doctrine of the Church.

Two elements combined to enable this resolution: (1) the unquestioned authority of the Apostles, specifically of Peter, and (2) the enlightenment of the Holy Spirit.

Although this process should have been a model for future councils, apostasy prevented the Church from continuing this inspired method.

Early theologians and some modern scholars have made much of a disagreement between Peter and Paul regarding the continuing tension over the issue of circumcision.[125] While visiting Antioch, Peter had no trouble dining with gentile members until certain Jews came from Jerusalem, whom he evidently feared to offend because they were of "the circumcision" (Galatians 2:12), not yet fully accepting the Council's former decision. If the text can be taken at face value, Paul rebuked Peter publicly, correctly censuring his senior Apostle. Thus, although Peter would have been wrong in this instance, there can be little doubt, given his character, that he would have reversed his position and sought to both exemplify and teach more vigorously the correct doctrine thereafter.

St. Jerome and St. John Chrysostom, fourth-century bishops, offered another viewpoint:

> The Apostles . . . permitted circumcision at Jerusalem, an abrupt severance of the law not being practicable; but when they came to Antioch, they no longer continued this observance, but lived indiscriminately with the believing Gentiles which thing Peter also was at that time doing. But when some came from Jerusalem who had heard the doctrine he delivered there, he no longer did so fearing to perplex them, but he changed his course, with two objects secretly in view, both to avoid offending those Jews, and to give Paul a reasonable pretext for rebuking him. For had he, having allowed circumcision when preaching at Jerusalem, changed his course at Antioch, his conduct would have appeared to those Jews to proceed from fear of Paul, and

his disciples would have condemned his excess of pliancy. . . . But in Paul, who was well acquainted with all the facts, his withdrawal would have raised no such suspicion, . . . Wherefore Paul rebukes, and Peter submits, that when the master is blamed, yet keeps silence, the disciples [holdouts to circumcision] may more readily come over.[126]

Regardless of which scenario is accurate, Peter held the "keys of the kingdom" on earth. He was the Lord's prophet. The real issue at stake was not a conflict between Peter or Paul but rather *the lack of obedience on the part of those still clinging to the law of Moses.* In essence, they turned their backs on the atonement of Christ and rejected the New Covenant he offered. The Church was striving to mature spiritually but having difficulty because of rebellion, or in other words, failure to follow the counsel of those called by God to preside.

The Tyranny of Rome

While Jewish persecution was bitter, it was minuscule compared to the tyranny of various Roman emperors. Some historians have improperly characterized Roman oppression as being sustained over many centuries; in fact, there were lengthy respites between waves of quite localized and sporadic repression. Nevertheless, even a little tyranny is tragic for the victims, and many cases of extraordinary mistreatment, exploitation, and execution persisted intermittently for nearly 250 years.

Roman Oppression Begins under Nero in A.D. 64

Roman persecution began to assert itself during the reign of Nero. The first five years of his reign were marked by peace and prosperity. General Corbulo was having good military success in Armenia. The governors in Rome were competent, and Nero granted the senate sufficient freedom to act unimpeded in its traditional role. Leaders such as Seneca and Burrus were effective and well liked. However, in approximately A.D. 59 Nero began to give way to his outrageous personal appetites. He exercised greater political power, openly disregarded the counsel of his ministers and restricted their authority, and murdered his own mother, Agrippina, and his wife, Octavia. He had already poisoned Britannicus, his only opposition in the imperial house, a few years earlier; Burrus may have also been poisoned, and Seneca fell from influence and withdrew into retirement, according to the Roman historian Tacitus. Nero next began to persecute the rich, the aristocratic, and the intellectuals. Such atrocities led all of Rome to disapprove of their emperor and his ways.

A catastrophic fire devastated Rome in A.D. 64. In an attempt to avert a recurrence of similar disasters in 23 B.C. and A.D. 6, a large fire brigade had been organized by Augustus. However, their efforts failed, and the city was left in ruins. In an attempt to soothe public opinion, Nero blamed the Christians for the tragedy. Tacitus recorded this effort as follows:

> To get rid of the report, Nero fastened the guilt and inflicted the most exquisite tortures on a class hated for their abominations, called Christians by the populace. Christus, from whom the name had its origin, suffered the extreme penalty during the reign of Tiberius at the hands of one of our procurators, Pontius Pilate, and a most mischievous superstition, thus checked for the moment, again broke out not only in Judea, the first source of the evil, but in Rome, where all things hideous and shameful from every part of the world find their centre and become popular. Accordingly, *an arrest was first made of all who pleaded guilty; then, upon their information, an immense multitude was convicted,* not so much of the crime of firing the city, as of hatred against mankind. Mockery of every sort was added to their deaths. Covered with the skins of beasts, they were torn by dogs and perished, or were nailed to crosses, or were doomed to the flames and burnt, to serve as a nightly illumination, when daylight had expired. Nero offered his Gardens for the spectacle, and was exhibiting a show in the Circus, while he mingled with the people in the dress of a charioteer or stood aloft on a car. Hence, even for criminals who deserved extreme and exemplary punishment, there arose a feeling of compassion; for it was not, as it seemed, for the public good, but to glut one man's cruelty, that they were being destroyed.[127]

Several modern scholars have set forth convincing arguments that Jewish-Christian factions were responsible for colluding with Nero in the death of many gentile Christians, including Peter and Paul, who were both strong supporters of a unified Church and presumably in Rome at this time. According to Garry Wills, who echoes Oscar Cullmann and Raymond Brown: "Nero first took some Christians prisoner, who explained they were not responsible for the fire *but informed on others who were.*"[128]

Wills, a widely published historian who is also Catholic, concludes that the first five decades of Christianity were embroiled in conflict between Christian Jews and Gentiles.[129] Although his case is built on circumstantial evidence, it is nonetheless consistent with the prophecies of the Apostles that wolves would enter the flock; it is an example of rebellion that precisely fits the model explained by Paul to the Thessalonians that a *falling away,* or mutiny, would occur (2 Thessalonians 2:1–3).

Paul's New Testament writings seem to characterize the Christian population in Rome as small, perhaps even an underground minority. Other contemporary writers, such as Josephus (A.D. 37–ca. 100) and the Roman biographer Gaius Seutonius Tranquillus (A.D. 69–140), seem to concur, making meager mention of the role of Christians in Roman society. Therefore, Tacitus's solitary record is important historically. According to Cheetham, the fact that Nero singled out Christians, distinguishing them as having sufficient numbers to isolate and persecute, suggests their numbers were greater than some historians may have thought.[130] On a more universal scale, the book of Acts attested that Christianity was spreading rapidly throughout the Eastern Hemisphere.

Though not constant, the periods of punishment and oppression that Rome inflicted on Christians were severe. Roman authorities speculated that if Christianity's leaders were eliminated, the religion itself might just go away. Subsequently, one by one the Apostles, who held the keys and the priesthood of God, were killed. They met together perhaps for the last time in A.D. 50–51, just a decade and a half after the Crucifixion. Inasmuch as the Apostles were scattered throughout the Mediterranean world preaching the gospel, they were unable to assemble as required to choose new Apostles to replace those who had fallen.

Some have confused Christ's statement to Peter "and the gates of hell shall not prevail against it" (Matthew 16:18) as evidence that the Church would never falter completely. However, inasmuch as the subject of this passage refers specifically to *revelation* and not the Church, it is more likely a reference to revelation itself. Christ's Church and kingdom would ultimately prevail, but a falling away

would occur first (2 Thessalonians 2:1–3), eventually to find in a future day a "restitution of all things" (Acts 3:21). The apostasy of the primitive Christian Church occurred as a result of the free agency of man. The will of the people was to "instruct" the Lord (1 Corinthians 2:16), to alter the Church, and to seek personal power rather than humble submission to the will of God. The passing of the Apostles was quickly followed by the passing of the Church. But God had not forgotten His promise to Abraham: He would again raise up righteous men—prophets—to prepare and warn the world of Christ's second coming.

The Fate of the Apostles

Although there are few fully dependable accounts regarding the later ministry and death of the Apostles, some material facts are known, including many romantic legends that have circulated through the centuries as to how they met their fates.

The New Testament records that **Judas** committed suicide (Matthew 27:3–5).

James, the son of Zebedee and brother of the Apostle John, was the first of the Apostles to be martyred (Acts 12:2). He was executed about A.D. 44 by King Herod Agrippa I of Judea. Eusebius reports that Clement of Alexandria recorded that the man who led James to his execution was so moved by the Apostle's testimony, he confessed to being Christian also. Both were now condemned to die, whereupon his former captor asked his forgiveness, after which they were beheaded together.[131]

Legendary accounts suggest that **Matthew** traveled to Ethiopia, where he became associated with Queen Candace (Acts 8:27) and was martyred in that country. Some writings indicate he was pinned to the ground and beheaded with a halberd (battle axe) at Nadabah, Ethiopia, in A.D. 60. In a letter attributed to Hippolytus, Matthew wrote his gospel in the "Hebrew tongue, and published it at Jerusalem, and fell asleep at Hierees, a town of Parthia."[132]

Matthias was called to take Judas's place (Acts 1:23–26), and according to Hippolytus, being "one of the seventy, was numbered along with the eleven apostles, and preached in Jerusalem." Although other legends exist regarding his death, the most prominent is that he was stoned at Jerusalem and then beheaded.[133]

Many legends surround the preaching and martyrdom of **Andrew**, the brother of **Peter.** While some apocryphal writings place his ministry in southern Russia at Scythia, others locate his teaching activities in Greece, while yet a third strong tradition pinpoints his evangelizing in Edessa in Asia Minor. According to several scholars, he may have preached in each of these locations. Although one account places his crucifixion at Edessa on an X-shaped cross, which came to be known as St. Andrew's Cross, Hippolytus locates Andrew's death at "Patrae, a town of Achaia." This tradition is supported in the Acts of Andrew which describes his labors as primarily in Greece or Macedonia and his martyrdom in "Patras."[134]

Hegesippus states that "when Peter was old," Nero planned to put him to death. When the disciples learned of this plot they urged him to flee the city (probably Rome), which he did after much pleading. But when he approached the city gate, he saw Christ walking toward him. Peter fell to his knees and said, "'Lord, where are you going?' Christ answered, 'I've come to be crucified again.'" From this vision Peter perceived it was his time to suffer "the death [by which] he should glorify God" (John 21:18), so he returned to

the city. After his arrest, he was taken to the place of his martyrdom where, according to Hippolytus, he was "crucified with his head downward," apparently because he elected not to be crucified in the same position as his Lord (approximately A.D. 66–67).[135]

Paul's conversion took place in approximately A.D. 33. Laboring in relative obscurity for about twelve years, his first recorded missionary experiences place him with Barnabas in Antioch in about A.D. 45 where they were both ordained to the ministry (Acts 13:1–4). His first epistle was probably written to the Galatians in A.D. 48, followed by his epistles to the Thessalonians in about A.D. 50, and to the Corinthians and Romans in the middle 50s. He was under house arrest from about A.D. 60 to 62, and while incarcerated wrote his prison epistles: Ephesians, Philippians, Philamon, and Colossians. He was released around A.D. 63 shortly before Rome burned, and according to many scholars Paul may have been able to visit western and eastern Europe and Asia Minor, during which time he also wrote his first epistle to Timothy and his epistle to Titus. After returning to Rome, he was imprisoned again, and he may then have written his second epistle to Timothy. A short time later, he was pronounced guilty of crimes against the emperor and condemned to death. In about A.D. 65, Paul was beheaded at Rome by order of Nero.[136]

Simon, the Canaanite, also known as the Zealot, is said to have been crucified in A.D. 61 in Lincolnshire, England. Legend asserts that Simon preached in Egypt, through North Africa to Carthage, then to Spain, and finally on to Great Britain.[137]

Philip lived in close proximity to John, who resided at Ephesus. He most likely performed missionary labors in France and Asia Minor. His place of death is confirmed by numerous sources to be Hierapolis in Phrygia. Hippolytus dates Philip's passing at the time of Domitian (A.D. 81–96) and states he was crucified "with his head downward."[138]

Although the Gospels tell us very little about **Bartholomew**, several apocryphal books suggest that he preached in many countries. The Gospel of Bartholomew states that he translated the Gospel of Matthew into the language of India and taught it in that country. Then, according to legend, he was cruelly beaten and crucified by pagan idolaters. The Martyrdom of St. Bartholomew offers an alternative version of his death near Armenia. In this account, the Apostle is placed in a sack and thrown into the sea.[139]

Thomas, called Didymus, preached in Babylon (Persia), Parthia, and India. Substantial documentation attests that Thomas was a "fearless evangelist," that he encountered great success in his missionary labors, and that he established the Christian religion in many parts of eastern Christendom. Legend maintains that "he endured various persecutions and consequently martyrdom for the belief and justice of our Lord, by a lance thrust by miscreants deputed by King Mizdi."[140]

Hippolytus records that **James**, the son of Alphaeus and brother of Matthew, preached in Jerusalem, "was stoned to death by the Jews, and was buried there beside the temple."[141]

Barnabas, the first of the Seventy, and possibly an Apostle who succeeded one of the original Twelve, is reported to have visited many countries to preach the gospel. Apparently, he returned to Cyprus, one of the original congregations he established with Paul, where he was killed by the Jews. Legend describes a secret burial with a copy of the Gospel of Matthew, written in his own handwriting, placed upon his chest.[142]

Accounts surrounding the identity of **Thaddaeus** called "Lebbaeus" (Matthew 10:3) are ambiguous and unclear. He is likely *Judas Thaddaeus Lebbaeus* (Luke 6:16; Acts 1:13), or he may be *St. Jude* or *St. Thaddaeus*. Various legends that support each of these names make it impractical and unproductive to speculate about the later life of this Apostle of the Lord.[143]

John the Beloved, the brother of James, while in Ephesus was arrested and sent to Rome. Legend maintains that he was cast into a large vessel filled with boiling oil but was unharmed. As a result he was released and banished by the Emperor Domitian to the Isle of Patmos, where he "saw the apocalyptic vision" and wrote the book of Revelation. Eventually, he was released from Patmos and returned to Ephesus, where, according to Hippolytus, "he fell asleep at Ephesus, where his remains were sought for but could not be found" (about A.D. 98–100).[144]

What Priesthood Authority Succeeded the Apostles?

Tradition tells us that Peter, who was given the mantle of authority when the Savior ascended into heaven, suffered martyrdom at Rome in A.D. 67. The Roman Catholic Church, as reported by Eusebius, alleges that St. Linus succeeded Peter that same year as bishop of Rome; Anencletus succeeded Linus in A.D. 78–79; and in A.D. 90–91 Clement succeeded Anencletus.[145] Declarations of rights to leadership made in later centuries, but not before the late fourth century, were based on the assumption that Peter himself was the bishop of Rome and that the Roman bishop held some sort of claim as the divinely appointed head of the Church. However, no credible documentation exists to support such a claim. Although there is no evidence that Peter founded the Church at Rome, there is limited evidence that he may have resided there before his death. A recent claim that Peter's tomb was discovered in Rome has been validated by some scholars and rejected by others.[146] More important, there is simply no credible evidence that his place of residence had anything to do with his divine calling as the earthly head of the Church, nor are there any records, histories, or legends.[147]

Christ clearly did choose Peter as His successor to administer the affairs of the Church. Peter's leadership is demonstrated throughout the book of Acts.[148] After his death, the Apostles would have gathered to officially select a successor to Peter. They were, after all, the ones entrusted with the keys and the authority of Jesus Christ to make such an appointment. However, no record suggests this event ever took place, and no documented, reputable findings support the Roman bishop replacing Peter *as the head of the Church*. While it is unknown as to whether or not Peter founded the Church in Antioch and later in Rome, as recorded by Eusebius,[149] his authority clearly extended beyond the boundaries of any one city. If a successor to Peter's authority had been appointed but not recorded, what of the other Apostles *still living* who all held the keys (Matthew 16:19; 18:18) to succeed Peter?

What of John the Beloved, the Son of Thunder? Most historians believe that John died in Ephesus in ca. A.D. 98–100, *some thirty-one years after Peter was martyred.* Of him the Savior said to His Mother, "Woman, behold thy son!" and to John, "Behold thy mother!" (John 19:26–27). John's ministry held a measure of importance over all but Peter and James. John would have been the senior Apostle after their passing and thus the rightful leader of the Lord's Church. Revelation intended for the entire Church has always come through the Lord's recognized and anointed prophets—it flowed through Adam, Enoch, Noah, Abraham, Moses, and

Jesus and His Apostles. Certainly revelation had not stopped with Peter, for John's most significant writings came to us from the lonely Isle of Patmos in the middle 90s. John, one of the original Twelve Apostles, was the one *still receiving literal, documented revelation* for the Church in general and would have been God's chosen oracle, not Linus, Cletus, or Clement, though they certainly held episcopal authority and received inspiration for their local congregations.

The Church Immediately Following the Death of the Apostles

Early Christianity was simple in its worship services, simple in its administration, full of faith and the power of the Lord, freely ministered to and directed by the Holy Spirit, and constantly working to retain the unblemished doctrines established by the Savior. The sayings of Jesus, Paul's letters, Peter's warnings, and James's exhortations were all designed to keep the flock of Christ on the straight and narrow path pertaining to doctrinal purity, simple and correctly performed ordinances, and commitment to living a Christlike life.

The anchor of the early Church was the example of its members. A unique harmony existed between the doctrine and commandments of the Savior and the genuine goodness and service rendered by the saints. Chastity before marriage and absolute fidelity after marriage were expected of all Christians. Marriage was a holy union, and the family was the foundation of all Christian communities.[150]

Baptized members of the Church, or saints, as they were called, referred to each other as "brother" or "sister,"[151] and the congregation was something of an extended family, united under the leadership of the bishop or presiding presbyter (elder). Baptisms of new converts were performed regularly under the direction of those in authority (usually the bishop). The ordinance was performed as was Jesus' baptism—by immersion—and symbolized the death and burial of sin through the death and resurrection of Christ. The English word *baptism* comes from a Greek word that means "to immerse, to sink, or to submerge." Baptism was performed for *the remission of sins* (Acts 2:37–38), the saints being "born again," as Jesus had witnessed to Nicodemus (John 3:5). The ordinance of baptism in the early Church was not just a symbol of obedience, akin to circumcision; rather it was an essential step in the salvation process. The author of the Clementine Recognitions credits Peter as having explained:

> But you will perhaps say, What does the baptism of water contribute towards the worship of God? In the first place, because that which hath pleased God is fulfilled. In the second place, because, when you are regenerated and born again of water and of God, the frailty of your former birth, which you have through men, is cut off, and so at length you shall be able to attain salvation; but otherwise it is impossible. For thus hath the true prophet testified to it with an oath: "Verily I say to you, that unless a man is born again of water, he shall not enter into the kingdom of heaven." Therefore make haste; for there is in these waters a certain power of mercy which was borne upon them at the beginning, and acknowledges those who are baptized under the name of the threefold sacrament, and rescues them from future punishments, presenting as a gift to God the souls that are consecrated by baptism.[152]

Each Sunday, the congregation came together in a worship service where those who were baptized received a sacred meal, partaking of bread and wine in commemoration of the sacrifice of the Son of God for their sins. Inasmuch as Jesus came forth from the grave on Sunday, the Sabbath day, a sign between God and His covenant people was ever after observed on the "first day of the week" (Acts 20:7). So holy was the sacramental experience that it became one of the deepest expressions of membership in the Lord's Church. Accordingly, those participating were required to be free of serious sin. Justin Martyr attests to the importance of the sacrament of the Lord's Supper:

> "And this food is called among us Eucharist, of which no one is allowed to partake except one who believes that the things which we teach are true, and has received the washing that is for the remission of sins and for rebirth, and who so lives as Christ handed down."[153] The emblems of bread and wine (sometimes mixed with water) were also taken by the deacons to the faithful who were ill and unable to attend services. Sabbath gatherings included readings from the ancient prophets, the Lord's sayings, and the memoirs of the Apostles, after which the presiding authority would exhort the members to "imitate these things." Prayers were also offered and hymns of praise.[154] Early Church writings indicate that these meetings were laden with the gifts of the Spirit: the sick were healed, and powerful testimonies were borne by the members.

The Apostles attempted, evidently under revelation (a forty-day teaching?), to form a unique kind of communal Church government wherein the saints "had all things in common":

> And they continued stedfastly in the apostles' doctrine and fellowship, and in breaking of bread, and in prayers. . . . And all that believed were together, and had all things common; and sold

their possessions and goods, and parted them to all men, as every man had need. And they, continuing daily with one accord in the temple, and breaking bread from house to house, did eat their meat with gladness. (Acts 2:42–46) And the multitude of them that believed were of one heart and of one soul: neither said any of them that ought of the things which he possessed was his own; *but they had all things common.* And with great power gave the apostles witness of the resurrection of the Lord Jesus: and great grace was upon them all. *Neither was there any among them that lacked:* for as many as were possessors of lands or houses sold them, and brought the prices of the things that were sold, and laid them down at the apostles' feet: and distribution was made unto every man according as he had need. (Acts 4:32–35; emphasis added)

Some have argued that this system was a temporary measure, but no evidence supports such a theory. Some have vainly attempted to label this approach as communism—an earthly social order rather than a community of saints acting in obedience to inspired apostolic authority. Nevertheless, it appears this practice did not last long in the Church; yet the earliest Christians continued to be generous with their means, contributing weekly offerings which were then distributed among the orphans, widows, strangers, those in bonds, or to the poor who were in need.[155] The venerable bishop Cyprian lamented the deterioration of unity and charity within the Church which this practice in earlier days had inspired: "They used to give for sale houses and estates; and that they might lay up for themselves treasures in heaven, presented to the Apostles the price of them, to be distributed for the use of the poor. But now we do not even give the tenths from our patrimony; and while our Lord bids us sell, we rather buy and increase our store. Thus has the vigor of faith dwindled away among us."[156]

Early Dissension and Schism— The Passing of the Primitive Church

What transformed such an orderly, unified, and loving environment into one of chaos, envy, and enmity? Scholars have been baffled for centuries regarding the many changes that transpired in the Church shortly after the death of the Apostles. Few records shed light on what happened between the fall of Jerusalem in a.d. 70 and the mid-second century. Nevertheless, something disastrous must have occurred, because we now find the Church raging in turmoil, contention, and apostasy. One cannot help pondering the full import of Peter's thoughts when anticipating the future: "But the end of all things is at hand: be ye therefore sober, and watch unto prayer. . . . Beloved, think it not strange concerning the fiery trial which is to try you, as though some strange thing happened unto you" (1 Peter 4:7–12).

Paul likewise appeared urgent after warning the saints of wolves in sheep's clothing: "Therefore watch, and remember, that by the space of three years I ceased not to warn every one night and day with tears" (Acts 20:31).

John, warning the faithful who yet remained, wrote: "Even now are there many antichrists; whereby we know that it is the last time. They went out from us, but they were not of us. . . . These things have I written unto you concerning them that seduce you" (1 John 2:18–26). "For many deceivers are entered into the world, who confess not that Jesus Christ is come in the flesh" (2 John 7).

Accordingly, about thirty years after Peter and Paul's warnings, the Lord, through the Apostle John, issued a call of repentance to the entire Church. To Ephesus, the Lord had said, "Repent, and do the first works; or else I will come unto thee quickly, and will remove thy candlestick out of his place" (Revelation 2:5); to Smyrna, "Be thou faithful unto death" (Revelation 2:10); to Pergamos, there are those "that hold the doctrine of Balaam, . . . [and] also them that hold the doctrine of the Nicolaitans, which thing I hate" (Revelation 2:14–15); to the saints at Thyatira, "Thou sufferest that woman Jezebel . . . to teach and seduce my servants to commit fornication. . . . as many as have not this doctrine . . . hold fast till I come" (Revelation 2:19–25); to Sardis, "I know thy works, that thou . . . art dead. . . . I have not found thy works perfect before God" (Revelation 3:1–2); to Philadelphia, "Because thou hast kept the word of my patience, I also will keep thee from the hour of temptation, which shall come upon all the world. . . . hold fast" (Revelation 3:10); to Laodicea, "I know thy works, that thou art neither cold nor hot. . . . So then because thou art lukewarm, . . . I will spue thee out of my mouth" (Revelation 3:15–16). Some congregations were failing quickly while others were striving to hold on. Yet John's message was clear to all: "Repent. . . . to him that overcometh will I give to eat of the tree of life" (Revelation 2:7).

Continuing problems among branches of the Church encouraged many of the first leaders to persevere in the practice established by Paul and other Apostles to write letters of exhortation and instruction. After another dangerous controversy at Corinth, brought on by "envy and strife," Clement of Rome, at about the same time as John (ca. A.D. 96), wrote an epistle urging those in sedition (apostasy) to submit to the authority of the presiding elders. Clement's epistle is held in high regard by Eusebius, who wrote: "Of this Clement there is one epistle extant, acknowledged as genuine, of considerable length and

of great merit, which he wrote . . . to . . . Corinth, at the time when there was a dissension in the latter. This we know to have been publicly read for common benefit, in most of the churches, both in former times and in our own; and that at the time mentioned a sedition did take place at Corinth, is abundantly attested by Hegesippus."[157]

Present-day Christianity also esteems Clement's letter because it is the earliest of the remaining Christian writings following the New Testament authors. Clement wrote:

Our apostles also knew, through our Lord Jesus Christ, there would be strife on account of the office of the episcopate [bishop]. For this reason, therefore, inasmuch as they had obtained a perfect fore-knowledge of this, they appointed those [ministers] already mentioned, and afterwards gave instructions, that when these should fall asleep, other approved men should succeed them in their ministry. We are of opinion, therefore, that those appointed by them, or afterwards by other eminent men, with the consent of the whole Church, and who have blamelessly served the flock of Christ in a humble, peaceable, and disinterested spirit, and have for a long time possessed the good opinion of all, cannot be justly dismissed from the ministry. For our sin will not be small, if we eject from the episcopate those who have blamelessly and holily fulfilled its duties. . . . But we see that you have removed some men of excellent behaviour from the ministry, which they fulfilled blamelessly and with honour.[158]

Clement observes weakening faith at Corinth witnessed first by Paul (1 Corinthians 11:18–19; 3:3–5). The Apostle censured them again in a letter at least one other time, as indicated earlier.[159] Now some thirty years later, the divisions and heresies first reported by Paul began to broaden because the Apostles were no longer in place to restrain escalating apostasy.

Ignatius also clearly confronted the problem of rebellion. In a revelation from God, by the Holy Ghost, he received inspired direction to counsel the members to follow their divinely chosen leadership: "For though some would have deceived me according to the flesh, yet my spirit is not deceived; for I received it from God. . . . having learned before hand the division caused by some among you, [God] is my witness, . . . the Spirit made an announcement to me, saying as follows: Do nothing without the bishop."[160]

Ignatius also pointed out the pattern of how apostasy actually begins. In the following example, certain members question the age of the bishop and begin holding private meetings without the authority of the bishop: "Now it becomes you *also not to despise the age of your bishop,* but to yield to him all reverence. It is right then, that we should be really Christians, and not merely have the name; even as there are some who recognize the bishop in their words, *but disregard him in their actions.* Such men seem to me not to act in good faith, since *they do not hold valid meetings* according to the commandment."[161]

The fact that Ignatius wrote similar letters of warning and admonition regarding the role and authority of the bishop to five of the six churches he addressed demonstrates the general problem of rebellion that the Church faced. Ignatius praised those at Smyrna for sending a delegate to Antioch with a letter (possibly from Polycarp), helping to restore unity in his own congregation at Antioch.[162] And although we must recognize the strength of the churches at Smyrna and Philadelphia, according to John's testimony near the end of the first century (Revelation 2:9; 3:10), Smyrna's fortitude came as a result of inspired

leadership (perhaps Polycarp), a devout and faithful servant who had been personally acquainted with some of the Apostles. After the humble and devoted bishops who succeeded the Apostles (Clement, Ignatius, and Polycarp) were martyred, *inspired* Church leadership appears to have decayed rapidly. One wonders why Ignatius in his letter to the Romans used words which seem to suggest that the authority of Christ was in the process of being taken from the earth:

"Remember in your prayers the Church in Syria [Antioch], which has God for its Shepherd in my room. Its bishop shall be Jesus Christ alone,—and your love."[163] It seems probable that if there was to be an earthly succession (as there always had been, dating back to Old Testament times), Ignatius would have mentioned this fact; instead, he seemed to say that since he would not be returning, the Lord Himself would take his place as bishop in Antioch. Although the people of Antioch elected a new bishop, did this presbyter possess the authority of Jesus? While no specific evidence exists to answer this question, the fact that Ignatius indicates that earthly leadership will not replace him (he said the *Lord alone* would be bishop *in his room*) may signify that priesthood authority was passing from the earth.

Ignatius's letters were written in captivity while he was traveling to Rome, where, according to Eusebius, he suffered martyrdom in A.D. 108.[164]

Finally, the Shepherd of Hermas, a series of visions, probably received at the turn of the first century,[165] was considered equally as orthodox as those in the Bible today and highly regarded by the early Church. The reason for its exclusion from the New Testament canon was not a lack of wide acceptance but rather failure of some third-century leaders to understand all its message; and the fourth-century Church demanded apostolic authorship since it no longer believed in continuing revelation. The angel's warning to the Shepherd, like John's revelation, centered on a "last call" to repentance. Unlike the apostolic charge from Jesus to "go ye therefore, and teach all nations" (Matthew 28:19), the angel directed her message only to *those who had already been baptized but were in sin* and surrounded by apostasy:

> But I say to you all, *as many as have received the seal,* keep simplicity and bear no malice, and do not remain in your guilt, or in remembrance of the bitterness of offences. *Be of one spirit and put away these evil schisms,* and take them away from yourselves that the Lord of the sheep may rejoice over them. But he will rejoice if all be found whole; but if he find some of them fallen away, it will be woe to the shepherds. *But if the shepherds themselves be found fallen away, what shall they answer to the Master of the flock?* That they have fallen away because of the sheep? They will not be believed.[166]

This passage is reminiscent of an earlier Old Testament time: "My people hath been lost sheep: their shepherds have caused them to go astray, they have turned them away on the mountains: they have gone from mountain to hill, they have forgotten their restingplace. All that found them have devoured them" (Jeremiah 50:6–7; see also Ezekiel 34:2–10).

The visions recorded in the Shepherd of Hermas must have been the final call to repentance to the baptized members of the Church *of that day.* Although the angel allowed that the "heathen" would be able to repent until the last, those who were already members would have only this one last chance to repent:

> Your seed, Hermas, have set God at naught, and have blasphemed the Lord, and have betrayed their parents in great wickedness, . . . they have added to their sins wanton deeds and piled up wickedness, and so their crimes have been made complete. . . . After you have made known these words to them, which the Master commanded me to reveal to you, all the sins which they have committed shall be forgiven to all the saints who have sinned up to this day, if they repent with their whole heart, and put aside doublemindedness. . . . For the Master hath sworn to his elect by his glory that if there be still sin after this day has been fixed, they shall find no salvation; for repentance for the just has an end; the days of repentance have been fulfilled for all the saints, but for the heathen repentance is open until the last day.[167]

The angel indicates that "up to this day," meaning the time of Hermas's vision, the saints may repent of their wickedness; however, she states that "after this day has been fixed," there will not be a second chance. Although the Shepherd's declaration of a single opportunity to repent may seem severe, this was actually the last of many warnings and is consistent with similar occurrences in preceding dispensations. Like the wicked in Enoch's time, the saints rejected John's first warning. Those who rejected Noah—when sin had become fully ripe (Genesis 6:3, 5)—were destroyed when the rains came and the earth was flooded. When the "crimes" of the early Christian Church had "been made complete," the Lord withdrew his priesthood as he had promised (Revelation 2:5). The saints had become deceived, as the Apostles had prophesied, and like Cain were attempting to serve God as *they* desired, not as the Lord had taught them (Genesis 4:5–7; Galatians 1:6).

However, the angel also sent her message to those who would yet be faithful: "You

. . . 'who work righteousness,' [and] remain steadfast . . . your passing [will] be with the holy angels. Blessed are you . . . [who] endure the great persecution which is coming."[168] Nevertheless, the angel declared that they must repent quickly. Those who had sinned but desired to change were among those stones rejected but not "cast far way from the tower":

> These are they who have sinned and wish to repent; for this reason they have not been cast far way from the tower, because they will be valuable for the building if they repent. Those, then, who are going to repent, if they do so, will be strong in the faith if they repent now, while the tower is being built; but if the building be finished, they no longer have a place, but will be cast away.[169]

In this passage, the angel states that there are those who "wish to repent"; although at this point they are rejected because of their sins, if they follow through with their righteous desires and repent, they will yet be included in the Church (tower). There is an unmistakable sense of urgency, for the angel insists they must "repent now, while the tower is being built." When would the tower be finished? Would it be before the passing of the Church of this age, or at Christ's second coming? The angel seems to refer to the saints of Hermas's day because the vision and warnings are plainly directed towards them. They were given one last chance to repent, remembering that *the days of repentance have been fulfilled for all the saints, but for the heathen repentance is open until the last day.* The tower would soon be completed and the period provided for repentance ended.

Later we learn that other stones, in contrast to those placed near the tower, were being cast far away. These, the angel said, were those who had once believed but "because of doublemindedness leave the true road. They think it possible to find a better road, and err."[170] The Shepherd desired to know whether those stones failing to repent at that time had the same opportunity of inclusion in the tower: "'Repentance,' she said, 'they have, *but they cannot fit into the tower*. But they will fit into another place much less honourable, and even this only after they have been tormented and fulfilled the days of their sins, and for this reason they will be removed, because they shared in the righteous word.'"[171] The majority, although members of the Church (those who shared in the righteous word), rejected Christ's pure teachings because of "doublemindedness," thinking "it possible to find a better road." These unrighteous saints would continue in the wicked world and would not receive the same reward at the Day of Judgment as those who repent before this "fixed time" spoken of by the angel.

Again reinforcing the previous conclusion, the Apostles (Acts 1:6), like the Shepherd, wanted to know about the "end times":

> And I began to ask her about the times, if the end were yet. But she cried out with a loud voice saying, "Foolish man, do you not see the tower still being built? Whenever therefore the building of the tower has been finished, the end comes. But it will quickly be built up; ask me nothing more. This reminder and the renewal of your spirits is sufficient for you and for the saints. But the revelation was not for you alone, but for you to explain it to them all, . . . these words which I am going to say to you. . . . I charge you . . . to speak them all into the ears of the saints, that they may hear them and do them and be cleansed from their wickedness."[172]

Just as Jesus had explained to His Apostles, "It is not for you to know the times or the seasons" (Acts 1:7), the angel instructed the Shepherd to "ask me nothing more." She informed the Shepherd that the Lord's "reminder" to repent was "sufficient" and that he must declare this message to all. The tower would soon be built, she said, and the opportunity to repent or, in other words, "the end," would soon come. The angel was not speaking of "the end" of the world because *the end did not come quickly*—the Savior has not yet returned in His glorious second coming. But the end did come for the Church of that age when a human church replaced the divine Church established by Jesus Christ. The most compelling evidence that the Church *did* pass away is that conditions failed to improve in the Church; instead, they grew significantly worse. Divisiveness, contention, and the alteration of sacred doctrines and rites escalated after this period.

The angel's final warning was addressed to the leaders of the Church: "Therefore I now speak to the leaders of the Church and those 'who take the chief seats.' . . . You are hardened, and will not cleanse your hearts. . . . See to it . . . that these disagreements do not rob you of your life"[173] (see also Jeremiah 12:10).

History documents that the leaders of the Church did not cleanse their hearts or repent but forged their own religion and their own path (see Jeremiah 8:20). Uncertainty as to doctrine and proper direction replaced the confidence inspired formerly by the Apostles.

John revealed that the individual churches were symbolized by candlesticks (Revelation 1:20). After warning various churches, he testified that if they did not repent, their *candlestick,* or church, would be removed from out of its place (Revelation 2:5). Did the churches repent or did things get worse? Hermas, about A.D. 100, and Hegesippus, around A.D. 140, testified that conditions had *deteriorated.*

Did the Church respond favorably to the *new* warnings given by the angel to the Shepherd? Justin Martyr recorded that controversies and false doctrines were escalating dramatically in his day.

Did the Church see any improvement after Justin in A.D. 155? Irenaeus in "Against Heresies" witnessed that corruption and apostasy within the Church had reached alarming proportions.

Did the Church finally repent after Irenaeus in A.D. 180? Bishop Cyprian in A.D. 251, responding to significant discord and faithlessness among the African saints, wrote his plainspoken exposition, *On the Unity of the Church:*

> This evil, most faithful brethren, had long ago begun, but now the mischievous destruction of the same evil has increased, and the envenomed plague of heretical perversity and schisms has begun to spring forth and shoot anew; . . . the Holy Spirit foretells and forewarns us by the apostle, saying, "In the last days," says he, "perilous times shall come. . . ." Whatever things were predicted are fulfilled. . . . Error deceives as the adversary rages more and more; senselessness lifts up, envy inflames, covetousness makes blind, impiety depraves, pride puffs up, discord exasperates, anger hurries headlong.[174]

Sadly, controversy and wickedness reached new heights during the reign of Constantine in the early fourth century, and the Church continued its downward spiral thereafter throughout the Middle Ages.

The Christian Reformer John Wesley, writing in the eighteenth century, explained:

> Soon after the pouring out of the Holy Ghost on the day of Pentecost, in the infancy of the Christian Church, there was indeed a glorious change. "Great

grace was then upon them all," Ministers as well as people. "The multitude of them that believed were of one heart and of one soul." But how short a time did this continue! How soon did the fine gold become dim! Long before even the apostolic age expired, St. Paul himself had grounds to complain, that some of his fellow laborers had forsaken him, having "loved the present world." And not long after, St. John reproved divers of the angels, that is, the ministers, of the Churches in Asia, because, even in that early period, their "works were not found perfect before God."

Thus did "the mystery of iniquity" begin to "work," in the Ministers as well as the people, even before the end of the apostolic age. But how much more powerfully did it work, as soon as those master-builders, the Apostles, were taken out of the way! Both Ministers and people were then farther and farther removed from the hope of the Gospel. In so much that when St. Cyprian, about an hundred and fifty years after the death of St. John, describes the spirit and behavior both of laity and Clergy that were round about him, one would be ready to suppose he was giving us a description of the present Clergy and laity of Europe. But the corruption which had been creeping in drop by drop, during the second and third century, in the beginning of the fourth, when Constantine called himself a Christian, poured in upon the Church with a full tide. And whoever reads the history of the Church, from the time of Constantine to the Reformation, will easily observe that all the abominations of the heathen world . . . overflowed every part of it. And in every nation and city the Clergy were not a whit more innocent than the laity.[175]

Finally, confirming fulfillment of the prophecy received by John the Revelator,

Wesley summarized:

> Such is the authentic account of "the mystery of iniquity" working even in the apostolic Churches!—an account given, not by the Jews or Heathens, but by the Apostles themselves. To this we may add the account which is given by the Head and Founder of the Church; Him "who holds the stars in his right hand"; who is "the faithful and true Witness." We may easily infer what was the state of the Church in general, from the state of the seven Churches in Asia. One of these indeed, the Church of Philadelphia, had "kept his word, and had not denied his name"; (Revelation 3:8;) the Church of Smyrna was likewise in a flourishing state: But all the rest were corrupted, more or less; insomuch that many of them were not a jot better than the present race of Christians; and our Lord then threatened, what he has long since performed, to "remove the candlestick" from them.[176]

As witnessed by the Apostle John and the Shepherd, the wicked world continued, but God's Church was taken from the earth for a season—as it had been from time to time during the patriarchal dispensations under similar conditions of apostasy. The candlestick, as attested to by John Wesley, had long since been removed.

Episcopal Elections or Ratification?

History was repeating itself. In previous dispensations, Israel had rejected and even killed its prophets (1 Kings 19:14), trusting instead in the arm of flesh (Jeremiah 17:5). Without the inspired leadership of the Apostles, the greatest problem confronting the Church was the question of priesthood authority. Jesus had revealed to the Apostles the doctrine of sustaining or ratifying those "called" to serve by revelation. When apostasy had run its course, priesthood officers were elected as in political contests, introducing quarrels and power struggles throughout the Church. The Apostles, Clement had said, "knew there would be strife on account of the office of the episcopate." Jude testified that "certain men crept in unawares, . . . ungodly men" (Jude 1:4). The incidents that began at Corinth and Galatia were not isolated—the Church itself was under attack.

Providing another example that early leaders were called of God and not merely elected by the voice of the people, Eusebius records that after the Apostle John was released from prison, he *appointed* worthy members to serve as bishops as God revealed them to him through the Holy Ghost. If New Testament tradition were followed, these men would then have been *ratified* by the voice of the members: "Coming from the isle of Patmos to Ephesus, he went also, when called to the neighboring regions of the Gentiles; in some to appoint bishops, in some to institute entire new churches, in others *to appoint to the ministry* some one of *those that were pointed out by the Holy Ghost.*"[177]

The procedure of "sustaining" or "ratifying" is scripturally based. However, the democratic method of selecting leaders was inspired by Plato and adopted by the second generation of Church Fathers after the death of the Apostles and later by the Reformers. The Christian historian Henry Chadwick wrote, regarding the democratic approach, "The process of electing a new bishop could be sharply divisive. Unanimity of choice was sufficiently *unusual* to be regarded as a 'special grace.' "[178] In contrast, no divisiveness existed when Mathias was chosen, nor when Stephen and his brethren were appointed, nor even when Saul (Paul) was identified as "a chosen

vessel unto me" (Acts 9:15), in spite of his notorious persecution of the saints, because each of these calls came by revelation through recognized priesthood authority.

The Rise of Heretical Christian Factions

Much in the early letters written by Ignatius to various branches of the Church exhorted them to avoid heresies that threatened the unity and progress of the Church. In order to achieve such unity, he counseled the saints to follow the bishop as the inspired representative of God. He particularly warned Church members about the growing problem of Gnosticism and Docetism: "For they alienate Christ from the Father, and the law from Christ. They calumniate His being born of the Virgin; they are ashamed of His cross; they deny His passion; and they do not believe His resurrection."[179]

We first become aware of Gnosticism through the admonitions of Paul: "O Timothy, keep that which is committed to thy trust, avoiding profane and vain babblings, and *oppositions of science* [*science* in Gr. = *gnosis*] *falsely so called:* which some professing have erred concerning the faith" (1 Timothy 6:20–21; emphasis added).

Paul further warned the Colossian saints: "Beware lest any man spoil you through philosophy and vain deceit, after the tradition of men, after the rudiments of the world, and not after Christ" (Colossians 2:8).

Current research indicates that Gnosticism's roots were founded on the fringes of the Jewish biblical tradition in approximately 200 BC. Mixed with oriental themes, originating from the area of Samaria-Palestine, Gnostic thought was also significantly influenced by the Hellenistic philosophy introduced by Philo Judaeus of Alexandria[180] (see pages

131, 150). Although *Gnosticism* in its various forms predated Christianity and existed while the Apostles were still alive, as Paul attests, Christian Gnosticism began to thrive early in the second century. The word *gnostic* derives from the Greek word *gnosis,* meaning knowledge, understanding, or science.[181] Apparently, Paul was seeking to protect the Church against human innovations and to keep the Church's doctrine from becoming entangled with worldly philosophies. Unfortunately, after the death of the Apostles, because Gnostic sects became predominantly Christian, the two ideologies were quickly meshed.

Gnostic Christians were no safer from revisionist theology than were orthodox Christians. Without the guidance of the Apostles, it appears that they combined sacred teachings, probably received during the forty-day ministry, with philosophical ideas, thus creating a counterfeit gospel. Because true doctrine was mixed with false doctrine, the whole became objectionable to early orthodox leaders who remained faithful to basic traditions but probably excluded many of the esoteric and essential parts of original Christianity as revealed by Jesus Himself.

Gnostic beliefs, as portrayed by portions of the Nag Hammadi Library discovered in Egypt in 1945, suggest that the Resurrection was only symbolic. Some of these writings imply that the divine spirit of Jesus Christ occupied the physical body of the man Jesus and that His body did not actually die on the cross; instead, the spirit of Jesus merely returned to the divine habitation whence He had come. Accordingly, Gnostic Christians repudiated the atoning sacrifice of Jesus and rejected His physical resurrection. Similarly, Christian Docetists taught that Christ was strictly a spiritual being, uncorrupted by a fleshly body. They insisted that Christ's physical appearance was merely an optical illusion.

Gnostics rejected the God of the Old Testament, whom they referred to as the demiurge, or the creator of the physical world. Matter, they said, was evil, and those who became awakened through gnosis were redeemed. In a Gnostic ritual designed to declare independence from the demiurge, the initiate reads: "I am a son of the Father—the Father who had a pre-existence. . . . I derive being from Him who is pre-existent, and I come again to my own place whence I came forth."[182]

According to Kurt Rudolph, the Gnostic obtained a "nearness to God through the idea of a divine kernel in man," thus, even the common man could have a close personal relationship with God "without priestly mediation."[183] Consequently, Gnostics rejected the authority of the bishop in favor of personal revelation and, according to Irenaeus, considered themselves beyond his judgment or censure.[184]

A Gnostic writing titled the Great Announcement explains one view of the origin of the universe. Referring to this book, Hippolytus recorded: "From the power of Silence appeared 'a great power, the Mind of the Universe, which manages all things, and is a male. . . . The other, . . . a great intelligence, . . . is a female which produces all things.'"[185]

Taken at face value, a careful reading of this passage might indicate the existence of both a male and a female power sharing in governance and creation. Perhaps reference to a "female producing all things" referred to "producing" the spirits of the universe. However, Gnostic teachers gave a strange and distorted interpretation to this passage, suggesting that God was the "great male-female power"; in other words, God is a male-female being: "There is in everyone [divine power] existing in a latent condition. . . . This is one power divided above and below; generating itself, making it grow, seeking itself, finding itself, being mother of itself, father of itself, sister of itself, spouse of itself, daughter of itself, son of itself—mother, father, unity, being a source of the entire circle of existence."[186]

Without the Apostles, one can see how these misunderstandings occurred. An Asian Christian by the name of Marcion (A.D. 144) was confused when comparing the God of the Old Testament, who seemed to demand justice and punished every violation of the law, with the New Testament God of love and forgiveness. In reality, the two Gods were really one and the same God, as indicated by Justin Martyr (see page 167). Writings containing truth (although subjected to scribal abuse) may have been distorted by Gnostic leaders who, like the orthodox, were fighting for power and for what they interpreted as original Christianity. Although the same principles contained in the Old Testament are present in the New Testament, the distinguishing difference is that in the New Testament Jesus Christ actually came in fulfillment of all Old Testament promises. Ancient Israel was so disobedient in the face of such great evidence that God often appeared stern and unforgiving, when in fact He had always been full of grace (Exodus 34:6) and consistent in His divine judgments (Hebrews 10:28–29). When Jesus came to establish the New Covenant, the outward performances of the Mosaic law were abolished, but the same basic principles pertaining to salvation survived, including the end-state of those who reject Him.

Gnostic leaders, it would appear, took many legitimate doctrines and teachings, altered them, and developed a counterfeit gospel. Regarding traditional Christianity's triumph over Gnosticism, Elaine Pagels has concluded:

> It is the winners who write history—their way. No wonder, then, that the viewpoint of the successful majority has dominated all traditional accounts of the origin of Christianity. . . . But the discoveries at Nag Hammadi reopen fundamental questions. They suggest that Christianity might have developed in very different directions. . . . Now that the Nag Hammadi discoveries give us a new perspective on this process, we can understand why certain creative persons throughout the ages, from Valentinus and Heracleon to Blake, Rembrandt, Dostoevsky, Tolstoy, Nietzsche, found themselves at the edge of orthodoxy. All were fascinated by the figure of Christ—his birth, life, teachings, death, and resurrection: all returned constantly to Christian symbols to express their own experience. And yet they found themselves in revolt against orthodox institutions.[187]

Pagel's conclusions, however, seem to strike at the branch rather than the root. Although history generously supports the problems associated with orthodox institutions, at stake was the preservation of *God's truth*. Because the mind of man, compared with God, is puny, *revealed truth* from God's duly appointed *living* servants was the only trustworthy safeguard of pure doctrine.

One of Gnosticism's central tenets, indicated by the Greek word *epinoia* (commonly referred to as the *luminous epinoia*), suggested that man can receive personal enlightenment from God. While this was in fact a true belief of the early Christians, ironically, Gnosticism's more radical viewpoints—the fruit of this teaching—was perhaps the major reason traditional Christianity eventually rejected this important doctrine altogether.

Without apostolic authority, no standard of *reliable* truth could be erected; thus, rather than risk losing what Irenaeus termed the apostolic tradition—basic principles of Christianity passed down from the Apostles—he and orthodox leaders who followed began to destroy faith in *continuing revelation*, making such statements as "For it is unlawful to assert that they preached before they possessed 'perfect knowledge,' as some do even venture to say, boasting themselves as improvers of the apostles."[188]

In other words, in an attempt to quell the influence of the Gnostic teacher Valentinus, Irenaeus taught his Christian community that no doctrine or knowledge existed beyond that which was revealed in apostolic writings. Unfortunately, both groups (the orthodox and the Gnostics), absent apostolic authority, missed the mark. Jesus *did* convey to His followers that they could receive inspiration and spiritual understanding from God through the Holy Spirit for their individual lives, for their families, and in comprehending scripture.[189] Jesus also taught them that He would reveal sacred and holy doctrines reserved only for the faithful (see pages 83–85). However, no member, individually, was responsible for revealing and defining doctrine *for the Church*. This responsibility had always been delegated to God's divinely chosen servants in order to keep the doctrine pure.[190] And as we have seen, prophets and the Apostles of the Lord Jesus Christ were removed from among the people because of widespread wickedness (as happened with ancient Israel), resulting in the loss of revelation, or the *luminous epinoia*, to the Church at large. Unfortunately, man-made doctrines cropped up in their stead.

Although Gnosticism was suppressed for many centuries during the Middle Ages, there has been a renewed interest in its teachings in recent years, due in large part to the discovery at Nag Hammadi. Many scholars, including James M. Robinson, Pagels, and Rudolph, have been fascinated sufficiently to revisit its origins and teachings. Unfortunately, portions of these recovered writings suggest wide divisions between the Apostles and the doctrines they established. For example, concerning the Resurrection (as well as with other doctrines), the Apostles are often seen at odds one with another.[191] Those who imply such discord between the Savior's chosen twelve have fallen prey to one of Satan's most clever ruses: He who fell from heaven seeks to destroy faith in the authority of Christ and God's chosen servants, whether they were the prophets of the Old Testament or the Apostles sent forth to administer the New Covenant. We remember Luke's testimony that the saints at Jerusalem were "of one heart and of one soul" (Acts 4:32) following the death of Jesus for at least a short period. There is little evidence to suggest anything but love and harmony between the Apostles themselves, both in doctrine and in leading the Church. Certainly this was the prayer Jesus offered so passionately to His Father prior to Gethsemane and Golgotha (John 17). Moreover, we also remember that Paul and others were instructed to keep the doctrine pure.[192] In what manner could such a commandment be fulfilled if Jesus' disciples themselves were unable to be united in basic Christian doctrines?

The fact that the Gnostics were just as divided as the orthodox suggests that both parties entered the postapostolic world in a similar fashion: each appears to have carried portions of the truth, *perhaps pure truth*, with them into the initial decades following the death of the Apostles. However, with no legitimate presiding authorities, the truth became clouded for both groups, and original Christianity passed from the earth.

In addition to Gnosticism, Hellenism

(Greek philosophy) in its various forms, known also as Platonism (the teachings of Plato) and Neoplatonism began to influence the Church's doctrine. Neoplatonism is the name given to a school of speculative scholars who attempted to expand and reconcile the metaphysical ideas of Plato and Aristotle with oriental themes. Included in this group was Hellenistic Judaism, as portrayed by the philosopher Philo Judaeus of Alexandria (20 B.C.–A.D. 50). Neoplatonist doctrine assumed that matter was basically evil and in direct opposition to the spiritual. To Neoplatonics, God was an unknowable being of pure, nonphysical matter who transcended anything that could be conceived and was known as "the highest abstraction."[193] Out of these philosophical ideas came the notion that salvation could be obtained through a strict ascetic discipline (self-denial). The Roman philosopher Plotinus (A.D. 205–70) was the founder of this new religion.

While the Apostles lived, they were able to suppress successfully such threats to unity and *true* orthodoxy. Eusebius, commenting on the apostasy of Simon the sorcerer, the same who was converted by Philip and reproved by Peter (Acts 8:1–24), testified:

> Nevertheless, that divine and celestial grace which co-operates with its servants, by their appearance and presence, soon extinguished the flame that had been kindled by the wicked one, humbling and casting down through them, "every height that elevated itself against the knowledge of God." Wherefore, *neither the conspiracy of Simon, nor any other one then existing, was able to effect anything against those apostolic times.* For *the declaration of truth prevailed and overpowered all,* and *the divine word itself,* now shining from heaven upon men, and flourishing upon earth, and *dwelling with his apostles,* prevailed and overpowered every opposition.[194]

Apostolic Authority No Longer Present in the Church

The Gnostics and other groups used the absence of the Apostles to raise the question of authority to their benefit. On what authoritative grounds, they queried, could their doctrines be discredited? Who was to interpret the true meaning of scripture? Who now presided over the Church and stood in the place of the Apostles? Because Ignatius wrote that the bishop of each local area possessed authority to administer the sacraments of the Church, some assumed that bishops had *inherited* apostolic authority. Inasmuch as Ignatius presided over Antioch at the turn of the first century, he and some of his contemporaries were undoubtedly ordained by Apostles who held keys. Such bishops possessed full authority to administer their particular offices, including ordinances such as baptism and the sacrament of the Lord's Supper. However, Ignatius states that he did not possess the keys of apostleship, implying he could not perpetuate the authority of Christ on earth. Says Ignatius, "I do not as Peter and Paul, issue commandments unto you. They were Apostles of Jesus Christ. But I am the very least [of believers]: they were free, as the servants of God; while I am, even until now a servant. But when I suffer I shall be the freedman of Jesus Christ, and shall rise again emancipated in Him."[195]

To the Philadelphians, Ignatius wrote: "I do not ordain these things as an apostle: for 'who am I, or what is my father's house,' that I should pretend to be equal in honour to them? But as your 'fellow soldier,' I hold the position of one who [simply] admonishes you."[196]

Polycarp was also a witness that bishops

such as himself and Ignatius did not possess the same authority as the Apostles: "These things, brethren, I write to you concerning righteousness, not at my own instance, but because you first invited me. For *neither am I, nor is any other like me*, able to follow the wisdom of the blessed and glorious Paul, who when he was among you in the presence of the men of that time taught *accurately* and steadfastly the word of truth."[197] Neither Ignatius nor Polycarp claimed the same authority as had the Apostles before them. Polycarp testified that no one, including himself, possessed the wisdom of the Apostles any longer. Conversely, nowhere in the history of the Old Testament can we find one prophet stating his own revelations from God to be of less efficacy than his predecessors.

Ignatius, like the Shepherd, did not seem concerned with the perpetuation of the Church; rather, he appeared to be consumed with warning those who were already baptized members and were being deceived. His writings indicate that he expected to suffer and die in defense of truth, as had the Savior and the Apostles before him: "Suffer me to be eaten by the beasts, through whom I can attain to God. I am God's wheat, and I am ground by the teeth of wild beasts that I may be found the pure bread of Christ. Rather entice the wild beasts that they may become my tomb, and leave no trace of my body. . . . Then shall I be truly a disciple of Jesus Christ. . . . I long for the beasts . . . and pray that they may be found prompt for me; I will even entice them to devour me promptly."[198] Because he understood the fate of the Church, Ignatius welcomed death but refused to divulge the mysteries of the kingdom:

> For might not I write to you things more full of mystery? But I fear to do so, lest I should inflict injury on you who are but babes [in Christ]. Pardon me in this respect, lest, as not being able to receive their weighty import, ye should be strangled by them. For even I, though I am bound [for Christ], and am able to understand heavenly things, the angelic orders, and the different sorts of angels and hosts, the distinctions between powers and dominions, and the diversities between thrones and authorities, the mightiness of the Aeons, and the pre-eminence of the cherubim and seraphim, the sublimity of the spirit, the kingdom of the Lord, and above all, the incomparable majesty of Almighty Go. . . . I am acquainted with these things.[199]

The Apostolic Fathers did not believe their authority to be equal to that of the Apostles and did not claim to have inherited the Apostleship. They understood the mysteries but elected not to share them with the general membership. Underscoring this fact, Ignatius testified that he was well acquainted with what Paul referred to as the "deep things of God" but declared that others would be *strangled* by them. Why has no one in historic Christianity since the time of the Apostolic Fathers claimed such an elevated understanding as explained by Ignatius in his epistle to the Trallians? Why was the authority of the Apostolic Fathers inferior to the authority of Peter and Paul, as testified by Ignatius? Why were the Apostolic Fathers *not* able to "issue commandments" as did the Apostles, but later bishops, such as Augustine, felt empowered to command and even destroy those not professing current orthodoxy? Why did the early Church Fathers favor martyrdom rather than seeking to build up the Church and continue the methodical evangelization of the world as had their predecessors? Would the death of the strong and mighty, such as Ignatius, advance the growth and maturity of the weak? Why were all the Apostolic Fathers permitted martyrdom, preventing them from passing along the unwritten traditions of Jesus? Why did the view of the early Church center almost exclusively on the "other side" rather than on its joy and triumph in the present or near future?

In the parable of the wicked husbandman, the Savior describes that His fate was to be the same as that of the prophets who had gone before him:

> And when the time of the fruit drew near, he sent his servants to the husbandmen. . . . And [they] took his servants [the prophets], and beat one, and killed another, and stoned another. Again, he sent other servants more than the first: and they did unto them likewise. But last of all he [God the Father] sent unto them his son [Jesus], saying, They will reverence my son. But when the husbandmen saw the son, they said among themselves, This is the heir; come, let us kill him, and let us seize on his inheritance. And they caught him, and cast him out of the vineyard, and slew him. (Matthew 21:34–39)

Jesus had testified to the Apostles, "Ye have heard how I said unto you, I go away, and come again unto you. . . . Hereafter I will not talk much with you: for the prince of this world cometh, and hath nothing in me."[200] Thus Jesus, who was "the light of the world," spoke of the coming night[201] and, as the "master of the house," had revealed to the Apostles, His "servants," that they were to suffer the same fate.[202] The Church also, after its message had been proclaimed to the world "for a witness unto all nations,"[203] was to experience the same outcome as had the Savior and His disciples.[204]

As prophesied, the Lord of the vineyard departed and was slain, and the "lord of this world" entered "and hath nothing in me";[205]

the wicked husbandmen then seized the vineyard for themselves until the Lord returns. No sooner was the good grain sown when immediately the adversary followed, sowing tares among the wheat; after the sheep, the wolves quickly followed, "not sparing the flock"; and after "sound doctrine" had been firmly planted came choking "fables" and "doctrines of devils";[206] after pure ears had heard and accepted truth, came worldly ears that "itched";[207] and after the gifts of the Spirit followed ordinary human qualities.[208] Only after a long season of anticipation,[209] when the Lord would finally return *and restore all* things,[210] could the wheat begin to be gathered[211] to effect a "divine re-ordering" of His Church once more in preparation for His "great and dreadful" second coming.[212]

Conclusion

Apostasy upended each dispensation that preceded the first advent of Jesus Christ. The New Testament declares that apostasy would also pervert the apostolic dispensation by changing its doctrines and replacing inspired leaders with those seeking power. The Old Covenant looked forward to Christ and, because of Israel's rebellion, contained many outward performances that were "fulfilled" and "done away" by the New Covenant introduced by Jesus Christ. This new law included the development of faith in the Savior, baptism by immersion for the remission of sins, receiving the gift of the Holy Ghost, and living a life in accordance with those principles taught in the Sermon on the Mount. Christ's atonement and resurrection unlocked the prison gates, permitting the gospel to be preached to both the living and the dead. Such practices must have been revealed to the Apostles during the forty days between the Savior's resurrection and ascension into heaven. These teachings were reserved for faithful followers who had proven their commitment to God.

The Apostles went forth proclaiming the everlasting gospel to the known world, in accord with the sacred stewardship received from Jesus Christ. These special disciples were subjected to all manner of persecutions, ultimately giving up their lives by way of violent deaths and becoming martyrs to the cause of Christianity. As eyewitnesses, they had borne testimony to mankind of the divine mission of their Lord and Savior Jesus Christ. Unfortunately, too many members of the Church rejected the New Covenant in favor of the "old ways" and united with worldly philosophies. A dark cloud lingered over Christianity as the Apostolic Fathers expected and welcomed the same fate as their predecessors. The Church that Christ had organized was entering an age of spiritual darkness, hiding in the wilderness in fulfillment of biblical prophecy (Revelation 12:6, 14).

Notes

1. The Apostles were commanded by the Savior to remain in Jerusalem until they received the Holy Ghost. Acts 2 describes the events of that day and testifies of the power the Apostles received through the Holy Ghost to minister and direct the Lord's Church.

2. Testament of Moses 11, in Charlesworth, *Old Testament Pseudepigrapha*, 1:933–34.

3. Epistula Apostolorum 17, 19 (Epistle of the Apostles), in Schneemelcher, *New Testament Apocrypha*, 1:259; parentheses in original; emphasis added. The Apostles petitioned the Savior: "Make known unto us what are the signs of thy Parousia [second coming] and of the end of the world, that we may . . . instruct those who come after us, to whom we preach the word of thy Gospel," Apocalypse of Peter, in Schneemelcher, *New Testament Apocrypha*, 2:625.

4. John 16:2; Matthew 24:9; 10:16–22, 28; 10:24–25; Mark 13:13; Luke 10:16; John 15:18–21.

5. Epistula Apostolorum 49–50 (Epistle of the Apostles), in Schneemelcher, *New Testament Apocrypha*, 1:277.

6. Schneemelcher, *New Testament Apocrypha*, 1:277.

7. Schneemelcher, *New Testament Apocrypha*, 1:278; see also Testament of Our Lord Jesus Christ 1:13. The idea that the just are going to be persecuted by the wicked is found in the Testament in Galilee, and Clement, First Epistle to the Corinthians 1:3–6, 45–47, 57, in *Apostolic Fathers*, 1:11, 85–91, 107–9.

8. Acts 20:29: "For in the last days the false prophets and corrupters will come in swarms; the sheep will turn into wolves, and love will turn into hate and persecute and betray one another." Didache 16, in *Ancient Christian Writers* 6, 24: "For there are many specious wolves who lead captive with evil pleasures the runners in God's race." Ignatius, Epistle to the Philadelphians 2, in *Apostolic Fathers*, 1:241; Clement of Rome, Second Epistle to the Corinthians 5, in *Apostolic Fathers*, 1:136–37. The same concept of the sheep being attacked by wolves is revealed at the time of apostasy during the days of Noah: 1 Enoch 89:13–27, 51–75, 90, in Charlesworth, *Old Testament Pseudepigrapha*, 1:65–72.

9. "He showed me many trees, without leaves, which appeared to me to be as if dry, for they were all alike. And he said to me: 'Do you see these trees?' 'Yes sir,' said I, . . . 'These trees which you see are they that dwell in the world.' 'Because . . . in the world, neither righteous nor sinners are apparent, but are all alike. For this world is winter for the righteous . . . In the winter the trees which have shed their leaves are alike, and it is not apparent which are dry and which are alive.' . . . He showed me again many trees, some budding and some withered, and said to me, 'Do you see, . . . these trees . . . which are destined to live in the world to come; for the world to come is summer for the righteous, but winter for the sinners. . . . In the summer the fruit of each individual tree is made plain.'" Shepherd of Hermas, sim. 3–4, in *Apostolic Fathers*, 2:147–51; Gospel of Philip 52:25–35, in James M. Robinson, ed., *Nag Hammadi Library in English* (San Francisco: HarperSanFrancisco,

1990), 142; Gospel of Philip 64:5–10, in *Nag Hammadi Library in English,* 148.

10. Ascension of Isaiah 3:19–4:5, in the Testament of Hezekiah, in Charlesworth, *Old Testament Pseudepigrapha,* 2:160–61.

11. Acts of Paul, in Schneemelcher, *New Testament Apocrypha,* 2:255.

12. Epistula Apostolorum 36–45 (Epistle of the Apostles), in *New Testament Aprocrypha,* 270–76; parentheses in original.

13. Clement of Rome, First Epistle to the Corinthians, in *Apostolic Fathers,* 1:13–17; Apostolic Constitutions 7.32, in *Ante-Nicene Fathers,* 7:471; Didache 16, in *Ancient Christian Writers,* 24. Documenting the history of corresponding types of apostasy that are repeated: "They will cast off my yoke, and they will accept a different yoke. And they will sow worthless seed." Secrets of Enoch in Slavonic 2 Enoch, 34, in Charlesworth, *Old Testament Pseudepigrapha,* 1:158–59; Testament of Moses 5:1–6, in Charlesworth, *Old Testament Pseudepigrapha,* 1:929–30; 1 Enoch 89:10–27, in Charlesworth, *Old Testament Pseudepigrapha,* 1:65–66. "And I asked the Truth, Who are these? And he said to me: This is the Deceiver and the Error. And they imitate the Beloved and his Bride, and they cause the world to err and corrupt it. And they invite many to the wedding feast and allowed them to drink the wine of their intoxication." Odes of Solomon 38:9–15, in Charlesworth, *Old Testament Pseudepigrapha,* 2:767.

14. "For the Lord said, 'Ye shall be as lambs in the midst of the wolves,' and Peter answered and said to him, 'if then the wolves tear the lambs?' Jesus said to Peter, 'Let the Lambs have no fear of the wolves after their death; . . . but fear him who after your death hath power over body and soul. . . . And be well assured, brethren, that our sojourning in this world . . . lasts a short time, but the promise of Christ . . . brings us rest, in the kingdom which is to come and in everlasting life.'" Clement of Rome, Second Epistle to the Corinthians, in *Apostolic Fathers,* 135. In answering the Apostle's query as to whether or not they can fulfill the mandate given them, especially when considering the wickedness to follow, Jesus promised, "Truly I say to you, preach and teach, as I will be with you. For I am well pleased to be with you,

that you may become joint heirs with me of the kingdom of heaven of Him who sent me. Truly I say to you, you will be my brothers and companions, for my Father has delighted in you and in those who will believe in me through you. . . . [S]o great a joy has my Father prepared (for you) that angels and powers desired . . . to view and to see it, but they will not be allowed to see the greatness of my Father." Epistula Apostolorum 19 (Epistle of the Apostles), in Schneemelcher, *New Testament Apocrypha,* 1:259–60. "Through their faithfulness unto death they will attain to the glory of God, which is their true destiny." Willem C. van Unnik, *Newly Discovered Gnostic Writings* (Naperville, Ill.: Allenson, 1960), 84.

15. Epistula Apostolorum 40 (Epistle of the Apostles), in Schneemelcher, *New Testament Apocrypha,* 1:272; see also, "And we said unto him again, 'O Lord, will the Gentiles then not say, Where is their God?'" Epistula Apostolorum 36, in Schneemelcher, *New Testament Apocrypha,* 1:269; cf. 1 Enoch 89:68–71, in Charlesworth, *Old Testament Pseudepigrapha,* 1:68–69; 4 Ezra 5:28–40; 7:46; 8:1–3, 14–15, in Charlesworth, *Old Testament Pseudepigrapha,* 1:533, 538, 542; 2 Baruch 55:2–8, in Apocalypse of Baruch, in Charlesworth, *Old Testament Pseudepigrapha,* 1:640.

16. Matthew 23:37, Jesus responded, "Believing in my name, they have done the work of sinners; they have acted like unbelievers." Further explaining, the Lord declared that "Adam was given the power that he might choose what he wanted of the two; and he chose the light . . . and left the darkness and withdrew from it. Likewise every man is given the ability to believe in the light." Epistula Apostolorum 36, 39 (Epistle of the Apostles), in Schneemelcher, *New Testament Apocrypha,* 1:270–71.

17. "I long for the beasts . . . and pray that they may be found prompt for me; I will even entice them to devour me promptly." Ignatius, Epistle to the Romans 4–5, in *Apostolic Fathers,* 1:231–33; Polycarp to the Philippians 9, in *Apostolic Fathers,* 1:295. "Says Paul, 'I am no deserter from Christ, but a lawful soldier of the living God. . . . I go to the Lord that I may come (again) with him in the glory of his Father.' His followers ask, 'How then

shall we live when thou art beheaded?' . . . Paul answers, 'Believe in the living God, who raises up from the dead both me and all who believe in him!'" Acts of Paul 11, in Schneemelcher, *New Testament Apocrypha*, 2:262. Says Justin: "Now it is evident that no one can terrify or subdue us who have believed in Jesus over all the world. For it is plain that, though beheaded, and crucified, and thrown to wild beasts, and chains, and fire, and all other kinds of torture, we do not give up our confession; but the more such things happen, the more do others and in larger numbers become faithful, and worshippers of God through the name of Jesus. For just as if one should cut away the fruit-bearing parts of a vine, it grows up again, and yields other branches flourishing and fruitful; even so the same thing happens with us. For the vine planted by God and Christ the Saviour is His people. But the rest of the prophecy shall be fulfilled at His Second Coming." Justin Martyr, Dialogue with Trypho 110, in *Ante-Nicene Fathers*, 1:254; Apocalypse of Paul, in E. A. Wallis Budge, ed. and trans., *Miscellaneous Coptic Texts in the Dialect of Upper Egypt* (New York: AMS, 1977), 540–42, 1060–61; Ephraim, Asketicon, in E. A. Wallis Budge, ed. and trans., *Coptic Martyrdoms, Etc., In the Dialect of Upper Egypt* (New York: AMS, 1977), 163–64, 415–16, resembles Clement's First Epistle to the Corinthians and the Shepherd of Hermas.

18. "These are the secret sayings which the living Jesus spoke," Gospel of Thomas 32:10, in *NHLE*, 126. "Even the canonical traditions record appearances only to believers" during the forty days (E. C. Rust, "Interpreting the Resurrection," in *Journal of Bible and Religion* 29 [1961]: 27–28); see also notes 19–24 below. A compelling thesis written by Hugh Nibley provides significant detail regarding the entire concept of the "40-day teachings" in "When the Lights Went Out" (Provo, Utah: FARMS, 2001), 49–90.

19. Clementine Recognitions 3.34, in *Ante-Nicene Fathers*, 8:123; see also Matthew 7:8; Gospel of Truth 19:4–18, in *Nag Hammadi Library in English*, 41; Gospel of Thomas 48:30–34, in *Nag Hammadi Library in English*, 136; Gospel of Thomas 81:10–14, in *Nag Hammadi Library in English*, 157; Gospel of Thomas 33:10–14, in *Nag Hammadi Library in English*, 126; Gospel of Thomas 40:16–18, in *Nag Hammadi Library in English*, 131; Gospel of Thomas 43:34–44:1, in *Nag Hammadi Library in English*, 133.

20. Clementine Recognitions 3.1, in *Ante-Nicene Fathers*, 8:117; see also, "'Shall . . . those be wholly deprived of the kingdom who have died before His coming?' Then Peter says: 'You compel me, O Clement, to touch upon things that are unspeakable. But so far as it is allowed to declare them, I shall not shrink from doing so.'" Clementine Recognitions 1.52, in *Ante-Nicene Fathers*, 8:91. Again, Peter to Clement: "And, behold, one of the scribes, shouting silt from the midst of the people, says: 'The signs and miracles which your Jesus wrought, he wrought not as a prophet, but as a magician.' Him Philip eagerly encounters, showing that by this argument he accused Moses also. For when Moses wrought signs and miracles in Egypt, in like manner as Jesus also did in Judaea, it cannot be doubted that what was said of Jesus might as well be said of Moses. Having made these and such like protestations, Philip was silent." Clementine Recognitions 1.58, in *Ante-Nicene Fathers*, 8:92; emphasis added. See also Ignatius, Epistle to the Trallians 5, in *Apostolic Fathers*, 1:217; Clement of Alexandria, Stromata 1.1, in *Ante-Nicene Fathers*, 2:299–303; Coptic Gnostic Apocalypse of Peter, in Schneemelcher, *New Testament Apocrypha*, 2:706–7; Apocryphon of James 1:8–25, in *Nag Hammadi Library in English*, 30.

21. Clementine Homilies 19:20, in *Ante-Nicene Fathers*, 8:336; emphasis added.

22. Ignatius, Epistle to the Trallians 5; emphasis added; brackets in original.

23. Hippolytus, Apostolic Tradition, 23:14, in R. P. C. Hanson, *Tradition in the Early Church* (London: SCM Press, 1962), 32.

24. 4 Ezra 14:37–48, in Charlesworth, *Old Testament Pseudepigrapha*, 1:555–56.

25. Abraham Cohen, *Everyman's Talmud* (New York: Schocken Books, 1995), 78.

26. "Sons" in this context refers to "descendent" or "offspring." See *Strong's Exhaustive Concordance*, ref. no. 1121, 1139. "Morning Stars" refers to those who "'early' served God," *Strong's Exhaustive Concordance*, ref. no. 1242, ref. no.

3556, 1371, 1402.

27. 3 Enoch 43:3, in Charlesworth, *Old Testament Pseudepigrapha*, 1:294.

28. 3 Enoch, Introduction, in Charlesworth, *Old Testament Pseudepigrapha*, 1:244.

29. 1 Enoch 39:10–12; 40:1, in Charlesworth, *Old Testament Pseudepigrapha*, 1:31.

30. Shepherd of Hermas, in *Apostolic Fathers*, 2:25.

31. 2 Clement 14:2, in *Apostolic Fathers*, 1:151.

32. Origen, De Principiis 2.9.1, in *Ante-Nicene Fathers*, 4:289.

33. *Ante-Nicene Fathers*, 2.9.2, 290.

34. *Ante-Nicene Fathers*, 2.9.3, 290.

35. *Ante-Nicene Fathers*, 2.9.6, 291.

36. Clementine Recognitions 1.24, in *Ante-Nicene Fathers*, 8:84.

37. 1 Enoch 48:2–7, in Charlesworth, *Old Testament Pseudepigrapha*, 1:35.

38. Testament of Adam 3:2–4, in Charlesworth, *Old Testament Pseudepigrapha*, 1:994.

39. Justin Martyr, Dialogue with Trypho 124, in *Ante-Nicene Fathers*, 1:262.

40. Irenaeus, "Against Heresies" 5, preface, in *Ante-Nicene Fathers*, 1:526.

41. Irenaeus, "Against Heresies" 4:38 (4), in *Ante-Nicene Fathers*, 1:522.

42. Hippolytus, Refutation of All Heresies 10:29, in *Ante-Nicene Fathers*, 5:152.

43. Hippolytus, Refutation of All Heresies 10:30, in *Ante-Nicene Fathers*, 5:153.

44. Clement of Alexandria, Exhortation to the Greeks 1, in *Ante-Nicene Fathers*, 2:174.

45. Clement of Alexandria, Instructor, 3.1, in *Ante-Nicene Fathers*, 2:271; see also Stromateis 23.

46. Clement of Alexandria, Stromata 7.10, in *Ante-Nicene Fathers*, 2:539.

47. Origen, Against Celsus 3.28, in *Ante-Nicene Fathers*, 4:475.

48. Origen, Commentary on the Gospel of John 2:2–3, in *Ante-Nicene Fathers*, 9:323–24.

49. Athanasius, Against the Arians 1.39, 3.34, in *Nicene and Post-Nicene Fathers*, 2:4:329, 412–13.

50. Athanasius, On the Incarnation 54, in *Nicene and Post-Nicene Fathers*, 2:4:65.

51. Augustine, On the Psalms 50.2, in *Nicene and Post-Nicene Fathers*, 1:8:178. Although Augustine's interpretation asserts that the elect are gods by grace, rather than by nature *and* grace, his theology is still consistent with the early Fathers, with the exception of the above notable distinction.

52. Clement of Alexandria makes mention in his Stromata and Exhortation to the Heathen several references relating to induction to the mysteries. See Clement of Alexandria, Stromata 1.12; 5.4; 7.2, in *Ante-Nicene Fathers*, 2:312, 449, 524; Clement, Exhortation to the Heathen 12, in *Ante-Nicene Fathers*, 2:205.

53. Ignatius, Epistle to the Trallians 9, in *Ante-Nicene Fathers*, 1:70; emphasis added.

54. Irenaeus, in Grant, *Irenaeus of Lyons*, 4:27:2, 158.

55. Clement of Alexandria, Stromata 6.6, in *Ante-Nicene Fathers*, 2:490; emphasis added.

56. Shepherd of Hermas, sim. 9:16, in *Apostolic Fathers*, 2:263.

57. Odes of Solomon 42:11–20, in Charlesworth, *Old Testament Pseudepigrapha*, 2:771; see also "He descended, indeed, into Hades alone, but He arose accompanied by a multitude," in John A. MacCulloch, *The Harrowing of Hell* (Edinburgh: Clark, 1930), chs. 15 and 16.

58. Didache, in *Ancient Christian Writers*, 15–18.

59. Ignatius, Epistle to the Magnesians 5, in *Apostolic Fathers*, 1:201. Free will is the key element in the Two Ways—choosing either life or death when one is faced with opposing choices: "And I pointed out to him [Adam] the two ways—light and darkness." 2 Enoch 30:12–15, in Charlesworth, *Old Testament Pseudepigrapha*, 1:152. "Now the world that is, and the world to come are two enemies. This world speaks of adultery, and corruption, and love of money, and deceit, but that world [where God is] bids these things farewell." Second Epistle to the Corinthians 6, in *Apostolic Fathers*, 1:135–36; brackets added; 1 Enoch 91–107, in Charlesworth, *Old Testament Pseudepigrapha*, 1:72–88.

60. Shepherd of Hermas, sim. 9:5–7, in *Apostolic Fathers*, 2:263.

61. Epistula Apostolorum 27 (Epistle of the

Apostles), in Schneemelcher, *New Testament Apocrypha*, 1:265. Odes and Psalms of Solomon 123 equates Christ's own baptism with the Decensus; cf. John H. Bernard, "The Descent into Hades and Christian Baptism," *Studia Sacra* (London: Hodder and Stoughton, 1917), 1–50.

62. Life of Adam and Eve 37:3, in Charlesworth, *Old Testament Pseudepigrapha*, 2:28990.

63. Augustine, Against Julian the Pelagian 57, in *Patrologia Latina*, 221 vols. (Paris: J. P. Migne, 1879), 45:1596–97, in Nibley, *Mormonism and Early Christianity*, 142.

64. Eusebius, Ecclesiastical History 24, 108.

65. 2 Enoch 61:2–3, in Charlesworth, *Old Testament Pseudepigrapha*, 1:187.

66. Fragments of Papias 5, in *Ante-Nicene Fathers*, 1:154. Papias was bishop of Hieropolos in about A.D. 140.

67. Irenaeus, "Against Heresies" 5.36.1–2, in Grant, *Irenaeus of Lyons*, 185.

68. Clement of Alexandria, Stromata 6.14, in *Ante-Nicene Fathers*, 2:506.

69. Origen, De Principiis 2.11.6, in *Ante-Nicene Fathers*, 4:299; cf. the doctrine of "stages of ascent," that is, three levels of enlightenment to which the Christian can aspire even during this life. H. P. Owen, "The Stages of Ascent in Hebrews 5:11 and 6:3," *New Testament Studies* 3 (1957): 243–53.

70. Shepherd of Hermas, sim. 9, in *Apostolic Fathers*, 2:217–97.

71. Testament of Levi 8:2–11, in Charlesworth, *Old Testament Pseudepigrapha*, 1:791.

72. 2 Enoch 22:8–10, in Charlesworth, *Old Testament Pseudepigrapha*, 1:138.

73. Shanks, ed., *Understanding the Dead Sea Scrolls*, 111–12. Those performing rites were "to wear the gar[ments . . .] in order to serve the children of Israel and they shall not die in this courtyard," in 11QTemple Scroll, Colossians 6:1, in Martinez, *Dead Sea Scrolls Translated*, 165.

74. J. G. Davies, *The Early Christian Church* (New York: Holt, Rinehart and Winston, 1965), 59.

75. Tertullian, On Baptism 2, in *Ante-Nicene Fathers*, 3:668.

76. Cyril of Jerusalem, Catechetical Lecture 20, in *Nicene and Post-Nicene Fathers*, 2:7:146–48.

77. Cyril of Jerusalem, Catechetical Lecture 21, in *Nicene and Post-Nicene Fathers*, 2:7:148–51.

78. Ambrose, On the Mysteries 7, in *Nicene and Post-Nicene Fathers*, 2:10:321.

79. Cyril of Jerusalem, Catechetical Lecture 22.8, in *Nicene and Post-Nicene Fathers*, 2:7:153.

80. Cyril of Jerusalem, Catechetical Lecture 23.2–3, in *Nicene and Post-Nicene Fathers*, 2:7:153.

81. Cyril of Jerusalem, Catechetical Lecture 23.4–8, in *Nicene and Post-Nicene Fathers*, 2:7:153–154.

82. Cyril of Jerusalem, Catechetical Lecture 23.9, in *Nicene and Post-Nicene Fathers*, 2:7:154.

83. 2 Jeu. 54 (40) in Carl Schmidt, *Gnostische Schriften in koptischer Sprache aus dem Codex Brucianus* (Leipzig: Hinrich, 1892), 99; and Gnostische Schriften in *koptischer Sprache*, 114–17, in Nibley, *Mormonism and Early Christianity*, 142.

84. Ignatius Ephraem II Rahmani, ed., *Testamentum Domini Nostri Jesu Christi* (Morguntiae: Kirchheim, 1899). The manuscript's date is established on ix–xiv, in Rahmani, *Testamentum*, in Nibley, *Mormonism and Early Christianity*, 47–48.

85. Rahmani, *Testamentum*, 36–37, 44, in Nibley, *Mormonism and Early Christianity*, 142.

86. Rahmani, *Testamentum*, 60, in Nibley, *Mormonism and Early Christianity*, 142.

87. Cyril of Jerusalem, Catechetical Lecture 23.21, in *Nicene and Post-Nicene Fathers*, 2:7:156.

88. Cyril of Jerusalem, Catechetical Lecture 23.22, in *Nicene and Post-Nicene Fathers*, 2:7:156.

89. Origen, De Principiis 2.11.2, in *Ante-Nicene Fathers*, 4:297.

90. Gospel of Philip, in Schneemelcher, *New Testament Apocrypha*, 1, vv. 76–77, 79, 122a, 127, 197–98, 204, 206.

91. Irenaeus, "Against Heresies" 1.21.3, in Grant, *Irenaeus of Lyons*, 85.

92. Ethiopic Apocalypse of Peter, in Schneemelcher, *New Testament Apocrypha*, 1:625.

93. Schneemelcher, *New Testament Apocrypha*, 1:626, vv. 1–2.

94. Schneemelcher, *New Testament Apocrypha*, 1:628, v. 6; 1:627, v. 4; 1:633, v. 14.

95. Epistle of Barnabas 21, in *Ante-Nicene Fathers*, 1:149.

96. Justin, Dialogue with Trypho 80, in *Ante-Nicene Fathers*, 1:239; brackets in original.

97. Irenaeus, "Against Heresies" 5.28.3, in *Ante-Nicene Fathers*, 1:557.

98. See Epistle of the Apostles 49, in *New Testament Apocrypha*, 1:277. "Now why will the judgement take place? That the wheat may be put in its barn and its chaff thrown into the fire."

99. Irenaeus, "Against Heresies" 5.28.4, in *Ante-Nicene Fathers*, 1:557.

100. Testament of Our Lord Jesus Christ 1:8; 12; 13, Adolf Von Harnack states that "this is a 40–day teaching," in *Texte and Untersuchungen zur Geschichte der altchristlichen Literatur* 9:16–17; cf. 2 Baruch 29:2–3; 70:7 in Charlesworth, *Old Testament Pseudepigrapha*, 1:631, 645; Testament in Galilee 7, in R. Graffin and F. Nau, ed., *Patrologia Orientalis* (Paris: Firmin-Didot, 1907), 9:184; Hippolytus, On Daniel 10, in *Patrologia Graeca* 10:685; On Daniel 12, in *Patrologia Graeca* 10:688; Clementine Recognitions 6.11, in *Ante-Nicene Fathers*, 8:145. The preparatory coming is not to be confused with the later coming. M. Feuillet, "Le sens du mot Parousia dans l'Évangile de Matthieu," in W. D. Davies and D. Daube, ed., *The Background of the New Testament and Its Eschatology* (Cambridge: Cambridge University Press, 1954), 262–269.

101. Life of Adam and Eve 14–16, in Charlesworth, *Old Testament Pseudepigrapha*, 2:262.

102. 2 Enoch 29:4; 31:3–6, in Charlesworth, *Old Testament Pseudepigrapha*, 1:148, 154; see also Tertullian, De Patientia 5; Irenaeus, "Against Heresies" 4.40.3; Augustine, de Genesi ad Litteram 11.18; Qu'ran: suras 2, 7, 15, 17, 18, 20, and 38.

103. Draper, *Opening the Seven Seals*, 129.

104. Draper, *Opening the Seven Seals*, 129.

105. Draper, *Opening the Seven Seals*, 130.

106. Draper, *Opening the Seven Seals*, 130.

107. Draper, *Opening the Seven Seals*, 132.

108. Draper, *Opening the Seven Seals*, 133.

109. Matthew 15:24.

110. Matthew 10:5–6.

111. Acts 4:4.

112. Acts 5:14; 6:7; 12:24.

113. Acts 6:7.

114. Acts 13:45.

115. Acts 8:3; 9:1.

116. Acts 13:50.

117. Acts 14:2, 5.

118. Acts 14:19.

119. Acts 21:27–36.

120. Josephus, Dissertation 1.

121. Justin, Dialogue with Trypho 17, in *Ante-Nicene Fathers*, 1:203.

122. Acts 28:30.

123. Romans 15:24, 28; Clement of Rome, First Epistle to the Corinthians 5, in *Ante-Nicene Fathers*, 1:6.

124. Acts 12.

125. Galatians 2:11–16. Garry Wills, in his publication *Papal Sin: Structures of Deceit* (New York: Doubleday, 2000), cites the conflicting accounts of Jerome and Augustine and of tension between the "separatists" (Jews), and "cosmopolitans" (Gentiles). In attempting to reconstruct history regarding truth telling between Augustine and Jerome, Wills misses the main point of Galatians 2:12, that of "rebellion." As with ancient Israel turning its back on authority, or in other words, the prophets (Deuteronomy 31:29), so when the Apostles departed, "grievous wolves" would enter the flock (Acts 20:29) because the saints refused to obey those whom God had invested with his divine authority. See Wills, *Papal Sin*, 277–83. Philip Schaff also shares the view taken in the present volume that the dispute between Peter and Paul is often overstated: "The unity of the apostolic church is quite conclusive against the modern invention of an irreconcilable antagonism between Paul and Peter." Schaff, *History of the Christian Church*, 1:341.

126. St. John Chrysostom, Commentary on Galatians, in *Nicene and Post-Nicene Fathers*, 1:13.18–19.

127. The Annals of Tacitus, trans. Alfred John Church and William Jackson Brodribb (Franklin Center, Pa.: Franklin Library, 1982), 343.

128. Wills, *Papal Sin*, 280.

129. Wills, *Papal Sin*, 281.

130. Nicholas Cheetham, *Keepers of the Keys: The Pope in History* (London: Macdonald, 1982), 5.

131. Eusebius, Ecclesiastical History 2.9, 58. John Foxe, *The New Foxe's Book of Martyrs*, rewritten

by Harold J. Chadwick (North Brunswick, N.J.: Bridge-Logos Publishers, 2001), 5; see also McBirnie, *Search for the Twelve Apostles*, 88–107.

132. McBirnie, *Search for the Twelve Apostles*, 174–82. Foxe, *Book of Martyrs*, 6; see also Hippolytus, Appendix, in *Ante-Nicene Fathers*, 5:255.

133. Hippolytus, Appendix, in *Ante-Nicene Fathers*, 5:255; *The International Standard Bible Encyclopedia*, ed. by Geoffrey W. Bromiley (Grand Rapids, Mich.: William B. Eerdmans, 1986), 697–719; Foxe, *Book of Martyrs*, 6.

134. McBirnie, *Search for the Twelve Apostles*, 80–81. Hippolytus, Appendix, in *Ante-Nicene Fathers*, 5:255.

135. Foxe, *Book of Martyrs*, 7. Hippolytus, Appendix, in *Ante-Nicene Fathers*, 5:255.

136. Hippolytus, Appendix, in *Ante-Nicene Fathers*, 5:255. Foxe, *Book of Martyrs*, 8; see also Eusebius, Ecclesiastical History 2.25, 80.

137. McBirnie, *Search for the Twelve Apostles*, 214, 230.

138. McBirnie, *Search for the Twelve Apostles*, 122–29; see also Eusebius, Ecclesiastical History 3.31, 116–17.

139. McBirnie, *Search for the Twelve Apostles*, 130–41. Foxe, *Book of Martyrs*, 8.

140. McBirnie, *Search for the Twelve Apostles*, 142–73, 172, 145.

141. Hippolytus, Appendix, in *Ante-Nicene Fathers*, 5:255.

142. McBirnie, *Search for the Twelve Apostles*, 260–61.

143. McBirnie, *Search for the Twelve Apostles*, 195–206.

144. McBirnie, *Search for the Twelve Apostles*, 108–21. Hippolytus, Appendix, in *Ante-Nicene Fathers*, 5:255. Tertullian testifies that John was "plunged, unhurt, into boiling oil, and thence remitted to his Island exile." Tertullian, "Prescription against Heresies" 36, in *Ante-Nicene Fathers*, 3:260.

145. Eusebius, Ecclesiastical History 3.4, 13, 15, 85, 100.

146. McBirnie, *Search for the Twelve Apostles*, 63–64, 74–75.

147. Richard P. McBrian, author of in an acclaimed, more recent publication writes: "There is no evidence that before his death Peter actually served the church of Rome as its first bishop. . . . Indeed there is no evidence that Rome even had a monoepiscopal form of government until the middle of the second century." *Lives of the Popes: The Pontiffs from St. Peter to John Paul II* (San Francisco: HarperSanFrancisco, 1997), 29.

148. Acts 3:6, 12–26; 4:8–12, 19–20; 5:1–10, 15, 29–32; 8:14–23; 9:32–41; 10; 11:2–18; 12:3–11.

149. Eusebius, Ecclesiastical History 3.36, 120. Ignatius succeeds Peter at Antioch. Eusebius, Ecclesiastical History 3.4, 85. Linus succeeds Peter at Rome.

150. Eberhard Arnold, *The Early Christians* (Farmington, Pa.: Plough Publishing House, 1997), 16.

151. Schaff, *History of the Christian Church*, 2:225; see also Chadwick, *Early Church*, 32.

152. Justin Martyr, First Apology 66, in *Ancient Christian Writers*, 70.

153. Clement of Rome, Clementine Recognitions 6.9, in *Ante-Nicene Fathers*, 8:155.

154. Justin Martyr, First Apology 65–67, in *Ancient Christian Writers*, 70–71.

155. Justin Martyr, First Apology 67, in *Ancient Christian Writers*, 71.

156. Cyprian, On the Unity of the Church 26, in *Ante-Nicene Fathers*, 5:429.

157. Eusebius, Ecclesiastical History 3.16, 101.

158. Clement of Rome, First Epistle to the Corinthians 44, in *Apostolic Fathers*, 1:81–83; emphasis added; brackets in original.

159. Acts of Paul, in Schneemelcher, *New Testament Apocrypha*, 2:255.

160. Ignatius, Epistles to the Philadelphians 7, in *Ante-Nicene Fathers*, 1:83.

161. Ignatius, Epistle to the Magnesians 3–4, in *Apostolic Fathers*, 1:199–201.

162. Ignatius, Epistle to the Smyrnaeans 11, in *Apostolic Fathers*, 1:263–65.

163. Ignatius, Epistle to the Romans 9, in *Apostolic Fathers*, 1:237.

164. Eusebius establishes the date of Ignatius' martyrdom in the tenth year of Trajan (A.D. 108), in Epistles of Ignatius, in *Apostolic Fathers*, 1:166.

165. Hahneman, "Muratorian Fragment," 410.

166. Shepherd of Hermas, sim. 9:31, in *Apostolic Fathers*, 2:293.

167. Shepherd of Hermas, vis. 2:2, in *Apostolic Fathers*, 2:19.

168. Shepherd of Hermas, vis. 2:2, in *Apostolic Fathers*, 2:21.

169. Shepherd of Hermas, vis. 3:5, in *Apostolic Fathers*, 2:39.

170. Shepherd of Hermas, vis. 3:7, in *Apostolic Fathers*, 2:45.

171. Shepherd of Hermas, vis. 3:7, in *Apostolic Fathers*, 2:45.

172. Shepherd of Hermas, vis. 3:8, in *Apostolic Fathers*, 2:49.

173. Shepherd of Hermas, vis. 3:9, in *Apostolic Fathers*, 2:52–53.

174. Cyprian, On the Unity of the Church 16, in *Ante-Nicene Fathers*, 5:426–27.

175. John Wesley, *The Works of John Wesley*, ed. Albert C. Outler, 24 vols. (Nashville: Abingdon Press, 1984), Sermon 104, 13–14, 7:177–78.

176. Wesley, *Works of John Wesley*, Sermon 61, 21, 6:259–60.

177. Eusebius, Ecclesiastical History 3.23, 105; emphasis added.

178. Chadwick, *Early Church*, 50.

179. Ignatius, Epistle to the Trallians 6, in *Ante-Nicene Fathers*, 1:68.

180. Kurt Rudolph, *Gnosis: The Nature and History of Gnosticism* (San Francisco: Harper San Francisco, 1987), 277–79.

181. *Strongest Strong's Concordance of the Bible*, ref. no. 1108, 1105.

182. Irenaeus, "Against Heresies" 1:21.5, in *Ante-Nicene Fathers*, 1:346.

183. Rudolph, *Gnosis*, 291.

184. Pagels, *Gnostic Gospels*, 38.

185. Hippolytus, Refutation of All Heresies 6:18, in *Ante-Nicene Fathers*, 5:82; see Pagels, *Gnostic Gospels*, 50–51.

186. Hippolytus, Refutation of All Heresies 6:17; Pagels, *Gnostic Gospels*, 51.

187. Pagels, *Gnostic Gospels*, 142, 150.

188. Irenaeus, "Against Heresies" 3:1 in, *Ante-Nicene Fathers*, 1:414.

189. Matthew 7:7; 11:27; 1 Corinthians 2:10; Ephesians 1:17–18; James 1:5.

190. John 7:16–17; Acts 2:42; Romans 16:17; 1 Timothy 1: 3–4, 10; 4:1, 16; 2 Timothy 3:14; 4:2–4; Titus 1:5, 9; 2:1; Hebrews 13:9; 2 John 1:7.

191. Pagels, *Gnostic Gospels*, 3–27, discusses controversial Gnostic writings that suggest the Apostles held differing views of the resurrection. While certain Gnostic writings are divisive on this important subject, biblical writings are wholly consistent, confirming the literal nature of the resurrection. The prophet Ezekiel was very clear in his remarkable revelation concerning the resurrection (Ezekiel 37:1–8). Moreover, Matthew testified "that many bodies of the saints which slept arose, and came out of the graves after his resurrection, and went into the holy city, and appeared unto many" (Matthew 27:52–53). Ignatius, in A.D. 108, also spoke plainly regarding his understanding of the precise nature of the resurrection (Ignatius, Epistle to the Smyrnaeans 3, in *Ante-Nicene Fathers*, 1:87). As we learn in 2 Corinthians 13:1, the law of witnesses is very clear. The Apostles were not divided as to the nature of the resurrection or any other critical doctrine.

192. See ch. 5, note 190.

193. Alfred Weber and Ralph Barton Perry, *History of Philosophy* (New York: Charles Scriber's Sons, 1925), 171.

194. Eusebius, Ecclesiastical History 2.14, 64; emphasis added.

195. Ignatius, Epistle to the Romans 4, in *Ante-Nicene Fathers*, 1:75.

196. Ignatius, Epistle to the Philadelphians 4, in *Ante-Nicene Fathers*, 1:81; brackets in original.

197. Polycarp to the Philippians 3, in *Apostolic Fathers*, 1:287; emphasis added.

198. Ignatius, Epistle to the Romans 4–5, in *Apostolic Fathers*, 1:231–33.

199. Ignatius, Epistle to the Trallians 5, in *Ante-Nicene Fathers*, 1:68; emphasis added.

200. John 14:28, 30.

201. John 9:4–5; Matthew 23:34–39; 17:12; Luke 11:51; Clementine Recognitions 3.61, in *Ante-Nicene Fathers*, 8:130.

202. John 16:2; Matthew 24:9; 10:16–22, 24–25, 28; Mark 13:13; Luke 10:16; John 15:18–21.

203. Matthew 24:14; 28:20; Mark 13:10.

204. 1 Peter 1:6–7; 4:12–14; Acts 20:28–30; 1 Timothy 4:1–3; 2 Timothy 3:1–7; 4:3–4; 2 Thessalonians 2:3; 2 Peter 2:1–22; Jude 1:4, 17–19; Galatians 1:6–7; Revelation 2:2, 4–5, 2 Corinthians 11:3–4; "Take up the epistle of the blessed Paul the Apostle. What did he first write to you at the beginning of his preaching? With true inspiration he charged you concerning himself and Cephas and Apollos, because even then you had made yourselves partisans. . . . But now consider who they are who have perverted you, and have lessened the respect due your famous love for the brethren. It is a shameful report, beloved, extremely shameful, and unworthy of your training in Christ." Clement of Rome, First Epistle to the Corinthians, in *Apostolic Fathers*, 1:89–91. Thus, Clement records the deepening problem of apostasy and the darkness that is shortly to come from the "prince of this world."

205. John 14:30.

206. 2 Timothy 4:1, 3–4.

207. Matthew 11:15; 2 Timothy 4:3.

208. 1 Corinthians 12:8–11, 31; 13:1–3, 8, 13. The corruption of the Church of the Middle Ages vindicates the assertion made by John Wesley that the gifts of the Spirit virtually disappeared after the ascent of Constantine to the throne of the Roman Empire. Inasmuch as Peter, Paul, John, and others testified of apostasy while they yet lived, it is probable that apostasy on many fronts was already well underway by the end of the first century. Beginning with Irenaeus, Clement of Alexandria, Tertullian, and Origen in the late second and early third centuries, there is more evidence that scholarship, philosophy, and human achievement replaced the simple gifts of the Spirit so prominent in New Testament Christianity. This period is comparable to the Jewish traditions of scribal erudition that replaced revelation, the Jews having killed the prophets.

209. 2 Thessalonians 2:1–3.

210. Jeremiah 16:16; Matthew 13:24–30, 38–40; v. 39 refers to the harvest at the end of the world.

211. Acts 3:19–21.

212. Malachi 4:1–2; 5–6.

CHAPTER SIX

COUNCILS AND CREEDS: EARLY CHRISTIANITY AFTER THE DEATH OF THE APOSTLES

We worship one God in Trinity, and Trinity in Unity, neither confounding the persons, nor dividing the substance. For there is one person of the Father, another of the Son, and another of the Holy Ghost. But the Godhead of the Father, Son, and Holy Ghost, is all one: . . . The Father incomprehensible, the Son incomprehensible and the Holy Ghost incomprehensible. . . . There are not three incomprehensibles, . . . but . . . one incomprehensible. . . . And yet they are not three Gods but one God.

—Excerpt from the Athanasian Creed

The Apostle Paul taught the importance of unity (1 Corinthians 1:13) within the body of Christ—a favorite metaphor for the Savior's Church. While history documents well the difficulty of living this commandment, Jesus' desires concerning it were very clear: He was on earth to perform His Father's will, and the Father expected His children to be unified (John 17). The historian Eusebius perceived that as long as the Apostles presided over the Church, they were able to suppress or often even extinguish heretical ideas. However, with the death of these humble servants, the prophesied wolves began to enter the flock. They came in many disguises, making it impossible for even the elect to extract the dross from legitimate

emerging theological ideas. Notwithstanding that a small group of spiritual noblemen sought to retain purity in the Church, it was a battle not to be won in this quarter of the world's annals. That victory would have to wait until the final period of the earth's history.

As if Satan were not content to watch the Church afflict itself, he enlisted the Roman Empire to torture the Church from without. Beginning with Nero in A.D. 64 and terminating with Diocletian's regime in A.D. 311, at times the Empire performed varying degrees of persecution, inhumanity, and extermination against the Christian faith. By contrast, other periods of this era observed relative calm. Tyranny and oppression finally relented when Galerius on

143

his deathbed (A.D. 311) signed the "edict of toleration." Notwithstanding such physical and political obstacles, apostasy within the Church in the absence of inspired leaders was responsible for the loss of priesthood authority and the alteration of pure doctrines early in the second century. Beginning in the fourth century, the cancerous corruption of Church hierarchy and doctrine spread quickly.

Persecution ended when the emperor Constantine declared Christianity to be the religion of the realm. It is difficult to assess the motives behind his decision—whether it was a spiritual manifestation from heaven as legend maintains or simply Constantine's genius in perceiving that Christianity represented the best opportunity for religious harmony within the Empire. Whatever the reason, the Church's fortune changed dramatically as Christianity now spread unimpeded throughout the Roman Empire. Unfortunately, Constantine and later emperors were not satisfied with *unity* of religion alone but wanted *control* over religious matters as well as those of state. The resulting secular influence destroyed critical similarities to New Testament Christianity as offices within the priesthood were purchased with money or influence. Councils and the development of doctrinal creeds replaced actual apostolic revelation, resulting in changed foundational doctrines and modified ordinances and sacraments.

Apostasy from within the Church

The first recorded Church historian was Hegesippus (ca. 110–180), writing in about the mid-second century. His account follows shortly on the heels of the Shepherd of Hermas, Ignatius, and the Epistle of Barnabas. Although much of his record has been lost, Eusebius was able to preserve a portion of it. Eusebius held him in high regard as a historian, as do many Christian scholars today. Hegesippus lamented:

> The Church continued until then as a pure and uncorrupt virgin; whilst if there were any at all that attempted to pervert the sound doctrine of the saving Gospel, they were yet skulking in dark retreats; but when the sacred choir of Apostles became extinct, and the generation of those that had been privileged to hear their inspired wisdom had passed away, then also the combinations of impious error arose by the fraud and delusions of the false teachers. These also, as there were none of the Apostles left, henceforth attempted, without shame to preach their false doctrine against the Gospel of truth.[1]

The testimony of Hegesippus is valuable in determining what took place following the death of the Apostles. After the Apostles and the generation who was "privileged to hear their inspired wisdom" were gone, then arose the false teachers and their fraudulent doctrines. Almost concurrent with the close of the mortal ministry of John, the last of the original Twelve, the purity of the gospel message as delivered by Jesus Christ and His Apostles was fading. The witness of John was followed by the warning of the angel to the Shepherd: "Your seed, Hermas, have set God at naught, and have blasphemed the Lord, and have betrayed their parents in great wickedness; . . . they have added to their sins wanton deeds and piled up wickedness, and so their crimes have been made complete."[2] The testimonies of the earliest Christian Fathers—Clement, Hermas, Ignatius, and Hegesippus—indicate that pure and original Christianity was declining, and history affirms that the Church became progressively more human and less divine.

To illustrate the effects of apostasy, Hegesippus describes how a man named Thebuthis sought a high Church position unrighteously:

But after James the Just had suffered martyrdom, as our Lord had for the same reason, Simeon, the son of Cleophas, our Lord's uncle, was appointed the second bishop [of Jerusalem] whom all proposed as the cousin of our Lord. Hence they called the Church as yet a virgin, for it was not yet corrupted by vain discourses. *Thebuthis made a beginning, secretly to corrupt it on account of his not being made bishop.* He was one of those seven sects among the Jewish people. Of these also was Simeon, whence sprang the sect of Simonians; also Cleobius, from whence came the Cleobians; also Dositheus, the founder of the Dositheans. From these also sprung the Gortheonians, from Gortheoeus; and also Masbotheans from Masbothoeus. Hence also the Meandrians, and Marcionists, and Carpocratians and Valentinians, and Basilidians, and the Saturnillians, *every one introducing his own peculiar opinions,* one differing from the other. From these sprung the false Christs and the false prophets and false apostles, *who divided the unity of the Church by the introduction of corrupt doctrines* against God and against His Christ.[3]

Eusebius further documented the existence of apostasy when he recorded the appearance of "insidious imposters and deceivers" during this early period:

The malignant spirit of iniquity, as the enemy of all truth, and always the most violent enemy to the salvation of men, was now devising every species of machination against the church, as he [Satan] had already before armed himself against it by former persecutions. When, however, cut off from those, he then waged a war by other methods, in which he employed the agency of wicked imposters as certain abandoned instruments and minions of destruction. Intent upon every course, he instigated these insidious imposters and deceivers, by assuming the same name with us (Christians) to lead those believers whom they happened to seduce to the depths of destruction, and . . . also [to] turn those who were ignorant of the faith, from the path that led to the saving truth of God.[4]

Gnosticism, in its diverse strains, was rapidly beginning to expand in Rome, Alexandria, and various other locations throughout the Empire. Without the authority of the Apostles, the ability of orthodox churches to check this pernicious offshoot was severely limited. The tares were now growing quickly among the wheat and were scarcely discernible by those pure in heart. Unfortunately, many of the humble and doctrinally sound Church leaders had already been martyred and in many cases replaced by charismatic, worldly minded individuals. According to Eusebius, the perversion had begun with Simon the sorcerer, followed by his successor Menander, and then Saturninus and Basilides. Irenaeus states that Basilides, "under the pretext of matters too deep to be divulged, stretched his inventions to a boundless extent, in his astonishing fictions of impious heresy."[5]

Dr. J. L. von Mosheim, a noted German scholar who produced an extensive work on ecclesiastical history in 1755, explained that such schisms and contentions caused severe conflicts within the Church in the latter part of the *first century:* "It will be easily imagined that unity and peace could not reign long in the Church, since it was composed of Jews and Gentiles, who regarded each other with

145

the bitterest aversion. Besides, as converts to Christianity could not extirpate radically the prejudices which had been formed in their minds by education, and confirmed by time, they brought with them into the bosom of the Church more or less of the errors of their former religions. Thus the seeds of discord and controversy were easily sown, and could not fail to spring up soon into animosities and dissensions, which accordingly broke out and divided the Church."[6]

Attempts to Defend Pure Christianity Fail

Lest we see only a one-sided and inaccurate picture, we should note that in the midst of these controversies wise and good men existed, striving to follow in the footsteps of the Apostles. Not everyone had taken up the cause of self-aggrandizement and power in lieu of truth and discipleship. In addition to fighting contention and impropriety within the Church, some men sought to defend and preserve Christianity against many forms of heresy. Among them were three particularly important groups known as Apostolic Fathers, Apologists, and Polemicists (see pages 8–9). Many of their doctrinal positions were presented in earlier chapters; nevertheless, it is worthwhile to look more carefully at their place in history, thus providing a more complete context to their teachings. In spite of the valiant efforts of these gifted and loyal Churchmen, apostasy by this time was widespread, and the unity and priesthood authority of the New Testament Church had already been taken from the earth.

Polycarp, Bishop of Smyrna (ca. A.D. 69–155)

In addition to the late first-century bishops Clement of Rome and Ignatius of Antioch, Polycarp, bishop of Smyrna for many years, worked as one of the Apostolic Fathers to preserve truth. For example, he wrote a letter to the Philippians in approximately A.D. 110 exhorting the saints against the heresies of Docetism that were beginning to infiltrate the Church at Philippi. He counseled them to live virtuous lives, to serve the Lord, and to endure faithfully to the end, even as Christ had. From Polycarp's correspondence with the saints, we know he was familiar with the writings of the Apostles John and Paul, and it is likely that Polycarp was personally acquainted with John. Although he may have been the "angel of the church in Smyrna" to whom it was written, "Be thou faithful unto death, and I will give thee a crown of life" (Revelation 2:8, 10), as some believe, it is also possible that Polycarp succeeded the individual spoken of by John. While Polycarp's epistle does not reflect the originality or authoritative apostolic style of leadership evident in the New Testament, it does reflect the inspired testimony of a righteous man fulfilling the duties entrusted him by God. Among many other noted conflicts, dissension and schism within the Church during Polycarp's day can be confirmed by the disputed election of Anicetus as bishop of Rome in A.D. 155. This democratic method of administering the affairs of the Church was widespread, and its divisive fruits were transparent. Instead of being called by prophecy (by the Holy Ghost) and by those who held the keys of Apostleship, the bishops were now *elected* by the voice of the people, giving rise to endless controversies. Polycarp traveled to Rome on Church business in A.D. 155 but while there was burned at the stake, following in the martyr's footsteps of the Apostles and many early Church Fathers.

Justin Martyr (ca. A.D. 100–165)

Born at Flavia Neapolis, a city of Samaria, Justin received his early education in Greek philosophy, receiving training from scholars in several fields. But it was the concepts of Plato that caught his attention and held it firm. Said he, "The perception of immaterial things quite overpowered me, and the contemplation of ideas furnished my mind with wings." He was converted to Christianity by an old man in about A.D. 130, about which conversion he later wrote, "A love of the prophets, and of those people who are friends of Christ, possessed me." He is well known for his defense of the Christian faith through academic letters he wrote to Antoninus Pius, a Roman monarch, with the purpose of disproving false charges—such as atheism, incest, and cannibalism—and contrasting Christianity with Judaism and pagan worship. In addition to his First Apology and Second Apology, Justin also composed Dialogue with Trypho, an Apologetic letter attempting to persuade Jews that Jesus was the Messiah. Justin was beheaded in Rome in A.D. 165.[7]

Irenaeus of Lyons (ca. A.D. 140–202)

Irenaeus is considered by many to be the most important Christian theologian between the Apostles and the third-century scholar Origen. We are given some insight into his early years from his most famous work, "Against Heresies," and from Eusebius's Ecclesiastical History. When he was perhaps fifteen years old, he came into contact with Polycarp at Smyrna. He wrote: "I remember the events of those days better than recent ones, for childhood learning grows up with the soul and is united with it, so that I can speak of the place where the blessed Polycarp sat and discussed, his entrances and exits and the character of his life, the appearance of his body, the discourses he made to the multitude, how he related his life together with John [the Beloved] and with the others who had seen the Lord, and how he remembered their words, and what he heard about the Lord from them, about his miracles and teaching."[8]

Irenaeus recalled the visit of Polycarp to Rome and wrote of a disagreement between this revered bishop and the Roman bishop Anicetus: "For neither could Anicetus persuade Polycarp not to observe what he had always observed with John our Lord's disciple and the other apostles with whom he had associated, nor did Polycarp persuade Anicetus to observe this, for he said that he ought to hold fast the custom of the presbyters before him."[9]

The discussion involved the day on which Easter should be celebrated. Until this time, the Roman church did not practice an annual observance of the Lord's resurrection but rather partook of the sacrament, or Eucharist, weekly in remembrance of this holy event. However, it is possible that Polycarp was suggesting that the Roman church incorporate the eastern tradition, purportedly established by the Apostles, of an annual celebration *in addition* to the weekly communion instituted by the Savior.

Irenaeus, following the pattern of his mentor, Polycarp, sought to stamp out the evils he observed in the Church, particularly Valentinian Gnosticism. He is identified with the Polemicists who challenged heretical factions, using intellectual arguments in an attempt to regain purity and unity within the Church. His "Against Heresies" was an extensive effort to expose the absurdity of the mystical mythology of Gnosticism. Using selected books from the Bible and the writings of earlier Church Fathers, Irenaeus demoralized the rationality of the demiurge (the evil spirit said to have created the material universe) and established his view that a loving God created this world, which later became corrupt because of the fall of Adam and Eve. In "Heresies," Irenaeus condemned such notable defectors as Marcion, who was excommunicated in A.D. 144, and Valentinian, who headed the school of Gnosticism at Rome. Irenaeus was elected bishop of Lyons in A.D. 177.

Tertullian of Carthage (ca. A.D. 150–220)

The foremost Apologist shaping the theology of the western Church was Tertullian, a lawyer by trade, proficient in Greek and Latin and intimate with the classics. He possessed unusual intellectual capacity, which he cleverly and passionately used to challenge the unreasonable tenets of polytheistic societies. His writings were so powerful that they continued to influence the theology of the Church throughout the Middle Ages, even up to and including the Reformers. Curiously, Tertullian became a member of a radical faction of the Church known as the Montanists, a group that organized *within* the Church in A.D. 156 when a man named Montanus in the province of Phrygia claimed to have received a divine revelation in concert with two women, Prisca and Maximilla. While the prophecy seemed suspicious to many, it appealed to others, including Tertullian.

The Montanist movement in Christian history was a watershed event. Previously, the Church had fully embraced the principle of continuing revelation. In other words, prophets had always revealed God's will in the past, and the early Christian Church believed that God continued to reveal His will through the Apostles and other righteous men who succeeded them. The Shepherd of Hermas is a prime example of postapostolic revelation

that was universally accepted by the ancient Church. However, the Montanist faction so troubled Church leadership that all Christian writings were now carefully scrutinized with regard to authentic apostolic authorship. Moreover, the belief in revelation turned a full 180 degrees, and Christian leaders in general began to claim that all revelation from the heavens ceased soon after the Apostles.

Tertullian sided with the Montanists because he rejected the idea that the Church was run by human leadership instead of the guidance of the Holy Spirit. He was attracted by the Montanist puritan ideals and condemned the Roman Church as being "unspiritual, institutionalized, and compromised by worldliness."[10] According to one writer, Tertullian eventually died "fulminating against his former Catholic brethren because they imagined that the Church was constituted by bishops rather than spiritual men."[11] Tertullian's departure from orthodoxy at this early date offers evidence that the Church was in apostasy. Had the Church of his day resembled the one described in the book of Acts, Tertullian and other faithful saints would not have rejected the orthodox leadership.

Hippolytus (ca. A.D. 165–ca. 235)

The leading theologian of the third-century Roman Church was Hippolytus. Although he was born in the Greek East, most of his ministry was in the western Church near Rome. His writings attacked the doctrines of such Roman bishops as Zephryinus (A.D. 198–217) and Callistus (A.D. 217–222). The election of the bishop of Rome was apparently disputed in 217, Callistus and Hippolytus each claiming to be the legitimate bishop of Rome; however, only Callistus is recorded in the official list of popes.[12] Hippolytus was clearly an orthodox bishop, following in the footsteps of Justin Martyr and Irenaeus. He studied directly under Irenaeus, who was a disciple of Polycarp, who was a disciple of John the beloved.[13] Thus, it may be said of Hippolytus that he exerted significant effort to carry on the apostolic tradition from the earliest fathers. According to one scholar, "Hippolytus brought into Rome the Catholic doctrine, and convicted two of its bishops of pernicious heresies and evil living. Accordingly, as Irenaeus teaches, the faith was preserved in Rome by the testimony of those *from every side resorting thither,* not by any prerogative of the See [Roman bishop] itself."[14] He suffered martyrdom in approximately A.D. 235–39.

Clement of Alexandria (ca. A.D. 155–ca. 220)

Like Tertullian, Clement of Alexandria was a renowned theologian of the early Church. No Christian writings exist from this time in Egypt until the sudden appearance of Clement's expositions near the end of the second century. Our only insights into Clement the man and his theology come from his well-known trilogy Exhortation to Conversion, the Tutor, and Miscellanies, in addition to a few other works of minor importance. Clement's writing reveals that he felt passionately about theology but was very careful when writing about the mysteries not to say much. For this reason, he never completed his intended treatise on Christian doctrine. According to Chadwick, Clement was unwilling to risk sharing pearls of truth with those who might not appreciate them:

> Clement's style . . . was to throw out exploratory hints for the reader to investigate and consider at leisure rather than to tell all that was in his heart and so cast pearls promiscuously before unworthy and swinish readers. The

content of the Stromateis (Micellanies) may certainly be taken to consist of as much dogmatic statement as Clement felt it safe to make, but the matter is wrapped in a deliberately misty and allusive style that prefers to put things in the form of a poetic reminiscence rather than in plain and straightforward prose.[15]

A transplant to Alexandria, Clement apparently put down roots there because of his fondness of Pantaenus, a convert from Stoicism who sought to abide the teachings of the apostolic tradition. Pantaenus was the first leader of the Alexandrian School of Theology; his star pupil, Clement, would follow him. The Christian world of this era was in a state of confusion. Paul once taught, "For if the trumpet give an uncertain sound, who shall prepare himself to the battle?" (1 Corinthians 14:8). Without the Apostles, conflicts flourished, and the Church foundered without clear direction.

Many forces were at work as Christianity expanded into Alexandria. Greek intellectuals had difficulty accepting the simple style employed in Christian scripture; the numerous and influential Valentinian Gnostics distrusted Greek philosophy yet persuasively advocated heretical ideas; and those who considered themselves orthodox—a decided minority—appeared reluctant to articulate precise theology. The Christian convert was introduced into a confusing climate without the harmony and strict moral code characteristic of the earliest Christians.

Clement, it seems, attempted to appease all parties while still preaching what he believed to be the true apostolic tradition. He accomplished this in some degree by reaching out to well-educated Greeks using the Platonic, Stoic, and Aristotelian philosophy with which they were familiar and then applying those themes to the scriptures. Clement employed philosophy as a rational approach to neutralize Gnosticism and to reclaim those seduced by its false appeal, using such philosophical rhetoric expressively to define orthodoxy. In the process of trying to resolve the serious dilemmas facing the early Church in Alexandria, Clement and his successors at the Alexandrian School unwittingly introduced philosophy into the mix, ultimately contributing to the Hellenization of Christian theology.[16]

Origen (A.D. 185–254)

Of the early theologians, perhaps the most remarkable was Origen. The sheer volume of his writings, perhaps six thousand works,[17] are staggering, and the impact of his thinking on modern Christian theology has been extraordinary. Origen's parents were faithful Christians. His father, Leonides, was slain during a Christian persecution when Origen was just seventeen. The Christian community at Alexandria was particularly devout during his youth, leading to a number of martyrs in that city. Origen thus became "an almost fanatical Christian," who in later years longed for the days when "there were few believers, but they really did believe, and they traveled the strait and narrow way that leads to life."[18]

Origen's education, funded by a wealthy Christian woman, enabled him to become a respected *grammateus,* a teacher of Greek literature. He was probably instructed by the acclaimed Platonist Ammonius Saccas, who also taught Plotinus, the founder of Neoplatonism. Origen also seems to have held Philo, the Jewish Hellenist, in high regard. Thus, it is little wonder that he used his extensive philosophic background to defend the Church against the growing threat of Gnosticism. In this respect, Origen followed the lead of Clement of Alexandria, who also

compared concepts from the Bible with views expressed in Greek literature and used them interchangeably to teach Christian doctrine and to refute Valentinian heresy. When Clement stepped down from his position during a time of renewed persecution, perhaps relocating to a new city, Origen, undaunted and unafraid of any consequences, openly served as a catechist, teacher, and benefactor not only to the Christian community at Alexandria in general but also to those imprisoned or sentenced to death.[19]

Origen's initial service as a catechist was unsanctioned. Perhaps reluctantly, Demetrius, the bishop of Alexandria, later endorsed him as a teacher in what was to be a stormy relationship between the two ever after. During this early period, Origen abandoned his secular teaching career, gave up his worldly goods, and zealously pursued a methodical study of inspired writings. Soon after, he replaced Clement as the head of the Alexandrian Theological School. Origen's youthful devotion to asceticism led him to a false interpretation of Matthew 19:12, by which he inflicted self-castration. Eusebius wrote that he later regretted this act as demonstrated by his specific repudiation of this practice in a commentary he wrote on Matthew. His ascetic lifestyle included such habits as praying and studying through much of the night; he owned only one coat and had not a single pair of shoes.[20]

Origen believed that God was an incorporeal Spirit, that the Son was His *Eternal Generation, Wisdom,* or *Word,* and that the Holy Ghost operated in unity and perfect harmony with the Father and the Son to accomplish the work of God the Father. Utilizing diverse scriptural references and explaining or relating them in Platonistic forms, Origen attempted to untangle how the Trinity could be three distinct beings, separate in rank and glory but united in harmony of will, and that God was incorporeal and the only uncreated class. In expounding his theology, it is important to note that Origen consistently used such words as "I am of [the] opinion," or, "I give it as my opinion," also making plain that certain doctrines were "not clearly indicated in our teaching," rather than quoting the words of the prophets, who said, "thus saith the Lord."[21]

As mentioned, Origen wrote that the soul or spirit was created prior to mortality. He believed that redemption was a gradual process, continuing after death, and was so taken with the ultimate victory of love, he concluded it was impossible for anyone to be totally depraved or completely stripped of free will and reason. He theorized that even Satan could repent at the very last.[22] Although most of his theology earned him the designation "The Father of Orthodoxy," some of Origen's biblical insights were later considered heresy in the sixth century. Imprisoned towards the end of his life during the great persecution of Decius in A.D. 250, he was released in broken health and died shortly thereafter.

Although Origen was fiercely opposed to pagan literature and the writings of Plato, he appeared less critical of the actual practice of Platonism (see pages 130–31). On the other hand, Clement of Alexandria was less inclined to advocate Platonism but held Plato himself in high regard, as had Justin Martyr before him.[23] What is true of this era, as of other ages, is that there was no shortage of truth or great men; but the *mixture* of truth with all the other combinations, spawned by apostasy and the resultant loss of priesthood authority, created a scarcity of the pure doctrines established by Jesus Christ. It produced a scene of turbulence, rivalry, and hostility which bred discord within the Church. In fact, so tense was the situation in the North African Church during this period that Cyprian, the learned bishop of Carthage, composed his celebrated exposition entitled On the Unity of the Church (251).

Eusebius, from a broader perspective and looking back, detailed the turmoil and divisiveness that prevailed throughout the Church during this time:

> But when by excessive liberty we sunk into indolence and sloth, one envying and reviling another in different ways, and we were almost, as it were, on the point of taking up arms against each other, and were assailing each other with words, as with darts and spears, prelates inveighing against prelates, and people rising against people, and hypocrisy and dissimulation had arisen to the greater heights of malignity, then the divine judgement, which usually proceeds with a lenient hand, whilst the multitudes were yet crowding into the Church, with gentle and mild visitations began to afflict its episcopacy; the persecution having begun with those brethren that were in the army. But some that appeared to be our pastors, deserting the law of piety, were inflamed against each other with mutual strifes, only anxious to assert the government as a kind of sovereignty for themselves.[24]

As spiritual and faithful Churchmen, early gospel writers such as Polycarp, Justin, Irenaeus, Tertullian, Hippolytus, Clement of Alexandria, and Origen sought to fight against the enemy *within*—heresy and apostasy—while they also fought the enemy *without*—severe persecution at the hands of the Roman Empire. The impact of these negative forces was so profound that it completely transformed the identity of the Church. Without *living* prophets and Apostles, it was impossible to disentangle the unfolding doctrines of

Christianity from the radical revisions forced upon them by Gnosticism, Neoplatonism, Hellenism, Judaism, and Paganism in combination with escalating corruption.

The Alliance of the Roman Empire with Christianity

Perhaps the greatest scourge that came upon the Savior's Church, thrusting it into utter apostasy while at the same time dramatically increasing its membership base, was the unholy partnership that took place between the Universal Church and the Roman Empire early in the fourth century. Persecution has a way of purging, purifying, unifying, and strengthening its members, while ease and prosperity tend to weaken and lull God's faithful into carnal security. Evidence of such decline was the moral and spiritual decay of the Church after Constantine's rise to power in A.D. 312.

The alliance between the Universal Church and the Roman Empire formally commenced when Constantine and a western general, Licinius, jointly issued the Edict of Milan in A.D. 313, granting religious freedom to the realm. Several key events transpired to make this decree possible.

In A.D. 284, Diocletian, considered one of Rome's great monarchs, became emperor. History honors him because of his genius in administration and leadership during the challenges of his time. He engineered a plan to reorganize the kingdom completely, dividing the Empire and designating Maximian emperor of the West while he remained emperor of the East. Galerius was appointed Caesar in the East, and Constantius Chlorus, Constantine's father, was appointed Caesar in the West, the Caesars being slated to succeed the emperors in twenty years. Galerius despised Christians, and inasmuch as the whole Empire was undergoing change—military, taxation, pricing, uniform currency, and political structure—the decision was made to also implement a uniform religious system. Galerius used his influence with Diocletian to target the abolition of Christianity in favor of pagan worship, and a significant assault against Christian worship was soon underway.

As the first order of business, in approximately A.D. 298, all Christians were removed from military and civil service. Beginning in A.D. 303 and timed to coincide with the feast of Terminalia on February 23, the "Great Persecution" began. Initially, laws were passed that banned services and destroyed houses of worship as well as nearly all Christian books. After two years of otherwise reserved oppression, a significant offensive was launched in the East, occasioned by the planned resignation of Diocletian and Maximian after twenty years of service. They were succeeded according to design by Galerius and Constantius in A.D. 305. Galerius intensified his efforts against Christians in the East, while Constantius was considerably less oppressive in the West. The crusade in the East was sustained until A.D. 311 when, on his deathbed, Galerius issued an edict of toleration, stating, "they had held their determination" and were thus allowed to meet freely if they remained orderly.

The death of Galerius set the stage for a power struggle to rule the Empire. Constantius had died in A.D. 306, and his son Constantine was named his successor by the loyal soldiers he commanded. However, Maximian and his son, Maxentius, attempted to regain leadership of the West when, in fact, Galerius had already appointed a powerful general, Licinius, as the western emperor. Constantine forged an alliance with Licinius, and in October, A.D. 312, Constantine marched toward Rome, where he fought the famous battle of Milvian Bridge. While marching, legend reports, Constantine looked up and saw a cross of light in the sky with an inscription stating, "Conquer by this sign." With the emblem of the cross displayed on their shields, Constantine's army crushed Maxentius; thus began the union of church and state.[25]

When Constantine became emperor of Rome, he began to involve himself in religious affairs, but his sons Constantius and Constans, who inherited the Empire, actually initiated control over matters of religion. Constantius, an outspoken Arian (see pages 157–59), relieved Athanasius of his position as bishop of Alexandria, in addition to many other Church leaders who shared the same orthodox views. Liberius, the new bishop of Rome, while considered courageous, was powerless to work against his Roman monarch. The Emperor's desire was that the Church should be Arian and subservient to the state, not only in matters of law but also in matters of doctrine and Church organization. According to Cheetham, Constantius, not his father, Constantine, may have been the real originator of "Caesaropapism."[26]

To evaluate accurately the fruits of this ill-fated alliance, let us compare some fundamental doctrines set forth by Jesus and the Apostles with the theology ultimately formulated by the fourth-century Church under Constantine and his successors.

The Christological Controversy: The Nature of the Godhead Altered

Ancient Israel had been chastened over and over again for relegating itself to the worship of false gods. Israel had been warned, "Thou shalt have no other gods before me" (Exodus 20:3). Additionally, God had declared through Isaiah, "I am the first, and I am the last; and beside me there is no God" (Isaiah 44:6). In both cases, the context is plain: "They that make a graven image are all of them vanity; and their delectable things shall not profit" (Isaiah 44:9). Similarly, Jesus reiterated the Old Testament commandment, "Thou shalt love the Lord thy God with all thine heart, and with all thy soul, and with all thy might" (Deuteronomy 6:5; Matthew 22:37). The New Testament saints were taught that there was one true God, even the Eternal Father; and Jesus Christ, His Only Begotten Son; and the Holy Ghost. They were instructed on the infinite harmony of will that existed within the Godhead and were commanded to worship the true and living God. On the other hand, while both Jews and Christians were commanded to worship the only true and living God, the God of Greek philosophy had become identified by Socrates and Plato as *the One*. The strict interpretation of the word *one* became the basis of perpetual confusion, speculation, and contention.

Significant changes overtook the Church in the early centuries after the death of the Apostles. The first significant alteration of theology was the most important: the true nature of God the Father and His Son, Jesus Christ, and the Holy Ghost. This simple and pure doctrine as taught by the Apostles was mystified by the generations of Church leaders who followed. Without the apostolic office to clarify gospel ideology, the rift in the Church over this one doctrine became preeminent. The question itself centered in reconciling the monotheistic beliefs of Hellenized Jews and Neoplatonics in *One* (immaterial and uncreated) God with the New Testament teaching that the Father is God, the Son is also God, as is also the Holy Ghost. The development of the Nicene Trinity was profoundly influenced by the recurring Old Testament theme "Thou art the God, *even thou alone*, of all the kingdoms of the earth."[27]

To demonstrate how quickly apostasy actually took root, we have only to look to the writings of Ignatius who, in his letter to the saints at Trallia, wrote as follows: "They introduce God as a Being unknown; they suppose Christ to be unbegotten; and as to the Spirit, they do not admit that He exists. Some of them say that the Son is a mere man, *and that the Father, Son, and Holy Spirit are but the same person,* and that the creation is the work of God, not by Christ, but by some other strange power."[28]

Ignatius was clearly troubled by those who perverted the pure teachings of Christ. He exposed those who claimed that God was unknown (incomprehensible; see John 17:3) and those who denied the existence of the Holy Ghost. He derided those who rejected the divinity of Christ and those who argued that members of the Godhead *are the same person.* Although historic Christianity does not cling to all of this perversion, misunderstandings linking Father, Son, and Holy Spirit as a single incorporeal entity eventually spawned the errant doctrine of "one substance" within the Trinity.

Trinitarian scholars recognize that "no doctrine of the Trinity in the Nicene sense is present in the New Testament."[29] Likewise, "there is no doctrine of the Trinity in the strict sense in the Apostolic Fathers,"[30] meaning that no one, before A.D. 150, attempted to define more than what was already provided in the text of the Old Testament, the Gospels, and the apostolic writings. What *can* be derived from the scriptures is that we worship God the Father, *in the name of* His Only Begotten Son in the flesh, Jesus Christ, who reveals truth to us *through* the Holy Ghost.

The Father, Son, and Holy Ghost are each identified as "God" but with differing respon-

sibilities. For example, in John 17 Jesus prays to His Father, stating "the hour is come," and pleads for His Apostles and for those who will believe on their words. This passage provides a witness that God, the Eternal Father, is the Supreme Ruler of the universe. Jesus Christ is identified as God the Son, our intercessor (Isaiah 53:12; Hebrews 7:25) and thus the Father's mediator (1 Timothy 2:5), as illustrated by John 1:1, where Jesus is described as the Word, the Word (also) being God, and that the Word was in the beginning with God. The Holy Ghost is portrayed as God when Peter censures Ananias, "Why hath Satan filled thine heart to lie to the Holy Ghost? . . . thou hast not lied unto men, but unto God" (Acts 5:3–4). Demonstrating the separate entity of the Holy Ghost, Jesus testified, "But the Comforter, which is the Holy Ghost, whom the Father will send in my name, he shall teach you all things" (John 14:26). The unity of the Godhead is explained in John 17:11–22: "Holy Father, keep through thine own name those whom thou hast given me, that they may be one as we are. . . . And the glory which thou gavest me I have given them; that they may be one, even as we are one." The scriptures teach that there are three separate and distinct Beings, perfectly united in purpose and harmony of will. Again, according to the scriptures, we worship God the Father, in the name of His Son Jesus Christ by the power of the Holy Ghost: "For though there be that are called gods, whether in heaven or in earth, (as there be gods many, and lords many,) but to us there is but one God, the Father, of whom are all things, and we in him; and one Lord Jesus Christ, by whom are all things, and we by him" (1 Corinthians 8:5–6).[31] The Bible gives no further explanation.

In the absence of prophets and Apostles, late second-century Christian scholars began to follow the pattern of Jewish intellectuals before the coming of Christ: They offered what they felt were scholarly answers to spiritual matters, seeking to define the Godhead as though they were pursuing some scientific discovery. Interpreting the Gospels and other inspired writings through the lens of Greek ideology and Hellenized Hebrew theology, they arrived at some fairly speculative conclusions when explaining the nature of God. Jesus told the Jews that the Father could *only* be revealed to them *through* the Son (Luke 10:22); thus, only revelation could provide the doctrinal answers Christians of this era sought. Neither the Bible authors nor the early Christian Fathers embraced Greek philosophy or Judaic scholarship; they rejected the perversions of Christian doctrine developed by Gnostic and Docetist defectors. The cause of this changing doctrine is ascribed to the apostasy explained by the Apostle John: "Thou hast left thy first love" (Revelation 2:4) and the angel to the Shepherd: "They think it possible to find a better road, and err" (see page 124). Not many years following Hermas's visions, quarrels over the nature of the Godhead intensified.

The doctrine of the orthodox Trinity *(one substance in three persons,* stemming from the Greek *homoousios,* and the Latin *consubstantialis)* began its evolution with Justin Martyr's writings in approximately A.D. 150, as he attempted to explain the *Logos* (Christ), meaning both "word" and "reason." In articulating his concept of the Logos, he used symbolic language, arguing that Christ was a part of God's essence, though separate, *"as fires kindled from a fire."*[32] Although later Christianity would construe Justin's words to imply that God and Jesus are one substance, his intent seems to indicate "offspring," not one substance. Accordingly, he also used the word *begotten:* "You perceive, my hearers, if

you bestow attention, that the scripture has declared that this Offspring was begotten by the Father before all things created; and that which is begotten is numerically distinct from that which begets, any one will admit."[33]

This was the beginning of comparisons and allegory as a replacement for precise interpretation of scripture to define true doctrine. From this point forward, a full theology of the nature of the Godhead would be developed, which produced a myriad of mystical elements *unexplainable by scripture.* While Justin was a man who loved and served God, he was a layman who may not have held ecclesiastical office. Although he believed that the Church still received revelation,[34] Justin himself provided no examples, nor did he mention those receiving current revelation.[35]

In approximately A.D. 200, Tertullian began to interpret and expand on Justin Martyr's ideas. Because of his legal training, Tertullian drew portions of his terminology from Roman courts of law rather than scripture. For example, he used the Latin word *substantia,* meaning "property rights," to express "material," or, in other words, God's *substantia* as his "domain." The word *Persona,* which actually referred to a party in a legal action, Tertullian used to denote a "person." Employed together in this manner, it seemed plausible that three *personae* could share one *substantia.*[36] Tertullian believed that God was a "corporeal" substance, though "purer than ours,"[37] but that the Godhead was "One, by unity of substance," such being a "mystery" that is "still guarded."[38] He held that Jesus and the Holy Ghost were subordinate to the Father. None of Tertullian's language can be found in scripture nor in any attempt by the Savior or the Apostles to explain the matter.

Although Tertullian's language provided a platform from which the Nicene Council would extrapolate, even third-century

155

theology *did not* describe the end eventually settled upon in Nicaea. Not many years after Tertullian, Origen began expressing his view of the Godhead. Like Justin, Origen believed in the separate nature of God and Jesus, insisting that they were separate persons or "subsistences."[39] He is also the first person to use the term *hypostasis,* a Stoic-Platonic term meaning "essence" or "real existence." He maintained that the Father was *ho theos,* meaning absolutely God, and that the Son was *theos,* or a second God subordinate to the Father. In the following excerpt from Against Celsus, Origen seemed to clarify the interpretation of his own statement regarding the separate but unified nature of the Father and the Son. First quoting Celsus, Origen then offers his response:

> "They pay excessive reverence to one who has but lately appeared among men, and they think it no offense against God if they worship also his servant." To this we reply, that if Celsus had known that saying, "I and My Father are one," . . . he would not have supposed that we worship any other besides Him who is the Supreme God. "For," says He, "My Father is in Me, and I in Him." And if any should from these words be afraid of our going over to the side of those who deny that the Father and the Son are two personages, let him weigh this passage, "And the multitude of them that believed were of one heart and of one soul," that he may understand the meaning of the saying, "I and my Father are one." . . . We worship, therefore, the Father of truth, and the Son, who is the truth; and these, while they are two, considered as persons or subsistences, are one in unity of thought, in harmony and in identity of will.[40]

Origen used the verse "And the multitude of them that believed were of one heart and of one soul" (Acts 4:32) to explain *how* the Father and the Son are one. The multitude did *not* become one substance: they became unified in love and one in righteous, unselfish desires. Origen also speaks of the Holy Ghost as a separate member of the Godhead, lower in hierarchal rank than the Father and the Son.[41] Although Origen's description to Celsus regarding the unity of the Godhead seems clear, others use his language (plainly dependent on Platonic theory) to support a Trinitarian view.[42] In the end, the Nicene Council took significant license when interpreting Origen's language in order to arrive at its eventual conclusion.

The Monarchian Controversy

The effort to define the Godhead provoked unending quarrels. The first such widespread conflict is known as the Monarchian Controversy. In this argument, there were those who revolted against Justin Martyr's bold statement of the Logos being "another God," not simply in will but also number.[43] Others believed in the view of Hellenized Jews who claimed that one could use the analogy of sun and sunlight to illustrate the "divine Logos." Justin underscored his belief that Jesus was separate and independent by using the metaphor of one torch being lit from another torch. The Monarchian creed insisted that the Father, Son, and Holy Ghost were the same person but that the three terms were used to describe the different roles God played to enable man's redemption. Thus, God was a single being whose three titles were simply *descriptive* and in no way altered his oneness. Monarchian ideology has also been termed *Modalism.* The architect of this theology is said to have been a Roman prelate from the eastern Church named Sabellius.[44]

Another theological perspective, Dynamic Monarchianism, or *adoptionism,* has been attributed to Paul of Samosata, who became bishop of Antioch in A.D. 260. This viewpoint claimed that although Christ's birth was miraculous, He was but a mere man until He was baptized, at which time the Holy Ghost made Him the Son of God by adoption. A heated debate continued for decades, marked by intellectual pride, divisiveness, subtleties, and the absence of the Holy Spirit. Tertullian authored a composition entitled Against Praxeas, in which he defended the concept of God as one substance consisting of three persons but attacked the biblical weaknesses of Sabellianism.

The Arian Controversy

As one debate subsided another began, this one being even more malicious and of much greater duration than the Monarchian dispute. In A.D. 318 a popular presbyter named Arius from the parish of Baucalis in Alexandria refused to support the concept of the Son being equal to the Father. Arius believed that only God the Father was "without beginning."[45] He reasoned that since the Logos, the preexistent Christ, was begotten, there was a time when "*he was not,*" and he must therefore necessarily be a creature (created out of nothing) and thus had a beginning. Accordingly, he asserted that Christ was clearly subordinate to the Eternal Father.[46] Following is the letter Arius later wrote to Constantine in defense of his belief:

> We believe in one God, the Father, all-sovereign; and in the Lord Jesus Christ his only-begotten Son who came into existence from him before all ages, God the Word, through whom all things in the heavens and on earth came into existence, who came down and assumed flesh and suffered, rose and went up into the heavens and comes again to judge the living and dead. And in the Holy Spirit and in the resurrection of the flesh and in the life of the future age and in the kingdom of heaven.[47]

This view was intensely disputed by Alexander, the bishop of Alexandria, who asserted that Christ, the Logos, was divine, eternally generated by the Father. However, he believed Christ was a separate *hypostasis* (person within the Trinity), sharing the same nature as the Father.[48] Arius petitioned the support of important bishops outside of Egypt, including Eusebius of Caesarea, and what began as a local dispute soon had the effect of dividing the eastern Empire.

Constantine dispatched his ecclesiastical advisor, Hosius, the bishop of Cordova, to investigate and intervene in the matter. After conferring with Alexander, Hosius aligned himself with the bishop and assembled a Church council at Antioch in which Eusebius was excommunicated. Displeased with the judgment, Constantine moved the greater council, which had been scheduled for Ancyra, to Nicaea and personally presided at the conclave. The meeting began in June 325 and was attended by more than three hundred bishops, primarily from the eastern provinces. The assembly, which later became known as the first ecumenical council of the Church, was directed by Constantine to resolve the dispute and bring harmony to the Roman Empire.

Surviving documents indicate that the delegates soon divided into three camps: those supporting the Arian position, those in agreement with Athanasius (the Nicene doctrine), and those who straddled the middle by embracing variations of the other two, known as Homoeousianism. This last group, which included Eusebius of Caesarea, held that there were three divine persons separate in rank and glory but united in harmony of will.[49] Representing the largest but least organized coalition, this doctrine had in fact been the prominent theology of the earliest Christians, as attested by Justin, Hippolytus, and Origen. Unfortunately, Arius pressed what was then considered a mildly heretical position; and in virtually a unanimous vote, the presbyters resolved to condemn the Arian view and compose a statement of belief or a creed that would render a precise definition of the nature of God and Jesus Christ. This declaration became known as the Nicene Creed. Following is the Nicene text in full:

Nicene Creed–A.D. 325 (*First Ecumenical Council*)
We believe in one God, the Father, Almighty, the maker of all things visible and invisible; and in one Lord, Jesus Christ, the Son of God, begotten of the Father, only begotten, (that is) of the substance of the Father; God of God, Light of Light; Very God of Very God; begotten not made; of the same substance with the Father, by whom all things were made, that are in heaven and that are in earth: who for us men, and for our salvation, descended and was incarnate, and became man; suffered and rose again the third day, ascended into the heavens and will come to judge the living and the dead; and in the Holy Spirit. But those who say there was a time when he [the Son] was not, and that he was not before he was begotten, and that he was made out of nothing, or affirm that he is of any other substance or essence, or that the Son of God was created, and mutable, or changeable, the Catholic Church doth pronounce accursed.

Although the Council's decision was nearly unanimous, it was marred by ambiguity. Many of the delegates understood differently the precise meaning "of one substance," *homoousios*, which affirms "identity"; yet it also implies that the Father and the Son are "the same." To some, the term indicated a personal or distinct identity, while to many others it referred to a much broader, generic identity.[50] William Rusch explains the confusion in this way:

It is not clear what the council intended to teach by the phrase "from the substance [ousia] of the Father" and homoousios with the Father. Both were unscriptural and employed with some reluctance. The latter phrase was placed in the creed by the emperor Constantine. . . . One of the assets of the word homoousios—and this led to its acceptance—was that different groups were able to interpret it in ways compatible with their own theology. As far as Constantine was concerned, this was agreeable.[51]

However, to soothe the continuing ill feelings of the Arians, Athanasius, the Nicene Creed's chief defender in the East, and Hilary, its foremost advocate in the West, agreed to include the term *homoiousios* (meaning similar substance), which had been refused at the Nicene Council. One scholar recorded the dispute in this manner:

Assailed by these difficulties, the most outstanding of the orthodox, an Athanasius, a Hilary, reached the point of conceding, in the interest of unity, that in order to judge of the faith, it was necessary to attach one's self less to words than to the expressed realities; without abandoning the *homoousios* (one substance), they admitted as catholic (orthodox) the *homoiousios* (like or similar substance), provided that one added "as to substance" or "in everything."[52]

Thus, matters of doctrine were *negotiated* in the same manner as political disputes.

The modifications offered by Athanasius and Hilary were never included in the Nicene text due to the negligence of a scribe. The eventual realization of the minute misunderstandings of definition later prompted a resurgence of fervor over the conflict. When Constantine died in 337, his son Constans, an Arian, overturned the Nicene Council's decision. The Arian controversy continued unabated until the Second Ecumenical Council at Constantinople in 381, at which time the Nicene Creed was reinstated. Nevertheless, this battle continued to rage for some four hundred years, while the Catholic Church maintained that the Holy Spirit had inspired the scribe to drop the *iota*.[53]

Postapostolic Christianity was feeling its way through the dark on a most important matter without the guidance of the Holy Spirit. The Savior had once mightily prayed to His Father in the famous intercessory prayer: "And this is life eternal, that they might know thee the only true God, and Jesus Christ, whom thou hast sent" (John 17:3). The Savior's testimony demonstrates the critical nature of the misconception of this formerly pure dogma. The earliest Christians did understand the nature of God, and Ignatius was unambiguous when he wrote, "I am able to understand . . . the incomparable majesty of Almighty God. . . . I am acquainted with these things" (see page 85). In times past, the Apostles filled the sacred role of clarifying doctrine; and since life eternal means knowing the true nature of God, a threatening breach occurred among the leadership of the Church, and the sheep of the fold were left in spiritual jeopardy.

God's Relationship to Man

The Apostles were eyewitnesses of the divinity of Jesus Christ: they were present at His baptism; they observed firsthand the power and fervency of His prayers; they experienced His mighty miracles; they heard the voice of God declare to them His Son on the Mount of Transfiguration; and they watched as He suffered in the garden and on the cross. The Apostles witnessed the empty tomb, and they examined the Savior's resurrected body, spending forty days in His presence. Jesus Christ was no mystery to them. Paul beheld the resurrected Lord on the road to Damascus. He was instructed by the Apostles, by those at Jerusalem, and by the Holy Spirit as later he discoursed many of the New Testament's most powerful sermons. He was "caught up to the third heaven," where he heard unspeakable words (2 Corinthians 12:2; see also vv. 1–4). When Paul observed the worship of idols and false gods while proclaiming the gospel in Greece, he testified:

"Ye men of Athens, I perceive that in all things ye are too superstitious. For as I passed by, and beheld your devotions, I found an altar with this inscription, TO THE UNKNOWN GOD. Whom therefore ye ignorantly worship, him declare I unto you" (Acts 17:22–23). God was not a mystery to Paul. As he continued to expound upon this theme, he revealed the divine heritage of mankind to the Athenians:

"For in him we live, and move, and have our being; as certain also of your own poets have said, For we are also his *offspring.* Forasmuch then as *we are the offspring* [Gr. *genos* = race, kindred, family][54] *of God,* we ought not to think that the Godhead is like unto gold, or silver, or stone, graven by art and man's device" (Acts 17:28; emphasis added). In this verse, Paul testifies of our *genetic* relationship with the Father. Paul later expounded on

159

our *adoptive* relationship with God, through Christ, when he testified to the Romans:

"The Spirit itself beareth witness with our spirit, that we are the children of God: and if children, then heirs; heirs of God, and joint heirs with Christ; if so be that we suffer with *him,* that we may be also glorified together" (Romans 8:16–17). Perhaps one of many reasons this subject was not a cloudy issue to the Apostles was the first-hand narrative they received from Mary regarding her encounter with Jesus at the empty tomb: "Jesus saith unto her, Touch me not; for I am not yet ascended to my Father: but go to my brethren, and say unto them, I ascend unto *my Father,* and *your Father;* and to *my God,* and *your God*" (John 20:17; emphasis added).

These scriptures demonstrate that we are the *spirit children* of God and that Jesus was also a spirit son of our Father, except in His case, Jesus is not just the firstborn spirit offspring but literally the *Only Begotten* Son of God in the *flesh.* When John declares, "For God so loved the world, that he gave his *only begotten* Son, that whosoever believeth in him should not perish, but have everlasting life" (John 3:16), he instructs us on the literal parent-child relationship between Jesus and the Father.

Evidence of this interpretation comes from a close examination of the Greek text. The word *offspring* as used in Paul's testimony to the Athenians comes from the Greek word *genos,* meaning *race.* This noun forms the basis for the English words *genetics* and *genes,* communicating that man is the same *species* as God himself. When Adam disobeyed God, mankind was cut off spiritually and physically from the presence of the Father; however, Christ was not. Accordingly, we learn from Paul's address to the Romans how we can be adopted back into the family of God. Paul uses two variations, describing the dif-

ference between the genetic and adoptive relationships. The word *sons* in Romans 8:14 derives from the Greek *huios,* meaning *sons by adoption.*[55] As the verses indicate, when men yield their hearts to God and are thus led by the Spirit of God, they become true disciples of Christ, worthy to be made heirs. The word *children* as used in verses 16 and 17 derives from the Greek *teknon,* meaning *offspring, descendant,* or, *fruit from seed*—in other words, one literally *related by birth.*[56]

A second scriptural example providing background for these two relationships is furnished by the Savior's teachings to the Pharisees. Acknowledging the Jews as the literal seed of Abraham, Jesus chides, "If ye were Abraham's children, ye would do the works of Abraham," and further, "Before Abraham was, I am!"[57] Although we are the literal offspring of God, we cannot overcome the Fall, becoming true disciples and thus heirs unless we learn *through Christ* to become like our Father. The foregoing verses testify that we enjoy a *fraternal* relationship with Jesus Christ, becoming *joint heirs* with Him, if it so be that we suffer with Him.

Paul taught the deeper import of our relationship to God when he affirmed: "Furthermore we have had fathers of our flesh which corrected us, and we gave them reverence: shall we not much rather be in subjection unto *the Father of spirits,* and live?" (Hebrews 12:9; emphasis added).

This verse reveals that God is the Father of the spirits of all men, but that by creating Adam and Eve *in His image,* God provided a lineage wherein He is not the natural parent of our physical bodies; rather, the literal parent-child relationship we experience in mortality is with fleshly parents who instruct and *correct* us. Paul reminded the Hebrews where their greater allegiance should lie and that it was far more important to submit themselves to "the *Father* [generator, nearest ancestor] of *spirits,* and live."[58]

Man's relationship to God was also well known to Old Testament authors. While praying to God for mercy, the Israelites petitioned, "O God, *the God of the spirits of all flesh,* shall one man sin, and wilt thou be wroth with all the congregation?" (Numbers 16:22). Likewise, Moses pleaded for guidance regarding who should lead Israel after him: "Let the Lord, *the God of the spirits of all flesh,* set a man over the congregation" (Numbers 27:16). Moreover, Zechariah, speaking of a former day, says, "The burden of the word of the Lord for Israel, saith the Lord, which stretcheth forth the heavens, and layeth the foundation of the earth, *and formeth the spirit of man* within him" (Zechariah 12:1; emphasis added). Further declaring our heritage, we are taught in Ecclesiastes concerning death: "Then shall the dust return to the earth as it was: *and the spirit shall return unto God who gave it*" (Ecclesiastes 12:7).

Although it is not explicit in these verses that God *begat* our spirits—as is clearly communicated by Paul—this relationship in concert with the Jewish belief in man's premortal existence implies this special relationship. Jesus taught, "Thou shalt love thy neighbour as thyself" (Matthew 19:19), knowing that one's neighbor is defined as all who need our assistance (Luke 10:30–36). He also commanded, "Love one another, as I have loved you" (John 15:12); in fact, the early saints referred to each other as *brother* and *sister.*[59] The prophet Malachi depicts this idea when he taught, "Have we not all one father? hath not one God created us? why do we deal treacherously every man against his brother, by profaning the covenant of our fathers?" (Malachi 2:10). When men were commanded to address God as "Our Father which art in heaven" (Matthew 6:9), a pattern was established as to the

nature of our eternal relationships and how we ought to conduct ourselves one towards another—for we are all the family of God.

The Foreordination of Jesus Christ, His Prophets, and All Mankind

Questions arise out of the claim that we are children of God, that we were begotten spiritually before we were created physically, and that we resided with our Eternal Father before we came to earth. What is the purpose of our physical birth and why are we born to certain parents in specific countries and under vastly different socio-economic circumstances? Why are we born into a particular lineage or race, such as chosen Israel? For reasons unknown to mankind, the Bible is silent on these subjects. The absence of such knowledge prompted the notable bishop of Hippo, Augustine, to develop the speculative and hitherto unknown doctrine of predestination later espoused by the Reformers Martin Luther and John Calvin. This dogma asserts that men do *not* have free will and that their fate is sealed before they ever come to earth, either to salvation or damnation, according to God's good pleasure. The Bible verses generally used to support this doctrine are drawn from Romans, chapter 9:

> Who are Israelites; to whom pertaineth the adoption, and the glory, and the covenants, and the giving of the law, and the service of God, and the promises. . . . In Isaac shall thy seed be called. . . . For this is the word of promise, At this time will I come, and Sara shall have a son. And not only this; but when Rebecca also had conceived by one, even by our father Isaac; (for the children being not yet born, neither having done any good or evil, that the purpose of God according to election

161

might stand, not of works, but of him that calleth;) it was said unto her, The elder shall serve the younger. As it is written, Jacob have I loved, but Esau have I hated. (Romans 9:4–13)

Inasmuch as revelation was given to Rebekah *before* the twins were born, we gain a greater perspective of God's foreknowledge: "And the Lord said unto her [Rebekah], two nations are in thy womb, and two manner of people shall be separated from thy bowels; and the one people shall be stronger than the other people; and the elder shall serve the younger" (Genesis 25:23).

Paul's use of the word *hate* stems from Malachi's revelation some thirteen hundred years *after* Jacob and Esau were born, when the actual deeds of Esau had already been accomplished: "I have loved you, saith the Lord. Yet ye say, Wherein hast thou loved us? Was not Esau Jacob's brother? saith the Lord: yet I loved Jacob, and I hated Esau, and laid his mountains and his heritage waste for the dragons of the wilderness" (Malachi 1:2–3). Only after Esau's evil (Hebrews 12–16) did the Lord use the language revealed through Malachi. God knew both Esau and Jacob before they were born; and *foreknowing* the righteous spirit of Jacob, God *elected* to send the chosen of Israel through the loins of Jacob. Accordingly, God's foreknowledge that Esau would serve Jacob neither destroyed free-will nor predestined those coming through Abrahamic descent to certain destruction or salvation.

Continuing in Romans 9, proponents of predestination quote Paul's reference to the potter and his clay: "Who art thou that repliest against God? Shall the thing formed say to him that formed it, Why hast thou made me thus? Hath not the potter power over the clay, of the same lump to make one vessel unto honour, and another dishonour?" (Romans 9:20–21). From this letter to the Romans, some believe that God (the potter) has the capacity to create one soul to honor and the other to dishonor using the same lump of clay. However, Paul clarifies his intent on this subject in a later communication to Timothy: "But in a great house there are not only vessels of gold and of silver, but also of wood and of earth; some to honour, and some to dishonour. If a man therefore purge *himself* from these, he shall be a vessel unto honour, sanctified, and meet for the master's use, and prepared unto every good work" (2 Timothy 2:20–21).

This passage asserts *free agency* when the man of his own *volition* chooses to purge *himself,* or rather, to grow and overcome the weaknesses of the flesh and thus be "prepared unto every good work." That men derive considerable strength from God to achieve such is certain; nonetheless, although He stands at the door and knocks, we, through our own agency, must choose to open the door (Revelation 3:20).

The interpretation of the foregoing verses also harmonizes with the parable of the talents, wherein one man is furnished ten talents, another five, and another one. They are then expected to labor and to earn a reasonable return based on the number of talents provided (abilities in combination with personal circumstances; Matthew 25:15–28).

Unlike later Churchmen, such as Augustine, Luther, and Calvin, the earliest Christian Fathers—Ignatius, Clement, and Justin Martyr, *those closest to Christ and the Apostles*—embraced the doctrine of free will and personal responsibility. They held to a different theology known in the Bible as *fore-ordination,*[60] a doctrine which suggests that men and women are preselected or "foreordained" to receive certain responsibilities, blessings, and opportunities based on prior acts of faith, obedience, and devotion to God as His spirit children before coming to earth. Although man may be foreordained to some blessing or responsibility based on previous decisions and deeds in his "first estate" (Jude 1:6), such honors are conditional on obedience in the face of conflicting choices (and thus free will) in mortality, our second estate.

The doctrine of foreordination originates with Jesus Christ. The term is first used by Peter when he testified that Christ was "fore-ordained" before the creation of this world to accomplish His redemptive work: "Forasmuch as ye know that ye were not redeemed with corruptible things . . . ; but with the precious blood of Christ . . . : who verily was fore-ordained before the foundation of the world, but was manifest in these last times for you" (1 Peter 1:18–20).

First Enoch testifies that Christ was chosen to perform His unique responsibilities before He came to earth (see page 89). Peter agrees with 1 Enoch on the meaning of foreordination when, at the beginning of his first epistle, he writes, "Elect according to the foreknowledge of God the Father" (1 Peter 1:2), which means that God made certain determinations based on the character of our spirits prior to our coming to earth. According to scripture, God blesses us to receive certain assignments in mortality, conditional on the righteous exercise of our free will. This idea begs the question, How does God obtain His foreknowledge? Paul provides an answer when he certifies that God will "not cast away his people [Israel] which he foreknew" (Romans 11:2), indicating that God knew intimately well those who had been pre-selected to come through the chosen lineage of Israel before they came to earth—just as any parent knows the habits and tendencies of his or her children. However, to claim those blessings, they must ultimately be obedient to the New Covenant through Jesus Christ. Once again, Justin confirmed this fact when he wrote:

> And you deceive yourselves while you fancy that, *because you are the seed of Abraham* after the flesh, therefore you shall fully inherit the good things announced to be bestowed by God through Christ. For no one, not even of them, has anything to look for, but *only those who in mind are assimilated to the faith of Abraham,* and who have recognized all the mysteries: for I say, that some injunctions were laid on you in reference to the *worship of God and practice of righteousness;* but some injunctions and acts were likewise mentioned in reference to the mystery of Christ, on account of the hardness of your people's hearts.[61]

Just as Jesus was foreordained to His earthly mission, God also revealed to the Old Testament prophet Jeremiah the nature of his important responsibility in mortality: "Before I formed thee in the belly *I knew thee;* and before thou camest forth out of the womb I sanctified thee, and I ordained [selected] thee a prophet unto the nations" (Jeremiah 1:5). It would seem that God knew Jeremiah and his valiant labors in his first estate—and it follows that God knew all the prophets—and *foreordained* them, or preselected them, to come forth at a specific time in the history of the world to accomplish their important role in God's plan. Likewise, it appears that God knew each of us and ordained many of His children to various responsibilities here on earth: "According as he hath chosen us in him before the foundation of the world, that we should be holy and without blame before him in love" (Ephesians 1:4).

Evangelical Christian scholar, David Bercot, addresses the seeming dichotomy of the Bible concerning predestination versus foreordination: "From what I have observed, many—perhaps most—evangelical Christians say they believe in predestination. Yet their prayers and actions show they really don't. Others simply throw up their hands, admitting, 'I don't know what I believe.' On the one hand, the scriptures teach that God is patient with us, 'not willing that any should perish, but that all should come to repentance' (2 Peter 3:9). But on the other hand, it says that God has 'mercy on whom he will have mercy, and whom he will he hardeneth' (Romans 9:18)."

Bercot then says: "I have wrestled with these seeming contradictory passages most of my adult life. So it was very comforting to discover that the early Christians had logical—and Scripturally sound explanations for these seeming contradictions. In fact, their understandings about God's foreknowledge and man's free will are among the most reasonable I've ever heard. By contrast, it was once again some of the Gnostic teachers who taught that humans are arbitrarily predestined for salvation and punishment."[62]

Another Evangelical writer, Clark Pinnock, explains his view of God's foreknowledge: "God, in order to be omniscient, need not know the future in complete detail. Were he to know it, we would have to suppose that it is already determined that human freedom is illusory. Our decisions would then settle nothing because there is nothing left to settle. We would have no 'say' in the way things turn out."[63]

Many Christians have been forced to reevaluate basic beliefs as more is learned of early Christianity. Bercot and Pinnock conclude that the traditional theology of the Reformers regarding predestination is unbiblical, and they defend the principle of free will and God's foreknowledge as taught

in the Bible and reenforced by early Christian writers.

God *foreknew* us based on acts associated with agency *before we came to earth*, explaining how God can deal with His children justly and mercifully in mortality. Earthly parents are given the opportunity to make informed judgments and decisions regarding *their* children which take into consideration mental, physical, spiritual, and social capacities. They have the prerogative, based on the foregoing, to consider the maturity and wisdom used by a child in making various life decisions in the exercise of free will, and thus to grant either greater privileges or restrictions as merited. Jesus offers salvation and eternal reward to all who will accept His grace and endure faithfully to the end of their lives. This invitation to salvation was extended by the Apostles, who were commanded to preach the gospel to the ends of the earth so that "he that believeth and is baptized shall be saved" (Mark 16:16). Although interested in the "ninety and nine," Christ was also uniquely interested in the "one" (Luke 15:4–7) and desired that *all* would come unto Him and be saved (1 Timothy 2:4), He being "no respecter of persons" (Acts 10:34). Moreover, those who are given greater gifts are also burdened with greater responsibility (Luke 12:48). Since God loves all His children and desires that *all* return to Him, it is incumbent upon those who have been so blessed to testify to all, through example and word, and to encourage all to come unto Christ.

Philosophical Creeds Replace Biblical Teachings

Although God was not a mystery to the Apostles nor to the early Apostolic Fathers, the true nature of our Heavenly Father became a mystery to those who followed. These bitter controversies can be traced to a lack of divine authority and the absence of revelation. The ensuing doctrinal debates over the natures of God and Jesus resulted in the historic gathering at Nicaea. Following the Nicene and succeeding councils, many doctrines were altered or eliminated and new credos introduced. The Apostles[64] and Athanasian Creeds[65] were statements of evolving theology developed over a period of centuries—the Apostles Creed not being fully defined in its present form until the eighth century. These creeds chose precise language in affirming that God was an incomprehensible and therefore an *unknowable* being, notwithstanding the verbiage to the contrary used in Jesus' intercessory prayer.

The Council of Constantinople— *A.D. 381 (Second Ecumenical Council)*

The Nicene Council did little to quell the Christological controversy. After the death of Constantius, Damasus, who succeeded Liberius as pope, was able to overturn the decisions of the deceased Arian emperor, reinstating deposed bishops who had failed to support Constantius's Arian theology. In A.D. 381, at the Second Ecumenical Council in Constantinople, the Church restored the creeds affirmed at the Nicene Council. At this council, Pope Damasus also forcefully asserted his primacy as head of the Catholic Church.

Council of Ephesus—*A.D. 431 (Third Ecumenical Council)*

The Christological quarrel did not end with the decisions of the Second Ecumenical Council. In A.D. 431, the patriarch of Alexandria, Cyril, was involved in a significant feud with Nestorius, the Patriarch of Constantinople. This controversy took place in Ephe-

sus at the Third Ecumenical Council. Cyril is said to have won the initial contest; but a serious rift still existed. Cyril's doctrine of the perfect union of the divine and human in Christ differed with Nestorius, who contended that these Natures were separate and that the divine will had been superimposed on the human. Thus, if Nestorius's view prevailed, it followed that Mary could not be accorded the honor of the Mother of God, only the mother of the *man* Jesus. His position offended many Christians both in the East and West.

Another notable contributor to the squabble was Eutyches, whose view was more modest and yet more fanatical. His claim was that Christ had one divine nature and no human nature at all. This heresy became known as *Monophysitism*.

Council at Chalcedon—*A.D. 451 (Fourth Ecumenical Council)*

The Monophysite and Eutychan issues were substantially resolved at the Fourth Ecumenical Council held at Chalcedon. After much debate, the Council reached a compromise, placing an emphasis on Christ's two natures (divine and human) in one person, which exist inseparably within Him. A letter written by Pope Leo I and read by his personal representatives to the delegates attending the council appears to have championed Cyril's cause, resulting in a consolidation of the new "revised" Christian view of God. Although the Christological debate was never unanimously decided (ongoing disputes culminated in the Monotheletism controversy in A.D. 638), Chalcedon marked a point at which the Church as a whole remained committed to the theology embraced by its Council. The Christian Reformers of the mid-sixteenth century also adopted the decisions rendered at Chalcedon.

Church councils replaced the Apostles

as the definers and custodians of pure doctrine. Unfortunately, they did not receive revelation, as the Apostles had; they were rife with contention, unlike the Apostles in their deliberations, and they no longer possessed the authority of God to act in His name. The basic doctrine of the true nature of God had been so altered as to render any competent understanding hopeless. Jesus' simple prayer to His Father, "And this is life eternal, that they might know thee the only true God, and Jesus Christ, whom thou hast sent" (John 17:3), was summarily frustrated. Ignatius expressed this concern in his epistle to the Trallians a few years after the death of the Apostles:

> The Lord says, "This is life eternal, *to know the only true God, and Jesus Christ* whom He has sent." And again, "A new commandment give I unto you, that ye love one another. On these two commandments hang all the law and the prophets." *Do ye, therefore, notice those who preach other doctrines, how they affirm that the Father of Christ cannot be known,* and how they exhibit enmity and deceit in their dealings with one another. They have no regard for love; they despise the good things we expect hereafter; they regard present things as if they were durable; they ridicule him that is in affliction; they laugh at him that is in bonds.[66]

An early Christian author, who purportedly recorded the words of the Apostle Peter, addressed this important subject. Responding to the heretic and apostate Simon the sorcerer (Acts 8:9), Peter testified that indeed the Father can be known by those who love and follow the Savior:

Then Peter says:

> You do not perceive that you are making statements in opposition to

yourself. For if our Jesus also knows Him whom ye call the unknown God, then He is not known by you alone. Yea, if our Jesus knows Him, then Moses also, who prophesied that Jesus should come, assuredly could not himself be ignorant of Him. For he was a prophet; and he who prophesied of the Son doubtless knew the Father. For if it is in the option of the Son to reveal the Father to whom He will, then the Son, who has been with the Father from the beginning, and through all generations, as He revealed the Father to Moses, so also to the other prophets; but if this be so, it is evident that the Father has not been unknown to any of them. But how could the Father be revealed to you, who do not believe in the Son, since the Father is known to none except him to whom the Son is pleased to reveal Him? But the Son reveals the Father to those who honour the Son as they honour the Father.[67]

The Bible and the Early Christian Fathers on the Godhead

What then is the true and transcendent nature of the Godhead, and how can mankind come to know this holy doctrine? Jesus taught, "Ask, and it shall be given you; seek, and ye shall find; knock, and it shall be opened unto you: for every one that asketh receiveth; and he that seeketh findeth; and to him that knocketh it shall be opened" (Matthew 7:7–8; see also Luke 11:10; Mark 11:24). He also testified, "I am the vine, ye are the branches. . . . If ye abide in me, and my words abide in you, ye shall ask what ye will, and it shall be done unto you" (John 15:4–7). Moreover, James, the Lord's brother, counseled, "If any of you lack wisdom, let him ask of God, that giveth to all men liberally, and upbraideth not; and it shall be given him. But let him ask in faith" (James 1:5–6). Jesus inquired of the Apostles, "Whom do men say that I the Son of man am," and Peter responded, "Thou art the Christ, the Son of the living God." Jesus then affirmed, "Flesh and blood hath not revealed it unto thee, but my Father which is in heaven" (Matthew 16:13, 16–17). We may know as Peter knew, independent of any other source, by revelation from God through the Holy Ghost, the truth about our Eternal Father and His Son, Jesus.

In John 1 we read, "In the beginning was the Word, and the Word was with God, and the Word *was* God. The same was in the beginning with God" (John 1:1–2; emphasis added). How, then, was the Word *with* God and at the same time God?

In the meridian of time, the Jews were in a state of apostasy. Israel rejected God in spite of the multitude of miracles and witnesses they were favored to receive, and as a result they were denied further light and knowledge which God might have revealed had they been more faithful (Isaiah 28:9–13). Similarly, pagan converts to early Christianity were also burdened by an abundance of polytheistic religions (the worship of many gods). Historic Christianity, without guidance from living prophets and relying solely on man's wisdom to comprehend the written word, could not decipher how Jesus could both be *with* God and *be* God. Justin Martyr *seems* to have understood this relationship and attempted to explain to Trypho the Jew that Jesus was separate and distinct from the Father, yet He was also *God the Son* from the beginning, acting in accordance and unity with the Father's will:

Then I replied, "Reverting to the Scriptures, I shall endeavour to persuade you, that He who is said to have appeared to Abraham, and to Jacob, and to Moses, and who is called God, is distinct from

Him who made all things,—*numerically, I mean.*"[68]

In addition to these words, I went on: "Have you perceived, sirs, that this very God whom Moses speaks of as an Angel that talked to him in the flame of fire, *declares to Moses that He is the God of Abraham, of Isaac, and of Jacob?*"[69]

I shall give you another testimony, my friends, said I, "from the scriptures, that God *begat* before all creatures a Beginning, [who was] a certain rational power [proceeding] from Himself, who is called by the Holy Spirit, now the Glory of the Lord, now the Son, again Wisdom, again an Angel, then God, and then Lord and Logos; and on another occasion He calls Himself Captain, when He appeared in human form to Joshua the son of Nave (Nun). *For He can be called by all those names, since He ministers to the Father's will, and since He was begotten of the Father by an act of will.*"[70]

Moreover, in the book of Exodus we have also perceived that the name of God Himself which, He says, was not revealed to Abraham or to Jacob, was Jesus, and was declared mysteriously through Moses. Thus it is written: "And the Lord spake to Moses, Say to this people, Behold, I send My angel before thy face, to keep thee in the way, to bring thee into the land which I have prepared for thee. Give heed to Him, and obey Him; do not disobey Him. For He will not draw back from you; for My name is in Him." *Now understand that He who led your fathers into the land is called by this name Jesus, and first called Auses (Oshea).*[71]

Justin describes a Father-Son relationship and the distinction of two separate beings. He asserts that Jesus is the God of Abraham, Isaac, and Jacob and that it was Jesus who led the children of Israel into the promised land. While later philosophers would distort the relationship and separateness of God and Jesus, Justin argues that they are Father and Son in the same context as we are the children of our parents. Thus, the Word was both *with* God (the Father) in the beginning, and *was* God (the Son)—the God of Abraham, Isaac, and Jacob.

The relationship of Christ, this world, and its inhabitants with the Father can be further established by a statement attributed to Paul the Apostle: "Giving thanks unto the Father . . . : who hath delivered us from the power of darkness, and hath translated us into the kingdom of his dear Son: . . . Who is . . . the firstborn of every creature: for by him were all things created, that are in heaven, and that are in earth . . . : all things were created by him, and for him" (Colossians 1:12–16).

The subject of the foregoing verses is Christ. By virtue of Jesus' sacrifice, we are indebted to the Father because He loved us enough to send His *Only Begotten Son* in order that we may be delivered from the chains of everlasting darkness and inherit eternal life. Jesus is the *firstborn* of *every* creature. He and the rest of humanity share the same Father—*spiritually*—in a genetic sense. Since Paul could not have been referring to the Savior's physical birth, the passage must necessarily refer to His *spiritual birth*. The unambiguous meaning of Paul's words is clear in the otherwise foolishness of his statement if he were referring to Christ's physical birth, inasmuch as He is the *only one born* of the Father in the flesh. Finally, Paul declares that all things were made "*for him*." Accordingly, this earth is His. He is the Creator *under the direction of the Father*. He effected the Atonement. He bought us with His blood. In this manner, Jesus is both Son and Father: Son because He is the Son of God the Eternal Father; and Father because He is the creator (Father) of this earth. As verified by Justin, Jesus is

the God who appeared unto Moses and is the God spoken of in the Old Testament. Christ *is* God, under the direction of and in harmony with the will of *His* Eternal Father; yet Christ and God are separate and distinct physical beings.

The scriptures and earliest Christian writings suggest that God the Eternal Father has a perfect, incorruptible physical body with a glorified, exalted spirit. His body is identical to Jesus' body, as described by the Savior's visit to the Twelve Apostles in the upper room after His resurrection. The Savior passed through material walls, yet His disciples could touch Him and He could eat and drink. Jesus informed them, "For a spirit hath not flesh and bones, as ye see me have" (Luke 24:39). The Apostolic Father Ignatius also cited this passage supporting these conclusions:

And I know that He was possessed of a body not only in His being born and crucified, *but I also know that He was so after His resurrection, and believe that He is so now.* When, for instance, He came to those who were with Peter, He said to them, "Lay hold, handle Me, and see that *I am not an incorporeal spirit.*" "For a spirit hath not flesh and bones, as ye see Me have." And He says to Thomas, "Reach hither thy finger into the print of the nails, and reach hither thy hand, and thrust it into My side"; and immediately they believed that He was Christ. Wherefore Thomas also says to Him, "My Lord, and my God." And on this account also did they despise death, for it were too little to say, indignities and stripes. Nor was this all; but also after He had shown Himself to them, that He had risen indeed, and not in appearance only, He both ate and drank with them during forty entire days. And thus was He, *with the flesh,* received up in their sight unto *Him* that sent Him.[72]

Ignatius refutes the authors of the Nicene Creed. He states that Jesus' testimony proclaims that He is not an incorporeal spirit and that Christ was received into heaven *with* His resurrected (glorified) flesh.

Because the Son is in the express image of His Father's person (Hebrews 1:3), resurrected and in possession of His incorruptible physical body (then and now), clearly both the Father and the Son have glorified, immortal, physical bodies complete with all the divine attributes characterized by the Catholic and Protestant orthodox Trinity (omniscient, omnipotent, omnipresent, infinite, and eternal), as described in early Christian writings. However, the New Testament suggests that the Holy Ghost does not have a physical body; rather, His purpose within the Godhead is to testify of the Father and the Son and of pure truth.[73] Accordingly, when we pray, we address our prayer to God the Father (Matthew 6:9). Our prayers are answered through Jesus Christ, the Son, our intercessor,[74] *through the ministration of the Holy Ghost, who is a spirit.*[75] Thus, the Godhead operates in perfect harmony, one with the other, as *One Eternal God* in divine purpose.

Explaining the early Christian view regarding the role of each person in the Godhead, Hippolytus wrote: "The Father decrees, the Word executes, and the Son is manifested, through [the Holy Ghost] whom the Father is believed on. . . . It is the Father who commands, and the Son who obeys, and the Holy Spirit who gives understanding: The Father who is above all, the Son who is through all, and the Holy Spirit who is in all."[76]

The divine conception of Christ occurred when the "power of the Highest" (Luke 1:35) overshadowed Mary. Christ inherited from His Eternal Father immortality, or power over death, and the capacity to effect the infinite atonement. From Mary, He inherited mortality, or the capacity to sin and experience humanity in every material respect. Jesus exercised His agency to reject sin and set for us an example of what we should strive to emulate (Hebrews 4:15). Through the centuries, Christianity has had difficulty resolving Christ's divine and human qualities and His relationship with the Father. Stephen Robinson explains:

> The orthodox view that the strict wall of separation between the human and the divine ("we aren't really his children; we can't really be like him") in my view is not really biblical but, once again, philosophical. It rests on the same objection to the clear sense of Scripture that led to the equally unbiblical doctrine of the two natures in Christ, which was added to historic Christianity by the Council of Chalcedon in A.D. 451. Scripture says that God in Christ became man, that "the Word was made flesh" (John 1:14), that "in all things it behooved him to be made like unto his brethren" (Hebrews 2:17). Nevertheless, Greek philosophy, the intellectual fashion of the day, demanded that the divine could not become truly human, and vice versa, since Plato had decreed that the human and the divine were mutually exclusive. So the Council of Chalcedon invented a second nature for Christ, something never stated in the Bible, to satisfy the philosophers by keeping the human and the divine separate in Christ as Plato insisted they must be. According to Chalcedon, Christ's divine nature never became human, never suffered, never died—the claims of scripture notwithstanding.[77]

Without revelation from the heavens to shed light on the explicit nature of God, Christianity is left with certain unresolved conflicts. Current orthodox Christian theology teaches the concept of three persons within one substance. The scriptural contradictions with this philosophy center in four major points:

First, the scriptures offer evidence of the physical resurrection of Christ with a perfect body, distinct from His mortal, corruptible body (Luke 24:36–46). With His resurrected physical body, he cannot share the same corporeal substance with the Father, *although He is the physical and spiritual offspring* of His Father in the same sense that we are the *spiritual* offspring of the Eternal Father.[78]

Second, explaining Christ's intercessory prayer in the context of current Christian orthodoxy is troublesome. Jesus prayed that the Apostles might be one, *as He and the Father are one.* The Savior prayed that *all believers in Christ might become one* as He and the Father are one (John 17:21). When the Godhead is viewed as three separate, exalted beings, without human weakness and prejudice and one in divine *thought, purpose, and action*, the Apostles and all true believers can be one in the same manner. The assertion of the orthodox Christian Trinity becoming one with the Apostles and all true believers is tenuous. The notion of Christ praying to another person within His own substance is equally difficult, as is obtaining wisdom and direction from Himself.[79]

Third, Christ declares that His Father is greater than He is (John 14:28), refuting the idea that Jesus is not subject to the Father within the Godhead. This is consistent with Christ's role as our intercessor with the Father (Hebrews 7:25; 1 Timothy 2:5) and with His teachings to the Apostles when He said, "The servant is not greater than his lord" (John 15:20). Significantly, the law of Moses commanded that at Passover all firstborn unblemished lambs and bullocks were to be offered as a sacrifice in similitude of the *firstborn of*

the Father who would ransom sinful man by the shedding of His own blood.[80] Even the Savior, the firstborn of every creature who attained an exalted position with His Father as God the Son before the dawn of physical life (1 Peter 1:20), was obedient and *subordinate* to His Father's will (John 6:38). Ignatius admonished the saints at Smyrna: "Let all things therefore be done by you with good order in Christ. Let the laity be *subject to* the deacons; the deacons to the presbyters; the presbyters to the bishop; the bishop to Christ, *even as He is to the Father.*"[81]

Several other verses indicate the subordinate role of the Savior to the Father *without minimizing* the literal Godhood of Jesus *or compromising their oneness*. Jesus testifies: "My doctrine is not mine, *but his that sent me.* If any man will do his will, he shall know of the doctrine, whether it be of God, or whether I speak of myself. He that speaketh of himself seeketh his own glory: but *he that seeketh his glory that sent him,* the same is true, and no unrighteousness is in him" (John 7:16–18; emphasis added). This passage clarifies that Jesus received revelation from His Father and that He was subordinate to His Father's will; and further, that Jesus desired to glorify His Father, not Himself.

The Savior, answering a question of the Pharisees, confirms both the separateness of person and oneness in purpose. Moreover, when Jesus uses the familiar law of Moses (the law of witnesses) to punctuate His declaration that the testimony of two men is true, He is not using subtlety or nuance: Christ's Father was one witness and He was the second witness: "The Pharisees therefore said unto him, Thou bearest record of thyself; thy record is not true. Jesus answered and said unto them, Though I bear record of myself, yet my record is true. . . . Ye judge after the flesh; I judge no man. And yet if I judge, my judgement is true: for I am not alone, but I and the Father that sent me. It is also written in your law, that the testimony of two men is true. I am the one that bear witness of myself, and the Father that sent me beareth witness of me" (John 8:13–18).

Finally, responding once more to the persistent questioning of the Pharisees, Jesus affirms His subordinate role (1), the separateness of personages (2), and oneness in unity (3): "Then said they unto him, Who art thou? And Jesus saith unto them, Even the same that I said unto you from the beginning. . . . and I speak to the world those things which I have heard of him [(1)(2)(3)] [the Father]. . . . When ye have lifted up the Son of man, then shall ye know that I am he, and that I do nothing of myself; but as my Father hath taught me, I speak these things [(1)(2)(3)]. And he that sent me is with me [(1)(2)(3)]: the Father hath not left me alone [(2)(3)]; for I do always those things that please him" [(1)(2)(3)] (John 8:25–29). When the Savior obediently says, "I do nothing of myself; but as my Father hath taught me, I speak these things," He attests to the subordination, the separateness of person, and the unity of the Godhead.

Fourth, the Bible maintains that we were created in God's "image, after our likeness" (Genesis 1:26). Scripture later declares, using precisely the same verbiage, that Seth was begotten in Adam's "own likeness, after his image" (Genesis 5:3), suggesting that both verses point to physical attributes. Further substantiating that we are created to look like our Father, Enoch revealed to his sons: "Understand that . . . he created man in the likeness of his own form, and put into him eyes to see, and ears to hear, and heart to reflect, and intellect wherewith to deliberate."[82] When Enoch used the word *form,* he implied that likeness and image refer to more than spiritual characteristics.

To understand what God declared when He used the phrase "Let *us*," we refer again to the Bible: John stated that Christ existed in the beginning with the Father, and Paul testified that Jesus created the heavens and earth. John furthered witnessed that the Word, or Jesus, was God the Son prior to the physical creation. Accordingly, it is consistent to assume that Christ was among those included in the word *us.* Justin Martyr likewise noted this example in his apology to Trypho the Jew:

God speaks in the creation of man with the very same design, in the following words: "Let Us make man after our image and . . . male and female created He them. And God blessed them, and said, increase and multiply, and fill the earth, and have power over it." And that you may not change the [force of the] words just quoted, and repeat what your teachers assert. . . . I shall quote again the words narrated by Moses himself, from which we can indisputably learn that [God] conversed with some one who was numerically distinct from Himself, and also a rational Being. These are the words: "And God said, Behold, Adam has become as one of us, to know good and evil." In saying, therefore, "as one of us,"[Moses] has declared that [there is a certain] number of persons associated with one another, and that they are at least two. . . . This Offspring, which was truly brought forth from the Father, was with the Father before all the creatures, and the Father communed with Him; even as the scripture by Solomon has made clear, that He whom Solomon calls Wisdom, was begotten as a Beginning before all His creatures and as Offspring by God.[83]

In his testimony, Justin declares that God conversed with someone numerically distinct from Himself and that this person (Jesus) was also a rational being. Justin further testifies that Jesus was the "offspring" of God, not some mystical "eternal generation." Justin also intimates that there may have been more than the Father and His Son, Jesus, when he states, "They are at least two."

In his discourse against the Noetians, the orthodox Hippolytus also describes the early Christian viewpoint that God and Jesus are two persons who are *one in purpose:*

> If, again, he allege His own word when He said, "I and the Father are one," let him attend to the fact, and understand that He did not say, "I and the Father am one, but are one." For the word *are* is not said of one person, but it refers to two persons, and one power. . . . What have the Noetians to say to these things? Are all one body in respect to substance, or is it that we become one in the power and disposition of unity of mind? In the same manner the Son, who was sent and was not known of those who are in the world, confessed that He was in the Father in power and disposition. For the Son is the one mind of the Father. We who have the Father's mind believe so (in Him).[84]

The testimony of Hippolytus is consistent with Justin Martyr's view: God and Jesus are separate and distinct beings who are "of one heart and of one soul" (Acts 4:32), united in divine will and purpose.

The Clementine Homilies record a classic confrontation, purportedly between Simon Magus and Peter, wherein Peter expresses his conviction of the nature of God:

> And Simon said: "I should like to know, Peter, if you really believe that the shape of man has been moulded after the shape of God." And Peter said: "I am really quite certain, Simon, that

this is the case. . . . It is the shape of the just God."[85] For He has shape, and He has every limb primarily and solely for beauty's sake, and not for use. For He has not eyes that he may see with them; for He sees on every side, since He is incomparably more brilliant in his body than the visual spirit which is in us, and He is more splendid than everything, so that in comparison with Him the light of the sun may be reckoned with darkness. Nor has He ears that he may hear; for He hears, perceives, moves, energizes, acts on every side. But He has the most beautiful shape on account of man, that the pure in heart, may be able to see Him, that they may rejoice because they suffered. For He moulded man in His own shape as in the grandest seal, in order that He may be the ruler and Lord of all, and that all may be subject to him.[86]

Although an understanding of the nature of God is necessary for salvation, and although we are commanded to come to know of His ways and attributes and to emulate them, the scriptures are also plain that God's ways are higher than our ways (Isaiah 55:9). Moreover, the Bible tells us that the depths of God are unsearchable (Romans 11:33), meaning that we cannot expect in this life to know *all* things about God and His plan for us. However, these verses once again fall far short of stating that God is incomprehensible and completely mysterious. In fact, He is only a mystery to those who fail to seek after Him and yield their hearts to Him. In contrast, the Bible affirms: "Beloved, now are we the sons of God, and it doth not yet appear what we shall be: but we know that, when he shall appear, we shall be like him; for we shall see him as he is" (1 John 3:2).

Early Jewish and Christian Belief in Anthropomorphism (Divine Embodiment of God)

In modern times, without reviewing the significant body of evidence contained in early Jewish writings, including at the time of Christ—thus relying exclusively on the Bible—it is difficult to explain such isolated verses as those that suggest God is solely a spirit.[87] Notwithstanding, scripture, taken as a whole, supports the doctrine that we are literally the offspring of God and that Jesus Himself was the firstborn spirit, *begotten of the Father,* prior to the physical creation. While the Bible alludes to the fact that *we* are the spiritual offspring of God, pseudepigraphal writings confirm that prior to coming to earth we were indeed preexistent with the Father and possessed bodies composed of spirit matter. Now our spirits are clothed in a mortal body, and what is most clear about John's testimony is *not* that God is an incorporeal Spirit but that we worship the Father *in spirit.* Interpretations made by ignorant translators, scribal errors, and willful text perversions must be placed in context with the canon *as a whole* in attempts to understand the nature of God. The Bible, early Jewish compositions, and the Pseudepigrapha contain many verses that illuminate the true nature of the Father's and Son's physical and spiritual composition.

The third-century and Nicene Fathers profoundly debated this subject, not finding general agreement until the fourth century, by which time Greek philosophy had completely enwrapped Christian doctrine. By contrast, most Jews and early Christians supported the doctrine of anthropomorphism (the divine embodiment of God).

According to a recently published study by Alon Goshen Gottstein, there should be no debate as to whether or not God has some kind of glorified body: "In all of rabbinic literature [covering both the tannaitic (a.d. 70–200) and amoraic (a.d. 220–500) periods] there is not a single statement that categorically denies that God has body or form. In my understanding, the question of whether the rabbis believed in a God who has form is one that needs little discussion. . . . Instead of asking, "Does God have a body?" we should inquire, "What kind of body does God have?"[88]

The significance of this research is underscored by the fact that the earliest Christian Church did not yet have the New Testament but relied *solely* on the Old Testament (Jewish scripture) as its revelatory handbook.

In first-century Alexandria, Greek thought had already penetrated the intellectual establishment through Philo Judeus, who often disputed the more literal interpretations of traditional Jewish schools. Notwithstanding Philo's opposition, most of the Jews in that city still widely believed in anthropomorphism. According to Harry Wolfson, the popular author of Philo's biography:

"The great mass of believers who will have not felt the impact of the foreign philosophy will see no need of any reconciliation between them [the opposing schools]. This great mass of believers will either remain indifferent to the innovations of the philosophic reconcilers, or will superciliously [haughtily] look upon them as mere triflers, or, if given provocation, will militantly oppose them as disturbers of the religious peace."[89] Wolfson acknowledges that Alexandrian Judaism was basically the same as Pharisaic Judaism in Palestine, which taught that God was indeed embodied.

The first Christian writers to assert plainly the philosophic concept of an incorporeal God were Clement of Alexandria and Origen, writing in the late second and early third centuries, respectively. Although they were incorporealists, their writings convey that most of the saints during that period believed in an embodied God, and that such doctrines as (1) the nature of God, (2) the origin of the human soul, (3) the existence of things before and after this world *were not specifically articulated* in the current teachings of the Church. Origen wrote:

> It is a subject of investigation how God Himself is to be understood,—whether as corporeal, and formed according to some shape, or of a different nature of bodies,—a point which is not clearly indicated in our teaching.[90]
> With respect to the soul . . . this beginning itself, whether it be by birth or not . . . is not distinguished with sufficient clearness in the teachings of the Church.[91]
> What existed before this world, or what will exist after it, has not become certainly known to the many, for there is no clear statement regarding it in the teaching of the Church.[92]

Because the doctrine concerning the embodiment of God was "not clearly indicated," even the learned Origen missed the mark in his attempt to explain what had become the mystery of God.

Demonstrating a gap in Origen's reasoned explanation of an incorporeal God, David Paulsen has recently explained the ambiguous text in John which states that "God is a Spirit" (John 4:24): "Pneuma (translated "spirit") literally meant air or breath—thus implying that spirit is composed of a material substance, *one of the four basic elements,* and since Christian Stoics believed that existence was confined to material bodies, God (being spirit) was only the purest of bodies."[93]

This explanation appears to harmonize with the description of God attributed to

Peter in the Clementine Homilies, Old Testament accounts, and early Jewish and Christian tradition.

Accordingly, the earliest Christians were *not* persuaded by philosophy, as we have seen; instead they were convicted by the holy scriptures and the earliest apostolic traditions. In Exodus we read: "Then went up Moses, and Aaron, Nadab, and Abihu, and seventy of the elders of Israel: and they saw the God of Israel [the premortal Jesus]: and *there was under his feet* as it were a paved work of a sapphire stone, and as it were *the body of heaven in his clearness*" (Exodus 24:9; emphasis added). Moses and seventy of the elders of Israel *saw* the God of Israel. This was Jesus Christ before He was born in the flesh; and the scriptures describe the heavenly nature of His spiritual body, including such attributes as His *feet*. Once again, a comparison of the account attributed to Peter in the Clementine Homilies with the Old Testament description provided above is warranted. Although the topic of this verse is Jesus' preexistent spirit body and not God the Father's exalted physical body, the similarities are striking.

In another related passage, scripture declares that Moses also spoke, *face to face,* with Jehovah: "And it came to pass, as Moses entered into the tabernacle, the cloudy pillar descended, and stood at the door of the tabernacle, and the Lord talked with Moses. And all the people saw the cloudy pillar stand at the tabernacle door: and all the people rose up and worshipped, every man in his tent door. *And the Lord spake unto Moses face to face, as a man speaketh unto his friend.* And he turned again into the camp: but his servant Joshua, the son of Nun, a young man, departed not out of the tabernacle" (Exodus 33:9–11; emphasis added).

Stephen's testimony also indicates the separateness of God and Jesus, thus confirming that if Christ has a physical body, His Father must likewise have a physical body, as is evident by the Savior standing on the Father's *righthand* side: "But he, being full of the Holy Ghost, looked up stedfastly into heaven, and saw the glory of God, and Jesus standing on the right hand of God, and said, Behold, I see the heavens opened, and the Son of man standing on the right hand of God" (Acts 7:55–56).

Furthermore, the Apostle Paul supplies additional witness to the physical nature and separateness of God and Jesus: "Who being *the brightness of his glory,* and *the express image of his person,* and upholding all things by the word of his power, when he had by himself purged our sins, *sat down on the right hand of the Majesty on high*" (Hebrews 1:3; emphasis added). Paul declares that Christ is both the *brightness of His glory* and the *express image* of His Father's *person*. Since the resurrected Christ has an incorruptible, *pure* physical body, this verse implies that His Father also possesses a glorified physical body *on whose right hand He sits.*

Evangelical theologian Clark Pinnock suggests that the Bible methaphors just cited are more than symbolic and that God may indeed have some type of corporeal body:

> If we are to take Bible metaphors seriously, is God in some way embodied? Critics will be quick to say that, although there are expressions of this idea in the Bible, they are not to be taken literally. But I do not believe that the idea is as foreign to the Bible's view of God as we have assumed.... Perhaps God's agency would be easier to envisiage if he were in some way corporeal. Add to that the fact that in the theophanies of the Old [and New] Testament God encounters humans in the form of a man.... Add to that the fact that God took on a body in the incarnation and Christ has taken

that body with him into glory. It seems to me that the Bible does not think of God as formless. . . . Most people, I suspect, think that God chooses to be associated with a body, while himself being formless. That may be so, but it is also possible that God has a body in some way we cannot imagine.[94]

Finally, 1 Enoch provides compelling testimony of the divine nature and separateness of God and Jesus Christ, including the Savior's role in man's redemption:

> At that place, I saw the One to whom belongs the time before time. And his head was white like wool, and there was another individual, whose face was like that of a human being. His countenance was full of grace like that of one among the holy angels. And I asked the one—from among the angels—who was going with me, and who had revealed to me all the secrets regarding the One who was born of human beings, "who is this, and from whence is he going as the prototype of the Before-Time?" And he answered me and said to me, "this is the Son of Man, to whom belongs righteousness, and with whom righteousness dwells. . . . The Lord of the Spirits has chosen him, and he is destined to be victorious before the Lord of the Spirits in eternal uprightness."[95]

This vision to Enoch establishes that the "One," the "Before-Time," the "Lord of the Spirits," is our Eternal Father in Heaven and, consistent with scripture, the Son of Man, or Jesus, was chosen by the Father from before the foundations of the world to redeem the rest of God's "spirit" children.

No clear tradition from the apostolic Church survived the human imprint (regarding several key doctrines) because of late first- and early second-century contention and rebellion. Without continuing revelation, *through prophets,* such questions as the nature of God could only be answered by Christian thinkers through scholarly speculation in the third century. This fact underscores the problem of apostasy. To all the ancient Patriarchs, *religion was revealed, not published in scholarly journals.* To answer the dilemmas created by apostasy in the past, the gospel was *re-revealed* by God numerous times, as chapter 2 documents, thus providing every dispensation with the same understanding of Heavenly Father's plan and was thus not solely reliant on past scripture or revelation. The apostolic period was the same: the saints received new revelation (however the same doctrine) coupled with the past revelations contained in the Old Testament. With the Church in apostasy *again,* the Church needed, even required, continuing revelation from God to reestablish its course.

Because Hellenized Judaism and Neo-platonic philosophy became entangled in the warnings of God, "Thou shalt have no other gods before me" (Exodus 20:3), and King Hezekiah's declaration, "Thou art the God" (Isaiah 37:16), second- and third-century theologians could not reconcile the unity of the Godhead; thus, belief in the divine embodiment of God disappeared from Christian theology. While some things about the nature of God may be *unclear,* absent prophetic utterance, what *is* clear is that such biblical statements, taken contextually and historically, referred to ancient Israel's propensity to worship idols rather than God. Polytheism *cannot* be described as worshiping God the Father *in the name* of His Son, Jesus Christ, by the power of the Holy Ghost—separate beings—who are One in divine purpose; rather, polytheism is the worship of idols and pagan gods.

The Doctrine of Biblical Inerrancy

Religious disagreements generated by opposing Christian theologies have plagued the unity sought by Jesus since the death of the Apostles. One of Satan's greatest ploys is combining significant truth with varying amounts of error. As early Christianity endeavored to preserve the truth in the midst of competing ideologies, unpolluted truth became elusive and obscure. Since scripture itself prophesies of the problems the early Church would face, it is obvious that Satan would attempt to alter the sacred record itself in order to aggravate the already significant theological discord facing the Church. Many Christian theologians have attempted to minimize the extent of tampering and intentional perversion of scriptural texts, however well meaning. Speculating that the Bible contains only trivial errors, insignificant to doctrinal understanding, is without reliable foundation. There are more than eight thousand manuscript copies of the New Testament, 5,366 alone in the Greek language—yet no two of them are identical.[96] The oldest surviving manuscript copy is from the late second century, at which point the theological controversies had been raging for at least one hundred years. All existing manuscripts have been copied numerous times—"copies of copies of copies"[97]; *there are no extant original autographs.* In fact, most manuscripts come from the eighth and ninth centuries with prized copies coming from the fourth century. Scholars admit that no one knows how many variations exist, but *they doubtless number in the hundreds of thousands.*[98]

The Catholic historian Henri Daniel-Rops asserts that because of errors by copyists and intentional changes, New Testament manuscripts were subjected to "numerous outrages." Quoting Origen, he adds:

"Today the fact is evident, that there are many differences in the manuscripts, either through the negligence of certain copyists, or the perverse audacity of some in correcting the text."[99]

Justin Martyr testified of intentional text revisions to the Old Testament by the Jews:

From the statements, then, which Esdras made in reference to the law of the passover, they have taken away the following:
"And Esdras said to the people, This passover is our Saviour and our refuge. And if you have understood, and your heart has taken it in, that we shall humble Him on a standard, and thereafter hope in Him, then this place shall not be forsaken for ever, says the God of hosts. But if you will not believe Him, and will not listen to His declaration, you shall be a laughing-stock to the nations."
And from the sayings of Jeremiah they have cut out the following:
"I [was] like a lamb that is brought to the slaughter: they devised a device against me, saying, Come, let us lay on wood on His bread, and let us blot Him out from the land of the living; and His name shall no more be remembered."
And since this passage from the sayings of Jeremiah is still written in some copies [of the scriptures] in the synagogues of the Jews (for it is only a short time since they were cut out), and since from these words it is demonstrated that the Jews deliberated about the Christ Himself, to crucify and put Him to death, He Himself is both declared to be led as a sheep to the slaughter, as was predicted by Isaiah. . . .
And again, from the sayings of the same Jeremiah these have been cut out:
"The Lord God remembered His dead people of Israel who lay in the graves; and He descended to preach to them

His own salvation."
And from the ninety-fifth (ninety-sixth) Psalm they have taken away this short saying of the words of David: "From the wood." . . . For when the passage said, "Tell ye among the nations, the Lord hath reigned from the wood," they have left, "Tell ye among the nations, the Lord hath reigned."[100]

Another ancient account substantiating the falsification of early writings and scripture comes from Dionysius, the bishop of Corinth in approximately A.D. 170:

For I wrote letters when the brethren requested me to write. And these letters the apostles of the devil have filled with tares, taking away some things and adding others, for whom a woe is in store. It is not wonderful, then, if some have attempted to adulterate the Lord's writings, when they have formed designs against those which are not such.[101]

A recent publication, *The Orthodox Corruption of Scripture,* by Bart Ehrman, is perhaps the most complete, thoroughly documented study outlining the oft-exercised practice of deliberately amending the New Testament original manuscripts for the purpose of making the text "more orthodox," according to a particular Christian group's manner of interpretation:

Theological disputes, specifically disputes over Christology, prompted Christian scribes to alter the words of scripture in order to make them more serviceable for the polemical task. Scribes modified their manuscripts to make them more patently "orthodox" and less susceptible to "abuse" by the opponents of orthodoxy.[102]

Ehrman quotes a 1934 publication

by Walter Bauer, who concluded that the "orthodox" group in the days of early Christianity was *not* a majority by any means but that their doctrines only won out over time: "Early Christianity embodied a number of divergent forms, no one of which represented a clear and powerful majority of believers against all others. In some regions, what was later termed 'heresy' was in fact the original and only form of Christianity."[103]

While subsequent studies disputed some of Bauer's conclusions, Erhman warns:

It would be a mistake to . . . think that the repudiation of Bauer's specific findings has freed scholars to return to the classical formulation. . . . Quite to the contrary, the opinio communis that has emerged is that despite the clear shortcomings of his study, Bauer's intuitions were right in nuce: if anything, early Christianity was even less tidy and more diversified than he realized.[104]

Thus, Ehrman queries, "Are the labels orthodoxy and heresy appropriate for describing early Christian movements?" He concludes, "Most scholars recognize that they cannot be used in any traditional sense, namely, to designate the true or original faith on the one hand and secondary aberrations from it on the other. . . . Looked at in socio-historical terms, orthodoxy and heresy are concerned as much with struggles over power as with debates over ideas."[105] Interestingly, such conclusions are right in line with the testimony of Clement of Rome to the Corinthians (regarding sedition and power), the other early Church Fathers, and also the historian Eusebius already quoted.

One of the tactics used by the competing factions was the practice of discrediting one's opponent. Ehrman states:

It is not certain in every case whether the heresiologists correctly understood the positions they attacked, or even, when they did, whether they presented them accurately. . . . The polemical literature of the second and third centuries comprises both tractates aimed directly at exposing and refuting heretical opinion (e.g., the lost works of Justin and Hegesippus, and the more familiar writings of Irenaeus, Hippolytus, and Tertullian). . . . But the question has become particularly perplexing since the discovery of the Nag Hammadi library, where Gnostics appear in some respects quite different from how they were depicted by their orthodox opponents.[106]

Ehrman, a highly regarded mainstream Christian scholar, describes the impossible task of filtering truth from error relative to the earliest Christian doctrines. He asserts that Church doctrine evolved over time, ultimately recasting the original and perhaps rejecting certain teachings of Jesus.

Demonstrating the control wielded by those who considered themselves orthodox, the bishop Serapion, who initially approved of the reading of the Gospel of Peter in his congregations, retracted his permission when he read the book for himself and discovered what *he* considered to be heretical Christology. According to Ehrman, "For him, and for them [the orthodox], this meant that the decisions concerning 'apostolicity' were ultimately based *not on claims of authorship* per se, but on a book's essential conformity to the *regula fidei*, that is, to the "apostolic" doctrine that orthodox Christians claimed as their own unique possession."[107]

Thus *it was power*, not apostolic authority, that defined Christian doctrine. Ehrman's research chronicles the widespread abuse of *intentional forgeries* by *all* parties, many of which were not discovered until modern times;[108] and yet the doctrines embraced were developed only on the basis of those few books ultimately incorporated into the orthodox canon—which books included a myriad of textual modifications! We do not know how many books were lost or fell into disuse because of fourth-century orthodox beliefs nor the full extent of tampering with original autographs. According to Ehrman, at this early date these texts were neither "*fixed in stone* nor *flawlessly reproduced* by machines capable of guaranteeing exact replication. They were copied by hand—one manuscript serving as exemplar of the next, copied by errant human beings of differing degrees of ability, temperament, and vigilance. The earliest scribes were by and large private individuals, not paid professionals, and in many instances their copies were not double-checked for accuracy. As we now know so well, mistakes—scores of them—were made."[109]

Finally, Ehrman underscores emphatically his contention why orthodox scribes altered the sacred texts:

> I nonetheless take my overarching thesis to be established: proto orthodox scribes of the second and third centuries occasionally modified their texts of Scripture in order to make them coincide more closely with the christological views embraced by the party that would seal its victory at Nicaea and Chalcedon. . . . [They] had to defend—at one and the same time—Christ's deity against adoptionists, his humanity against docetists, and his unity against separationists. This, and primarily this, I would argue, is why scribes modified the New Testament text.[110]

Bruce Metzger's acclaimed book *The Text of the New Testament* agrees with Ehrman's findings when Metzger lists the methods of intentional text corruption used by scribes, i.e., deliberate changes in spelling and grammar, harmonistic corruptions, the addition of natural complements (the embroidering and embellishment of simple gospel truths), harmonizing historical and geographical discrepancies, and the practice of *conflation* (the merging of variant texts). In addition, unconscious errors were made from faulty eyesight, faulty hearing, errors of the mind, and errors of judgment.[111]

As these studies reveal, fallible and biased men determined which books were to be included in the final canon of scripture, and neither Athanasius nor any other early Church leader ever claimed divine intervention in the eventual selections. No doubt there were questions and lively debate over which epistles were genuinely written by the Apostles and other inspired authors and those which were known or thought to be manipulated by the Gnostics and other apostate groups. Significantly, many manuscripts are known not to have survived due to manipulation by the prejudiced views of orthodox leaders and the massive persecution and book burnings during the reign of Diocletian.

Little evidence exists to support the claim of *Bible inerrancy*. Inasmuch as the accepted canon contains flaws, and no one knows to what extent those flaws have corrupted interpretation, it is difficult to use the Bible alone as a standard to discern the voice of God in the present dispensation. Christians today stand in an isolated position, and the Bible cannot answer the critical question why this would be so.

Floyd Filson seemed to recognize this fact in his work *Which Books Belong in the Bible:*

> It is possible, however, to stress the Bible so much and give it so central a place that the sensitive Christian conscience must rebel. We may illustrate such overstress on the Bible by the

often-used (and perhaps misused) quotation from Chillingworth: "The Bible alone is the religion of Protestantism." Or we may recall how often it has been said that the Bible is the final authority for the Christian. If it will not seem too facetious, I would like to put in a good word for God. It is God and not the Bible who is the central fact for the Christian. When we speak of "the Word of God" we use a phrase which, properly used, may apply to the Bible, but it has a deeper primary meaning. It is God who speaks to man. But He does not do so only through the Bible. He speaks through prophets and apostles. He speaks through specific events. And while his unique message to the Church finds its central record and written expression in the Bible, this very reference to the Bible reminds us that Christ is the Word of God in a living, personal way which surpasses what we have even in this unique book. Even the Bible proves to be the Word of God only when the Holy Spirit working within us attests the truth and divine authority of what the Scripture says. . . . Our hope is in God; our life is in Christ; our power is in the Spirit. The Bible speaks to us of the divine center of all life and help and power, but it is not the center. The Christian teaching about the canon must not deify the Scripture.[112]

Bible inerrancy, as defined by *The Chicago Statement*, composed in recent years by a large group of influential Evangelical theologians, is abbreviated as follows:

1. When all the facts are known . . . (meaning, if all the facts were known, the Bible would be shown to be inerrant).

Reviewing the data just presented, one may conclude:

- There probably were genuine and authentic Christian books and writings that have been lost in their original form or are less valued than they were by the earliest Christians.
- There is an absence of reliable, substantial Christian religious history from approximately A.D. 68–150.
- What original Christianity really *was* is not clear today.
- Vast numbers of textual variations place a perplexing cloud over what the true facts really may be for some doctrines.
- Christian scholars admit the significant differences in today's version of Christianity compared with New Testament Christianity.

When all the facts are known is a hollow statement in light of the *fact* that the facts are not reliably known.

2. In their original autographs . . .

This might be a true statement—except that none of the scriptures in their original autographs exist today. Changes do not need to be significant to alter the meaning of doctrine as we know so well from Augustine in his development of the doctrine of original sin. Since we cannot know how extensively they were changed, *in their original autographs* once again seems hollow. After all, what Christian would argue that were we to have the original autographs we would not hold them to be self-evident and unqualifiedly true? Since we do not have the scriptures in their original autograph and material textual variations are certain, without the guidance of *living* prophets as in ages past, how are Christians to determine in many cases what pure doctrine really is?

3. Properly interpreted . . .

The standard rules of *hermeneutics*, the guidelines for interpreting interpersonal communication, would be an acceptable place to start in arriving at proper interpretations. Understanding historical/cultural background, literary context, and rules of grammar are helpful to achieve literal and accurate interpretations, as well as treating parables and proverbs as they were intended, which is to illustrate an important lesson without necessarily being construed to denote authentic history, prophecy, or law. Because we do not have the original autographs and the texts *were* altered in a material way, the rules of hermeneutics are insufficient when applied to the Godhead, salvation, and apostolic authority. Hermeneutics have been *unsuccessfully* used in applications as apparent as simple acts of morality, exemplified by some mainstream Christian denominations that condone homosexual activity, including recognition and acceptance to serve in the ministry, while the scriptures do not appear to equivocate on such issues. These conditions magnify the need for living prophets to interpret previous scripture and to reveal God's word in the present day based on our inability to do so for ourselves.

4. In everything they affirm . . .

This conclusion also seems vague, since we cannot distinguish between the lesson or principle a biblical author is trying to convey without *also* accepting the incidental facts or *pieces of the puzzle* the author may present in the process. Most Christians believe *everything the scriptures affirm, when properly translated and interpreted.* Without original autographs and unaltered texts, we can be certain of what the Bible affirms in key instances only with the help of living prophets because we have no way of knowing otherwise what is properly translated and interpreted.

5. Whatever that has to do with doctrine or morality or with the social, physical, or life sciences . . .

The scriptures serve as a guide to every aspect of our lives: they should influence our spiritual development; they should enlighten us as to the doctrines of salvation; they should help us learn and develop family values; they should influence decisions we make in our private and public lives; they should inspire the cultivation of a strong moral code; they should influence the criteria used to develop one's professional and business ethics; and finally, they should create a lens to how we view science and make related ethical and moral decisions. All these statements hinge upon accurate biblical interpretations, which hinge on accurate texts, which hinge on the capacity of man to render inspired interpretations, an impossibility without apostolic authority or the voice of prophets.

The Bible *is* the word of God and contains the fullness of the everlasting gospel; but it is *not* inerrant in its current form. Notwithstanding its documented errors, the Bible contains the inspired teachings of God's Apostles and prophets throughout the ages. The Bible will bring happiness and joy in this life and eternal life in the world to come to those who follow its precepts, for so the scriptures testify. Under the direction of the Holy Ghost, we are promised that we can understand scripture, just as inspiration flowed to the Apostles and all worthy members of the early Church. Nevertheless, the inaccurate interpretation of scripture, beginning with the loss of the Apostles, has created divergent belief systems at odds with many truths taught in the New Testament. Errors of interpretation must be discovered in order that we may fully live the abundant life Jesus offered.

The Closing of the Bible Canon

Many modern Christians argue that John's Apocalypse is evidence that the Bible canon is closed: "If any man shall add unto these things, God shall add unto him the plagues that are written in this book: and if any man shall take away from the words of the book of this prophecy, God shall take away his part out of the book of life" (Revelation 22:18–19).

Modern Bible scholars recognize that "the book of this prophecy" refers to the book of Revelation, not the entire modern canon. They also agree that the "Bible" did not exist in the late A.D. 90s when many scholars believe John recorded this revelation and was not "fixed" until the late fourth century. The book of Deuteronomy states, "Ye shall not add unto the word which I command you, neither shall ye diminish ought from it" (Deuteronomy 4:2). Accordingly, the book of Revelation contains no valid argument that God was finished speaking to man, but both verses *do* say that God's word (from any dispensation) must not be altered.

Paul warned the Galatian saints, "But though we, or an angel from heaven, preach any other gospel unto you than that which we have preached unto you, let him be accursed" (Galatians 1:8). Paul referred to the fact that Church members in Galatia were still clinging to Judaism and had not fully embraced original Christian teachings. Additional scripture or revelation from the heavens *was not* the topic of Paul's address; instead, his concern was that *the gospel*, or in other words, *pure doctrine*, ought not to be modified—*even by an angel*. If an angel came bearing doctrines that revised those taught by Jesus or the Apostles, the angelic source would probably be of Satanic origin. However, if an angel came bearing the same pure doctrines as New Testament Christianity or revealed anew esoteric rites or sacraments that had been lost due to apostasy, such a revelation would be perfectly legitimate. What history seems to document so well is that the Christianity passed down from Nicaea to modern times was *dramatically different* from the Christianity revealed by Jesus. Paul could just as emphatically preach

to the Nicene Council, "I marvel that ye are so soon removed from him that called you into the grace of Christ unto another gospel" (Galatians 1:6).

According to Metzger, the saints in Edessa were not contaminated as quickly as those at Rome:

> Christianity seems to have reached the Euphrates valley about the middle of the second century, that is, while the country was still an independent state. Its people, unlike the Greek-speaking Syrians in the west with their headquarters at Antioch, used Syriac as their mother tongue. It is not surprising that the Christianity of Edessa began to develop independently, without the admixture of Greek Philosophy and Roman methods of government that at that early date modified primitive Christianity in the West and transformed it into the amalgam known as Catholicism.[113]

Metzger (and every other informed scholar) understands that Greek philosophy was blended into pure Christianity; Catholicism became an "amalgam." According to Paul's definition, Christianity actually became *another gospel* shortly after the revelation to Hermas.

The overarching motivation for closing the Bible canon was the fear of heretical doctrines making their way into the Church mainstream. Without the Apostles, Church leaders were not confident in their ability to distinguish between divine and false revelations. The disputed Montanist revelation in A.D. 156 occasioned intense scrutiny of the debate, and solid lines began to replace those that had been dotted. Nevertheless, the only real claim made by the Montanists was that the spiritual gifts enumerated by Paul ought still to be valid. Quoting Campenhausen,

Metzger writes:

> Nowhere do we hear that these writings were described as a "New Gospel," were cited as "Scripture," or were combined as a third section with the old Bible to form a new Montanist canon. . . . The real authority to which appeal was made in the Montanist camp was not a new canon, but the Spirit and his "gifts"; and it was recognition of these which was demanded from the Catholic church [by the Montantists].[114]

Because Tertullian believed the Church had lost its spirituality, he joined the Montanist faction which was, in his day, still part of the Universal Church. Until this time, the Church considered itself a Church of revelation. The Shepherd of Hermas, a post-apostolic revelation, forcefully attested that God continued to speak to man from yonder heaven. Justin Martyr also claimed that the Church received revelation in his day.[115] It would appear that revelation ceased because man rejected God's warnings, evidence that the Church itself was in apostasy.

Many Bible scholars conclude that although there may be other authentic books of some value, they do not add material value to the testimony already included in the present canon.[116] Others suggest that some of the early Fathers themselves cited that no revelation was necessary in addition to that revealed by Jesus or the Apostles. As evidence, statements made by Irenaeus and Tertullian are offered.[117] Paradoxically, it was Tertullian who left the mainstream in search of the spiritual gifts reminiscent of the early Christian Church. By Tertullian's day, New Testament Christianity no longer existed but had been replaced by what was becoming a Hellenized adaptation. When scholars make such statements, they conclude that revelation from the heavens is no longer necessary

because all that is required for man's salvation is contained in the Bible. Although the basic message of the gospel is complete in the Bible, without ongoing communication from heaven to clarify its contents, the same confusion, conflict, and lack of unity experienced by the early Christian Church *after the Apostles* will continue. Some intellectuals, both early and modern, teach that the Apostles received the fullness of the gospel (which they did) and that the Apostles shared the fullness of the gospel with *all* Christians (which they did not). Ignatius, an earlier and more reliable witness than either Irenaeus or Tertullian, wrote that he understood things about the gospel which he elected not to share with the general membership. In the early Christian Church, sacred things were not written; instead, they were transmitted orally *to the faithful*. Moreover, without continuing revelation, the higher teachings of Jesus will not be understood. According to the testimony of the earliest Christian writers, these teachings contribute to man's ability to gain eternal reward and are therefore of considerable importance.

Philosophical and Errant Allegorical Interpretations Responsible for Corrupt Theology

Early Church writers were not oblivious to the threat that Greek philosophy and other religious cultures posed in maintaining pure Christian doctrine. Tertullian queried, "What indeed has Athens to do with Jerusalem? What concord is there between the academy and the Church?" Answering his rhetorical questions, he asserted, "Our instruction comes from 'the porch of Solomon,' who himself taught that 'the Lord should be sought in simplicity of heart.'" Tertullian then declared,

"Away with all attempts to produce a mottled Christianity of Stoic, Platonic, and dialectic composition."[118]

Thus, two obstacles exist that seem insurmountable in achieving accurate interpretations of the Bible: (1) the loss or corruption of original scriptural text, and (2) allegorical and philosophical misinterpretations caused by the Hellenization of Christianity. Although parables and allegory were usefully employed by the Savior and others to teach true believers the mysteries of the kingdom, without prophetic guidance, interpretations became speculative rather than authoritative.

Christian author Earl E. Cairns explains in his widely published book *Christianity Through the Centuries* how philosophy and man's wisdom became intermingled with Christian theology. Already well underway, the integration of philosophy into Christianity was significantly advanced by the Alexandrian School, opening in approximately A.D. 185. Cairns says:

Its earliest leader was Pantaenus, an able convert from, according to some, Stoicism. Clement (of Alexandria), and then Origen succeeded him as leaders of that influential school of Christian thought. The men of the Alexandrian school were anxious to develop a system of theology that by the use of philosophy would give a systematic exposition of Christianity. They had been trained in the classical literature and philosophy of the past and thought it could be used in the formulation of Christian theology. . . . Thus, instead of emphasizing a grammatico-historical interpretation of the Bible, they developed an allegorical system of interpretation that has plagued Christianity since that time. . . . This method of interpretation has done much harm to the cause of correct interpretation of the Scriptures.[119]

An example of how quickly philosophical tendencies began is found in a pagan analogy used by Clement, the bishop of Rome in A.D. 95, in his first epistle to the Corinthians:

Let us consider that wonderful sign [of the resurrection] which takes place in Eastern lands, that is, in Arabia and the countries round about. There is a certain bird which is called a phoenix. This is the only one of its kind, and lives five hundred years. And when the time of its dissolution draws near that it must die, it builds itself a nest of frankincense, and myrrh, and other spices, into which, when the time is fulfilled, it enters and dies. But as the flesh decays a certain kind of worm is produced, which, being nourished by the juices of the dead bird, brings forth feathers. Then, when it has acquired strength, it takes up that nest in which are the bones of its parent, and bearing these it passes from the land of Arabia into Egypt, to the city called Heliopolis. And, in open day, flying in the sight of all men, it places them on the altar of the sun, and having done this, hastens back to its former abode. The priests then inspect the registers of the dates, and find that it has returned exactly as the five hundredth year was completed.

Do we then deem it any great and wonderful thing for the Maker of all things to raise up again those who have piously served Him in the assurance of a good faith, when even by a bird He shows us the mightiness of His power to fulfil His promise?[120]

In an attempt to give authority and potency to his communication, Clement used Greek and pagan allegory rather than relying solely on the scriptures and the influence of the Holy Spirit. At this early stage, it is doubtful that Clement himself mixed Greek thought with actual doctrine. However, most of the Christian Apologists came from Platonic and Stoic (philosophical) backgrounds. Clement's use of Greek allegory was merely the beginning of the escalating use of Platonic thought to explain Christian doctrine. Philosophy became hopelessly entangled in Christian teachings as theologians sought to define a precise expression of Church doctrine without apostolic or prophetic enlightenment.

The Nicene Council convened more than two centuries after the passing of the Apostles. The Twelve had fought valiantly to retain the unblemished teachings of their Master and to expose heretical "wolves." No historian denies the Hellenistic influences that sought to exert themselves on the postapostolic Church; and just as the children of Israel were seduced into worshiping the golden calf, the philosophies of men captivated the hearts of the masses, ultimately recasting Christianity. This did not develop overnight; rather, pride, envy, contention, and greed increasingly infiltrated the Church until Christ's Church was removed from the earth, at some point very early in the second century, to be nourished in the wilderness "for a time" (Revelation 12:14). The effect of apostasy was the loss of influence by the Holy Ghost and the counsel of living Apostles and prophets, leaving early ecumenical councils and creeds to define *inaccurately* the nature of the Godhead.

The Ordinance of the Sacrament Is Altered

Paul once taught the Corinthian saints to "keep the ordinances, *as I delivered them to you*" (1 Corinthians 11:2; emphasis added). Unfortunately, in addition to mystifying the true nature of God, the Church also altered the sacred ordinance of the sacrament of the Lord's Supper. Christian philosophers

attempted speculative explanations where the scriptures alone offered only modest or seemingly incomplete answers. Throughout the ensuing centuries, impurities began to infiltrate almost every aspect of Christian life. Alterations in the sacrament began early in the second century, escalating in the third century when lengthy prayers were authorized and the ceremony itself was aggrandized. The most corrupting provision of the new dogma was teaching that the emblems themselves were transformed into the literal body and blood of Christ, the belief that Christ was daily and literally crucified anew for the sins of those present. This doctrine, later known as *transubstantiation*, was formally canonized by Pope Innocent III in 1215. The basis for the doctrine is the interpretation of the phrase "this is my body," wherein the emblems themselves, or "host," were worshiped, creating within the ordinance of the sacrament itself a form of idolatry.

The sacrament was first instituted in an upper room by the Savior with the Twelve Apostles. The Savior washed the feet of his disciples, then blessed bread and offered wine:

And [Jesus] took bread, and gave thanks, and brake it, and gave unto them, saying, This is my body which is given for you: *this do in remembrance of me.* Likewise also the cup after supper, saying, This cup is the new testament in my blood, which is shed for you. (Luke 22:19–20; emphasis added)

The sacrament *was a representation* of the body and blood of Jesus Christ, just as the unblemished lamb had been a representation of Jesus before the Savior's offering of His life on the cross. When the Savior instructed his Apostles in the proper observance of this ordinance, Jesus had not yet suffered for man's sins. He had not yet sweat great drops of blood in the lonely Garden of Gethsemane, nor had he hung and suffered on the cross at Calvary. Those original emblems of bread and wine were *not* transformed by Jesus into portions of His own body and blood *prior* to His suffering and death on the cross. Jesus was preparing his disciples to partake of the sacrament of the Lord's Supper *in the place of* animal sacrifice. Rather than continuing to obey the old law, they would now offer up a broken heart and a contrite spirit.[121] By partaking of the sacrament, we promise to *remember the Lord Jesus Christ,* thereby remembering His atoning sacrifice. In this way, we are prompted to repent regularly of individual sin, which allows us to remain in the Savior's covenant grace. Without the Apostles to clarify doctrine, there was no one to redirect the Church in its desire to embellish the ordinances and sacraments pertaining to salvation.

Besides accounts furnished in the New Testament, the earliest known documents containing information regarding the sacrament of the Lord's Supper came from Justin Martyr in the mid-second century. In his First Apology, Justin wrote:

> There is brought to the president of the brethren bread and a cup of water and [a cup] of wine mixed with water, and he taking them sends up praise and glory to the Father . . . through the name of the Son and the Holy Spirit, and offers thanksgiving. . . . When he has concluded the prayers . . . all the people present assent by saying, Amen. . . . Those who are called by us deacons give to each of those present a portion of the bread and wine and water, and they carry it away to those who are absent.[122]

The simplicity expressed by Justin in A.D. 155 is similar to what is conveyed in the New Testament. Over the next several decades,

many changes would occur.

In the mid-third century, new nomenclature and additions to the ceremony were introduced. Terms such as the *Preface,* the *Sanctus,* the *Institution Narrative,* and the *Our Father* became common in the West. Surviving accounts indicate that during this period uniformity in practice among the congregations of the Church was lacking, particularly from east to west. According to Davies, the tendency throughout the Empire was to "overlay the primitive pattern with *elaborations,* consisting of prayers and litanies."[123] After the fifth century, an entrance chant was also invented.[124]

Although wording used by the earliest Christian writers was similar to New Testament accounts, such as "take, eat this is my body," later theologians would embellish biblical language and develop lengthy speculative doctrinal treatises around them. For example, Bishop John Chrysostom (354–407) wrote of *eating* Christ and insisted that the wine was identical to the blood that flowed from Jesus' side.[125] Bishop Ambrose (333–397) advanced the question "The word of Christ could make out of nothing that which was not; cannot it change the things which are into that which they are not?"[126] Ultimately, these ideologies and philosophies were canonized and accepted throughout the Church of Rome. Mosheim portrayed the problem of adopting such a literal interpretation:

> The comparison of the Christian oblation with the Jewish victim and sacrifice, produced a multitude of unnecessary rites, and was the occasion of introducing that erroneous notion of the Eucharist, which represents it as a real sacrifice, and not merely as a commemoration of that great offering that was once made upon the cross for the sins of mortals.[127]

In addition to exposing doctrinal error, Mosheim also correctly implied that the sacrament (the Lord's Supper) replaced the Jewish sacrifice. The sacrifice of Jesus was performed only once, replacing the daily sacrifices required under the Mosaic law which were intended to point men towards Christ. Accordingly, baptism was also performed *only once,* signifying that the initiate was born again and had entered into a covenant with Jesus Christ always to remember Him and to keep His commandments. A correct understanding of the purpose of the sacrament resolves the apparent dilemma recorded in Hebrews 6:4–6 regarding the problem of the sins we commit *after* baptism. God never required Israel to be perfect; He required them to keep the covenant they had made with Him and not to turn their back on Him by worshiping other gods. The performance of the daily sacrifice (and their best effort in being obedient to God's commandments) was sufficient. Similarly, the Lord's Supper was instituted to help the saints keep their baptismal covenant with God and to receive forgiveness of sins on a frequent basis. That is why the sacrament was offered to the saints weekly in the early Church, why they had to be free of serious sin, and why they took the emblems of Lord's Supper to the elderly and sick who were unable to attend.[128]

Unfortunately, the simple way in which the Church initially commemorated our Lord's sacrifice was turned into an elaborate process very different in practice *and* meaning. Davies concludes that such changes "arose both from a psychological need and from a change of circumstances. The laity came to worship and wanted that note to be sounded from the outset; they demanded and were eventually given some kind of devotional preparation to the sacrament proper."[129]

The Ordinance of Baptism Is Changed

Another modification occurred with the ordinance of baptism. The word *baptism* derives from the Greek word *baptizo,* meaning "to immerse, submerge, or to sink." The Apostle John records:

And John [the Baptist] also was baptizing in *Aenon* near to Salim, *because there was much water there:* and they came, and were baptized. (John 3:23; emphasis added)

Aenon is the Hebrew term for "spring"; thus, John was baptizing in a spring because there was "much water there," suggesting baptism by immersion. The Savior's baptism in the River Jordan, also with much water, implies that His baptism was performed by immersion. The Ethiopian eunuch was baptized in a wayside pool (Acts 8:36–39), Lydia, in a river (Acts 16:13–15), both consisting of sufficient water for immersion. The simple nature of baptism without fanfare is intimated in every New Testament example. Furthermore, the Bible indicates three purposes for baptism: (1) to fulfill all righteousness (Matthew 3:15); (2) to be "born again" in order to enter into the kingdom of God (John 3:5); (3) for the remission of sins (Acts 2:37–38). Inasmuch as baptism is for the *remission of sins,* doctrines which suggest that baptism is necessary for infants or those otherwise incapable of sin are not scripturally based.

To the Romans, Paul writes:

Know ye not, that so many of us as were baptized into Jesus Christ were baptized into his death? Therefore we are buried with him by baptism into death: that like as Christ was raised up from the dead by the glory of the Father, even so we also should walk in newness of life.

(Romans 6:3–4)

Paul was instructing the Romans not only in the proper manner of baptism but also in the symbolism associated with this sacred ordinance. According to Paul, if we have repented and complied with the Savior's command to be baptized, we are buried with Him *(figuratively)* in the water as He was buried in the tomb. When we come forth out of the water, we are cleansed of our sins, "our old man is crucified with him, that the body of sin might be destroyed," and we then press forward in "newness of life," even as the Savior died and was then resurrected (Romans 6:6, 4; see also vv. 3, 5; Colossians 2:12–13).[130]

Enhancements to the baptismal ceremony began early in the second century and multiplied as the century progressed. By the time of the Nicene Council, simplicity had been replaced by an elaborate and mystical service. Justin Martyr, writing in the mid-second century, described baptism in his day as follows:

> As many as are persuaded and believe that the things we teach and say are true, and undertake to live accordingly, are instructed to pray and ask God with fasting for the remission of their past sins, while we pray and fast with them. They are then brought by us where there is water, and are born again in the same manner of rebirth by which we ourselves were born again, for they receive washing in the water in the name of God the Father and Master of all, and of our Savior, Jesus Christ, and of the Holy Spirit. For Christ also said, "Except you are born again, you will not enter into the Kingdom of heaven." Now it is clear to all that it is impossible for those who have once come into being to enter into their mothers' wombs.[131]

Justin Martyr's account closely mirrors baptism as described in the New Testament.

No special requirements were necessary for baptism other than a change of heart and a desire to serve God. Baptism was performed on any occasion and without fanfare or elaboration. The initiate was simply taken to "where there is water" and then baptized. The only feature in Justin's commentary not mentioned in the New Testament was the practice of fasting and praying in preparation to receive the ordinance. He clarifies in his First Apology noted above (1) the qualifications for baptism: instruction, a testimony of that which has been taught, and prayer and fasting [repentance] to ask God for forgiveness of their "past sins"; (2) the proper mode of baptism: by immersion and performed in the name of the Father, Son, and Holy Spirit; and (3) the purpose of baptism: for the remission of sins, i.e., to be "born again." Justin's account, including the practice of immersion, is almost identical to Irenaeus's description some twenty years later.[132]

The Didache, or the Teaching of the Twelve Apostles, indicates that the preferred method of baptism was by immersion, "in the name of the Father and of the Son and of the Holy Spirit."[133] Further, the Didache instructs the baptizer and the baptized to fast for one or two days prior to the baptism. An allowance seems to be made if there was no "living or running water"; then the act of pouring water (aspersion) three times upon the head of the baptized in the name of the Father, Son, and Holy Spirit was acceptable.[134] While some academics believe the Didache was written in the first century, others note it may have "suffered some revision" or that its origin may be as late as the third century.[135] Nevertheless, this notable addition to New Testament practices seems to have opened the way for man to take additional license to modify the ordinance of baptism, removing the symbolism taught by Paul and exemplified by the

Savior's own baptism.

In the third century, Tertullian describes the performance of baptism in his treatise De Baptismo (On Baptism):

> There is absolutely nothing which makes men's minds more obdurate than the simplicity of the divine works which are visible in the act [of baptism], . . . that with so great simplicity, without pomp, without any considerable novelty of preparation, . . . a man is dipped in water, and amid the utterance of a few words is sprinkled and then rises again.[136]

Although Tertullian characterizes baptism in his day as "without pomp," preparations nevertheless required "repeated prayers, fasts and the bendings of the knee, and *vigils all night through.*"[137] After the water was blessed, the initiates "descended," after which they were "anointed immediately upon their ascent, and the bishop then laid his hands upon them for the reception of the Holy Spirit."[138] In spite of the fact that Tertullian's account demonstrates the basic simplicity of a century earlier, the addition of "vigils all night through" and the anointing seem to be the beginning of increasing embellishments not present in the New Testament accounts.

Tertullian resided in Carthage (in modern-day Morocco) located in the western section of the Roman Empire. Interestingly, western narratives, written in approximately the same time frame, detail greater ornamentation than their eastern counterparts. Paraphrasing Hippolytus, who lived in Rome, Davies explains:

> The preparation is to take three years and is to include instruction, prayers, and exorcisms. On the Thursday before Easter the candidates are to take a bath and are to fast on Friday and Saturday. On the final day they are brought before the bishop, who exorcizes them and breathes in their faces for the expulsion of spirits. There follows a vigil for the reading of the Scriptures and further instruction. At the cockcrow, the water is blessed, clothes are removed and there is a renunciation of "Satan, and all thy servants and all thy works," whereupon they are anointed with the Oil of Exorcism. Descending to the water, answers are given to interrogations. Before putting on their clothes, the newly baptized receive the Oil of Thanksgiving; then the bishop lays his hand upon them, consecrated oil is poured on their heads and the kiss exchanged.[139]

The method of baptism varied from east to west, from congregation to congregation, and was undergoing change. Immersion previous to the third century appears to have been the standard mode of baptism. Cyprian, bishop of Carthage in the mid-third century, endorsed sprinkling in the place of immersion in special cases of physical infirmity. Novatus, apparently near death, was the first recorded person baptized by sprinkling. Infant baptism also became common during this period, and the symbolism associated with baptism, along with one of its primary purposes, the remission of individual sins, was essentially destroyed. The criteria for baptism explained by the New Testament and Justin Martyr cannot be met by infants who cannot believe because they have not yet developed cognitive ability (Acts 2:37–38), cannot exercise faith for the same reason, and cannot confess sins because they have none. The very definition of sin presupposes knowledge (Romans 5:13; James 4:17). Additionally, no record exists of the Savior ever claiming man is responsible for Adam's sin, and no apostolic writings exist of man being held answerable for it. However, there is ample testimony of man being held accountable for his own sins—thus the need for baptism. As the scriptures declare, Christ Himself paid the penalty of Adam's sin (1 Corinthians 15:22).

Such early writings furnish evidence that indeed the ordinance of baptism had been altered. The New Testament contains no record of elaborations such as sprinkling, infant baptisms, fasting as a requirement for baptism, baptism being performed only during certain days of the year, exorcisms, and anointing with oil—specifically as related to the ordinance of baptism itself. Baptism in the early Church was performed throughout the year, with the only requirements being to obtain sufficient knowledge as to make a cognitive choice, demonstrate faith in Jesus Christ, and repent of one's sins; furthermore, the rite was to be performed by one holding genuine priesthood authority.

Initially, the Church of Rome was responsible for altering this once pure doctrine. The Reformers further clouded the doctrine of baptism when they professed that baptism was an *outward sign of an inward conversion*, teaching that profession of faith in Christ alone without the ordinance of baptism was sufficient for salvation, contrary to the recorded commandments regarding the necessity for baptism (Mark 16:16) and in spite of the great emphasis the Reformers placed on *Sola Scriptura*, or (translated) *the Bible being the sole authority for Christians*.

The Church in General Apostasy

The chaos resulting from general apostasy was enormous. Contrasting the unity of doctrine and practices evident in the early Christian Church (Acts 2:42), the Church had been in considerable turmoil for many generations. What began as divisiveness and pride escalated into corruption and grave

sin. The condition of Christianity following Nicaea was such that many honest and courageous men recognized that the Church was in general apostasy. Referring to Paul's prophecy in 2 Thessalonians 2:3–10, Cyril, bishop of Jerusalem in the mid-fourth century, wrote:

> Thus wrote Paul, and now is the falling away. For men have fallen away from the right faith; and some preach the identity of the Son with the Father, and others dare to say that Christ was brought into being out of nothing. And formerly the heretics were [plainly] manifest; but now the Church is filled with heretics in disguise. For men have fallen away from the truth, and have itching ears. . . . Most have departed from the right words, and rather choose the evil, than desire the good. This, therefore, is falling away.[140]

Theodoret, bishop of Cyrrhus, wrote of significant discord early in the fifth century:

> The storm tossing the churches has not suffered us to take our share of unalloyed gladness. If, when one member is in pain the whole body is partaker of the pang, how can we forbear from lamentation when all the body is distressed? And it intensifies our discouragement to think that these things are the prelude of the general apostasy. May your piety pray that since we are in this plight we may get the divine succor, that, as the divine Apostle phrases it, we may "be able to withstand the evil day." But if any time remain for this life's business, pray that the tempest may pass away, and the churches recover their former calm, that the enemies of the truth may no more exult at our misfortunes.[141]

Not many years later, Theodoret wrote another letter to John, the bishop of Germanicia, on the same subject:

Immediately on receipt of your holiness's former letter I replied. About the present state of affairs, it is impossible to entertain any good hope. I apprehend that this is the beginning of the general apostasy. For when we see that those who lament what was done as they say, by violence, at Ephesus, show no signs of repentance, but abide by their unlawful deeds and are building up a superstructure at once of injustice and of impiety; when we see that the rest take no concerted action to deny their deeds and do not refuse to hold communion with men who abide by their unlawful action, what hope of good is it possible for us to entertain?[142]

Gregory of Nyssa also wrote of the great problem of doctrinal speculation and apostasy:

In speculative inquiry fallacies readily find place. But where speculation is entirely at rest, the necessity of error is precluded. And that this is a true account of the case, may be seen if we consider how it is that heresies in the churches have wandered off into many and various opinions in regard to God, men deceiving themselves as they are swayed by one mental impulse or another; and how these very men with whom our treatise is concerned have slipped into such a pit of profanity.[143]

The eastern churches were under no less strain. Basil, bishop of Caesarea in A.D. 370, recorded that the "conflagration which has devoured a great part of the East is already advancing by slow degrees into our own neighborhood."[144] In addition, when the fame of the righteous bishop Barsus of Edessa reached the emperor Valens, he banished him to Egypt, "depriving the flock of their shepherd" and placing "in his stead a wolf."[145] Basil addressed the exiled bishop, praying that "the Mighty One" would "restore us to the peace of the beginning—unless indeed the apostasy is nigh at hand, and the events that have lately happened are the beginnings of the approach of Antichrist."[146]

John had already testified that "even now there are many antichrists" (1 John 2:18), and although it appears the Church had been without priesthood authority since the middle of the second century, it was only now, in a day of general apostasy, that this condition began to be evident to many.

Conclusion

The achievements of man are self-evident and of little worth compared to the divine works of God, illustrated by the manner in which man placed his imprint on the pure work of Christ. Councils and creeds replaced divinely appointed authority, and scholarship replaced revelation, resulting in man's understanding of the true nature of God being modified and mystified. The sacrament of the Lord's Supper became a literal and daily sacrifice rather than a commemoration of the one and only sacrifice offered as an atonement for the sins of humankind. The essential ordinance of baptism was changed as Church leaders altered the inspired method taught by John the Baptist and Jesus, removing its sacred symbolism and meaning. Centuries later, the Reformers would pronounce baptism unnecessary for salvation. The words of the prophet Isaiah had been fulfilled: "They have transgressed the laws, changed the ordinance, broken the everlasting covenant" (Isaiah 24:5).

Notes
1. Eusebius, Ecclesiastical History 3.32, 118.
2. Shepherd of Hermas, vis. 2:2, in *Apostolic Fathers,* 2:19.

3. Eusebius, Ecclesiastical History 4.22, 157; emphasis added; brackets in original.

4. Eusebius, Ecclesiastical History 4.7, 132.

5. Quote in Eusebius, Ecclesiastical History 4.7, 133.

6. Johann Lorenz Mosheim, *An Ecclesiastical History, Ancient and Modern, from the Birth of Christ to the Beginning of the Eighteenth Century* (West Jordan, Utah: n.p., 1980), Cent. 1, part 2; ch. 3:11.

7. Introductory note on Justin Martyr, *Ante Nicene Fathers*, 1:159–61.

8. Grant, *Irenaeus of Lyons*, 2.

9. Grant, *Irenaeus of Lyons*, 3.

10. Chadwick, *Early Church*, 92.

11. Chadwick, *Early Church*, 53.

12. Cheetham, *Keepers of the Keys*, 13; Glenn E. Hinson, *The Church Triumphant: A History of Christianity up to 1300* (Macon, Ga.: Mercer University Press, 1995), 144; see also Eusebius, Ecclesiastical History 6.22, 242–43, for information about Hippolytus' various works.

13. Introductory Notice to Hippolytus, in *Ante-Nicene Fathers*, 5:7.

14. *Ante-Nicene Fathers*, 5:5.

15. Chadwick, *Early Church*, 95.

16. Chadwick, *Early Church*, 95–96.

17. "Few authors were as fertile as Origen. St. Epiphanius estimates at six thousand the number of his writings, counting separately, without doubt, the different books of a single work, his homilies, letters, and his smallest treatises. . . . This figure, repeated by many ecclesiastical writers, seems greatly exaggerated. St. Jerome asssures us that the list of Origen's writings drawn up by St. Pamphilus did not contain even two thousand titles . . . ; but this list was evidently incomplete. Eusebius . . . had inserted it in his biography of St. Pamphilus, and St. Jerome inserted it in a letter to Paula" (*The Catholic Encyclopedia*, vol. 11 [New York: Robert Appleton Co., 1911]).

18. Homily on Jeremiah 4:3, in Joseph Trigg, *Origen* (New York: Routledge, 1998), 5.

19. Trigg, *Origen*, 9, 12, 14.

20. Trigg, *Origen*, 14; Eusebius, Ecclesiastical History 6.8, 226–27; see also Chadwick, *Early Church*, 109. On Origen's ascetic habits see Eusebius, Ecclesiastical History 6.3, 222.

21. Origen, De Principiis 1.1–3, in *Ante-Nicene Fathers*, 4:242–56.

22. Origen, De Principiis 2.8.3, in *Ante-Nicene Fathers*, 4:287–88; see also Trigg, *Origen*, 16; and Chadwick, *Early Church*, 107.

23. Chadwick, *Early Church*, 101.

24. Eusebius, Ecclesiastical History 8.1, 318.

25. History of Sozomen, ch. 3, in *Nicene and Post-Nicene Fathers*, 2:2:241–42.

26. Cheetham, *Keepers of the Keys*, 21.

27. Exodus 20:3; 2 Kings 19:15; Isaiah 37:16; 43:11; 44:6–9. The recurring theme of "one God" has more to do with Israel's perpetual disobedience as demonstrated by rebellion and the worship of idols and false gods. If we are the children of God by birth (Acts 17:29; Hebrew 12:9) and by adoption (Romans 8:16), and if Jesus is the firstborn spirit of the Father (Colossians 1:15), thus making Jesus our Elder Brother as well as God the Son; if God delegated His authority to Jesus and crowned Him God before the world was (1 Peter 1:20), all of which scripture verifies, then there is no need to integrate false Jewish tradition into the pure theology introduced by Jesus and the Apostles.

28. Epistle of Ignatius to the Trallians 6, in *Ante-Nicene Fathers*, 1:68; emphasis added.

29. *The Trinitarian Controversy*, trans. and ed. William G. Rusch (Philadelphia: Fortress Press, 1980), 2.

30. *Trinitarian Controversy*, 3.

31. Origen expressed his early third-century viewpoint of this passage: "And thus the first-born of all creation, who is the first to be with God, and to attract to Himself divinity, is a being of more exalted rank than the other gods beside Him, of whom God is the God, as it is written, 'The God of gods, the Lord, hath spoken and called the earth.' It was by the offices of the first-born that they became gods, for He drew from God in generous measure that they should be made gods, and He communicated it to them according to His own bounty. The true God, then, is 'The God,' and those who are formed after Him are gods, images, as it were, of Him the prototype. . . . Now it is possible that some may dislike what we have said representing the Father as the one true God, but admitting other beings besides

the true God, who have become gods by having a share of God. They may fear that the glory of Him who surpasses all creation may be lowered to the level of those other beings called gods. We drew this distinction between Him and them that we showed God the Word to be to all the other gods the minister of their divinity. . . . As then, there are many gods, but to us there is but one God the Father, and many Lords, but to us there is one Lord, Jesus Christ." Origen, Commentary on the Gospel of John 2:2–3, in *Ante-Nicene Fathers*, 9:323–24.

32. Justin, Dialogue with Trypho 128, in *Ante-Nicene Fathers*, 1:264.

33. Justin, Dialogue with Trypho 129, in *Ante-Nicene Fathers*, 1:264.

34. Justin, Dialogue with Trypho 82, in *Ante-Nicene Fathers*, 1:240.

35. It seems odd that Church leaders would have accepted as genuine or authoritative interpretations from those not possessing the "keys" of apostolic priesthood authority, as was the case with Moses, Joshua, and Peter; see 1 Corinthians 4:1; Amos 3:7; Numbers 12:6; 2 Timothy 3:4; 2 Peter 3:2.

36. A. Kenneth Curtis, J. Stephen Lang, and Randy Petersen, *The 100 Most Important Events in Christian History* (Grand Rapids, Mich.: Revell, 1998), 24; cf. Chadwick, *Early Christian Church*, 89–90.

37. Tertullian, On the Resurrection of the Flesh 51, in *Ante-Nicene Fathers*, 3:584.

38. Tertullian, Against Praxeas 2, in *Ante-Nicene Fathers*, 3:598.

39. Origen, On Prayer 15.1; Against Celsus 8.12, in *Ante-Nicene Fathers*, 4:643.

40. Origen, Against Celsus 5.39, in *Ante-Nicene Fathers*, 4:561.

41. Origen, Fragment 37 on the Gospel of St. John, in *Trinitarian Controversy*, 15.

42. William Rusch concludes that one should not assume that Origen "teaches a triad of disparate beings rather than a Trinity." He acknowledges, however, that Origen "draws upon his Platonic and Philonic philosophy," and then by this, he interprets Origen's conclusion, stating, "It is possible to see how he is holding to a genuine trinitarianism" (14–15). Unfortunately, there is little evidence to reach an emphatic or empirical determination. Instead, this passage by Origen seems to explain not only the Son's relationship to His Father, but also to us. Origen recorded: "Now it is possible that some may dislike what we have said representing the Father as the one true God, but admitting other beings besides the true God, who have become gods by having a share of God. . . . We drew this distinction between Him and them that we showed God the Word to be to all the other gods the minister of their divinity, . . . but to us there is but one God the Father, and many Lords, but to us there is one Lord, Jesus Christ." Commentary on John 2.3, in *Ante-Nicene Fathers*, 9:323–24. Origen's language in this commentary harmonizes perfectly with Paul, who taught that the faithful shall be "heirs of God, and joint-heirs with Christ" (Romans 8:16). Just as Christ has already partaken of God's divinity and is God's heir, so shall we, if faithful, be heirs of God, and partakers of His divinity, and joint heirs with Jesus Christ who, according to Origen, will be the minister of our divinity. But we shall still worship one God, the Father of all, and one Lord, even Jesus, who has redeemed us from our sins. We should always remember how God in the Old Testament operated, when through His prophets he declared, "Thus saith the Lord." Such heavenly statements eliminate the kind of confusion under discussion.

43. Chadwick, *Early Church*, 85–86.

44. Chadwick, *Early Church*, 87.

45. Arius' Letter to Eusebius of Nicomedia, in Rusch, *Trinitarian Controversy*, 30.

46. Socrates, Ecclesiastical History 5, in *Nicene and Post-Nicene Fathers*, 2:2:3.

47. Arius and Euzoius, Letter of the Presbyter Arius and Euzoius to the Emperor Constantine, in Rusch, *Trinitarian Controversy*, 61.

48. Rusch, *Trinitarian Controversy*, 18.

49. Kelly, *Early Christian Doctrines*, 247–48; Rusch, *Trinitarian Controversy*, 19.

50. Chadwick, *Early Church*, 130.

51. Rusch, *Trinitarian Controversy*, 19–20.

52. Jacquin, *Histoire de l'Eglise*, 1:664.

53. E. Royston Pike, *Encyclopedia of Religion and Religions* (New York: Meridian, 1958), 29.

54. See Grimm, *Thayer's Greek-English*

Lexicon, ref. no. 1085, 13, and *Strong's Exhaustive Concordance*, ref. no. 1085, 1487.

55. Grimm, *Thayer's Greek-English Lexicon*, ref. no. 5207, 5206, 634; *Strong's*, ref. 5207, 5206, 1538.

56. Grimm, *Thayer's Greek-English Lexicon*, ref. no. 5043, offspring to be regarded as true, genuine children, 617—derived from ref. no. 5088, to bring forth, bear, produce (fruit from seed) of women giving birth, 623. *Strong's Exhaustive Concordance*, ref. no. 5043, child, offspring, descendent—derived from ref. no. 5088, to give birth, delivered, born, 1536–57.

57. John 8:37–44, 58; emphasis and interpretation added. In this verse, Jesus testifies of His premortal existent nature and status as the firstborn of the Father. He was the God of Abraham, Isaac, and Jacob, and He was Moses' lawgiver. Justin Martyr testified that Jesus Christ, appearing in human form, was the God of the Old Testament. See Dialogue with Trypho 56, 59, 61, 75, 113, 126, and 127, in *Ante-Nicene Fathers*, 1:223–24, 227–28, 236, 256, 262–63, 263).

58. *Strong's Exhaustive Concordance*, ref. no. 3962, 1522; Grimm, *Thayer's Greek-English Lexicon*, 494.

59. Schaff, *History of the Christian Church*, 2:225; see also Eberhard Arnold, *The Early Christians: Selected and Edited from All the Sources of the First Centuries*, trans. and ed. Society of Brothers at Rifton, N.Y. (Grand Rapids, Mich.: Baker Book House, 1979), 10.

60. Justin Martyr wrote: "But if the word of God foretells that some angels and men shall be certainly punished, it did so because it foreknew that they would be unchangeably [wicked], but not because God had created them so." Justin, Dialogue with Trypho 141, in *Ante-Nicene Fathers*, 1:270; emphasis added; see ch. 2 herein, note 22.

61. Justin, Dialogue with Trypho 44, in *Ante-Nicene Fathers*, 1:216–17; emphasis added.

62. David W. Bercot, *Will the Real Heretics Please Stand Up: A New Look at Today's Evangelical Church in the Light of Early Christianity*, 3d ed. (Henderson, Texas: Scroll, 1999), 75.

63. Clark H. Pinnock, *Most Moved Mover: A Theology of God's Openness* (Grand Rapids, Mich.: Baker Academic, 2001), 100.

64. Apostles' Creed: "I believe in God the Father Almighty, Creator of Heaven and earth; and in Jesus Christ, His only Son, our Lord; who was conceived by the Holy Ghost, born of the Virgin Mary, suffered under Pontius Pilate, was crucified, died, and was buried; He descended into hell; the third day he rose again from the dead; he ascended into Heaven, sitteth at the right hand of God, the Father Almighty; From thence he shall come to judge the living and the dead; I believe in the Holy Ghost, the Holy Catholic Church, the communion of saints, the forgiveness of sins, the resurrection of the body, and Life everlasting."

65. Athanasian Creed: "We worship one God in Trinity, and Trinity in Unity, neither confounding the persons, nor dividing the substance. For there is one person of the Father, another of the Son, and another of the Holy Ghost. But the Godhead of the Father, Son, and Holy Ghost, is all one: the glory equal, the majesty co-eternal. Such as the Father is, such is the Son; and such is the Holy Ghost. The Father uncreate, the Son uncreate, and the Holy Ghost uncreate. The Father incomprehensible, the Son incomprehensible and the Holy Ghost incomprehensible. The Father eternal, the Son eternal, and the Holy Ghost eternal. And yet there are not three eternals; but one eternal. As also there are not three incomprehensibles, nor three uncreated; but one uncreated, and one incomprehensible. So likewise the Father is Almighty, the Son Almighty, and the Holy Ghost Almighty; and yet there are not three Almighties, but one Almighty. So the Father is God, the Son is God, and the Holy Ghost is God, and yet they are not three Gods but one God."

66. Ignatius, Epistle to the Trallians 6, in *Ante-Nicene Fathers*, 1:68; emphasis added.

67. Peter, in Clementine Recognitions 2.48, in *Ante-Nicene Fathers*, 8:110.

68. Justin, Dialogue with Trypho 56, in *Ante-Nicene Fathers*, 1:223.

69. Justin, Dialogue with Trypho 59, in *Ante-Nicene Fathers*, 1:226–27.

70. Justin, Dialogue with Trypho 61, in *Ante-Nicene Fathers*, 1:227.

71. Justin, Dialogue with Trypho 75, in *Ante-Nicene Fathers*, 1:236.

72. Ignatius, Epistle to the Smyrnaeans 3, in

Ante-Nicene Fathers, 1:87; emphasis added.

73. John 15:26; 16:13–16.

74. Hebrews 7:25; 1 Timothy 2:5.

75. "When he, the Spirit of truth is come, he will guide you into all truth: for he shall not speak of himself; but whatsoever he shall hear, that shall he speak" (John 16:13; emphasis added; see also Nehemiah 9:20; Mark 13:11; Luke 12:12; John 14:26; 15:26.

76. Hippolytus, Against the Heresy of One Noetus 14, in *Ante-Nicene Fathers,* 5:228.

77. Craig L. Blomberg and Stephen E. Robinson, *How Wide the Divide: A Mormon and an Evangelical in Conversation* (Downers Grove, Ill.: InterVarsity Press, 1997), 83.

78. John 20:17; Acts 17:29; Romans 8:16; Hebrews 12:9.

79. John 5:19–20, 30; 17:1–26.

80. Deuteronomy 15:19–21; Hebrews 10:1–17.

81. Ignatius, Epistle to the Smyrnaeans 8, in *Ante-Nicene Fathers,* 1:89; emphasis added.

82. Secrets of Enoch 65, in Platt, *Forgotten Books of Eden,* 103.

83. Justin, Dialogue with Trypho 67, in *Ante-Nicene Fathers,* 1:229; emphasis added; brackets in original.

84. Hippolytus, Against the Heresy of One Noetus 7, in *Ante-Nicene Fathers,* 5:226.

85. Clementine Homilies 16.19, in *Ante-Nicene Fathers,* 8:316.

86. Clementine Homilies 17.7, in *Ante-Nicene Fathers,* 8:319–20.

87. John 4:24; Colossians 1:15.

88. Alon Goshen Gottstein, "The Body as Image of God in Rabbinic Literature," *Harvard Theological Review* 87 (1994): 172; see also Arthur Marmorstein, *The Old Rabbinic Doctrine of God,* 3 vols. (New York: Ktav, 1968), in David Paulson, "The Doctrine of Divine Embodiment," in *Early Christians in Disarray* (Provo, Utah: Brigham Young University Press, 2005), 250.

89. Harry Austryn Wolfson, *Philo: Foundations of Religious Philosophy in Judaism, Christianity, and Islam,* 2 vols. (Cambridge: Harvard University Press, 1948), 1:72

90. Origen, De Principiis, Preface 9, in *Ante-Nicene Fathers,* 4:241.

91. Origen, De Principiis, Preface 5, in *Ante-*

Nicene Fathers, 4:240.

92. Origen, De Principiis, Preface 7, in *Ante-Nicene Fathers,* 4:240–41.

93. See Gedaliahu Strousma, "The Incorporeality of God: Context and Implications of Origen's Position," *Religion* 13 (1983), 345–58; see also Jantzen, in Paulson, "The Doctrine of Divine Embodiment," in *Early Christians in Disarray,* 259.

94. Pinnock, *Most Moved Mover,* 33–34.

95. 1 Enoch 46:1–4, in Charlesworth, *Old Testament Pseudepigrapha,* 1:34.

96. Ehrman, *Orthodox Corruption of Scripture,* 27.

97. Ehrman, *Orthodox Corruption of Scripture,* 27.

98. Ehrman, *Orthodox Corruption of Scripture,* 27.

99. Henri Daniel-Rops, *L'eglise des ap otres et des martyrs* (Paris: A Fayard, 1949), 313.

100. Justin, Dialogue with Trypho 72–73, in *Ante-Nicene Fathers,* 1:234–35.

101. Dionysus, To the Roman Church 4, in *Ante-Nicene Fathers,* 8:765.

102. Ehrman, *Orthodox Corruption of Scripture,* 4.

103. Ehrman, *Orthodox Corruption of Scripture,* 7.

104. Ehrman, *Orthodox Corruption of Scripture,* 8.

105. Ehrman, *Orthodox Corruption of Scripture,* 12.

106. Ehrman, *Orthodox Corruption of Scripture,* 15.

107. Ehrman, *Orthodox Corruption of Scripture,* 18.

108. Ehrman, *Orthodox Corruption of Scripture,* 23–24.

109. Ehrman, *Orthodox Corruption of Scripture,* 25.

110. Ehrman, *Orthodox Corruption of Scripture,* 275, 278.

111. Metzger, *Text of the New Testament,* 186–206.

112. Floyd V. Filson, *Which Books Belong in the Bible?* (Philadelphia: Westminster Press, 1957), 20–21.

113. Metzger, *Canon of the New Testament,* 113.

114. Campenhausen, in Metzger, *Canon of the New Testament,* 104.

115. Justin, Dialogue with Trypho 82, in

Ante-Nicene Fathers, 1:240.

116. Metzger, *Canon of the New Testament,* 287–88.

117. Irenaeus wrote: "For it is unlawful to assert that they preached before they possessed 'perfect knowledge,' as some do even venture to say, boasting themselves as improvers of the apostles" ("Against Heresies" 3.1, in *Ante-Nicene Fathers,* 1:414; Tertullian said, "Since the Lord Jesus Christ sent his apostles to preach, (our rule is) that no others ought to be received as preachers than those whom Christ appointed" ("Prescription against Heresies" 21, in *Ante-Nicene Fathers,* 3:252). Both of these men were striving to protect the Church against the rise of Gnosticism and escalating apostasy. Although Irenaeus and Tertullian were both wonderful men, the Church, as established by Christ, had already passed away before the middle of the second century. This is attested to by the Apostle John and the Shepherd of Hermas. Of note, even though apostasy was already rampant in the Church during the time of John the Revelator, Clement of Rome, and Ignatius of Antioch (as each of their epistles and letters witness), none of these gospel writers echo the later claims of Irenaeus and Tertullian. Instead, they spoke of rising apostasy; and John and Ignatius both intimated that the Church was already on the way out; see ch. 5 herein.

118. Tertullian, "Prescription against Heresies" 7, in *Ante-Nicene Fathers,* 3:246.

119. Earle Edwin Cairns, *Christianity through the Centuries: A History of the Christian Church,* rev. and enlarged 2d ed. (Grand Rapids, Mich.: Zondervan, 1981), 108; emphasis added.

120. Clement of Rome, First Epistle to the Corinthians 25–26, in *Apostolic Fathers,* 1:53–54.

121. Epistle of Barnabas 2:10, in *Ancient Christian Writers,* 39; cf. Psalm 34:18; 51:17.

122. Justin, First Apology, in *Ancient Christian Writers,* 58, ch. 65, 70.

123. Davies, *Early Christian Church,* 266.

124. Davies, *Early Christian Church,* 266.

125. Davies, *Early Christian Church,* 268.

126. Davies, *Early Christian Church,* 268.

127. Mosheim, *Ecclesiastical History,* Cent. II, Part II, ch. 4:4.

128. Justin Martyr, First Apology 65–66, in *Ancient Christian Writers* 56, 70–71. Henry Chadwick has written, "To share in this sacred meal was so deeply felt to be the essential expression of membership of the society that fragments of the broken bread were taken round to any who were absent through illness or imprisonment. A serious moral fault entailed exclusion from sharing in the meal," in Chadwick, *Early Church,* 32.

129. Davies, *Early Christian Church,* 267.

130. Chadwick confirms this early interpretation: "The rite of baptism by which they were admitted to the Church was both a commemoration of the moment at the river Jordan . . . , and . . . a powerful metaphor described as being 'buried with Christ,'" in Chadwick, *Early Church,* 32.

131. Justin Martyr, First Apology 61, in *Ancient Christian Writers,* 56, 66–67.

132. Apuleius, Metamorph, 11.4.

133. Didache, in *Ancient Christian Writers* 6, 19.

134. Didache, in *Ancient Christian Writers* 6, 19.

135. Didache, in *Ancient Christian Writers* 6, 4. Henry Chadwick dates the Didache as late first century but suspects revisions. See Chadwick, *Early Church,* 47.

136. Tertullian, On Baptism 2, in *Ante-Nicene Fathers,* 3:668.

137. Tertullian, On Baptism 20, in *Ante-Nicene Fathers,* 3:678–79.

138. Davies, *Early Christian Church,* 103.

139. Davies, *Early Christian Church,* 148.

140. Cyril of Jerusalem, Catechetical Lectures 15.9, in *Nicene and Post-Nicene Fathers,* 2:7:107–8.

141. Theodoret, in *Nicene and Post-Nicene Fathers,* 2:3:268–69.

142. Theodoret, in *Nicene and Post-Nicene Fathers,* 2:3:323.

143. Gregory of Nyssa, Against Eunomius, in *Nicene and Post-Nicene Fathers,* 2:5.

144. Basil of Caesarea, To the People of Chalcis, Letter 222, in *Nicene and Post-Nicene Fathers,* 2:8:261.

145. Theodoret 14–15, in *Nicene and Post-Nicene Fathers,* 2:3:117.

146. Basil, To Barsus, Bishop of Edessa, in Exile, Letter 264, in *Nicene and Post-Nicene Fathers,* 2:8:303.

CHAPTER SEVEN

THE CHURCH OF THE MIDDLE AGES: AN ERA OF DIVIDED FRUITS

Ye shall know them by their fruits. . . . A good tree cannot bring forth
evil fruit, neither can a corrupt tree bring forth good fruit.
Wherefore by their fruits ye shall know them.

—Matthew 7:16–20

After the death of the Apostles, the Church began to argue about the meaning of primary doctrinal points. Understandably, without the central leadership of the Apostles, the Church soon began to fracture. The writings of the early Apostolic Fathers did not focus on providing an official and systematic explanation of Church doctrine; instead, they centered on sustaining those called of God, by prophecy, and by the laying on of the hands of the presbytery. For example, Clement of Rome warned the Corinthian Church to avoid sedition, envy, and strife and to "be subject to the presbyters." He called upon these saints to repent, follow the example of Christ, develop faith, and perform good works. Similarly, Igna-tius repeatedly admonished Church members (as did Paul in Hebrews 13:17) to follow the counsel of the bishop, seek unity in Christ, beware of false teachers, meet together often to hear the word of God, develop faith in the Savior, and be examples of His love. Sadly, the early saints and leaders in general, analogous to Israel, did not follow this counsel.

Although the Apologists and Polemicists were good and honorable men, their writings show a tendency to become progressively *less* inspired and more speculative. The Christian group considering itself *orthodox* began to build a stronger base of support, contending for the faith through Apologetic and Polemical treatises. The Christological controversy had shaken the Church to its very foundations; thus, even before the Roman emperors exerted their powerful influence on the Church, the highest ranks of ecclesiastical leadership were divided and filled with contention. The early records indicate that the influence of the Holy Ghost, so crucial to the success of the primitive Church, was lost. With the ascension of Constantine to the imperial throne, a new phenomenon was introduced into the Church known as Caesaropapism, a term referring to the control wielded by emperors and kings over the pope. Thus, in addition to the alteration of important salvation doctrines and sacraments, such as the proper mode and purpose of baptism, the corrupt practices of simony (the sale of Church leadership positions) and nepotism (promoting family members to high-ranking positions) began to raise their ugly twin heads. The Christological doctrines were politicized, negotiated, and decided in this uninspired setting.

Christianity during the Middle Ages

The fall of the Roman Empire, occasioned by the invasions and conquest by the northern barbarians, wrought in civilization a decline in human progress. Before 410, when Rome was first sacked by the West Goths, and before 455, when even greater humiliation was inflicted by the Vandals, prosperity prevailed throughout much of the Empire. Excellent road systems and effective communication methods were conducive to trade; large estates speckled the Italian landscape and surrounding provinces, particularly around the Mediterranean; even the poor enjoyed adequate living standards, furnished in part by government food programs and the opportunity to view public games.[1]

One of the positive developments that

came from these nomadic incursions was the conversion of the Goths and other Germanic peoples to the Arian form of Christianity. They received not only a knowledge of Christ's atonement but also a written language prompted by the determination to translate the Bible into the Gothic language. However, in addition to tragic loss of life, one of the obvious negative consequences of war was the disruption of trade and commerce, resulting in a dramatic decline in living standards, which in turn put an end to education for the masses. In a spiraling effect, the lack of education produced ignorance, which in turn prevented the genius necessary for economic recovery. Ignorance also produced societies that embraced superstition, and the Church was not spared in this development which, along with the rest of the western world, accepted as truth a multitude of falsehoods. In spite of this notable decline, it would be a mistake—in view of modern scholarship—to continue characterizing the Middle Ages as *dark*.[2]

This chapter does *not* detail a chronology of the nearly one thousand years beginning with the fall of Rome until the Renaissance; rather, it demonstrates that Christianity in its pure form no longer existed on the earth much beyond the first century. *Careful emphasis is made here to distinguish the behavior of the Church of the Middle Ages from the modern Catholic Church.* Moreover, it is not my aim simply to point out obvious behavioral flaws to the exclusion of noteworthy achievements that are just as apparent. However, owing to space considerations, our discussion of this period will be limited mainly to investigation of various aspects of apostasy rather than a balanced historical perspective. Accordingly, seven fundamental manifestations of apostasy that existed during this age will be explored: (1) military force was used to evangelize, purge nations of non-Catholic belief, and conduct *holy wars;* (2) simony and nepotism replaced divinely appointed ecclesiastical responsibility; (3) the "gifts of the Spirit" so evident in the New Testament Church were lost (1 Corinthians 12:1–11); (4) the partnership ultimately forged between church and state opposed the teachings of scripture; (5) substantial modifications were made to the churchly organization and priesthood structure established by Jesus; (6) corruption of existing doctrines and the development of speculative theology, unfounded in sacred writings, increased, (7) the papacy thrust censure upon itself.

The absence of divine light, resulting from apostasy, ushered the world into an age of spiritual bewilderment.

Military Force Used to Quell Theological Differences

A striking corollary exists between Israel during the time of the Savior and Christianity after the death of the Apostles. Jewish leaders in the meridian of time were convinced that Israel was striving to follow God and sincerely believed that Jesus had profaned time-honored notions about their God and Judaism's relationship with Him. When Stephen was stoned for what the Jews interpreted as blasphemy (Acts 7:54–60), Jewish leaders may not have been murderers any more than was Pope Innocent III (see page 201) in his determination to exterminate the "heretical" Albigenses during the Crusades. Both parties were wrong yet did what each believed was right.

However, the Savior never authorized such methods as brutality or compulsion in proclaiming the gospel, nor did the Apostles. In fact, the earliest Christians believed that *free will* was an essential element in man's

redemption—neither the Jews, represented by the Sanhedrin, nor the Christians, represented by the papacy, had any God-given right to demand or compel obedience from others. Both were in apostasy from truth as it had been revealed in its pure form.

Numerous examples of coercion or military force can be substantiated during the Middle Ages. Beginning with the Donatists in the fourth century, continuing with the Crusades in the eleventh century onward, and ending when the activities of the Inquisition ceased in the eighteenth century, physical force was used to compel people to comply with the orthodox beliefs of the Universal Church. Although past historians have not always painted an accurate portrait of these events, each of these conflicts did in fact involve the unnecessary loss of many thousands of lives and opposed the teachings and pattern of peace established by Jesus.

The Donatists

Donatism was founded in the early fourth century on the premise that those serving in the priesthood must be holy men who followed the patterns of right living established by the Apostles. With Bishop Cyprian (ca. 250), they held that the validity of baptism and the other sacraments of the Church were conditional upon the worthiness of the minister.[3] They further claimed that the Church had ceased to be holy and thus had forfeited its assertion of being the body (congregation) of Christ when it permitted unworthy bishops to continue in office.[4] The Donatist conflict arose over those who remained valiant while facing intense persecution under the Roman emperor Diocletian and those suspected of renouncing their Christian views during the same period. This schism, ultimately lasting more than four hundred years, divided the

African Church and was the cause of much bitterness and bloodshed.

While Augustine opposed the use of force early in his career as bishop, he changed his thinking when the Church began gaining new converts because of pressure from the civil government and when his fellow bishops pressured him to go along with this direction. In January 412, the emperor Honorius formally condemned Donatism and levied fines against its supporters according to social class. He confiscated property and exiled the Donatist clergy. Augustine approved of compulsion as a means of building the Church from this point on.

Seeking scriptural justification for this new position, Augustine referred the parable of the marriage supper, wherein Christ had said, "Compel them to come in" (Luke 14:23). However, the historical context of this passage does not support Augustine's interpretation. In Jesus' day, marriage invitations would already have been delivered and accepted. On the day of such an event, a servant would have been sent to remind the guests of the wedding. According to the Savior's parable, covenant Israel (the invited guest) rejected Christ's request to attend. The invitation was then extended to the Gentiles, who were described as the poor, maimed, halt, and blind. Still later, even the pagans beyond the walls and strangers in the gates of the holy city would be bidden to the feast. Not expecting such an invitation, they would naturally hesitate until, by gentle urging and genuine assurance that they were sincerely included among those bidden, they would then feel *compelled or constrained* to come. Clearly, the notion of driving people into the wedding feast like cattle would never have entered Christ's mind nor His teachings. The possibility of discourteous late guests, who were once invited but attended first to other matters they viewed

as more important, is indicated in the Lord's closing words, "For I say unto you, that none of those men which were bidden shall taste of my supper."[5] Understanding the parable of the marriage feast reveals that Augustine's rationalization for compelling men's souls is false and that robbing man of his free will is foreign to the true doctrine of Christ. Augustine had difficulty deciding whether compelled converts were fully justified when they returned to the "orthodox" fold; he left the problem of sincerity and honesty to God.[6] Coercion thus entered into Christianity and became the rule of the faith for more than twelve hundred years.

The Crusades

The Crusades were first organized by Pope Urban II in 1095. Initially established in response to the conquest of Syria and Palestine by the Muslim Seljuks and the concern of western Christians in losing the Holy Lands to "infidels," later crusades expanded to include forced conversions, territorial expansion, and, sadly, the looting and plundering of conquered areas.

Although the aim of the Church was voluntary conversion, a "programme of conversion" in the eyes of the papal hierarchy presupposed territorial expansion. In fact, a leading expert has suggested that during the late Middle Ages the spread of Christianity was *more* about territorial expansion than the actual conversion of the mind.[7]

Although initiated by the popes, the Crusades became exceedingly popular with the people, who, unfortunately, included the Teutonic knights, who reveled more in war and spoils than in expanding the borders of Christianity.[8] Historians chronicle seven crusades of varying length between 1095 and 1271. The original goals of checking the advance of Islam and repairing relations with Constantinople (the eastern Church) proved miserable failures.

In 1208, Pope Innocent III ordered a crusade against the Albigenses (Cathari), a religious group in Southern France that intermingled Gnosticism with Christianity. The Cathars had organized their own priesthood, settled many of the doctrinal dilemmas creating tension in the Church, and advocated a life of greater simplicity and privation. According to Swanson, they rejected "an institutionalized church which appeared incapable of living according to its own precepts."[9]

To their credit, the Catholic Church initially attempted to reconvert the Cathars through peaceful methods; however, when one of the pope's representatives was murdered, military might replaced diplomacy. Working hand in hand with the Inquisition, the crusaders, under the direction of Innocent III, determined to stamp out what they considered a dangerous heresy. In a decisive battle fought at Muret in 1213, the Cathari were crushed by the invading papal armies. Another full-scale offensive was conducted in 1226. Lasting nearly twenty years, these military incursions were the cause of much bloodshed. Notwithstanding the pope's crusade, the Inquisition, and the work of aggressive preaching missions, small groups of Cathars survived in localized areas and were hunted by the Church as late as the fourteenth century.

The Church's decision to use such means as the Crusades to spread Christianity, to stop the advance of Islam, and to destroy heretical strains of belief was not necessarily an indictment against itself nor of civilization during the Middle Ages. Despite their failure, and although such methods seem barbaric by today's standard, they were, given the Church's view of its mission, understand-

able—especially in the context of the period under discussion. What the Crusades clearly did demonstrate is that the guiding principles of Christianity had changed. There can be little doubt of the Church's *original* doctrine of free agency. Had the Church of the Middle Ages not been in apostasy, it would have remained true to its founding precepts, radiating like a beacon from a lighthouse established upon the rock of living prophets and Apostles, and upon the cornerstone, Jesus Christ. Sadly, this was not the case.

The Inquisition

In addition to the Crusades, which were used as full-scale measures, the Inquisition was the instrument used to crush isolated heresy and later the Protestant reform movement. Ironically, the reactions of the Church to opposing ideology demonstrated a certain level of insecurity. Although Catholicism in the late Middle Ages had become a dominant force in the world, it was still surrounded by enemies, was still defining its doctrine, and was still uncertain of the timing of the Second Coming. Accordingly, in the Church's zeal to maintain a unified Church as instructed by Christ, without revelation from heaven it departed from the original teachings of its founder. The Inquisition especially focused on men of thought and reason who differed with the theology or practices of the Church and who gathered followers after them, the earliest Reformers receiving the harshest penalties.

The impact of the Inquisition depended on the local support of government officials. For example, in many provinces, secular leaders denied its admission into their territories. In other areas, limited resources strained its ability to achieve widespread effectiveness. However, in nation states such as Spain, with the full support of powerful rulers, the Inquisition had devastating results. Thousands were executed and tens of thousands exiled, specifically Jews and Moorish Muslims. So successful was the Spanish Inquisition that Spain had little difficulty maintaining Catholic orthodoxy as late as the eighteenth century.

In the mid-sixteenth century, the Holy Office was established for the express purpose of maintaining the orthodoxy of the writings of Catholic theologians and high Churchmen. In the beginning, the activities of the Roman Inquisition were somewhat restrained; however, in 1555 Pope Paul IV initiated an intense pursuit of those suspected of heresy. He demanded that a list of offensive books be produced and then authorized the printing of a work entitled the *Index of Forbidden Books*. Although later popes tempered the zeal of the Roman Inquisition, they began to see it as the customary instrument of papal government for regulating Church order and doctrinal orthodoxy. In this way, they behaved in the same manner as some of the early Roman emperors, such as Diocletian, who in A.D. 303 had mandated the destruction of all Christian books and writings.

Unfortunately, most people today still have a distorted understanding of the Inquisition, its role, and the force with which it was normally administered. Henry Kaman and others have done much to balance the traditional viewpoint. We now know that the Inquisition was much less violent, authoritarian, and oppressive than previously thought. Nevertheless, the object of the Crusades and the Inquisition, designed to compel men's souls, clearly ran counter to the teachings of Jesus: "This is my commandment, That ye love one another, as I have loved you. Greater love hath no man than this, that a man lay down his life for his friends" (John 15:12–13). The Lord's divine Church had become a human church, no longer behaving as Christ had, instead resembling the condition of Israel before the meridian of time.

Simony and Nepotism Replace Inspiration from the Holy Spirit

Although Constantine saved Christians from a martyr's doom, he opened wide the floodgates of escalating apostasy until little remained of the Church Jesus had organized. Pride, power, and greed—habitual problems in ancient Israel—also became commonplace in Christianity as ecclesiastical position became the surest means to royal favor. A practice known as *simony* (named after Simon Magus, Acts 8:18–24) enabled men to purchase ecclesiastical appointments from political rulers and later from leaders of the corrupt Church hierarchy. Such men sold their souls for power and influence rather than developing Christlike attributes and obtaining genuine authority through receiving an inspired call from the Lord.

Unlike Peter and John, who said to the author of this evil practice, Simon, "Thy money perish with thee, because thou hast thought that the gift of God may be purchased with money" (Acts 8:20), clerics gladly accepted priestly position in return for supporting the rulers who secured their election. That support, however, too often meant that they became mere pawns to the kings or emperors who brought them to power.

Simony began with the Edict of Milan in 313 and soon became widespread under Constantius, the son of Constantine, a vigorous supporter of Arian doctrines. Some Catholic historians depict Pope Liberius (352–60) as a man of courage but conclude that he was powerless to act against the emperor. This fact is made evident when, in Milan, Constantius succeeded in inducing all but three bishops to adopt the Arian position; those refusing were deposed and replaced with Arian successors.[10] Accordingly, control of the Church by the state prevented the influence of the Holy Spirit from making known the mind and will of God to His servants, and many clergymen began to compromise principle in exchange for promotion within the Church.

An example of such compromise occurred during the administration of Pope Vigilius in the mid-sixth century. He had been exiled by the Emperor Justinian for refusing to denounce the famous Three Chapters, a widely accepted work of three fifth-century theologians. However, the Deacon Palagius, who had joined Vigilius in exile, accepted the papal crown in 556 from the emperor in exchange for his condemnation of these writings. According to McBrian: "The Roman clergy were very unhappy about having to accept Palagius without even an election. . . . Many religious and nobles broke communion with Palagius, and his consecration had to be delayed for several months because no bishop would agree to officiate."[11] The emperor hoped this compromise would create harmony in the Empire, but it was instead merely the beginning of centuries of political maneuvering between both the state and the Church, each one using the other to achieve political and personal goals.

Simony soon became rampant throughout Christendom. When discussing the papal reign of Gregory I, the Great (590–604), Cheetham explains, "Simony, the traffic in ecclesiastical offices, was *universal* and laymen were commonly promoted by royal favours to the most lucrative [positions as bishop]."[12] He later describes the progression of this evil in 752:

Corruption and simony were even more rampant than in Brunhilde's day, with the Kings rewarding their lay supporters with lucrative bishoprics and abbeys. Pluralists abounded and according to a letter from Boniface to the Pope, "although they say they do not commit adultery, some bishops are nevertheless drunken and unreliable, or go hunting or fight in the army." As for the lower clergy, "as deacons they have had four or five or more concubines at night in bed and are not yet ashamed to read the Gospel."[13]

Along with simony, nepotism played a disastrous role in the corruption of Church hierarchy. All too often appointments and elections to high clerical positions, including pope, produced tragic results. In the late tenth and early eleventh centuries, two rival Roman families, the Crescentii and the Counts of Tusculum, controlled papal elections. These clans dominated both secular rule and the papacy. At the death of John XIX, the Tusculum family decided to separate civil affairs from Church governance. One family member, Gregory, was crowned king while another, an immature fifteen-year-old, was elected pope. Known as Benedict IX, he made no attempt to hide his violent and immoral behavior: "Naturally, the spectacle of the Pope carousing and whoring his way around Rome aroused chroniclers to heights of indignation. . . . He had a bad name for corruption and violence."[14]

Nepotism, like simony, was also the cause of degeneracy throughout the Church. Men elected or appointed in this manner were not called of God, nor did they possess the gift of the Holy Ghost or the authority of Jesus Christ; these actions exposed the absence of genuine priesthood authority and the gifts of the Spirit.

Although the Roman Church attempted to reform itself from time to time, corruption had been firmly embedded for centuries and would not dislodge itself easily from the Church's core. Leo IX was one such reforming pope. Traveling throughout the Empire in the mid-eleventh century, he sought to control nepotism and simony. While consecrating a new basilica at Reims, he staged an exhibition designed to showcase his reforms. He placed the shrine of St. Remigius on the altar and called upon the bishops and abbots present to testify publicly that their offices had not been obtained by simony. Suspecting a snare, many senior clerics refused to attend the synod, including the king, who was often an accomplice to simony. Those who did attend were caught unawares—many confessed and were excommunicated or otherwise punished.[14] Although attempts were made to continue reforms, simony was entrenched throughout the Universal Church for centuries to come; not until the modern age would this vice be substantially eliminated from its ranks.

Although the widespread presence of simony and nepotism in the Church throughout the Middle Ages is not disputed, neither should one assume that Catholic Christians during this period were all corrupt. The point of discussing these polluted practices within the hierarchy is to demonstrate clearly the presence of apostasy at the Church's center. Had the pure religion of Christ actually survived, an authoritative remnant possessing inspired leadership—called in the same manner as the original Apostles—could be identified. During the Counter-Reformation in the mid-sixteenth century, the two major abuses of simony and nepotism came under scrutiny, standing as compelling evidence that the authority of Christ no longer existed and that the Church was in apostasy, these practices being found nowhere in the primitive Christian Church.

The Church and Its Leaders Were Devoid of the Holy Ghost

The scriptures clearly specify the requirements that qualify one to serve God and to be eligible to enjoy the gifts of the Spirit. The term *sanctification*—or living a life of holiness, chastity, and piety—has always been associated with receiving the fruits or blessings of the Spirit. *Possession of the Holy Spirit was essential to the Apostles in directing the Church of Jesus Christ.* One cannot expect to have the Holy Ghost without living a life in harmony with the teachings of Jesus; during the Middle Ages, many of the pastorate became ambitious and self-serving and thus devoid of such spiritual endowments.

The scriptures confirm the importance of love, righteous living, and receiving the "gift" of the Holy Ghost to direct the course of the Christian life:

By this shall all men know that ye are my disciples, *if ye have love one to another.* (John 13:35; emphasis added)

And we are his witnesses of these things; and *so is also the Holy Ghost, whom God hath given to them that obey him.* (Acts 5:32; emphasis added)

He that hath my commandments, and keepeth them, he it is that loveth me: and he that loveth me shall be loved of my Father, and I will love him, and will manifest myself to him. . . .

But the Comforter, which is the Holy Ghost, whom the Father will send in my name, *he shall teach you all things, and bring all things to your remembrance,* whatsoever I have said unto you. (John 14:21–26; emphasis added)

And I will pray the Father, and he shall give you another Comforter, . . . even the Spirit of truth; whom the world cannot receive, because it seeth him not, neither knoweth him: but ye know him; for he dwelleth with you, and shall be in you. (John 14:16–17)

The Savior reveals in these passages that He is the mediator and intercessor between God and man, and that He will petition the Father to send the Holy Ghost to come upon the Apostles. Jesus described the Holy Ghost as the *Spirit of truth* and taught His disciples that the world would not receive the Holy Ghost because they did not qualify, for they did not know the Savior nor did they obey His commandments.

Modern Christians recognize the power of the Holy Ghost as received by the Apostles at the day of Pentecost. Before being endowed with the Spirit, Peter denied Jesus (Luke 22:34), cut off a centurion's ear (John 18:10), and was fishing unclothed, embarrassed when he recognized the Lord (John 21:3–7). After the forty-day experience with Jesus and receiving the Holy Ghost at Jerusalem, Peter and the Apostles were filled with a power and steadiness they had not enjoyed previously:

And when the day of Pentecost was fully come, they were all with one accord in one place. And suddenly there came a sound from heaven as of a rushing mighty wind, and it filled all the house where they were sitting. And there appeared unto them cloven tongues like as of fire, and it sat upon each of them. *And they were all filled with the Holy Ghost,* and began to speak with other tongues, as the Spirit gave them utterance. (Acts 2:1–4; emphasis added)

Prior to receiving the Holy Ghost, the Apostles had queried Jesus, "Why could we not cast him out"? (Matthew 17:19); afterward, they were confident in the role given

them by the Savior. This change was noticeable on the occasion when Peter and John, walking toward the temple, beheld a lame man requesting alms. Peter's powerful and faith-filled response was, "Silver and gold have I none; but such as I have give I thee: In the name of Jesus Christ of Nazareth rise up and walk" (Acts 3:6).

In addition to increased faith, Peter and the other Apostles now possessed great courage. Contrasting Peter's weakness in denying Jesus before the Resurrection and forty-day ministry, *after the day of Pentecost,* we read:

Then Peter, *filled with the Holy Ghost,* said unto them, Ye rulers of the people, and elders of Israel, if we this day be examined of the good deed done to the impotent man, by what means is he made whole; be it known unto you all, and to all the people of Israel, that by the name of Jesus Christ of Nazareth, *whom ye crucified,* . . . doth this man stand here before you whole. (Acts 4:8–10; emphasis added)

Members of the Sanhedrin recognized this change and were astonished: "Now when they saw the boldness of Peter and John, and perceived that they were unlearned and ignorant men, they marvelled" (Acts 4:13).

The Apostles were no longer afraid of what would happen to them, even if their lives were to be taken. The Jewish leaders were furious with the Apostles for openly charging them with crucifying Jesus, so they cast their Christian counterparts into prison. The Apostles were released by a miracle and fearlessly continued their ministry:

And [the Sanhedrin] laid their hands on the apostles, and put them in the common prison. But the angel of the Lord by night opened the prison doors, and brought them forth, and said, Go, stand and speak in the temple to the people all the words of this life. (Acts 5:18–20)

The Apostles obeyed the angel and in unveiled defiance to the chief priests taught openly at the temple. When they were rebuked by the Jewish Sanhedrin for proclaiming the gospel, Peter, at the peril of his own life, exclaimed: *"We ought to obey God rather than men.* The God of our fathers raised up Jesus, *whom ye slew and hanged on a tree.* Him hath God exalted with his right hand to be a Prince and a Saviour"* (Acts 5:29–31; emphasis added).

Not only the Apostles but the Seventy also received great power from the gift of the Spirit. Stephen, called and set apart to this special office, is said to have been full of faith and power, performing great wonders and miracles (Acts 6:5–8). Likewise, Paul after his conversion demonstrated many gifts of the Spirit and preached with unparalleled power and authority. The writings of all New Testament authors reflect deep spirituality, humility, and love; and they convey the determination each held to obey the commandments. *The fruit of righteous living endowed these men with profound faith and spiritual power,* allowing them to perform mighty miracles and *continuously* to receive divine direction in guiding the Church.

All Church members who followed Peter's counsel to be baptized and receive the gift of the Holy Ghost (Acts 2:38), and who "continued stedfastly in the apostles' *doctrine* and *fellowship,* and in *breaking of bread,* and in *prayers"* (Acts 2:42; emphasis added), received many of the same spiritual gifts witnessed of Peter, Stephen, and others. Paul wrote about spiritual endowments in his letter to the Corinthians:

No man can say that Jesus is the Lord, but by the Holy Ghost. . . . the mani-

festation of the Spirit is given to every man to profit withal. . . . to one is given by the Spirit the word of wisdom; to another the word of knowledge by the same Spirit; to another faith . . . ; to another the gifts of healing . . . ; to another the working of miracles; to another prophecy. (1 Corinthians 12:3, 7–10)

Such gifts depended on one's faith, hope, and charity and continuing one's godly walk (1 Corinthians 13:13; Hebrews 6:1–6).

Soon after the death of the Apostles, the gifts of the Spirit began to diminish. The failure of the Church as a whole to follow and sustain those called of God, restrain heresy, and preserve pure motives later prevented the outpouring of the Spirit so prevalent in the early Church. Paul's testimony to the Thessalonians documents why the ancient Church was blessed with the Spirit and alludes to why these gifts disappeared in later Christianity:

"Ye are witnesses, and God also, how holily and justly and unblameably we behaved ourselves among you that believe: as ye know how we exhorted and comforted and charged every one of you, as a father doth his children" (1 Thessalonians 2:10–11).

When the Church hierarchy became corrupt following the death of the Apostles, the spiritual gifts ceased to exist among them. Centuries later the Christian Reformer and founder of Methodism, John Wesley, wrote:

It does not appear that these extraordinary gifts of the Holy Ghost were common in the Church for more than two or three centuries. We seldom hear of them after that fatal period when the Emperor Constantine called himself a Christian; and, from a vain imagination of promoting the Christian cause thereby, heaped riches and power and honour upon Christians in general, but in particular upon the Christian

Clergy. From this time they almost totally ceased; very few instances of the kind were found. The cause of this was not, (as has been vulgarly supposed,) "because there was no more occasion for them," because all the world was become Christians. This is a miserable mistake; not a twentieth part of it was then nominally Christian. The real cause was "the love of many," almost of all Christians, so called, was "waxed cold." The Christians had no more of the spirit of Christ than the other heathens. This was the real cause; the Christians were turned heathen again, and had only a dead form left.[16]

Wesley concluded that the gifts and fruits of the Holy Ghost did not survive in the Church of the Middle Ages, the cause being the failure of the later Church to uphold the teachings and doctrines set forth in the New Testament Church.

The Partnership of Church and State Not Aligned with Biblical Principles

When Constantius succeeded his father, Constantine, as emperor of Rome, he began to embroil Christianity in doctrinal controversy. Forcing the Arian view of God on the Church, he deposed bishops, including Athanasius, of their priestly positions when they refused to accept his theology. His quest for power demanded that the Church be subservient not only in the affairs of state but also in matters of doctrine and ecclesiastical organization, creating an unholy and unprincipled relationship between the papacy and secular governments. The following are a few examples of the consequences, recognizing that a multitude of others could be presented as this unhealthy and unauthorized relationship continued for more than twelve centuries.

When the Emperor Justinian sought to influence the election of Palagius as pope, the action bore corrupt fruits. Although it is common in political affairs to compromise in order to accommodate diverse views, God's truth cannot be arbitrated. The emperor's goal was peace within his realm: since conflicts continued to flare between Monophysites and orthodox Catholics, he sought an amicable solution. Theodore Ascidas, the bishop of Ceasarea and Justinian's advisor in religious matters concerning the Republic, suggested that if the famous *Three Chapters*, a work by three fifth-century theologians, would be discarded from orthodoxy, the Monophysites might be subdued. His recommendation was carried out in 544 against the vehement protests of Pope Vigilius. The emperor therefore abducted the pope and placed him in exile for several years until he acquiesced. Unfortunately, the pope died of kidney failure when his ship reached port in Syracuse. The deacon Palagius had been a vigorous supporter of the pope's strong stance in championing the *Three Chapters*. However, Justinian correctly judged the aspiring Palagius and offered him the papal chair in exchange for publicly denouncing those works. Palagius set aside his personal convictions and accepted the emperor's offer.[17]

Palagius's purchase of the papal office was an obvious fraud. The Savior explained, "For what is a man profited, if he shall gain the whole world, and lose his own soul? or what shall a man give in exchange for his soul?" (Matthew 16:26). From 556, beginning with Palagius, until 741 a pope could not be formally elected without consent from the emperor in Constantinople.[18] Accordingly, the process for choosing Church leaders was no longer inspired by the Holy Ghost but by the political objectives of secular rulers.

This unholy and strained partnership of

church and state would get worse before it got better. As mentioned, beginning in the sixth century, a pope could not be elected without the approval of the emperor. Increasing his grip still further, in the late ninth century, the temporal ruler alone appointed a pope. According to Bryce in his history of the Holy Roman Empire, during the reign of Henry III, the empire "attained the meridian of its power." He records that "The Roman Priesthood" was "forced to receive German after German as their bishop at the bidding of a ruler so powerful, so severe and so pious." Under these less than favorable circumstances, not only the papacy but the entire Roman clergy entered an era of unparalleled degeneracy, steeped in immorality, ruthless violence, and open participation in the traffic of clerical offices and Church property.[19]

A final illustration of government intervention epitomizes the problems caused by combining the interests of church and state. King Henry of Germany deposed Pope Gregory VII over a rift that occurred between them in about 1077; Gregory returned the favor by excommunicating the king. After much intrigue and various counterplots, King Henry deposed Gregory a second time and assembled a synod of bishops who, yielding to political pressures, elected the archbishop of Revenna, an "anti-pope," as Clement III.[20] Dissension between monarch and pope, and the yielding by bishops to political pressures rather than the Holy Ghost divided what once had been Christ's Church upon the earth. Schisms in the Universal Church had been notorious for many centuries. Notably, the eleventh century experienced a marked increase in such divisions underscored by the election of three popes in 1045, each claiming legitimacy.[21]

Although the Church had little control over decisions made by secular monarchs, the internal corruption of the priestly hierarchy, including the behavior of administrative clerics and the lower priesthood, was solely the Church's responsibility. The Savior once said to Pilate, "My kingdom is not of this world" (John 18:36); the Church, having lost its moral compass, could not make this necessary separation. The resulting schisms, anti-popes, irregular ordinations, secular control, and degeneration and immorality within the clergy all point to unfortunate apostasy from original Christianity.

Uninspired Revisions in Church Government

As documented in chapter 3, the Savior organized His Church with specific offices and responsibilities. The Apostles, particularly Paul, explained the purpose of these offices. The Church would ultimately grow and require increased ecclesiastical support. The Savior implied to Peter that the Apostles would need continuous revelation to respond appropriately to such growth. Said He, "Blessed art thou, Simon Bar-jona: for flesh and blood hath not revealed it unto thee [not miracles, not because you've seen me], *but my Father which is in heaven.* And I say also unto thee, That thou art Peter, and upon *this rock* [revelation or living prophets] I will build my church; and the gates of hell shall not prevail against it" (Matthew 16:17–18). Although the Savior may have been referring partly to Peter, whose name means "rock" (Gr. *petra* = rock) in Peter's apostolic and prophetic role, and to Himself as the cornerstone of the Church (Ephesians 2:20), the actual subject Christ addressed in this passage was revelation given to the one whom He had chosen to lead His Church after His ascension. The Savior testified to Peter that the reason Peter was *certain* of the divinity of Jesus Christ was that the Father had revealed it to him *through prayer, by the power of the Holy Ghost*. It was *continuous revelation* which Jesus declared the gates of hell could not prevail against.

When the Church condoned sin and error, the Apostles were taken from the earth, revelation ceased, and the Church fell into apostasy. Without revelation, the earthly leadership had only earthly means for coping with growth and other related problems. Persecution, heresy, impure motives within the clergy, sin, and, equally important, the changing landscape when Constantine asserted primacy over the Church—all were variable and demanding forces to oversee. Only revelation could ensure that God's will was done. Revelation was His method of governing through prophets before the birth of Christ,[22] it was His method during Christ's earthly ministry,[23] and it was His method after the Savior's death through the Apostles.[24] God's nature does not change (Hebrews 13:8–9; James 1:17).

When we compare and contrast the Church leadership structure in the Middles Ages to the New Testament hierarchy, the differences are easily evident. The Church established by Jesus included deacons, teachers, and priests; it contained elders, seventies, and high priests; and it consisted of evangelists, bishops, and Apostles. The Roman Church altered this organization to include popes, cardinals, sub-deacons, abbots, friars, monks, exorcists, acolytes, and others. Organizational modifications in connection with significant membership growth are typical and necessary in any enterprise. However, God established His Church with an organization that could accommodate growth, and that growth should occur within its original, inspired structure and follow its revealed pattern of selecting leaders. The role of the exorcist and the monastic movement of the Middle Ages significantly departed from the tradition and revelation contained in the New Testament.

Jesus and His Apostles exorcized evil spirits on several occasions. Who are these evil spirits? They are the disobedient spirits who were cast out of heaven for rebellion and apparently who will never receive a physical body. Since the days of Adam, these wicked souls have influenced mankind to sin and reject God. On occasion they attempt to briefly inhabit mortal bodies in their efforts to torment man. By the authority of the Melchizedek Priesthood, held by Jesus and delegated to the Apostles, such spirits were cast out of several individuals mentioned in scripture (Matthew 4:24; 8:16). In the New Testament Church, *all* who were duly ordained to the priesthood of the New Covenant (Hebrews 7:12) could command in the name of Jesus and rebuke the hosts of Satan (Luke 10:17; Mark 9:1; 16:17). This act was accomplished by a combination of priesthood authority, faith, and spiritual purity. During the Middle Ages, the Roman Church conferred specific authority on certain priests to cast out devils, thus limiting such power to those called exorcists, a notable contrast to the primitive Church. The role of an exorcist was a human addition to the Church, not introduced by revelation and not authorized by God.

Monastic societies also emerged in postapostolic Christianity. Although not really connected to the priesthood itself, they were organizations sponsored by the Church whose origins cannot be found in New Testament Christianity.

Monks presumably withdrew from society to avoid all earthly excesses. They fasted, prayed, studied, wrote, and went to great lengths to affirm total virtue and piety. However, in doing so and in spite of their best intentions, they were deceived by the father of lies. They became spiritually blind (Romans 11:25) by being overzealous (Romans 10:2–3). This method of deceit (overzealousness) had long been practiced by Satan with great success among the children of Israel. Many historians believe that the Essenes at Qumran practiced disciplines similar to those of the monastic societies of the Middle Ages; yet no concrete evidence supports this claim. Christ never organized or discussed orders similar to those established by monks, nor did holy writ furnish any instructions to institute such societies. Although not speaking directly about the addition of priesthood offices, such statements as "whatsoever is *more* than these cometh of evil" (Matthew 5:37), or "though we, or an angel from heaven" (Galatians 1:8), or "if any man shall add" or "any man shall take away" (Revelation 22:18–19), suggest that man cannot alter God's work. Such gospel laws were clearly established in ancient times, demonstration that the gospel has always been the same. From Moses, the Israelites learned, "What thing soever I command you, observe to do it: thou shalt not add thereto, nor diminish from it" (Deuteronomy 12:32). The Savior knew that some would want to do more than they were commanded and that it would bring evil upon them. His instruction to be a light to the world and not put it under a bushel (as happened in monasteries) was confused by some (Matthew 5:14–15).

The monastic societies prevalent in the Middle Ages may have been popularized by the third-century monk St. Anthony. Born of wealthy parents in approximately 251, Anthony grew up knowing the good things of the world. However, Anthony's parents died when he was about twenty years old; having read portions of the Savior's teachings to "the rich young man," Anthony divested himself of all his possessions and gave them to the poor. Becoming overzealous in his desire to follow Christ, he practiced excessive self-denial. Legend maintains that he lived on one meal a day of bread and water and slept on the bare ground. Anthony isolated himself from the world, withdrawing to an abandoned fort, where he lived for twenty years without seeing the face of another human being. Even his food was handed to him over the wall of the fort.[25] While no one should doubt Anthony's pious devotion to God, his reclusive lifestyle finds no origin in the teachings of Jesus.

These kinds of sacrifices may sound inspiring, but they are not scriptural, and they are not productive according to the commandments of God. God instructed Adam and Eve, "Be fruitful, and multiply, and replenish the earth" (Genesis 1:28). This command has never been rescinded. To assume that we must sacrifice or endure difficulties during certain periods of our lives because of agency, economic decline, or political influences is defensible. Enduring these times teaches us patience and gratitude for God's gifts as we experience the contrasts of happiness and joy, pain and sorrow. For reasons known only to God, conditions in certain countries make it virtually necessary for some to despair perpetually. Free will and God's non-interference in man's agency, coupled with His grace in making things equitable in the end (Luke 16:25), seem to play a role in man's suffering. Such circumstances furnish opportunities for Christian service and charity. But it is inconsistent with the will of God as revealed in scripture for a righteous man to sacrifice continually and needlessly or to suffer without cause.[26]

Monastic societies, in addition to other offices and organizations, were improperly incorporated into the Church structure originally established by Jesus and supply further evidence that New Testament Christianity no longer existed. Again, there is no questioning the show of devotion that many monks possessed for God, then or now, but there is simply no scriptural justification for this particular avenue of showing that devotion.

Further Corruption and Additions to Church Doctrines

The Speculative Doctrines of Augustine (354–430)

Doctrinal speculation escalated during the Middle Ages. Although begun much earlier, the desire to create a rigid theological system flowered with Augustine, and many of his tenets were actually canonized in later centuries. Considered by many to be the greatest of the Latin Fathers and among the most revered western doctors of the Church, his influence in Christian doctrine persists today in both Catholic and Protestant teachings. His father was a pagan who later converted to Christianity, while his mother, devoutly Christian, exerted a powerful influence over his life. He was well educated in rhetoric and experimented with several philosophic systems, including the religion known as Manichaeism.[27] For approximately nine years, Augustine was associated with this sect, being a "hearer" but not a full-fledged member, before converting to Christianity in 387. Although for approximately fifteen years he lived with a woman, who bore him a son, Augustine entered the clergy and was ordained in 391, becoming bishop of Hippo in 395, which office he held until his death.

Augustine lived during a tumultuous period in evolving Christianity. His theology matured in the midst of the Donatist controversy, the Pelagian conflict, and the Manichaean heresy. While Augustine was a dynamic Church leader, apostasy was already deeply entrenched in the Church. He considered Christianity the successor to pagan worship and was himself significantly influenced by Neoplatonic thought. Augustine unwittingly crystallized and fused Greek philosophy into Christianity, eliminating the last remnants of pure Christianity as taught by the Apostles. In addition to his concept of *original sin,* two of the major theological themes he engaged in during his ministry dealt with predestination and creation ex nihilo.

Predestination Verses God's Foreknowledge, Foreordination, and Free Will

Augustine's theory of predestination stands in stark contrast to early Christian doctrine. His speculative teaching relies on Greek philosophy rather than the Bible. The following excerpt from The City of God, one of Augustine's most celebrated works, established his position on the subject:

> Wherefore our wills also have just so much power as God willed and foreknew that they should have; and therefore whatever power they have, they have it within most certain limits; and whatever they are to do, they are most assuredly to do, for He whose foreknowledge is infallible foreknew that they would have the power to do it, and would do it.
>
> Therefore, whatsoever a man suffers contrary to his own will, he ought not to attribute to the will of men, or of angels, or of any created spirit, but rather to His will who gives power to wills. It is not the case, therefore, that because God foreknew what would be in the power of our wills, there is for that reason nothing in the power of our wills.[28]

Augustine believed that because God

foreknows what a person will do prior to an act of commission or omission, man has no power over his own will. From this conclusion, Augustine necessarily extrapolates that God arbitrarily, or at least in some fashion known only to God, chooses His elect children to be saved while the rest are damned. For Augustine there was no such thing as true self-determination—everything or anything good happened because God foreknew *and willed it to be so.* Thus, Augustine believed that mankind's fate was sealed before birth, either to election or damnation.

J. N. D. Kelly summarizes Augustine's position in the following manner:

> It is for God to determine which shall receive grace and which shall not. . . . The number of elect is strictly limited, being neither more or less than is required to replace fallen angels. Hence he [Augustine] has to twist the text "God wills all men to be saved" (1 Timothy 2:4), making it mean that He wills the salvation of all the elect, among whom men of every race and type are represented. God's choice of those to whom grace is given in no way depends on His foreknowledge of their future merits, for whatever good deeds they do will themselves be the fruit of grace.[29]

Answering the inevitable accusations of favoritism, Augustine replied as follows:

> There can in the end, be no answer to this agonizing question. God has mercy on those whom He wishes to save, and justifies them; He hardens those upon whom He does not wish to have mercy, not offering them grace in conditions they are likely to accept it. If this looks like favoritism, we should all remember that all are in any case justly condemned, and that if God decides to save any it is an act of ineffable compassion.[30]

Satan's greatest ploy is half-truths. We recall Satan's deceitful statement to Eve, "Ye shall not surely die: for God doth know that in the day ye eat thereof, then your eyes shall be opened, and ye shall be as gods, knowing good and evil" (Genesis 3:4–5). The fallen state of man brought about not only physical death but also spiritual death, separating us from God and necessitating the atonement of Jesus Christ. Augustine would have us believe that only a small number of God's children are elect before they are born into this world and thus automatically saved, while the masses come to earth, including innocent children, predestined to damnation. This concept is foreign to scripture and cannot be supported by religious history. While God's foreknowledge allows Him to know eternal outcomes before they actually occur, that He actually wills some of His children to election and others to damnation is a doctrine borne of a source other than God.

Augustine's theology of predestination was not the doctrine of the early Christian Church, nor was it the belief of many others in fourth-century Christianity. Semi-Pelagians, as they were called, believed that the initial movement of faith came from the sinner's own choice to come unto God. They believed that grace assisted a man who had begun to will his own salvation[31] and that God meant what He said when He inspired the words "Who will have *all* men to be saved, and to come unto the knowledge of the truth" (1 Timothy 2:4). Notwithstanding that Augustine's theories were at odds with those of early Christianity and many other Churchmen of his own day, they eventually won out, becoming the dominant thought of the Universal Church and the Protestant movement when it arose.

The earliest Christian communities strongly believed in free will, while Christianity in the fourth century began to speculate

212

significantly and to alter the pure teachings of the prophets and the Apostles.

Doctrine attributed to Peter in the Clementine Recognitions was recorded as follows:

Whether any one, truly hearing the word of the true Prophet; is willing or unwilling to receive it, and to embrace His burden, that is, the precepts of life, *he has either in his power, for we are free in will.* For if it were so, that those who hear had it not in their power to do otherwise than they had heard, there were some power of nature in virtue of which it were not free to him to pass over to another opinion. Or if, again, no one of the hearers could at all receive it, this also were a power of nature which should compel the doing of some one thing, and should leave no place for the other course. *But now, since it is free for the mind to turn its judgment to which side it pleases, and to choose the way which it approves, it is clearly manifest that there is in men a liberty of choice.*[32]

The Christian teacher next described the burden of responsibility upon hearing the truth:

Before any one hears what is good for him, . . . he is ignorant; and being ignorant, he wishes and desires to do what is not good for him; wherefore he is not judged for that. But when once he has heard the causes of his error, and has received the method of truth, then, if he remain in those errors with which he had been long ago preoccupied, he shall rightly be called into judgment, to suffer punishment, because he has spent in the sport of errors that portion of life which was given him to be spent in living well. But he who, hearing those things, willingly receives them, and is thankful that the teaching of good things has been brought to him, inquires more eagerly, and does not

cease to learn, . . . gives thanks to God because He has shown him the light of truth; and for the future directs his actions in all good works, for which he is assured that there is a reward prepared in the world to come.[33]

This early Christian writer, perhaps recording Peter's views, informs us that we will be judged according to our response to hearing the truth. His discourse validates the basic premise of free will: men are provided the Two Ways (life or death), whereupon they must choose for themselves the path they will take.

Justin Martyr added his testimony regarding free will:

God, wishing men and angels to follow His will, resolved to create them free to do righteousness; possessing reason. . . . And with a law that they should be judged by Him, if they do anything contrary to right reason. . . . [34] Since God made . . . men in the beginning with free will, in eternal fire they will justly suffer the punishment of whatever sins they have committed. And this is the nature of all that is made— to be capable of vice and virtue. For neither would any of them be praiseworthy unless there was power to turn to both.[35]

Continuing, Justin recorded:

In the beginning He made the human race with the power of thought and of choosing the truth and of acting rightly, so that all people are without excuse before God; for they are born capable of exercising reason and intelligence.[36]

Finally, for Justin, free will was a critical element concerning man's salvation:

But lest some may infer from what has

been said by us that whatever things happen, happen according to inevitable destiny, because they were foretold as foreknown, this too we explain. We have learned from the prophets . . . that punishments . . . and good rewards are given according to the merit of each person's actions. . . . For if it be destined that one person be good and another wicked, neither is the former meritorious nor the latter blameworthy. And again unless the human race has the power by free choice to avoid evil and to choose good, there is no responsibility for actions of whatever kind they be. . . . But this we assert is irrevocable destiny, that those who choose the good have deserved rewards, and those who choose the opposite have their just punishment. For God did not make a man or a woman like other things, such as trees and animals, which cannot act by choice. . . . Through Moses God spoke to the first formed man: "Behold before your face are good and evil, choose the good."[37]

As one of the Fathers closest to the Apostles, Justin Martyr was a strong proponent of the doctrine of free will, for it was a central part of the apostolic tradition. But Justin was not alone in this regard. Methetes (in his Epistle to Diognetus), Irenaeus, Hippolytus, Clement of Alexandria, Origen, and every other writer within the *early* Christian community were all in harmony regarding the principle of free will as a basic Christian tenet.

Methetes taught, "He sent Him; as to men He sent Him; as a Savior He sent Him, and as seeking to persuade, not to compel us; for violence has not place in the character of God."[38]

Calling free will the "ancient law of human liberty," Irenaeus explained:

This expression [of our Lord], "How often I would have gathered thy children together, and thou wouldest not," set forth the ancient law of human liberty, because God made man a free [agent] from the beginning, possessing his own power, even as he does his own soul, to obey the behests (ad utendum sentenia) of God voluntarily, and not by compulsion of God. For there is no Coercion with God. . . . And in man, as well as angels, He has placed the power of choice, so that those who had yielded obedience might justly possess what is good. . . . On the other hand, they who have not obeyed shall . . . receive condign punishment.[39]

The learned Hippolytus wrote, "Man possesses the capacity of self-determination, inasmuch as he is able to will and not to will, *and* is endued with power to do both."[40]

Finding full agreement with his early Christian brethren, Clement of Alexandria stated, "In no respect is God the author of evil. But since free choice and inclination originate sins, and a mistaken judgement sometimes prevails, . . . punishments are rightly inflicted."[41]

Origen too believed that we are rational beings and participate with God's grace in the salvation process: "God the Father bestows upon all, existence; and participation in Christ, in respect of His being the word of reason, renders them rational beings. From which it follows that they are deserving either of praise or blame, because capable of virtue and vice."[42]

Punctuating the profound belief Origen held regarding man's free agency, Joseph Trigg has written:

Origen presents grace and free will not as mutually exclusive, but as complimentary. We see this in his interpretation of another problematic text, "So it depends not on man's will or exertion, but on God's mercy" (Romans 9:16). He argues that Paul is not denying human agency but appropriately indicating God's share in our salvation far exceeds ours. [According to Origen] Paul is like a sailor who, at the conclusion of a safe voyage, ascribes all the credit to God. The Sailor does not for a moment suppose he could have arrived safe at harbor without his own skill at navigation. Even so, he is far more impressed by God's role in giving favorable winds, hospitable weather, and the stars as a guide.[43]

The collective weight of the earliest Christian Fathers as proponents of free agency is nearly overwhelming. It is certainly unmistakable. In stark contrast, Augustine's speculative doctrine of *election* does not find harmony with the Old or New Testament, with the tenets of the early Christian Fathers, or with ancient pseudepigraphal writings. Misguided interpretations of a few isolated verses led Augustine to create entire theoretical discourses on the subject of predestination. By contrast, when faced with a similar doctrinal dilemma, Peter, as the Lord's prophet, was given a dream clarifying God's will to the membership of the Church (Acts 10:9–48). Augustine attempted to construct a doctrine based alone on intellectual arguments. In the final analysis, we are left to ponder the reality that the earliest Christian writers are closer to the original teachings of Jesus than theologians writing in the fifth century, an era of escalating corruption.

Creation ex Nihilo

Creation *ex nihilo* is the term used by historic Christianity to describe the method by which God created the earth and universe. It theorizes that God created the earth and everything on it out of absolutely nothing.

There has been some speculation about the early Fathers' teachings regarding creation,[44] but Basilides, a Gnostic philosopher in the early to mid-second century, is generally credited with originating this theory.[45] In approximately 170, it began spreading in Christian circles through the writings of Tatian, a pupil of Justin Martyr who later became Gnostic.[46] However, Judaism and the earliest Christian communities held to the tradition that God *organized* preexistent matter or created the earth from a *watery chaos*. It was later Christians, influenced by Greek philosophy, who taught that the earth was created *out of nothing*. The orthodox Church of the fourth century adopted the theology of Gnostic philosophers in spite of all the polemics written against them in the second century.[47] Once again, speculation and scholarship replaced revelation as the means of defining this doctrine. The danger of speculation is that when one doctrine becomes errant or impure it is often intertwined in other related doctrines, changing the nature of the Church itself from a divine institution into a human organization.

No passages in the standard canon exist that provide a credible reference to the doctrine of creation ex nihilo. The only scriptural verse providing some foundation is found in the Apocrypha. A traditional rendition of this translation reads, "So I urge you, my child, to look up to the sky and the earth. Consider everything you see there, and realize that God made it all from nothing" (2 Maccabees 7:28).

Christian scholars cannot agree on the translation of the most crucial phrase "from nothing." According to Torchia, this phrase may be translated from the Greek as either "from the non-existent" or "from things which did not exist" (preexistent but unformed matter).[48] Because the translation is uncertain, it is impossible to know precisely the author's intent. The difference between God's prophets of the past and Tatian and those who followed was that prophets—in contrast to philosophers—did not speculate but expressed doctrine in such terms as "thus saith the Lord" (Exodus 5:1; 20:22–24).

Torchia states that the second most compelling passage cited, the Genesis creation account, is admissible as evidence of God creating matter out of nothing: "In the beginning God created the heaven and the earth. And the earth was without form, and void; and darkness was upon the face of the deep. And the Spirit of God moved upon the face of the waters" (Genesis 1:1–2).

Although Christian scholars admit to no direct evidence of God creating matter out of nothing, they also assert that there is no explicit evidence that God simply *organized* preexisting matter.[49] Because there is no evidence of a *two-step creation process,* the creation of physical matter first, then its ultimate organization, in Genesis or any other scripture, the statements that "the earth was without form and void; and darkness was upon the face of the deep" and that "the spirit of God moved upon the face of the waters" clearly indicate the existence of water and thus unorganized land mass, which God then began to frame. Supporting this conclusion, the *Interpreter's Bible* holds that the Hebrew term *bere' sit,* translated in the King James Version as "in the beginning," would be more correctly rendered "in the beginning *of.*" This interpretation appropriately merges verses 1 and 2, validating the opinion of E. A. Speiser, who has proposed a more correct reading: "When God set about to create heaven and earth, the world being then a formless waste."[50] Clark Pinnock writes, "I agree with process theology exegetically that Genesis 1 does not itself teach ex nihilo creation but presents God as

imposing order on chaos.[51]

Additionally, Frank Moore Cross contends that the *tradition* of creation ex nihilo improperly influenced the translation found in Genesis 1:1.[52]

In contrast to 2 Maccabees, other apocryphal writings defend the concept of God organizing the earth out of preexistent matter: "For thy almighty hand *that made the world out of shapeless matter,* lacked not means to send among them a multitude of bears and fierce lions" (Wisdom of Solomon 11:17).

Supporting *Wisdom,* the view of the early Christian Church was also creation out of chaos. Justin Martyr wrote, "And we have been taught that in the beginning He of His goodness, for people's sakes, formed all things out of unformed matter."[53]

Justin further recorded in his First and Second Apologies: "But we all hold this common gathering on Sunday, since it is the first day, on which God transforming darkness and matter made the Universe. . . ."[54] His son, . . . is begotten before the creation, when in the beginning God created and set in order everything through Him."[55]

Although some scholars refuse to accept Justin's statements as supporting creation from preexisting matter, it is quite likely, given his Middle Platonist background, that he would have clearly stated, as others later did, the precise Hellenistic view.

Similarly, Clement of Alexandria reflected the same understanding in his *Hymn to the Paedagogus:* "Out of a confused heap who didst create this ordered sphere, and from the shapeless mass of matter didst the universe adorn."[56]

While the early Christian Fathers expressed belief in creation from preexisting matter, conflicting accounts from the Shepherd of Hermas, itself an early record, were used by Origen as evidence for his third-century view in support of creatio ex nihilo. For example, in one instance the Shepherd recorded that God "made out of nothing the things that exist."[57] On the other hand, *Hermas* declared, "By his mighty word [He] 'fixed the Heaven and founded the earth upon the waters,' "[58] describing creation from watery chaos.

Origen seemed to inply a two-step creation process: first, the creation of physical matter itself, and second, its ultimate organization:

> And I cannot understand how so many distinguished men have been of [the] opinion that this matter . . . was uncreated, i.e., not formed by God himself, who is the Creator of all things, but that its nature and power were the result of chance.[59]

Origen then uses the ambiguous testimony of Hermas to defend his view of creation ex nihilo: "In the book of the Shepherd also, in the first commandment, he speaks as follows: 'First of all believe that there is one God who created and arranged all things, and made all things to come into existence, and out of a state of nothingness.' "[60]

Nevertheless, Origen recognized that many educated Christians in his day believed in the Jewish position of creation from watery chaos:

> Very many, indeed, are of the opinion that the matter of which things are made is itself signified in the language used by Moses in the beginning of Genesis: "In the beginning God made heaven and earth; and the earth was invisible and not arranged": for by the words "invisible and not arranged" Moses would seem to mean nothing else than shapeless matter.[61]

Origen's view of creatio ex nihilo is an extension of his belief that members of the Godhead were the only uncreated class. His rationale was that matter is unstable and changeable and that God, by definition of scripture, is *unchangeable.* Through apostasy, the *pure* knowledge of man's preexistence and the knowledge that man was the same species as God was lost. Also lost was the knowledge that even as Jesus proceeded from and was first spiritually begotten of the Father, we also proceeded from and were begotten of the Father. Accordingly, just as Jesus was in a changeable state until after His resurrection, we also will remain in a changeable state until after the resurrection. In time, if we have kept the New Covenant offered by the Savior, we will progress to a perfected condition and become essentially unchangeable beings, "heirs of God, and joint-heirs with Christ" (Romans 8:16).

The preponderance of evidence from scripture and the earliest Christian Fathers suggests that God *organized* existing matter rather than generated matter from nothing. Einstein's theory of relativity posits that matter cannot be created or destroyed but that it changes form—a view supported by the scientific community today. Ironically, Plato himself, from whom later Christians borrowed extensively, believed in the eternity of matter. Although science is not a compilation of absolutes, true science and true religion will always be entirely compatible. In the absence of divine revelation, scholarship replaces scripture and direct communication from God. Unlike religious scholarship, too often fraught with speculation, pure doctrine is always precise.

The writings of Philo Judeaus, a Jewish theologian contemporary with Jesus Christ, well known for blending Greek philosophy into Judaism; Basil, bishop of Caesarea in the late fourth century; and Ambrose, bishop of

Milan, are credited with forming the foundation upon which Augustine later constructed his speculative creation ex nihilo theories.[62] The reason this subject is important is not whether the earth was either created out of nothing or organized out of preexistent matter but how it contributed to false doctrines about the Godhead. As with Origen, Philo Judeaus also taught that only God is uncreated and that nothing can be coeternal with God, including matter.[63] Both of these doctrines are speculative and *cannot be substantiated by an appeal to the Bible.*

Theophilus of Antioch, when extolling the power of the Christian God over the god of the philosophers, best illustrates the thought patterns of *later* Christian Churchmen when he wrote:

> And what great thing is it if God made the world out of existent materials? For even a human artist, when he gets material from some one, makes of it what he pleases. But the power of God is manifest in this, that out of things that are not He makes whatever He pleases.[64]

Man's need to embellish and adorn seems to be well supported by history. Unfortunately, such doctrinal enhancements led Church leaders such as Ambrose to use the speculative dogma of creation ex nihilo to legitimize the doctrine of transubstantiation (see pages 185–87). As Paul so aptly prophesied, the time did come when men did not endure sound doctrine, "but after their own lusts" they did "heap to themselves" false teachers, turning away their ears from the truth, and the truth was turned into fables (2 Timothy 4:3–4).

The Doctrine of Papal Infallibility

During the period of the Chalcedonian Council (451), Leo I desired to authenticate the authority of the Roman See (bishop's seat) as the successor to St. Peter's divine authority. He wrote that, although he personally could not hope to attain the virtues attributed to St. Peter nor any other pope, the papacy itself was infallible; thus, the pope was entitled to perform his duties as "the most organizationally, morally, and intellectually perfect individual." Moreover, Leo asserted that the pope could not be judged by any outside power, that he was in effect "infallible."[65] Of these assertions, Cheetham explains:

> Leo's claim stemmed not only from the text in Matthew xvi, but from an utterly spurious letter from the first century Pope Clement informing James, the brother of Jesus, at Jerusalem, that St. Peter had passed on his powers to Clement and his successors in the presence of the Christian community at Rome. For all its apparent flimsiness it was not questioned by Leo's contemporaries.[66]

These excerpts from Leo's surviving letters raise two questions: (1) What legitimate evidence exists that the Roman bishop was to be Peter's successor? (2) Does the papacy's claim to infallibility—in spite of historically proven facts to the contrary—actually invalidate the office?

The Apostles once asked the Lord:

> Who is the greatest in the kingdom of heaven? And Jesus called a little child unto him, and set him in the midst of them, and said, Verily I say unto you, Except ye be converted, and become as little children, ye shall not enter into the kingdom of heaven. Whosoever therefore shall humble himself as this little child, the same is greatest in the kingdom of heaven. (Matthew 18:1–4)

The Savior, in an effort to train His Apostles for their future assignment, next

218

related the following story:

> Then came to him the mother of Zebedee's children with her sons, worshipping him, and desiring a certain thing of him. And he said unto her, What wilt thou? She saith unto him, Grant that these my two sons may sit, the one on thy right hand, and the other on the left, in thy kingdom. But Jesus answered and said, Ye know not what ye ask. . . . [It]is not mine to give, but it shall be given to them for whom it is prepared of my Father.
>
> . . . You know the princes of the Gentiles exercise dominion over them, and they that are great exercise authority upon them. But it shall not be so among you: but whosoever will be great among you, let him be your minister; and whosoever will be chief among you, let him be your servant. (Matthew 20:20–27)

The abuses of papal authority during the Middle Ages are well documented. In spite of the fact that Jesus instructed the Apostles, "It shall not be so among you," some popes of this era exercised power equal to their temporal monarchs. The bishops of Rome and Constantinople had disputed equal authority since the Emperor Constantine set himself up as head of the Church and moved his residence to Constantinople, the city named in his honor. A decisive rift between the East and West occurred in 1054 and has divided the Universal Church since that time. In light of the foregoing scriptural verses, it is important to note the power struggles that have characterized the Church of Rome, beginning with the reign of Constantine. From the papacy to the cardinals, from the cardinals to the archbishops, and on down the line of priestly influence, the cravings for power, wealth, and fame, fed by the partnership of the state, created an atmosphere within the Church that encouraged avarice and pride and resembled anything but the innocence of a little child.

The doctrine of the infallibility of the pope has long been questioned. The list of offenses over the centuries is extensive and includes such atrocities as murder, mutilation, homosexuality, fornication, adultery, abortion, greed, dishonesty, and so forth. Although legend has probably embellished some of the deeds attributed to the papacy, many of the charges are substantially documented.

The history of the papacy is a mixed bag of capable and pious men interspersed with pontiffs who brought dishonor on the Church. This fact is punctuated by the Catholic historian, McBrian, when writing about the papacy during the height of the Carolingian Empire:

> Although there have been many low periods in the history of the papacy, the period between the beginning of the Carolingian Empire (800) and the end of the pontificate of Damasus II (1048) was undoubtedly its lowest, some happy exceptions to the rule notwithstanding. The period was marred by papal corruption (including simony, ie., the buying and selling of church offices, nepotism, lavish lifestyles, concubinage, brutality, even murder).[67]

The only purpose in this book of bringing attention to the scandals perpetrated by many popes is to demonstrate that they were neither infallible nor morally or intellectually superior to other men. They led what had become a human church; while many popes were exemplary individuals, some were either regrettable or patently evil, consistent with secular rulers throughout history but inconsistent with the character of the prophets and Apostles of God.

From the time of Constantine, Roman emperors, against the wishes of Church hierarchy, involved themselves in spiritual matters. It should be no surprise to learn that in time the reverse also occurred: in the eighth century, *the papacy began to wield its influence in civil concerns,* producing an unhealthy interest by the nobles in papal elections. At the death of Paul I in 767, Toto of Nepi entered Rome with armed supporters who frightened the city into electing his brother Constantine. After one year in office, the Roman clergy rose up against the new pope with the help of Lombard troops. An attempt to rig the next election failed, and the clergy, according to custom, consecrated Stephen III. The example of this pope characterizes the problems encountered with a number of pontiffs during the Middle Ages and Renaissance periods:

> His was a miserable pontificate, the climax of excitable barbarism and political ineptitude. A weak and shifty character, the Pope was . . . manipulated [and] unleashed a rancorous and savage persecution against all possible rivals. Constantine . . . and many others were blinded and mutilated.[68]

In another scandal some years later, serious charges of immorality and perjury were levied against Pope Leo III (795–816). Because the charges were disregarded, Paschalis, the pope's nephew, and some of his friends knocked Pope Leo off his horse during a St. Mark's day procession and then attempted to blind him and cut out his tongue. Somehow he escaped mutilation and was carried into a nearby monastery. King Charles helped Leo get safely back to Rome with intentions of helping him restore order and authority, but the king's advisor warned him that the charges were true and presented to him a detailed list of offenses. The king was so shocked that he burned the record but ordered an investigation. Leo apparently had to wait nearly a year to resolve this most embarrassing situation.

Charles came personally to Rome to consider the charges with other representatives of the clergy:

> After three weeks of discussion, the principle that a Vicar of Christ could not be judged by his fellow men was held to prevail; all the same Leo was required to mount the pulpit of St. Peter's and to read, *under oath,* a statement formally exculpating himself from the accusations brought against him.[69]

The final year of Paschal I's pontificate (819–24) was disgraced by his explicit involvement in a capital crime. Two senior officials in his court, known to have pro-Frankish affections, were found blinded and beheaded inside the precincts of the Lateran. Although the Emperor ordered an immediate investigation, Paschal evaded authorities by taking the same oath that had exonerated Leo III.[70]

In 974 the Crescentii family elevated a little-known deacon named Franco to the papal chair. Known as Boniface VIII, a future pope described him as a "horrendous monster, surpassing all men in wickedness." Among the many crimes he committed was the strangling of his predecessor. With imperial commanders approaching, the pope fled to Constantinople with as much booty as he could carry.[71]

Prior to the Reformation, papal corruption reached a peak. One reason was that the sale of ecclesiastical offices was rampant throughout the Church. Men were not appointed to Church offices because of their piety or love for God, nor were they called of God by prophecy as were the Apostles before them. They were selected because of their ability to pay. For example, Alexander VI (1492–1503) created eighty new offices and received 760 ducats (about $19,000) from each appointee. Julius II (1503–13) formed a bureau of 101 secretaries who cumulatively paid him 74,000 ducats for the honor. Leo X (1513–23) nominated 60 chamberlains and 141 squires to the papal household and received from them 202,000 ducats. So lucrative was the office of the pope at this time that Alexander VI is said to have received from a variety of sources an income of 70,000 ducats (est. $1,750,000) per year.[72] Additionally, nepotism was widespread; for example, Alexander elevated five family members to cardinalships.[73]

Thus, Isaiah's prophecy, "Forasmuch as this people draw near me with their mouth, and with their lips do honour me, but have removed their heart far from me, and their fear toward me is taught by the precept of men" (Isaiah 29:13), was fully realized in both the papacy and the general clergy.

Paul details the qualifications of a bishop in his epistles to both Timothy and Titus (1 Timothy 3:1–7; Titus 1:7–9). Such attributes as being blameless, holy, the husband of one wife, vigilant, sober, of good behavior, not given to wine, and temperate do not describe the majority of popes during the Middle Ages. While it goes without saying that Jesus is mighty to save and to forgive when we truly repent, contrition and remorse do not imply there is no consequence for sin. Any ecclesiastical leader involved in sexual transgressions, corruption, or other serious sin would be removed from his position of authority to protect the integrity and trust of the Church, which is scriptural. The examples of Judas Iscariot, Esau, and the Old Testament prophet Balaam offer evidence that the Lord requires obedience from those who would be His chosen servants. Ironically, the papacy and Church hierarchy had a history of dealing severely with the laity and lower clergy when convicted of serious sin.

Notwithstanding the papacy's colorful past, the doctrine of infallibility was actually canonized at the Vatican I Council of 1869–70. In accordance with the desires of Pope Pius IX, "the question of infallibility was promoted to a higher place on the agenda."[74] After a spirited debate, the American and English delegations—dissenting in two previous votes—withdrew from the proceedings. A final ballot was taken on July 18, 1870, and was approved by the remaining 533 bishops still in attendance. Although the approved wording was such that infallibility was only recognized when the pope spoke *ex cathedra*, meaning in the exercise of his pastoral office,[75] in order to agree with such a verdict, one had to determine that the depravity of the papacy during the Middle Ages did not destroy its authority.

No evidence exists to support Pope Leo's claim that the papacy inherited Peter's authority. To the contrary, changing doctrines and speculative theology demonstrate that man's authority, not God's, succeeded the Apostles. Nor can Leo's assertion of papal infallibility be supported by scripture, evidence from the early Christian era, or the actions of the papacy during the Middle Ages. God's prophets and Apostles have never been infallible, not even when acting in the "exercise of their pastoral office." Notwithstanding they have not been perfect, true prophets and true Apostles would never lead the Church astray, a claim the papacy cannot make.

Worship of the Virgin Mary

In both the third and fourth Church councils, held in Ephesus and Chalcedon respectively, the divine and human natures of Jesus were hotly debated. At this time, the Greek title *theotókos* (Mother of God) was first introduced in theological writings. Nestorius, patriarch of Constantinople, contested the term, insisting that Christ was two persons, one divine and one human, and that Mary was mother of Christ but not of God.

In 431, the Ephesian Council condemned Nestorianism and proclaimed that Mary was to be called *theotókos,* a title that has been used since that time in the Orthodox and Roman Catholic Churches.

An unhealthy and unscriptural devotion began to be attached to Mary as the mother of God *after the fourth century.* False doctrines, like falsehoods of any kind, must breed additional corruption in order to retain harmony. Such is the case with the false dogmas surrounding Mary. Beginning with Augustine's theology of *original sin,* disobedience for partaking of the forbidden fruit was construed as merely euphemistic—the real sin was deemed to be sexual intercourse. Inasmuch as the first commandment from God was to multiply and replenish the earth (Genesis 1:28), Augustine's interpolation seems unfounded; nevertheless, this assumption formed the basis for what became a very complex philosophy. The mistaken view that Adam's sin was sexual misconduct became the justification for infant baptism, because it was imagined that infants were tainted from birth as a result of "original sin." From this errant ideology came the concept of celibacy, which, it was reasoned, made the unmarried more holy than those entering the covenant of matrimony. Logic next dictated that Mary must have been perfect in order to give birth to the Son of God, and for her to be perfect she could not have been conceived in original sin. Thus, it was rationalized that she must have been conceived through the intervention of the Holy Spirit; therefore, she must have also been perfect and not subject to death as the unavoidable result of sin. Accordingly, rather than suffering an ordinary human death, she fell into a deep sleep and was taken instantly to heaven where she came into direct contact with her son, Jesus, making her the ideal intermediary for prayer. Of course, none

of these doctrines can be found in scripture.

Just before the Reformation period, in the fourteenth and fifteenth centuries, reverence for Mary increased remarkably. The cause of this devotion seems due to the Christian proselyting of tribal communities such as the Goths and others in central and northern Europe. However, these peoples were strongly influenced by Arianism, the doctrine that denied Christ was also God. But if Christ was not God, who would represent man to God the Father? Mary was the logical candidate to fill that void and intercede for sinners, actually becoming the "co-redeemer."[76] Historians writing about this era suggest that Mary's prayers and petitions were construed to appease the severe justice of Christ. The rosary was first introduced during this period as a devotion employed to count prayers and litanies (invocations of Mary), later to include hymns and psalms. Such human innovations had been common in the Church since the demise of the Apostles. Thus, *special interest groups* often dictated the Church's direction, folklore, and its subsequent acceptance into the mainstream, including devotional practices, the introduction of new religious orders, and certain doctrinal innovations, all of which were "demand-led, by the spirituality and desires of the laity."[77]

The chronology of theological devotion to Mary may be summarized as follows: In the thirteenth century, the doctrine of the *immaculate conception* was introduced. This is the theological concept that Mary was conceived without original sin. While many opposed this idea, contending that it diminished Christ's role as our Redeemer, Pope Sixtus IV (1471–84) endorsed it and established the Feast of the Immaculate Conception in 1477 to be celebrated on December 8. Formalization of this doctrine came much later on the anniversary on this date under Pope Pius IX, when he issued his *Ineffabilis Deus* on December 8, 1854.[78] Finally, Pope Pius XII in 1950 added to Mary's acclaim when he designated the doctrine of the *bodily assumption of Mary into heaven* an article of faith for all Roman Catholics.[79] None of these decrees stemmed from traditions of antiquity, and none can be attributed to the primitive Christian Church or to scripture. According to the Bible, Jesus is the *only* name given under heaven whereby man can be saved (Acts 4:12).

Jesus inherited genetic traits from each of His parents, just as we do. From Mary, Jesus inherited the full range of human tendencies; and from the Eternal Father, Jesus inherited God's full range of immortal attributes, including dominion over all human frailties and power over death. Notwithstanding, Jesus was already God the Son from before the foundations of the world, being the firstborn of every creature under heaven, thus existing before Mary's spiritual or physical conception. Mary *is* the earthly mother of Jesus Christ's corruptible body but not His eternal Spirit; she is *not* the mother of God in the sense attributed to Mary by the Chalcedonian Council.

The women of God have played significant roles in all ages of the world. When we stand before the bar of God, we will each know for ourselves that motherly influence chiefly molded mankind. Not only as mothers but in countless other capacities will we see the majesty of women's influence upon the world. Likewise, Mary should be accorded every honor due her celebrated status as the earthly mother of our Lord and Savior Jesus Christ. Only one woman in the history of the world has filled such a role as she did. However, we owe to apostasy and error the allegiance that would have us worship Mary or believe she stands as an intercessor between Christ and mankind. No scriptural evidence to support such a belief exists.

Supererogation and Indulgences

The doctrine of supererogation, or, Treasury of Merits, was unknown in early Christianity or during the patriarchal dispensations; it was first introduced by the Roman Church at the end of the eleventh century. R. N. Swanson has summarized the development of this theology as follows:

> The possibility of purging sins after death offered new incentives to prepare for the after-life which were rapidly exploited. . . . Prayers and masses for the dead would assist the soul by reducing its torment, . . . The idea of the Treasury of Merits was formally adumbrated [vaguely outlined] by Pope Clement VI in 1343; although it had been partially worked out by others earlier. The saints, and pre-eminently Christ by His Passion, had built up a super-abundance of merit before God which the church could direct to other causes; a theory which allowed the . . . pope to distribute indulgences which remitted the pains to be incurred after death. The idea of indulgences grew massively, haphazardly, and almost spontaneously, from what seems to be its first appearance . . . in 1095. Indulgences were marketed as remissions [of sin] . . . time off purgatory . . . bought to aid the souls of those already dead.[80]

Indulgences were first offered as motivation to those participating in the Crusades and were known as "plenary [comprehensive] indulgences." By the time of the Reformation, indulgences could be acquired by the laity through undertaking pilgrimages, contributing to building programs, or "buying" confessional letters.[81] The purchase of *remitted sins* was plainly an antibiblical idea, but it quickly gathered steam when its effectiveness was proven during the Crusades; however, its practice was the straw that broke the camel's back, inspiring Martin Luther to inaugurate the Reformation.

The patriarchal dispensations and the New Testament Church required the repentant sinner to confess his sins, forsake the behavior, and make restitution where possible.[82] By contrast, the postapostolic Church after Constantine imposed severe physical penalties. Instead of the grace of Christ being sufficient to enable forgiveness, special fasts, floggings, and even death were administered to those guilty of serious sin. In effect, they denied the atonement of Jesus Christ by requiring individual acts of atonement from the sinners.

As mentioned, just prior to the Reformation greater abuses began to surround the practice of granting purchased indulgences: they were now said to bestow immediate spiritual relief *even without personal repentance.* This perversion led Martin Luther and others of the clergy to abandon the Church and undertake Protestant reforms. One of the participants in this historic epoch was an individual by the name of Johann Tetzel who became the center of conflict when, in the course of selling indulgences near Wittenberg, his sermons came to the attention of Martin Luther. Preying upon fear and ignorance, Tetzel preached:

Listen to the voices of your dear dead relatives and friends, beseeching you and saying, "Pity us, pity us. We are in dire torment from which you can redeem us for a pittance." Do you not wish to? Open your ears. Hear the father saying to his son, the mother to the daughter, "We bore you, nourished you, brought you up, left you our fortunes, and you are so cruel and hard that now you are not willing for so little to set us free. Will you let us lie here in flames? Will

you delay our promised glory?"[83]

Then, with suprising audacity, Tetzel would say:

*As soon as the coin in the coffer rings,
The soul from purgatory springs.*[84]

Money collected from the sale of indulgences went to fund the new St. Peter's Cathedral in Rome. Under an arrangement made with Pope Leo X, half of the proceeds went to rebuild St. Peters and half went to the archbishop of Mainz to fund the cost of his appointment as archbishop of that city.

In the Gospel of John, we are told that God the Father delegated to His Son Jesus Christ power to forgive sins (John 5:22, 27). Following the Resurrection, Jesus declared to His Apostles, "Whose soever sins ye remit, they are remitted unto them; and whose soever sins ye retain, they are retained" (John 20:23). Notwithstanding the authority given by the Savior to His Apostles, *the doctrine of repentance was never withdrawn.*

The scriptures teach that in order to repent, a man must recognize his sins, confess them (with sincere sorrow) and forsake them (Proverbs 28:13; 2 Corinthians 7:10), make restitution (Ezekiel 33:15–20), and strive to live a righteous life (Hebrews 6:6). These laws were established from the foundation of the world, and the very God who ordained these laws does not disobey or circumvent them. Money cannot buy the "gift of God" (Acts 8:20), and it cannot buy forgiveness. The doctrine of indulgences, first proposed a thousand years after the apostolic period, was presented to and embraced by the papacy, an institution that had undergone centuries of continuous corruption. No balance can be found between the teachings of scripture and the reality of what the Church was endeavoring to promote. In the end, forgiveness is granted by Him who atoned for our sins, bought us with His own blood, and stood as proxy for our failings. Jesus prayed to the Father that the Apostles might be one with Him and the Father. The papacy of the Middles Ages was not in harmony with God. Did not Jesus say to His Apostles, "I am the vine, ye are the branches. . . . If ye abide in me, and my words abide in you, ye shall ask what ye will, and it shall be done unto you" (John 15:5–7). The popes of this age could not qualify to remit sins in the manner extended by Jesus to His Apostles; quite simply the Church no longer possessed priesthood authority. If so, the popes would not have offered forgiveness of sin purchased with money.

Although the foregoing prose seems harsh, it is not intended to denigrate Catholics who hold great faith in the power of the Church and in its priests. The purpose in presenting the voice of scripture (God's truth) is to indicate what the early Christians believed and practiced. Notwithstanding, the mystic practice of indulgences cut the Christian Church asunder, and although it was simplified in 1967 and certain reforms introduced, the Catholic Church still grants (purchased) indulgences today, one of the evidences of the apostasy of the Church of Rome.

The Church Imposes Celibacy upon Its Clergy

Celibacy was never taught and never practiced by the New Testament Church. Although recorded history of the apostolic age is sparse, Eusebius writes that Peter, Philip, and Paul were all married but that Paul "did not take [his wife] about with him, in order to expedite his ministry the better."[85] Celibacy was apparently first practiced by some Christians early in the second century; thereafter,

monastic societies began to emerge in the mid-third century with St. Anthony. Celibacy soon became more common in the Church's priesthood, and it was proposed at the counsel of Nicaea that priests and deacons should refrain from marriage and be compelled to a life of self-denial. However, according to Sozomenus and others, "the law was opposed openly and decidedly by Paphnutius, bishop of a city of the Upper Thebais in Egypt."[86] Paphnutius was a *highly respected* bishop who survived severe persecution under Maximian during the regime of Emperor Diocletian: He had lost an eye during this time and was well known as a man of considerable faith and miracles. In rejecting this law, he implored the council:

> Not to impose so heavy a yoke on the ministers of religion: asserting that 'marriage itself is honorable, and the bed undefiled'; urging before God that they ought not to injure the Church by too stringent restrictions. "For all men," said he, "cannot bear the practice of rigid continence."[87]

Through this wise bishop's counsel, the measure failed.

Although celibacy was not formally passed into canon law until 1074, pressure continued to mount throughout the Church and was—in actual practice—mandatory near the end of the sixth century. Monastic societies substantially expanded during this period under the leadership of Benedict of Nursia, who established the Benedictine Rule. Notable clergymen such as Gregory the Great, pope from 590 to 604, were disciples of this order. However, corruption within these reclusive societies became commonplace in the ensuing centuries with the rampant practice of simony, nepotism, widespread immorality, and an easily discernible change from being devotees of discipline, study, and service to becoming patrons of indolence, sloth, and wealthy monasteries. Consequently, the natural and productive state of matrimony was replaced by unnatural celibate communes.

After centuries of corruption, monastic reforms were finally initiated at Cluny in eastern France in the early tenth century. A charter was granted to a reform-minded abbot named Berno who came from another monastery to establish the new one at Cluny. The charter granted liberal authority to the new order, providing freedom from government and religious authority and self-rule under the protection of the pope. Reform spread quickly through both the Benedictine Rule as well as the more than eleven hundred monasteries established under Cluniac leadership by the twelfth century. The major elements of reform included a crackdown on simony, nepotism, and the absolute celibacy of all clergymen. In addition to the Benedictine and Cluniac societies, the Franciscan Order was established by St. Francis of Assisi, achieving remarkable growth in the early thirteenth century. Celibacy became universal among the clergy by the pope's order, and the growth spawned by these directives created an increased demand for monastic societies, but corruption returned in later years. One historian recorded:

> Of the four orders of friars founded in the thirteenth century—Franciscans, Dominicans, Carmelites, Augustinians—all but the last had become scandalously lax in piety and discipline. . . . Absolved by their great wealth from the necessity of manual labor, thousands of monks and friars neglected religious services, wandered outside their walls, drank in taverns, and pursued amours [sexual liaisons].[88]

The general clergy had become so despotic due to the unnatural state of celibacy that Erasmus was led to say, "Many convents of men and women differ very little from public brothels."[89]

The Roman Church professes that the practice of celibacy by the clergy is supported by scriptural passages from the New Testament, specifically 1 Corinthians 7:6–7, 25 and Matthew 19:12. The Church contends that celibacy was established so that "the clergy may serve God with more freedom and with undivided heart"; thus, "being called to serve Jesus Christ, the clergy may embrace the holier life of self-restraint." And while the Church maintains that matrimony is itself a holy state, official doctrine declares that celibacy is "a state of greater perfection."

The Bible reveals that such doctrines were never subscribed to or taught by Jesus and the Apostles, and no communal orders were ever established during New Testament Christianity. First Corinthians 7 is widely misunderstood because precise interpretations have been applied to answers which Paul gave to specific Corinthian questions (v. 1) *which we no longer have access to!*

A critically acclaimed modern publication, *Cultural Literacy* by E. D. Hirsch, examines the importance of understanding basic events from world history in order to comprehend other basic interrelated subjects without requiring an author to dissect and explain the layers of key historical details. Hirsch uses the example of reading a newspaper. He illustrates that if a journalist had to stop to interpret every fact without assuming the reader comprehended the most basic and general information, the article would become lengthy and boring to the average reader. To individuals lacking such basic knowledge, reading a simple newspaper article and properly interpreting the message would be difficult if not impossible. Hirsch writes:

> The recently rediscovered insight that literacy is more than a skill is based

upon knowledge that all of us unconsciously have about language. We know instinctively that to understand what somebody is saying, *we must understand more than the surface meanings of the words; we have to understand the context as well.* The need for background information applies all the more to reading and writing. To grasp the words on the page *we have to know a lot of information that isn't set down on the page.*[90]

Many details germane to understanding Paul's response to the Corinthians simply are not available to us, such questions as what did Paul's audience know regarding the Lord's doctrines of marriage, *or what his audience assumed Paul already knew, or what Paul assumed it already knew,* when certain questions were asked about very isolated aspects of marriage. An example of such a unique question might be when the Sadducees petitioned the Savior regarding which husband would belong to a woman in the hereafter of the seven she married under very unique circumstances.[91] Paul's answers would have been carefully prepared responses directed at very specific inquiries. Such a significant and far-reaching doctrine and practice as celibacy unfortunately was built around obscure, limited, and uncertain passages of scripture.

Finally, a number of compelling verses can be cited as clearly opposing such theology. As an example of coming apostasy, Paul observes the following: "Now the Spirit speaketh expressly, that in the latter times some shall depart from the faith, giving heed to seducing spirits, and doctrines of devils; . . . forbidding to marry" (1 Timothy 4:1–3).

In the beginning, God Himself counseled, *"It is not good that the man should be alone; I will make an help meet for him"* (Genesis 2:18; emphasis added). Further, God said, "Therefore shall a man leave his father and his mother, and shall cleave unto his wife: and

they shall be one flesh" (Genesis 2:24). Jesus, answering a question from the Pharisees, responded, "For this cause shall a man leave father and mother, and shall cleave to his wife: and they twain shall be one flesh? Wherefore they are no more twain, but one flesh. What therefore God hath joined together, let not man put asunder" (Matthew 19:5–6). Paul teaches that the woman is created for the man and that "neither is the man without the woman, neither the woman without the man, in the Lord" (1 Corinthians 11:9). Paul also instructed the Hebrews that marriage was "honourable in all" (Hebrews 13:4). Lastly, Paul carefully advised those who were bishops how they should treat a wife and children (1 Timothy 1:2–5; Titus 1:6). Undeniably, bishops of New Testament Christianity were not celibate.

If the record and evidence of history can be used to validate the wisdom offered by the early fourth-century bishop Paphnutius, then we may easily establish that celibacy was not inspired of God but by men. Modern historian and Catholic Garry Wills has recently compiled a significant case as to why the Catholic Church ought to amend its canon law and permit the marriage of priests. In the context of Church doctrine (not his own opinion which is decidedly liberal), he catalogues the current *widespread* problem of homosexuality, fornication, adultery, and worse yet, the abuse of children and adolescents, both male and female.[92] He concludes:

The Pope has made the number of priests dwindle sharply by insisting on celibacy, and he has ended up not only with a smaller number of priests but with a diminished band that is *less* celibate. Almost all the priests who left in the massive hemorrhage of the 1970s and 1980s left to marry. The homosexual priests stayed, which meant that their proportion of the whole went up even when their absolute numbers stayed the same. And now even that absolute number is rising.[93]

There is no record of celibacy ever being practiced during the dispensations of Adam, Enoch, Noah, Abraham, or Moses. The only evidence of celibacy prior to the meridian of time is displayed when Judah was in apostasy. No celibacy can be substantiated during the lifetime of the Savior or His Apostles. Only when the inspired wisdom of the oracles of God were silenced (due to apostasy as we may suppose) did the practice of celibacy begin.

Pope Proclaims That He Is the Vicar of Christ

Akin to the doctrine of infallibility, the papal claim of being the Vicar of Christ is without reliable foundation. Admittedly, many popes were highly skilled administrators and capable ministers who led moral and spiritual lives; however, as we have seen, many possessed no such redeeming qualities. Soon after the death of the Apostles, the bishops of major cities became the presiding authorities over large geographical regions, with no one bishop exercising authority over another. Victor, bishop of Rome near the end of the second century, thought that other cities should observe Easter on the same day as the Roman church. And in the mid-third century, in a dispute over baptism between Bishop Stephen of Rome and Cyprian of Carthage, Stephen used the text of Matthew 16:19 to buttress the Roman position.[94] As we have seen, Hippolytus vehemently denied that Rome had such authority and opposed false doctrines taught by both Zephyrinus (198–217) and Callistus (217–23), as had Polycarp with Anicetus (155). Nonetheless, beginning in the mid-third century there is some sentiment towards Rome, the alleged

seat of St. Peter, as the center of Christianity and attempting to exert some measure of primacy over the other bishops. Whatever convictions may have been held by various local leaders, no general policies existed within the Church for many centuries after the death of the Apostles. For example, the sacraments (Eucharist, baptism, marriage, etc.) were performed differently all over the Roman Empire. However, after Constantine became emperor and his successors were heavily involved in matters of religion, greater emphasis on uniformity and central leadership emerged.

There are no reliable writings produced by the Apostolic Fathers recognizing any primacy of the Roman bishop, nor were any validations supplied by the Apologists or Polemicists. No early communication exists that would lead us to conclude any superior authority was held by the Roman bishop. Although Clement of Rome wrote two surviving letters of exhortation to the Corinthians, Ignatius of *Antioch* has by far the most extant letters addressed to various congregations, including a letter of instruction and counsel he wrote to the Church at Rome. No trustworthy evidence exists suggesting that any bishop had authority over another bishop or region. Notwithstanding, by the late fourth century, Roman bishops were claiming absolute supremacy over the Church. Cheetham writes of Pope Damasus (366–84), "He proclaimed in the firmest terms the primacy of his apostolic see at the precise moment when the Catholic faith became indisputably the empire's official religion."[95]

At the same time Damasus was strongly advocating his central leadership from Rome, the patriarch of Constantinople—the new seat of the imperial government—was claiming equal status to the bishop of Rome. This rift would ultimately divide the Universal Church.

A few decades later during very turbulent political times for the Empire, another Roman bishop, Leo I, again reasserted Rome's position of authority over all Christendom. Cheetham explains:

> As his 150 surviving letters show, he insistently reminded them [other bishops] of their dependence upon the [seat] of St. Peter as the fount of all authority, of their duty to obedience to it, and of its own duty of caring for them. When Hilarius, bishop of Arles, tried to assert the independence of the Gallican church against Rome, Leo obtained from the pliant Valentinian [emperor of Rome] a decree confirming the absolute primacy of the Apostolic See and forbidding the bishops of Gaul or any other imperial province, under threat of legal penalties, to contravene its ordinances. At the same time he was working out a theory of papal monarchy. He wished to establish that the powers conferred upon St. Peter by Christ himself were automatically handed down to the Apostle's successors and all future bishops of Rome who were, at least in principle, elected by the city's clergy and laity.[96]

Notwithstanding Leo's claims, the Fourth Ecumenical Council, held at Chalcedon, declared the patriarch of Constantinople to be equal with Rome itself and superior to those bishops at Antioch and Alexandria.[97]

The tradition of Roman primacy matured in 607, when Pope Boniface III, who with his predecessor had pushed tirelessly in acquiring the recognized title of pope, finally persuaded the Emperor Phocus to confer the ecumenical title upon him. Bonaface rewarded Phocus by erecting a gilded statue in the Roman forum.[98] Although the title of "pope," meaning father, is typically identified with the Roman bishop, it was also used by prelates in other cities. Even today, the patriarch of the Coptic Church in Alexandria bears this designation.

Perhaps the boldest and most troubling assertion from any pope came from Gregory VII in the late eleventh century. In his zeal to reform the Church, Gregory (given name Hildebrand) sought greater supremacy over secular, temporal, and spiritual matters than any pontiff preceding him. In a document attributed to him entitled the *Dictatus Papae,* he declared that the Roman Church had "never erred and would never err." He claimed that its bishop was alone to be called universal, having power and authority over all other bishops, and that he himself could be judged by no one. Gregory asserted that he had power even to depose emperors, having authority to release subjects from allegiance to their sovereign.[97] Beginning with the rise of Hildebrand to the papal chair, the temporal authority of the pope became greater than kings and emperors during the twelfth and thirteenth centuries.

This claim was underscored by one of Gregory's highly regarded successors, Innocent III. In a particularly dangerous political situation where two German kings had been simultaneously elected, Otto had been crowned emperor by Innocent, only to have Otto attempt to exercise control over the Church. Innocent found himself in the precarious circumstance of having to join in a political alliance with Frederick of the House of Hohenstaufens. The Hohenstaufens historically had assumed not only the right of leadership of Germany but also of Italy, along with the misleading title "King of the Romans," assuming automatic coronation over such, including the papal state and the city of Rome. Of this situation, Cheetham observes:

> Innocent was determined to rebut that contention. For him there was no doubt

at all that only a pope could choose and make an emperor; the latter was simply the sworded arm of the universal church; *the pope was the sun and the Emperor, shining with reflected light, the moon.*[100]

Accordingly, Innocent viewed even his temporal authority as higher than that of the emperor. However, in the centuries just preceding him, the papacy hardly resembled the Vicar of Christ that it claimed to be. From 757, with some few exceptions, to 1045 a period of corruption, murder, immorality, intrigue, lavish indulgence, and nearly every other depravity conceivable emerged.[101] Although historians attempt to explain this period as befitting the times due in part to the interruption of learning and culture invoked by the invasions of the Northern Barbarians, crimes of the papacy of that era are far too egregious to ignore. While such behavior may be best understood in the context of "the times," the real reason was far more simple: the Church and its leaders had strayed from the authority and principles of original Christianity. Noah did not vacillate in his age (Genesis 6:9); despite Abraham's idolatrous father, he was faithful (Apoc. of Abraham 8); Moses, Joshua, Caleb, and others did not fall into sin with the majority—only when God was fully rejected after lengthy periods of intervention, as with Noah, prior to Moses, and after King Josiah (following many wicked generations) did God partly withdraw Himself for periods of time.

In a similar period of apostasy, the pope represented himself as Christ's spokesman on earth charged to act in His name. Fortunately, the Savior gave us a key by which all men can judge accurately both good and evil. Said He to his Apostles:

Ye shall know them by their fruits. Do men gather grapes of thorns, or figs of thistles? Even so every good tree bringeth forth good fruit; but a corrupt tree bringeth forth evil fruit. A good tree cannot bring forth evil fruit, neither can a corrupt tree bring forth good fruit. . . . Wherefore by their fruits ye shall know them. (Matthew 7:16–20)

Jesus could not have spoken more plainly. While many popes, including Gregory VII and Innocent III, were capable and well-meaning leaders, their policies, doctrines, and overzealous and unbiblical approach to nonbelievers (as manifest in the Crusades and the Inquisition) were far from the teachings set forth by the Son of God whom they claimed to represent. One cannot conclude that the pope was either infallible, intellectually superior, or more morally perfect than other men, given the undeniable tradition and character of the papacy, nor that these men were the Vicars of Christ invested with the apostolic authority of Peter.

During this period, the tradition began whereby the pope was no longer elected by the voice of the people but by what became known as the College of Cardinals. Remembering the words of the Apostolic Father, Clement of Rome, regarding the pattern established by the Savior and the Apostles, bears repeating in this section:

Our apostles also knew, through our Lord Jesus Christ, there would be strife for the title of bishop. For this cause, therefore, since they had obtained a perfect fore-knowledge of this, they appointed those already mentioned, and afterwards gave instructions, that when these should fall asleep, other approved men should succeed them in their ministry. *We are of opinion, therefore, that those appointed by them, or afterwards by other eminent men, with the consent of the whole Church . . . cannot be justly dismissed from the ministry.*[102]

Moreover, the book of Acts explains that revelation for selecting new leaders was received by the Apostles through the Holy Ghost and ratified by the common consent of the people (see pages 126–27). This pattern established by the Savior and the Apostles had not been observed for centuries by the Church of Rome. Because the Church was not receiving revelation from the Holy Ghost and was now rejecting the voice of the people, Christianity moved even further away from the original teachings of Jesus Christ.

Another disturbing event involving the papacy was the troubling schism which took place at Avignon, France, in the fourteenth century. Pope Clement V, a Frenchman elected by the College of Cardinals in 1305, moved the papal headquarters from Rome to Avignon in 1309. A weak administrator who was timid in the exercise of his authority, Clement and many of his successors introduced further blight upon the credibility of the office of the pope while the people of Europe became very uncomfortable with the Roman See operating under the influence of powerful French rulers.

In 1377, after the diplomatic intervention of Catherine of Sienna, Gregory XI returned the papal office to Rome, ending what some historians term the "Babylonian captivity." Upon Gregory's death the next year, the cardinals elected Bartolomeo Prignano, the archbishop of Bari, as Pope Urban VI. It was believed that Urban would be a moderate force who might mend the rift between the Italians and the cardinals from France. This quarrel had escalated over the many decades the papacy had resided in Avignon, with French cardinals holding a majority in the electoral college. Unfortunately, Urban's behavior was highly offensive and created significant contention and animosity between the cardinals

and the pope, causing the French cardinals to leave Rome in small groups during the summer of 1378. They assembled in Anagni and attempted to coerce Urban to resign. In frustration, the thirteen French cardinals declared Urban's election "uncanonical" and elected Robert of Geneva as Clement VII. Each pope promptly excommunicated the other pope, whereupon Urban appointed twenty-nine of his own cardinals.

Just when it appeared that order and the authority of the papacy had been restored to Rome, Clement VII, seeking safety from the angry Italians, moved his regime back to Avignon. Thereafter a division of allegiance occurred. England, Germany, Northern Italy, and Scandinavia followed Urban in Rome. France, Scotland, Spain, and Southern Italy followed Clement VII in Avignon. Numerous attempts to end the schism were pursued by governments from both sides, warring factions abounded, but no resolution to the problem could be secured. Because each pope had his own college of cardinals, instead of unifying after his death, each elected a new competing pope. Power and corruption embraced the papacy of this era, and neither side would acquiesce.

Circumstances took an even more bizarre turn when a council was convened in Pisa in 1409 by a majority of cardinals and Churchmen from both sides. The council voted to depose the two existing popes, Gregory XII and Benedict XIII, and to elect a new conciliar pope, Alexander V, who died shortly thereafter and was followed by Pope John XXIII. However, the authority of the cardinals' actions was not recognized by either of the contending popes nor some of the secular governments who supported one pope or the other, so now there were three popes who had been formally elected by three separate colleges of cardinals.

The great schism finally came to an end in 1417 under the leadership of Sigismund, the Holy Roman Emperor. Pope John was tried, convicted, and deposed. Pope Gregory, by now a man in his late eighties, resigned and accepted a cardinal's position until his death. Refusing to concede, Pope Benedict died in exile. The newly elected Pope Martin had the responsibility of repairing years of damage to the papacy and of restoring order to the Church. And yet an even greater challenge would face the Universal Church in the years ahead—a demand for reformation and the advent of the Protestant revolution.

The Bible itself stands as a witness that the popes were not the Vicars of Christ. The comparison of rebellious Israel and the Church of the Middle Ages, often used in this book, equally fits in this instance. The Lord prophesied through Jeremiah:

"The house of Israel and the house of Judah have been utterly unfaithful to me" declares the Lord. They have lied about the Lord; they said, "He will do nothing! No harm will come to us; we will never see sword or famine. The prophets are but wind and the word is not in them; . . ." The [false] prophets prophesy lies, and the priests rule by their own authority, and my people love it this way. . . . From the least to the greatest, all are greedy for gain; [false] prophets and priests alike, all practice deceit. They dress the wound of my people as though it were not serious. "Peace, peace," they say, when there is no peace. Are they ashamed of their loathsome conduct? No, they have no shame at all; they do not even know how to blush. (Jeremiah 6:13–15 NIV)

Israel was plainly rejected by the Lord during this period (Jeremiah 6:30). False prophets, priests, and the people alike had turned their backs on God. The condition

of the priesthood during the Middle Ages was no different: it had rejected the Master in favor of worldly ambition. And like Israel who "love[d] it this way," so also the laity had demanded many of the changes that altered original Christianity.[103] Israel was in apostasy when Christ came; the Universal Church during the Middle Ages clearly resembled Israel during the days of Isaiah and Jeremiah. Would Israel during Jeremiah's time be rejected while Christianity in the Middle Ages be accepted?

Conclusion

The Catholic Church today in no way resembles the Church of the Middle Ages. Although doctrines such as celibacy continue to plague the Church, great good is being done by its schools and ministries throughout the world. Moreover, Christianity is indebted to the Roman Church for the preservation of the canon and for many truths that survived the human imprint. While the Church organization itself languished in sin during those many centuries of spiritual confusion and despair, people of faith lived who trusted in God and followed Him according to the dictates of conscious. God-fearing sons and daughters during wicked periods of apostasy in the patriarchal dispensations also remained virtuous and true, in spite of the corrupt environment in which they lived.

Nevertheless, the legacy of erring doctrine and the absence of divine authority remains from that early period when the Apostles died and their successors were rejected by aspiring men. Although the Church attempted to regain its course, apostasy escalated throughout the centuries, beginning with the rise of Constantine to the imperial throne and achieving its peak just before the Counter Reformation. The Church abused its power and authority by exercising control over men through such means as the Crusades and the Inquisition; and the widespread practice of simony and nepotism was man's uninspired and corrupt system of replacing and selecting Church leaders. Furthermore, contrasting the ministry of the Apostles, the clergy and papacy deteriorated into an ecclesiastical body devoid of the Spirit and unable to call upon the inspiration of heaven.

The marriage of church and state was doomed from the outset. The laws of God and *His truth* cannot be politicized or negotiated; His standards and teachings are absolute and have been from the beginning. The modifications made to the priesthood organization of the Church were human innovations, as were the adornments to sacred ordinances and sacraments. Such alterations were reminiscent of apostasy in earlier dispensations. When the heavens became silent and there were no longer "open visions" as in the days prior to Samuel's divine appointment, scholarly speculation replaced revelation from the heavens and the Lord's divine Church became a human church. Finally, the decline of the papacy and the entire priesthood hierarchy furnishes powerful evidence that the Lord was no longer directing the work of the Church. Notwithstanding, God had not forgotten His children and was steadily working His will *through the agency of man* and according to His eternal and unchangeable laws.

Notes

1. Brian Tierney and Sidney Painter, *Western Europe in the Middle Ages, 300–1475* (New York: McGraw-Hill, 1998), 21–22; see also Cheetham, *Keepers of the Keys,* 24.

2. C. H. Haskins has written, "[T]he continuity of history rejects . . . sharp and violent contrasts between successive periods, . . . [M]odern research shows us the Middle Ages [were] less dark and less static, the Renaissance less bright and sudden, than was once supposed," in Wallace K. Ferguson, *The Renaissance in Historical Thought* (New York: Houghton Mifflin, 1975), 333.

3. Kelly, *Early Christian Doctrines,* 410.

4. Kelly, *Early Christian Doctrines,* 410.

5. James E. Talmage, *Jesus the Christ: A Study of the Messiah and His Mission According to Holy Scriptures Both Ancient and Modern* (Salt Lake City: Deseret Book, 1990), 452.

6. Chadwick, *Early Church,* 223.

7. Robert N. Swanson, *Religion and Devotion in Europe, c. 1215–c. 1515* (Cambridge: Cambridge University Press, 1995), 264.

8. Swanson, *Religion and Devotion in Europe,* 266.

9. Swanson, *Religion and Devotion in Europe,* 14.

10. Cheetham, *Keepers of the Keys,* 21.

11. McBrian, *Lives of the Popes,* 94.

12. Cheetham, *Keepers of the Keys,* 43.

13. Cheetham, *Keepers of the Keys,* 58.

14. Cheetham, *Keepers of the Keys,* 84.

15. Cheetham, *Keepers of the Keys,* 87; see also McBrian, *Lives of the Popes,* 174–75.

16. Wesley, *Works of John Wesley,* sermon 89, 7:26–27.

17. Cheetham, *Keepers of the Keys,* 35.

18. Cheetham, *Keepers of the Keys,* 36.

19. Cheetham, *Keepers of the Keys,* 85.

20. Cheetham, *Keepers of the Keys,* 96–97.

21. Cheetham, *Keepers of the Keys,* 84.

22. Revelation given to Adam, Genesis 1:28–30; to Noah, Genesis 6:13; 9:8–17; to Abraham, Genesis 17:1–5; to Isaac, Genesis 26:1–5; to Jacob, Genesis 48:2–4; to Joseph, Genesis 40:8–19; to Moses, Exodus 3:2–6. God works His will through prophets, see Amos 3:7.

23. Revelations of the Father come through the Son: Luke 6:12–13; John 5:20; 7:16; 14:31; 15:15.

24. Revelation continued to guide the Church through the Apostles: Acts 1:24; 5:19–20; 9:10–16; 10:11–15; 13:2–3. At the same time such bishops as Clement in Rome and Ignatius in Antioch are currently ministering; all but John of the original Twelve have perished, yet he (John) continues to receive revelation in the mid to late

A.D. 90s (Revelation 1:1–3). This revelation issued a stern warning to the Church to repent (Revelation 2:5). It was followed a few years later by the vision to the Shepherd of Hermas with an urgent "last call." There is nothing in John's revelation—or the entire canon—to imply that the heavens will thereafter close until the second coming of Jesus. In fact, it is a strange and inexplicable phenomenon that God would not continue to operate today as in ages past. On the other hand, history attests that apostasy, as witnessed at various times throughout the Old Testament, will occur: notice the gap between Ephraim and Moses, probably caused by idol worship (Joshua 24:14); Samuel 3:1; Psalm 74:9; Jeremiah 5:31; 1 Maccabees 4:46; 9:27; no prophets between Malachi and John the Baptist due to wickedness (Malachi 2:8), perfectly accounted for heavenly silence after the apostolic age.

25. Curtis, Lang, Petersen, *100 Most Important Events in Christian History*, 30–31.

26. Compare the prosperity of Abraham, Isaac, Jacob, Joseph, and even Job. These and many other examples do not square with Anthony or any of the ascetics of the postapostolic period. Also see Job 38:7; Ecclesiastes 9:9; Isaiah 12:3; John 15:11; 16:21; 3 John 1:4.

27. Manichaeism was founded in the third century by the philosopher Mani. He claimed several visions that placed him in a succession of the prophets Buddha and Jesus, ending with himself. The doctrine of Mani was similar in nature to Gnostic religions, dividing the universe into the evil material world ruled by Satan and the righteous spiritual realm governed by God. Augustine eventually wrote expositions condemning Manichaeism.

28. Augustine, City of God 5.9–10, in *Nicene and Post-Nicene Fathers*, 1:2:90–93.

29. Kelly, *Early Christian Doctrines*, 368–69.

30. Kelly, *Early Christian Doctrines*, 369.

31. Kelly, *Early Christian Doctrines*, 370–71

32. Clementine Recognitions 5.6, in *Ante-Nicene Fathers*, 8:144.

33. Clementine Recognitions 5.7, in *Ante-Nicene Fathers*, 8:144; emphasis added.

34. Justin Martyr, Dialogue with Trypho 141, in *Ante-Nicene Fathers*, 1:270; emphasis added.

35. Justin, Second Apology 7, in *Ancient Christian Writers* 56, 78–79.

36. Justin, First Apology 28, in *Ancient Christian Writers* 56, 43.

37. Justin, First Apology 43–44, in *Ancient Christian Writers* 56, 52–53; emphasis added.

38. Epistle of Methetes to Diognetus 7, in *Ante-Nicene Fathers*, 1:27.

39. Irenaeus, "Against Heresies" 4.37.1, in *Ante-Nicene Fathers*, 1:518.

40. Hippolytus, Refutation of All Heresies 29, in *Ante-Nicene Fathers*, 5:152.

41. Clement, Stromata 1.17, in *Ante-Nicene Fathers*, 2:319.

42. Origen, De Principiis 8, in *Ante-Nicene Fathers*, 4:255.

43. Origen, Peri Archon 3.1.19, in Trigg, *Origen*, 29.

44. N. Joseph Torchia, *"Creatio ex nihilo" and the Theology of St. Augustine: The Anti-Manichaean Polemic and Beyond* (New York: Peter Lang Publishing, 1999), 5–8.

45. Edwin Hatch, *The Influence of Greek Ideas on Christianity* (Gloucester, Mass.: P. Smith, 1970), 195–96.

46. Torchia, *"Creatio ex nihilo,"* 9–10.

47. Irenaeus, Clement of Alexandria, Tertullian, and Origen all wrote lengthy discourses against the various Gnostic sects flourishing within Christianity of the second and third centuries.

48. Torchia, *"Creatio ex nihilo,"* 2. Philo believed that the world was created out of "formless stuff" (*amorphou hyles*) rather than from nothing. He appears to say this in De Opificio Mundi 9. Philo agrees with the Book of Wisdom on this matter (Wisdom 11:17). Philo and Wisdom are sometimes pitted against 2 Maccabees 7:28, however, according to Gerhard Kittel, Gerhard Friedrich, and Geoffrey W. Bromiley, *The Theological Dictionary of the New Testament* (New York: William B. Eerdmans, 1985), 3:878, 2 Maccabees says that the world was made "not from things" rather than from nothing. Thus, 2 Maccabees is not necessarily inconsistent with Philo or Wisdom.

49. Kittel, Friedrich, and Bromiley, *Theological Dictionary of the New Testament*, 3:2–3.

50. Cuthbert A. Simpson, *The Book of Genesis:*

Introduction and Exegesis, in The Interpreter's Bible, 12 vols. (New York: Abington Pess, 1952–57), 1:466.

51. Pinnock, *Most Beloved Mover,* 146; see also P. Copan, "Is Creatio ex Nihilo a Post Biblical Convention? An Examination of Gerhard May's Proposal," *Trinity Journal* 17 (1996): 77–93.

52. Keith Norman, "Ex Nihilo: The Development of the Doctrines of God and Creation in Early Christianity," *BYU Studies* 17, no. 3 (1977). Speiser's translation means literally, "In the beginning of God's creating" (see Cuthbert A. Simpson, *The Book of Genesis: Introduction and Exegesis, in the Interpreter's Bible,* 12 vols [New York: Abington Press, 1952–57], 1:466).

53. Justin Martyr, First Apology 10, in *Ancient Christian Writers* 56, 28.

54. Justin Martyr, First Apology 67, in *Ancient Christian Writers* 56, 71.

55. Justin Martyr, Second Apology 6, in *Ancient Christian Writers* 56, 77.

56. Clement of Alexandria, Instructor 3:12, in *Ante-Nicene Fathers,* 2:296.

57. Shepherd of Hermas, vis. 1:6, in *Apostolic Fathers,* 2:9.

58. Shepherd of Hermas, vis. 3:4, in *Apostolic Fathers,* 2:15.

59. Origen, De Principiis 2:1:4, in *Ante-Nicene Fathers,* 4:269.

60. Origen, De Principiis 2:1:5, in *Ante-Nicene Fathers,* 4:270.

61. Origen, De Principiis 4:1:33, in *Ante-Nicene Fathers,* 4:379.

62. Torchia, *"Creatio ex nihilo,"* 33–36.

63. Torchia, *"Creatio ex nihilo,"* 34.

64. Theophilus, Theophilus to Autolycus 2:4, in *Ante-Nicene Fathers,* 2:95.

65. Cheetham, *Keepers of the Keys,* 26.

66. Cheetham, *Keepers of the Keys,* 26.

67. McBrian, *Lives of the Popes,* 127

68. Cheetham, *Keepers of the Keys,* 60.

69. Cheetham, *Keepers of the Keys,* 65; emphasis added.

70. Cheetham, *Keepers of the Keys,* 66–67.

71. Cheetham, *Keepers of the Keys,* 80.

72. Will Durant, *The Reformation: A History of European Civilization from Wyclif to Calvin, 1300–1564* (New York: Simon and Schuster, 1957), 19.

Durant's book was published in 1957 and the estimates provided reflect that date.

73. Cheetham, *Keepers of the Keys,* 188.

74. Cheetham, *Keepers of the Keys,* 265–66.

75. Cheetham, *Keepers of the Keys,* 266.

76. Euan Cameron, "The Power of the Word: Renaissance and Reformation," in *Early Modern Europe: An Oxford History,* ed. Euan Cameron (New York: Oxford University Press, 1999), 86.

77. Swanson, *Religion and Devotion in Europe,* 9.

78. Swanson, *Religion and Devotion in Europe,* 264.

79. Swanson, *Religion and Devotion in Europe,* 291.

80. Swanson, *Religion and Devotion in Europe,* 37–38.

81. Cameron, *Early Modern Europe,* 87.

82. Leviticus 6:4, "[B]ecause he hath sinned, and is guilty, that he shall restore that which he took"; Psalm 38:18, "I will declare mine iniquity; I will be sorry for my sin"; Proverbs 28:13, "whoso confesseth and forsaketh them shall have mercy"; Matthew 9:2, "Seeing their faith"; 2 Corinthians 7:10, "godly sorrow worketh repentance to salvation."

83. Roland H. Bainton, *Here I Stand: A Life of Martin Luther* (Nashville, Tenn.: Abingdon Press, 1978), 59.

84. Bainton, *Here I Stand,* 60.

85. Eusebius, Ecclesiastical History 3.30, 115.

86. Hefele, in *Nicene and Post-Nicene Fathers,* 2:14:51. Socrates wrote, "There were among the bishops two of extraordinary celebrity, Paphnutius, . . . and Spyridon," in *Nicene and Post-Nicene Fathers,* 2:2:8.

87. Socrates on Paphnutius, in *Nicene and Post-Nicene Fathers,* 2:2:18.

88. Durant, *Reformation,* 20; brackets added.

89. Erasmus, Epistle 94, in James Anthony Froude, *Life and Letters of Erasmus: Lectures Delivered at Oxford 1893–1894* (New York: C. Scribner's Sons, 1894), 352.

90. Ed Hirsch, *The Dictionary of Cultural Literacy,* ed. E. D. Hirsch Jr., Joseph F. Kett, and James Trefil (Boston: Houghton Mifflin, 1991),

3; emphasis added.

91. Matthew 22:30. In the resurrection "they neither marry, nor are given in marriage," referencing that marriage is an earthly ordinance and must be authoritatively performed in mortality, that "whatsover thou shalt bind on earth shall be bound in heaven" (Matthew 16:19). Deuteronomy 25:5–6 sets forth Israel's law concerning such. Thus, the example used by Jesus may have been a real-life situation found in one of the twelve books of the Apocrypha, the book of Tobit (Tobit 3:17; Tobit 6:17), where we read of a woman named Sara who had married seven brothers in succession, each of whom died on the wedding night. The angel Raphael was sent to ensure that one of her cousins, Tobit, for whom she had been destined all along, arrange for them to meet and marry, suggesting that she was married or "sealed" to Tobit but not the other seven men. That may be one of the reasons why Jesus told the Sadducees that they did not know the scriptures; they left out the information about the eighth husband. See John Tvednes, "A Much Needed Book That Needs Much," review of *One Lord, One Faith*, by Michael T. Griffith, *FARMS Review of Books* 9 (1997): 41

92. Wills, *Papal Sin*, 175–202.

93. Wills, *Papal Sin*, 190–92. Chadwick, *Early Christian Church*, 237.

94. Chadwick, *Early Church*, 237.

95. Cheetham, *Keepers of the Keys*, 22.

96. Cheetham, *Keepers of the Keys*, 26. See Letters of Leo the Great, letter 10, in *Nicene and Post-Nicene Fathers*, 2:12:8–9. Letter 11, An Ordinance from the Roman Emperor Valentinian, supports Leo's ouster of Hilary and confirms Leo's supremacy over all other Catholic bishops.

97. Cheetham, *Keepers of the Keys*, 27.

98. Cheetham, *Keepers of the Keys*, 48.

99. Cheetham, *Keepers of the Keys*, 94.

100. Cheetham, *Keepers of the Keys*, 127; emphasis added.

101. Cheetham, *Keepers of the Keys*, 59–85.

102. Clement of Rome, First Epistle to the Corinthians 44, in *Apostolic Fathers*, 1:83–84; emphasis added.

103. Swanson, *Religion and Devotion in Europe*, 9; see also Davies, *Early Christian Church*, 267.

CHAPTER EIGHT

THE RENAISSANCE AND REFORMATION PERIOD

Since Your Majesty and your lordships desire a simple reply, I will answer without horns and without teeth. Unless I am convicted by Scripture and plain reason—I do not accept the authority of popes and councils, for they have contradicted each other—my conscience is captive to the Word of God. I cannot and will not recant anything, for to go against conscience is neither right nor safe. Here I stand, I cannot do otherwise. God help me. Amen.

—Martin Luther

Secular, Protestant, and Catholic historians view differently the causes that propelled the Middles Ages into the modern era. In fact, the term *Renaissance* may itself be outdated and insufficient to explain this age. One historian has termed it a *reevaluation* rather than a rebirth of classical antiquity. The old viewpoint "owes something to the propaganda of the Renaissance men themselves, just as the Protestant Reformers, a century or so later, would claim to have 'rediscovered' the text and message of the Bible."[1] Thus, one's perspective plays a large role in the interpretation of history and events. Truth seeking—especially seeking God's truth—must transcend narrow personal views.

Secular historians have suggested that "Europe gradually emancipated itself, however, incompletely, from the superstition of organized religion."[2] They allege that religion began to break away from ritual purification to a manner of worship more reflective, personal, and rational; and yet they marvel at the speed with which the Reformation advanced. In just a few short decades, more change occurred in religious ideology than in the previous five centuries of intermittent reform and constant tumult. Faithful religious historians nevertheless recognize that ritual purification was revealed by God throughout the patriarchal dispensations and was accepted as *God's truth*. The New Covenant, offered by Jesus Christ, *extended* ritual purification but in a different, simpler form: baptism, receiving the Holy Ghost, and partaking of the Lord's Supper. Superstition is man's creation—a product of apostasy; thus during the Middle Ages when civilization experienced a crisis in education, the ravages of war, economic distress, and significant family health issues, corrupt theology infiltrated the Church as man turned to irrational beliefs in order to face such unrelenting hardship.

From a secular point of view, the Reformation often gives credit to the developing nation states, such as England and France, and their insistence on self-rule without interference from the Church. Issues such as papal taxation, large national land tracts owned by the Church, and the subjection of clergy only to Church courts rather than state courts combined to inspire the rising middle class to oppose secular interference by the Roman hierarchy. This sentiment, they say, soon spread throughout all of Europe. The secular outlook attempts to explain that economic motives were the major impetus for the Reformation.

From a Protestant perspective, the Church had become corrupt, having strayed from the pure doctrines and pattern of worship described in the New Testament and inspired God-fearing men to institute reforms.

From a Catholic viewpoint, Martin Luther and others created heresy and schism within the Church, stemming from such motives as an impure desire to marry. Nevertheless, the Catholic Church did recognize an urgent need to rehabilitate itself, as manifest by the *Counter-Reformation* that commenced at the Council of Trent in 1545.

Recent scholarship points to five principal reasons for the success of the Reformation: (1) because many secular leaders no longer desired to be a part of the Church, the old blackmailing "tactics of excommunication and interdict no longer worked"; (2) the

contest between France, Spain, and Germany over the "prizes of Milan and Naples" following the French invasion of Italy in 1494 forced papal involvement; (3) "sensitive times," wrote Euan Cameron, "needed politically adept popes like Alexander VI or Julius II, who were manipulators and managers of people"; during such times, he said, "a spiritual leader was a luxury"; (4) significant contention existed within the College of Cardinals, while at the same time the Church itself was strapped for cash and "heavily dependent on the sale of offices"; and (5) the Church had yet to resolve its own doctrinal dilemmas and could not authoritatively respond to the Protestant's theological challenges.[3] Although it is clear that a number of factors converged to influence reforms, the common thread motivating all of them was the depravity of popes and clerics and the unrighteous power they exercised in temporal and spiritual domains. The Reformers did not initially protest ritual worship or even superstitious doctrines; they rebelled against corrupt authority.

The translation of the Bible into native languages was a leading element that encouraged reforms. As access to education increased and men's reasoning became armed with the written word, increasing numbers of people noticed obvious discrepancies between existing Church doctrines, the practices of the priestly organization, and the word of God as recorded in scripture. Even though scripture recitation was a fundamental element of early Christian worship, the common man was kept from reading the Bible in earlier centuries through a lack of education and beginning in 1078 because of strict papal decrees. Although St. Jerome published his Latin Bible in the fourth century, basically only monks and clergymen benefited because of the poor education levels. For example, even King John, who signed the Magna Carta, could not read or write but had been taught to sign his name.

The Forerunners of the Reformation

Just as the Bible contains many prophecies predicting a general apostasy, it equally supplies passages promising a restoration of divine truth. Inasmuch as apostasy, with its attendant problems, did not occur overnight, neither would a new dispensation come into being without significant groundwork. Many inspired individuals would perform important preliminary responsibilities in preparation for a long-promised, latter-day restoration. The combined efforts of these Reformers would crack the religious strongholds that had existed for centuries and would inspire a resurgence of scriptural discovery, particularly for the common man. Innovation would increasingly illuminate learning of all kinds, and a spirit of new life would begin to permeate society. While the Church of Rome was trying to suppress the translation of the Bible into common languages, these inspired men, coupled with new discoveries and inventions, would hasten the day of the Reformation.

The Waldensians

The first notable religious rebellion was initiated by a wealthy French merchant from Lyons named Peter Waldus or Valdes in 1173.[4] He experienced a life-changing event when he apparently witnessed the sudden death of a prominent citizen. About this same time, he heard a minstrel singing in the town square about St. Alexis, a wealthy young man who had left home and family and spent many years teaching and ministering to the poor. After a long period, the now weary and feeble son returned home to his parents, seeking shelter; sadly, they did not recognize

him, and he soon died.

The result of these two events wrought in Waldo a change of heart. He sought the advice of a parish priest, who rehearsed with him the parable of the rich man. After placing his two daughters in the abbey at Fontevrault, he established an endowment for his wife, sold all he had, and distributed his remaining wealth to the poor. He hired two priests, Bernard Ydros and Stephen of Ansa, to translate into the vernacular the Gospels and other portions of the Bible, and began to gather followers who went out *two by two* preaching the gospel.[5] Known as the Waldensians, they memorized large portions of the Bible and taught the message of scripture to the common man, eventually planting roots of independent Christian thought throughout Europe.

Although they did not immediately oppose the Catholic Church and actually sought its authority to preach at the Third Lateran Council in 1179, Alexander III denied the request. For the Church, the decision to permit the laity to preach was simple: "The untrained should not aim to train the untrained."[6] Theology was difficult to understand, even for the well educated, the Church concluded. Thus, when considering such mystical Catholic doctrines as the Eucharist (whether or not the bread and wine were actually changed into the flesh and blood of Jesus, and the question of Christ's physical presence at communion), if *theologians* had been debating this doctrine for centuries, how were *lay people* to resolve such complex issues?

Unfortunately, twelfth-century Christianity was mired in the false tradition of force imposed after Constantine, having long since abandoned the inspired position of the New Testament Church: "He sent Him; as to men He sent Him; as a Savior He sent Him, and as *seeking to persuade*, not to compel us; *for*

239

violence has not place in the character of God."[7] Thus, although the Church viewed itself as reasonable and completely within its right to maintain unity of doctrine, it forgot that God would not rob man of free will. Initially, Waldo and his supporters were excommunicated for their preaching activities. When this extreme measure failed to stop them, the Inquisition sought to destroy them, often burning them as heretics. At various trials, they were convicted of

> translating the New and Old Testament into the vulgar tongue and this they teach and learn. For I have heard and seen a certain countryman who used to recite Job word for word, and many others who knew the whole New Testament perfectly.[8]

These kinds of injustices caused people to question the authority and correctness of the Universal Church. While the Inquisition persecuted, imprisoned, and executed the Waldensians and others like them,[9] a general hunger to possess and comprehend the scriptures began to rise throughout Europe.

Whereas the Waldensian movement originated and flourished completely outside Church control, another important undercurrent, begun in Germany and England, actually commenced within the Church. Its founder, John Wycliffe, unlike the unlettered Waldensians, was the leading scholar and clergyman of his day.

John Wycliffe (1320–84)

At the height of his popularity, Wycliffe was the pride of prestigious Oxford University and the most influential clergyman in England. He was a professor at Oxford for more than eighteen years before he earned his doctorate of theology in 1372. He was well versed in the scriptures, both the Latin Vulgate and Greek Bibles, and matured into a prolific author. He was also known as the most gifted and moving preacher in England before the Reformation.[10]

Out of Wycliffe's intellectual understanding of the Bible sprouted his objections to the Church practices and doctrines of the day. Specifically, Wycliffe believed all saints shared the "keys" with Peter; that the teachings of scripture prevail when in conflict with Church doctrine; that the wafer and wine did not become the body and blood of Jesus; that popes, like Christ, ought not to interfere with secular authority; that the Church had no right to tax; that priests had no authority to grant forgiveness of sin—true contrition was sufficient; and that "straight truth-telling" should not be compromised, even to promote a worthy cause.[11] These were bold statements audaciously proclaimed against such powerful and established bodies as the papal and clerical institutions.

However, Wycliffe was also realistic about his chances of motivating reforms from within the Church; rather, his intent was to align himself with the nobles against the corrupt clergy. When he viewed the plight of the common person's circumstances and compared it with the widespread excesses of educated priests, he stated that his "inmost soul was stirred to its depth by the spectacle of social wretchedness which was rife."[12]

Despite the evil he observed *within* the Church, including its ill effects on the poor, the most significant motivating factor influencing Wycliffe's revolutionary activities was the famed schism between Avignon and Rome in 1378.[13] Additionally, although his extensive education and understanding of the Latin Vulgate gave Wycliffe confidence in his distinctive theological views, they were not the cause of his later efforts to bring about reform. When he observed the negative effects of the rivalry between competing papal governments, he became disillusioned with the Universal Church, concluding that the Bible was the only authoritative source of God's law to man. Wycliffe spent the remainder of his life taking its message to the people.

A significant obstacle hindered his progress: no English version of the Bible existed, and most people could not understand the Latin, including a majority of the priests. Wycliffe resolved that if the people did not have the law because they did not have access to it, they could not be held accountable. He undertook the formidable task of translation, beginning with selected pages and sections of the Bible. Each page was handwritten, including all the copies used by those who helped him preach. These individuals, called "poor priests," or Lollards, were typically students or clerks working during vacations or breaks.

Although Wycliffe remained in the Church his entire life, he and his followers were greatly persecuted. False charges were levied against him, and many attempts were made to place Wycliffe on trial. Although these efforts failed, he was often attacked publically and was ultimately condemned as a heretic by the archbishop of Canterbury, resulting in his dismissal as a professor at Oxford. With that action, all but his most loyal supporters abandoned him. Notwithstanding, Wycliffe remained convinced that his work would ultimately prevail.

Believing that every man had the right to read the Bible in his own language, Wycliffe turned his attention to translating the Latin Vulgate into English. Prior to beginning the work of translation, he and his assistants studied copies of the old Latin texts. Most scholars today believe that he had access to the oldest, most dependable Latin Vulgate manuscript in England. Additionally, he and his colleagues studied the commentaries and writings of many well-known Bible scholars. During the process of translation, they were often subjected to many forms of persecution. Some of Wycliffe's associates were tried, excommunicated, and imprisoned. Despite such great opposition, he completed the initial work of translating the New Testament in 1382. Wycliffe died of a stroke December 31, 1384, shortly after his monumental project was completed—"having lit a fire which shall never be put out."[14]

Almost prophetically, the seeds Wycliffe planted were sowed in fertile soil and began to reap a bounteous harvest. Interest in the English Bible became so widespread that anyone who had been associated with Wycliffe was excommunicated, hunted, imprisoned, tortured, and burned. Scores of Lollards were burned at the stake, their Bibles fastened around their necks.[15] Wycliffe's ultimate victory, through John Hus and many others, produced so much venom within the Church that the Council of Constance ordered his bones to be exhumed and burned thirty-one years after his death. His enemies, thinking that perhaps now he had been silenced forever, were shocked to read a poem that began circulating in England:

> *The Avon to the Severn runs,*
> *And Severn to the Sea;*
> *And Wycliffe's dust shall spread abroad*
> *Wide as the waters be.*[16]

Wycliffe's greatest crime was that he challenged the abuses of the Church and desired that the common man have access to the Holy Bible in his own language.

John Hus (1369–1415)

At the same time the Council of Constance was issuing its edict seeking vengeance upon the remains of Wycliffe, another forerunner to the Reformation, John Hus, was being burned at the stake by that same conclave. In 1396 Hus began lecturing Aristotelean philosophy prior to becoming a deacon in 1398. He was ordained to the priesthood in 1401 after receiving bachelor's and master's degrees at the University of Prague. He became acquainted with Wycliffe's writings before he was ordained, reading four of his primary works. Hus was so moved by them that he wrote in the margin of a copy he was reading, "Wyclif, Wyclif, you will unsettle a man's mind."[17] Hus was commissioned to preach at the Bethlehem Chapel in 1402 and became an effective exponent of Roman doctrine early in his career as a priest. Although no trace of Wycliffe's ideology can be found in Hus's early discourses,[18] many of his later sermons spoke against the evils of the Church, and the idea of reform gained popular acceptance in his native Bohemia. Hus wrote:

Our bishops and priests of today, and especially our Cathedral canons, and lazy Mass celebrators, hardly wait for the close of the service to hurry out of the church, one to a tavern, and the other . . . to engage in amusements unworthy of a priest.[19]

Hus agreed with Wycliffe that Christ, not Peter, was head of the Church and that the scriptures served as the sole source of faith and doctrine for the believer. Hus also asserted that some popes had been heretics. He was consequently branded a heretic himself, excommunicated, and his writings suppressed. He found refuge outside Prague, where he continued to preach, write, and study. "The supreme aim of religion," he taught,

"was to love God absolutely." He denounced pride, luxury, avarice, and immorality, both among the lay and clerical members of the Church.[20] The chief product of Wycliffe's pen, *Concerning the Church*, developed Hus's teachings pertaining to what is termed by the Reformers as "the universal priesthood of all believers."

In 1414 Hus was promised safe conduct by the pope and Emperor Sigismund to the Council of Constance to present his views. Instead of hearing Hus, the Council had him arrested, gave him a mock trial without the benefit of an advocate, and condemned him to death as a heretic. Among other spurious charges, such as selling the head of John the Baptist for 50,000 ducats, committing adultery with his brother's wife, raping nuns, and sodomy,[21] it was alleged that Hus "wished to be and is the fourth person in the Godhead."[22] According to Novotny:

This was a fantastically absurd charge that represents a twisted deduction from philosophical realism, alleging that there could be more than three hypostates in the Trinity—although he neither made any such deduction nor claimed to be the fourth hypostasis of the Godhead.[23]

While the sentence was being read, Hus knelt and prayed:

Lord Jesus Christ, I implore thee, forgive all my enemies for Thy great mercy's sake; and Thou knowest that they have falsely accused me and have produced false witnesses and concocted false articles against me! Forgive them for Thy boundless mercy's sake![24]

He was kept in prison for seven months before he was burned. As he stood before the stake and was asked to recant, he looked heavenward and said:

242

God is my witness, that those things that are falsely ascribed to me and of which the false witnesses accuse me, I have never taught nor preached. . . . And in the truth of the Gospel that I wrote . . . I am willingly gladly to die today.[25]

As the executioner lit the fire, Hus immediately began to sing in a loud voice, "Jesus Christ, Thou son of the Living God, have mercy on me."[26] As the flames rose high around the face and body of the martyr, Hus began to sing again: "thus praying within himself and moving his lips, . . . he expired in the Lord."[27] The Council at Constance had dismissed its own broken promise of safe conduct to Hus, stating that "no brief of safe-conduct in the case of a heretic is binding. No pledge is to be observed which is prejudicial to the Catholic faith and ecclesiastical jurisdiction."[28]

Savonarola (1452–98) and Erasmus (1466–1536)

While Wycliffe, Hus, and others sought reform outside the Church hierarchy, not believing in the authority of the pope, notable clergy such as Girolamo Savonarola and Desiderius Erasmus attempted reform from within by denouncing the wickedness of priesthood leadership but maintaining allegiance to the Church itself. After the French army expelled the Medici from Florence in 1495, Savonarola, a Dominican monk, became the city's new political and religious leader. A powerful orator and prophetic preacher, Savonarola introduced rigid moral and ethical reforms, initially gaining wide acceptance from the citizenry in his outspoken criticism of the corruption of Church hierarchy. He was particularly vocal in his pronouncements against the scandalous pope Alexander VI (1492–1503), whose extreme moral failures

were punctuated by his numerous illegitimate children. Indeed, the Florentine historian Guicciardini seems quite generous in stating he was "most sensual towards both sexes" and guilty of "sensuality, avarice, cruelty, injustice, and duplicity."[29] Although Savonarola was excommunicated in 1497, he continued to speak out against the pope. When Pope Alexander placed the city of Florence under an interdiction, Savonarola was turned over to papal ambassadors, who ensured that he was tried and publicly executed.

Erasmus, known as a biblical humanist, received an unusually diverse and broad education due to his initial training at the school of the Brethren of Common Life in Diventor, as well as continuing education at various schools throughout Europe, mainly in England. Perhaps the most popular theologian of the Church, Erasmus was in communication with virtually every recognized scholar in Europe. Early in adult life, he recognized the problems confronting the Church and was particularly opposed to theological scholasticism:

> By their stammering and by the stains of their impure style they disfigure theology which had been enriched and adorned by the eloquence of the ancients. They involve everything whilst trying to resolve everything.[30]

According to Erasmus, the world was "overloaded with human constitutions and opinions and scholastic dogmas, and overburdened with the tyrannical authority of orders." Faith, he taught, required simplification.[31] Consequently, he argued that the Church must return to its original roots: "All that is not yet overgrown or has not passed through many hands, has such a potent charm."[32] He opposed "remote philosophical systems" that neglected the sources of Christianity itself.[33]

Erasmus's conception of the Church "was no longer purely Catholic"[34]; thus he wrote popular satire about its hierarchy and corrupt institutions. However, he was also a serious writer who attempted to effect serious change. He had a passion for theology, and his crowning achievement was the completion of a critical edition of the Bible from various Greek manuscripts. Erasmus felt that errors had crept into the Vulgate based on quotations he had read from Jerome, Augustine, and Ambrose.

Although many opposed his view, he favored the right of the people to read the scriptures:

> I totally disagree with those who are unwilling that the sacred Scriptures, translated into the vulgar tongue, should be read by private individuals, as if Christ had taught such subtle doctrines that they can with difficulty be understood by a very few theologians, or as if the strength of the Christian religion lay in men's ignorance of it.[35]

He was astonished by those who felt their authority would be threatened if the laity were permitted to read the scriptures in their "purified form" and to attempt to "understand them in the original."[36]

Although he was a staunch supporter of Church reforms, Erasmus nevertheless did not fully embrace the Reformation when it arose, instead trying to preserve peace by taking the middle ground. Near the end of his life, he wrote, "On no other account do I congratulate myself more than on the fact that I have never attached myself to any party."[37] He believed in the principle of "spiritual liberty." Erasmus is remembered as a voice of reason, both by Protestant and Catholic historians.

Two secular events took place in the fifteenth century that had a profound influence on the Reformation.

First, the invention of the printing press enabled new translations of the Bible to be reproduced in great numbers. Johann Gutenberg began printing experiments in the late 1430s. Although he did not possess the resources required to complete his project alone, through partnerships he was able to fund and design the world's first printing press. One of the early publications was the Bible that bears his name. In addition to the Bible, this new printing capability expanded other publications, leading to increased literacy and educational opportunities.

The second event was the fall of Constantinople to the Turks in 1453. Since the time of Constantine's ascension to the throne, Rome had shared some of its stature with this prominent eastern capital. Now that Constantinople was in the hands of non-Christian rulers, the centers of learning in Europe began to shift, attracting to the Roman Church and its areas of influence some of the brightest minds from the East. Intellectualism and enlightenment were expanding throughout Europe, and the Bible was at the core of human interest.

William Tyndale (1492–1536)

Following in the tradition of Wycliffe and encouraged by the work of Erasmus, William Tyndale was one of the dominant figures of the English Reformation. Whereas Wycliffe's English rendering of the New Testament was taken from the Latin Vulgate, Tyndale achieved a more accurate translation using the Greek Bible. Although Erasmus was instrumental in both Bible translations and in championing Church reform, Tyndale completed the work of bringing *both* the Old and New Testaments to English-speaking people. Inasmuch as English conquest and colonization during this period were extensive, his influence proved profound.

Born in 1492, Tyndale was educated

244

at Oxford University, where he received his master's degree. After his ordination in 1515, he attended Cambridge University, where he was probably influenced by the teachings of Erasmus. Tyndale worked single-mindedly his entire life to translate and publish a worthy Greek translation of the Bible in English. Earlier in his career, Tyndale was denounced by an overzealous Catholic who said to him, "It would be better to be without God's law"—i.e., the Bible—"than without the pope's," to which Tyndale replied, "If God spare me life, ere many years I will cause the boy that driveth the plow to know more of the Scripture than you do."[38]

Although he received support from Luther and many others, opposition at every turn required Tyndale to relocate from London to Wittenburg, to Hamburg, to Cologne, and finally to Worms, evading the authorities of the Church by using great care and frequent movements. He published his first translation of the New Testament while at Worms in about 1526. In the years to come, he continued to translate and retranslate in order to achieve the accuracy he desired.

Using a network of merchant contacts he had established early on, Tyndale achieved a wide distribution of the new English Bible, in spite of untiring exertions by both church and state to thwart this effort. Finally in 1535, while living in a rented home in Antwerp provided by his merchant friends, he was quietly betrayed by an English acquaintance with whom he had developed a close friendship. Tyndale was taken to Vilvorde Castle near Brussels, where, after being imprisoned for sixteen months in a cold and damp cell, he was tried, publicly stripped of his ecclesiastical authority, and led to the stake, where he was strangled and burned. His last words before he died were, "Lord, open the King of England's eyes."[39]

While Tyndale was in prison, one of his gifted assistants, Miles Coverdale, worked quietly behind the scenes to continue the work of translating the first complete Bible, all the Old and New Testament. With the help of Sir Thomas More, a one-time opponent, and Thomas Cromwell, a minister in Henry VIII's court, this project was concluded in 1536.

Notwithstanding the initial success of finishing the translation, more than seventy-five years would pass before complete freedom to own and read the English Bible without fear of retribution would occur. During this period, however, freedom to own a Bible depended on the whim and religious convictions of current royalty.

The Great Bible, published in 1539, was placed in most churches and in the homes of those affluent enough to afford it. The Geneva Bible was published in 1560, and because it was smaller, with easier-to-read type, it became the common family Bible for the next fifty years. By the time the authorized King James Version was published in 1611, the question of making the English Bible available to all people was put to rest forever. The scholars responsible for the King James Version were the finest of the day, and the work was accomplished with the blessing and energetic encouragement of James I. In the end, the worthy aims of both Wycliffe and Tyndale bore sweet fruit, and Tyndale's dying prayer, "Lord, open the King of England's eyes," was finally realized.

The New Testament declares that the mission of John the Baptist was to serve as the *forerunner* of Jesus Christ. His teachings and the followers he amassed prepared the way for greater acceptance of the Messiah. Likewise, inspired men such as Peter Waldo, John Wycliffe, John Hus, and William Tyndale played significant roles in the eventual success of the Reformation. However, heaven

245

seems to have reserved the leading role for a man who combined intellect with spirituality, determination with courage, and a boisterous personality with uncommon leadership.

First-Generation Reformers

Martin Luther (1483–1546)

Martin Luther was born of free peasant parents on November 10, 1483, in Eisleben, Saxony. His father obtained an interest in several copper mines and two smelting operations, becoming very wealthy by 1511. Luther obtained his initial schooling at the Brethren of the Common Life in Magdeburg, later relocating to a school in Eisenach from 1498–1501. In Eisenach, Luther learned Latin, which qualified him for acceptance to the University of Erfurt in 1501, where he came under the influence of William of Ockham, who believed revelation was important to matters of faith. Luther seems to have spent a great deal of time pondering salvation for his soul. Upon graduation from Erfurt in 1505 with his master of arts degree, he began to study law at the urging of his father. However, Luther seems to have experienced a change of heart when he encountered a severe thunderstorm near Stotternheim and was knocked to the ground by lightning. Fearing for his life, he promised to become a monk if he were to be spared; two weeks later, in July 1505, he joined the Augustinian monastery at Erfurt. In 1507 Luther was ordained a priest and later sent to Wittenburg, where he continued his studies and lectured in theology.

Luther experienced his first grievances with the Church while on assignment to Rome in 1510, representing his order. Here he witnessed the spurious papal government of Julius II at its worst and observed firsthand the corruption of the Roman clergy and the luxury to which it had become accustomed.

He was shocked by the laxity and superficial expressions of faith he witnessed. Although Luther was wrong in assuming that the Church was prosperous when it was at this point in debt, St. Peter's Cathedral still presented an outward appearance of opulence and prosperity. These scenes were particularly troubling to one who spent so much time considering the salvation of his own soul rather than the acquisition of material wealth.

In 1511 he was reassigned at Wittenberg, where he completed his doctor of theology degree and was appointed professor of scripture. Here Luther began developing the theology that would initiate lasting reforms in Christianity. He spent considerable time studying the writings of Paul, becoming convinced that salvation came through faith in Christ alone and not through justification by works. Included in his unfolding theological system was his belief that the scriptures were the only source of authority for sinful people seeking salvation and that the priesthood belonged to all believers, not just the ordained clergy. Inasmuch as the Catholic priesthood hierarchy was corrupt, Luther developed a speculative doctrine, hitherto unknown, that allowed for any Christian to perform the rites and sacraments of the Church, notwithstanding the firm testimony of the Apostolic Fathers to the contrary.

Luther might never have found an opportunity to vent his frustrations so effectively had it not been for the severe conflict of opposing interests between the archbishop of Mainz and Frederick the Wise, the elector of Saxony, over the sale of indulgences. In 1517 Pope Leo X began selling indulgences to finance the building of St. Peter's Cathedral in Rome. This arrangement was particularly corrupt in that the archbishop had borrowed a large sum of money in order to pay Pope Leo for the privilege of holding more than one see. The archbishop was to share in fifty percent of the proceeds from the sale of these indulgences to repay his bank loan. To further complicate the situation, the archbishop's sale of indulgences on the borders of Frederick's territory were in direct competition with Frederick's sale of indulgences, which monies were meant to fund the purchase of religious relics that adorned the castle church at Wittenburg and also to subsidize other projects (such as the university at Wittenburg employing Luther) specifically beneficial to the German people rather than the Italians. Even though it was not in his best interest personally, Luther spoke out against this issue because he believed the eternal welfare of his parishioners was threatened by the false promises associated with the practice of purchasing indulgences.[40]

Luther and Pope Leo had a chilly discussion on the subject of indulgences in which Leo disregarded the scriptural objections raised by Luther. Consequently, Luther, aware of his support from Frederick, the German humanists such as Erasmus, and the German people themselves, penned his famous Ninety-Five Theses and nailed them to the main door of the castle church at Wittenberg. The Ninety-Five Theses were concise statements of Luther's profound opposition to the practice of indulgences. Luther's bold action was a challenge to debate the issue and bring reason to a corrupt policy. News of the list of grievances spread quickly, becoming a source of controversy.

Luther's first opposition came from the feisty agent for the archbishop, Johann Tetzel. Inasmuch as Luther was receiving crucial support from his Augustinian brethren, Tetzel sought an alliance with the Dominican monks, attempting to quell Luther's growing influence. In 1518 Luther was summoned to appear before a diet at Augsburg, where he was confronted by Cardinal Cajetan of Gaeta. Luther courageously held to his convictions, stating he would not concede unless evidence was presented from scripture supporting the papal position. He later debated the renowned theologian John Eck over a lengthy period extending eighteen days. The proceedings were widely circulated throughout Europe and had the effect of increasing his support among the German masses. Luther was quietly championed by Frederick, the Elector of Saxony, who protected him on many occasions when his life was threatened. He had already won initial support from the influential Erasmus and his colleagues at Wittenburg.

To better comprehend Frederick's support of Luther, we have only to understand the groundswell that was beginning to form throughout Germany. In a letter written September 11, 1520, by Ulrich von Hutten to the Elector, we read:

We see that there is no gold and almost no silver in our German land. What little may perhaps be left is drawn away daily by the new schemes invented by the council of the most holy members of the Roman Curia. What is thus squeezed out of us is put to the most shameful uses. Would you know, dear Germans, what employment I have myself seen that they make at Rome with our money? It does not lie idle! Leo X gives a part to nephews and relatives (these are so numerous that there is a proverb at Rome, "As thick as Leo's relations"). . . . Does Your Grace perceive how many bold robbers, how many cunning hypocrites commit repeatedly the greatest crimes under the monk's cowl and how many crafty hawks feign the simplicity of doves, and how many ravening wolves simulate the innocence of lambs? And although there be truly a few pious among them, even they cling to superstition and pervert the law of life which Christ laid down for us.[41]

Thus, with growing sympathy, in 1520, Luther took his case to the people. He wrote several expositions, still acknowledged as his primary works, which presented his views for reforms. Luther's first treatise was *The Sermon on Good Works* published in May, followed by *The Papacy at Rome* in June, *The Address to the German Nobility* in August, *The Babylonian Captivity* in September, and *The Freedom of the Christian Man* in November. His conclusions not only denounced indulgences but also criticized some of the core beliefs of the Church, such as the priesthood hierarchy, the Eucharist (the sacrament of the Lord's Supper), and the authority of the Roman priesthood, by virtue of extolling his view that all who were baptized received what he termed the *priesthood of the believers.*

Luther claimed that the papal government had become corrupt and that clerical abuses had unjustly separated and made unscriptural distinctions between the clergy and laity. His conclusion was that God's authority was not in the hierarchy of the Catholic priesthood but rather in the scriptures themselves, which contained the word of God. Moreover, Luther rejected the basic premise of transubstantiation, which stated that "the elements retain their accidents of shape, taste, color, and so on, but lose their substance, for which is substituted the substance of God."[42] Luther, based on 1 Peter 3:18 ("For Christ also hath *once* suffered for sins"), believed that Christ was sacrificed once and for all upon the cross; thus the Eucharist as performed by the Roman priesthood was in error according to scripture, due to its claim that the Savior was crucified anew with each ceremonial Mass. Other theologians, including Erasmus, also believed the concept of substance was not biblical but rather a "scholastic sophistication."[43]

Finally, Luther differed with the Universal Church on the sacrament of baptism. He objected once again to the power of the clerics and declared that the efficacy of baptism depended on the faith of the individual rather than on the authority of the priest.[44] Unfortunately, Luther's view here raised serious biblical problems, for how could an infant exercise faith? Unlike the earliest Christians who clearly opposed infant baptism because baptism was for the *remission of sins* (not Adam's fall), Luther sought to rationalize his position by comparing the "faith of a man in his sleep with the *figment* of an implicit faith in the baby"; or as he later taught, "that infants were sponsored by the faith of their parents."[45]

In response to Luther's essays, Leo X issued a papal bull against him on June 15, 1520, resulting in his excommunication. When Luther's publications were openly burned by the priests and friars at Cologne, he returned the compliment by publicly burning the pope's official decree on December 10, 1520. Luther took his final stand against the abuses and errors of the Church when he was summoned to the diet at Worms in the spring of 1521. Here Luther gave his now famous and inspiring defense:

> Since Your Majesty and your lordships desire a simple reply, I will answer without horns and without teeth. Unless I am convicted by Scripture and plain reason—I do not accept the authority of popes and councils, for they have contradicted each other—my conscience is captive to the Word of God. I cannot and will not recant anything, for to go against conscience is neither right nor safe. Here I stand, I cannot do otherwise. God help me. Amen.[46]

From this point on, Luther's break with the Church gained increasing momentum. The Reformation was now solidly underway.

Luther was aided in his quest of reforming Christianity by a bright young scholar named Philipp Melanchthon, a twenty-one-year-old professor of Greek who joined the staff of the University at Wittenberg in 1518. More thoughtful and deliberate than Luther, Melanchthon was a good match for his fiery companion. In order to preserve Luther's life, Frederick the Wise placed him in seclusion at the Wartburg Castle from 1521–22. Luther later referred to this season of his life as his *Patmos*, alluding to the Apostle John's imprisonment upon that lonely isle.[47] During this period, Melanchthon worked out the basic theological tenets of the Reformation while Luther translated the Greek Bible into his native German language. Both of these activities eventually helped them take the message of the Reformers to the people. While at Wartburg, Luther also wrote a thesis entitled *On Monastic Vows*, in which he encouraged monks to renounce their oaths and to marry as God had ordained in the holy scriptures.

In 1526 Luther wrote two more doctrinal works called the *German Mass* and *Order of Service*. Further progress included the *Short Catechism* in 1529, affirming brief statements of doctrine, including the Ten Commandments, the Apostles' Creed, and the Lord's Prayer. The *Augsburg Confession* in 1530, written by Melanchthon and approved by Luther, was the first of many creeds of the Reformation, rivaling those of the fourth-century Church, such as the Nicene Creed in 325. Finally, in 1535, ministerial candidates began to be examined and ordained, creating a final ecclesiastical separation with the Church of Rome.

In the fall of 1529, Luther met the Swiss Reformer Ulrich Zwingli at the Marburg Castle of Phillip of Hesse. They agreed on more than fourteen of fifteen propositions but were unable to resolve differences on how Christ was present in the elements of the Communion. While Zwingli held to his belief that the emblems of the sacrament were partaken *in remembrance* of Jesus Christ, Luther maintained there was yet a tangible, physical presence of Christ in the Communion, though the substance did not actually change as claimed by the Universal Church. Also, very early on, the Anabaptist movement arose with which Luther broke openly in 1535.

The extraordinary growth of Lutheranism in Northern Germany was sustained in large part by the wars being waged against the Turks and the French. The Schmalkaldic League was formed by the Protestant princes in 1531 to protect the new religion, but when conflict with neighboring countries occupied the energies of the emperor and the Catholic princes, the league's services were never required and the Lutheran movement was allowed to grow unchecked. When those wars officially ended in 1546, the emperor at last turned his military efforts to the Protestants in an attempt to restore unity of faith. Military engagements failed to halt the steady progress of the Reform effort, however, and an agreement was finally achieved in 1555 known as the *Peace of Augsburg*. This compromise gave Lutheranism legal rights equal to Catholicism in Germany.

Luther was a man for his times. Many Christians believe that he was inspired by God. Historical accounts project him to be a man of spirituality and integrity. The reforms he initiated took major steps forward in ending corruption and amending some of the doctrines that had strayed so far from New Testament Christianity. On the other hand, other of his doctrines, such as predestination, differed greatly from early Christian teachings. Notwithstanding Luther's remarkable achievements in reforming the Church, serious problems yet existed: Protestant leaders were unable to obtain a unity of theology. As a princely sovereign seeking peace for his subjects, Frederick the Wise became frustrated over this lack of harmony:

> As a prince he was responsible for the public peace. As a Christian he was concerned for the true faith. He wished to be enlightened as to the meaning of Scripture, and appointed a committee. But the committee could not agree. No group in Wittenberg could agree, neither the university, nor the Augustinians, nor the chapter at the Castle Church. "What a mess we are in," said Spalatin (a Luther colleague), "with everybody doing something else."[48]

During the next century of reform, numerous factions would break from Lutheranism because they could not agree on the true doctrines of Jesus. They never achieved the unity that the Savior prayed so mightily for at the conclusion of His ministry (see John 17).

Besides a clear lack of unity, Luther's reforms failed to achieve religious freedom; thus, systems of worship outside the boundaries of those accepted by the state were still subjected to serious persecution, including the death of tens of thousands of Anabaptists during the decades to come. Ironically, while some of Luther's reforms, such as removing corruption from the clergy, brought Christianity closer to its original roots, others, such as predestination and the denial of priesthood authority, poignantly described by Ignatius and the earliest Christians, were abandoned, taking the Reformers further away from New Testament doctrines. When Luther died in 1546, his faithful companion, Philipp Melanchthon, carried on their work.

Ulrich Zwingli (1484–1531)

Switzerland was unique at the time of the Reformation because it enjoyed a greater measure of religious freedom than any of its neighbors. The country itself was organized politically into what were known as cantons. Each canton was a self-governing unit that was part of a larger confederacy. Because of Switzerland's strong democracy, young Swiss men were employed by the pope as mercenaries to safeguard his special interests.[49]

Ulrich Zwingli was born in 1484 to parents of reasonable affluence. His father not only farmed but also served as the chief magistrate of Wildhaus, the city where Zwingli was raised. Zwingli graduated with his bachelor of arts degree in 1504 and his master of arts in 1506 from the University of Basil. During the next ten years, Zwingli served as a parish priest in Glarus, acting twice as chaplain to some of the Swiss mercenaries. When he witnessed many of these young men killed on foreign soil, he began openly to oppose the mercenary system.

Public officials thereafter made life difficult for Zwingli, and he sought and obtained an appointment at Einseideln near Zurich in 1516. During this period of service, Zwingli began to doubt some of the practices within the Church. He came into contact with the teachings of Erasmus and researched his Latin translation of the Greek New Testament, and his studies soon led him to challenge such Church doctrines as indulgences and the adoration of relics and saints. The acclaim he received for his scriptural knowledge and straightforward interpretations led to an appointment as pastor in Zurich at the Great Cathedral in 1519. The spread of the Protestant movement in Switzerland really got underway in 1522 when one of Zwingli's parishioners, Christopher Froschauer, served meat to his workmen during Lent, openly disregarding canon law. Zwingli had also instigated certain reforms in the worship service, deviating from the established patterns of the Church. He asserted that the Bible was the only authoritative source that ought to be binding on Christians. These actions led the city fathers to hold a public debate, inviting those who opposed Zwingli's views to challenge him in an open forum. In preparation for the debate, Zwingli published what became known as the *Sixty-Seven Articles*, defending such beliefs as salvation by faith alone, Christ's position as the head of the Church, the Bible as sole authority, and the right of priests to marry. His articles also criticized unscriptural Church traditions.

The debate was held in January 1523. Zwingli's ideology prevailed, and the city council of Zurich voted to accept it. Thus, both Zurich and Bern were now firmly Protestant. Over the next several years, Zwingli's movement expanded to include all the northern Swiss cantons as well as French-speaking Geneva. Fighting eventually erupted between the Protestant and Catholic cantons, which was settled by a peace agreement at Cappel in 1530. Unfortunately, fighting broke out again in 1531 when Zwingli attempted to force reform in Catholic cantons. Zwingli was mortally wounded in the battle and his body was taken by his captors and brutally mutilated. His work, however, was continued by Heinrich Bullinger, who ultimately joined forces with John Calvin in 1549.

Second-Generation Reformers

John Calvin (1509–1564)

After Martin Luther, perhaps no Reformer wielded more influence than John Calvin. Millions of Reformed Faith Christians worldwide accept the basic theological ideas he developed. Born in 1509, Calvin

is considered to be the leader of the second generation of Reformers. He was educated at the University of Paris, receiving his master of arts degree in 1528. Thereafter, his father arranged for him to attend the University of Orleans to study law. Calvin transferred to the University of Bourges in 1529, where he completed his law degree in 1532. Sometime in 1533, Calvin was converted to the ideas of the Protestant Reformation, and this change of heart led him to leave his homeland of France to settle in Switzerland.

In 1536 Calvin completed *The Institutes of the Christian Religion*, the work that would eventually place Calvin at the head of the Christian Reformation. Like the Apologists of second-century Christianity who sometimes addressed their writings to secular leaders, Calvin addressed a copy of his *Institutes* to Francis I of France, hoping he would accept the ideas of the Reformation and stop the persecution of those suffering for their beliefs. Evangelical Christian seminaries today use the acronym TULIP to describe the five basic tenets Calvin developed: "T" depicts his belief in the *total depravity* of man, meaning that all men born upon this earth have inherited the guilt of Adam's sin, and they can do nothing to save themselves because their will is totally corrupt.[50] The "U" expresses Calvin's belief that salvation is *unconditional* to those whom God has "elected" or saved because of God's foreknowledge; thus, salvation has nothing whatsoever to do with human responsibility or merit. Simply put, God will save His elect and condemn the rest.[51] The "L" denotes his belief in the *limited atonement* of Jesus Christ, referring to Calvin's conviction that Christ's atonement is limited to those whom He elects to save.[52] The "I" indicates that God's grace is *irresistible*, and the elect will be saved separately from their own first desire to know God, as the Holy Spirit irresistibly draws them to Christ.[53] Finally, the "P" embodies Calvin's belief in the *perseverance* of the saints. Essentially, Calvin believed that the elect, who are irresistibly saved by the work of the Holy Spirit, will never finally be lost.[54] In other words, paraphrasing the popular evangelical aphorism, *once saved, always saved,* or that man, once saved, cannot fall from grace.

Although an abbreviated version of Calvin's salvation theology, this is the heart of what he taught. Later in this chapter we will address such issues as authority, origin, and doctrine, and compare these issues with the history and problems of the Roman Church that Calvin sought to reform. These will also be compared with scripture and the original form of Christianity the Reformers sought to replicate. But for now, let us continue with the story.

As a result of Calvin's work, Reformed Christianity spread in Switzerland and expanded to Scotland, Holland, and North America. Calvin's theological influence was cast ultimately almost everywhere Christianity existed. The city of Geneva flourished under his leadership, which combined a strict ethical, moral, and doctrinal code with the establishment of civil laws to ensure adherence to this nearly theocratic ideal of government. The establishment of an excellent educational system and devotion to a strong work ethic can also be attributed to Calvin's vision and administration. His philosophy would ultimately inspire democracy, education, and hard work in establishing the principles and ideals of New England America. Like other religious leaders of the Reformation period, many believe John Calvin was an inspired man. From the time

of his conversion to reformed principles until his death in 1564, he preached tirelessly his view of the message of salvation in Jesus Christ.

After John Calvin's death, other leaders continued to extend the influence of the Reformed Faith. The Waldenses of southern France accepted the Protestant faith, and the Huguenots became a dynamic and well-organized force within France's borders. Unfortunately, French determination to unify religious worship caused more than 200,000 Huguenots to be exiled from France. They settled in Switzerland, England, Holland, Prussia, South Africa, and the United States, and reform never really took hold in France.

John Knox (1514–72)

John Knox, also a noteworthy second-generation Reformer, became a student and follower of the principles taught by John Calvin and provided forceful and decisive leadership in establishing reforms throughout Scotland. Led by Knox in 1560, the Scottish Parliament instituted laws that abolished the Mass and instituted the Reformed Faith with only slight refinements, leading to the emergence of Presbyterianism.

Although both Scotland and Wales united with England in the Reformation, the Irish revolted against their British conquerors during this same period. To retaliate, in 1557 the English Parliament seized two-thirds of Irish rebel lands and transferred ownership to English settlers. This action led to the sharply divided Ireland that persists today—northern Ireland giving allegiance to the British crown and Protestantism, and southern Ireland remaining faithful to Catholicism.

The final country in Europe won to

Protestantism during this period was Holland. Opposed to Spanish domination, several northern provinces of the Netherlands revolted against their oppressors. This conflict was not simply political but also religious; and when the Dutch finally prevailed, they embraced the Reformed Faith.

Jacobus Arminius (1560–1609)

The only opposition to Calvinist views came from Jacobus Arminius, considered by some an unorthodox Reformer. Arminius was educated at Leyden and Geneva under the tutelage of the renowned theologian Theodore Beza. A highly respected scholar, Beza became Protestant in 1548, shortly thereafter joining Calvin in Geneva and succeeding Calvin at his death. Arminius spent the next fifteen years as a pastor in Amsterdam, and in 1603 he returned to Leyden as a professor of theology. Owing to Beza the primary instruction he received, Arminius became an authority on Reformed Faith principles. Arminius's passionate research and careful scrutiny of Calvin's theology led him to reach subtle but important differences on a number of key points:

1. Both Calvin and Arminius believed that because of the Fall, man inherited Adam's sin. Whereas Calvin reasoned that man's will had been so corrupted *(total depravity)* that salvation was entirely a matter of divine grace, Arminius believed in the agency of man to initiate acceptance of Jesus Christ in cooperation with God's grace, as had the Apostolic Fathers before him.[55]

2. Calvin believed that election was *unconditional* and that God, based solely on His sovereign will, would save His elect and condemn the rest. Arminius held that election was according to the foreknowledge (not predestination) of God and conditional

upon man's faith in Christ. Arminius's position agreed with Justin Martyr and the Apostolic Fathers.[56]

3. Calvin *limited* the Atonement to those who had been elected or saved; Arminius affirmed that Christ's suffering was available to all but operative only in those who developed faith in Christ and chose to accept Him.[57]

4. Calvin asserted that Christ's grace was *irresistible;* Arminius believed that man could reject grace, again finding firm agreement with those closest to the ministry of Christ.[58]

5. Finally, Calvin contended under his doctrine of *perseverance* that once elected by God, man could not fall from grace; Arminius concluded that God gave men grace so that they need not fall, but the scriptures seemed to indicate that it was possible for men to fall from grace.[59]

A review of these differences uncovers an interesting Protestant paradox. The earliest Christian doctrines following the Apostles paralleled in many respects those of Arminius, while Calvinist doctrines grafted most of their roots in Augustine, whose speculative doctrines were far removed from original New Testament Christianity. Since none of the Reformers claimed divine revelation or authority from God, such divergent views in Christian theology could not be reconciled.

When Arminius died, a group of ministers organized and developed a theology around his convictions. These articles, entitled *A Remonstrance,* published in 1610, were debated at the Synod of Dort in 1618 but were defeated by the Calvinist delegation. Arminians were persecuted for many years but continue today as an accepted faith within Christianity. The Arminian influence was significant to the Methodist movement under John Wesley in the eighteenth century.

Henry VIII: Self-Indulgence Gives Rise to the Church of England

When the English Reformer William Tyndale uttered his last words, praying "Lord, open the King of England's eyes," little did he know how close his petitions were to being answered. Only a few years earlier in 1522, Henry was honored by Pope Leo X with the distinguished title "Defender of the Faith" for writing a theological treatise that championed the papacy in its campaign against Luther. However, King Henry became entangled in a quarrel with Pope Clement VII over a request that his marriage with Catherine of Aragon be dissolved in order that he might marry Anne Boleyn. King Henry desperately desired a male heir to assume his throne; and since Catherine had been unable to fulfil that wish, he sought the divorce. Henry contemplated divorcing Catherine as early as 1514 but waited through her child-bearing years in hopes of raising a legitimate heir through the Tudor line. Henry contended that he and Catherine were never legally married, since she was first married to his brother Arthur. Catherine and Arthur married when they were just sixteen and fifteen respectively, and Arthur died six months after their marriage. According to Catherine, the marriage was never consummated. Because the dowry she brought with her from Spain was so large, and in order to maintain the marital alliance with Ferdinand, Henry the VII was determined to wade through the necessary legal and ecclesiastical wranglings to have her betrothed to his son Prince Henry. Twenty-four years later in 1527, Henry sought to use the original contrived legal process as grounds to annul his marriage with Catherine.

Unfortunately for Henry, Pope Clement was beholden to powerful Charles V, Catherine's nephew, who succeeded Ferdinand to the throne of Spain and became the Holy Roman Emperor in 1519. Charles refused to sanction the divorce unless Catherine willingly consented. When Clement unwisely delayed his response to Henry, Henry became impatient and took matters into his own hands. In January 1531, Henry summoned a convocation of bishops in Canturbury with the intent of severing ecclesiastical ties to Rome. Threatening to confiscate their "property and benefices [position and income]," if they did not consent to his demand to be accepted as head of the Church in England, the bishops negotiated and finally yielded. During the meeting, the bishops had avowed to Henry that "Christ is head of the Church" whereupon the king replied, "Very well, I consent. If you declare me *head of the Church* you may add *under God*."[60] By March 1532, Henry obtained sufficient support from a majority of bishops to declare independence of the English Church from Rome. He secretly married Anne Boleyn in January 1533 and, unable to obtain a last-minute annulment from Pope Clement, received approval for divorce in April from the now independent English convocation of bishops. On May 23, Thomas Cranmer, the archbishop of Canterbury, declared Henry's marriage to Catherine void and five days later pronounced Anne Boleyn his lawful wife. Hence, by manipulation and the exercise of kingly power, Henry achieved his desires to marry Anne.

Ironically, Henry's scheme to marry Anne prepared the way for the English Bible to be published. She was the daughter of a wealthy merchant and diplomat with close ties to the king. Years earlier, Anne had attended school in Paris, where she served for a time as a lady-in-waiting to Marguerite of Navarre, from whose influence she may have developed Protestant leanings. Consequently, Anne favored an English Bible, paving the way for Tyndale's Bible to be published and distributed in the churches shortly after his death in 1536.

In response to Henry's defiance, he was excommunicated by Pope Clement. Henry countered by persuading Parliament to pass the Act of Supremacy in 1534, formally severing England from all papal ties and placing him firmly at the head of the Church in England. Numerous events collided nearly simultaneously, making such reforms possible. The rising middle class had replaced feudal lords only a few decades earlier, bringing greater stability to the realm and creating a strong independent nation that sought secular autonomy from the pope. Issues of papal taxation, large land tracts owned by the Church, and intellectual and spiritual resurgence brought about in part by Wycliffe, the Lollards, and the translation and distribution of Tyndale's English Bible—these factors combined to make Henry's sweeping changes popular with the people. In order to ensure the continuing success of his policies, Henry closed most of the monasteries, seized some of the property for himself, and sold the rest at bargain prices to the middle class in exchange for support among those of influence and nobility.

The actions of a secular king were responsible for redirecting the spiritual compass of an entire nation. Unfortunately, this king was not an honorable ruler but one driven by personal appetites. He also lacked God-given authority to select those who would guide the English Church. Although Britains were required to obey the king instead of the pope in spiritual as well as temporal matters, their theology remained largely Roman Catholic.

The Anglican Church differed from the religions established by the European Reformers because they continued to assert the importance of a priesthood hierarchy rather than the "priesthood belonging to all believers." In an attempt to claim apostolic authority, Matthew Parker was ordained archbishop of Canterbury by three bishops who had been banished by Mary Tudor, the staunch Catholic daughter of Henry VIII and Catherine of Aragon. "Parker," it was asserted, "in turn, consecrated the newly appointed bishops, and thus the succession was preserved."[61]

Demonstrating the feeble position taken by the Anglican Church regarding apostolic authority, in 1896 the Church of England, under the leadership of Lord Halifax; and the Catholic Church, under Pope Leo XIII, explored unification of the two faiths. This request was ultimately denied under a papal decree that refused to recognize the authority of the Anglican priesthood. Because the Catholic Church itself had been in apostasy for centuries and was no longer vested with the authority of Jesus, regardless of how it is viewed, the Church of England lacked any authority whatsoever to act in the name of God or perform any of the ordinances or sacraments of the Savior's Church.

Protestantism became firmly rooted in Germany, Switzerland, France, Scandinavia, England, Scotland, and Holland. Four major groups had been formed since Martin Luther first tacked his Ninety-Five Theses to the door of the Wittenberg church: Lutheranism, Calvinism or Reformed Faith churches, the Anglican Church in

England, and the Anabaptists, who favored clear separation of church and state and were somewhat more radical in their departure from Catholic doctrine. The Roman Church faced the difficulty of responding to the overwhelming losses it had sustained in a few short years.

The Counter-Reformation and the Reformation of the Catholic Church (1545–64)

The pontiffs of the early Protestant Reformation were weak men who lacked the vision and courage necessary to resolve the mounting difficulties politically and spiritually caused by centuries of corruption. They failed to hear the genuine and legitimate concerns of those who were well educated, spiritually enlightened, and eager to see the Church reform itself. The failure of the popes—including the Church's central leadership machinery—to heed these repeated warnings inspired widespread revolution and a subsequent exodus from the Church. Conversely, the popes of the Counter-Reformation and of Reforming Catholicism were generally devoted to the faith and characterized by hard work, resilience, and determination to implement necessary course corrections.

During the papacy of Paul III (1535–49), the call for internal reforms was the central focus of his ministry. He appointed a committee of nine cardinals to study the abuses of the clergy. In 1537 the delegation submitted its findings and reported a straightforward list of abuses by the clergy in general and of the papacy in particular, including numerous recommendations for reform. Many of the suggested internal reforms were effected immediately. Pope Paul proposed a general Church council be

held at Trent to deal with external issues and questions of Church doctrine that divided Lutheranism and Catholicism.

Internal reforms had already begun within many of the monastic orders. The Augustinians, the Barnabites, the Theatines (established in 1524), the strict Capuchin branch of the Franciscans formed in 1525, the Ursuline Order for women organized in 1535, and the newly formed Jesuits approved by Paul III in 1540 had all demanded reform and had made significant contributions in effecting change throughout the Church. In 1545 Pope Paul finally succeeded in bringing political entities sufficiently together to convene the Council of Trent and against great odds achieved remarkable progress. In 1547 the Council moved to Bologna, Italy, and was temporarily disbanded in 1548 shortly before Pope Paul died in 1549.

Paul's successor, Julius III (1550–55), was one of three leading cardinals who presided at the Council of Trent. He recalled the Council of Trent in 1551 but was forced to adjourn the assembly after only one year when Maurice, the Duke of Saxony (southern Germany), turned his allegiance to the Protestants and away from the Holy Roman Emperor, Charles V, who was a vigorous supporter of Catholicism. Maurice's alliance with Henri II of France set the stage for a treaty with the Protestants in 1552 called the Peace of Passau. This accord was later reenforced and formalized as the Peace of Augsburg in 1555. While Julius endured several setbacks during his rule, he remained staunchly devoted to reform.

One of the more notable popes of the Counter-Reformation was Gian Putro Carafa, titled Paul IV (1555–59). A fiery personality, Paul IV was the most zealous of all the reforming popes. Clerical and curial abuses of the papal treasury were eliminated, the elevation of cardinals due to foreign influence came to an abrupt halt, and simony was treated as heresy. Pope Paul was ruthless in his punishment of such crimes and developed a reputation of being severe and unforgiving. However, such a temperament was probably necessary to correct this enormous, unwieldy institution that had gone largely untended for centuries.

Paul IV prepared a list of "forbidden books," seeking to curtail free thought in an effort to bring order and greater harmony to the Church he loved. The Inquisition was resurrected under Paul III, and Paul IV had been its leader. As pope he increased its activities and intensity. He became so fanatical in his reforms that he was known as a "harsh bigot," untrusting of even close advisors. When he died, the mob razed the Inquisition's headquarters.

The last pope of the Counter-Reformation was Pius IV (1559–65). Although equally committed to reform, Pius discontinued the oppressive and severe approach of his predecessor. Reconvened in January 1562, the Council of Trent finished its work in December 1563, reaching agreement on every doctrinal and reform issue brought before them. Following the Council, Pius moved quickly to institute all reforms. Cheetham writes:

> He appointed a special committee of Cardinals to put the decrees into effect, refashioned the Curia, abolished all clerical privileges incompatible with Tridentine reform, cut the index down to size and dismissed 400 superfluous members of the papal household.[62]

Last, the Catholic Church initiated a significant missionary movement through its monastic orders. As the known world began to expand through the great Spanish and French explorers of the day, the Universal Church expanded its reach to Latin America, Quebec, and Southeast Asia. The sixteenth century is remembered as the great century of Roman Catholic missions.

The Counter-Reformation was Catholicism's response to the Protestant challenge. Before the internal reforms of the Universal Church and the initiatives during the Counter-Reformation, the expansion of ideas begun by Martin Luther took root in numerous countries throughout the Eastern Hemisphere. So effective were the countermeasures taken by the Church of Rome that Protestant advances were virtually stopped in their tracks. After 1560 no other country except Holland was won to Protestantism. In fact, both Poland and Belgium returned to the Catholic fold through the efforts of Jesuit preaching and education.

Although the Peace of Augsburg stabilized Europe, and although the Roman Church succeeded to some degree in cleaning its own house, religious tensions were still high throughout Europe. Several of the German princes were persuaded to embrace Protestant ideals, and in open defiance of the compromises reached at Augsburg, they converted the people of their provinces to the Protestant faith. Fearing a collapse of the Peace of Augsburg, the German princes organized the Protestant Evangelical Union in 1608; the Catholic princes followed by organizing the Catholic League in 1609. With state and religious lines firmly drawn, the only thing preventing open war was the absence of a lighted match. This was kindled in 1618 when the Protestants of Bohemia, outraged by the aggressive policies of the Catholic hierarchy, stormed the royal castle of the Holy Roman Emperor, Ferdinand II, and threw two of his ministers out of a tower window. Led by Count Heinrich

Matthias von Thurn, the Protestant armies scored several early victories, deposing Ferdinand and installing Frederick V, Elector of the Palatinate, as ruler of Bohemia. Until that moment, Pope Paul V had favored peace but finally sided with Ferdinand, and a bloody war followed that would span three decades.

The Thirty-Years War disrupted life all over Europe but was especially catastrophic in Germany. During this period, Germany lost approximately one-fourth of its population; in some regions, as many as two-thirds of the inhabitants were killed. Incalculable property was destroyed and great human suffering resulted. The conflict finally ceased in October 1648 when a treaty was signed at Munster, known as the Peace of Westphalia. It ended the religious wars of Europe.

Analysis of the Reformation

Harry Emerson Fosdick wrote: "In 1572 a picture was published in a Bohemian psalter representing Wycliffe striking the spark, Hus kindling the coals, and Luther brandishing the flaming torch."[63] Beginning with Wycliffe and Hus, Martin Luther succeeded in obtaining the necessary political as well as ecclesiastical support to effect reform when he nailed his Ninety-Five Theses to the door of the Wittenberg chapel. What began as objection to the sale of indulgences grew into a number of distinct theological differences. The heavy emphasis placed by the Catholic Church on works, specifically when dealing with confessions to clergy, and the methods imposed by the Church to bring about repentance, such as fasting, pilgrimages, and floggings, were also of critical concern.

The Protestants—composed of Lutherans, Calvinists, Anglicans, and Anabaptists—generally agreed on the concepts of justification by faith, the Bible as the sole authority for Christians, and the priesthood held by all believers. However, broad disagreement existed regarding most other doctrines. The problems with the Catholic Church had centered on corruption within the clergy and papacy and doctrinal errors that had crept into the Church. The problems with the Protestants stemmed from a lack of unity in both organization and theology, doctrines at odds with early Christianity, and the crucial question whether they possessed any divine authority to administer the ordinances and sacraments of the Savior's Church.

Luther was convinced that salvation through faith alone in Jesus Christ, not works, would reconcile man with God. He witnessed firsthand the evil practices of the papal court and had access to the historical records of the disgraces of the past. He concluded that the Bible alone could stand as the sole authority between God and man. Luther was well acquainted with the Universal Church's claim as the successor to the apostolic authority of St. Peter and advocated a new doctrine he called the priesthood equality of all believers, minimizing the obstacle that the Protestant faith might lack the authority of Christ to administer the Lord's sacrament and other ordinances. What started as a few concerns blossomed into many as the Protestants disagreed with other Universal Church doctrines such as transubstantiation, supererogation, the worship of the virgin Mary, and purgatory.

However, the answers to doctrinal questions were not as simple as either side professed. In a frank discussion regarding the theory of predestination with Luther, Erasmus quipped, "Is it not unjust that God should create man incapable of fulfilling the conditions for salvation and then at whim save or damn for what cannot be helped?" Luther admitted this was a "stumbling block," but then quoted from the story of Esau and Jacob, which seemed to suggest that their fates were sealed before birth. Erasmus replied that "other passages of Scripture bear a different sense, and the matter is therefore not clear. If it were, why should debates over it have continued for centuries?" "Scripture" he argued, "needs to be interpreted, and the claim of the Lutherans to have the Spirit by which to interpret is not confirmed by the fruits of the Spirit in their behavior."[64]

In this exchange, Erasmus points out a major flaw in how Reformation theology developed. Doctrinal controversy had shaken the Church since the death of the Apostles. The Lutherans, he suggested, did not conduct themselves any better than Catholics and therefore could not qualify to receive a more inspired interpretation. Was Reformation theology inspired or interpreted by human wisdom? Did God ordain us to remain in such a state of ambiguity and controversy for hundreds of years; rather, did Paul teach (1 Corinthians 1:10, 13) and Jesus pray (John 17) that we ought to be unified?

In addition to unresolved doctrinal debates, the question of priesthood authority persisted. The scriptures testify that priesthood authority is necessary to administer the sacraments of the Church, exert power over unclean spirits, call down the grace of heaven to heal sickness and disease, and gather the lost sheep of the house of Israel.[65] Great disparity existed between the teachings of the early Christian Church regarding priesthood authority and the doctrine referred to by the Reformers as *the Priesthood*

of the Believers. Apostolic teachings, as well as those of Ignatius and Clement, furnish evidence of the special authority bestowed upon the bishops and presbytery in presiding over local branches of the Church. The doctrine surrounding the transfer of priesthood authority was communicated to the earliest Church Fathers but later corrupted and lost to future generations. Like Augustine, the Reformers would have also been required to "twist" numerous Biblical references, examined in chapter 3, regarding the need for literal priesthood authority in order to dismiss them outright as the Protestants ultimately did.

Another confusing dichotomy left behind by the Reformers was their decision to subscribe to several early tenets set forth in the Nicene and Chalcedonian Councils, while rejecting other doctrines established by that same generation of Christian leaders. For example, the Reformers embraced the doctrine of the Trinity but rejected the authority of the pope and his legates, largely responsible for crafting and supporting this doctrine. Pope Leo I, as has already been mentioned, was writing his dissertation on the infallibility of the bishop of Rome at the same time he was advocating his version of the Trinity. Because the Reformers were attempting to return to the principles of New Testament Christianity, their greater faith in such men as Augustine and the leaders of his day, rather than the teachings of Ignatius and Clement, the earliest Christian leaders, is bewildering.

Over time, the Reformers did achieve remarkable success in rescuing the Church from immediate moral and spiritual decay, triggering the Counter-Reformation and ultimately returning to some of the principles and devotion characterized by New Testament Christianity. The Protestant clergy were professionally trained, but they were no longer viewed as authoritatively superior to the lay membership; thus clerical abuses diminished. Scripture reading and sincere worship were more commonplace. Certain doctrinal innovations, such as transubstantiation, Mary as intercessor to Jesus, indulgences, and papal infallibility were eliminated. Importantly, monetary abuses were also greatly reduced.

Justification by Faith

Through the centuries following the death of the original Apostles, the Church had moved increasingly away from the pure teachings of Jesus. During the late Middle Ages, the Catholic Church characterized Jesus as an austere figure and placed Mary in an unscriptural intercessory position of worship, adoration, and mercy. Instead of the grace of Christ being sufficient to forgive—including the biblical repentance process of godly sorrow, confession, and forsaking one's transgressions—the sinner was required to participate in special fasts, pilgrimages, and floggings, with death being administered to those guilty of serious sin.

The Reformers were influenced by such apostasy when they crafted the doctrine of justification by faith. Additionally, they were influenced by the Apostle Paul's emphasis on grace in contrast to works, *according to the law of Moses*. Paul was a Jew who lived by the Jewish law and was devout, if not overzealous, in its adherence. When properly instructed by the Savior through His Apostles and the Holy Spirit, Paul placed a contextually related emphasis on the role of grace in order to combat the false traditions of Jewish converts. The law of Moses had been fulfilled. Animal sacrifice and the

strict practices of the preparatory gospel were no longer expected. God now required a broken heart and a contrite spirit, and men were commanded to develop faith in Jesus, not adhere blindly to the works of the law of Moses. However, neither Paul nor any other New Testament author diminished the importance of righteous living, a very different thing than obedience to the exacting discipline of the Mosaic Law. While biblical testimony implied that good works alone will not save us, *agency* in accepting the Savior's grace and *following* His teachings were equally understood in the determination of eternal reward or punishment. For example, if anyone were to commit even a single sin, his need for the Atonement was equally great as that of the most wretched man: "For all have sinned, and come short of the glory of God" (Romans 3:23). Men were saved not by good works but by the grace of Jesus. Yet the scriptures were plain that our eternal outcome depended on not just believing, not just confessing, but also on obeying the laws and ordinances of the gospel.[66] However, the Reformers eliminated individual responsibility in the role of salvation, despite biblical teachings and testimony from the Apostolic Fathers clearly to the contrary.

Jacobus Arminius, a lone dissenting Reformer, recognized the importance of individual responsibility in the salvation process and maintained that it was possible for a man to fall from grace once saved. This view, later echoed by John Wesley and captured in his essay entitled *A Letter to a Roman Catholic*, stated:

> I believe God forgives all the sins of them that truly repent and unfeignedly believe his holy gospel; . . . If a man sincerely believes thus much, and practices accordingly, can anyone possibly persuade you to

think that such a man will perish everlastingly? But does he practice accordingly? If he does not, we grant that all his faith will not save him.[67]

The scriptures indicate that by *faith* we are made whole, by *faith* our sins are justified, and by *faith* we will receive salvation. Faith by its scriptural definition implies action and presupposes effort. A person may fully *believe* in Jesus Christ and accept the fact that He is the Savior of mankind. However, a person of *genuine faith*, through individual agency, will *choose* to follow Jesus and apply Christian principles in his life. Likewise, where little faith fails to produce a single miracle, significant faith inspires mighty miracles. The more an individual *elects* to align his life with that of the Master *and thus participate in His grace*, the more faith he is able to exercise. The Bible is filled with scripture specific to the requirement of righteousness and obedience to gospel law, and thus *free will*, in the role of salvation and eternal reward:

Not every one that saith unto me, Lord, Lord, shall enter into the kingdom of heaven; *but he that doeth the will* of my Father which is in heaven. (Matthew 7:21; emphasis added)

If ye keep my commandments, ye shall abide in my love; *even as I have kept my Father's commandments,* and abide in his love. (John 15:10; emphasis added)

Teaching us that . . . we should live soberly, righteously, and godly, in this present world; looking for that blessed hope, and the glorious appearing of . . . our Saviour Jesus Christ; who gave himself for us, that he might redeem us from all iniquity, and purify unto himself a peculiar people, zealous of good works. (Titus 2:12–14)

They profess that they know God; *but in works they deny him.* (Titus 1:16)

If a man . . . purge himself from these, he shall be a vessel unto honour, sanctified and meet for the Master's use (2 Timothy 2:21).

For as the body without the spirit is dead, *so faith without works is dead also* (James 2:26; emphasis added).

If ye continue in my word, then are ye my disciples indeed; and ye shall know the truth, and the truth shall make you free. (John 8:31; emphasis added)

Though he were a Son, yet learned he obedience by the things which he suffered; and being made perfect, he became the author of eternal salvation unto *all them that obey him.* (Hebrews 5:8–9; emphasis added)

He that hath an ear, let him hear what the Spirit saith unto the churches; *to him that overcometh* will I give to eat of the tree of life, which is in the midst of the paradise of God. (Revelation 2:7; emphasis added)

The dead were judged out of those things which were written in the books, *according to their works.* (Revelation 20:12; emphasis added)

Perhaps the clearest of all scriptures testifying of the combined role of faith and works *as to eternal reward* is found in the book of James. He offers a compelling argument that true faith is actually demonstrated by one's works:

What doth it profit, my brethren, though a man say he hath faith, and have not works? can faith save him? If a brother or sister be naked, and destitute of daily food, and one of you say unto them, Depart in peace, be ye warmed and filled; notwithstanding ye give them not those things which are needful to the body; what doth it profit? Even so faith, *if it hath not works*, is dead, being alone. Yea, a man may say, Thou hast faith, and I have works: shew me my faith without thy works, and *I will shew thee my faith by my works*. Thou believest that there is one God; thou doest well: *the devils also believe*, and tremble. But wilt thou know, O vain man, that *faith without works is dead*? (James 2:14–20; emphasis added)

James begins his remarks by asking a rhetorical question, "Though a man say he hath faith, and have not works, can faith save him?" He then illustrates his position with an unambiguous story or analogy: If you simply tell a hungry man to be warmed and filled but do not feed him, will his hunger be satisfied? James insists it will not, stating he will demonstrate *his* faith *by* his works, that is, he will feed him and be an instrument in the hands of God in applying "pure religion" (James 1:27). Designating the difference between mere belief and genuine faith, James declares that "the devils also believe" (James 2:19). Before the creation of the earth, the devils were disobedient;[68] in spite of a perfect knowledge of the position and status of the Son of God before the foundations of the world were laid, they rejected truth, choosing evil instead. Works are the manifestation of faith and cannot be separated.

Finally, James articulates in plain language the true principle of faith regarding how men are justified by the Savior: "Ye see then how that by works a man is justified, *and not by faith only*" (James 2:24; emphasis added).

No conflict exists between faith and works. They are interdependent on one another. While our works are not capable of

saving us—Jesus Christ alone being mighty to save—the lack of works will doubtless influence our eternal rewards. Furthermore, this point of view echoes the ideology of the Apostolic Fathers and the documentation of the Two Ways so prevalent in early Christian writings. In view of how far from the truth the Universal Church strayed from the Savior's plan for our redemption, most Reformers moved to the other end of the spectrum, disregarding the evidence of the role of works contained in holy writ.

Although Luther discounted the book of James, declaring it was "an epistle of straw compared to [Paul's epistles], for it has nothing in the nature of the Gospel about it,"[69] the earliest Christians revered James's epistle, and its doctrine is consistent with the teachings contained in the four Gospels. Paul himself taught:

Know ye not that the unrighteous shall not inherit the kingdom of God? Be not deceived: neither fornicators, nor idolaters, nor adulterers, nor effeminate, nor abusers of themselves with mankind, nor thieves, nor covetous, nor drunkards, nor revilers, nor extortioners, shall inherit the kingdom of God. (1 Corinthians 6:9–10)

Modern Christianity is just beginning to understand the important combination of *faith* and *works* in God's plan for our salvation. After detailing the early Christian writings from Clement of Rome, the Shepherd of Hermas, Ignatius, Polycarp, the Epistle of Barnabas, Justin Martyr, Clement of Alexandria, Origen, Hippolytus, Cyprian, and Lactantius—all of whom affirm the important role of works in salvation—David Bercot concludes:

Nevertheless, we also play a role in our own salvation, according to Scripture and the early Christians. First, we have to repent and believe in Christ as our Lord and Savior in order to avail ourselves of God's grace. After receiving the new birth [baptism], we also have to obey Christ. . . . So salvation begins and ends with grace, but in the middle is man's faithful and obedient response. Ultimately, salvation depends upon both man and God. For this reason, James could say we are saved by works and not faith alone.[70]

Another confusing aspect of the doctrine of justification by faith alone can be found in the Reformers' view that baptism is not an essential qualification for entrance into the kingdom of heaven. If baptism is not required to enter the kingdom of heaven, how are the following verses to be interpreted?

Then cometh Jesus from Galilee to Jordan unto John, to be baptized of him. But John forbad him, saying, I have need to be baptized of thee, and comest thou to me? And Jesus answering said unto him, Suffer it to be so now: *for thus it becometh us to fulfil all righteousness.* Then he suffered him. (Matthew 3:13–15; emphasis added)

Go ye therefore, and teach all nations, baptizing them in the name of the Father, and of the Son, and of the Holy Ghost: Teaching them to observe all things whatsoever I have commanded you. (Matthew 28:19–20)

He that believeth [has faith, which is signified by true repentance] *and is baptized* shall be saved; but he that believeth not shall be damned. (Mark 16:16; emphasis added)

Now when all the people were baptized, it came to pass, that *Jesus also being baptized,* and praying, the heaven was opened, and the Holy Ghost descended

in a bodily shape like a dove upon him, and a voice came from heaven, which said, Thou art my beloved Son; *in thee I am well pleased.* (Luke 3:21–22; emphasis added)

But the Pharisees and lawyers *rejected the counsel of God* against themselves, *being not baptized of him.* (Luke 7:30; emphasis added)

Jesus answered and said unto him, Verily, verily, I say unto thee, *Except a man be born again, he cannot see the kingdom of God.* Nicodemus saith unto him, How can a man be born when he is old? can he enter the second time into his mother's womb, and be born? Jesus answered, Verily, verily, I say unto thee, *Except a man be born of water and of the Spirit,* he cannot enter into the kingdom of God. (John 3:3–5; emphasis added)

Some theologians interpret the Savior's answer to verse 4 as referring to: (1) "*Except a man be born of water*" = our live physical birth, and (2) "*. . . and of the Spirit*" = a subsequent spiritual rebirth or awakening. Instead, Jesus teaches Nicodemus that being *born again* consisted of two parts. First, when we are baptized, we undergo a physical *rebirth*—symbolically—as we are immersed in the water and come forth again out of the water. We are born into mortality through water, clean and pure, having just come from the presence of God. Because of the fall of man and our fallen environment, we develop flaws and human weaknesses that would prevent us from coming back into the presence of God without the atonement of Jesus Christ. The Savior ransoms those who accept His atonement, who are baptized, and who strive to follow Him. Baptism, as taught by the early Christian Church, is in similitude of the Savior's death on the cross and subsequent resurrection. We are born *again* "of the water," going down into the water unclean, even as the mortal body of Jesus was corruptible and placed in the grave after He offered up His life for us. We come forth out of the water, clean again as when we were born an infant—innocent and pure—just as Jesus came forth from the empty tomb on the third day with a perfect, incorruptible, and immortal body.

The second part of being *born again*, our spiritual *rebirth*, is the receipt of the gift of the Holy Ghost by the laying on of hands, as illustrated so precisely in Acts 8:14–20. This rebirth is the quickening of our spirit as we spiritually mature and desire God's influence to guide us toward sanctification. When we receive the gift of the Holy Ghost, we are promised the companionship of God's spirit to guide us through the tests and trials of this mortal experience as we repent regularly of our sins and strive to follow Jesus.

Confirming this interpretation, Justin Martyr taught:

> Then they are brought by us where there is water, and are born again in the same manner of rebirth by which we ourselves were born again. . . . For Christ also said, "Except you are born again, you will not enter into the Kingdom of heaven." Now it is clear to all that it is impossible for those who have once come into being to enter into their mothers' wombs.[71]

Justin, one of the earliest Christians, equated water baptism as the rebirth required to enter heaven, precisely as explained to Nicodemus by Jesus.

Another early Christian witness pronouncing the essential nature of water baptism is attributed to Clement of Rome or one of his followers. Recording words credited to Peter, he explains:

> When you have come to the Father, you will learn that this is His will, that you be born anew by means of waters. . . . For he who is regenerated by water, having filled up the measure of good works, is made heir of Him by whom he has been regenerated in incorruption. . . . And do you suppose that you can have hope towards God, even if you cultivate all piety and righteousness, but do not receive baptism? . . . Now God has ordered everyone who worships Him to be sealed by baptism; but if you refuse, and obey your own will rather than God's, you are doubtless contrary and hostile to his will.[72]

Perhaps the strongest language used by an early Christian leader affirming the critical role of baptism pertaining to salvation comes from Hippolytus:

> If, therefore, man has become immortal, he will also be God. And if he is made God by water and the Holy Spirit after the regeneration of the laver he is found to be also joint-heir with Christ after the resurrection from the dead. Wherefore I preach to this effect: Come all ye kindreds of the nations, to the immortality of baptism. . . . And how, saith one, shall we come? How? By water and the Holy Ghost.[73]

Gratefully, we need not rely solely upon the early Christian writings to comprehend the need to receive the ordinance of baptism. Consider the strength of other New Testament verses that illustrate this important doctrine:

> Now when they heard this, they were pricked in their heart, and said unto Peter and to the rest of the apostles, Men and brethren, what shall we do? Then Peter said unto them, *Repent*, and *be baptized every one of you* in the name of Jesus Christ *for the remission of sins,*

and ye shall receive *the gift of the Holy Ghost.* (Acts 2:37–38; emphasis added)

Note that Peter does *not* say, "Oh, just believe on Christ, accept him as your Savior, confess his name, and your salvation shall be assured." Augmenting Peter's injunction, Paul recounts his own conversion and the direction he personally received from Ananias, to whom he was sent specifically by the Savior:

And now why tarriest thou? *arise, and be baptized,* and *wash away thy sins,* calling on the name of the Lord. (Acts 22:16; emphasis added)

Not by works of righteousness which we have done, but according to his mercy he saved us, *by the washing of regeneration* [baptism], and *renewing of the Holy Ghost.* (Titus 3:5; emphasis added)
The like figure *whereunto even baptism doth also now save us* (not the putting away of the filth of the flesh, but the answer of a good conscience toward God,) by the resurrection of Jesus Christ. (1 Peter 3:21; emphasis added)

Baptism follows repentance, and repentance follows faith. Repentance *and* baptism are essential elements in man's redemption. They are part of what it means to exercise faith and be *born again.* When we examine the historical background of baptism, we observe its central place in the plan of salvation in the earliest Christian communities and with the Apostolic Fathers.

As with justification by faith, modern Protestant Christianity is *beginning* to understand that baptism is not just an outward performance to an inward conversion. David Bercot reflects:

I still remember the first time I read Jesus' words to Nicodemus: "Truly I say to you, unless one is born of water and the Spirit, he cannot enter into the kingdom of God" (John 3:5 NAS). I was a young boy . . . reading that verse in a small Bible study group. The teacher asked . . ."What does it mean to be born of water?" "Water baptism," I blurted out, feeling proud of myself for having figured this out. However, to my chagrin, the teacher explained that this was a common misconception. . . . Through the years I was able to correct others who [were] mistaken [and] to explain the "correct" view. So it took the wind out of my sails when I discovered that the early Christians universally understood Jesus' words to refer to water baptism. And once again, it was the gnostics who taught differently from the church—saying that humans can't be reborn or regenerated through water baptism. Irenaeus wrote about them: "This class of men have been instigated by Satan to a denial of that baptism which is regeneration to God."[74]

Bercot then describes how the early Christians believed in baptism *for the remission of sins,* the *symbolism and reality of the new birth,* and the *"spiritual illumination"* attained through receiving the gift of the Holy Ghost.[75] Urging a call for reform he writes:

Since we feel the need to associate our spiritual rebirth with a fixed day and hour, why don't we tie it to baptism, rather than the alter call? Actually the alter call and associate prayers are a product of the revival movements of the eighteenth and nineteenth centuries, and they were unknown to any Christians before that time.[76]

Finally, Bercot points out that infants do not need baptism and that God has a fair plan for those who do not have the opportunity to receive the gospel in mortality. Bercot says,

One thing that particularly impresses me about the early Christians is that they never put God in a box. For example, they always believed that God would do what was loving and just towards pagans who never had the opportunity to hear about Christ. . . . They believed that unbaptized babies who died in infancy could still be saved. It was Augustine, writing centuries later, who taught that all unbaptized infants are damned.[77]

The Reformation occurred as Christians everywhere began to have greater access to the Bible through translations into their native languages, and they objected to the discrepancies between the doctrines being practiced and those taught in the holy scriptures. As modern Christianity obtains more of the early writings, another doctrinal reformation of sorts is underway as some branches of Christianity attempt to correct erroneous, unbiblical teachings.

The parable of the talents explains another dimension in the role of the Savior's grace in our ultimate eternal outcome. In this parable, the Savior illustrates that He will do for us what we cannot do for ourselves. We are not judged equally but according to the talents we have been blessed with and the difficulties we have been required to endure in mortality. Simply put, nurturing righteous desires and putting forth our best efforts, according to our talents and circumstances, is what the Savior expects. His grace (not our works) is sufficient to make up the difference. Hence the verse "For unto whomsoever much is given, of him shall much be required" (Luke12:48). The early Christians clearly did understand this concept. Justin Martyr wrote in his First Apology:

> We believe, . . . that every person will suffer punishment in eternal fire according to the merit of his actions, and will give account according to the ability he has received from God, as Christ reminded us when He said, "To whom God has given more, from him more will be required."[78]

Finally, the testimony of Paul bears witness to the importance of endurance in faith (not perfection) to the end of our lives: "For I am now ready to be offered, and the time of my departure is at hand. *I have fought a good fight,* I have finished my course, *I have kept the faith:* Henceforth there is laid up for me a crown of righteousness" (2 Timothy 4:6–8; emphasis added).

Original Christianity was unknown to the world during the Middle Ages; thus, the salvation doctrine taught by the Catholic Church had strayed so far from apostolic teachings that the Reformers' task of repairing the essential aspects of Christian worship was impossible. Yet, a thorough investigation of the Bible reveals that the Savior taught us the way, the truth, and the life, and we cannot come unto the Father except through Him (John 14:6). He commanded that we exercise faith, repent of our sins, and be baptized for the remission of sins. The Apostle Paul explained the beauty and symbolic nature of baptism. The Bible testifies that baptism consummates the faith we have expressed in Jesus Christ through genuinely repenting of our sins and explains that we are then under covenant obligation, as was ancient Israel (Deuteronomy 28:1–9, 15), to persist in obeying the gospel to the best of our ability, regularly repenting of our sins, partaking of the emblems of the Lord's Supper, and thereby keeping our *faith* firm to the end of our lives.

The Bible as the Sole Authority for Christians

Just as the apostasy of the Universal Church contributed to the development of the doctrine of justification by faith, it also left its mark upon the origin of *sola scriptura*. The corrupt traditions of the Roman hierarchy and its claims of absolute authority and infallibility created contradictions between what was taught in New Testament Christianity and what was being practiced in the Church. The reigns of Pope Alexander VI (1492–1503), Julius II (1503–15), and Leo X (1513–15) are characterized by objective historians as among the most despotic years of an already colorful papal history.

When Martin Luther traveled to Rome on Church business in 1510, he was shocked by the character of Julius II. And perhaps he was thinking about Jesus cleansing the temple when he nailed his Ninety-Five Theses to the door of the Wittenberg church in opposition to the sale of indulgences in 1517. No wonder Martin Luther was so resolute when he said at the Diet of Worms in 1521, "Unless I am convicted by Scripture and plain reason—I do not accept the authority of popes and councils, for they have contradicted each other—my conscience is captive to the Word of God. . . . Here I stand, I can do no other, may God help me! Amen!"[79]

The Reformers placed great emphasis on the Bible as the sole authority for sinful Christians seeking salvation. They truly had no other honest options. The papal governments were completely defiled at this point, and the Bible is clear that the Holy Spirit will not reside with those who are unworthy. The only remnant of reliable Christianity remaining was the Bible itself. No other source could be trusted. Confirming this conclusion, Luther himself wrote:

The chief cause that I fell out with the pope was this: the pope boasted that he was the head of the Church, and condemned all that would not be under his power and authority; for he said, although Christ be the head of the Church, yet, notwithstanding, there must be a corporal head of the Church upon earth. With this I could have been content, had he but taught the Gospel pure and clear, and not introduced human inventions and lies in its stead. Further, he took upon him power, rule, and authority over the Christian Church, and over the Holy Scriptures, the Word of God; no man must presume to expound the Scriptures, but only he, and according to his ridiculous conceits; so that he made himself lord over the Church, proclaiming her at the same time a powerful mother, and empress over the Scriptures, to which we must yield and be obedient; this was not to be endured. They who, against God's Word, boast of the Church's authority, are mere idiots. The pope attributes more power to the Church, which is begotten and born, than to the Word, which has begotten, conceived, and born the Church.[80]

Notwithstanding these unusual circumstances and despite the apparent sound logic of the Reformers' argument, if studied, the doctrine of *sola scriptura* shows itself as unbiblical. It was not the scriptures *themselves* that the gates of hell could not prevail against. The Bible does not speak of itself as the foundation or the cornerstone of the Church, nor did it even exist when Paul and Peter wrote their epistles. The Bible probably did not exist as a volume in any form until the fourth century. Responsible scholars acknowledge that a much larger number of esteemed scriptural books or epistles were widely used by the earliest Christians. The Codex Sinaiticus, Codex Alexandrinus, and Codex Claromontanus page 10) are only a few of the various versions compiled alongside our current canon. The Church of that age, already in error, disclaimed any notion of revelation from the heavens, so the final decisions regarding the canon must be automatically questioned. The foundation of the Church was the living prophets and Apostles. It was *continuous* revelation through Jesus Christ's *authorized servants* that the gates of hell could not prevail against, and it was the *living*, undefiled authority of the holy priesthood that was missing from the earth (Matthew 16:17–19).

If the Church itself had not embraced apostasy centuries before, Martin Luther and the other Reformers would have had nothing to reform. Luther would never have developed the doctrine of *sola scriptura* because he would have accepted the unbroken chain of priesthood authority descended from Christ rightfully and righteously passed on from one Christian generation to the next. Rather than trusting popes and councils, many of whose lives were marred by sin and corruption, the Reformers would have easily sustained the interpretations of living prophets and Apostles and found current teachings consistent with ancient ones. Martin Luther could have rejoiced in his ministry rather than fighting through painful reforms in the Church he had loved since his youth. However inspired the work of the Reformers, the hand of God was just beginning to bring spiritual light to a yearning world, hungry for the original message of faith and hope found in Christ Jesus.

Only by the providence of God were Frederick the Elector of Saxony and other German princes moved to support Luther's reforms. In spite of a vast groundswell of support, the Protestant campaign nearly suffered defeat at the hands of the Holy Roman Empire. Had the complete and everlasting truths of the gospel, reserved to come forth in the *dispensation of the fulness of times* (Ephesians 1:10), appeared in Martin Luther's day, they would surely have been smothered. There was as yet no appetite for genuine freedom of religious thought.

The Priesthood of the Believers

The Reformers valiantly attempted to reconstruct early Christian practices when they developed the doctrine of the *priesthood of the believers*. In the New Testament, abundant examples provided evidence of those who—when they demonstrated faith in Jesus Christ, repented of their sins, were baptized, received the gift of the Holy Ghost, and displayed a continuing willingness to follow the Savior—became "a chosen generation, a royal priesthood, an holy nation" (1 Peter 2:9). This promise was originally given to Moses and the children of Israel when God declared to Moses that He would make them a "peculiar treasure" and a "kingdom of priests" (Exodus 19:5–6). However, because of disobedience, this promise mentioned in Exodus (as testified to by the author of the Epistle of Barnabas) was withheld until the advent of Jesus Christ.[81] This is also documented by the fact that only one tribe, the Levites, received the priesthood under the law of Moses. When apostasy overcame the early Christian Church at some point after the death of the Apostles, God's priesthood, or the promise of becoming a "kingdom of priests," was withdrawn for a season, *just as in earlier dispensations.*

During the apostolic dispensation, Christ introduced a very specific method of making men a "royal priesthood" by ordaining them deacons, teachers, elders, and bishops. The Apostles were ordained and given power and authority to act in their callings (Mark 3:13–15). Likewise, Stephen and his companions were ordained in the same manner (Acts 6:6), as were Saul and Barnabas (Acts 11:22–25; 13:2–3). Elders were ordained from every church and every city (Acts 14:23; 16:4; Titus 1:5).

The "keys" and authority of the priesthood, given to Peter and the Apostles to perform the sacraments of the Church (see pages 56–59), were taken from the earth when wickedness became so widespread that God no longer spoke through the remnant of His former priesthood hierarchy; inevitably, the original authority of Jesus Christ was lost from the earth. As the Reformers examined New Testament Christianity, comparing the earliest Greek and Hebrew translations, and as they researched the earliest Christian communities, they discovered that a prominent lay priesthood was responsible for building the kingdom of God and that no professional clergy had ever legitimately existed. Moses once complained to the Lord:

> Who am I, that I should go unto Pharaoh, and that I should bring forth the children of Israel out of Egypt? (Exodus 3:11)

> I am not eloquent, neither heretofore, nor since thou hast spoken unto thy servant: but I am slow of speech, and of a slow tongue. (Exodus 4:10)

Moses was not a professional clergyman. As it had been with God's prophets, so it was with His Apostles: they were fishermen, tax collectors, tent makers, and carpenters—men of common occupations but uncommon faith. Not only the Apostles but also the Seventy and others who were called to the ministry received priesthood authority and were modest, humble men who loved the Lord and desired to follow Him. Taught Paul:

> For ye see your calling, brethren, how that not many wise men after the flesh, not many mighty, not many noble, *are called:* but God hath chosen the foolish things of the world to confound the wise; and God hath chosen the weak things of the world to confound the things which are mighty. (1 Corinthians 1:26–27)

Qualifications to receive the priesthood did not rest with advanced theological degrees or philosophical rhetoric but simply in man being called of God, as was Aaron (Hebrews 5:4).[82]

The Reformers recognized that the Catholic priesthood was defiled and without legitimate authority. However, they failed to understand in their development of *sola scriptura* and the *priesthood of the believers* the significance the New Testament authors placed on literal priesthood authority being essential to act in His name, to perform the rites and sacraments of the Church, and to administer the affairs of the kingdom of God. Although they acknowledged the potential of faithful believers to be a part of this "royal priesthood," they ignored the process recorded in scripture by which such authority was conferred and then passed on. The New Testament is specific that the priesthood was not given to man indiscriminately but only to one who was qualified by the Holy Spirit, being baptized and receiving the gift of the Holy Ghost, being humble and obedient, and persevering in a godly walk. Worthy and prepared, such men were called of God by revelation and then ordained properly by one who already held the priesthood, such as one of the Apostles. The Reformers knew there were no Apostles to ordain them, yet they recognized priesthood authority as an important concept in Christ's Church.

Many people of the Reformation era and, subsequently, the Great Awakening, believed in and looked forward to the day when Jesus would restore original Christianity once again upon the earth. History calls these men and women "seekers." One such man was Roger Williams, credited with founding the first Baptist Church in America. Williams said, "There is no regularly constituted church on earth, nor any person authorized to administer any church ordinance; nor can there be until new apostles are sent by the Great Head of the Church for whose coming I am seeking."[83]

Another striking figure was none other than one of our nation's founding fathers, Thomas Jefferson. In a letter to John Adams, Jefferson wrote:

> Their Platonising successors indeed, in after times, in order to legitimate the corruptions which they had incorporated into the doctrines of Jesus, found it necessary to disavow the primitive Christians, who had taken their principles from the mouth of Jesus himself, of his Apostles, and the Fathers contemporary with them. They excommunicated their followers as heretics. . . . We must leave therefore to others, younger and more learned than we are, to prepare this euthanasia for Platonic Christianity, and its restoration to the primitive simplicity of its founder.[84]

In the late nineteenth century, a group of seventy-three noted theologians expressed their views concerning the Church of the modern era compared with New Testament Christianity:

> We must not expect to see the Church of Holy Scripture actually existing in its perfection on the earth. It is not to be found, thus perfect, either in the collected fragments of Christendom, or still less in any one of these fragments.[85]

In 1956 a highly regarded Protestant minister, J. B. Phillips, who translated the most widely distributed private rendition of the New Testament, published his views about the modern Church after he completed his translation of the book of Acts:

> Yet we cannot help feeling disturbed as well as moved, for this surely is the Church as it was meant to be. It is vigorous and flexible, for these are the days before it ever became fat and short of breath through prosperity, or musclebound by over organization. These men did not make "acts of faith," they believed; they did not "say their prayers," they really prayed. They did not hold conferences on psychosomatic medicine, they simply healed the sick. We in the modern Church have unquestionably *lost* something. Whether it is due to the atrophy of the quality which the New Testament calls "faith," whether it is due to a stifling churchiness, whether it is due to our sinful complacency over the scandal of a divided Church, or whatever the cause may be, very little of the modern Church could bear comparison with the spiritual drive, the genuine fellowship, and the gay unconquerable courage of the Young Church.[86]

Conclusion

The Reformation was inspired by God and was part of His plan from the beginning. Inasmuch as the agency of man is inviolate, God the Father knew from the foundations of the world how His children would respond initially to His Son's simple message of salvation from sin and error. He knew that the preaching of the Apostles would ultimately fail to prevent apostasy because of human pride and vain ambition. He knew the philosophies and sophistries of sinful man would smother the plain and unadorned truths presented by the Savior and that man would surrender to such temptations as power, greed, and earthly pleasures. Notwithstanding His open arms (Matthew 23:37), God knew He would be rejected for a season and that He would "set his hand again the second time to recover the remnant of his people" (Isaiah 11:11).

Martin Luther and the other Reformers came forth at a singular time in man's history, chosen by God from before the foundations of the world to lay the groundwork for a restoration of original Christianity. Their work was not the culminating work heralded by scripture but rather one of many preliminary steps necessary for God to reveal Himself again to man. True democracy had yet to pierce the veil of sovereign monarchies. The execution of Michael Servetus by the Calvinists in 1553,[87] the slaughter of thousands of Anabaptists by the Lutherans, the repressive activities of the Catholic Inquisition, and the control sought by kings and emperors in religious matters all combined to demonstrate that religious tolerance did not yet exist. Conditions of a spiritual awakening coupled with continuing religious intolerance point to the preparatory nature of the mission of the Reformers.

Yet the progressive attributes of eminent men such as the great English statesman and philosopher of science Sir Francis Bacon (1561–1626), the master playwright William Shakespeare (1564–1616), the physicist and astronomer Galileo (1564–1642), the French mathematician and philosopher Rene' Descartes (1596–50), and the English poet John Milton (1608–74), author of such transcendent poems as *Paradise Lost* and *Paradise Regained,* were only a sample of the great minds giving rise to what would become known as the Age of Intellectual Reason or Rationalism. From these would sprout the seeds of lasting

democracy and ultimately religious freedom.

As we consider the Reformation—its cause, purpose, and result—we must examine the Savior's teachings to His Apostles relative to such. We read in Matthew:

No man putteth a piece of new cloth unto an old garment, for that which is put in to fill it up taketh from the garment, and the rent is made worse. Neither do men put new wine into old bottles: else the bottles break, and the wine runneth out, and the bottles perish: but they put new wine into new bottles, and both are preserved. (Matthew 9:16–17; see also Mark 2:21–22; Luke 5:36–37)

Jesus had just been queried by the Pharisees as to why He dined with publicans and sinners and why they (the Pharisees) fasted but Jesus' disciples did not. Jesus answered that the time would come when He would no longer be with His disciples, and then they would fast. He then related the parable of the new wine in an old bottle, signifying that one could not put the teachings of the new law revealed by Jesus into the old bottle of the Mosaic law; the old law could not be *reformed,* it had to be *restored* to its original intent and purity *by revelation* through Jesus Christ. Similarly, the Reformation was new wine being poured into old bottles. The outcome was easily predictable: "The new wine will burst the bottles, and be spilled" (Luke 5:37). So it was with the rise of Protestant denominationalism: The new wine burst the old bottles and the resultant splinters spilled forth without finding agreement in crucial doctrinal foundations. Thus, religious quarrels persisted, and with religious freedom more than two centuries away, governments continued to oppress. Nevertheless, the Reformation was part of the Father's plan—a forerunner, as John the Baptist was before the advent of Jesus Christ, and John Wycliffe before the Reformation.

Notes

1. Cameron, "Power of the Word," 67.
2. Cameron, "Power of the Word," 81.
3. Cameron, "Power of the Word," 96.
4. Various writers of the thirteenth century have given several versions of Peter's name: Valdesius, Valdensius, or Waldunus. See Schaff, *History of the Christian Church*, 5:493n1.
5. Schaff, *History of the Christian Church*, 5:495.
6. Swanson, *Religion and Devotion in Europe*, 12.
7. Epistle of Methetes to Diognetus 7, in *Ante-Nicene Fathers*, 1:27, written in ca. A.D. 130.
8. Margaret Deanesly, *The Lollard Bible and Other Medieval Biblical Versions* (Cambridge: Cambridge University Press, 1920), 61.
9. Other lay preaching groups such as the Humiliati in north Italy suffered like the Waldenses until they were reconciled by Innocent III, who sought creative ways to meet the demands of the laity while still keeping them in the orthodox fold. Swanson, *Religion and Devotion in Europe*, 69.
10. H. W. Hoare, *The Evolution of the English Bible* (London: John Murray, 1902), 77.
11. According to Loserth and Arnold, in Schaff, *History of the Christian Church*, 6:328.
12. Schaff, *History of the Christian Church*, 6:332–41.
13. Schaff, *History of the Christian Church*, 6:86; Harry Emerson Fosdick, *Great Voices of the Reformation* (New York: Random House, 1952), 3; F. F. Bruce, *History of the Bible in English* (New York: Oxford University Press, 1978), 12.
14. A statement credited to John Horn, Wycliffe's assistant, in Schaff, *History of the Christian Church*, 6:323.
15. Fosdick, *Great Voices of the Reformation*, 8.
16. Deanesly, *Lollard Bible*, 365.
17. Matthew Spinka, *John Hus and the Council of Constance* (New York: Columbia University Press, 1965), 30.
18. Spinka, *John Hus*, 30.
19. John Hus, in Harry Emerson Fosdick, *Great Voices of the Reformation*, 38.
20. Spinka, *John Hus*, 31.
21. Spinka, *John Hus*, 32.
22. Fosdick, *Great Voices of the Reformation*, 39.
23. Spinka, *John Hus*, 229.
24. Spinka, *John Hus*, 229.
25. Spinka, *John Hus*, 233.
26. Spinka, *John Hus*, 233.
27. Spinka, *John Hus*, 233.
28. Schaff, *History of the Christian Church*, 6:386.
29. Cheetham, *Keepers of the Keys*, 190.
30. Johan Huizinga, *Erasmus and the Age of Reformation* (New York: Harper and Rowe, 1957), 22–23.
31. Huizinga, *Erasmus and the Age of Reformation*, 109.
32. Huizinga, *Erasmus and the Age of Reformation*, 109.
33. Huizinga, *Erasmus and the Age of Reformation*, 110.
34. Huizinga, *Erasmus and the Age of Reformation*, 102.
35. Edgar J. Goodspeed, *The Making of the English New Testament* (Chicago: University of Chicago Press, 1925), 3.
36. Huizinga, *Erasmus and the Age of Reformation*, 111–12.
37. Huizinga, *Erasmus and the Age of Reformation*, 107.
38. Charles Beard, *The Reformation of the 16th Century in Its Relation to Modern Thought and Knowledge* (Westport, Conn.: Greenwood Press Reprint, 1980), 305.
39. Bruce, *History of the Bible in English*, 51–52.
40. Bainton, *Here I Stand*, 55–56.
41. Lewis W. Spitz, ed., *The Protestant Reformation, 1517–1559* (St. Louis, Mo.: Concordia, 2003), 34.
42. Bainton, *Here I Stand*, 107–8.
43. Bainton, *Here I Stand*, 108.
44. Bainton, *Here I Stand*, 110.
45. Bainton, *Here I Stand*, 110.
46. Bainton, *Here I Stand*, 144.
47. Bainton, *Here I Stand*, 149–52.

48. Bainton, *Here I Stand,* 157; parentheses added.

49. The Swiss Guard continues to serve at the Vatican. Its members serve for two years, and they must be Catholic and Swiss. Also, they must have already completed their military training in the Swiss army.

50. John Calvin, *The Institutes of Christian Religion,* ed., Tony Lane and Hillary Osborne (Grand Rapids, Mich.: Baker Academic, 1987), 88–91.

51. Calvin, *Institutes of Christian Religion,* 213–16.

52. Calvin, *Institutes of Christian Religion,* 216.

53. Calvin, *Institutes of Christian Religion,* 96–102.

54. Calvin, *Institutes of Christian Religion,* 222–23.

55. Ch. 2 herein, note 21, names some of the early Christian leaders who ascribe to the principle of free will; see also James Arminius, *The Writings of James Arminius,* trans. W. R. Bagnall, 3 vols. (Grand Rapids, Mich.: Baker Book House, 1956), 1:247–48, 329; 2:470–73; 3:459.

56. Arminius, *Writings of James Arminius,* 1:248.

57. Arminius, *Writings of James Arminius,* 1:316–17.

58. Arminius, *Writings of James Arminius,* 1:254.

59. Arminius, *Writings of James Arminius,* 1:254, 281; see also Galatians 5:4; 1 Timothy 1:19; Hebrews 6:4–6; 10:26; 2 Peter 2:2.

60. J. H. Merle d'Aubigne, *The Reformation in England,* 2 vols. (Carlile, Pa.: Banner of Truth Trust, 1963), 2:57.

61. Albert H. Newman, *A Manual of Church History,* 2 vols. (Philadelphia: American Baptist Publication Society, 1933), 2:269.

62. Cheetham, *Keepers of the Keys,* 211.

63. Fosdick, *Great Voices of the Reformation,* 3.

64. Bainton, *Here I Stand,* 197.

65. Matthew 10: "And when he had called unto him his twelve disciples, he gave them power against unclean spirits, to cast them out, and to heal all manner of sickness and all manner of disease [v. 1]. . . . Go . . . to the lost sheep of the house of Israel [v. 6]. Heal the sick, cleanse the lepers, raise the dead, cast out devils: [v. 8]. And if the house be worthy let your peace come upon it: . . . [T]ake no thought how or what ye shall speak [v. 19]."

66. Obedience: Matthew 7:21; Luke 11:28; John 7:17; 14:15; 1 John 2:3–4, 6. Different rewards: John 14:2; 8:17.

67. Wesley, "Letter to a Roman Catholic," in *Works of John Wesley,* 10:82–83.

68. See Matthew 8:28–32; Mark 1:23–26; Luke 4:33–35; 8:27–33; see also treatment in chapter 5.

69. Holman's Editions of Luther's Works, vol. 6, "Preface," translations by Dr. C. M. Jacobs, and this in turn by William Harrison Bruce Carney, "Luther and the Bible, Its Origin and Content," ch. 2 in O. M. Norlie, ed., *The Translated Bible 1534–1934, Commemorating the 400th Anniversary of the Translation of the Bible by Martin Luther* (Philadelphia: United Lutheran Publishing House, 1934); see also Filson, *Which Books Belong in the Bible,* 34.

70. Bercot, *Will the Real Heretics Please Stand Up,* 65.

71. Justin Martyr, First Apology, in *Ancient Christian Writers* 56, ch. 61, 66–67.

72. Clementine Recognitions 6.8, in *Ante-Nicene Fathers,* 8:154–55

73. Hippolytus, Discourse on the Holy Theophany 8, in *Ante-Nicene Fathers,* 5:237.

74. Bercot, *Will the Real Heretics Please Stand Up,* 77–78; see "Against Heresies", bk I, ch. 21.1 for Bercot's quote of Irenaeus refuting the Gnostics in approximately A.D. 170.

75. Bercot, *Will the Real Heretics Please Stand Up,* 78–80.

76. Bercot, *Will the Real Heretics Please Stand Up,* 82.

77. Bercot, *Will the Real Heretics Please Stand Up,* 81.

78. Justin, First Apology 17, in *Ancient Christian Writers* 56, 35.

79. Bainton, *Here I Stand,* 144.

80. Luther, Anti-Christ.

81. Epistle of Barnabas, ch. 14, in *Apostolic Fathers,* 1:391.

82. See also ch. 3 herein for a fuller treatment of this doctrine. Moreover, we remember the Savior's teaching, "Ye have not chosen me, but I have chosen you, and ordained you, that ye should go and bring forth fruit" (John 15:16). The Savior instituted an orderly method for conferring upon his servants priesthood authority to act in his name.

83. William Cullen Bryant, ed., *Picturesque America; or, the Land We Live In* (New York: D. Appleton, 1872), 1:502.

84. Thomas Jefferson to John Adams, October 12, 1813, in *Jefferson Writings* (New York: Library Classics of the United States, 1984), 1302.

85. William Smith, *Smith's Dictionary of the Bible* (Boston: Houghton, Mifflin and Company, 1896).

86. J. B. Phillips, *The Young Church in Action: A Translation of the Acts of the Apostles* (New York: Macmillan, 1955), vii, xvi.

87. Michael Servetus (1511–53), while a law student at Toulouse, had a deeply moving religious experience and became a serious student of Christianity, including the doctrine of the Trinity, which he came to oppose. E. M. Wilbur wrote:

"He [Servetus] turned against the traditional formulations of the nature of Christ and the relation of the persons of the Trinity. He believed that such terms as hypostases or persons, substance, essence, and the like were imposed upon Biblical conceptions from Greek metaphysics and as such were abstract, speculative, artificial, and unrelated to the living God. Having failed to convince the Reformers in Basel and Strasburg of the propriety of his views, Servetus in 1531 published his treatise On the Errors of the Trinity." *Harvard Theological Studies* 16, 6–10, by E. M. Wilbur, in Spitz, *Protestant Reformation,* 102. Servetus was burned to death in an execution presided over by John Calvin in 1553. Those who suggest that Calvin acted out of what he considered a self-imposed duty in cleansing the world of heretics are probably correct; such activities were indeed typical of the age. However, this type of response was not representative of primitive Christianity, a clear indication that the New Testament Church had not yet been restored.

FREEDOM IN AMERICA AND RELIGIOUS TOLERANCE INSPIRE THE GREAT AWAKENING

The summer soldier and the sunshine patriot will, in this crisis, shrink from the service of their country; but he that stands it now, deserves the love and thanks of man and woman. Tyranny, like hell, is not easily conquered; yet we have this consolation with us, that the harder the conflict, the more glorious the triumph. What we obtain too cheap, we esteem too lightly: it is dearness only that gives everything its value. Heaven knows how to put a proper price upon its goods; and it would be strange indeed if so celestial an article as freedom should not he highly rated.

—Thomas Payne

God revealed to Moses that he was to lead the children of Israel to a choice land flowing with milk and honey (Deuteronomy 26:9). The republic of America was likewise destined to become a promised land. Indeed, Christopher Columbus wrote many times that he felt the inspiration of the Almighty in his historic discovery of San Salvador. When large numbers of people began emigrating to the New World 120 years later, many were God-fearing men and women who desired to worship Him according to the dictates of conscience. They were fleeing the tyrannical and oppressive rule of European monarchs who were still striving to maintain the so-called "divine right of kings." Although the Reforma-

tion had unlocked the door of religious freedom in the Old World, by no means was the door yet open, nor were people free to worship as they pleased. Generally, an individual was relegated to participate in the Church of whatever state he happened to live in, regardless of his own personal religious convictions. However, the march of freedom continued its onward trek, albeit slowly, and not without significant setbacks and persecution along the way.

The religious wars of Europe took a toll on the faith of its citizens; consequently, men of thought rather than belief emerged, ushering in a new age of reason and intellect. Religious myths and errant ideologies were gradually dispelled by fresh discoveries made by the new philosophers of science and industry. While some questioned God due to an increasing reliance on intellect and continuing dissatisfaction with the poor example of institutionalized religion, many people of faith were galvanized by adversity and fought to return to a personal understanding of primitive Christianity. Unfortunately, those groups seeking to worship outside the state-sanctioned religion were subjected to barbarous treatment; accordingly, some groups sought religious liberty outside of the motherland, even risking dangerous journeys across the Atlantic to the newly discovered Americas.

Notwithstanding that those emigrating to the New World came seeking freedom—both economic and religious—they were not predisposed to offer such liberties to others with differing views. The American colonies were initially intolerant, each new settlement seeking to establish and preserve a single and unified religious culture. In the mid-eighteenth century, an extraordinary spiritual awakening occurred, beginning in New England and spreading quickly throughout the colonies, producing greater religious diversity. Gradually, intolerance gave way to tolerance as the pursuit of economic freedoms and emancipation from England impelled the colonists to set aside religious differences. The Declaration of Independence was signed, the American Revolution was won, and a new constitution, inspired by God, was written and adopted by the thirteen colonies.

The Inspired Mission of Christopher Columbus

The discovery of the Americas was no accident. Although Christopher Columbus was not the first from the Eastern Hemisphere to navigate the Atlantic successfully, he was the first to bring solid information back to Europe about its inhabitants, perform serious exploration, attempt colonization, introduce Christianity to the native peoples, and discover both of the best sailing routes to cross the Atlantic. His primary motivation for sailing to the Indies was his love of God and his desire to spread Christianity. The historian Las Casas shares this perspective of Columbus's sincere yearning for such a mission:

He was extraordinarily zealous for the divine service; he desired and was eager for the conversion of these people [the native inhabitants], and that in every region the faith of Jesus Christ be planted and enhanced, . . . ever holding great confidence in divine providence.[1]

In spite of his monumental preparations, Columbus never accepted any credit or claimed the voyage was of his own doing. Columbus ascribed all of the glory to God and to fulfillment of scripture, particularly Isaiah. Wrote Columbus:

I have searched out and studied all kinds of texts: geographies, histories, chronologies, philosophies and other subjects. With a hand that could be felt, the Lord opened my mind to the fact that it would be possible to sail from here to the Indies, and he opened my will to desire to accomplish the project.[2]

Recounting the sustained effort required to convince Ferdinand and Isabella, Columbus continued to reenforce his theme of divine providence:

I spent seven years here in your royal court discussing this subject with the leading persons in all learned arts, and their conclusion was that it was vain. . . . But afterwards it all turned out just as our Redeemer Jesus Christ has said, and as he had spoken earlier by the mouth of his holy prophets.[3]

The feat of locating the two best sailing routes to the Americas without prior trans-Atlantic sailing experience cannot be attributed merely to good fortune. According to one noted historian, "There can be no doubt that the faith of Columbus was genuine and sincere, and that his frequent communion with forces unseen was a vital element in his achievement."[4] To that end, Columbus recorded, "I pointed out that for the execution of the journey to the Indies I was not aided by intelligence, by mathematics or by maps. It was simply the fulfillment of what Isaiah had prophesied."[5]

Finally, as to the inspired purpose of his journey, Columbus was always consistent. When writing to Amerigo Vespucci, he once declared:

> I feel persuaded by the many and wonderful manifestations of Divine Providence in my especial favour, that I am the chosen instrument of God in bringing to pass a great event—no less than the conversion of millions who are now existing in the darkness of Paganism.[6]

In the context of being a chosen instrument in introducing the gospel to the New World, Columbus nearly always quoted from the Gospel of John: "And other sheep I have, which are not of this fold: them also I must bring, and they shall hear my voice; and there shall be one fold, and one shepherd" (John 10:16).[7]

The founding of America was providential. Not only would the message of Christianity be preached to its inhabitants as Christopher Columbus desired, but the land of North America would become a haven for those seeking truth and freedom to worship God according to the dictates of conscience. This freedom would ultimately inspire the finest creativity and productivity the world would ever know and would eventually produce the political climate necessary for God to establish the fullness of His gospel once more among men.

A New Age of Rationalism and Intellectualism Begins

As the Reformation advanced, a reborn interest in knowledge and progress began to attack myths that had been widely believed for centuries, ultimately giving rise to what has been christened by historians as an age of enlightenment.

Life in medieval and early modern Europe was high risk: injuries and inexplicable illnesses resulted in steep mortality rates; infertility, unpredictable weather, crop failures, and other anomalies made mere existence a daily struggle. Support systems to cope with such realities included a plethora of mysticisms and superstitions. Amulets, herbs, and religious recitations—used to ward off bad luck—were common throughout Europe. When such methods became exhausted during a crisis, help was often sought from the parish priest or a folk healer. According to one writer's research:

> Sixteenth-century ecclesiastical visitation records show that peasants had no sense of any meaningful division between religion and magic in their strategies for coping with the vagaries of life. To them, the idea that a cure for toothache consisted of the saying of five our Fathers and five creeds, or that a crumbled mass wafer and the intercession of saints were seen as guarantors of the fertility of the local soil, was eminently logical: the end result justified any means employed to obtain it.[8]

Folk-healers were also widely used to find lost items, heal illnesses, or lift spells. For example, using salves for ailments, the assistance of a crystal stone to locate stolen property, and herbs to protect livestock from witches, Georg Kissling became renowned in his German village.[9]

Following the Reformation, superstition and mystic practices were greatly frowned upon by both Protestant and Catholic clergy, and parishioners were encouraged to report unseemly conduct. Peasants believed that witches were the cause of personal misfortune which, by 1560, led to public accusations, civil trials, and thousands of executions—many of which were probably groundless.

Underscoring the widespread nature of mystic belief, King James VI of Scotland (James I as king of England) published a book in 1597 entitled *Demonologie* which Will Durant referred to as "one of the horrors of literature."[10] James claimed that witches had supernatural powers to kill, haunt houses, cause ravaging storms, and produce such emotions as love and hate. Accordingly, he advocated the death penalty for suspected witches, including patrons paying for such services as palm reading. After a near disaster at sea when returning from Denmark with his new bride, he caused four individuals whom he suspected of conspiring against him by use of wizardry to be tortured into admissions of guilt. One of the accused, John Fain, was burned at the stake but not before being subjected to inhuman atrocities.[11]

According to Alison Rowlands, approximately 60,000 people—most of them women—were executed in Europe during the early modern period.[12] In Britain even learned physicians, such as William Harvey and Sir Thomas Brown, believed in witchcraft.[13] In an effort to temper superstition and expose the horrors of those falsely accused, Reginald Scot, an Englishman, bravely penned a treatise in 1584 entitled *The Discouerie of Witchcraft*. Although little changed immediately, sometime later James moderated his extreme approach by demanding fair trials and ending forced confessions. From this environment of fear and superstition, science and the age of reason slowly emerged.

Growing economic pressures, caused by the expansion of business and industry, became the stimulus for discovery, invention, and new quantitative processes. Systems for logarithms and computation were developed by John Napier (1614) and Henry Briggs (1616). Versions of the slide rule were devised by William Oughtred (1622) and Edmond Gunter (1624). Such discoveries aided the advancement of astronomy, navigation, and engineering. Thomas Harriot achieved important progress in mathematics, establishing innovative processes that developed the standard form of modern algebra. William Gascoigne (1639) designed and constructed a device called the micrometer, allowing scientists to adjust the telescope with remarkable precision. Speculations surrounding the forces of moving planets aided Newton in the development his theory of gravity. Ongoing studies surrounding the earth's magnetism led to advances with the compass, the discovery of the magnetic poles, and energy associated with electricity. Such progress spawned greater interest in exploration for commercial purposes. Sir Humphrey Gilbert, Sir Martin Frobisher, John Davys, and Henry Hudson all sought new navigational passageways through the Northwest, and Thomas Cavendish explored southern South America, successfully completing the third circumnavigation of the globe.

The most important scientific discovery of the age may have been made by Sir William Harvey in 1615 when, through extensive experimentation, he established the theory of the circulation of blood from the heart through the body and back again to the heart. Ultimately, Harvey's historic discovery shed new light on every facet of physiology, including the relationships between body and mind.

Perhaps the brightest star contributing to the ushering in of this new age of science and discovery was Sir Francis Bacon. Born in 1561 to Sir Nicholas Bacon, the Lord Keeper of the Great Seal in the English courts, young Francis was raised in privileged circumstances. Being slight of frame and lacking in physical attributes, he turned his attention to the development of his mind, becoming well known for his scholarship and intellect. After three years of university studies at Cambridge, he was sent by his father to France to learn the ways of politics. Nicholas unexpectedly passed away, leaving Francis with little means to support himself, and he returned to London to study law. In 1584, at age twenty-three and against great odds, he was elected to Parliament. His service would span nineteen years, earning him a reputation for broad learning, insightful and resourceful thinking, and persuasive oratory skills.

Bacon's expertise as a lawyer enabled him to achieve a comfortable level of affluence. He established a magnificent estate at Gorhambury, complete with competent servants and secretaries. His gardens provided for physical therapy, and the secluded retreat offered the privacy he required for research and philosophical compositions.

Learning and ambition provided little time for personal relationships. Although he did marry later in life (at forty-five years of age), he had no children. His persistence in seeking office in the king's court finally paid off when James appointed him solicitor general in 1607; in 1613, attorney general; in 1616, a member of the privy council; in 1617, Lord Keeper of the Great Seal; and in 1618, Chancellor. Bacon's loyalty and effectiveness brought additional titles: in 1618 he was named the first Baron Verulam, and in January 1621, Viscount St. Albans.[14]

Later, in 1621 a disaster occurred that would actually enable a lasting benefit to humanity. The incoming parliament that year was enraged over James's policy regarding monopolies. Inasmuch as Bacon had vigorously defended the king's programs and had used his influence as attorney general to secure desired judicial verdicts, Parliament investigated him in hopes they could uncover improprieties that might remove him from office. Public officials were poorly paid, and, although technically against the law, gifts were often furnished from those being aided. Twenty-three separate charges of corruption were levied against Bacon for accepting such gifts. After consulting with James, he decided to plead guilty, but he denied that his verdicts had been influenced by such. In fact, in many cases he had ruled against the giver. Although a substantial fine and imprisonment were levied against him, the king pardoned him from both judgments, and Bacon retired to his estate in Gorhambury. After Bacon's death, Rawley, his first biographer, discovered the famous lines "I was the justest judge that was in England these 50 years. But it was the justest censure in Parliament that was these 200 years."[15]

Ironically, the impeachment produced a positive result. In his reclusive chateau, Bacon redirected his energy, intellect, and skill away from public service to his equally great love of science and philosophy. In this setting, Bacon would "ring the bell that called the wits together," and, as well stated by Durant, he "would proclaim, in majestic prose, the revolt and program of reason."[16]

Of Bacon it was said that "he wrote philosophy like a lord chancellor" and "planned it like an imperial general."[17] In *The Advancement of Learning,* he called for a dramatic increase and support for colleges, libraries, laboratories, biological gardens, museums of science and industry, increased communication and collaboration throughout Europe, better pay for teachers and researchers, and the classification of all fields of learning. His *Novum Organum* recommended a new system of thought, including the inductive study of nature itself through experience and experiment. In all of this, however, we must remember that he was not a scientist but rather a philosopher of science. In spite of his significant education and noteworthy achievements, recent scholarship has demonstrated that even Bacon "was influenced by the magical tradition."[18]

Nonetheless, Francis Bacon played a critical role in a critical age in the earth's temporal and spiritual history. In the end, the collective influence of the era he led—in transition to the modern world—impelled both. Bacon helped to free Renaissance Europe from remaining too constricted by the conclusions and thought patterns of antiquity. His method was to start by doubting everything; accordingly, he insisted on an "expurgation of the intellect" as the beginning of renewal. He wrote, "Human knowledge as we have it is a mere medley and ill-digested mass, made up of much credulity and much accident, and also of childish notions which are at first imbibed."[19] In others words, we cannot rely necessarily, when striving to discover truth, on the belief systems with which we are raised.

Religious Persecution and Intolerance in England

During the reign of James I, England enjoyed a lengthy economic expansion; unfortunately, under his son Charles I, that trend took a downturn. Unrest in religious matters persisted for decades: The conflict between Catholicism and the Anglican Church was fierce, and by the late sixteenth century the controversy expanded to include Presbyterians and Puritans. A small group seeking religious freedom within a sect of the Puritans, known as Separatists or Pilgrims, had already migrated to the Americas in 1620. In 1630 a much larger Puritan company landed in present-day Boston. The flagging economy, combined with religious oppression in their homelands, would soon bring a flood of immigrants to North America.

In the early seventeenth century, the Church of England enjoyed the government's full protection. By 1628 its Thirty-nine Articles passed Parliament and were legally enforceable. Anglican bishops claiming apostolic succession rejected the Puritan and Presbyterian practice that others besides bishops could authoritatively ordain ministers. Although most Puritans sought reforms and acceptance rather than outright separation from the English Church, events taking place during this period removed all hope of reconciliation. Catholicism was making a comeback in Britain, and a leading Anglican in the English government, William Laud, determined to reinstate some of the complex ceremony of the Anglican liturgy in order to establish a certain harmony of religious practice. To the Puritans, these reversals threatened the simplicity of their faith and represented a relapse into Catholicism, including the prominence of the priest presiding over the congregation. Laud was ruthless in implementing his new directives. Ministers not in compliance were stripped of their position and income. Those writing in opposition were in danger of losing their ears or suffering other forms of brutal punishment.[20]

One Puritan minister, Alexander Leighton, in 1628 confessed his authorship of a treatise that labeled the institution of bishops as anti-Christian and satanic. He was placed in irons and imprisoned in solitary confinement for fifteen weeks in a cold, damp cell "full of rats and mice, and open to snow and rain." Conditions were so desperate that his "hair fell out, and his skin peeled off." He was tied to a stake, "receiving thirty-six stripes with a heavy cord upon his naked back; he was placed in a pillory (a wooden framework securing head and hands) for two hours in November's frost and snow; he was branded in the face, had his nose slit and his ears cut off, and he was condemned to life imprisonment."[21]

Amazingly, Laud's principal adversaries, the Puritans, agreed with him on the practice of intolerance. They concluded that the origin of Christianity was so self-evident that anyone disputing a religion so founded must be a "criminal or fool," and society should be safeguarded from the damnations that would follow from his teaching.[22] Puritans resolved that intolerance was preferred to individual freedom of religion and independent thought. Paradoxically, there were so many sects among the Puritans themselves that it was a "rare generalization that [could] hold of them all."[23] Suppression of free will and intolerance within Christianity, including the Thirty-Years War between Catholics and Protestants, resulted in diminishing faith as many began to deny the divinity of Christ or the possibility of an eternal hell.

The events of this era were evidence that the Reformation had not yet returned Christianity to its form as it had existed during the apostolic ministry. Intolerance was never a tenet of the Savior's Church. Free will (the Two Ways) was documented in the Bible, the Pseudepigrapha, the Apocrypha, and by the earliest Christian Fathers; however, it was not to be found in any of the sects professing Christianity during this period. Nevertheless, the hand of God presided over all. His pattern has never been to usurp man's agency. When Jesus came to fulfill His earthly ministry, the Jewish Sanhedrin rejected Him because of pride and overzealous adherence to the law of Moses. According to Jesus, they did not understand the scriptures (Matthew 22:29) and killed the prophets (Luke 13:34). Because He appeared as other men, He went unrecognized by many. Jesus could have compelled the Jews at any time, but like Adam and Eve, they were allowed to choose for themselves. God would work His will, but it would be done through men who were receptive to the promptings of the Holy Spirit, individuals who, like Columbus, filled small but crucial roles in the unfolding of His work. Wycliffe, Luther, Calvin, Bacon, and a multitude of others would be used by God in very natural ways to effect the end that He desired. Similarly, He would convert the acts of wicked men such as Henry VIII into outcomes that would ultimately accomplish His purposes. In neither case would God rob man's agency.

Colonizing America

Although people of faith are usually willing to suffer rather than submit to tyranny, the prospect of seeking religious freedom in America became increasingly appealing. In some cases, religion was not the only motivating factor: poor economic conditions in England and throughout much of Europe also played a role. Thus, while the majority of early immigrants were poor, they brought with them the attributes of their rich European heritage. Included in this legacy were the major religions of western Europe, the

Catholic and Protestant creeds, the Bible, the writings of the Reformers, and various political ideologies. Separation of church and state was yet a foreign concept to most; the majority supported a unified state-sponsored religion. Most believed that any voluntary religious system would fail, breeding a disorderly society, and result in the damnation of many souls.

The first permanent English settlement on American soil, Jamestown, Virginia, was founded on the James River by the Virginia Company of London. Shortly thereafter, two of the well-remembered epics of American religious colonization followed: the Brownist *Mayflower* immigrants, settling in what is now Plymouth, Massachusetts; and the Puritans, locating near present-day Boston. The histories written about these settlements, as well as those that would later be known collectively as the Thirteen Colonies, tell the story of the gradual evolution of American culture from a seventeenth-century European lifestyle to a culturally blended system shaped by isolation, increased freedom, and the rugged frontier. The importance of these early settlements was that they brought to America an incomparable value system of morality and inspiring work habits that eventually would lead to greater religious liberty and free enterprise than the world had ever known.

Jamestown, Virginia

Established in 1607, the settlement at Jamestown was the scene of significant hardship over the course of its nearly one-hundred–year existence. The colony endured disease, starvation, Indian massacres, and several devastating fires, including Bacon's rebellion in 1676, when it was burned to the ground.

Remaining loyal to the crown, Jamestown instituted the Anglican Church as its faith.

Upon arrival in the New World, the Reverend Robert Hunt organized and presided over the first religious services. According to John Smith, prayers were offered morning and evening, two sermons were delivered each Sunday, and the sacrament of the Lord's Supper was administered during services once every three months.[24]

In 1609 a new charter was issued by James I, transferring political authority from the king to the Virginia Company of London. Laws and civil ordinances were then drawn up in England by company directors and provided to the new acting governor, Thomas Gates, for enforcement. Among the statutes was the directive to obey canon law as prescribed by the Church of England. This charter became the basis for Britain's state-sponsored religion, to be imposed upon all colonists, and it provided authority to exercise severe penalties on those indulging in any kind of moral or ethical failure. Moreover, those endeavoring to organize and participate in competing denominations were also subject to harsh treatment, including exile.

In spite of lingering old customs and laws, the settlers at Jamestown would distinguish themselves as God-fearing people of ability and character. As with the Puritan settlements to come, the spirit, energy, and resilience required to tame the frontier and to endure considerable suffering would lay the foundation for a remarkable new country and political process.

The Mayflower Compact

During the reign of Elizabeth I, religious oppression was severe. Installed by Elizabeth as the archbishop of Canterbury, John Whitgift dedicated his ministry to silencing the new sect known as Puritans (so called because of their determination to purify English Protestantism from all practices not found in the New Testament). A resolute minority from this group openly severed ties with the Anglican faith, establishing self-governing congregations that elected their own clergy and no longer recognized state-sponsored episcopal authority. The sect became known as Congregationalist or Separatist. Its principal leader, Robert Browne, published two leaflets in 1581 that summarized a new democratic constitution for Christianity. Two members of the group, judged to be in defiance of the queen's religious authority, were hanged in 1583. Persecution and executions intensified in the coming years.

Presented with the choice of loyalty to country or faith, many of the Brownist movement took refuge in the Netherlands at Leyden. Their motto, "Reformation without tarrying for any," was taken from one of the pamphlets by their founder.[25] Facing the loss of their English cultural heritage and desiring to preach the gospel to the Indians, thirty-five members of the community chose to immigrate to America. A group of London investors financed the voyage in exchange for most of the crop harvests for a period of six years. Unfortunately, the English merchant backers were not of the same high moral character so cherished by the Separatists, and they later defrauded the immigrants for more than the amount agreed to in the contract. Furthermore, because only a small group determined to make the journey, the investors insisted on recruiting additional passengers not of the Leyden company who later in the voyage created disturbances with mutinous speeches. The *Mayflower* set sail from Plymouth, England, on September 20, 1620, intending to land in Virginia. However, strong winds drove the *Mayflower* north just before reaching the American coast, into Provincetown Harbor at the end of Cape Cod. Facing disunity from the "strangers," Governor William Bradford wrote:

This day, before we came to harbour, observing some not well affected to unity and concord, but gave some appearance of faction, it was thought good there should be an association and agreement, that we should combine together in one body, and to submit to such government and governors as we should by common consent agree to make and choose, and set our hands to this that follows, word for word. . . .
In the name of God, Amen. We whose names are underwritten, the loyal subjects of our dread sovereign Lord, King James, by the grace of God, of Great Britain, France and Ireland king, defender of the faith, etc., having undertaken, for the glory of God, and advancement of the Christian faith, and honor of our king and country, a voyage to plant the first colony in the Northern parts of Virginia, do by these presents solemnly and mutually in the presence of God, and one of another, covenant and combine ourselves together into a civil body politic, for our better ordering and preservation and furtherance of the ends aforesaid; and by virtue hereof to enact, constitute, and frame such just and equal laws, ordinances, acts, constitutions, and offices, from time to time, as shall be thought most meet and convenient for the general good of the colony, unto which we promise all due submission and obedience.

In witness whereof we have hereunder subscribed our names at Cape-Cod the 11th of November, in the year of the reign of our sovereign lord, King James, of England, France, and Ireland the eighteenth, and of Scotland the fifty-fourth. Anno Domine 1620.

John Carver
Stephen Hopkins

William Bradford
Digery Priest
Edward Winslow
Thomas Williams
William Brewster
Gilbert Winslow
Isaac Allerton
James Chilton
John Tilly
John Craxton
Francis Cooke
John Billington
Thomas Rogers
Joses Fletcher
Thomas Tinker
John Goodman
John Ridgate
Samuel Fuller
Edward Fuller
Christopher Martin
Richard Clark
William Mullins
Richard Gardiner
William White
John Allerton
Richard Warren
Thomas English
John Howland
Edward Doten
Edward Liester
Edmund Margesson
Miles Standish
Peter Brown
John Alden
Richard Bitteridge
John Turner
George Soule
Francis Eaton
Edward Tilly

According to one of William Bradford's biographers, the intent of the Leyden group's immigration was more than just religious freedom and preaching to the Indians:

Bradford, . . . was utterly convinced that from the beginning of time God had foreseen and forordained that a devout band of

Separatists from England and Holland would sail across the Atlantic Ocean and establish a purified Christian Church in the desolate wilderness of North America. . . . He knew . . . that its consequences would last until the end of time.[26]

In fact, Bradford's feelings about the Seperatist's mission were so strong, New England historian Perry Westbrook wrote:

The ultimate assumption, and one that Bradford readily made, was that the Plymouth venture was a part—and an important part—of God's overall plan to restore true Christianity to the world.[27]

Finally, Bradford connected the goals and mission of the Pilgrims with both ancient Israel and apostolic Christianity:

Bradford [with] his wandering band of "saints" was reliving the lives of both the ancient Israelites and the Apostles. Assuming these roles, the "saints" were seeking a promised land, attempting to return to Zion, and struggling to reestablish the primitive Christian Church.[28]

Although the Separatists had left England to escape religious oppression and to restore the ancient Christian Church, they soon found their new environmental hardships more deadly than British rulers. Disease spread throughout the colony, and nearly half the settlers did not survive the first winter. Thirteen heads of family perished, in addition to twenty mothers. Only a small number of able-bodied men and youth were available to help with the spring planting. Had it not been for the significant faith and devotion of the survivors, the colony would almost certainly have been abandoned. Although the influence of the Pilgrims upon the development of the United States is often overstated by its historians, these colonists were nonetheless representative of the character and fiber of those inspired by God to people the promising new frontier known as America. And as for Bradford's original dream, history must judge whether or not his small band was instrumental in paving the way for the return of original Christianity to the earth.

The Massachusetts Bay Colony— A Bible Commonwealth

The first Puritan migration to the Massachusetts Bay area was led by John Endecott, whose group settled in Salem in 1628. Two years later, another Puritan organization of approximately 700 souls under the administration of John Winthrop sailed from Yarmouth, England, in March, 1630, and landed in Boston, Massachusetts, on June 12. The charter granted to the Massachusetts Bay Company entitled the settlers to establish a significant level of self-government within the colony itself rather than from London. While the Puritan colonies attempted no control over a man's private views, public expressions of what were considered heretical doctrines were not tolerated. Accordingly, the Puritan government was established upon biblical principles and laws that were very narrow and harsh. According to Winthrop, the governor of the new settlement, the intent of the Puritans was to "be as a city upon a hill."[29]

Winthrop was educated at the University of Cambridge and studied law at Gray's Inn in London. He was a prosperous attorney in the Court of Wards and Liveries from 1623 until he was terminated from that position in 1629, most likely due to his Puritan affiliations. Winthrop's political philosophy, consistent with his religious beliefs, was that the new colony could be governed most effectively by a small number of educated and devout leaders. Consequently, he opposed an unlimited democracy. This ideology guided Puritan settlements for nearly a century, and little opposition to the prevailing religious beliefs was countenanced during this period.

The declining economy in England, coupled with significant political turmoil under Charles I, prompted an exodus of those suffering religious oppression from their homeland. Often referred to as the Great Migration, an estimated 20,000 English Puritans settled in America by 1642, mainly in New England.[30] They established a Bible commonwealth that eventually annexed Plymouth and expanded into Connecticut. Ironically, although they left Britain in the pursuit of religious freedom, the Puritan settlers did not extend this privilege to others not sharing the same biblical views. Accordingly, its magistrates wielded great power and were revered as "public ministers of God," using the authority of government to accomplish the design of the Church.[31] The result was, in the words of James Hutson, that "today some of the things the Puritans said and did seem ugly."[32] The society of New England did not celebrate the doctrine of free agency so prized by the early Church; rather, they were "professed enemies of it [toleration]."[33]

In spite of Puritan intolerance, a great good was effected by the strict moral code invoked by the democratic theocracy they aspired to establish. Puritan ideals included absolute sexual purity, an industrious work ethic, honesty and integrity, a strong sense of self-reliance, prudence, thrift, and courage. While the acquisition of wealth was supported, idle luxury, like nobility, was disdained. Furthermore, they advocated parliamentary government and trial by jury, all of which established a sturdy foundation for the building of America. In light of the fruits of such a productive system, it is difficult to ignore its positive attributes. Notwithstanding, God would not compel men to choose Him, and as prophesied, the wheat would grow beside the tares until His coming. At that time, men will have chosen for themselves whether to follow Jesus. Those following Jesus will remain, and those denying Him will be destroyed (Matthew 25:31–34). Only then will a theocracy flourish and bloom as the Savior of mankind reigns in righteousness as King of Kings. Men will follow obediently, not because they have been commanded but because they have *chosen* Him over worldly pleasures.

Religious Intolerance in Early America

As demonstrated, the early colonies did not tolerate multiple religions. Leaders embraced the idea of religious uniformity, believing that disunity would disrupt the peace and create a disorderly society. The Massachusetts Bay Colony is specifically remembered for its strict intolerance; however, intolerance was widely experienced throughout all the early settlements. Rather than offer an exhaustive history of intolerance in early America, I have chosen to demonstrate its harsh reality by discussing the uncompromising treatment encountered by some of the early settlers in Virginia; by Roger Williams, founder of the Baptist movement in America; by Anne Hutchinson, an early American Reformer; and by the men and women who were executed in the Salem witch trials of the late seventeenth century. In order for a restoration of New Testament Christianity to be achieved, as many hoped, intolerance would have to be tempered and state control of religious affairs abolished.

Religious Persecution in Virginia

When Thomas Dale became governor of Jamestown in 1611, he enforced a series of laws that had been drafted in England and were particularly severe. For example, certain offences, such as speaking profanely about the Trinity or the Thirty-nine Articles of the Church of England, were regarded as capital crimes punishable by death. Harsh penalties were also inflicted on adulterers and those breaking other laws associated with the Ten Commandments. On a smaller scale, monetary fines were issued for missing church services, and non-conformists were beaten until they recanted.[34]

Initially, Puritans were not regarded as having left the Anglican fold; therefore, they were not persecuted and were allowed to live peacefully among their brethren. However, laws passed in England altered that classification, prompting a wave of persecution that spanned many decades. In 1642 a group of Puritan Separatists settled Nansemond County south of the James River. Their numbers began to grow, and in 1645 the state banished the Reverend Thomas Harrison, a former Anglican minister. The congregation appealed to Puritan leaders in England who, at this time during the English Civil War (1642–49), were in control of Parliament. Oliver Cromwell ordered Governor Berkeley to reinstate Harrison, who declined to return. Unfortunately, during this interim period, the Separatists in Nansemond were subjected to barbarous treatment. Many were imprisoned, some had their arms removed, and all were ordered by the local court to cease meeting.[35]

Similarly, Quaker missionaries began preaching in the mid-seventeenth century, attempting to establish adherents in Virginia. They were met with stiff resistance by established religionists who declared that the Quakers promoted "lies, miracles, false visions, prophecies and doctrines," which would have the effect of "destroy[ing] religion, laws, communities, and all bonds of civil societie."[36] Because the Quakers were viewed as a secret society, refusing to pay tithes to the state-supported church or to assist in the defense of their families or the colonists, they were heavily persecuted by the Virginia courts and legislature.[37]

The enactment of secular laws that attempted to control man's religious agency runs counter to the revealed laws of God. Inasmuch as free will is perhaps God's greatest gift to man, excepting the Atonement, the suppression of that gift caused much harm to spiritual growth. The inhumane treatment of some, and the general persecution observed in Virginia with Puritans, Quakers, and others, is not indicative of New Testament Christianity. Clearly, apostasy from the principles and teachings of Jesus had not yet been resolved.

The Exile of Roger Williams

Roger Williams, like many of the notable leaders of his day, was educated at Cambridge University in England. His close association with John Winthrop, Oliver Cromwell, and Thomas Hooker led to his complete separation with the Anglican Church and his immigration to Boston in February 1631. In 1632 he left Boston to settle in Plymouth over a disagreement with authorities concerning the regulation of religious matters, but he returned in 1633 to accept a teaching post in Salem. Williams was a proponent of religious freedom, and his statement that "forced worship stinks in God's nostrils,"[38] ultimately led to his exile from the colony in 1635. He publicly challenged the validity of the Massachusetts Bay charter's authority to grant politically appointed leaders the power to confiscate Native American lands without compensation and to establish a uniform faith and worship service among the colonists.

Leaving Boston, Williams made his way to Rhode Island, where he purchased land from the friendly Narragansett Indians and founded Providence in 1636, establishing a society based on religious liberty labeled by orthodox Puritans as "the latrina of New England."[39] He rejected the view that lawlessness would prevail in settlements that granted freedom of conscience. He was rebaptized by a layman in 1639. Whether the baptism was performed by immersion, pouring, or sprinkling is uncertain; however, he baptized a small group who shared the same view of religious freedom and the separation of church and state. Williams is credited with organizing the first Baptist Church in America in which only sincere believers were permitted baptism and entrance into the church. Curiously, he soon withdrew from the congregation, pronouncing himself a *seeker*, or in other words, one who believes in the basic doctrines of Christianity but does not belong to a particular denomination.

Although Williams's religious ideology was basically Calvinist, he dismissed claims of priesthood authority by Catholic or Protestant religions. He believed that apostasy had destroyed the primitive Church and that the authority to perform the sacraments and ordinances no longer existed. He anticipated that Christ's Church would be restored by divine means, and he searched without success for this truth the rest of his life. One of his former associates, John Winthrop, wrote, "Williams concluded that the Protestants were 'not . . . able to derive the authority . . . from the apostles.' . . . [He] conceived God would raise up some apostolic power."[40]

Concerning the separation of church and state, Williams later wrote, "If none but true Christians, members of Jesus Christ, must be civil magistrates, and publicly entrusted with civil affairs, then none but Christians should be husbands of wives, fathers of children, . . . but against this doctrine the whole creation, the whole world may rise up in arms."[41]

Like many notable men, Roger Williams did not receive acclaim during his lifetime. However, several years before the American Revolution, his writings were widely distributed, and he is remembered by some historians as the great American prophet of religious liberty.

The Banishment of Anne Hutchinson

Anne Hutchinson attained notoriety in Boston for her stirring sermons on the doctrine of a salvation attained through the intuition of God's indwelling in grace (also referred to as inner-light). At first Hutchinson's preaching was confined to women, but community leaders later attended meetings. Because her doctrines seemed to refute local religious beliefs (specifically her Calvinistic leanings that favored grace over works), she came under attack from the Puritan clergy for criticizing the rigid moral and legal codes of the Puritan faith in the New England area.

Hutchinson's doctrines introduced divisions into the settlement, resulting in her being charged in the General Court of Massachusetts with "traducing [maligning] the ministers." The court, presided over by Governor John Winthrop, has been called by many historians a travesty of justice. She was judged guilty, excommunicated, and banished from the colony, later seeking refuge in Rhode Island. Sadly, in spite of the noteworthy achievements of the Puritan settlements, religious tolerance was no better in the Massachusetts Bay Colony than in England, where they themselves had been the subjects of inscrutable law.

The Salem Witch Trials

Irrational mysticism permeated society during the Renaissance and Reformation periods, as well as in the century that heralded the Age of Reason. The well-remembered drama in Salem was typical of those during the European witch epidemic. The commotion began with hysteria among young girls. A physician charged the unusual behavior to demoniac possession. The situation was complicated by public tension over political instability, fueled by a minority discontent over Puritan theocracy, specifically dealing with the persecution of Quakers and those still belonging to the Anglican Church. Under these difficult circumstances, suspected witches were prosecuted, often at the encouragement of many in the ministry. Following the old European pattern, confessions were obtained and prosecution began. Initially, evidence such as dreams and hallucinations was permitted, making it unnecessary for the accused to be present at the scene of the crime. Admission of such weak exhibits prevented fair and balanced trials, rendering defense of the accused impossible. Many of those suspected were esteemed members of their communities. Nevertheless, thirteen men and six women were hanged in 1692 for refusing to testify: one man was pressed to death. The barbarous nature of the entire spectacle incited public outrage, finally compelling the governor to stop the trials.

So piercing was the sorrow of those participating in the hearings that later in 1697 the entire jury, including the judge and one of the "tormented girls," acknowledged their error publicly and begged forgiveness from the families of the condemned. Nevertheless, witch trials were later resumed, although spectral evidence was no longer permitted, reversing prior trends and making conviction essentially hopeless. Witchcraft trials ceased after 1711 in America.

Intolerance and unreason stand as evidence that apostasy from Christ's Church endured beyond the Reformation. Execution, dismemberment, imprisonment, whipping, general persecution, and banishment are clearly foreign to the teachings of Christ. Jesus dispelled unreasonable thinking in His day, demonstrating that religious and political diversity can comfortably coexist.[42] Indeed, He stands unequaled in wisdom by any person of any age. The Apostles, through the Holy Spirit, likewise prevented heresy and unsound doctrines from taking hold in the Church during their lifetimes. All doctrine, counsel, and practices in the New Testament are consistent with intelligent reasoning and functional logic. Intolerance and unbalanced responses to diverse Christian viewpoints and mystic beliefs were not only detectible in Christian practices of this century but common. Notwithstanding, divine will was beginning to make itself manifest in the progress of freedom. A glimmer of light was barely discernible on the horizon as a new dawn of hope emerged in the American Colonies.

The Rise of Tolerance and Religious Freedom

Religious tolerance in America was achieved only by degrees over an extended period. Tolerance began to increase as economic pressures influenced the establishment of new colonies, such as Maryland. Following the English Civil War, immigrants from other countries were encouraged by England to settle in British-owned colonies. During the reign of Charles II (1661–85), six new colonies were founded in North and South Carolina, New York, New Jersey, Pennsylvania, and Delaware. Tolerance was promised

in each of these colonies from the outset for both economic and defensive reasons. Moreover, legislation, both in England and America, that granted greater religious freedom was passed in the late seventeenth century. In spite of these gains, persecution persisted in most areas, including the latter colonies, until the Declaration of Independence was signed in 1776.

The first formal statute providing for religious tolerance in the Thirteen Colonies was enacted by the Roman Catholics in Maryland. This measure, known as the Toleration Act of 1649, provided legal protection to any Trinitarian Christian denomination but still authorized the colony to inflict severe penalties on anyone preaching against the orthodox Trinity or its unity. Charles I had granted a charter to Cecil Calvert, but too few Catholic emigrants were recruited to validate the charter; religious toleration was thus necessary to attract Protestants to build up their numbers. Although governed by fair and charitable leaders, the religious passions aroused by the English Civil War in the 1640s pitted Catholics against much larger numbers of Protestants, thus threatening Calvert's charter. Accordingly, he directed the Maryland Assembly to pass the Toleration Act. Its protection was short-lived, however, and war broke out just five years later when Protestant assemblymen repealed the equalizing legislation. Intermittent persecution of the Catholics continued in Maryland until independence from England was declared by representatives from each of the Thirteen Colonies.

Originally settled by the Dutch, New Netherlands was conquered by England in 1664 and renamed New York. Included in the conditions of surrender was the guarantee of religious freedom. Once again, economic forces fueled the movement from uniformity to religious pluralism. If the old settlers elected to leave the colony, its financial stability would collapse; thus, toleration was the only means of sustained growth and prosperity. Likewise, the Dutch settlers, who were Reformed Faith Calvinists, were obliged to allow Anglican worship services. Moreover, Jewish colonists, regarded as important to capital investment, were permitted to remain in spite of the perception that mammon was their god. Lutherans and Quakers, also repressed prior to English rule, now worshiped unmolested, built meetinghouses, and successfully recruited ministers to lead their congregations.

Following England's Glorious Revolution in 1688, Parliament passed the Toleration Act of 1689, a pivotal event in religious history. The liberties endowed by this law in Britain were essentially granted in America inasmuch as colonial laws were not to be in conflict with English statutes. Although the English legislation, when interpreted by the letter of the law, protected only Trinitarian Protestants, in practice the same freedom of worship was extended to Christians in general. The effects of the Toleration Act gradually rippled throughout the colonies. During the first half of the eighteenth century, toleration improved almost universally throughout the colonies. While isolated incidents of persecution and oppression persisted, freedom of religion gradually gained ground.

The beginning of religious pluralism in New England was occasioned by the consolidation of all colonial charters north of the Delaware River under one government in 1688. Uniformity had been preserved in New England until that time when the new governor, Edmond Andros, demanded that Anglicans be permitted to worship peacefully and requested the right to share meeting space with the Congregationalists. In 1691 a new charter combining Plymouth Colony with the Massachusetts Bay Colony was formed. New laws contained within the charter granted limited toleration to all Protestant sects. Although the English law of toleration was generally acknowledged throughout New England, religious liberty was as yet many years away.

Unwittingly, Native Americans contributed to the advance of religious pluralism in the Old Dominion. An attack by the Tuscarora Indians in 1711 on frontier settlers in North Carolina resulted in 120 civilian casualties. Neighboring Virginia, awakened by this tragedy, resolved to provide protection to border settlements. A buffer zone was created between Indian camps and the English colonists. Land grants, tax exemptions, and other incentives were offered to attract immigrants willing to take up arms and defend their countrymen. Many Reformed Faith German families, at the governor's invitation, settled above the falls of the Rappahannock River. A fort was built near the wilderness homes, and other Germans settled along the river in the ensuing years. These pioneers were offered religious liberty, which began the decline of intolerance and the ascent of pluralism in Virginia. A few years later, German Lutherans settled near the Blue Ridge Mountains. Colonial leaders offered aggressive land promoters the same generous terms in encouraging settlement in the Shenandoah Valley. This resulted in the migration of many German Protestants and Scotch-Irish Presbyterians who came to farm these fertile glens and brought with them diverse Christian beliefs and worship practices.

The late sixteenth and early seventeenth centuries were a defining period for religious liberty. New laws were passed, both in England and America, that promoted religious pluralism. While economic and defensive influences were instrumental in the decline of state-controlled religion, theological diversity lay at the root. Scholars and lay people alike, when reading the same Bible, interpreted its words and history differently. Accordingly, Catholics, Congregationalists, Anglicans, Presbyterians, Baptists, Quakers, and others could not be placed in a single mold and coerced to worship God in a manner that conflicted with personal conscience. Ultimately, the combination of conscience, commerce, and defense in colonial America proved too great an obstacle, and uniformity gave way to the free exercise of worship and religious pluralism.

The Great Awakening

The primary stimulus that initially inspired the Great Migration from England to America was the pursuit of religious freedom. Although intolerance traveled with it, the same forces that caused Luther's colleague, Spalatin, to conclude "What a mess we're in, with everybody doing something else"[43] eventually paved the way for increased acceptance of divergent religious views. This divergence, or rather the continuing quarrels over biblical interpretations, compelled many to look inward and to determine for themselves which doctrinal beliefs they accepted. Perhaps the most significant religious debate of the eighteenth and early nineteenth centuries centered on the Arminian concept of free will, or man's agency to initiate a relationship with God, and Calvin's theology of total election (predestination) and grace apart from any effort made by man. This conflict, and the energetic and spirited conviction of certain revivalist preachers, inspired what historians have termed the Great Awakening.

Revivalism in America may have had its beginning in Northampton, Massachusetts, with the Reverend Solomon Stoddard. Over

a period of sixty years, he claimed that five "harvests" or "reformations" had occurred in his congregation: in 1679, 1683, 1696, 1712, and 1718.[44] Of these religious stirrings, Jonathan Edwards wrote:

> Some of these times were much more remarkable than others, and the ingathering of souls more plentiful. . . . But in each of them, I have heard my grandfather say, the bigger part of the young people in the town seemed to be mainly concerned for their eternal salvation.[45]

The yearning to receive eternal salvation for those seeking reconciliation with God has been a consistent theme since the Reformation. Luther, Calvin, and large numbers of the general population attributed Christian conversion to an inward conviction of sins and the recognition that without the grace of Jesus individuals could not overcome the natural man and receive forgiveness for their sins. This inward desire, coupled with passionate sermons delivered by itinerant preachers and congregational ministers, led to sweeping conversions all over colonial America.

Jonathan Edwards and George Whitefield

Although there were many effective ministers during the Awakening period, the initiation of this spiritual revolution is often attributed to Jonathan Edwards and George Whitefield. Jonathan Edwards was the grandson of Solomon Stoddard and replaced Stoddard as pastor of the church at Northampton at age twenty-six. His ideology was staunch Calvinism with slight Arminian leanings. He was a powerful orator, and the discourses he delivered during 1734–35 brought some three hundred souls into his congregation. However, some of those converted became unusually obsessed by his fiery illustrations of eternal damnation to the point of considering suicide. In spite of the fact that the primary motivation of conversions in many instances was fear, Edwards's sermons were popular, and the town requested that they be published at the expense of the citizenry. The work was titled:

> Discourses on Various Important Subjects, Nearly Concerning the Great Affair of the Soul's Eternal Salvation, Viz.
> I. Justification by Faith Alone
> II. Pressing into the Kingdom of God
> III. Ruth's Resolution
> IV. The Justice of God in the Damnation of Sinners
> V. The Excellency of Jesus Christ
> Delivered at Northampton, Chiefly at the Time of the Late Wonderful Pouring Out of the Spirit of God There.[46]

Edwards believed that his sermon on justification, although threaded throughout each of the others, was the sermon most penetrating in the minds of his listeners:

> By the noise that had a little before been raised in this country concerning that doctrine, people here seemed to have their minds put into an unusual ruffle. . . . The following discourse of Justification that was preached at the two lectures seemed to be remarkably blessed. . . . So that this was the doctrine on which this work in its beginning was founded, as it evidently was in the whole progress of it.[47]

Disaster struck Northampton when Joseph Hawley, the town's leading merchant, committed suicide, apparently over his desire to know conclusively of his "saved" condition. Edwards and others, bewildered for a time, could only ascribe the blame to Satan.[48]

One of the difficulties encountered with the Calvinist doctrine of justification was,

quite naturally, the question of one's personal assurance of salvation. There were some who, in their view of this doctrine, reasoned that if they were in fact saved, then they were ready to meet God; on the other hand, if they were not saved, they probably never would be, and their guilt would only increase over time. In such a frenzied state of mind, several attempted suicide, some successfully.[49] Confusion over this incident halted religious fervor for a few years, and Edwards lamented the loss of the days when Northampton was "a city set on a hill."[50]

In 1740 Edwards met with George Whitefield, a well-known itinerant preacher from Britain. Whitefield landed in Newport, Rhode Island, in September and preached several times before heading to Boston, where he was warmly welcomed by the local clergy and civic leaders. Over a period of several weeks, Whitefield experienced stunning success in moving the hearts and minds of the people he addressed. By mid-October he reached Northampton, where he became acquainted with Edwards and spoke to the local congregation. Edwards was deeply touched by Whitefield's stirring sermons. He "wept during the whole time of the exercise. The people were equally affected."[51] From town to town and from region to region, Whitefield made his way throughout New England and the Middle Colonies. Not only was he an effective revivalist, he was also tireless. His journal indicates that he was in New England for forty-five days, during which time he called upon forty towns and delivered ninety-seven sermons.[52]

Why was Whitefield so successful? James Hutson has advanced several compelling reasons: (1) Calvinist doctrine during this period was at the height of its popularity. To Congregationalist and Presbyterian audiences, whom Whitefield often addressed as "half beast and half devils,"[53] this style of preaching was "music to [their] theological ears."[54] (2) Whitefield often vocalized his defiance for England's Church hierarchy, so resented by America's non-Anglican Christians. (3) He introduced and mastered revolutionary techniques for attracting and appealing to the masses. For example, Whitefield understood the power of advertizing; he spoke extemporaneously, simply, and passionately; and he employed effective stage methods that mirrored a theatrical performance.[55] In fact, one scholar recently compared his revivals to "the civil rights demonstrations, the campus disturbances, and the urban riots of the 1960s combined."[56]

Unfortunately, Whitefield was a tough act to follow. His colorful style and ability to connect with his audience were not well duplicated by his self-appointed successor, Gilbert Tennent, who was caricatured as an "awkward and ridiculous Ape of Whitefield."[57] Not only did Tennent offend some people sympathetic to the evangelical cause, he was particularly venomous in his attacks against opposing ministers. A rift occurred in as many as 125 Congregationalist Churches, ultimately dividing ministerial groups into two factions, known as "Old Lights" and "New Lights."[58] Thus, although the discourses preached by Edwards, Whitefield, and others initiated a renewal of religious zeal throughout the American colonies, they also fostered contention.

The Old Lights considered themselves more orthodox and rejected the emotional outbursts inspired by the revivalist movement. Such criticism had a foundation in fact. Revivalist sermons preyed on the fears and limited scriptural understanding of parishioners. Shouting, moaning, weeping, and sighs were common during services: "Alas, I am undone; I'm undone! O, my sins! How

they prey upon my vitals! What will become of me? How shall I escape the damnation of hell, who have spent away a golden opportunity under Gospel light, in vanity?"[59] Old Light ministers were also more experienced in counseling and assisting parishioners through difficult times. Their theology included some Arminian precepts, eventually evolving into the Unitarian movement of the nineteenth century.

New Lights, on the other hand, pointed to the stunning numbers of conversions and enthusiasm for God kindled by the powerful preaching of the revivalist movement. They contended that ministerial education was not necessarily mandatory and downplayed "convulsions and hysteria" on the part of the converted. New Light ideology was strictly Calvinist and was the precursor of the Evangelical crusades that followed a century later.

The Great Awakening was a giant step forward in religious freedom and in galvanizing America's passion for independence. Like the Reformation, the Revivalist movement was inspired of God. It had the effect of drawing people closer to Christ and living according to His teachings; however, New Testament Christianity had not yet been rediscovered. While the revivalist movement had positive effects on society, it also had clear shortcomings when compared with the fruits described by Jesus. The New Testament generously supported the doctrine of love. Moreover, research in recent decades has confirmed that providing consistent training and unconditional love to children yields more fruit than stern rebuke and fear. The unnatural emotions evoked by thunderous preaching, rather than the "still small voice" described by Elijah (1 Kings 19:12), stand as a witness of the human element in the revivalist approach.

The basic doctrine of free will was still being disputed. Notwithstanding the numerous writings supporting man's agency to choose life or death in the Bible, the Pseudepigrapha, the Apocrypha, and the early Christian Fathers, the doctrine of election was plainly the prevailing view. Man's agency does not diminish God's omnipotence or grace, nor does God's grace deny man's accountability. In the past, prophets provided clarity to doctrines that Satan had distorted or perverted. The Bible affirms that prophets and angels would be sent again to the earth in order to prepare mankind for the return of Jesus Christ; otherwise, the world would be "smitten with a curse" at His coming.[60]

The ability of independent denominations to grow in the same town or area, spurred by the many doctrinal viewpoints vigorously debated by various Christian factions, led to a religious pluralism in America not previously sanctioned anywhere in the rest of the world. Before the Great Awakening, Congregationalists, Anglicans, and Quakers were the three largest Christian sects in America. They were soon replaced by the Presbyterians, Methodists, and Baptists. Revivalism encouraged both layman and clergy to unite with a particular sect. Because no one church was dominant, intolerance began to diminish. Predictably, when the colonies faced the prospect of revolution against their native homeland, religious differences were set aside in the pursuit of achieving an independent democracy.

A New Birth of Freedom

Soon after independence from England was formally announced, laws protecting individual rights, including religious liberty, were enacted. The Church of England was formally disestablished in the Americas, and constitutions were being written throughout the colonies that provided freedom to assemble and worship, including equal political treatment.

Old laws requiring state-supported taxes for the Church were repealed, and each congregation became responsible for its own financial support. In 1785 Thomas Jefferson composed legislation that brought still greater reforms in Virginia. The new law stated that "no man shall be enforced, restrained, molested or burdened . . . on account of his religious opinions or belief; but . . . all men shall be free to profess . . . their opinions in matters of religion . . . and the same shall in nowise . . . affect their civil capacities."[61] In 1787 at the Constitutional Convention held in Philadelphia, thirty-nine delegates representing their respective states signed the Constitution of the United States. By June 1788, nine states had ratified the Constitution, making it binding upon all states. The first presidential and congressional elections were held in January and February 1789 and the Bill of Rights (the first ten amendments) was adopted in 1791. The United States of America was born, and with it a monumental experiment in democracy. Included in this sacred constitution was the freedom to worship God according to one's own understanding and conscience. The laws of man concerning free expression of thought, worship, and self-determination finally matched the laws of God as revealed in scripture and as taught by the early Christian Fathers.

Conclusion

Beginning with Christopher Columbus, we see the inspiration of the Almighty in the establishment of political freedom and religious tolerance in America. Because God works in natural ways without inhibiting the will of man, a great work was yet to be accomplished in unlocking the old shackles still remaining from the dredges of the Middles Ages and binding humanity. Men like Sir Francis Bacon introduced new patterns of thought; indeed, they led humankind into a new age of reason and intellectual discovery. This enlightenment coincided with a slow but steady increase in spiritual light sparked by the Renaissance and Reformation in breaking the grip of the Church over state, ultimately bringing Christians closer to the principles and teachings of their Founder. With divine forces at work, the Great Migration was inspired by both economic and religious stimuli. A vast wilderness was tamed, and colonial America turned its diversity into productivity and a unique kind of harmony. Significant intolerance ultimately gave way to religious liberty, and the Christian message, albeit a fractured one, spread throughout the colonies. God inspired honorable men to form a new system of government that relied upon individual liberty and personal responsibility. The success of the Constitution is evidence it was written under celestial guidance. God's hand had been set to the plow, the field had been finely tilled and the soil prepared, seed had been cast, and a divinely appointed harvest yet to come had been foretold.

Notes

1. Samuel Eliot Morison, *Admiral of the Ocean Sea,* 2 vols. (Boston: Little, Brown and Co., 1942), 1:63–64.

2. Delno C. West and August Kling, *The Book of Prophecies of Christopher Columbus* (Gainesville: University of Florida Press, 1991), 105.

3. West and Kling, *Book of Prophecies of Christopher Columbus,* 107.

4. Morison, *Admiral of the Ocean Sea,* 1:65.

5. West and Kling, *Book of Prophecies of Christopher Columbus,* 111.

6. C. Edwards Lester, *The Life and Voyages of Americus Vespucius* (New York: New Amsterdam Book Company, 1903), 79.

7. West and Kling, *Book of Prophecies of Christopher Columbus,* 229.

8. Alison Rowlands, "The Condition of Life for the Masses," in Cameron, *Early Modern Europe,* 40–42.

9. Rowlands, "Condition of Life for the Masses," in Cameron, *Early Modern Europe,* 41.

10. Will Durant, *The Age of Reason Begins: A History of European Civilization in the Period of Shakespeare, Bacon, Montaigne, Rembrandt, Galileo, and Descartes: 1558–1648* (New York: Simon and Schuster, 1961), 162.

11. Durant, *Age of Reason,* 162.

12. Rowlands, "Condition of Life for the Masses," in Cameron, *Early Modern Europe,* 42.

13. Durant, *Age of Reason,* 163.

14. Durant, *Age of Reason,* 170.

15. Francis Bacon, *The Works of Francis Bacon,* ed. James Spedding, Robert Leslie Ellis, and Douglas Denon Heath, 15 vols. (New York: Hurd & Houghton, 1862–72), 2:463.

16. Durant, *Age of Reason,* 171.

17. Durant, *Age of Reason,* 174.

18. Robin Briggs, "Embattled Faiths: Religion and Natural Philosophy in the Seventeenth Century" in Cameron, *Early Modern Europe,* 173.

19. Bacon, Novum Organum, i, 97.

20. Perry Miller, *Errand into the Wilderness* (Cambridge: Harvard University Press, 1956), 14, in James H. Hutson, *Religion and the Founding of the American Republic* (Washington: Library of Congress, 1998), 4.

21. John Lingard, *History of England* (London, 1855), 7:181; Hippolyte Taine, *History of English Literature,* trans. H. Van Laun (Philadelphia: A. Altemus, 1908), 265; see also Durant, *Age of Reason,* 189–90.

22. Durant, *Age of Reason,* 190.

23. Durant, *Age of Reason,* 190.

24. John Smith, *Captain John Smith Works,* ed. Edward Arber, 2 vols. (Westminster, 1895), 2:957–59.

25. Robert Browne, "Reformation without Tarring for Any," (London, 1583), in Hutson, *Religion and the Founding,* 3.

26. Perry D. Westbrook, *William Bradford* (Boston: Twayne Publishers, 1978), 18.

27. Westbrook, *William Bradford,* 86.

28. Westbrook, *William Bradford,* 88.

29. John Winthrop, "A Modell of Christian

Charity," in Perry Miller and Thomas Johnson, *The Puritans* (New York: American Book Company, 1938), 199.

30. Hutson, *Religion and the Founding*, 7.

31. Hutson, *Religion and the Founding*, 7.

32. Hutson, *Religion and the Founding*, 7.

33. Miller and Johnson, *Puritans*, 185.

34. Peter Force, ed., *Tracts and Other Papers, Relating Principally to Origin, Settlement, and Progress of the Colonies in North America*, 4 vols. (New York: Peter Smith, 1947), 3:10–19.

35. Edward W. James, ed., *The Lower Norfolk County Virginia Antiquary*, 4 vols. (New York: Peter Smith, 1951), 2:12–14.

36. Philip Alexander Bruce, *Institutional History of Virginia in the Seventeenth Century*, 2 vols. (New York: Putnam, 1910), 1:222–26.

37. William Waller Hening, ed., *The Statutes at Large: Being a Collection of All the Laws of Virginia from the First Session of the Legislature, in the Year 1619*, 13 vols. (New York: R. & W. & G. Bartow, 1819–23), 1:532–33.

38. Patricia Bonomi, *Under the Cope of Heaven* (New York: Oxford University Press, 1986), 35; see also Hutson, *Religion and the Founding*, 8.

39. Hutson, *Religion and the Founding*, 20.

40. John Winthrop, *History of New England*, ed. James Kendall Hosmer, 2 vols. (New York: Barnes and Noble, 1946), 1:309; see also chapter 7 quotation from Roger Williams, 270.

41. Roger Williams, "The Bloody Tenet of Persecution," in Harry Emerson Fosdick, *Great Voices of the Reformation*, 445.

42. The example of Jesus' question, "Woman, where are those thine accusers?" (John 8:10) shows the Savior's merciful and reasoned approach. He did not condone her action but directed her to "go, and sin no more." When the Pharisees attempted to back the Savior into a corner regarding loyalty to the government of God verses the government of heaven, Jesus wisely responded, "Render therefore unto Caesar the things which are Caesar's; and unto God the things which are God's" (Matthew 22:21). Jesus was not a dictator; He was a teacher. The Day of Judgment was not yet but would wait until the end of the world when He would return in His glory. Until then, individuals must exercise agency to choose whether or how they will follow God.

43. Bainton, *Here I Stand*, 157.

44. Jonathan Edwards, *The Great Awakening*, ed. C. C. Goen (New Haven, Conn: Yale University Press, 1972), 4–5.

45. Robert G. Pope, *The Half-Way Covenant: Church Membership in Puritan New England* (Princeton, N.J.: Princeton University Press, 1969), 146.

46. Goen, *Great Awakening*, 19.

47. Goen, *Great Awakening*, 19.

48. Goen, *Great Awakening*, 46.

49. Goen, *Great Awakening*, 47.

50. Goen, *Great Awakening*, 47.

51. Goen, *Great Awakening*, 49.

52. Goen, *Great Awakening*, 49.

53. Benjamin Franklin apparently heard Whitefield address a congregation in this manner, in Hutson, *Religion and the Founding*, 29.

54. Hutson, *Religion and the Founding*, 29.

55. Hutson, *Religion and the Founding*, 29.

56. Richard Bushman, ed., *The Great Awakening Documents on the Revival of Religion* (New York: Atheneum, 1970), 129–30.

57. Hutson, *Religion and the Founding*, 30.

58. Hutson, *Religion and the Founding*, 30.

59. Goen, *Great Awakening*, 51. Jonathan Parson's letter dated April 14, 1744, in the *Christian History*, 2:135. He was describing an experience at East Lyme, Connecticut, in April 1741.

60. Malachi 4:5–6. That Elijah is prophesied to perform some mission prior to the second coming of Christ is certain. Malachi was not referring to Elijah's appearance at the Mount of Transfiguration, as this event had nothing to do with the "great and dreadful day of the Lord." Accordingly, Elijah's appearance and mission have to do with preparations prior to the Second Coming; see also Revelation 14:6–7, "And I saw another angel fly in the midst of heaven, having the everlasting gospel to preach unto them that dwell on the earth." These verses testify of an important event to take place preceding the Second Coming. Further commentary is provided in ch. 11.

61. Backman, *Religious Revolt in Virginia*, 128–29.

Chapter Ten

The Second Great Awakening and Doctrinal Reformation of the Nineteenth Century

Every one is so full of his own wisdom, that there might be found as many reformers as heads, if any were allowed to take upon themselves the task of mending them, except those whom God has constituted the supreme rulers of his people or to whom he has given sufficient grace and zeal to be prophets.

—Rene Descartes, *Discourse on Reason*

The religious freedom offered by the United States Constitution at last opened the door for the development and spread of diverse theological ideas. Whereas the Reformation had the effect of reducing corruption and of making inroads towards a return to primitive Christian values, relatively few denominations had been able to emerge from its core. State control of religion throughout Europe had continued to hold its grip on organized worship services. The latter part of the eighteenth century and the opening of the nineteenth century witnessed a second spiritual awakening fueled by political independence and a new doctrinal revolution. Religions built on creeds such as the Nicene and Chalcedonian canons of

Catholicism, the Augsburg Confession of the Lutherans, the Westminster Confession of the Reformed Faith churches, and the Thirty-nine Articles of the Church of England evolved into a frenzy of denominationalism.

Although some scholars have felt that religion in America was on the decline in the eighteenth century, new studies indicate that religion was probably healthy and was actually expanding throughout the colonies. Gathering in homes and barns, many "dissenters" worshiped outside the state-established system.[1] As democracy exerted its powerful influence on the fledgling nation, religious activity continued to grow but in different directions. In addition to the spread of Calvinism, the Arminian concept of free will found significant renewal through the teachings of John Wesley. And as the Age of Reason continued to flower, significant objections to fourth- and fifth-century religious creeds began to sprout among America's educated class. Many rejected the Trinitarian concept of God in favor of views held by some of the earlier Christians. Revivalist furor increased, and the new concept of open-air camp meetings began to penetrate the American frontier. The convergence of these influences provided the setting and the circumstances necessary for God to begin to fulfill biblical prophecies made millennia ago.

The Age of Reason Inspires a Second Doctrinal Reformation

In the mid-eighteenth century, American colonists still widely believed in the creeds of the European Reformers. At this juncture, belief in the Nicene Trinity was nearly universal; with the exception of Quakers, other Christian faiths generally agreed on major points of theology, mostly dividing on such issues as Church governance and minor doctrinal beliefs. For example, excluding Quakers and Catholics, the Bible was the sole authority for sinful Christians seeking salvation. While virtual agreement existed regarding the doctrine of the Fall, Americans were divided on the Atonement and man's role in agency and the exercise of faith. This divergence in thought was the primary argument between Arminianism and Calvinism. The concepts of life after death and of hell and the judgment were also similar among all faiths besides Quakers and Catholics. Likewise, excluding Catholics, baptism and the Lord's Supper were considered principally symbolic and not necessary for salvation. During this period, all but Quakers denied the possibility of "open visions" because they believed the

canon to be closed, insisting that it contained all the revelation necessary for man's salvation. Continuous innovations in science and a rise in rationalism in the opening of the nineteenth century dramatically altered this picture. Just as uniformity had been elusive during the Protestant Reformation, this second doctrinal revolution was more diverse and theologically contentious than the first. Thus, in addition to Catholicism and Calvinist Protestantism, growing denominationalism, fueled by intellectual diversity, became a battleground of doctrinal ideas. A more organized campaign to gather converts into both new and traditional churches began.

The Deist Movement

In the midst of what Thomas Paine called the Age of Reason, a new religious ideology known as deism gathered followers, particularly among well-educated Americans. Deism was borne of liberal intellectuals in Europe during that explosive period of enlightenment and discovery between 1650 and 1800 and was adopted by many framers of the Constitution. They believed that humanity was not inherently evil but that people were born innocent and untainted by Adam's sin. Like the early Christian Father Irenaeus, they taught that man becomes corrupt over time by the environment in which he is raised. Accordingly, deists were enthusiastic proponents of education, of separating church and state, and of high moral values. The Englishman Edward Herbert, Baron of Cherbury, crystalized the deist view into five points:

1. There is chiefly one supreme God.

2. He is chiefly to be worshiped.

3. Piety and virtue are the primary aspects of worship.

4. We must repent of our sins; if we do so, God will forgive us.

5. There are rewards for good men, and

punishment for sinners in the next life.[2]

Because the domination of traditional Christianity prevailed, most of the Founding Fathers who embraced deism were reticent to publicly reveal their beliefs or to openly oppose orthodoxy. However, several, such as John Adams, Thomas Jefferson, and Benjamin Franklin, wrote or spoke privately about their views. John Adams, in a letter to Thomas Jefferson declared, "The Ten Commandments and the Sermon on the Mount contain my religion."[3] Jefferson, the most outspoken of those who wrote letters and kept journals, asserted that "Calvinism has introduced into the Christian religion more new absurdities than its leaders had purged it of old ones."[4] Jefferson further described to John Adams his opposition to historic Christianity when, opposing the doctrine of the orthodox Trinity, he reasoned:

> Three are one and one is three; and yet the one is not three, and the three are not one. . . . This constitutes the craft, the power and profit of the priests. Sweep away their gossamer fabrics of factious religion, and they would catch no more flies.[5]

Commenting further on this theme, William Cobbett, an English journalist who lived in the colonies for ten years as a political fugitive, explained, "A Christian worships three Gods in the person of one God, and in defiance to the science of numbers contends that, three times one is one, and that, once one is three. . . . They tell us that their God is his own son; that this son is his own father, and that he was born unbegotten, being four thousand years older than his mother."[6]

Benjamin Franklin also held some deist views. He developed a creed similar to the one expressed by English deists, stating that although the doctrines of Jesus had undergone "various corrupting changes," his religion and system of ethics were, "as he left them to us, the best the world ever saw or is likely to see."[7]

Although these celebrated leaders opposed traditional Christianity, they possessed strong convictions of Jesus Christ as a great prophet; though they denied the divinity of Jesus, they advocated His moral code and teachings. Like other Christians, uncertainty surrounding the Godhead was just as apparent as had been the case since not long after the passing of the Apostles. The Church had been in apostasy for many centuries and the fruit of this rebellion was not only an absence of the gifts of the Spirit but also the presence of many errant doctrines, widespread confusion, and contention as to what primitive Christian theology may have been. Nevertheless, like other seekers, deists like John Adams, Thomas Jefferson, and Benjamin Franklin were among the more honorable men of their day. They exercised faith in God and believed in the values taught by scripture. Jefferson himself seems to have experienced a religious change of heart in the 1790s which altered his earlier views and significantly influenced his presidency.[8] In a letter to Charles Thompson, he wrote:

> I . . . have made a . . . book . . . , which I call the philosophy of Jesus; it is a paradigma of his doctrines, made by cutting the texts out of the book, and arranging them on the pages of a blank book, in a certain order of time or subject. A more beautiful or precious morsel of ethics I have never seen; it is a document in proof that I am a real Christian, that is to say, a disciple of the doctrines of Jesus, very different from the Platonists, who call me infidel and themselves Christians and preachers of the Gospel while they draw all their characteristic dogmas from what its author never said nor saw. They have compounded from

the heathen mysteries a system beyond the comprehension of man, of which the great reformer [Jesus] . . . , were he to return on earth, would not recognize one feature.[9]

Regardless of the Founding Fathers' actual beliefs, it seems clear that they (including America in general) did not follow the path of European deists who drifted into anti-clericalism; instead, they integrated with traditional churches. Although the beliefs of these esteemed men were not considered orthodox by most religious leaders of the day, the Framers aptly evaluated shortcomings of early nineteenth-century Christian churches. Just as Martin Luther could observe the corruption of the Roman Church, Jefferson and others of his day could decipher the alteration of doctrines and practices evident in modern Christianity as compared with those of the early Christian Church. Nevertheless, they did not claim nor did they have superior inspiration to their Christian brethren as to what original Christianity was. Uniquely, as with the Reformers, God performed a marvelous work through the framers of the Constitution. Whatever private religious ideas they may have held, they were inspired by God in developing and refining the laws pertaining to democracy and freedom.

The Rise of Unitarianism

Like other religious ideologies, Unitarianism was transplanted from Europe. The distinctive feature of this new faith was its opposition to the doctrine of the Trinity, its belief in a supreme and unified God, and its teaching that Jesus Christ, although inspired, was merely a man. The first Unitarian Society in America was founded in Philadelphia in 1796 by the noted scientist and educator, Joseph Priestly. Due to controversial politi-

cal tracts he had written in England, Priestly became unpopular and left his homeland in 1794, establishing himself in Pennsylvania. Unitarianism was later made fashionable in America through the advocacy of Henry Ware. Selected as the Hollis Professor of Theology at Harvard in 1805, he promoted the ideas of this more liberal form of Christianity to his students. Upon graduation, many of these well-cultured and educated young Americans introduced Unitarianism into the Congregational parishes where they settled. Other influential Unitarians included the orthodox Congregationalist reverend John Sherman, who wrote, *One God in One Person Only: and Jesus Christ a Being Distinct From God, Dependent upon Him for His Existence, and His Various Powers, Explained and Defended* in 1805, and the New Hampshire minister, Noah Worcester, who published in 1810 the anti-Trinitarian work entitled *Bible News of the Father, Son, and Holy Spirit.*[10]

Universalists

In addition to the establishment of Unitarian Societies, Universalism, another anti-Calvinist sect, found its way across the Atlantic to America. Its predominant feature was its liberal view of salvation. Not many decades after the passing of New Testament Christianity, Origen had expressed the idea of God's love being so profound that eventually all would be able to repent, suffer for their sins, and receive some level of eternal reward. During the Reformation, a form of this doctrine was revived by a few Protestants, including some Anabaptists, who believed that the suffering of devils and those consigned to hell would at some point have an end. This doctrine was rejected at the Augsburg Confession; however, with the advent of the Age of Reason and Enlightenment, its acceptance began to rise.

Liberal Congregationalists

The Universalist view of Adam's fall was similar to a liberal movement that was gaining momentum inside New England Congregationalist churches. As religious liberty evolved following the birth of America, an increasing number of liberal Congregationalists determined that man did not become totally depraved as a result of the Fall. This view, championed by Charles Chauncy, taught that although the Fall created within man a disposition to sin, Adam's sin was not inherent in his descendants. Accordingly, Murray believed in free will and man's capacity to choose good or evil.

Free-Will Baptists

While most Baptists in the nineteenth century followed Calvinism, a large number began to accept the idea that man participates in the salvation experience. Known as Freewill Baptists, they advocated the fundamental principles taught by James Arminius. As with the other sects emerging in this new doctrinal revolution, Free-will Baptists denied that Adam's sin was inherited by man. They taught that mankind is accountable for his own actions and not Adam's transgression. All humans commit sin and consequently will suffer death, they explained; however, Christ's atonement paid the penalty resulting from the Fall, thus making one responsible only for one's own sins. Those who repent of individual sin and accept Jesus Christ receive complete forgiveness. Uniquely, they believed that "all who die short of the age of accountability are rendered sure of eternal life."[11]

American Methodist Societies

The Christian Reformer responsible for the rise and widespread acceptance of the doctrines expounded by James Arminius was the well-known clergyman John Wesley. Born in 1703 in Epworth, Lincolnshire, Wesley was one of ten living children raised by Samuel and Susannah Wesley. The Wesley children were taught the principles of economy and provident living, which perhaps explains his passion for helping the poor, visiting the sick, and educating children. He attended school at the Charterhouse in London at the age of thirteen, where he received his foundation in the ancient languages of Greek, Hebrew, and Latin. Wesley's keen mind and academic success earned his acceptance and a scholarship to attend the prestigious Oxford University in 1720, where he graduated in 1724. The next year in recognition of uncommon discipline and remarkable intellect, John was ordained a deacon in the Anglican Church; three years later, in 1728, he was ordained a priest. During this period, Wesley continued his studies at Oxford when, in 1726, having completed his Master of Arts, he became a fellow at Lincoln College lecturing in the subjects of Greek and logic.

In about 1730, Wesley assumed leadership of a small organization designed to instill greater devotion to the sacraments. Scornfully referred to as the "Holy Club," this group later became known as the Methodists due to the methodical manner in which they approached Bible study, prayer, and regular visits to various special needs groups. Out of this association emerged the larger denomination Wesley later founded.

In 1735 Wesley volunteered to preach the gospel in the American colonies, representing the Society for the Propagation of the Gospel in Foreign Parts. Originally expecting to teach the Native Americans of Georgia, after observing religious indifference in the European settlers, Wesley determined to alter his plans and to establish organized religion among the colonists. Unfortunately, his ritualistic approach, strict conventions, and candor in his discourse with women were rejected; after three years, Wesley returned home to England, discouraged. Shortly after his arrival, Wesley had a profound experience that entirely changed the course of his life. On the evening of May 24, 1738, he attended an informal Sabbath meeting in which the Bible and commentaries on the scriptures were read. While listening to Martin Luther's preface to the Epistle on Romans, John claimed that he was suddenly converted. "I felt my heart strangely warmed," he witnessed. "I felt I did trust in Christ, Christ alone, for salvation; and an assurance was given me, that he had taken away *my* sins, even *mine,* and saved *me* from the law of sin and death."[12]

In addition to this very personal experience, Wesley was also influenced by a group of humble Germans who called themselves Moravians. Perhaps his only beneficial experience in America, John noted the peaceful calm exhibited by these people during a terrifying storm. Consequently, after his spiritual conversion, he visited Herrnhut to study the Moravian Church in greater depth. His time with the Moravians influenced his theology and commitment thereafter to preach the gospel of Jesus Christ.

Wesley's newfound zeal, in combination with his rigid doctrinal positions, strained relations with Anglican leaders, and his unorthodox preaching disturbed the parishioners in many congregations he visited. However, he experienced great success in helping the poor and downtrodden. This led to his first open-air revival meeting, to which the common people flocked by the thousands. John's penchant for organization enabled him quickly to establish his converts into societies, similar to the one he headed while teaching at Lincoln College. Beginning in Bristol in 1739, he expanded his organization to London in 1740 and Newcastle in 1742. From these centers, the movement spread to smaller townships and country districts. The appeal to Wesley's unique approach was his compassion for the poor, the benefits derived from being organized into small groups, and the strict discipline expected of its members. Meeting together weekly for prayer and worship, members were able to teach, train, and lift each other in living the principles espoused in the Bible as interpreted by Wesley. Because the Church of England did not recognize any other religious organization until after 1791, the Methodist Church was not formally established during Wesley's lifetime. Accordingly, the doctrines he advocated were very similar to those of the Anglican Church's Thirty-Nine Articles; he simply reduced the number to twenty-five, eliminating all Calvinist tenets relating to predestination. By the time Wesley died in 1791, Methodist societies numbered more than 75,000, expanding rapidly thereafter.

The organizational system established by Wesley was infused into the leadership of the entire church. Methodism spread quickly in England, making its way to America just before the Revolutionary War. In 1784 Thomas Coke and Francis Asbury were appointed by Wesley to be superintendents of the Methodist Societies in America. Following the usual pattern employed in England, itinerant ministers preached in open-air meetings, eventually organizing their converts into local congregations. In this manner, Wesley's upstart faith rapidly penetrated the American frontier. By 1820 Methodism was established throughout the new republic, including the rural countryside bordering the edge of civilization.

One of the principal doctrines emphasized by Wesley and the Methodists of early America was the Arminian belief that God's grace is open to everyone. Similar to the early Christian Church, Wesley also championed the doctrine of free will and man's ability to accept or reject God's grace once offered. Although man does not initiate grace, he taught, man has the power to resist it. The primary consideration is the individual's decision to accept or reject this gift. Consequently, man determines his own destiny. He explained that the process of regeneration occurs when one is cleansed from sin through the Atonement. In this way, men receive the strength to obey God's commandments and submit themselves to His will. Sanctification, Wesley declared, is a much longer process, springing from man's inner character and righteous desires. This higher level of obedience and virtuous thought, he advised, is also a gift from God, for although God desires all men to be saints, few allow themselves to be chosen.[13]

Non-Traditional Nineteenth-Century Christian Groups

In addition to familiar and long-debated religious ideologies, several new religious groups emerged in the early nineteenth century. Although the Reformers aspired to return to the doctrines and ideals of New Testament Christianity, many nevertheless felt this end had not yet been achieved. They continued to search for truth and anticipated the time when God would restore again the primitive Church. In addition to Catholic, Calvinist, Arminian, and Arian views, a number of communal (Acts 2:42–46; 4:32–35) and restoration (Acts 3:21) denominations emerged, seeking to reestablish the ancient Church.

Communal Societies

One of the best-known communal experiments was undertaken by a group commonly recognized as the Shakers. Formally named The United Society of Believers in Christ's Second Appearing or the Millennial Church, its founder, Ann Lee, initially established a small sect in England. Migrating to America in 1774, she purchased a wilderness tract of land near Albany and began to attract followers. Although she died in 1784, her work was carried on for a time by others. By 1828 a total of nineteen small communities had been established. One of the general characteristics of early communal religious orders was the charismatic personality of its founder and claims to divine revelation. For example, when Ann Lee was released from prison in England, she declared to her followers that she had seen a vision:

> I saw Adam and Eve engage in the very transgression that led to the fall of all mankind. But in the midst of my anguish, Christ appeared to me, comforted my soul and commissioned me to preach the Gospel of the stainless life. "I am Ann the Word," she testified. "I feel the blood of Christ running through my soul and body."[14]

Shakers believed that Christ was infused in Mother Ann Lee, that she was His special instrument, and that when she spoke, it was the "Christ spirit" dwelling in her who was speaking. Additionally, they claimed that God is bisexual in nature, first appearing in the form of a male (Jesus) and later in the form of a female (Mother Ann Lee).

In addition to the Shaker movement, several other religious groups established communal societies early in the nineteenth century. The Harmonites were founded by George Rapp, an immigrant from Germany who settled in Harmony, Pennsylvania. After attracting a number of followers in 1805, he organized a type of communistic theocracy in which the members unitedly built homes, shops, mills, factories, churches, and schools. Another group characterizing this type of society emigrated from Germany and was called the Separatists of Zoar. In 1817 they established a cooperative system in a wilderness area in eastern Ohio.

Providing additional substance to the examples used by the ancient Jewish leader Gamaliel, these societies virtually disappeared in the twentieth century; very few Shakers remain today:

> For before these days rose up Theudas, boasting himself to be somebody; to whom a number of men, about four hundred, joined themselves: who was slain; and all, as many as obeyed him, were scattered and brought to nought. After this man rose up Judas of Galilee in the days of the taxing, and drew away much people after him: he also perished; and all, even as many as obeyed him, were dispersed. (Acts 5:36–37)

Thomas and Alexander Campbell Seek to Restore the Ancient Christian Church

In addition to religious communal societies trying to imitate New Testament Christian practices, several other religious leaders sought a restoration of primitive Christianity. The most prominent movement within this group was led by Thomas and Alexander Campbell. Thomas Campbell migrated from Ireland to America in the first years of the nineteenth century, locating thirty miles south of Pittsburgh, Pennsylvania, where he was appointed pastor in a Presbyterian parish. Campbell was released from his position in 1809 for teaching heretical doctrines—he had rejected the authority of the Church to forbid communion to those not professing the Westminster Confession of Faith. Moreover,

he taught that faith was the fruit of "an intelligent response of the mind to evidence," rather than a spirit-filled emotional experience.[15]

While still in Pennsylvania, Thomas Campbell continued to preach his distinctive views and was successful in gathering a number of followers. His supporters were organized into a self-governing society called the Christian Association of Washington. The charter for this association was summarized in the principles recorded in Thomas Campbell's charismatic work *Declaration and Address* (1809). Campbell desired that his organization promote "a pure Gospel Ministry, that shall reduce to practice that whole form of doctrine, worship, discipline, and government, expressly revealed and enjoined in the word of God [Bible]." Not claiming any particular church affiliation, Campbell recorded that the organization was instituted "for the sole purpose of promoting simple evangelical Christianity" and a return to "that simple original form of Christianity."[16]

After completing one year at the University of Glasgow, Alexander joined his father in Pennsylvania soon after his dismissal as pastor. He became deeply involved with his father's new ministry, assuming leadership of the movement shortly thereafter. In 1811 Alexander was converted to the doctrine of baptism by immersion. He was immersed by a Baptist and was appointed pastor of the Brush Run church in Bethany, West Virginia, later that year. He and his father launched a new program of reform designed to end sectarian divisions and to unite Christians by conceding freedom in all matters of opinion and imposing no qualifications for fellowship other than those revealed in the primitive Church.

Although vaguely affiliated with the Baptists until 1830, Alexander traveled frequently, preaching his unorthodox restorationist views. In 1823 he founded a publication titled the *Christian Baptist,* which he later changed, in consequence of his formal break with the Baptist Church, to the *Millennial Harbinger.* He asserted that missionary, tract, and Bible societies were unbiblical. He declared that synods, associations, and theological seminaries were not a part of the early Church. Alexander's controversial approach was at odds with many in the clergy, particularly his contention that they preached for hire. With the inauguration of his organization, the *Disciples of Christ* (later Churches of Christ), he claimed the eventual need of a restoration of New Testament Christianity. This idea was captioned in the title page of his newly renamed *Harbinger,* which included John's prophecy in the book of Revelation: "And I saw another angel fly in the midst of heaven, having the everlasting gospel to preach unto them that dwell on the earth, and to every nation, and kindred, and tongue, and people" (Revelation 14:6).

Campbell believed in the Reformers' concept of *sola scriptura,* rejecting new revelation or doctrinal clarifications in his theological system.[17] He rejected the Nicene and Reformer's Creeds, claiming instead to "speak where the Bible speaks and remain silent where the Bible is silent." Accordingly, they partook of the Lord's Supper each Sabbath and baptized by immersion.

While the Reformation in the sixteenth century resulted in some theological changes and a repudiation of corruption, the second doctrinal revolution of the late eighteenth and early nineteenth centuries produced a dramatic reorientation of Christian thought. The traditional theology of the Trinity was challenged by deists, Unitarians, and most Universalists; these groups also opposed the conventional doctrine that man was utterly depraved because of Adam's sin. The idea that the Bible was inerrant was also rejected by several religious groups. Many communal societies believed that revelation had been intended by God to be ongoing and argued that the Bible canon was not closed. Importantly, almost every denomination originating during the Revolutionary generation emphasized the essential role of free will in the salvation process. The frightening picture that unbelievers were tormented eternally in a lake of fire and brimstone diminished in influence, while baptism by immersion for the remission of sins and preoccupation with the Second Coming increased.

The sheer number of those who followed nontraditional Christian leaders, including the venerable framers of the American Constitution, provides evidence that numerous Americans and Christians throughout the world recognized the need for a restoration of New Testament Christianity. The effect of this second doctrinal revolution was that many Protestants were brought into greater harmony with the teachings of the ancient Church. With freedom of religion taking root throughout the world, particularly in America, conditions were ripe for the God of heaven to open a new dispensation and to restore the primitive Church of Jesus Christ, precisely as Peter had promised millennia ago (Acts 3:21).

The State of Organized Religion in the Eighteenth Century

Past historians have characterized religion in the eighteenth century as in a declining state after its initial zeal in helping to establish colonists in America. Traditional accounts have portrayed religion in New England and larger townships as "cold and formal" and virtually nonexistent along the expanding frontier. James Hutson recently summarized conventional views as follows:

The Great Awakening is represented as giving Christianity a temporary boost, but, after the Awakening spent its force, religion is pictured as sinking back into a rut. By the time of the American Revolution, an indifferent population is seen as acquiescing in the program of leaders, nominally Christian, but committed to the agenda of the Enlightenment, who proceeded to send religion to the sidelines of American life.[18]

Current scholarship demonstrates that religious fervor actually increased during the colonial period. The former misconception of religious inactivity or indifference has been due in part to biased or incomplete views expressed by frontier clergy or organizations such as the Society for the Propagation of the Gospel in Foreign Parts. When reports made by returning Anglican missionaries of "unruly beasts" and "heathens and heretics" are read in full, such "monsters" turned out to be Quakers and Presbyterians—stiff dissenters who were accused of teaching corrupting doctrines at variance with those espoused by the Church of England.[19]

We now know that a large percentage of colonial Americans gathered in farm homes or barns rather than traditional houses of worship. When George Keith reported to Anglican officials that in New Jersey there "was no face of any public Worship of any sort," in fact, forty-five congregations were meeting in private homes under the leadership of a dedicated lay person or schoolmaster.[20] Hutson maintains that such groups "existed in every colony," although more numerous south of New England. In Maryland, a number of Lutheran and German Reformed congregations had been meeting together for decades until they were finally discovered by ordained ministers who were greeted by these Christians with "tears of joy." Scotch-Irish Presbyterians, well known for their solid

piety and zeal, were perhaps the largest group that established frontier churches. As many as 250,000 may have emigrated to America before the Declaration of Independence. According to one expert, these settlers probably "introduced as much religious energy into the eighteenth-century middle and southern colonies as the Puritans did in seventeenth-century New England."[21]

Organized religion itself, not religious worship, may have suffered some setbacks in the eighteenth century. Sparsely populated areas in frontier settlements and a shortage of ministers available to pastor churches were very real problems for institutional churches. This was especially true of the Anglican sect, because none of its bishops resided in America. Because the Church of England required its clergy to be ordained by duly constituted bishops, few ministers were willing to make the dangerous transatlantic voyage. Another genuine problem encountered in wilderness areas was the lack of education and affluence of those emigrating, initially accounting for the paucity of cultural and religious refinements typical of the upper class in England. Consequently, many farmers and backwoodsmen on the American frontier could neither read nor write.

Even in New England, earlier historians suggested that church activity was declining in the eighteenth century. As evidence, they cited dwindling membership rolls, parishioners pursuing worldly goods, and the rise of rationalism and science. Religious enthusiasm was not diminishing; however, Americans were simply exploring new theology. Unitarianism and other break-offs, not well liked by traditional clergymen, claimed many converts, thus weakening the Congregationalist establishment. A Church synod had been organized as early as 1662 to consider solutions to declining membership rolls. The "Half-Way

Covenant," a compromise to the original strict requirements of Church membership, was the outcome of these discussions. Under this arrangement, grandchildren whose parents had not declared their faith were granted partial membership rights in most Congregationalist churches if the grandparents were full members. However, they were denied the privilege of communion until after true conversion and public testimony warranted full membership. This innovation was added to by the Reverend Solomon Stoddard in about 1700 when he proposed that those who were righteous but not yet "born again" be permitted to partake of the Lord's Supper. Although this recommendation was controversial, it proved too popular to ignore and was adopted in most New England churches.[22] And while religious turmoil engulfed the entire region, resulting in splinter groups and dividing the Congregationalist churches, religiosity was not waning but growing.

Documenting the rise in Church membership throughout the eighteenth-century, Hutson's research concludes:

> Anglican churches increased from 111 in 1700 to 406 in 1780; the Baptists from 33 to 457; Congregationalists from 146 to 749; German and Dutch Reformed from 26 to 327; Lutherans from 7 to 240; and Presbyterians from 28 to 475. And the colonists crowded these churches, estimates being that between 1700 and 1740, between 74.7 and 80 percent of the population attended with some frequency.[23]

Church membership rolls continued to swell throughout the Great Awakening and the American Revolution and into the nineteenth-century. Baptist and Presbyterian missionaries streamed into the southern colonies, conducting missions, setting up revivals, and preaching the fiery brand of revivalistic Christianity popularized during the Awakening. The Anglican Church was greatly impacted by the success of these missionaries. One Anglican priest, resentful of Presbyterian evangelist tactics, wrote:

> [They preach] the terrors of the law, cursing & scolding, calling old people Grey headed Devils, and all promiscuously, Damn'd doubled damn'd. . . . Lumps of hell fire, incarnate Devils, 1000 times worse than devils, etc.[24]

Baptist and Presbyterian growth was later joined by the Methodist movement in 1774. Although the first American Methodist congregation was not established until the eve of the Revolution, by 1780 they had 106 churches, and by 1790 the number had surged to 712.[25] The doctrinal reformation of the late eighteenth century was well underway, and although creedal religions established early in America were declining, religious worship in America was healthier than ever.

Revivalism Spawns a Second Great Awakening

Evangelicalism, first experienced during the Great Awakening, continued to gain momentum during the American Revolution. According to one writer, "The nation had seen nothing yet, for, during the first half of the nineteenth century, it became such a dominant force that historians have used terms such as golden day to describe its sovereignty in American religious life."[26] Methodist circuit riders, Baptist farm preachers, and Presbyterian mission programs combined to combat deism, effectively halting its spread early in the nineteenth century. Revivalist camp meetings were also popularized during this time, profoundly affecting the behavior of many Americans. Evangelicalism and revivalist camp meetings combined to spark what history calls the Second Great Awakening.

Within only a few decades of its inception, the Methodists had organized a unique system for preaching its brand of the Christian message throughout the American settlements. Geographical areas called circuits were established so that eventually a single itinerant minister could preach the gospel to virtually every family in his area. Preaching stations in homes, schools, or public buildings were located throughout the network so that sermons could be scheduled at regular times and dates, informing the farmers and frontiersmen of Methodist services.

The stunning success of this approach can be attributed to many factors. First, the requirements to ordain a Methodist minister were not nearly as rigorous as had been mandated by many other faiths. To enter the ministry, a Methodist clergyman had to express his conversion and his willingness to abide by the rules of the society, demonstrate that he could preach effectively, and own a horse. Although his education was generally higher than that of the average citizen Methodist ministers were not required to hold formal degrees. Second, the Methodists were less rigid in doctrinal beliefs, a freedom that appealed to independent-minded Americans. The basic emphasis of Methodist theology was that man was sinful and that Christ had died for all who would accept Him, develop faith in Him, and repent of their sins. Third, the Methodist circuit riders were tireless and weathered every condition and season. Whereas there were few clergyman in the colonial era, settlers now had ready and consistent access to spiritual leadership. Fourth, because the circuit riders experienced so many conversions, they developed a strong commitment to their work. Despite exceptionally low wages, they believed they were performing an important labor and receiving many blessings from the Lord. The Methodist Church was the fastest growing religion before the Civil War.[27]

Although not as effective as the Methodist circuit riders, Baptist farm preachers nevertheless enjoyed significant success. Similar in education to Methodist preachers, the Baptist elders were not formally trained. In addition to being husbands, fathers, and farmers, these devoted men preached regularly in their own communities and in the outlying areas surrounding them. Upon converting several families in a particular area, they organized a congregation, occasionally ordaining another farm preacher. Because no central authority directed their efforts, no regular schedules were employed. Thus, when the Baptist faith had been planted in a given area and a desire to organize had been established, ministers from other faiths sometimes reaped the waiting harvest.

The Presbyterian missionary program also contributed to the gathering of converts during the Second Great Awakening. To address the acute shortage of ministers in colonial America, they established theological schools in the mid-eighteenth century. Although obtaining a measure of success in population centers, frontier settlements could not afford a full-time preacher. At the commencement of the nineteenth century, Presbyterian leadership attempted to resolve this dilemma by sending preachers into outlying districts for one- or two-month assignments. Summer circuit riders were employed to preach in these areas.

One of the most fruitful methods in the conversion of farmers on the American frontier was the revivalist camp meeting. The success of this phenomenon began in Kentucky in 1796 when a popular Presbyterian minister,

James McGready, organized such an event to accommodate the large numbers wishing to hear his sermons. From this start, Methodists, Baptists, and Presbyterians all conducted camp meetings in rural settlements. This form of preaching became so popular that farmers would travel as much as fifty miles with their families to participate. According to Peter Cartwright, one of the best known circuit riders, "ten, twenty, and sometimes thirty ministers, of different denominations would . . . preach night and day, four or five days together; and indeed, I have known these camp-meetings to last three or four weeks."[28]

Although somewhat controversial, camp meetings had a significant influence in the lives of many participants who desired to live a more godly life and unite with a particular sect. Hundreds, sometimes thousands, gathered, carrying lighted candles, singing, and listening to stirring sermons. As with the first Great Awakening, emotional outbursts were common during the meetings. Cartwright observed, "I have seen more than a hundred sinners fall like dead men under one powerful sermon," and "I have seen and heard more than five hundred Christians all shouting aloud the high praises of God at once."[29] Witnesses described this falling down as if being struck by lightning. Some would remain prostrate on the ground for a period of time while others would jump up and be struck down again. Still others convulsed and jerked or even crouched in a canine position, barking like a dog. Crawling up to a tree—snarling, growling, and barking—some believed that such antics would "tree the devil."[30] While many viewed such hysteria as manifestations of the power of God, others condemned them as unhealthy and unnatural.

The effect of the Second Great Awakening on American life was dramatic. Whereas previous European visitors viewed the colonists as uncultured, unlettered, and irreligious, the Frenchman Alexis de Toqueville judged after his visit to the United States in the 1830s, "There is no country in the world where the Christian religion retains a greater influence over the souls of men than in America."[31] Methodist circuit riders, Baptist farm preachers, Presbyterian missionaries, and other groups all vied for new members in an attempt to gather converts to their specific views of Christianity. Competition for converts and contention over various doctrines espoused by the Reformers Calvin and Arminius many times cast a shadow over the otherwise good feelings accompanying conversion.

Revivalism in Western New York

While Revivalism's influence was felt throughout the entire country, some areas were exposed repeatedly to camp meetings and itinerant preachers. One such area of religious activity was in western New York, commonly referred to as a "burned over district." Sparsely populated until the 1790s, settlers began pouring into this fertile region at the close of the century and in the opening decades of the nineteenth century. During this period of significant influx, a number of revivals were responsible for large numbers of converts joining the various sects.

Many of the early settlers to this section of the republic were farmers and backwoodsmen who neglected organized religion but who were Christians by belief. In the winter of 1799, that picture began to change. Hundreds of ministers representing many denominations traveled long distances to this area ripe for the message of salvation. Many converts were gathered that year, which generated even more excitement and expanded efforts by the clergy. Similar success was achieved in 1807;

and following the War of 1812, with continuous migration from New England, the frontier began to recede and congregations of various denominations were established. Converts joining churches during this period exceeded previous awakenings, with significant revivals occurring in 1815, 1818, and 1821.[32]

One of the most popular preachers of the day, Charles G. Finney, continued this flurry of excitement in 1825. Finney began his career as a lawyer and was critical of many religious teachings. Although he was not formally trained as a minister of any particular faith, a deeply spiritual experience altered his life's work, and he began to preach his own unique interpretations of the Bible. He initiated a religious revival in 1824 that soon achieved remarkable success. Rather than emphasizing doctrine, Finney focused on the same kind of spiritual conversion he had experienced. Although he too was criticized by some for promoting emotional and unnatural outbursts, he invited settlers to make the important decision of accepting Christ. Many accepted his challenge and later joined with the Presbyterians.[33]

Conclusion

Religious liberty, guaranteed by the Constitution, permitted freedom of expression, now being manifest in greater spirituality, devotion to God, and sectarian diversity. Revivalism was also instrumental in motivating Americans to unite in large numbers with a specific church and to evaluate individual religious convictions. Although its tactics and expressions were controversial, the result was positive. Many sought to align themselves more closely with the teachings of the Master.

If America, like Canaan, was to be a promised land, perhaps the God of heaven was pouring out His Spirit upon its people, leading this country to become an ensign to other nations (Isaiah 5:26). Western New York, a "burned-over district," was a hotbed of religious activity and a scene of intense competition to win new converts to various denominations in that region.

Notes

1. Hutson, *Religion and the Founding*, 22

2. Leslie Stephen and Sidney Lee, ed., *The Dictionary of National Biography*, 22 vols. (London: Oxford University Press, 1917), 9:630; Hannah Adams, *An Alphabetical Compendium of the Various Sects which Have Appeared in the World from the Beginning of the Christian Era to the Present Day* (Boston: B. Edes and Sons, 1784), xxiv.

3. Lester J. Cappon, ed., *The Adams-Jefferson Letters*, 2 vols. (Chapel Hill: University of North Carolina Press, 1959), 2:361, 373, 494.

4. Saul K. Padover, ed., *Thomas Jefferson on Democracy* (New York: New American Library, 1958), 166.

5. Thomas Jefferson to John Adams, August 22, 1813, *The Works of Thomas Jefferson*, ed. Paul Leicester Ford, 12 vols. (New York: G. P. Putnam's Sons, 1904–5), 11:328–30.

6. Peter Porcupine [William Cobbett], *Christianity Contrasted with Deism; or, The Present Religion of France: To Which Is Added, an Address to the Society for Promoting Christian Knowledge and Piety* (Philadelphia, 1796), 23–24, Evans No. 30192.

7. James Madison Stifler, *The Religion of Benjamin Franklin* (New York: D. Appleton and Company, 1925), 61–62.

8. Hutson, *Religion and the Founding*, 73–74.

9. Jefferson to Charles Thompson, January 9, 1816, in *Jefferson Writings*, 1372–73.

10. Milton V. Backman Jr., *American Religions* (Salt Lake City: Deseret Book, 1965), 207–8.

11. Porter S. Burbank, *Freewill Baptists, Rupp's Original History*, 59, 65–66; see also N. A. Baxter, *History of the Freewill Baptists* (Rochester: American Baptist Historical Society, 1957).

12. John Wesley, *The Journal of the Rev. John

Wesley, 4 vols. (London: J. M. Dent and Co., n.d.), 1:102.

13. For Wesley's belief in salvation offered to all, see *Works of John Wesley,* sermon 1, 7, 5:14–15. Wesley's explanation of how we are justified, see *Works of John Wesley,* sermon 5, 2.1–3.9, 5:56–64. On sanctification, see *Works of John Wesley,* 1:224–25, sermon 63, 6:49–54; sermon 76, 6:414–24.

14. Hinds, 355; Andrews, 11–12, 97, in Daryl Chase, "The Early Shakers," Ph.D. diss., University of Chicago, 1936, 14, 143, in Backman, *American Religions.*

15. W. E. Garrison and A. T. DeGroot, *The Disciples of Christ* (St. Louis, Mo.: Bethany Press, 1958) 133–39.

16. Garrison and DeGroot, *Disciples of Christ,* 146–48.

17. Royal Humbert, ed., *A Compend of Alexander Campbell's Theology* (St. Louis: Bethany Press, 1961), 90–91.

18. Hutson, *Religion and the Founding,* 19.

19. Hutson, *Religion and the Founding,* 19–20.

20. Hutson, *Religion and the Founding,* 22.

21. Hutson, *Religion and the Founding,* 22.

22. Goen, *Great Awakening,* 55–56; Backman, *American Religions,* 268–69.

23. Hutson, *Religion and the Founding,* 24.

24. Hutson, *Religion and the Founding,* 34–35.

25. Hutson, *Religion and the Founding,* 35.

26. Hutson, *Religion and the Founding,* 35.

27. John O. Gross, *The Beginnings of American Methodism* (New York: Abingdon Press, 1961), 66–69; see also Backman, *American Religions,* 285–86.

28. Peter Cartwright, *Autobiography of Peter Cartwright,* ed. W. P. Strickland (New York: Carlton and Porter, 1857), 45.

29. Cartwright, *Autobiography,* 45–46.

30. Cartwright, *Autobiography,* 49–51; *Autobiography of Rev. James B. Finley: Or, Pioneer Life in the West,* ed. W. P. Strickland (Cincinnati: Cranston and Curtis; New York: Hunt and Eaton, n.d., 166–67; cf. Bernard A. Weisberger, *They Gathered at the River* (Boston: Little, Brown and Co., 1958).

31. Alexis de Tocqueville, *Democracy in America,* trans. Henry Reeve, 2 vols. (Cambridge: 1864), 1:388; see also Hutson, *Religion and the Founding,* 114.

32. Whitney R. Cross, *The Burned-Over District: The Social and Intellectual History of Enthusiastic Religion in Western New York, 1800–1850* (Ithaca, N.Y.: Cornell University Press, 1982), 9–13.

33. Charles G. Finney, *Memoirs of Rev. Charles G. Finney* (New York: F. H. Revell, 1876), 77–80, 144–147, 164–65, 288–89.

CHAPTER ELEVEN

A RESTORATION OF THE PRIMITIVE CHRISTIAN CHURCH?

And he shall send Jesus Christ, which before was preached unto you: Whom the heaven must receive until the times of restitution of all things, which God hath spoken by the mouth of all his holy prophets since the world began.

—Acts 3:20–21

In earlier dispensations, the prophets of God were divinely chosen. In the midst of great wickedness, it was written of Noah that he "found grace in the eyes of the Lord" (Genesis 6:8). To trembling Enoch, God said, "Do not fear righteous man, . . . come near to me and hear my voice" (1 Enoch 15:1). To young Abraham, a voice from heaven called, twice speaking his name, "Abraham, Abraham!" He responded, "Here I am." Then the Lord said, "You are searching for the God of gods, the Creator. . . . I am he" (Apocalypse of Abraham 8:1–3). God called the name of that prophet who was to become Israel's deliverer, "Moses, Moses," whose reply was the same, "Here am I." At another time in Israel's history God, called a young prophet, "Samuel," who responded, "Here am I." When Samuel finally understood it was the voice of the Lord, and not Eli's, he answered, "Speak, Lord; for thy servant heareth," to which God replied, "Samuel, Behold, I will do a thing in Israel, at which both the ears of every one that heareth it shall tingle" (1 Samuel 3:4–11).

From Adam to Malachi, the Lord called prophets to help guide and direct His chosen people. Prophets of all ages revealed doctrines relating to salvation (such as ordinances and commandments), not only to reveal future happenings but also to minister to current events and current problems. This pattern can be found in the teachings of practically every Old Testament prophet. The same motif can be traced in the New

Testament to Jesus and the Apostles. As this volume has documented, however, apostasy throughout history has either limited God's prophecies to man, or for certain periods has stopped them altogether. Nevertheless, the book of Acts testified that Jesus Christ Himself would return to the earth to "restore all things" prior to His second coming when the wicked will be destroyed (Acts 3:20–21).

More recent scholarship translates Acts 3:21, cited as the epigraph to this chapter, as a "restoration" instead of "restitution," as found in the King James Version.[1] Derived from the Greek word *apokatastasis,* when broken into its roots, *apo,* meaning "away from or separation," and *kathistemi,* indicating "to set in order," means literally "to set in order or reestablish something lost by separation"; it also implies "to be appointed or ordained," signifying the role of authority in restoration.[2] Thus a "reformation" simply will not do—according to scripture. When Jesus came to earth in His first advent, the gospel was not reformed, i.e., corruption corrected; rather, it was restored and re-introduced sparkling new—by revelation. Peter, speaking prophetically, suggests that this scenario will be replayed prior to, and in preparation for, the Savior's return in His glory to redeem the righteous and destroy the wicked. Obviously, this is no small event, but when would such a refreshing come and what was to be restored? Peter's prophecy at the temple speaks of the "times" (*kairos*) of refreshing (Acts 3:19), meaning "appointed time," and the "times" (*chronos*) of restoration (Acts 3:21), meaning "period of time," or in other words, restoration carried out over a period of time.[3] Peter, in these same verses, had said this future event was prophesied "by the mouth of all his holy prophets since the world began" (Acts 3:21). The father of John the Baptist, "filled with the Holy Ghost" (Luke 1:67), prophesied that Israel was to be

recovered, or "saved from our enemies . . . ; to perform the mercy promised to our fathers . . . ; the oath which he sware to our father Abraham" (Luke 1:71–73). Although the Jews initially rejected Christ, Peter prophesied that they could be forgiven in the future (Acts 3:19). Thus, notwithstanding that Jesus predicted that during the appointed time or season of the Gentiles, the Jews would be scattered and Jerusalem would be "trodden down" (Luke 21:24),[4] he also revealed on the same occasion that He would "send his angels" to "gather together his elect" (Matthew 24:31). This subject was already on the Apostles' minds as they asked the Savior, "Wilt thou at this time restore again the kingdom to Israel" (Acts 1:6). Of course, restoring Israel would require revelation from God through prophets, as had been His pattern at all other times when "restoring" the everlasting covenant lost by apostasy. Accordingly, the Lord referred to Malachi's prophecy (Malachi 4:5), explaining to Peter that Elijah would yet come "and restore all things" (Matthew 17:11), this being the same verbiage as that received by Peter at the temple (Acts 3:19–21). The long series of historical events that followed Peter's prophecy chronicle this journey from apostasy to restoration.[5]

Prophecy declares and history accords that a general apostasy of the Church that Jesus founded took place following the ministry of the Apostles. Although the apostasy was unrecognizable by most in the beginning, it became obvious to many in later centuries. So corrupt had the Church become that the Protestant Reformation significantly divided Christianity in the sixteenth century. However, no Reformer ever claimed a divine manifestation to restore what many already acknowledged had been lost to apostasy from the principles and practices of New Testament Christianity.

The fruits of the Reformation were plainly mixed. The divided Church and the inability of any sect to restore to Christianity its primitive organization, priesthood, and vitality is evidence that the mission of the Reformation was preparatory, designed to break the heavy yoke of religious oppression. More groundwork followed. The millstone of intolerance was finally shed when the American Constitution guaranteed religious liberty. In addition, the enlightenment that began with the Renaissance and Reformation continued to swell as freedom expanded and caused thinking men and women everywhere to revisit both biblical teachings and the theology handed down by the Reformers. This re-orientation of much Christian doctrine early in the nineteenth century resulted in many new religious denominations—faiths that sought to align themselves with biblical truths in an attempt to return to the Church that Christ had founded, faiths such as Methodists, Baptists, Seventh-Day Adventists, Jehovah's Witnesses, Christian Scientists, and Mormons (officially The Church of Jesus Christ of Latter-day Saints). Revivalism brought religion closer to thousands of people, and large numbers sought a return to the practices and beliefs of the ancient Church. In this setting, many were searching for truth and seeking for the welfare of their souls.[6]

A Claim Worth Examining

Suppose that into this revivalist-rich, truth-seeking environment God inserted a modern Moses, a prophet assigned once again the stewardship for directing God's household on the earth. If such an event were to happen, it would be the most significant spiritual outpouring in centuries. It would be important to investigate it as thoroughly as we have investigated the series of apostasies in recorded history.

One claim to such a prophetic appointment that is worth examining is that of Joseph Smith Jr., founder of The Church of Jesus Christ of Latter-day Saints. This book has neither space nor resolve to put forth his entire case, but the doctrine and organization that came forth under his direction is remarkable in both its comprehensive breadth and pinpoint accuracy relative to what was lost through apostasy.

Because much of his story is connected with the coming forth of the Book of Mormon and Joseph's several visions associated with it, the next few pages will cover what this controversial book of sacred writing is, how it came into Joseph's possession, and what he did with both the book and the knowledge it contained. Then we will look at several key doctrines that this "American prophet" restored to Christianity. Again, this is hardly more than a snapshot of a fascinating portrait, but the success of what Joseph Smith contributed is so overwhelming that we would be amiss if we didn't at least offer a smattering of information with the suggestion that further study would not be out of line.

Over the years many stories have circulated, speculating as to how a young boy with neither sophistication nor education could possibly produce a volume as complex as the Book of Mormon, a volume of scripture that he translated from golden plates revealed to him by an angel of God. Further complicating this picture is the amount of actual translation time Joseph was afforded to accomplish the work. Moreover, "Smith's Golden Bible," as hostile neighbors were wont to call it, contained a great deal of information which could not be proved or disproved in 1830, the vast majority of which has now been successfully verified. Of recent interest has been the critically studied language patterns, proven to be the ancient styles and Middle Eastern patterns it purports to be. Most important, informed scholars have been astonished by the message of the book and its finely detailed theology, consistent with the Bible and matching precisely the theology of the earliest Christians.[7]

During the period of translating the Book of Mormon, primarily four individuals served as scribe to Joseph: Martin Harris, a prosperous local farmer; Joseph's wife, Emma; Oliver Cowdery, a school teacher who became acquainted with Joseph and assisted in the bulk of the translation; and John Whitmer, from Fayette, who acted as scribe in translating a separate but parallel account of the first 116 pages which were lost by Martin Harris. Translation of the plates first began in mid-April 1828 and concluded in early July 1829, a finished product of nearly six hundred pages. However, due to many setbacks and the necessity of laboring for daily maintenance, the actual translation took only about sixty-five to seventy-five days![8]

Joseph soon learned that translating consisted of more than just possessing the Urim and Thummim and the plates. Using the interpreters as an aid and then working towards a translation, Joseph began to understand how the process worked. Although he never shared the intimate details of the procedure, in a revelation given in behalf of Oliver Cowdery to Joseph, the Lord said, "Behold, you have not understood; you have supposed that I would give it unto you [the power to translate], when you took no thought save it was to ask me. . . . You must study it out in your mind; then you must ask me if it be right, and if it is right I will cause that your bosom shall burn within you." Apparently the work of translation, consistent with God's expectation in other areas, required all of Joseph's own mental exertions and talents; the Lord would overcome human

deficiency and fill the gaps.[9]

With Emma's help, between December 1827 and February 1828, Joseph copied numerous characters from the plates and translated them using the Urim and Thummim. Through a series of events, Martin Harris began to acquire some faith in Joseph's veracity, in his prophetic role, and in the project of translation. Joseph and Emma had recently moved to Harmony, Pennsylvania, to escape persecution and those possessing evil designs concerning the plates. Martin Harris joined them in February and, taking some of the translated characters, traveled to New York for the purpose of meeting with experts in the field of Middle Eastern languages.

While in New York, he visited with at least three men who were highly regarded linguists. Luther Bradish, a widely traveled New York assemblyman, was also noted for his expertise in the Middle East. Evidently, Bradish referred Martin Harris to the acclaimed scholar Samuel Latham Mitchill, often called a "living encyclopedia," or a "chaos of knowledge." It is unclear whether he first saw Mitchill or Professor Charles Anthon of Columbia College; but according to Harris, Mitchill confirmed the translation. Probably referred by Mitchill, Harris then went to see Charles Anthon, a prominent classical studies professor who was to become the leading scholar in his day.[10]

According to Martin Harris, Anthon said that the translation was correct, "more so than any he had before seen translated from the Egyptian." Then Martin showed Anthon those characters which had not yet been translated, which Anthon identified as Egyptian, Chaldaic, Assyrian, and Arabic and purportedly gave Harris a certificate to the people of Palmyra affirming the same. Curious as to the origin of the plates, Anthon queried as to how they came into Smith's possession. When Martin explained that an angel had revealed the location, the professor took back the document and tore it up. Apparently, he offered to translate the plates himself if Martin would bring them to him. He was informed that "part of the plates were sealed" and that he was forbidden to bring them, whereupon Anthon replied, "I cannot read a sealed book." In 1834 and again in 1841, Anthon wrote two conflicting versions of his encounter with Harris to Mormon critics. In the first account, he stated that he had refused to provide Harris a written opinion; in the second letter, he wrote that he gave the opinion "without any hesitation" in an attempt to uncover the fraud.[11]

Although it is impossible to ascertain with accuracy what actually transpired, circumstantial evidence provides support for Harris's story. First, he had nothing to gain and everything to lose by sponsoring Joseph. At risk were his family, his fortune, his time, and his reputation. Second, he went to New York, in part, to satisfy his own curiosity about the plates and Joseph Smith. Harris's devotion to Joseph thereafter, including *substantial* financial support, provides a basis to believe Martin's version. Third, the content of Anthon's conflicting accounts, as communicated to Mormon critics, is by itself suspicious. The prevailing traditional view of angels was such that Anthon's own credibility and reputation might be impugned.[12]

Sometime in the succeeding months, Joseph and his associates became aware that Martin Harris and Professor Anthon unwittingly fulfilled Bible prophecy. Isaiah predicted:

And the vision of all is become unto you as the words of a book that is sealed, which men deliver to one that is learned, saying, Read this, I pray thee: and he saith, I cannot; for it is sealed:

and the book is delivered to him that is not learned, saying, Read this, I pray thee: and he saith, I am not learned. (Isaiah 29:11–12)

The fact that he could not immediately translate in 1827, that he was in reality unlearned, must have profoundly impacted Joseph when he connected Harris's experience with this passage. Joseph Knight, one of Smith's associates, recalled: "He being an unlearned man did not know what to do. Then the Lord gave him power to translate himself. Then were the learned men confounded, for he, by the means he found with the plates . . . could translate those characters better than the learned."[13] Moreover, Isaiah's prophecy provided further context and meaning to the words Joseph testified he heard from the Savior in his First Vision:

Wherefore the Lord said, Forasmuch as this people draw near me with their mouth, and with their lips do honour me, but have removed their heart far from me, and their fear toward me is taught by the precept of men. (Isaiah 29:13)

In consequence of this condition, Isaiah had previously revealed that prophets and seers had been removed from among them, consistent with the theme and evidence contained in this book: "For the Lord hath poured out upon you the spirit of deep sleep, and hath closed your eyes: the prophets and your rulers, the seers hath he covered" (Isaiah 29:10).

Accordingly, Isaiah predicted a future day, involving "a sacred book," when prophets would again speak in the name of God the Lord:

Therefore, behold, I will proceed to do a marvellous work among this people, even a marvellous work and a wonder: for the wisdom of their wise men shall perish, and the understanding of their prudent men shall be hid. (Isaiah 29:14)

As to the origin of the "book," a key theme of the entire chapter, verse 4 reveals:

And thou shalt be brought down, and shalt speak out of the ground, and thy speech shall be low out of the dust, and thy voice shall be, as one that hath a familiar spirit, out of the ground, and thy speech shall whisper out of the dust. (Isaiah 29:4)

According to the angel Moroni, the plates had been buried and sealed up unto the Lord late in the fourth century. Its message was familiar, parallel to that contained in the Bible, and it seemed to come forth out of the ground, by divine appointment, into the hands of Joseph Smith. Its language, from centuries of righteous prophets, whispered out of the ground. Like the prophets of the Bible, these American seers had passed on, but their message survived and would now be proclaimed by living prophets in this new dispensation preceding the coming of Christ.

When Martin Harris returned from New York, he was eager to assist the young prophet in bringing forth this book to the world. References to his experience with the linguists in New York were published in newspapers, both in Rochester and Palmyra, in August 1829. Martin was genuinely amazed that Joseph's ability to translate appeared greater than these eminent men from the eastern United States with whom he had visited. Pomeroy Tucker, a local Episcopal priest in Palmyra and later historian, wrote that Martin concluded from his experience that "God hath chosen the foolish things of the world to confound the wise." He remembered him saying, "The very

fact that Smith was an obscure and illiterate man" was proof to him that Joseph "must be acting under divine impulses."[14]

Although Harris's wife was deeply opposed to his involvement with Joseph and the plates, his commitment and belief in the project would not be swayed. From about April 12 until June1 14, 1828, Martin labored diligently to help Joseph with the translation. To preclude him from viewing the plates, a curtain was used to divide the two men while Joseph translated on one side, with the aid of the interpreters or a seer stone, while Martin acted as scribe. According to Martin, when the two became weary, they would venture down to the river to exercise "by throwing stones out on the river, etc." Finding a stone that closely resembled the one Joseph used for translation, he exchanged the seer stone with the false imitation. "The prophet remained silent, unusually and intently gazing in darkness. . . . Much surprised, Joseph exclaimed, 'Martin! What is the matter? All is as dark as Egypt!' " His look betrayed him, and when questioned as to his motive, Martin said he had done so "to stop the mouth of fools who told [him] that the prophet had learned those sentences and was merely repeating them." During this two month period, 116 pages were translated.[15]

Shortly thereafter, a disaster occurred which had profound influence on all who became associated thereafter with the translation but particularly on the prophet Joseph. Although Martin had received a number of assurances and witnesses of the divine authenticity of the work, he was constantly badgered by his wife, Lucy, and others who thought him a fool for trusting Joseph. To help quiet the skeptics, Martin asked Joseph if he might take the manuscript to show his wife and a few close family members. Due to his close relationship with Martin, and the fact that he had helped him when he seemed to have "no earthly friend," Joseph sympathized with his friend's feelings and prayed to the Lord for permission to grant his request. The Lord refused, but Martin persisted. Upon further inquiry, the answer was the same, but still Martin pled with the prophet for consent. On Joseph's third attempt, the Lord authorized Martin to take the manuscript under specific conditions: first, that he only show the writings to his wife, his brother, his father and mother, and his wife's sister; and second, that Joseph assume full responsibility for the manuscript's safety. After binding him with an oath, Joseph allowed Martin to depart.[16]

Although the work of translation was of utmost importance, it was not Joseph's only concern. The day after Martin left, Emma gave birth to their first child; tragically, the newborn son, named Alvin after Joseph's dear departed brother, died within a few hours of his birth. Emma herself came very close to death, but after two weeks she began to improve, thus allowing Joseph to turn his attention once again to the manuscript. To facilitate his trip to Palmyra, Emma's mother agreed to care for her daughter during his absence, enabling him to leave at once.

Joseph was exhausted when he arrived in Palmyra at dawn and, after having received some refreshment from his mother, he requested that Martin be sent for "with all possible speed." Martin was expected around 8:00 A.M. but did not arrive until half past twelve. Lucy then reported, "We saw him walking with a slow and measured tread toward the house, his eyes fixed thoughtfully upon the ground. When he came to the gate, he did not open it but got upon the fence and sat sometime with his hat drawn over his eyes." When he finally entered the house, he sat down as if to eat with the family, taking a knife and fork in his hand but then suddenly dropped them. Pressing his hand upon his temples, he cried out in agony, "Oh! I have lost my soul. I have lost my soul." Having suppressed his fears to this point, Joseph "sprang from the table," exclaiming, "Oh Martin, have you lost the manuscript? Have you broken your oath and brought down condemnation upon my head as well as your own?" Deeply distressed, Martin admitted his failure, not knowing how or where the manuscript had disappeared. In utter anguish Joseph rebuked himself: "Oh my God, my God," he sobbed, clenching his hands, "All is lost, is lost! What shall I do? I have sinned. It is I who tempted the wrath of God by asking him for that which I had no right to ask, as I was differently instructed by the angel." Weeping bitterly, he paced the floor.[17]

Joseph returned to Harmony in July 1828 and commenced at once to humble himself before God and to plead with Him "in mighty prayer" for mercy and forgiveness. An angel appeared to Joseph saying he had sinned and that because he had allowed himself to be responsible for "this man's faithlessness," he was required to return the Urim and Thummim to the angel. The heavenly messenger then revealed to Joseph that if he would be "very humble and penitent," he might receive them again.[18] Shortly thereafter, he received the following revelation:

> Behold, you have been entrusted with these things, but how strict were your commandments; and remember also the promises which were made to you, if you did not transgress them. And behold, how oft you have transgressed the commandments and the laws of God, and have gone on in the persuasions of men. . . . Behold, thou art Joseph, and thou wast chosen to do the work of the Lord, but because of transgression, if thou art not aware thou wilt fall. But remember, God is merciful; therefore, repent of

that which thou hast done; . . . thou art still chosen, and art again called to the work.[19]

Commenting about this dark period of Joseph's life, Richard Bushman, an acclaimed Columbia University history professor, offers the following insight:

This revelation gave the first inkling of how Joseph would speak in his prophetic voice. With a few exceptions, the revelations are not reports of experiences written in the first person by the author, as in Joseph's narratives of his life. The speaker stands above and outside Joseph, sharply separated emotionally and intellectually. . . . There is no effort to conceal or rationalize, no sign of Joseph justifying himself to prospective followers. The words flow directly from the messenger to Joseph and have the single purpose of setting Joseph straight. . . . At age twenty-two Joseph knew how to speak prophetically.[20]

The external events that occurred in 1828 were only a part of the story of Joseph's life. His internal world was continually being shaped by divine influence, giving him the breadth and depth to accomplish the enormous work that lay ahead.

The plates and interpreters were returned to Joseph in September 1828. During the fall, he was required to work the farm he was renting from his father-in-law, Isaac Hale, and to prepare for winter. Amid all the activities competing for his time, Joseph resumed translation. Emma wrote for Joseph during this period and always exhibited a deep faith in the work to which her husband had been called. During the course of translation, the plates often lay on a table, wrapped in a linen cloth. Later in life, in a conversation with her son, Joseph Smith III, she explained what the plates felt like "when tracing their outline and

shape." "They seemed to be pliable like thick paper," she said. And they "would rustle with a metallic sound when the edges were moved by the thumb, as one does sometimes thumb the edges of a book." Apparently Joseph III, who was only twelve when his father was martyred, wondered whether he might have written the manuscript previously, or perhaps memorized what he dictated. Emma replied that during this time of Joseph's life he "could neither write nor dictate a coherent and well worded letter; let alone dictating a book like the Book of Mormon." Providing even more assurance, she added, "he had neither manuscript nor book to read from. . . . If he had had anything of the kind he could not have concealed it from me." Then she testified to her son:

I am satisfied that no man could have dictated the writing of the manuscripts unless he was inspired; for when acting as scribe, your father would dictate to me hour after hour; and when returning for meals, or after interruptions, he would begin at once where he had left off, without either seeing the manuscript or having any portion of it read to him. This was a usual thing for him to do. It would have been improbable that a learned man could do this; and for one so ignorant and unlearned as he was, it was simply impossible.[21]

In April 1829, Joseph was introduced to Oliver Cowdery, who became acquainted with the Smith family when boarding with them while teaching at the district school in Palmyra. The story of the gold plates had gained wide circulation in the area, arousing a deep curiosity in the young teacher. He first learned of Joseph Smith and the ancient record through twenty-four-year-old David Whitmer but was unable to elicit much information from the elder Smiths. After a lengthy period, Oliver obtained the trust of Joseph Sr., who then offered a brief sketch of some of the events that had taken place. He became preoccupied with the plates and the work of the young prophet, meditating upon the testimonies he had heard, and thus determined to make the matter a subject of sincere prayer. Approaching the Smiths he reported, "I have now resolved what I will do. . . . I firmly believe that if it is the will of the Lord that I should go, and that there is a work for me to do in this thing, I am determined to attend to it." Accordingly, after completing his teaching term in March, he traveled the 150 miles to Harmony with Joseph's brother Samuel.[22]

Unaware of the events taking place in Palmyra, Joseph had been praying diligently that the Lord might send him a scribe. Given Emma's demanding responsibilities, she could write but little for him, and Joseph felt a great sense of urgency to complete the translation. When Oliver and Samuel arrived in Harmony, Oliver addressed the prophet, "Mr. Smith, I have come for the purpose of writing for you." Conversing late into the evening on Sunday, Joseph rehearsed the entire history, according to Lucy, "as far as it was necessary," and then they "commenced the work of translation" the next morning. Starting on April 7, 1829, the work progressed rapidly, with few interruptions, until it was complete in early July.[23]

As with Emma, Oliver became thoroughly convinced of the divine calling of Joseph. He later reported in 1834: "These were days never to be forgotten—to sit under the sound of a voice dictated by the inspiration of heaven awakened the utmost gratitude of this bosom! Day after day I continued, uninterrupted, to write from his mouth, as he translated with the Urim and Thummim." He maintained that no man "could translate and write directions" given to these ancient cul-

tures, "from the mouth of the Savior, of the precise manner in which men should build up His Church, and especially when corruption had spread uncertainty over all forms and systems practiced among men."[24]

One of the unique experiences Oliver encountered with Joseph that strengthened his witness of the divinity of the work was a revelation that Joseph received in April 1829 on his behalf. In this revelation, he was informed of two experiences that he had never shared with Joseph or anyone else. After Joseph conveyed to Oliver the heavenly message, Oliver acknowledged that the prophet was inspired and "that the work was true, because no being living knew of the thing alluded to in the revelation, but God and himself."[25]

Shortly before the translation was complete, Joseph applied for and received a copyright from the clerk of the Northern District of New York. After lengthy negotiations with Egbert B. Grandin of Palmyra—which required as security a note against the farm of Martin Harris—5,000 copies of the Book of Mormon were printed and offered for sale on March 26, 1830, for the sum of $3,000. What began as a vision in September 1823 from the angel Moroni had now culminated in the publication of a sacred volume of ancient scripture comparable to the Bible. The title page declared its purpose:

> The Book of Mormon, an account written by the hand of Mormon . . . to the convincing of the Jew and Gentile that JESUS IS THE CHRIST, the ETERNAL GOD, manifesting himself unto all nations.

Joseph Smith never professed that the purpose of the Book of Mormon was, in any way, to replace the Bible. The Bible, he taught, was the *word of God* as far as it was translated correctly. Although he did not have the kind of evidence in his day that is currently available, the Lord revealed to him that many plain and precious parts had been removed. In spite of any errors it may hold, the Bible contains the central drama of God's chosen people and instructs those who love God in how they should conduct their lives and receive salvation. The Book of Mormon, Joseph revealed, was another testament of Jesus Christ and of His divine mission. Joseph explained that the Bible contained the history of God's communication to those who lived in the ancient world in what is often referred to as the Eastern Hemisphere. He taught that the Book of Mormon was a record of God's dealings with those who lived primitively on the American continents, or the Western Hemisphere. The book chronicles the history of several groups of people who migrated from the Old World, under the inspiration of God, to the New World and contains His revelations among them. The most important account contained in the Book of Mormon was the appearance of Jesus Christ, after His resurrection, to those on the American continent. He established His Church among them, exactly as He had done in Jerusalem. One of Joseph's primary teachings was that together, these two volumes of scripture could bring people unto Christ and His salvation—if they would elect to receive and obey these sacred and divinely inspired writings.

The Restoration of the "Keys" of the Aaronic and Melchizedek Priesthoods

When Jesus fulfilled His earthly ministry, He established, by revelation from His Father, a formal priesthood and Church organization. This priesthood was perpetuated for a short period of time by the Apostles and those who followed. Clement and Igna-

tius, perhaps the most reputable and reliable witnesses of the early Church, testified to the need for the bishop to perform the sacraments and ordinances revealed by the Savior and the Apostles. As we saw in chapter 5, when the Church passed away, early in the second century, the priesthood died with it, and the organization that remained became largely a corrupt, human counterfeit.

While Joseph and Oliver were translating the Book of Mormon, they found many things in the sacred writings that caused them to seek additional understanding. One such experience occurred while they translated the section titled Third Nephi, an account of the Savior's visit to the Americas after His resurrection in Jerusalem. Unlike the Savior's obscure entry into the world as the Babe of Bethlehem, Jesus descended from the clouds in glory near the temple in the land known as Bountiful, just as He had ascended into heaven in the midst of about five hundred in Jerusalem (1 Corinthians 15:6). Thus, His acceptance by those who witnessed this miraculous event was universal. When the Savior began teaching the people there, who were called "Nephites," He immediately gave authority to twelve disciples to baptize, and He explained to them the manner and importance of baptism. Joseph and Oliver wondered about the special authority that seemed necessary to perform this holy sacrament. Oliver recalled, "It was easily to be seen, that amidst the great strife and noise concerning religion, none had authority from God to administer the ordinances of the Gospel." The two men were sufficiently troubled that they ceased translating and decided to make their question a matter of prayer.[26]

On May 15, 1829, they repaired to the woods near the banks of the Susquehanna River. While they prayed, a "messenger from heaven descended in a cloud of light." He identified himself as John the Baptist and said that he was acting under the direction of Peter, James, and John, who held the "keys of the Priesthood of Melchizedek." Placing his hands upon their heads, he ordained them, saying:

> Upon you my fellow servants, in the name of Messiah, I confer the Priesthood of Aaron, which holds the keys of the ministering of angels, and the Gospel of repentance, and of baptism by immersion for the remission of sins; and this shall never again be taken from the earth until the sons of Levi do offer again an offering unto the Lord in righteousness.[27]

According to Joseph and Oliver, John the Baptist advised them regarding the limits of authority they had just received. The Aaronic Priesthood, he said, had license to administer the ordinance of baptism but not to lay on hands for the gift of the Holy Ghost. He explained that they would receive this authority at a later time. John directed them to baptize each other and to ordain one another to the Aaronic Priesthood again, "for so were we commanded," wrote Joseph.[28]

Following the instructions they received, they baptized each other by immersion in the Susquehanna River:

> Immediately on our coming up out of the water after we had been baptized, we experienced great and glorious blessings from our Heavenly Father. No sooner had I baptized Oliver Cowdery, than the Holy Ghost fell upon him, and he stood up and prophesied many things which should shortly come to pass. And again, so soon as I had been baptized by him, I also had the spirit of prophecy, when standing up, I prophesied concerning the rise of this church, and many other things connected with

the Church, and this generation of the children of men. We were filled with the Holy Ghost, and rejoiced in the God of our salvation.[29]

Once again, God had answered the prayers of His humble servants. Step by step, line upon line, the process of the restoration was being revealed to the young prophet. After being baptized, Joseph recorded, "Our minds being now enlightened, we began to have the Scriptures laid open to our understandings, and the true meaning and intention of their more mysterious passages revealed unto us in a manner which we never could attain to previously, nor ever before had thought of."[30]

Although Joseph was brief and plain-spoken in his account, careful not to draw attention from the essence and the singular importance of this event, Oliver, in his usual gift for eloquence, later expressed the extraordinary joy they both experienced on this occasion:

> The Lord, who is rich in mercy, and ever willing to answer the consistent prayer of the humble, after we had called upon him in a fervent manner, aside from the abodes of men, condescended to manifest to us His will. On a sudden, as from the midst of eternity, the voice of the Redeemer spake peace to us, while the veil was parted and the angel of God came down clothed with glory and delivered the anxiously looked for message, and the keys of the Gospel of repentance. "What joy! what wonder! what amazement! While the world was racked and distracted—while millions were groping as the blind for the wall, and while all men were resting upon uncertainty, as a general mass, our eyes beheld—our ears heard." As in the "blaze of day"; yes, more—above the glitter of the May sunbeam, which then shed its brilliancy

to see my own father baptized into the true Church of Jesus Christ,' and covered his face in his father's bosom and wept aloud for joy as did Joseph of old when he beheld his father coming up unto the land of Egypt." For Lucy and Joseph Sr., this was a wonderful time. Lucy's dream had been fulfilled in which her husband, unwilling to join with any church before the Restoration, now became the flexible and beautiful tree accepting the fullness of the gospel as revealed through their son. And Joseph Sr.'s dreams were also fulfilled. After seeing a desolate and barren field covered with dead fallen timber and devoid of any vegetation or life, after searching for his salvation and finding in his last dream that "there is but one thing which you lack," finally, from his prophet-son he learned that "the last thing" was to receive the ordinance of baptism and the gift of the Holy Ghost. This essential step had now been taken.[35]

The Church of Jesus Christ was once again organized among men. Although in its infancy, the authorized structure was in place and the restored Church, with its prophet, was in the same position as the early Christian Church when the Apostles guided it according to revelation. Just as the primitive Church enjoyed remarkable growth and suffered intense persecution, so also did the restored Church. In the ancient Church, the organization and doctrines unfolded line upon line and precept upon precept; this was also the case in the restored Church of Jesus Christ.

The Calling of the Twelve Apostles

In reading the New Testament, it becomes apparent that much of the structure of the Church of Jesus Christ was introduced by the Apostles after the ascension of the Savior. Although He called and appointed the Twelve and the Seventy, we learn nothing about the ordination of teachers, priests, elders, bishops, or evangelists until the apostolic ministry. The accounts of the calling of Stephen and his brethren, and of Saul and Barnabas, permit us to understand the depth of the authority and flexibility given by Jesus to His Apostles to administer the affairs of a dynamic and growing Church. Aided by the Holy Ghost, appointments could be made, by revelation, to ensure that God's will continued to be performed as it had been when the Savior exclaimed, "I came down from heaven, not to do mine own will, but the will of him that sent me" (John 6:38). The organization and structure of the restored Church matured in precisely the same manner.

In 1833 a large number of men called to travel from Kirtland, Ohio, to Independence, Missouri, to aid their brethren who were suffering greatly from persecution. By all outward appearances, it was a difficult mission that failed in its objectives. Several were disappointed and left the Church. However, a number of men distinguished themselves as obedient, faithful servants, learning to trust in those whom the Lord had called, rather than in the "arm of flesh." One brother, "too weak in faith," refused to go. Meeting Brigham Young as he was returning from Missouri, he remarked, "Well, what did you gain on this useless journey to Missouri with Joseph Smith?" Brigham responded, "All we went for." Then, explaining his answer, he said, "I would not exchange the experience I gained in that expedition for all the wealth in Geauga county."[36] Little did this man realize what the Lord already knew. The Saints would suffer and be driven from place to place: from New York, to Ohio, to Missouri, to Illinois, and finally, west to the Salt Lake Valley. This early experience not only trained men in obedience and sacrifice but also prepared them to guide the Saints as they encountered unprecedented persecution, physical deprivation, and spiritual trials.

Joseph had known as early as June 1829 that twelve Apostles would be chosen whose responsibility would be to preach the gospel to the nations of the earth, precisely as their ancient counterparts had. These men were to be "special witnesses of the name of Jesus Christ in all the world and would be selected by the Three Witnesses of the Book of Mormon, acting under divine revelation from God. They were to constitute a traveling, presiding high council, operating under the direction of three presiding high priests, consisting of the prophet and two counselors, and forming a quorum or "Presidency of the Church." Additionally, other men were to be appointed to serve as members of the quorums of Seventy and would be given responsibilities parallel to those of Christ's day. They also were to be "especial witnesses to the Gentiles and in all the world."[37]

On February 14, 1835, a carefully planned two-day conference of the Church was held, leading to the selection and ordination of the Twelve Apostles. The meetings began with a special address by the prophet Joseph, who used John 15 as the theme for his remarks. Emphasizing the necessity of one's union with Jesus, he used Christ's image of a branch's dependence on the vine if it would have life. "And greater love hath no man than this, that a man lay down his life for his friends." Love must become so great, he taught, that it will not withhold life as a sacrifice to friendship. "The Apostles," Joseph said, "are declared to be the friends of Christ." He counseled them regarding the Savior's words, "Ye have not chosen me, but I have chosen you and ordained you that you may bring forth much fruit." He instructed them that Jesus had

commanded them "to love one another" and to remember "that if the world hate you, ye know that it hated me before it hated you." Of humility he said, "The servant is not greater than his Lord," and then cautioned them, "If they persecuted me, they will persecute you." "But when the Comforter is come, even the Spirit of truth, he will testify of me," thus teaching those who would be called, "Ye also shall bear witness."[38]

After this stirring sermon, the prophet asked if they would sustain those called to be Apostles, under divine inspiration, and if they would be satisfied in carrying forward the plan that these men be chosen by the Three Witnesses as appointed by revelation. The proposal was unanimously approved. The conference then adjourned for a one-hour recess. The afternoon session began with a hymn and prayer, after which the Three Witnesses were called on in turn to pray, in the same order as they received their witness. The prophet and his two counselors then laid their hands upon the Three Witnesses and blessed them, after which the witnesses selected the Twelve Apostles and ordained them. Then the newly called Apostles received instructions and exhortations, principally from Oliver Cowdery. Following are two short excerpts:

The Lord gave us a revelation that, in process of time, there should be twelve men chosen to preach His Gospel to Jew and Gentile. Our minds have been on a constant stretch, to find who these twelve were; when the time should come we could not tell; but we sought the Lord by fasting and prayer to have our lives prolonged to see this day, to see you, and to take a retrospect of the difficulties through which we have passed; but having seen the day, it becomes my duty to deliver to you a charge; . . . You have many revelations put into your hands—revelations to make you acquainted with the nature of your mission; you will have difficulties by reasoning of your visiting all the nations of the world. You will need wisdom in a ten-fold proportion to what you have ever had; you will have to combat all the prejudices of all nations.

You have been indebted to other men, in the first instance, for evidence; on that you have acted; but it is necessary that you receive a testimony from heaven for yourselves; so that you can bear testimony to the truth of the Book of Mormon, and that you have seen the face of God. That is more than the testimony of an angel. When the proper time arrives, you shall be able to bear this testimony to the world. . . . Never cease striving until you have seen God face to face. Strengthen your faith; cast off your doubts, your sins, and all your unbelief; and nothing can prevent you from coming to God. Your ordination is not full and complete till God has laid his hand upon you. We require as much to qualify us as did those who have gone before. God is the same. If the Savior in former days laid His hands upon His disciples, why not in latter days?[39]

That God would reveal Himself to man is a foreign concept to a sectarian world. Yet Jacob had seen God "face to face" (Genesis 32:30); Moses and seventy elders of Israel saw God (Exodus 24:9–10); Moses knew the Lord "face to face" (Dueteronomy 34:10); and Isaiah also saw the Lord (Isaiah 6:5). The Apostles too were eyewitnesses of the Savior—of His ministry, of His miracles, of His atonement, of His suffering on the cross, and of His resurrection. They became special witnesses to all the world. Like the prophets of old, Joseph Smith also received many glorious visions, seeing both the Father and the Son. Similarly, the Apostles of this new dispensation, Oliver Cowdery taught, were

under no less obligation to become acquainted with God.

The Seventy were chosen two weeks later, on February 28, 1835. As with the Apostles, they were also selected from among those men who had offered up their lives by going to Missouri. "He could not organize His kingdom," Joseph taught, "unless they were a body of men . . . who had made as great a sacrifice as did Abraham."[40] Together, these two quorums would be responsible for opening up the preaching of the restored gospel to the entire world.

The Esoteric Meaning and Purpose of Temples Revealed Anew

Throughout the history of the world, temples have served a vital role in religious, political, cultural, social, and artistic settings. Upon Israel's release from Egypt, a revelation was given to Moses regarding the building of a tabernacle, its design, materials, and purpose. This sacred edifice was a central place of worship for the Israelites and included an outer court called the Holy Place and an inner sanctuary called the Holy of Holies. This portable house of God became permanent when Solomon constructed a magnificent temple at Jerusalem in about 1005 B.C. Unfortunately, because of Israel's wickedness, the temple became defiled and was destroyed in about 587 B.C. during the Babylonian siege. Judah was released by Cyrus of Persia in 537 B.C., and he permitted the Israelites to return to the Holy Land to rebuild the temple, which was completed in 515 B.C. Once again, apostasy was responsible for the physical and spiritual decay of God's temple. The Temple Scroll, recovered at Qumran, is now widely believed to be as credible and as important as any book in the Torah. About sixteen years before the

Savior's birth, the temple began to be rebuilt by Herod (taking nearly eighty years) and was later regarded by Jesus as His Father's house. The temple was considered sacred not only by Jesus during His lifetime but also by the Apostles, who continued "daily with one accord in the temple."

Although the specific location of Mount Sinai cannot be verified, the events that transpired there are considered holy by Jews, Muslims, and Christians. In this elevated, secluded setting, God appeared to Moses and revealed His law. Synonymous with the "mountain of the Lord's house" (Isaiah 2:2), the tabernacle and temples of ancient Israel, likewise, were places of worship where God could commune with His people. By definition, the idea of the temple itself embraced the specific characteristics of the root *QDS and the terms *bayit* and *templum*.[41] According to scholars, "the temple as *bayit* first and foremost became a 'house' where Deity 'tented' or 'tabernacled' among the people,"[42] becoming the "House of Yahweh," or the house of God. Isaiah had prophesied that in the last days "the mountain of the Lord's house" would be established "in the top of the mountains," that it would "be exalted above the hills" and that "all nations" would flow unto it (Isaiah 2:2). Shortly after the restoration of the Savior's Church, the purpose and meaning of temples was revealed anew.

In 1832 Joseph received the first-known revelation concerning temple building in this new dispensation:

Organize yourself; prepare every needful thing; and establish a house, even a house of prayer, a house of glory, a house of order, a house of God. . . . Verily I say unto you, it is my will that you should build a house. . . . Therefore, let it be built after the manner which I shall show unto three of you.[43]

Church members began construction on a temple at Kirtland, Ohio, in June 1833. At a staggering cost of about $200,000, the sacrifice required to fulfill this commandment from the Lord was enormous. The impoverished Saints, willing to offer all they possessed in order to be obedient, donated the required labor and money. In the final stages of construction, many women of the Church donated their treasured china, which was then ground and added as texture to the surfaces of the plaster and stucco walls, providing sparkle and luster. The design of this edifice was given by way of revelation, as with the tabernacle and with Solomon's temple (Exodus 25:8–9; 1 Chronicles 28:11–12); however, its full purpose had not yet been made known.

The temple was dedicated on Sunday, March 27, 1836, and was attended by nearly one thousand members of the Church. "A multitude were deprived of the benefits of the meeting" due to space limitations. A great Pentecostal scene unfolded at the end that was made all the more remarkable because there were so many witnesses. The meeting commenced at 9 A.M. with a scripture reading by Sidney Rigdon, followed by a hymn, the invocation, and another hymn. After addressing the congregation, Rigdon called for a sustaining vote of the prophet Joseph Smith, which was unanimously approved. This was followed by two more hymns and a short sermon by the prophet urging the members to sustain local authorities who had been called of God to serve.[44] After yet another hymn, Joseph Smith offered the dedicatory prayer by revelation. Following are some excerpts:

Thanks be to Thy name, O Lord God of Israel, who keepest covenant and sheweth mercy unto Thy servants who walk uprightly before Thee, with all their hearts; Thou who hast commanded Thy servants to build a house to Thy name in this place. And now Thou beholdest, O Lord, that Thy servants have done according to Thy commandment, And now we ask Thee, Holy Father, in the name of Jesus Christ, the Son of Thy bosom, in whose name alone, salvation can be administered to the children of men, we ask Thee O Lord, to accept this house, the workmanship of the hands of us, Thy servants, which thou didst command us to build; for Thou knowest that we have done this work through great tribulations; and out of our poverty we have given of our substance, to build a house to Thy name, that the Son of Man might have a place to manifest Himself to His people. . . . Remember Thy Church, Oh Lord, . . . that [it] may come forth out of the wilderness of darkness, and shine forth fair as the moon, clear as the sun, and terrible as an army with banners; And be adorned as a bride for that day when Thou shalt unveil the heavens, and cause the mountains to flow down at Thy presence. . . . O hear, O hear, O hear us O Lord! And answer these petitions, and accept the dedication of this house unto Thee, the work of our hands, which we have built unto Thy name.[45]

Following this stirring dedicatory prayer, the choir sang "The Spirit of God Like a Fire Is Burning," a hymn written for this occasion. Following is a portion of the hymn:

The Spirit of God like a fire is burning!
The latter-day glory begins to come forth;
The visions and blessings of old are returning,
The angels are coming to visit the earth.

After singing this six-verse hymn, the

prophet asked the congregation if they would accept the dedicatory prayer, and a unanimous vote approved the measure. Joseph then declared the building dedicated, and the Lord's Supper was blessed and distributed to the congregation. Many prominent elders, including the prophet, bore testimony, and the dedication session ended with a benediction.[46]

At a special meeting with priesthood leaders in the evening, at which 416 were present, Joseph proceeded to instruct the brethren in the ordinance of washing the feet. During the dedication, many had witnessed the presence of angels, and Joseph began to teach them about the spirit of prophecy. Following the prophet, George A. Smith, then a member of the Seventy, was speaking when, according to Joseph Smith's account, "a noise was heard like the sound of a rushing mighty wind, which filled the Temple, and all the congregation simultaneously arose, being moved upon by an invisible power; many began to speak in tongues and prophecy; others saw glorious visions; and I beheld the Temple was filled with angels, which fact I declared to the congregation. The people of the neighborhood came running together (hearing an unusual sound within, and seeing a bright light like a pillar of fire resting upon the Temple), and were astonished at what was taking place. This continued until the meeting closed at eleven P.M."[47]

Stunning parallels exist between the account recorded in the New Testament regarding the day of Pentecost and the Kirtland Temple experience: (1) both were observed by a multitude of witnesses; (2) both were viewed skeptically by the popular sectarian religions of the day; (3) both demonstrated the power of God, e.g., the spirit of prophecy, the gift of tongues, and visions; (4) both resulted in numerous converts; (5) both resulted in increased religious commitment and devotion to God; (6) both demonstrated the power of the Holy Ghost and the *rushing of a mighty wind that filled all the house;* (7) both shared an experience involving the *appearance* of fire: the cloven tongues of fire at the day of Pentecost and the pillar of fire resting on the temple at Kirtland; and (8) both confirmed the authority of God's chosen leadership to its existing members. As remarkable as this outpouring of the Spirit was, greater miracles and blessings were yet to follow.

On Sunday, April 3, 1836, after the afternoon worship service, Joseph and Oliver withdrew from the congregation and went to the west end of the temple on the lower floor to the Melchizedek Priesthood pulpits. Lowering a canvas partition, referred to as a veil, in order to secure privacy, they bowed their heads "in solemn, silent prayer." Rising from his knees, Joseph recorded that "the veil was taken from our minds, and the eyes of our understanding were opened. We saw the Lord standing upon the breastwork of the pulpit." Joseph then described the appearance of the Savior, saying that "his eyes were as a flame of fire; the hair of his head was white like the pure snow; his countenance shown above the brightness of the sun; and His voice was as the sound of the rushing of great waters." The resurrected Lord bore witness of His divine ministry, saying, "I am your advocate with the Father. Behold, your sins are forgiven you." Expressing His acceptance of the temple, the Savior said, "My name shall be here; and I will manifest myself to my people in mercy in this house. . . . And the fame of this house shall spread to foreign lands."[48]

After the vision of the Savior had closed, immediately the heavens again opened and Moses appeared, conferring upon Joseph and Oliver the keys of the *gathering of Israel.* Following this, another angelic messenger appeared committing to them the dispensation of Abraham, saying that "in us and our seed all generations after us should be blessed."[49]

When these visions had closed, Joseph testified that yet another "great and glorious vision burst upon us." Elijah the prophet appeared to them, saying, "Behold, the time has fully come, which was spoken by the mouth of Malachi—testifying the he [Elijah] should be sent before the great and dreadful day of the Lord come—To turn the hearts of the fathers to the children, and the children to the fathers, lest the whole earth be smitten with a curse." According to Joseph and Oliver, Elijah then said, "By this ye may know that the great and dreadful day of the Lord is near, even at the doors."[50]

The significance of these visions to Joseph and Oliver and the infant Church were staggering. Piece by piece, the fullness of the gospel was being restored. What began with the Book of Mormon continued with the restoration of the priesthood, the organization of the Church, and the establishment of the priesthood leadership structure, including "priesthood quorums." Now the keys that were originally given by Jesus to the Apostles of old were gradually being transferred to Joseph. The keys of the Melchizedek Priesthood had already been received from Peter, James, and John. With the keys received from Moses, the gathering of dispersed Israel could begin; with the "keys" associated with the promises made to Abraham, those accepting the gospel could now be adopted into the house of Israel and claim the promises given to Abraham. Finally, with the return of Elijah (Malachi 4:5–6), the hearts of the fathers would soon be turned to the children, and the children to the fathers. But what did that mean?

The Mission of Elijah and Baptism for the Dead

The secular world has long questioned the possible interpretation of "turning the hearts of the fathers to the children" and vice versa. In other words, what could be so important that if Elijah did not return, as Malachi prophesied, the whole earth would be "utterly wasted" at the Savior's second coming. As the restoration unfolded, doctrinal revelations to the prophet Joseph Smith restored such truths, known to the ancient Church but lost because of apostasy. The early Christians believed the gospel would be taught to those who had died but who perished without the law, meaning without having known of the Savior and His teachings. They believed that such deceased persons, based upon the principle of the Two Ways, would be able to exercise agency and thus choose to either accept or reject the Savior and His teachings. The primitive Church also performed baptisms for the dead. From the Shepherd of Hermas, we recall that the New Testament Church believed in the joining together of dispensations, that all true believers, from every age, would have the opportunity of receiving the "seal" of baptism.

In 1842 Joseph received a revelation that brought clarity to all that had been revealed previously during the Restoration. Beginning with the account of Peter receiving the "keys of the kingdom" (Matthew 16:19) from Jesus, Joseph taught that this power "to bind on earth" and have the action bound in heaven had significant meaning. "Binding," he explained, also referred to "recording," thus "whatsoever you record on earth shall be recorded in heaven, . . . for out of the books shall your dead be judged, according to their own works." Joseph realized that this doctrine would be considered "bold" to modern Christians. "Nevertheless," he said, "in all ages of the world, whenever the Lord has given a dispensation of the priesthood to any man (prophet), by actual revelation, or any set of men, this power (to bind on earth and in heaven) has always been given."[51]

Illuminating the connection between baptism for the living and the dead, Joseph recorded: "The ordinance of baptism by water, to be immersed therein in order to answer to the likeness of the dead, that one principle might accord with the other; to be immersed in the water and come forth out of the water is in the likeness of the resurrection of the dead in coming forth out of their graves; hence, this ordinance was instituted to form a relationship with the ordinance of baptism for the dead, being in the likeness of the dead." Insight from a prophet of God helps us to see that the symbolism associated with being born again reaches out to and embodies both baptism for the living and the dead. "Consequently," Joseph taught, "the baptismal font was instituted as a similitude of the grave."[52]

Explaining the importance of this teaching, Joseph testified, "And now my dearly beloved brothers and sisters, let me assure you that these are principles in relation to the dead and the living that cannot be lightly passed over, as pertaining to our salvation. For their salvation is necessary and essential to our salvation, as Paul says concerning the fathers—that they without us cannot be made perfect—neither can we without our dead be made perfect" (Hebrews 11:40).[53] Malachi's prophecy now begins to assume new meaning. Inasmuch as vast numbers have died "without the law," and since Christ died for all, everyone must have the opportunity, either in mortality or after death, to hear the gospel plan. Subsequently, upon the principle of the Two Ways, men must choose, either to accept God's plan, or reject it. If they accept it, they must be "born again," either in mortality, or by proxy after death. Hence, the mission of Elijah was to turn the hearts of the fathers to the children, or in other words, to plead with heaven that the hearts of their descendants would be softened and inspired to perform this earthly work for them, which they had been denied in mortality. In the matter of turning the hearts of the children to the fathers, Joseph explained that genealogical research must be performed and, in this manner, the living could *seek after* their departed ancestors in order to perform for them the work they could not perform for themselves. In this manner, the "seal" of baptism could be placed upon all the righteous who love God and desire to serve Him through the gift of His Son Jesus.

In summary, Joseph revealed, "There is a welding link . . . between the fathers and the children." This link, he taught, is baptism for the dead. The cumulative effect of this process, he prophesied, is that "a whole and complete and perfect union, and welding together of dispensations, and keys, and powers, and glories shall take place." Through these sacred ordinances, all those who loved righteousness, from Adam through the end of the world, would be sealed to Christ, who bought us with His own blood. This was the essence of the teachings of the early Christian Church, revealed anew in the dispensation of the fullness of times.[54]

Eternal Marriage

The Gospel of Philip provides an incomplete and controversial account of eternal marriage. Marriage was considered a mystery by the early Church and little is written about the subject in the standard canon or the Apocrypha. Matthew 22:30 is often used as evidence that "eternal marriage" is

not a true Christian tenet. Further research demonstrates that this position is weak. The example used by Jesus may have been a real-life situation found in one of the twelve books of the Apocrypha, the book of Tobit, where we read of a woman named Sara who had married seven brothers in succession, each of whom died on the wedding night. The angel Raphael was sent to ensure that one of her cousins, Tobit, for whom she had been destined all along, arrange for them to meet and marry, suggesting that she was married or "sealed" to Tobit but not the other seven men. That may be one of the reasons why Jesus told the Sadducees that they didn't know the scriptures; they left out the information about the eighth husband.[55]

Marriage, like baptism, Joseph explained, is an earthly ordinance and must be authoritatively performed in mortality, that "whatsoever thou shalt bind on earth shall be bound in heaven" (Matthew 16:19). The priesthood authority to "bind," he said, is the critical factor. For "whatsoever things are not by me shall be shaken and destroyed." Consequently, those married without the same authority given to Peter, marry only for the duration of mortality: "If a man marry him a wife in the world, and he marry her not by me nor by my word, and he covenant with her so long as he is in the world and she with him, their covenant and marriage are not of force when they are dead, . . . therefore, when they are out of the world they neither marry nor are given in marriage; but are appointed angels in heaven." This revelation is consistent with Matthew 22:30 and also with marriage vows that state "until death do us part," or "as long as you both shall live."[56]

Joseph Smith brought clarity to a sacred, and yet "mysterious," teaching. In his doing so, God revealed through him one of the most touching and pleasing doctrines ever imparted from heaven to man. Marriage, as ordained of God, is the most profound of all relationships on earth. The potential for true affection, trust, selfless service, companionship, and joy—in short, love—is enormous. The blessing of bringing children into the world, of teaching them, loving them, and serving them has no worldly equal. To imagine a separation at death when a godly couple has sought the unity taught in the Bible is unscriptural and unthinkable. The Lord, clarifying what was *unclear* in the Gospel of Philip, revealed through Joseph:

> If a man marry a wife by my word, which is my law, and by the new and everlasting covenant, and if it is sealed unto them by the Holy Spirit of promise, by him who is anointed, unto whom I have appointed this power and the keys of this priesthood; and it shall be said unto them—ye shall come forth in the first resurrection; and . . . it shall be done unto them in all things whatsoever my servant hath put upon them, in time, and through all eternity; and shall be of full force when they are out of the world.[57]

Families, Joseph explained, could be sealed together forever by the priesthood, which is the power to bind authoritatively in heaven what has been bound on earth.

The temple dedication at Kirtland was an important event in the progression of the Restoration. Once again, an authorized house of the Lord had been established in His name. Soon, ordinances familiar to the early Christians would be revealed anew in this latter-day dispensation. Another temple would shortly be built in Nauvoo, Illinois, and then, by divine design, the Saints would ultimately locate in the midst of the Rocky Mountains. There they would dedicate another temple to God; it would become the mountain of the Lord's house, and as a result of missionaries traveling the world over, all nations would flow unto it.

The Dispensation of the Fulness of Times

The prophet Daniel prophesied concerning the end the world. In the well-known dream that he both identified and interpreted for King Nebuchadnezzer, he beheld a great image or idol, with a head of gold, the breast and arms made of silver, the belly and thighs were brass, the legs were made of iron, and the feet consisted of a combination of iron and clay. Daniel observed that a stone smote the image, breaking it into pieces, and that the stone became a mountain that filled the earth. Daniel's prophetic interpretation said that the various materials comprising the image were kingdoms of the earth that would eventually break into pieces:

> And in the days of these kings shall the God of heaven set up a kingdom, which shall never be destroyed: and the kingdom shall not be left to other people, but it shall break in pieces and consume all these kingdoms, and it shall stand for ever. Forasmuch as thou sawest that the stone was cut out of the mountain without hands, and that it brake in pieces the iron, the brass, the clay, the silver, and the gold; the great God hath made known to the king what shall come to pass hereafter. (Daniel 2:44–45)

The early Christian bishop Hippolytus explained his view of Daniel's prophecy: The "lion" coming up "from the sea" (Daniel 7:4, 3), he taught, symbolized the Babylonian dynasty and is the head of gold referred to by Daniel. The "eagle's wings" (Daniel 7:4) portrayed Nebuchadnezzar's pride in exalting himself above God; thus, his wings were plucked and his glory was destroyed. The second beast that Daniel saw was "like to a bear" (Daniel 7:5), it denoted the Persians who followed Babylonia to power. In depicting "three ribs in the mouth of it" (Daniel 7:5), the prophecy pointed to three nations—the Persians, Medes, and Babylonians—represented by the silver following the gold. The third beast was "like a leopard" (Daniel 7:6), meaning the Greeks; "for after the Persians," Hippolytus said, "Alexander of Macedon obtained the sovereign power on subverting Darius," being shown by the brass on the image. In explaining the "four wings of a fowl," the prophecy alluded to the "four heads" (Daniel 7:6), or, rather, four kingdoms, which were partitioned from Alexander's kingdom at his death. The fourth beast was described as "dreadful and terrible," with "iron teeth" (Daniel 7:7). This powerful political kingdom, depicted by the iron, was the Roman Empire, which controlled Asia and Europe during Hippolytus's life. This mighty nation, Hippolytus predicted, would be followed by the toes of the feet made of iron and clay and from which other kings would arise. "The ten toes of the image," he said, "are in the future . . . and are equivalent to (so many) democracies." Finally, Hippolytus, concluded:

> After a little space the stone will *come from heaven* which smites the images and breaks it in pieces, and subverts all the kingdoms, and gives the kingdom to the saints of the Most High. This is the stone which becomes a great mountain, and fills the whole earth.[58]

Joseph Smith declared that the dispensation he ushered in was the great latter-day kingdom prophesied by Daniel. All of the other kingdoms, he said, were made with hands and were earthly political governments. By contrast, the restoration of primitive Christianity, effected by God Himself, was made without hands and would one day "fill the whole earth."

Recently, Harold Bloom, an acclaimed American literary critic, has written a compelling thesis entitled *The American Religion: The Emergence of the Post-Christian Nation.* Recognizing the significant achievements of the prophet Joseph Smith, he wrote:

> I . . . do not find it possible to doubt that Joseph Smith was an authentic prophet. Where in all of American history can we find his match? . . . I can only attribute to his genius or daemon his uncanny recovery of elements in ancient Jewish theurgy that had ceased to be available either to normative Judaism or to Christianity, and that survived only in esoteric traditions unlikely to have touched Smith directly. . . . As an unbeliever, I marvel at his intuitive understanding of the permanent religious dilemmas of our country.[59]

No one in 1830 would have predicted the rise of The Church of Jesus Christ of Latter-day Saints as it has unfolded. What began in humble circumstances in the Whitmer home in Fayette, New York, with six official members, has ballooned to more than twelve million members worldwide (2004) and is projected to grow to 265 million by 2080.[60] This, Joseph asserted, is the dispensation that was prophesied by Paul (Ephesians 1:10) and all the holy prophets since the world began (Acts 3:21), wherein all of the knowledge from every previous dispensation would be "gathered together in one" and called the "dispensation of the fullness of times." Two years before his martyrdom, Joseph, writing to a Chicago journalist, prophetically proclaimed:

> The standard of truth has been erected; no unhallowed hand can stop the work

from progressing; persecutions may rage, mobs may combine, armies may assemble, calumny may defame, but the truth of God will go forth boldly, nobly, and independent, till it has penetrated every continent, visited every climb, swept every country, and sounded in every ear, till the purposes of God shall be accomplished, and the Great Jehovah shall say the work is done.[61]

Conclusion

Reason and evidence combine to demonstrate that God revealed a single plan for man's salvation following Adam's fall. Heavenly Father's plan contained instructions and commandments that would be required from His household on earth, including the development of faith in Jesus Christ and participation in covenants involving ritual ordinances also necessary for salvation. This plan has been revealed to man in every dispensation through God's stewards, known as prophets and seers. Apostasy has been described in many ways in this volume but perhaps most vividly as man turning his back on God by breaking his covenant with deity and choosing to follow his own selfish desires rather than the inspired course revealed through God's prophets.

Apostasy has certainly occurred in every dispensation, including that period following the death of the Apostles. However, the resolution of such apostasy is a matter of opinion and most will draw their own conclusions, which may differ from those in this volume. Happily, we know that God is a loving God who loves *all* of His children and desires that each of us returns to His presence. Thus, this book does not condemn any religion, knowing that many faiths contain significant truth that is pleasing to God. By the same token, it attempts to emphasize in a positive light

those whose teachings seem to align most closely with the teachings of Jesus Himself and whose practices resemble the Church He established anciently.

In the not-too-distant future, the Savior of mankind will surely return to earth in His glorious second coming. Although we do not know God's timing, we would be unwise to put off this most important search for truth, in light of the Savior's parable regarding the five unfaithful virgins who did not keep their lamps trimmed and filled with oil. Whether we are Catholic or Protestant, Mormon or Jew, Muslim or Budhist, we are *all* the children of the same loving God and He desires, even *yearns,* that we will heed the voice of *His* prophets, past and present.

The Bible, filled with the love of God and in harmony with other ancient inspired writings, indicates that *all* of the Father's children who know and love Jesus Christ, and who follow Him according to the dictates of conscience, including that portion of revealed truth which each has received, will be caught up to meet the Savior when He comes again. Paul taught us that we must prove all things and hold fast to that which is good (1 Thessalonians 5:21). The Bible is plain that God will answer the prayer of the humble and those who have sufficient faith to follow the promptings of the Holy Spirit when He calls us, as it were, *by our own name* (Isaiah 43:1). Prophets have revealed God to man on earth for millennia; prophets are once again upon the earth, declaring the fullness of His gospel as in dispensations past.

Notes

1. Apokatastasis, *Strong's Exhaustive Concordance,* ref. no. 605, 1482.

2. Apo, ref. no. 575 and Kathistemi, ref. no. 2525 (2596+2476), in *Strong's Exhaustive Concordance,* 1481, 2513; see also Grimm, *Thayer's Greek-*

English Lexicon, 314.

3. Kairos, ref. no. 2540 and Chronos, ref. no. 5550, in *Strong's Exhaustive Concordance*, 1506, 1542; see also 318.

4. Kairos, ref. no. 2540 in Grimm, *Strong's Exhaustive Concordance*, 1506, and 318.

5. This idea is described in Richard L. Anderson, *Guide to Acts and the Apostles' Letters*, 3d ed. rev. (Provo, Utah: Foundation for Ancient Research and Mormon Studies, 1999), 5.

6. Like Martin Luther, John Calvin, John Wesley, and many others of the Reformation and Great Awakening periods, Joseph Smith was concerned with the welfare of his own soul when he was a young man. See Richard L. Bushman, *The Beginnings of Mormonism* (Urbana: University of Illinois Press, 1984), 53; see ch. 2, 204 n30, in Bushman's work for a detailed origin of Joseph's statement.

7. See John W. Welch, ed., *Reexploring the Book of Mormon* (Salt Lake City: Deseret Book; Provo, Utah: Foundation for Ancient Research and Mormon Studies, 1992), and Donald W. Parry, Daniel C. Peterson, and John W. Welch, ed., *Echoes and Evidences of the Book of Mormon* (Provo, Utah: Foundation for Ancient Research and Mormon Studies, 2002), for a full treatment of modern scholarship not known in 1830 but documented in recent years.

8. Welch, *Reexploring*, 1–5.

9. D&C 9:7–9; Bushman, *Beginnings of Mormonism*, 86.

10. Bushman, *Beginnings of Mormonism*, 87.

11. Joseph Smith, *History of the Church of Jesus Christ of Latter-day Saints*, ed. B. H. Roberts, 2d ed. rev., 7 vols. (Salt Lake City: The Church of Jesus Christ of Latter-day Saints, 1932–51), 1:64–65; Bushman, *Beginnings of Mormonism*, 87–88.

12. For a more complete account refuting Charles Anthon's version of his encounter with Martin Harris, see Welch, *Reexploring the Book of Mormon*, 73–75.

13. Jessee, "Joseph Knight's Recollection," 35, in Bushman, *Beginnings of Mormonism*, 89.

14. Pomeroy Tucker, *Origin, Rise, and Progress of Mormonism* (New York: D. Appleton and Co., 1867), 42; Bushman, *Beginnings of Mormonism*, 89.

15. Bushman, *Beginnings of Mormonism*, 90; Edward Stevenson, "Incidents in the Life of Martin Harris," *Millennial Star* 44 (February 6, 1882): 86–87.

16. Lucy Mack Smith, *The History of Joseph Smith by His Mother*, rev. George A. Smith and Elias Smith (American Fork, Utah: Covenant Communications, 2000), 160; Bushman, *Beginnings of Mormonism*, 90–91.

17. Smith, *History of Joseph Smith by His Mother*, 164–66.

18. Smith, *History of Joseph Smith by His Mother*, 173–74.

19. Smith, *History of Joseph Smith by His Mother*, 174–75; D&C 3:5–9.

20. Bushman, *Beginnings of Mormonism*, 93.

21. Porter, "Study of Origins of The Church of Jesus Christ of Latter-day Saint in the States of New York and Pennsylvania, 1816–1831" (Ph.D. diss., Brigham Young University, 1971; Provo, Utah: BYU Studies and Joseph Fielding Smith Institute for Latter-day Saint History, 2000), 151–53; Lucy Mack Smith, *Biographical Sketches of Joseph Smith the Prophet: And His Progenitors for Many Generations* (Orem, Utah: Grandin, 1995), 124. Emma gave this account in an interview February 4–10, 1879, with her son Joseph Smith III, published in *Saints Herald* (Plano, Iowa, October 1, 1879): 289–90; cf. Bushman, *Beginnings of Mormonism*, 96.

22. Smith, *History of Joseph Smith by His Mother*, 180–82.

23. Smith, *History of Joseph Smith by His Mother*, 184; Bushman, *Beginnings of Mormonism*, 97.

24. Oliver Cowdery, *Messenger and Advocate* 1 (October 1834): 14–16.

25. D&C 6:14, 22–23; Smith, *History of the Church*, 1:35.

26. Oliver Cowdery.

27. *Messenger and Advocate* 1 (October 1834); Joseph Smith, *History of the Church*, 1:39; D&C 13.

28. Smith, *History of the Church*, 1:40–41.

29. Smith, *History of the Church*, 1:42–43.

30. Smith, *History of the Church*, 1:44.

31. *Messenger and Advocate* 1 (October 1834).

32. D&C 27:5.

33. D&C 128:20; 27:5, 7, 12–13.

34. Smith, *History of the Church,* 1:77–79; David Whitmer reports that about twenty came from Colesville, fifteen from Manchester, and twenty from the Fayette area. Journal of Edward Stevenson, January 2, 1887.

35. Smith, *History of Joseph Smith by His Mother,* 223; Lucy's dream, 59–60; Joseph Sr.'s dreams, 63–66, 88–90, 94.

36. B. H. Roberts, *A Comprehensive History of The Church of Jesus Christ of Latter-day Saints, Century One,* 6 vols. (Salt Lake City: Deseret News Press, 1930), 1:370–71.

37. Regarding the calling of the Apostles by the Three Witnesses; see D&C 18:27, 37. Regarding the organization of the priesthood and apostolic responsibilities; see D&C 107.

38. Roberts, *Comprehensive History,* 1:373.

39. Smith, *History of the Church,* 1:186; 195–96.

40. Smith, *History of the Church,* 1:182, notes, under Joseph Young's recording of Joseph Smith's address to the Seventy.

41. Donald W. Parry, ed., *Temples of the Ancient World: Ritual and Symbolism* (Salt Lake City: Deseret Book; Provo, Utah: Foundation for Ancient Research and Mormon Study, 1994), xiv.

42. Parry, *Temples of the Ancient World,* xiv.

43. D&C 88:119; 95:8, 14.

44. Smith, *History of the Church,* 2:410–19.

45. Smith, *History of the Church,* 2:420–26.

46. Smith, *History of the Church,* 2:426–28.

47. Smith, *History of the Church,* 2:428; see also Milton V. Backman, *The Heavens Resound: A History of the Latter-day Saints in Ohio, 1830–1838* (Salt Lake City: Deseret Book, 1983), 300.

48. Smith, *History of the Church,* 2:434–35; see also D&C 110:1–10.

49. Smith, *History of the Church,* 2:435; see also D&C 110:11–12.

50. Smith, *History of the Church,* 2:436; see also D&C 110:13–16.

51. D&C 128:8–9.

52. D&C 128:12–13.

53. D&C 128:15.

54. D&C 128:18.

55. Tobit 3:17; 6:17; early Christian scholar John Tvedtness has suggested that this is a plausible answer.

56. D&C 132:15.

57. D&C 132:19.

58. Hippolytus, Treatise on Christ and Antichrist, in *Ante-Nicene Fathers,* 5:208–9.

59. Harold Bloom, *The American Religion: The Emergence of the Post Christian Nation* (New York: Simon and Schuster, 1992), 95, 101, 127.

60. Jeffrey L. Sheler, "The Mormon Moment," *U.S. News and World Report,* November 13, 2000. According to Rodney Stark, professor of sociology and religion at the University of Washington, "If current trends hold, . . . Latter-day Saints [would be] second only to Roman Catholics among Christian bodies."

61. Smith, *History of the Church,* 4:540.

A BRIEF HISTORY OF JOSEPH SMITH JR.

Beware of false prophets, which come to you in sheep's clothing, but inwardly they are ravening wolves. Ye shall know them by their fruits. Do men gather grapes of thorns, or figs of thistles? Even so every good tree bringeth forth good fruit. . . . A good tree cannot bring forth evil fruit, neither can a corrupt tree bring forth good fruit. . . . Wherefore by their fruits ye shall know them.

—Matthew 7:15–18, 20

Joseph Smith Jr. was a remarkable man. Of that there seems to be little room for doubt. But a prophet? That is perhaps a more important question than appears on the surface. While a portion of his major doctrinal and organizational contributions have been covered in the main text, in order to acquaint the curious with a more complete history of this man whom millions believe to have been a prophet of God, the following provides additional information about his environment, his family, and the man himself.

The First Vision of an American Prophet

Joseph's preoccupation with salvation began about the age of twelve, during the winter of 1817 or early in the spring of 1818. This interest probably followed the revivals of 1816–17 in western New York, the effects of which were still being felt in Palmyra. Joseph stated that his keen interest in religion and salvation led him to "searching the Scriptures."[1] In July 1819, the Methodist clergy in the region held a conference lasting one week, which drew about 110 ministers from a five-hundred-mile radius, where they received instruction and policy from Bishop R. R. Robert. Typically during such conferences, people gathered from miles away to hear various ministers preach in between sessions. Joseph later recalled:

Some time in the second year of our

339

of his great uneasiness on the subject of religion and his significant desire to be saved, he had never before attempted an audible prayer. Wanting complete seclusion, he looked around to make certain he was alone. Then, kneeling down, he began to "offer up the desires of [his] heart to God." Suddenly, Joseph was "seized upon" by some force from the unseen world which began to overpower him, binding his tongue so that he could not speak. "Thick darkness," he said, "gathered around me, and it seemed to me for a time as if I were doomed to sudden destruction." Joseph exerted all his mental ability to call upon God to release him from this unseen enemy. Just at the moment when he was ready to give up in despair, he was released from this dark enemy when he saw "a pillar of light" directly over his head. Joseph then testified:

> When the light rested upon me I saw two Personages, whose brightness and glory defy all description, standing above me in the air. One of them spake unto me, calling me by name and said, pointing to the other—*This is My Beloved Son. Hear Him!*[13]

One would hardly expect that Joseph would be given God's entire plan regarding the last times in one setting—God had never done so in the past. But there had been two pressing questions on Joseph's mind. In 1832, when he first recorded his vision, he was still a very young man, only twenty-six years of age. Thus, this early written account is from a limited and more personal perspective. Joseph wrote that when "the pillar of light" came down "he was filled with the Spirit of God." "The Lord opened the heavens upon me and I saw the Lord and he spake unto me saying, Joseph my son thy sins are forgiven thee, go thy way, walk in my statutes and keep my commandments. Behold, I am the Lord

of glory. I was crucified for the world that all those who believe on my name may have Eternal life."[14] Joseph now had the answer to the question of his eternal salvation.

The other object that troubled Joseph was the sins of the world, contention, and the divided churches. To this the Lord replied, "The world lieth in sin at this time and none doeth good, no not one. They have turned aside from the Gospel and keep not my commandments. They draw near to me with their lips while their hearts are far from me and mine anger is kindling against the inhabitants of the earth."[15] Plainly, the Lord was *not* saying to Joseph that all of His children (including Joseph) were evil; rather, that none were worshiping Him in a pleasing manner—nor could they until His authority and truth had been restored once again. That God would be displeased with error and incorrect forms of worship, such as with Cain's feigned sacrifice, is self-evident. Joseph now had the answer he sought as to which church he should join: The Lord told him that none of the churches on earth contained a fulness of truth.

Several years later, Joseph's understanding of the scope of the restoration had increased. Accordingly, an account he wrote in 1835 revealed additional details of his first vision:

> "My tongue was swollen in my mouth, so that I could not utter. . . ." Hearing a noise behind him, Joseph became concerned: "I strove again to pray, but could not; the noise of walking seemed to draw nearer, I sprang upon my feet and looked round, but saw no person."[16]

By 1838 Joseph recognized the true significance of his vision. Although Joseph's eternal salvation and his question as to which church he should join were of personal significance, they paled in comparison to God's grand design. The vision was a parting of the heavens, the opening of a new dispensation. This vision was not about Joseph, it was about God's plan to restore the fulness of the gospel once more upon earth; it was a prelude to the final gathering of Israel in the last days in preparation for the second advent of Jesus Christ. Thus, in 1838, Joseph recorded that God the Father appeared *with* His Son Jesus Christ. For nearly seventeen hundred years, Christianity had misunderstood the very nature of God. In Joseph's vision, the distortion of that fundamental truth was made clear once and for all, as the same clarity of doctrine that was available to Jesus' Apostles now was restored. In his *finished* narrative, he did not refer to personal forgiveness; instead, he focused on the Savior's message of apostasy and restoration. When Joseph inquired as to which church was right, the Lord informed him:

> I must join none of them, for they were all wrong, and the Personage who addressed me said that all their creeds were an abomination in his sight: that those professors were all corrupt; that: "they draw near to me with their lips, but their hearts are far from me, they teach for doctrines the commandments of men, having a form of godliness, but they deny the power thereof.[17]

As the vision closed, Joseph found himself lying on his back looking up toward heaven. Joseph reported that he "had no strength" but soon recovered sufficiently to walk back to his house. He did not immediately tell anyone of his experience; however, as he was leaning upon the fireplace, his weakness must have been evident. His mother asked him if anything was wrong, to which he replied, "Never mind, all is well—I am well enough off. . . . I have learned for myself that Presbyterianism is not true."[18] When Luther, Calvin, and Wesley became converted to the Lord and

were prevailed upon by the Holy Spirit, each received a personal assurance of God's love for them and of His forgiveness of their sins. Similarly, Joseph now received this same conviction. "My soul was filled with love and for many days I could rejoice with great joy and the Lord was with me."[19]

Several days later, he related his experience to a Methodist minister. Being young and naive, Joseph was surprised at the preacher's consequent ridicule and instant rebuke. What he may not have known is how the Christian world viewed visions. Richard Bushman offered the following perspective:

> The preacher reacted quickly, not because of the strangeness of Joseph's story but because of its familiarity. Subjects of revivals all too often claimed to have seen visions. In 1825 a teacher in a Palmyra Academy said she saw Christ descend "in a glare of brightness exceeding tenfold the brilliancy of the meridian Sun." The *Wayne Sentinel* in 1823 reported Asa Wild's vision of Christ in Amsterdam, New York, and the message that all denominations were corrupt.[20]

Nevertheless, at Joseph's young age, he could scarcely believe the contempt with which he was being treated by this clergyman and by many others who later learned of his claim:

> I soon found, however, that my telling the story had excited a great deal of prejudice against me among professors of religion, and was the cause of great persecution, which continued to increase; and though I was an obscure boy, only between fourteen and fifteen years of age, and my circumstances in life such as to make a boy of no consequence in the world, yet men of high standing would take notice sufficient

to excite the public mind against me, and create a bitter persecution; and this was common among all the sects—all united to persecute me.[21]

Although the mainstream clergy lumped Joseph's vision together with many others they attributed to charlatans, there is an interesting contrast between the examples listed above, including the account of Mother Ann Lee of the Shakers, and the experience of Joseph Smith. Many of those purporting unusual visions used them as a licence to commit immoral acts or to significantly alter established biblical doctrines.[22] Joseph, on the other hand, was not a party to any such unrighteous behavior, nor did the doctrines he eventually taught depart from any scriptural text. In fact, the theology later revealed through the young prophet was virtually identical to the doctrines of the early Church, which doctrines were not known to him or published at this early date. The writings of the early Roman bishop Hippolytus testified that the antichrist impersonates the Savior in every detail and "seeks to liken himself in all things to the Son of God."[23] But Joseph's message was always consistent and unspectacular; it did not contain any elements of hysteria and emotionalism common with revivalism. Rather, it was very much like any Old Testament account, such as at Stephen's death (Acts 7:55–56), or comparable to Paul's experience on the road to Damascus (Acts 9:3–6):

I had actually seen a light, and in the midst of that light I saw two Personages, and they did in reality speak to me; and though I was hated and persecuted for saying that I had seen a vision, yet it was true; and while they were persecuting me, reviling me, and speaking all manner of evil against me falsely for so saying, I was led to say in my heart: Why persecute me for telling the truth?

I have actually seen a vision; and who am I that I can withstand God, or why does the world think to make me deny what I have actually seen? For I had seen a vision; I knew it, and I knew that God knew it, and I could not deny it; neither dared I do it; at least I knew that by so doing I would offend God, and come under condemnation.[24]

In every dispensation, or whenever a prophet of God has been chosen, His pattern has been clear and unmistakable to the faithful. The Lord had called out on many previous occasions: "Abraham, Abraham"; "Moses, Moses"; "Samuel, Samuel." Now God spoke the name of Joseph. Like Samuel, Joseph was a young man holding few preconceived notions of God and His ways. His was a blank book on which God could begin to write and thus to mold and shape His young prophet so that the Savior's Church and priesthood could be restored once again upon the earth. But Joseph was not alone. He was blessed by a wonderful family who were deeply religious and who had carefully trained each child in principles of hard work, personal responsibility, patriotism, and independent thinking. With such support and with the Spirit of God upon him, he would marshal the extraordinary strength of character that would be required of him in becoming an instrument in the hands of God to bring forth a restoration of primitive Christianity.

Joseph Smith's Ancestry

Joseph Smith Jr. was born of God-fearing, noble ancestors who were respected and productive citizens. These character traits were diffused into Joseph and his siblings, creating strong family bonds and a love of life and liberty. Like the majority of unchurched Christians in western New York, they were not always affiliated with a particular denomination but lived according to the Savior's teachings as revealed in the New Testament.

During the height of the Puritan migration, Joseph's third-great-grandfather, Robert Smith, sailed from England to Boston in 1638 when he was just fifteen years old. He later wed Mary French and, after a short time, settled a few miles north of Salem in the farm village of Topsfield, Massachusetts, where they became the parents of ten children. At Robert's death in 1693, his estate was valued at 189 pounds, a large sum in those days. Samuel Smith was born in 1666. He and his wife, Rebecca, had nine children and were well regarded in the community at Topsfield. Evidently, Samuel had been a public servant, and it was recorded on the town and country records that he was a "gentleman."[25]

Joseph's great-grandfather, Samuel Jr., was born in 1714. He was a popular community leader and a strong supporter of America's war for independence. Priscilla Gould, Samuel's wife, was a descendent of the founder of Topsfield, and together they bore five children. When Priscilla died unexpectedly, Samuel married her cousin, also named Priscilla, and she raised the children, one of whom was Asael, Joseph's grandfather, born in 1744. Through his industry and integrity, Samuel was repeatedly elected to public office. He served as assessor, selectman, town clerk, representative to the General Court (legislature), and as a delegate to the Provincial Congress. Perhaps his greatest honor was that he was selected as moderator of the town meeting twenty times, a recognition that was "reserved for one who commanded universal respect." He was actively involved in the Revolution, during which time he served on the Committee of Safety. When Samuel Jr. died on November 14, 1785, his obituary in the *Salem Gazette* read that he "was esteemed

a man of integrity and uprightness, . . . a sincere friend to the liberties of his country, and a strenuous advocate for the doctrines of Christianity."[26]

Asael Smith wed Mary Duty at age twenty-three and moved from Topsfield to Tunbridge, Vermont, in June 1791. With his eleven children, they established four farms, cut from more than three hundred wilderness acres, in a ten-year period. Like his fathers before him, he was admired by the townspeople where he lived. Beginning in 1793, he was elected to nearly every office in the community during the nearly thirty-year period they resided in Tunbridge.[27]

Asael's religious views were similar to those of the Universalists. In an address to his family, he wrote:

> The soul is immortal. . . . Do all to God in a serious manner. When you think of him, speak of him, pray to him, or in any way make your addresses to his great majesty, be in good earnest. . . . And as to religion, study the nature of religion, and see whether it consists in outward formalities, or in the hidden man of the heart.[28]

Moreover, he believed that "God was going to raise up some branch of his family to be a great benefit to mankind."[29] Asael fully accepted Joseph's testimony of the First Vision and the events that transpired thereafter before his death in 1830.

Solomon and Lydia Mack were Joseph's maternal grandparents. Solomon was an adventurer, prone to accident and misfortune. Nevertheless, he was a hard-working and God-fearing man. Over many years, he had sought to provide well for his family but had encountered every kind of obstacle. During his productive years he showed little interest in church attendance or scripture reading. However, in 1810 a bout with rheumatism caused a change of heart. "After this I determined to follow phantoms no longer but to devote the rest of my life to the service of God and my family."[30] Later that year, he read the Bible and began praying frequently and sincerely. For the next ten years, before his death, he admonished his family and others to serve the Lord and to avoid the pursuit of worldly gain at the expense of serving God and family. Due to Solomon's many travels, Joseph's grandmother, Lydia, had borne the brunt of raising and teaching their large family. Lucy Mack, Joseph's mother, was Lydia and Solomon's youngest daughter. She attributed to her mother "all the religious instructions as well as most of the educational privileges which I had ever received."[31]

Joseph's parents, Joseph Sr. and Lucy, were also endowed with many of the virtues ascribed to their forebearers. Shortly before meeting Joseph, Lucy was mourning the death of her sister Lovina. In some despair, she sought the "change of heart" so often spoken "from the pulpit." She began reading the Bible regularly and "prayed incessantly." During her meditations, she was greatly perplexed about the course she should take:

> If I remain out of any church, the rest will all declare that I am in the wrong. No church will say I am right unless I unite with them, and this makes them witnesses against each other. How shall I decide, inasmuch as the Church of Christ in former days was not like any of them?[32]

After her marriage to Joseph on January 24, 1796, they obtained part ownership on one of the farms he had helped to build with his father, Asael. Additionally, they received a $1,000 gift from Lucy's brother, Stephen, and his business partner John Mudget. By all accounts, the young couple was off to a wonderful start. For the next six years, they continued farming in Tunbridge, during which time three children were born: a first son who died in childbirth; the second, Alvin, born February 11, 1798; and the third, Hyrum, born February 9, 1800.[33]

In 1802 Joseph and Lucy decided to rent out their farm and start up a mercantile operation in nearby Randolph, Vermont. The venture was funded by a Boston company that supplied $2,000 worth of goods on a line of credit. Although inventory sold quickly, it was bartered for commodity payments promised at harvest. During this same period, Joseph became interested in the ginseng root which grew wild in Vermont and held great value in China for its perceived health benefits. He obtained a substantial supply for which he was offered $3,000 from a merchant named Stevens. However, Joseph elected to bypass the middleman and handle the entire shipment himself in order to collect the retail price. Unfortunately, he was defrauded by Stevens's son, who collected the entire amount from the Chinese for both his father's crop and Joseph's. The sham was discovered by Stephen Mack; however, when Joseph pursued the swindler, he fled to Canada. Joseph and Lucy were now in desperate circumstances: the note on the mercantile goods he had purchased was due, the store shelves were empty, and his customers were unable to make good on their debts. Consequently, the Smiths were forced to sell the farm and to use the $1,000 wedding gift Lucy had saved in order to repay financial obligations. According to Lucy, they took this extreme step in order to escape the "embarrassment of debt" but soon found themselves under the "embarrassment of poverty." This series of financial misfortunes reduced the Smiths from farm ownership to farm tenancy, which required frequent moves.[34]

During this period, Lucy became critically ill. One physician diagnosed her with tuberculosis, the same disease that had taken her sisters, Lovisa and Lovina. Joseph came to her bedside, sobbing and in great distress. Taking her hand in his, he cried: "Oh Lucy! My wife! You must die. The doctors have given you up, and all say you cannot live." A woman of great faith, Lucy recalled that she "begged and pled" with the Lord that He would "spare her life" so that she could raise her children and comfort her husband. She made a covenant with God that she would serve Him and find religion, "whether it was in the Bible or wherever it might be found, even if it was to be obtained from heaven by prayer and faith." These thoughts regarding her husband, children, and "heavenly things" troubled her mind the entire night. Then, toward morning, she records that a voice spoke to her, saying, "Seek and ye shall find; knock, and it shall be opened unto you. Let your heart be comforted. Ye believe in God, believe also in me." Lucy immediately began to recover and resolved that she would never forget her promise to God.[35]

Without delay, Lucy continued her search for truth and salvation. She visited with numerous ministers and listened to many sermons, but her hunger and thirst remained. After a lengthy period, she learned of a minister "noted for his piety" who would be preaching the next Sabbath at the Presbyterian Church. Lucy attended, anxious in her "expectation of obtaining that which alone could satisfy my soul—the bread of eternal life." As the minister began preaching, she said, "I fixed my mind with breathless attention on the spirit and matter of the discourse, but all was emptiness, vanity, [and] vexation of the spirit." She wrote that his words fell upon her heart "like the chill" of a late winter blast upon an ear of ripening corn. "It did not fill the aching void," Lucy remembered, nor did it "satisfy the craving hunger of my soul."

Lucy determined to hold to her course of following the example given by Jesus and His Apostles. "I will hear all that can be said, read all that is written, but particularly the word of God shall be my guide to life and salvation, and I will endeavor to obtain if it is to be had by diligence and prayer." She followed this standard of discipline for many years but was eventually baptized by a minister who agreed to perform the rite without officially requiring her to become a member of his church. Lucy did not join with any denomination until 1820 during the period of the religious revivals in Palmyra, at which time she joined the Presbyterian church.[36]

In 1803 Lucy had a peculiar dream. In it she observed two beautiful and majestic trees standing at the edge of a lovely and spacious meadow with a pure and clear stream running by them. One of the trees was surrounded by a "bright belt that shone like burnished gold, but far more brilliantly." This particular tree appeared lively and animated, bending gracefully in the gentle breeze as if to express great joy and happiness in its motion. The belt also "partook of the same influence," moving in unison with the motion of the tree, continually increasing in "refulgence and magnitude until it became exceedingly glorious." In stark contrast, the other tree was like a pillar of marble and would not bend no matter how hard the wind blew. In her dream, she wondered about the meaning of these representations. While thus pondering, Lucy was given to know that the trees represented her husband and his older brother Jesse Smith:

> The stubborn and unyielding tree was like Jesse; the other, more pliant and flexible, was like Joseph my husband; that the breath of heaven, which passed over them, was the pure and undefiled Gospel of the Son of God, which Gospel Jesse would always resist, but which

Joseph, when he was more advanced in life, would hear and receive with his whole heart and rejoice therein; and unto him would be added intelligence, happiness, glory, and everlasting life.[37]

This dream was a great comfort to Lucy, because her husband, Joseph, was repulsed by the traditional churches of the day. On several occasions, she had been successful in convincing him to attend a Methodist church, but Asael, with his Universalist leanings, opposed his son's attendance at churches that limited God's grace to only some sinners.

Although Joseph Sr. refused to join any particular denomination, he was deeply religious. He insisted on having family prayer both morning and evening, he exercised faith when his children were ill, and he endeavored to abide biblical principles in his daily walk. His son William recalled: "My father's religious habits [were] strictly pious and moral." In spite of his attitude regarding existing denominations, he was influenced by the several revivals that occurred between 1799 and 1820. During the time of Lucy's father's conversion in 1810–11, Joseph Sr. "became much excited upon the subject of religion" but still held out for "the ancient order, as established by our Lord and . . . his Apostles."[38]

While in this period of heightened spiritual awareness, Joseph received a series of unusual dreams. Sometime in April 1811, after retiring to bed in a state of reflection about the "situation of the Christian religion," Lucy records that "he soon fell asleep" and experienced a vivid dream, which she wrote down "just as he told it to me the next morning." He found himself traveling in a barren field. Looking to the north, south, east, and west, he saw nothing except "dead, fallen timber." There was no evidence of life, either of animals or vegetation, and there prevailed a "deathlike" silence. Finding himself alone,

"with the exception of an attendant spirit, who kept constantly at my side," he inquired as to the meaning of what he saw. The spirit answered: "This field is the world which now lieth inanimate and dumb in regard to the true religion, . . . but travel on and . . . you will find . . . a box, the contents of which, if you eat thereof, will make you wise, and give you wisdom and understanding." As soon as Joseph came to the box and began tasting its contents, "all manner of beasts, horned cattle, and roaring animals rose up on every side in the most threatening manner possible, tearing the earth, tossing their horns and bellowing most terrifically all around me." Joseph perceived his dream to mean that the religions of the day were either barren and silent or wildly hostile to true wisdom and understanding; thus the beasts had prevented him from partaking of the contents of the box. According to Lucy, Joseph Sr. concluded "that there was no order or class of religionists that knew anymore concerning the kingdom of God" than those who "made no profession of religion whatever."[39]

From the period of the first financial setbacks in 1803 until 1812, many other family and temporal events shaped the future of the Smith family. Joseph was born on December 23, 1805, in Sharon, Vermont; Samuel Harrison was born in Tunbridge on March 13, 1808; another son, Ephraim, was born in March 1810 when the family resided in Royalton, but he died in his infancy; and William was born on March 13, 1811. Soon after William's birth, the family moved to Lebanon, New Hampshire, and Joseph and Lucy were in high spirits over the success that had attended their recent exertions. They felt to congratulate themselves for overcoming, against great odds, numerous challenges, and they now found themselves in comfortable and relatively prosperous circumstances.[40]

Optimism and abundance did not last long, however; calamity struck in 1812. Typhoid fever swept through the upper Connecticut Valley, leaving some six thousand dead in its wake. When the dreaded disease came into Lebanon, it "raged there horribly," afflicting the Smith children one by one. Only Joseph Sr. and Lucy escaped its ravages. Sophronia was critically ill for three months. The attending physician finally declared that "she was so far gone" it would be impossible for her to recover and, suspending care, he left. As the child lay "utterly motionless" with eyes wide open exhibiting the "hue of death," Joseph and Lucy fell upon their knees and began to pray, pouring out their "grief and supplication" into the ears of Him "who hath numbered the hair upon our heads." Lucy wrote: "Did the Lord hear our petition? He did hear it." However, when they arose, they observed that Sophronia was not breathing. Lucy wrapped the young child in a blanket and, holding her tightly in her arms, began pacing the floor. Those present attempted to persuade her that the child was dead. With tender emotion, Lucy recorded: "My reader, are you a parent? . . . Feel for your heart-strings. Can you tell me how I felt with my expiring child strained to my bosom, which thrilled with all a mother's love. . . . Would you then feel to deny that God had power to save, to the uttermost, all who call on him? I did not then and I do not now." Soon the child sobbed and looked up into her mother's eyes, having the "appearance of natural life" and breathing freely. With the fever now broken, Sophronia began to mend immediately until she fully recovered.[41]

All the children recovered; however, seven-year-old Joseph developed complications from the fever. Pain in his shoulder was incorrectly diagnosed as a sprain. Within a couple of weeks, a sore had formed in his armpit which, when the doctor lanced the site, immediately discharged a quart of purulent matter. Young Joseph said that upon receiving relief from his shoulder the pain "shot like lightening" down his side and into the marrow of the bone in his leg. In great anguish, the boy cried out, "Oh Father, the pain is so severe! How can I bear it?" During this period, a lifelong bond began to form between Joseph and his older brother Hyrum, who rarely left his side and often pressed the affected area, providing temporary relief. After three weeks, Joseph's condition became grave and this time a surgeon was called in, whereupon he made an eight-inch incision between his knee and ankle. The procedure relieved the pain immediately; however, as soon as the wound began to heal, the pain returned "as violent as ever." Another incision was made, this time to the bone, and once again relief was only passing. The swelling soon returned. A council of surgeons was called to determine what options existed, and it was decided that amputation was the only safe course open at this juncture. Refusing the idea of amputation, Lucy huddled the seven physicians together in a room separate from Joseph's and asked if any alternative procedures could be considered. Fortunately for Joseph, he was attended by Nathan Smith, one of the most acclaimed surgeons in New England, from the Dartmouth Medical College, who had developed an advanced procedure in removing only the diseased portion of the bone. Although amputation was recommended as the best and safest course, Lucy's will prevailed. During the surgery, young Joseph refused to be bound or to be given any brandy to sooth him, permitting only the presence and comfort of his father. According to Lucy, the surgeons cut nine large chunks of bone from his leg, and although Joseph cried out because of pain, he remained still, and the surgery was soon complete. This time he finally began to recover although, because of a number of complications, convalescence continued for nearly three years.[42]

The period spanning 1814–19 was extremely difficult for the Smiths. A series of setbacks and crop failures converged, finally compelling the family to leave New England and settle in western New York. Medical expenses arising from typhoid fever and Joseph's ordeal had left the family destitute once again. Under these difficult circumstances, Joseph Sr. decided to move the family to Norwich, Vermont. Successive crop failures in 1814 and 1815 persuaded him that he would attempt a successful harvest only one more year, but if that failed, the family would go to New York, "where farmers raise wheat in abundance." Summer never did arrive in 1816. Lucy wrote of an "untimely frost"; almanac records indicate that on June 8 that year several inches of snow covered the highlands of northern New York and New England. The temperature became so cold that ice formed on the ponds, and chilly, dry weather persisted throughout the summer. "This was enough." A firm decision was made to move to New York. After making arrangements to pay his debts, Joseph Sr. set out in advance for Palmyra. Lucy encountered considerable hardship in making the journey alone with her eight children. Debt repayment had left her with less than $80, and by journey's end, the only item of value remaining with which to pay the innkeeper was Sophronia's eardrops. Lucy was so emotionally spent by the time the family arrived in Palmyra, she recalled:

> The joy I felt in throwing myself and my children upon the care and affection of a tender husband and father doubly paid me for all that I had suffered. The children surrounded their father,

clinging to his neck, covering his face with tears and kisses that were heartily reciprocated by him.[43]

Through tireless labor, the family soon established themselves in Palmyra. By 1818 they owned their own farm and had erected a two-room log cabin. Utilizing every available skill and constant energy, they sold burned ash, cord wood, cakes, maple, and sugar; additionally, they manufactured and sold such small items as black ash baskets and birch brooms. Moreover, Alvin was now old enough to obtain labor, and it was by his achievement that the Smiths were able to make their second land payment. Accordingly, they now found themselves better off than any period preceding the misfortune of 1803.[44]

During this time, Joseph Sr. had two more dreams, or a total of seven, as recorded by his wife. In the sixth dream, Joseph was walking alone and much fatigued but seemed to realize he was going to a meeting, the Day of Judgment, and he realized that it was he who was to be judged. Upon arriving at the meetinghouse, he knocked to obtain admission but was informed that he was too late. "Presently," Joseph recalled, "I found that my flesh was perishing." Despite fervent prayer, his flesh continued to wither upon his bones. In a state of total despair, a porter or angel asked if Joseph had done all that was necessary in order to receive admission. "It then occurred to me to call upon God, in the name of his Son Jesus; and I cried out, in the agony of my soul, 'Oh, Lord God, I beseech thee, in the name of Jesus Christ, to forgive my sins.' After which I felt considerably strengthened and I began to mend." The angel then remarked that it was "necessary to plead the merits of Jesus, for he was the advocate with the Father" and the Mediator between God and man.[45]

Joseph's final dream was received in 1819. He met a man carrying a peddler's backpack who addressed him, saying, "Sir, will you trade with me today? I have now called on you seven times, I have traded with you each time, and have always found you strictly honest in all your dealings. . . . I have now come to tell you that this is the last time I shall ever call on you, and there is but one thing which you lack in order to secure your salvation." Joseph arose to get some paper, but in his excitement, he awoke.[46]

The Smith family history is one of success and triumph, but it is also laden with hardship and adversity. From the earliest ancestors coming from England to the time of Joseph's first vision, the Smiths were people of character, integrity, and industry. Although deeply religious, many family members had chosen not to join any of the sects of the day; instead, they read the Bible, discussed its teachings, prayed consistently, lived morally, and accepted the Savior and His atonement, always seeking after salvation. They were people of profound faith who had been carefully tempered and seasoned through distinctive trials. Asael, Lucy, and Joseph had each received inspired dreams that prepared them to accept the message Joseph Jr. would soon bring them. As with Joseph the carpenter and Mary, the Smith family were prepared by heaven in order that they might accept the great responsibilities that would be placed on their shoulders.

Heavenly Instruction

Joseph Smith's first vision occurred sometime in the spring of 1820, when he was just fourteen years old. Although he was subjected to continuous ridicule after relating his vision to one of the local ministers, and subsequently by many townspeople when his

experience became common knowledge, he never gave up his cheery disposition. Importantly, the Lord allowed for the development of the young prophet as he was tutored by heaven and prepared to carry out his future role. Not surprising, everyday life was basically the same for Joseph, who wrote, "I continued to pursue my common vocation." Responsibility for clearing land, planting and harvesting crops, chores in the barnyard, and earning additional income away from the farm during the growing season—these were all a part of Joseph's daily work week. He was entering the age of his greatest productivity at home, where he was capable of heavy labor and earning additional income for the family that was not yet being laid away for his adult years.[47]

Little is recorded of Joseph's spiritual meditations, thoughts, or experiences in the years immediately following his first vision. Although still a boy, his world was now filtered through a different lens, and he was keenly aware of his actions and personal weaknesses. Joseph later recalled, "I was left to all kinds of temptations; and mingling with all kinds of society, I frequently fell into many foolish errors, and displayed the weakness of youth, and the foibles of human nature; which, I am sorry to say, led me into divers temptations offensive, in the sight of God." However, Joseph was careful to point out that he had never possessed a disposition to commit any type of serious sin. But he did confess that he "was guilty of levity" and that he "sometimes associated with jovial company, not consistent with the character of one who was called of God." At times, Joseph felt condemned for his "weaknesses and imperfections," insomuch that he desired to receive forgiveness anew and to know of his state and standing before God.[48]

A little more than three years after his

initial communication with heaven, on September 21, 1823, Joseph retired to his bed and, with great faith and feeling, prayed "to Almighty God for forgiveness" of his "sins and follies." He also prayed for a divine manifestation, having full confidence that he would receive such, inasmuch as he had already been given one previously. While Joseph was praying, he recalled:

> I discovered a light appearing in my room, which continued to increase until the room was lighter than at noonday, when immediately a personage appeared at my bedside, standing in the air, for his feet did not touch the floor. He had on a loose robe of most exquisite whiteness . . . beyond anything earthly I had ever seen; . . . his whole person was glorious beyond description, and his countenance was truly like lightning. The room was exceedingly light, but not so very bright as around his person.[49]

The angel, reassuring Joseph that he was forgiven of his sins and of his favor with God, identified himself as Moroni, a prophet who had lived on the American continent in the late fourth-century A.D. He said that God had a work for him to do and that his "name should be had for good and evil among all nations, kindreds, and tongues." He informed Joseph about an ancient book, "written upon gold plates," and explained that it contained an account of the former inhabitants of the American continent. This book, Moroni said, also contained the "fullness of the everlasting gospel" as it was "delivered by the Savior" to those who lived upon this land shortly after His death and resurrection in Jerusalem.[50]

John the Revelator once testified that he saw "another angel fly in the midst of heaven, having the everlasting gospel to preach unto them that dwell on the earth, and to every nation, and kindred, and tongue, and people"

(Revelation 14:6). Bible scholars have often speculated on the meaning of this passage. However, no interpretations have been offered that seem to conform to the specific language John used. The early Christian writer Origen, when commenting on this passage, implied three different dispensations:

> And as in His coming now He fulfilled that law [of Moses] which has a shadow of good things to come, so also by that [future] glorious advent will be fulfilled and brought to perfection the shadows of the present advent. . . . At the time . . . when He will more worthily transfer all the saints from a temporal to an everlasting Gospel, according to the designation, employed by John in the Apocalypse, of "an everlasting Gospel.[51]

In the foregoing commentary, Origen describes the dispensations of Moses and of the Apostles and also a future dispensation—preparatory to the return of Jesus Christ—in which an angel will come bearing the "everlasting Gospel." Furthering interpreting John 14:6, he posits: "For at the end an exalted and flying angel, having the Gospel, will preach it to every nation, for the good Father has not entirely deserted those who have fallen away from him."[52]

Joseph's description of the angel Moroni and the message he bore find full agreement with the Revelator's text and with Origen's interpretation.

Moroni began immediately to provide initial instruction to Joseph. He informed him that included with the plates was a translation instrument that consisted of two stones in silver bows, fastened to a breastplate. Moroni called this device the Urim and Thummim[53] and said that the possession and use of these stones in former times constituted a "seer" and that they had been "prepared for the purpose of translating the book." The angel next began quoting selected Old and New Testament prophecies, some of which, he said, were about to be fulfilled. Each of these scriptures either made specific reference to the restoration of the gospel, the final days of the earth's existence, or preparations which had to precede the second coming of Christ. Moroni told Joseph that when the time should come, he would be permitted to retrieve the plates and the Urim and Thummim, which he was forbidden to show to anyone and that if he did he would be destroyed. While the angel was yet present, it was clearly shown to Joseph, in a vision, the precise location of the plates so that he knew exactly where to obtain them. With this initial communication complete, he observed that the light in the room gathered immediately around Moroni's person; he saw a conduit open right up into heaven, through which Moroni ascended until he finally disappeared, and the room was once again completely dark.

Joseph lay "musing on the singularity" of the experience, and he marveled at the things he had just been told. While meditating, he was surprised when once again his room began to fill with light, and the same messenger appeared, rehearsing the entire vision, word for word, as he had received it the first time. In addition to repeating the same information, Moroni informed Joseph of great judgments that were soon to come upon the earth, by means of "famine, sword, and pestilence." The vision closed, and he ascended as before. So riveted to his mind was this communication that sleep now fled, and he lay awake "overwhelmed in astonishment." Then, to his utter amazement, the angel appeared at his bedside for a third time, restating verbatim the entire message. Moroni then cautioned Joseph, "in consequence of the indigent circumstances" of his family, that Satan would

try to tempt him "to get the plates for the purpose of getting rich." He was told forcefully that he "must have no other object . . . in getting the plates but to glorify God."[54]

Shortly after the third visit, daylight began to break, and Joseph realized that the interviews must have taken the whole of the night. He dressed and, with the rest of the family, began the day's work of reaping wheat alongside his brothers. He said nothing of the visions to his family, but his weakened condition from lack of sleep must have been apparent. Lucy records that Joseph stopped working and seemed to be in a "deep study." Alvin attempted to hurry him, and he worked diligently for a time and then stopped as before. His father, noticing how pale Joseph was, advised him to go back to the house and tell his mother he was sick. In attempting to cross a fence on his way home, Joseph collapsed in exhaustion. His first recollection as he came to was the same messenger, who called him by name. Moroni asked him why he hadn't related the experience to his father. Joseph replied that "he was afraid his father would not believe him." The angel assured him, "He will believe every word you say to him." Moroni then related the entire contents of the communication as before, after which Joseph obeyed the messenger and told his father of the "vision and the commandments" he had received. Joseph's father had learned to trust in the divine nature of his own dreams and, as the angel had promised, he believed every word. His father assured Joseph that the revelation was "of God" and told him to obey the instructions he had received.[55]

Joseph went immediately to the place that the angel had shown him in vision. He recorded: "Owing to the distinctness of the vision . . . , I knew the place the instant that I arrived there." He described the location as "convenient to the village of Manchester,

Ontario county, New York," explaining that there was "a hill of considerable size, and the most elevated of any in the neighborhood. On the west side of this hill, not far from the top," Joseph found the large stone as revealed by the angel. He dug away the earth from around the edges and, finding a lever, was able to remove the stone. Inside a box, made of stones positioned in "some kind of cement," lay hidden the gold plates, the Urim and Thummim, and the breastplate. Joseph attempted to remove the plates but was severely shocked. The angel appeared and rebuked him, reminding him that he must have no other object than to glorify God. Apparently, in spite of having been warned, the value of the gold was too much for Joseph and his thoughts reflected such.[56]

Joseph, forgiven for his impropriety, received instructions from the angel on that occasion that he never forgot:

> While Joseph remained here, the angel told him, "Now I will show you the distance between light and darkness, and the operation of a good spirit and an evil one. An evil spirit will try to crowd your mind with every evil and wicked thing to keep every good thought and feeling out of your mind, but you must keep your mind always staid upon God, that no evil may come into your heart." The angel showed him by contrast, . . . the consequences of both obedience and disobedience to the commandments of God, in such a striking manner, that the impression was always vivid in his memory until the very end of his days; . . . he remarked that ever afterwards he was willing to keep the commandments of God.[57]

This graphic experience had a profound influence upon Joseph. Later in his life, in 1834, Joseph recorded his thoughts about his utterly hectic schedule: "No month ever found me more busily engaged than November; but

as my life consisted of activity and unyielding exertions, I made this my rule: *When the Lord commands, do it.*"[58]

After his chastisement, the angel informed Joseph that the time of bringing forth the plates had not yet arrived and directed him to return to the hill each year for the next four years, on the same appointed day, September 22. He would receive additional instructions with each visit.

Having received the assurance of his father's confidence, Joseph now felt free to relate the entire experience to the rest of his family members. He warned them that the angel had commanded him "not to proclaim these things or to mention them abroad, for we do not any of us know the weakness of the world, which is so sinful, and that when we get the plates they will want to kill us for the sake of the gold, if they know we have them." Lucy reported that Joseph received instruction periodically and that every evening they gathered together to listen to his orations: "I think that we presented the most peculiar aspect of any family that ever lived upon the earth, all seated in a circle, father, mother, sons, and daughters, listening in breathless anxiety to the religious teachings of a boy eighteen years of age who had never read the Bible through by course in his life. For Joseph was less inclined to the study of books than any child we had, but much more given to reflection and deep study."[59]

Joseph returned to the hill each succeeding year, as he had been commanded: "Each time I found the same messenger there, and received instruction and intelligence from him at each of our interviews, respecting what the Lord was going to do, and how and in what manner his kingdom was to be conducted in the last days." Although Joseph's spiritual experiences were sublime, these were exceedingly difficult years for him and his family, filled with tragedy, persecution, and the daily exertion required just to survive. In spite of the Lord's towering expectations from Joseph, he was not spared one wit from life's toil and troubles. Arriving home three hours late one evening, he threw himself into a chair, utterly exhausted. When his parents expressed obvious concern—after taking a few moments to recover—he replied, "Father, I have had the severest chastisement that I ever had in my life." Not knowing from whom the reproach had come, Joseph Sr. became indignant. Joseph managed to smile at his father, appreciating his love and protective nature. "It was the angel of the Lord," Joseph responded. "He says I have been negligent, that the time has now come when the record should be brought forth, and that I must be up and doing. . . . I know what course I am to pursue, and all will be well." His initial training was over. The time had come for him to remove the plates from their ancient hiding place.[60]

Eyewitnesses to a Prophet's Works

Important to the account of the coming forth of the Book of Mormon were credible witnesses. Similar in principle to the lesson conveyed by Jesus to the Apostle Thomas (John 20:26–29), Joseph Smith taught that man must walk by faith in this life. Nevertheless, in all dispensations of the world, God had used the law of witnesses to verify His word. For example, Paul taught that "in the mouth of two or three witnesses shall every word be established" (2 Corinthians 13:1). The law of witnesses was also included in the Mosaic covenant (Deuteronomy 17:6; 19:15). The Pseudepigrapha affirms that there were more witnesses than Noah in testifying of the world's impending destruction.[61] The Lord sent Aaron with Moses to Pharaoh. When

Jesus was baptized, among others who may have been there, God the Father spoke from the heavens and the Holy Ghost descended "like a dove" (Matthew 3:16; see also vv. 15–17). And when Jesus went into the holy mount, he took with Him Peter, James, and John (Matthew 17:1–5). Likewise, the Lord instructed Joseph that He would reveal to him special witnesses who would have the privilege of seeing the angel Moroni, hearing the voice of God, and handling for themselves the golden plates from which the Book of Mormon was translated. Additionally, eight other men would be permitted to handle the plates, to leaf through them, to lift them, to view the engravings, and to attest to the ancient workmanship. These men would then, according to the revelation given to Joseph, be required to bear witness to the world of the things which the Lord had shown them.

In a court of law, witnesses play a crucial role in determining the innocence or guilt of those accused of breaking the law. Empirical data, such as DNA and fingerprints, are given far more credence than circumstantial evidence. In the case of multiple witnesses, testimony becomes more powerful when, although coming from various points of view, the individuals relate essentially the same story, without conflicting (material) details. Moreover, witnesses are viewed as more credible when they possess a character and reputation above reproach, when there is no personal bias, when no conspiring connection exists between them, and when there is no potential for personal gain, enrichment, or power. In standing the test of time, witnesses are doubly trustworthy if the story remains the same, in spite of disaffection or even a complete severance in association. Indeed, one of the ultimate tests is whether the story itself can endure the passage of time, the discovery of new technology, and advances in science and learning. Accordingly, as Book of Mormon witnesses are introduced hereafter, they will be judged in the light of these exacting standards.

For many years, the burden of attesting to the divine nature of Joseph's work, of the appearance of the angel Moroni, and of the existence and authenticity of the gold plates fell solely and squarely on the young prophet's shoulders. This was a lonely period for him, and he was constantly at the mercy of a loving and kind Father in Heaven to furnish both major and minor miracles to his associates in order to retain their faith, allegiance, and commitment. While translating the Book of Mormon, Joseph and his scribes noted several instances in which the Lord indicated that additional witnesses would be called on to bear testimony to the world. Inquiring as to the meaning of these passages, he received the following revelation: "In addition to your testimony, the testimony of three of my servants, whom I shall call and ordain, unto whom I will show these things, and they shall go forth with my words that are given through you."[62]

The final portion of the translation of the Book of Mormon occurred at the Peter Whitmer Sr. residence in Fayette, New York. As mentioned, Oliver Cowdery had first been introduced to Joseph through David Whitmer, one of Peter's sons. Knowing of the prophecy of the witnesses and having been intimately involved during translation, Martin Harris, Oliver Cowdery, and David Whitmer began to wonder if the privilege of viewing the plates would be theirs. When the manuscript was completed in early July 1829, Joseph requested the company of his parents in nearby Waterloo. The good news was also communicated to Martin Harris, who was deeply interested in the progress of the work, particularly because his loss of the early man-

uscript had delayed its completion. The three immediately departed for Waterloo, arriving shortly before sunset. They spent the evening reading the manuscript and greatly rejoicing, not yet understanding the magnitude of the work that lay ahead. Joseph alone, Lucy recalled, comprehended that a dispensation of the gospel had been committed to him, "of which the starting bud had scarcely yet made its appearance."[63]

When they arose the next day, after breakfast and the usual morning service—which included reading, singing, and prayer—Joseph stood and, turning to his friend, said, "Martin Harris, you have got to humble yourself before God this day and obtain, if possible, a forgiveness of your sins. If you will do this, it is God's will that you and Oliver Cowdery and David Whitmer should look upon the plates." David was plowing in his fields when he learned from Joseph and Oliver that they were to seek a witness that day. He quickly tied his team of horses to a fence, and when Martin arrived, the four men retired to the nearby woods together. "According to previous arrangement," they each prayed in turn, pleading with "Almighty God" for the divine manifestation they sought and which had been promised. The first attempt yielded nothing, and so they tried again—but to no avail. Before making a third attempt, Martin realized that his unworthiness was preventing the group from receiving the desired witness. Consequently, he withdrew from his friends to find solitude and forgiveness. According to their account, not many minutes later, they beheld a light above them "of exceeding brightness." An angel of the Lord stood before them and held in his hands the plates they had been praying to view. "He turned over the leaves one by one," so that the engravings could be distinctly viewed. The angel addressed himself to David Whitmer directly, saying, "Blessed is the Lord and he that keeps his commandments." Then they heard a voice from out of the bright light say, "These plates have been revealed by the power of God, and they have been translated by the power of God; the translation of them which you have seen is correct, and I command you to bear record of what you now see and hear."[64]

After receiving this glorious vision, Joseph left Oliver and David in search of Martin. Finding him some distance away "fervently engaged in prayer," he knelt with him, and they soon received precisely the same manifestation. Martin Harris then cried out in "ecstacy of joy." Jumping to his feet, he said, "'Tis enough; mine eyes have beheld." Then he shouted, "Hosanna," blessing God and rejoicing.[65]

Soon after this extraordinary vision, the witnesses recorded their testimony, which appeared in the initial publication of the Book of Mormon in its opening pages and in each succeeding edition:

Be it known unto all nations, kindreds, tongues, and people, unto whom this work shall come: That we, through the grace of God the Father, and our Lord Jesus Christ, have seen the plates which contain this record, which is a record of the people of Nephi, and also the Lamanites, their brethren, and also of the people of Jared, who came from the tower of which hath been spoken. And we also know that they have been translated by the gift and power of God, for his voice hath declared it unto us; wherefore we know of a surety that the work is true. And we also testify that we have seen the engravings which are upon the plates; and they have been shown unto us by the power of God, and not of man. And we declare with words of soberness, that an angel of God came down from heaven, and he

brought and laid before our eyes, that we beheld and saw the plates, and the engravings thereon; and we know that it is by the grace of God the Father, and our Lord Jesus Christ, that we beheld and bear record that these things are true. And it is marvelous in our eyes. Nevertheless, the voice of the Lord commanded us that we should bear record of it; wherefore, to be obedient unto the commandments of God, we bear testimony of these things. And we know that if we are faithful in Christ we shall rid our garments of the blood of all men, and be found spotless before the judgement seat of Christ, and shall dwell with Him eternally in the heavens. And the honor be to the Father, and to the Son, and to the Holy Ghost, which is one God. Amen.

Eight additional witnesses were identified by the Lord to the prophet Joseph, who were given the opportunity to view the plates but did not see the angel. David's brothers—Christian, Jacob, Peter Jr., and John—all received this blessing. Hiram Page, Joseph's father, and Joseph's brothers, Hyrum and Samuel, were also privileged to examine the plates and to be special witnesses. They recorded their testimony as follows:

Be it known unto all nations, kindreds, tongues, and people, unto whom this work shall come: That Joseph Smith, Jun., the translator of this work, has shown unto us the plates of which hath been spoken, which have the appearance of gold; and as many of the leaves as the said Smith has translated we did handle with our hands; and we also saw the engravings thereon, all of which has the appearance of ancient work, and of curious workmanship. And this we bear record with words of soberness, that the said Smith has shown unto us, for we have seen and hefted, and know of a surety that the said Smith has got the plates of which we have spoken. And we give our names to the world, to witness unto the world that which we have seen. And we lie not, God bearing witness of it.

Substantial documentation exists to verify the character and reputation of the Book of Mormon witnesses. The following facts strengthen the position of these individuals as witnesses: (1) they all joined the Church Joseph founded; (2) they devoted substantial time and material resources to building up a new and unpopular religious organization; (3) they became early leaders of the Church; (4) they all experienced substantial financial loss accumulated from Church participation, frequent moves, and bitter persecution; (5) they were subjected to slanderous criticism and social ostracism; (6) some were subjected to mob violence, including the prophet's brother, Hyrum, who suffered martyrdom with him at Carthage, Illinois; (7) many of the witnesses became personally disaffected from the prophet, including each of the three witnesses, who, for various offenses were excommunicated (two of them, Martin Harris and Oliver Cowdery returned to the Church, were rebaptized, and died in full faith and fellowship); and (8) each of the three witnesses reconfirmed their testimonies just prior to death.[66] Throughout their lives, the witness they bore never faltered, changed, or diminished in any way. Likewise, although several of the eight witnesses left the Church, they never recanted their original testimony. In short, Joseph Smith and the other witnesses of the Book of Mormon were like the Apostles and early Christian martyrs in *the defense of individual testimony*. They were unwilling to yield to any type of pressure, whether physical, emotional, social, financial, or even death. As documented by the fore-going facts, the Book of Mormon witnesses serve as reliable notaries and could bear up under the most stringent requirements of the law as material witnesses in any civilized court on earth.

Martin Harris was a mature man of forty-six years when he met the prophet Joseph. In order to properly assess his character and nature, we must know him as the people of Palmyra knew him for nearly thirty years *before* his introduction to the plates. Well documented is the fact that no person in the early Palmyra period exceeded him in achievement or reputation for honesty and responsibility. Before his involvement in bringing forth the Book of Mormon, Martin was known as a farmer and citizen of recognized ability. In addition to owning more than 240 acres of productive land, he was also noted for his expertise in raising animals, such as swine and sheep; and for his production of textiles, such as linen, cotton, blankets, and flannel. Martin also served his community a number of times as an elected official. He was chosen seven times in his district to be the "overseer of highways and fence viewer," including 1829, the year the Book of Mormon translation was completed. His repeated selection for this type of service indicated his diplomacy in working with people and the universal trust he had earned among the citizenry.[67]

One of Martin's contemporaries, an opponent of Mormonism, wrote of him, "He was considered an honest, industrious citizen by his neighbors." Echoing this view, the *Palmyra Courier* printed a five-installment series dedicated to Martin and his father. While the Church itself was viewed by the townspeople as regrettable, of the younger Harris it was recorded he "was an industrious, hard-working farmer, shrewd in his business calculations, frugal in his habits, and was termed a prosperous man in the world."

Another respected non-Mormon, Pomeroy Tucker, an eminent politician and editor in western New York for more than forty years, appraised Martin as "honest and benevolent" and credited him with being "a prosperous, independent farmer, strictly upright in his business dealings."[68]

Perhaps Stephen S. Harding, a territorial (non-Mormon) governor of Utah during the Civil War, captured best the essence of how the people of Palmyra felt about Martin Harris. Harding, born in Palmyra, returned as a young man in 1829 in the midst of the stir created by the Book of Mormon. He recalled that the affair "excited a good deal of curiosity and comment" chiefly because "such a man as Martin Harris" believed in it and financially supported it. To a prejudiced community, it was "truly phenomenal" that he "should abandon the cultivation of one of the best farms in the neighborhood."[69]

From all that is recorded, we may conclude that although many considered Harris to be deluded by the prophet Joseph Smith, he was nevertheless considered honest, trustworthy, responsible, and reputable prior to his involvement with the Book of Mormon. An impartial observer of this period wrote that no early citizen of Palmyra "received so many rebuffs" or suffered "so many unfeeling comments" as did Martin Harris.[70] In spite of such cruelty, he defended his witness and testimony until death. In 1871, shortly before his passing, he made the following statement:

I have never failed to bear testimony to the divine authenticity of the Book of Mormon. I know of a surety that the work is true. It is not a matter of belief . . . but knowledge. Just as surely as the sun is shining on us and gives us light, and the moon and stars give us light by night, just as surely as the breath of life sustains us, so surely do I know that Joseph Smith was a true prophet of God, chosen of God to open the last dispensation of the fulness of times; so surely do I know that the Book of Mormon was divinely translated. I saw the plates; I saw the angel; I heard the voice of God. . . . I might as well doubt my own existence as to doubt the divine authenticity of the Book of Mormon or the divine calling of Joseph Smith. . . . My testimony . . . has not varied . . . in 41 years.[71]

Oliver Cowdery was also a faithful witness of the Book of Mormon until his passing. Having become separated from the Church for a period because of differences with some of its leaders, he was later rebaptized in Kanesville (now Council Bluffs), Iowa, in November 1848, when the Church was still in the process of heading west.

In order to appraise accurately Oliver's character and reputation, one must become acquainted with his activities and pursuits during the period he was estranged from the Church. From 1838 to 1848, he became a highly respected attorney, politician, journalist, and civic servant. Moving to Ohio in 1839, he was elected that year as one of thirteen delegates to represent Geauga County at the bicounty senatorial convention and in 1840 was initially selected as editor of a Democratic campaign newspaper. Unfortunately, when it was learned that he was one the of the Three Witnesses to the Book of Mormon, he was dropped from consideration. In spite of this rebuff, he remained in Tiffin, Ohio, for seven years, during which time he earned an impeccable reputation. One of Oliver's many advocates, William Lang, was a prominent citizen who served as a prosecuting attorney, probate judge, mayor of Tiffin, county treasurer, and a two-term Ohio senator. In a work entitled *History of Seneca County,* authored by Lang later in his life, he expressed sincere praise and admiration for the "noble and true manhood"[72] exhibited by Oliver Cowdery:

Mr. Cowdery was an able lawyer and a great advocate. His manners were easy and gentlemanly; he was polite, dignified, yet courteous. He had an open countenance, high forehead, dark brown eye, Roman nose, clenched lips and prominent lower jaw. He shaved smooth and was neat and cleanly in his person. He was of light stature, about five feet, five inches high, and had a loose, easy walk. With all his kind and friendly disposition, there was a certain degree of sadness that seemed to pervade his whole being. His association with others was marked by the great amount of information his conversation conveyed and the beauty of his musical voice. His addresses to the court and jury were characterized by a high order of oratory, with brilliant and forensic force. He was modest and reserved, never spoke ill of any one, never complained.[73]

From this quotation, and numerous others that could be cited,[74] we can easily discern the integrity, character, and good name earned by Oliver in providing distinguished service to his community. Nevertheless, one may also imagine the melancholy he must have felt from time to time having witnessed such marvelous and miraculous events, only to be separated from that organization he was instrumental in founding and from which he had derived so much joy. Suffering from an incurable lung disease, he died on March 3, 1850, almost eighteen months after rejoining The Church of Jesus Christ of Latter-day Saints.

When the community of Tiffin learned of Oliver's passing, the *Seneca Advisor* reported:

His numerous acquaintances at this place will receive the tidings of his decease with much regret. He was a man of more than ordinary ability, and during his residence among us had endeared himself to all who knew him in the private and social walks of life.[75]

Before his death, Oliver repeated to David Whitmer the testimony he had expressed to others on so many occasions :

I was present at the deathbed of Oliver Cowdery in 1850. . . . Oliver died the happiest man I ever saw. . . . His last words were, "Brother David, be true to your testimony to the Book of Mormon, for we know that it is of God and that it is verily true." After shaking hands with the family and kissing his wife and daughter, he said, "Now I lay me down for the last time, I am going to my Savior," and died immediately, with a smile on his face. Many witnesses yet live in Richmond, who will testify to the truth of these facts, as well as to the good character of Oliver Cowdery.[76]

David Whitmer, like his associates Martin Harris and Oliver Cowdery, was esteemed as a man of high character and integrity by all who knew him. According to one historian, David Whitmer was an "individualist" who bordered on the edge of "stubborn." "Whether in Mormon society or not," he wrote, "he stood like a rock for his principles. This outspoken and utterly honest personality would have been the first to detect fraud and expose it. During eight years in the Church and fifty years of strict separation from it, he maintained without compromise that he had seen the angel and the plates."[77] Not given to frivolous statements, Whitmer had a stern reputation for saying what he meant, and meaning what he said.

David's father was characterized by his family as a "hard-working, God-fearing man," "a strict Presbyterian" who "brought his children up with rigid sectarian discipline."[78]

Although somewhat tempered by his experiences with the Book of Mormon and the Restoration, David was often described in a similar manner by those who knew him best. As a young man, he demonstrated uncommon responsibility and natural leadership. Consequently, he was elected sergeant of the newly formed Seneca County militia in 1825 at the age of twenty. Two letters written to him by Oliver Cowdery, expressing a firm conviction of Joseph's prophetic role, initiated his interest in the Book of Mormon. The work of translation moved to his father's home shortly thereafter and by June 1829, he had become a witness to the world of the divine authenticity of the plates, the appearance of the angel, and of hearing the voice of God bear record that the translation was correct.

His involvement in the Church was at the highest levels for eight years between 1830 and 1838. According to David, concerns over new revelations and a growing and changing Church polity began to influence his thinking negatively. This condition, combined with the growing influence of Sidney Rigdon, a former Campbellite preacher, widened his disaffection from the prophet. David wrote "Rigdon was a thorough Bible scholar, a man of fine education, and a powerful orator. He soon worked himself deep into Brother Joseph's affections, and had more influence over him than any other man living."[79] Although all three Book of Mormon witnesses separated from the Church, only David never returned.

Locating in Richmond, Missouri, Whitmer soon became involved in a number of diverse business interests but was known primarily for his delivery company called The Old Reliable Livery and Feed Stable. His great-granddaughter, in summarizing the business, wrote: "They filled hauling contracts, rented out carriages and buggies, and met two trains a day at Lexington junction with a beautifully decorated yellow bus. . . . Side lines were feed and grain, sand and gravel."[80] In addition to his businesses, he served on fair boards, was elected to several terms as a city councilman, and was chosen to fill an unexpired mayoral term in 1867–68. The *Ray County Atlas of 1877* featured him as one of the region's twenty most influential citizens.[81]

Jacob T. Child, the prominent editor of the *Richmond Conservator*, was one of many who held David Whitmer in high esteem. Serving at various times as both mayor of Richmond and state assemblyman, he was also elected president of the Missouri Press Association by his peers and was appointed Ambassador to Siam by President Grover Cleveland. Child's respect for Whitmer impelled him to defend this honored citizen when he was criticized because of his connection to the Book of Mormon. On one occasion an anti-Mormon lecturer, Clark Braden, visited Richmond and publicly denounced Whitmer as disreputable. The *Conservator's* rebuttal was published on the front page and, while unsupportive of Mormonism, it was resolute in its opinion that in view of David Whitmer's "forty-six years of private citizenship . . . in Richmond, without stain or blemish," his public credibility was fully warranted. The respected journalist readily acknowledged that theological views were open to debate but insisted that this man's character was not. "If a life of probity," he wrote, "of unobtrusive benevolence and well doing for well nigh a half century, marks a man as a good citizen, then David Whitmer should enjoy the confidence and esteem of his fellowmen."[82]

David Whitmer's last written testimony was recorded in a pamphlet he published shortly before his death, in part to explain his separation from the Church. In this booklet, he confirmed the witness he had consistently given throughout his life:

I will say once more to all mankind, that I have never at any time denied my testimony or any part thereof. I also testify to the world, that neither Oliver Cowdery or Martin Harris ever at any time denied their testimony. They both died reaffirming the truth of the divine authenticity of the Book of Mormon. I wish now, standing as it were, in the very sunset of life, and in the fear of God, once [and] for all to make this public statement: That I have never at any time denied that testimony or any part thereof, which has so long since been published with that Book, as one of three witnesses. Those who know me best, will know that I have always adhered to that testimony. And that no man may be misled or doubt my present views in regard to the same, I do again affirm the truth of all my statements, as then made and published. "He that hath an ear to hear, let him hear"; it was no delusion! What is written is written, and he that readeth let him understand. Beware how you hastily condemn that book which I know to be the word of God; for his own voice and an angel from heaven declared the truth of it unto me, and to the two other witnesses who testified on their death-bed that it was true.[83]

Neither the Three Witnesses nor any of the Eight Witnesses ever recanted their original testimonies as published in the Book of Mormon. Moreover, individually and collectively, they exceeded the precise legal standards that would be required to make them credible to any reasonable and impartial jury. They were well known to the non-Mormon world; they were universally respected as men of honesty and integrity; although each of the Three Witnesses and several of the Eight Witnesses became disaffected from the prophet Joseph Smith, they all reaffirmed their testimonies throughout their lives; they suffered personally and professionally for remaining true to their witness; there was never any personal gain, or any hope for such, either in the beginning or at any time during their mortal existence; and finally, the testimony they championed has stood the test of time. The religious organization they helped found has flourished throughout the world, and its people, taken as a whole, are a powerful testament of its truth.

Notes

1. Bushman, *Beginnings of Mormonism,* 53.
2. Joseph Smith–History 1:5, from Smith, *History of the Church,* vol. 1, chs. 1–5.
3. Bushman, *Beginnings of Mormonism,* 53.
4. Lucy was baptized in 1803 but did not join a specific church. Her history records that she continued to read the Bible until her oldest son was twenty-two years of age. Alvin turned twenty-two in 1820; see also Bushman, *Beginnings of Mormonism,* 205n32.
5. Joseph Smith–History 1:8, from Smith, *History of the Church,* vol. 1, chs. 1–5.
6. Tucker, *Origin, Rise, and Progress of Mormonism,* 28; Turner, *History,* 214, in Bushman, *Beginnings of Mormonism,* 54.
7. Milton V. Backman, *Joseph Smith's First Vision: Confirming Evidences and Contemporary Accounts* (Salt Lake City: Bookcraft, 1980), 177.
8. Joseph Smith–History 1:6, from Smith, *History of the Church,* vol. 1, chs. 1–5.
9. Turner, *History,* 213–14; John Alonzo Clark, *Gleanings by the Way* (Philadelphia: W. J. and J. K. Simon, 1842), 225; Joseph Smith, *History of the Life of Joseph Smith, Jr.,* 156. Pomeroy Tucker stated that "as Joseph grew up he learned to read comprehensively," including the Bible; see Tucker, *Origin, Rise, and Progress of Mormonism,* 17, in Bushman, *Beginnings of Mormonism,* 54.
10. Smith, *History of the Life of Joseph Smith Jr.,* 156.
11. Joseph Smith–History 1:9, from Smith, *History of the Church,* vol. 1, chs. 1–5.
12. Joseph Smith–History 1:12–13, from Smith, *History of the Church,* vol. 1, chs. 1–5.

13. Joseph Smith–History 1:15–16, from Smith, *History of the Church,* vol. 1, chs. 1–5.

14. Joseph Smith–History 1:17, from Smith, *History of the Church,* vol. 1, chs. 1–5.

15. Smith, *History of the Life of Joseph Smith, Jr.,* 157; Dean C. Jessee, *The Early Accounts of Joseph Smith's First Vision* (Sandy, Utah: Mormon Miscellaneous, 1984), 283–87; in Bushman, *Joseph Smith and the Beginnings of Mormonism,* 57, 206n44.

16. The quotations are from an interview with Robert Mathias, who called himself "Joshua the Jewish Minister," recorded in Manuscript History, November 9, 1835, 120–22, in Bushman, *Beginnings of Mormonism,* 57. This account is reprinted in Jessee, *Early Accounts,* 284–85, and Backman, *Joseph Smith's First Vision,* 158–59.

17. Joseph Smith–History 1:19, from Smith, *History of the Church,* vol. 1, chs. 1–5.

18. Joseph Smith–History 1:20, from Smith, *History of the Church,* vol. 1, chs. 1–5.

19. Smith, *History of the Life of Joseph Smith Jr.,* 157; Jessee, *Early Accounts,* 283–87.

20. Bushman, *Beginnings of Mormonism,* 58, cf. ch. notes, 207n50.

21. Joseph Smith–History 1:22, from Smith, *History of the Church,* vol. 1, chs. 1–5.

22. Bushman, *Beginnings of Mormonism,* 59.

23. Hippolytus, Treatise on Christ and Antichrist, in *Ante-Nicene Fathers,* 5:6:206.

24. Joseph Smith–History 1:25, from Smith, *History of the Church,* vol. 1, chs. 1–5.

25. *Church History in the Fulness of Times* (Salt Lake City: The Church of Jesus Christ of Latter-day Saints, 1989) 16; Bushman, *Beginnings of Mormonism,* 20.

26. *Church History in the Fulness of Times,* 16; Bushman, *Beginnings of Mormonism,* 20.

27. *Church History in the Fulness of Times,* 16–17; Bushman, *Beginnings of Mormonism,* 20–21.

28. *Church History in the Fulness of Times,* 17, citing Richard Lloyd Anderson, *Joseph Smith's New England Heritage: Influences of Grandfathers Solomon Mack and Asael Smith* (Salt Lake City: Deseret Book, 1971), 124, 125, 129.

29. *Church History in the Fulness of Times,* 17, citing George A. Smith, *Memoirs of George A. Smith,* 2; see also Anderson, *Joseph Smith's New England Heritage,* 124, 125, 129.

30. Smith, *History of Joseph Smith by His Mother,* 11; Bushman, *Beginnings of Mormonism,* 18.

31. Smith, *History of Joseph Smith by His Mother,* 40; Bushman, *Beginnings of Mormonism,* 18.

32. Smith, *History of Joseph Smith by His Mother,* 42.

33. Smith, *History of Joseph Smith by His Mother,* 46.

34. Smith, *History of Joseph Smith by His Mother,* 51–53; see also Bushman, *Beginnings of Mormonism,* 30.

35. Smith, *History of Joseph Smith by His Mother,* 48.

36. Smith, *History of Joseph Smith by His Mother,* 48–50.

37. Smith, *History of Joseph Smith by His Mother,* 59–60.

38. William is cited in Richard Lloyd Anderson, "Joseph Smith's Home Environment," *Ensign* 1 (July 1971): 58. Joseph Sr.'s first dream is recorded in Smith, *History of Joseph Smith by His Mother,* 63–64; see also Bushman, *Beginnings of Mormonism,* 38–39.

39. Smith, *History of Joseph Smith by His Mother,* 64–65; see also Bushman, *Beginnings of Mormonism,* 39.

40. Smith, *History of Joseph Smith by His Mother,* 68; see also Bushman, *Beginnings of Mormonism,* 31–32.

41. Smith, *History of Joseph Smith by His Mother,* 69–71; see also Bushman, *Beginnings of Mormonism,* 32.

42. Smith, *History of Joseph Smith by His Mother,* 72–76; see also Bushman, *Beginnings of Mormonism,* 32–33.

43. Smith, *History of Joseph Smith by His Mother,* 81–86; see also Bushman, *Beginnings of Mormonism,* 40–42.

44. Smith, *History of Joseph Smith by His Mother,* 86–87; see also Bushman, *Beginnings of Mormonism,* 48–49.

45. Smith, *History of Joseph Smith by His Mother,* 89–90.

46. Smith, *History of Joseph Smith by His Mother,* 94.

47. Smith, *History of the Church,* 1:27; Bushman, *Beginnings of Mormonism,* 59.

48. Smith, *History of the Church,* 1:28.

49. Smith, *History of the Church,* 1:29–32.

50. Smith, *History of the Church,* 1:33–34.

51. Origen, De Principiis 4.25, in *Ante-Nicene Fathers,* 4:375.

52. Origen, Commentary on John 1.14, in *Ante-Nicene Fathers,* 10:305.

53. Smith, *History of the Church,* 1:35–43. Other biblical passages referring to the Urim and Thummim are: Exodus 28:30; Leviticus 8:8; Numbers 27:21; Deuteronomy 33:8; 1 Samuel 28:6; Ezra 2:63; Nehemiah 7:65. For further discussion relating to the revelatory nature of the Urim and Thummim, see Cornelius Van Dam, *The Urim and Thummim: A Means of Revelation in Ancient Israel,* rev. ed. (Winona Lake, Ind.: Eisenbrauns, 1997); Ann Jeffers, *Magic and Divination in Ancient Palestine and Syria* (New York: E. J. Brill, 1996); Appendix, "Glowing Stones in Ancient and Medieval Lore," in John Tvednes, *The Book of Mormon and Other Hidden Books: Out of Darkness unto Light* (Provo, Utah: Foundation for Ancient Research and Mormon Studies, 2000).

54. Joseph Smith–History 1:46, from Smith, *History of the Church,* vol. 1, chs. 1–5.

55. *History of Joseph Smith by His Mother,* 108–9; Joseph Smith–History 1:49–50, from Smith, *History of the Church,* vol. 1, chs. 1–5.

56. Joseph Smith–History 1:50–52, from Smith, *History of the Church,* vol. 1, chs. 1–5. Lucy's preliminary manuscript contains the account of Joseph's thoughts as he attempted to lift the plates from the box. Joseph Knight and Oliver Cowdery also recorded the events as they understood them. These accounts are published in Bushman, *Beginnings of Mormonism,* 209n65.

57. Smith, *History of Joseph Smith by His Mother,* 109.

58. Smith, *History of the Church,* 2:170.

59. Smith, *History of Joseph Smith by His Mother,* 111.

60. Smith, *History of the Church,* 1:54; Smith, *History of Joseph Smith by His Mother,* 134–135. The important history associated with the events preceding the removal of the plates can be read in the above *History of Joseph Smith by His Mother,*

111–35. For a complete and balanced view of Joseph's early years, see Bushman, *Beginnings of Mormonism,* 64–78.

61. Enoch declared repentance and predicted the Flood before his translation. The righteous men Enos, Cainan, Mahalaleel, Jared, Methuselah, and Lemech were all contemporary with Noah.

62. D&C 5:11.

63. Smith, *History of Joseph Smith by His Mother,* 197–99.

64. *Times and Seasons* 3 (September 1, 1842): 897–98; David Whitmer also gave his account in the *Kansas City Daily Journal* (June 5, 1881).

65. Smith, *History of the Church,* 1:55.

66. See also Backman, *Eyewitness Accounts of the Restoration,* 133.

67. Palmyra Town Record, 1811, 1813, 1814, 1815, 1825, 1827, 1829, in Richard Lloyd Anderson, *Investigating the Book of Mormon Witnesses* (Salt Lake City: Deseret Book, 1981), 99.

68. Eber D. Howe, *Mormonsim Unvailed: or, a Faithful Account of That Singular Imposition and Delusion, from Its Rise to the Present Time* (Painesville, Ohio: By the author, 1834), 13; *Palmyra Courier* (May 24, 1872); Pomeroy Tucker, *Origin, Rise, and Progress of Mormonism;* see Anderson, *Investigating the Book of Mormon Witnesses,* 95–96.

69. Letter of S. S. Harding to Thomas Gregg, February 1882, Milan, Indiana, cit. Thomas Gregg, *The Prophet of Palmyra* (New York: J. B. Alden, 1890), 36–37, in Anderson, *Investigating the Book of Mormon Witnesses,* 97.

70. *Palmyra Courier* (May 24, 1872). Compare note with Anderson, *Investigating the Book of Mormon Witnesses,* 95n3.

71. Stevenson, "Incidents in the Life of Martin Harris," 470, in Backman, *Eyewitness Accounts of the Book of Mormon,* 159.

72. Anderson, *Investigating the Book of Mormon Witnesses,* 41.

73. William B. Lang, *History of Seneca County: From the Close of the Revolutionary War to July, 1880; Embracing Many Personal Sketches of Pioneers, Anecdotes, and Faithful Descriptions of Events Pertaining to the Organization of the County and its Progress* (Springfield, Ohio: Transcript

Printing, 1880), 365. In critiquing Lang's commentary, Anderson writes: "In evaluating Lang's opinion of Cowdery, it must be admitted that he shows a distinct critical ability in appraising the qualities of his fellow attorneys in the Seneca County bar." Cited in Anderson, *Investigating the Book of Mormon Witnesses*, 41.

74. Richard Anderson's *Investigating the Book of Mormon Witnesses* provides a thorough, balanced historical treatment of this subject.

75. *Seneca Advisor* (November 1, 1850).

76. David Whitmer, *An Address to All Believers in Christ: By a Witness to the Divine Authenticity of the Book of Mormon, David Whitmer* (Nauvoo, Ill.: New Nauvoo Neighbor Press, 1976), 8; see also Backman, *Eyewitness Accounts of the Restoration*, 163.

77. Anderson, *Investigating the Book of Mormon Witnesses*, 66.

78. *Chicago Tribune* (December 17, 1885).

79. Whitmer, *Address to All Believers in Christ*, 35, in Anderson, *Investigating the Book of Mormon Witnesses*, 69.

80. Blankmeyer, *David Whitmer*, 50, in Anderson, *Investigating the Book of Mormon Witnesses*, 72.

81. See *Richmond Conservator* (April 9, 1858; April 5, 1861; and April 7, 1864). He lost by a 48–49 vote in 1858. *Illustrated Historical Atlas of Ray County, Missouri. Compiled, Drawn and Published from Personal Examinations and Surveys by Edward Brothers, of Missouri* (Richmond, Mo.: Richmond News, 1971), in Anderson, *Investigating the Book of Mormon Witnesses*, 72.

82. *Richmond Conservator* (August 22, 1884) in Anderson, *Investigating the Book of Mormon Witnesses*, 73.

83. Whitmer, *Address to All Believers*, 8–9, 43. Also published in Backman, *Eyewitness Accounts of the Book of Mormon*, 155–56.

Selected Bibliography

Abegg, Martin, Jr., Peter Flint, and Eugene Ulrich, trans. *The Dead Sea Scrolls Bible.* San Francisco: HarperSanFrancisco, 1999.

Adams, Hannah. *An Alphabetical Compendium of the Various Sects.* Boston, 1784.

The Annals of Tacitus. Translated by Alfred John Church and William Jackson Brodribb. Franklin Center, Pa.: Franklin Library, 1982.

Ancient Christian Writers. Translated by Leslie William Barnard. Mahwah, N.J.: Paulist Press, 1948.

Anderson, Richard Lloyd. *Guide to Acts and the Apostles' Letters.* Provo, Utah: Foundation for Ancient Research and Mormon Studies (FARMS), 1999.

———. *Joseph Smith's New England Heritage: Influences of Grandfathers Solomon Mack and Asael Smith.* Salt Lake City: Deseret Book, 1971.

———. *Investigating the Book of Mormon Witnesses.* Salt Lake City: Deseret Book, 1981.

The Apocrypha KJV. Iowa Falls, Iowa: World Bible Publishers, n.d.

The Apostolic Fathers. Translated by Kirsopp Lake. 2 vols. Cambridge, Mass.: Harvard University Press, 1997.

Arminius, James. *The Writings of James Arminius.* Translated by W. R. Bagnall. 3 vols. Grand Rapids, Mich.: Baker Book House, 1956.

Bacon, Francis. *The Works of Francis Bacon.* Edited by James Spedding, Robert Leslie Ellis, and Douglas Denon Heath. 15 vols. New York: Hurd & Houghton, 1862–72.

Backman, Milton V., Jr. *American Religions and the Rise of Mormonism.* Salt Lake City: Deseret Book, 1965.

———. *Eyewitness Accounts of the Restoration.* Salt Lake City: Deseret Book, 1986.

———. *The Heavens Resound: A History of the Latter-day Saints in Ohio, 1830–1838.* Salt Lake City: Deseret Book, 1983.

———. *Joseph Smith's First Vision: The First Vision in Its Historical Context.* Salt Lake City: Bookcraft, 1971.

Bainton, Roland H. *Here I Stand.* New York: Penguin Group, 1995.

Barker, James L. *Apostasy from the Divine Church.* Salt Lake City: Deseret News Press, 1960.

Baxter, N. A. *History of the Freewill Baptists.* Rochester, N.Y.: American Baptist Historical Society, 1957.

Beard, Charles. *The Reformation of the Sixteenth Century in Its Relation to Modern Thought and Knowledge.* Westport, Conn: Greenwood Press Reprint, 1980.

Bercot, David W. *Will the Real Heretics Please Stand Up: A New Look at Today's Evangelical Christian Church in the Light of Early Christianity.* Tyler, Texas: Scroll Publishing, 1989.
———. *A Glimpse of Early Christian Life.* Tyler, Texas: Scroll Publishing, 1991.

Bernard, John H. *The Descent into Hades and Christian Baptism.* London: Hodder & Stoughton, 1917.

Bet ha-Midrash. 6 vols. Jerusalem: Wahrmann Books, 1967.

Bickmore, Robert Barry. *Restoring the Ancient Church.* Phoenix: Cornerstone Publishing, 1999.

Black, Matthew. *Apocalyptus Henochi Graece.* Leiden: E. J. Brill, 1970.

Blankmeyer, Helen Van Cleave. *David Whitmer, Witness for God.* Springfield, Ill.: 1955.

Blomberg, Craig, and Stephen E. Robinson. *How Wide the Divide.* Downers Grove, Ill: InterVarsity Press, 1997.

Bloom, Harold. *The American Religion: The Emergence of the Post-Christian Nation.* New York: Simon and Schuster, 1992.

The Book of Prophecies of Christopher Columbus. Translated by Delno C. West and August Kling. Gainesville: University of Florida Press, 1991.

Bright, John. *A History of Israel.* 3d ed. Philadelphia: Westminster Press, 1981.

Bromiley, Geoffrey W., ed. *The International Standard Bible Encyclopedia.* 4 vols. Grand Rapids, Mich.: William B. Eerdmans, 1956.

Bruce, F.F. *History of the Bible in English.* New York: Oxford University Press, 1978.

Bruce, Philip Alexander. *Institutional History of Virginia in the Seventeenth Century.* 2 vols. New York: G. P. Putnam's Sons, 1910.

Bryant, William Cullen, ed. *Picturesque America; or, the Land We Live In.* New York: D. Appleton and Co., 1872.

Bushman, Richard L. *The Beginnings of Mormonism.* University of Illinois Press, 1984.

Cairns, Earle E. *Christianity through the Centuries.* 3d ed. Grand Rapids, Mich.: Zondervan, 1996.

Cameron, Euan, ed. *Early Modern Europe.* New York: Oxford University Press, 1989.

Calvin, John. *The Institutes of Christian Religion.* Grand Rapids, Mich.: Baker Book House, 1999.

Cannon, William R. "John Wesley's Doctrine of Sanctification and Perfection." *Mennonite Quarterly Review* 35, no. 2 (April 1961).

Cappon, Lester J., ed., *The Adams-Jefferson Letters.* 2 vols. (Chapel Hill: University of North Carolina Press, 1959.

Cartwright, Peter. *Autobiography of Peter Cartwright, the Backwoods Preacher.* Edited by W. P. Strickland. New York: Carlton and Porter, 1857.

Chadwick, Henry. *The Early Church.* Revised ed. New York: Penguin Group, 1993.

Chadwick, Owen. *A History of Christianity.* New York: St. Martin's Press, 1995.

Charles, R.H. *The Book of Enoch.* London: Oxford University Press, 1913.

———, ed. *Apocrypha and Pseudepigrapha of the Old Testament.* 2 vols. Oxford: Clarendon Press, 1912.

Charlesworth, James H. *Authentic Apocrypha.* Richland Hills, Texas: Bible Press, D. & F. Scott Publishing, 1998.

———. *Jesus and the Dead Sea Scrolls,* New York: Doubleday, 1992.

———. *The Old Testament Pseudepigrapha and the New Testament.* Harrisburg, Pa.: Trinity Press International, 1998.

———, ed. *Old Testament Pseudepigrapha.* 2 vols. New York: Doubleday, 1983.

Chase, Daryl. "The Early Shakers." Ph.D. dissertation, University of Chicago, 1936.

Cheetham, Nicholas. *Keepers of the Keys.* New York: Charles Scribner's Sons, 1983.

Church History in the Fulness of Times. Salt Lake City: The Church of Jesus Christ of Latter-day Saints, 1989.

Clark, John Alonzo. *Gleanings by the Way.* Philadelphia: W. J. and J. K. Simon, 1842.

Clement of Alexandria. *Stromateis 1–3.* Translated by J. Ferguson. Washington, D.C.: The Catholic University of America Press, 1991.

Cohen, Abraham. *Everyman's Talmud.* New York: Schocken Books, 1949, 1995.

Cohen, Daniel. *The Spirit of the Lord: Revivalism in America.* New York: Four Winds Press, 1975.

Cobbett, William. *Christianity Contrasted with Deism.* 2d ed. Philadelphia, 1796.

Cowdery, Oliver. *Messenger and Advocate* 1 (October 1834).

Cross, Whitney R. *The Burned-Over District.* Ithaca, N.Y.: Cornell University Press, 1950.

Curtis, A. Kenneth, J. Stephen Lang, and Randy Petersen. *The 100 Most Important Events in Christian History.* Grand Rapids, Mich.: Fleming H. Revell, Baker Book House, 1991.

Daniel-Rops, Henri. *L'eglise des ap otres et des martyrs.* Paris: A Fayard, 1949.

d'Aubigne, J. H. Merle. *The Reformation in England.* Edinburgh: Banner of Truth Trust, 1963.

Davies, W. D., and D. Daube. *The Background of the New Testament and Its Eschatology.* Cambridge: Cambridge University Press, 1956.

Davies, John G. *The Early Christian Church.* Grand Rapids, Mich.: Baker Book House, 1965.

Deanesly, Margaret. *The Lollard Bible and Other Medieval Biblical Versions.* Cambridge: Cambridge University Press, 1920.

Draper, Richard E. *Opening the Seven Seals.* Salt Lake City: Deseret Book, 1991.

Durant, Will. *The Reformation.* Vol. 6 of *The Story of Civilization.* New York: Simon and Schuster, 1957.

Durant, Will, and Ariel Durant. *The Age of Reason Begins.* Vol. 7 of *The Story of Civilization.* New York: Simon and Schuster, 1961.

Edwards, Jonathan. *The Great Awakening.* Edited by C. C. Goen. New Haven, Conn.: Yale University Press, 1972.

Erhman, Bart D. *The New Testament and Other Early Christian Writings.* New York: Oxford University Press, 1988.

———. *The Orthodox Corruption of Scripture: The Effect of Early Christological Controversies on the Text of the New Testament.* New York: Oxford University Press, 1993.

———. *Lost Christianities.* New York: Oxford University Press, 2003.

Eusebius Pamphilus. *Ecclesiastical History.* Grand Rapids, Mich.: Baker Book House, 1995.

Ferguson, Wallace K. *The Renaissance in Historical Thought.* Cambridge, Mass.: The Riverside Press, 1948.

Filson, Floyd V. *Which Books Belong in the Bible.* Philadelphia: Westminster Press, 1957.

Finney, Charles G. *Memoirs of Rev. Charles G. Finney.* New York: F. H. Revell, 1876.

Force, Peter, ed. *Tracts and Other Papers, Relating Principally to Origin, Settlement, and Progress of the Colonies in North America.* 4 vols. New York: Peter Smith, 1947.

Ford, Paul L., ed. *The Works of Thomas Jefferson.* 12 vols. New York: G. P. Putnam's Sons, 1904–05.

Fosdick, Harry Emerson. *Great Voices of the Reformation.* New York: Random House, 1952.

Foxe, John. *The New Foxe's Book of Martyrs.* Rewritten by Harold J. Chadwick. North Brunswick, N.J.: Bridge-Logos Publishers, 1997.

Froehlich, Karlfried. *Biblical Interpretation in the Early Church.* Philadelphia: Fortress Press, 1984.

Froude, James Anthony. *Life and Letters of Erasmus: Lectures Delivered at Oxford, 1893–1894.* New York: C. Scribner's Sons, 1894.

Garrison, W. E., and A. T. DeGroot. *The Disciples of Christ.* St. Louis, Mo.: Bethany Press, 1958.

Golb, Norman. *Who Wrote the Dead Sea Scrolls.* New York: Scribner, 1995.

Goodspeed, Edgar J. *The Making of the English New Testament.* Chicago: University of Chicago Press, 1925.

Gonzalez, Justo L. *The Story of Christianity.* Peabody, Mass.: Prince Press, 2004.

Gottstein, Alon Goshen. "The Body as Image of God in Rabbinic Literature." *Harvard Theological Review* 87 (1994).

Grant, Robert M. *Irenaeus of Lyons.* New York: Routledge, 1997.

———. *Second Century Christianity.* London: Society for Promoting Christian Knowledge, 1946.

Gregg, Thomas. *The Prophet of Palmyra.* New York, 1890.

Grimm, Carl Ludwig Wilibald. *Thayer's Greek-English Lexicon of the New Testament.* Translated by Joseph H. Thayer (Milford, Mich.: Mott Media, 1982.

Gross, John O. *The Beginnings of American Methodism.* New York: Abingdon Press, 1961.

Hale, John. *The Civilization of Europe in the Renaissance.* New York: Macmillan, 1993.

Hatch, Edwin. *The Influence of Greek Ideas and Usages upon the Christian Church.* London: Williams and Norgate, 1914.

Hening, William Waller, ed. *The Statutes at Large: Being a Collection of All the Laws of Virginia.* 13 vols. Richmond, Va., 1819–23.

Hirsch, E. D., Jr. *Cultural Literacy.* New York: Random House, Vintage Books, 1988.

Hoare, H.W. *The Evolution of the English Bible.* London: John Murray, 1902.

Howe, Eber D. *Mormonsim Unvailed; Or, a Faithful Account of That Singular Imposition and Delusion, from Its Rise to the Present Time.* Painesville, Ohio: The author, 1834.

Hughes, Philip. *The Reformation in England.* 2 vols. London, 1952.

Humbert, Royal, ed., *A Compend of Alexander Campbell's Theology.* St. Louis, Mo.: Bethany Press, 1961.

Huizinga, Johan. *Erasmus and the Age of Reformation.* New York: Dover Publications, 2001.

Hutson, James H. *Religion and the Founding of the American Republic.* Washington, D.C.:

Library of Congress, 1998.

Hippolytus. *The Apostolic Tradition.* Edited by Gregory Dix and Henry Chadwick. Ridgefield, Conn.: Morehouse Publishing, 1991.

Ignatius. *Testamentum Domini Nostri Jesu Christi.* Edited by Ephraem II Rahmani. Morguntiae: Kirchheim, 1899.

Josephus. *The Complete Works of Josephus.* Translated by William Whiston. Grand Rapids, Mich.: Kregel, 1981.

Jackson, Kent P., and Robert L. Millet, eds. *Studies in Scripture.* 8 vols. Deseret Book, 1984–88.

James, Edward W., ed. *The Lower Norfolk County Virginia Antiquary.* 4 vols. New York: Peter Smith, 1951.

Jeffers, Ann. *Magic and Divination in Ancient Palestine and Syria.* Leiden: E. J. Brill, 1996.

Jefferson, Thomas. *Writings.* New York: Library Classics of the United States, 1984.

Jessee, Dean C. *Personal Writings of Joseph Smith.* Salt Lake City: Deseret Book, 1984.

Justin Martyr. *Ancient Christian Writers.* Translated by Leslie William Barnard. Mahwah, N.J.: Paulist Press, 1997.

Kelly, J. N. D. *Early Christian Doctrines.* Rev. ed. New York: Harper Collins, 1978.

Kittel, Gerhard, Gerhard Friedrich, and Geoffrey W. Bromiley. *The Theological Dictionary of the New Testament.* New York: William B. Eerdmans, 1985.

The Lost Books of the Bible and the Forgotten Books of Eden. Cleveland: World Bible Publishers, 1963.

Lester, C. Edwards. *The Life and Voyages of Americus Vespucius.* New York: New Amsterdam Book Company, 1903.

Lynch, Joseph H. *The Medieval Church.* New York: Longman Group, 1998.

Marmorstein, Arthur. *The Old Rabbinic Doctrine of God.* 3 vols. New York: Ktav, 1968.

Martinez, Florentino Garcia, ed. *The Dead Sea Scrolls Translated: The Qumran Texts in English.* Translated by Wilfred G. E. Watson. 2d ed. Grand Rapids, Mich.: William B. Eerdmans, 1996.

McBirnie, William Stuart. *The Search for the Twelve Apostles.* Living Books ed. Wheaton, Ill.: Tyndale House Publishers, 1973.

McBrien, Richard P. *Lives of the Popes: The Pontiffs from St. Peter to John Paul II.* New York: Harper Collins, 2000.

MacCulloch, Diarmaid. *The Reformation.* New York: Penguin Group, 2004.

McDonald, Lee Martin, and James A. Sanders, eds. *The Canon Debate.* Peabody, Mass.: Hendrickson Publishers, 2002.

Metzger, Bruce M. *The Text of the New Testament.* New York: Oxford University Press, 1992.
———. *The Canon of the New Testament.* New York: Oxford University Press, 1997.

Migne, J. P. *Dictionaire des Apocryphes.* 2 vols. Paris: 1856.
———, ed. *Patrologia Graeca,* 161 vols. Paris: 1857.

Morison, Samuel Eliot. *Admiral of the Ocean Sea: A Life of Christopher Columbus.* 2 vols. Boston: Little, Brown, 1942.

Mosheim, Johann Lorenz. *An Ecclesiastical History, Ancient and Modern, from the Birth of Christ to the Beginning of the Eighteenth Century.* West Jordan, Utah: n.p., 1980.

Newman, Albert H. *A Manual of Church History.* 2 vols. Philadelphia: American Baptist Publication Society, 1933.

Nibley, Hugh. *Enoch the Prophet.* Salt Lake City: Deseret Book and Provo, Utah: Foundation for Ancient Research and Mormon Studies (FARMS), 1986.

―――. *Mormonism and Early Christianity—Collected Works of Hugh Nibley, Vol. 4.* Salt Lake City: Deseret Book and Provo, Utah: FARMS, 1987.

NIV Study Bible. Rev. ed. Grand Rapids, Mich.: Zondervan Press, 2002.

Norlie, O. M., ed. *The Translated Bible, 1534–1934, Commemorating the 400th Anniversary of the Translation of the Bible by Martin Luther.* Translated William Carney and C. M. Jacobs. Philadelphia: United Lutheran Publishing House, 1934.

Norman, Keith. "Ex Nihilo: The Development of the Doctrines of God and Creation in Early Christianity." *BYU Studies* 17, no. 3 (1977).

Oberman, Hieko A. *Luther.* New York: Doubleday Dell, 1992.

Pagels, Elaine. *The Gnostic Gospels.* New York: Random House, Vintage Books, 1989.

―――. *The Origin of Satan.* New York: Vintage Books, 1995.

―――. *Beyond Belief.* New York: Random House, 2003.

Padover, Saul K., ed. *Thomas Jefferson on Democracy.* New York: New American Library, 1958.

Parrinder, Geoffrey, ed. *World Religions: From Ancient History to the Present.* New York: Facts on File, 1983.

Parry, Donald W., ed., *Temples of the Ancient World: Ritual and Symbolism.* Salt Lake City: Deseret Book; Provo, Utah: Foundation for Ancient Research and Mormon Study (FARMS), 1994.

Parry, Donald W., Daniel C. Peterson, and John W. Welch, eds. *Echoes and Evidences of the Book of Mormon.* Provo, Utah: Foundation for Ancient Research and Mormon Studies (FARMS), 2002.

Phillips, J. B. *The Young Church in Action: A Translation of the Acts of the Apostles.* New York: Macmillan, 1955.

―――. *The New Testament in Modern English.* New York: Simon and Schuster, 1995.

Pike, E. Royston. *Encyclopedia of Religion and Religions.* New York: Meridian, 1958.

Pinnock, Clark H. *Most Moved Mover.* Grand Rapids, Mich.: Baker Book House, 2001.

Pope, Robert G. *The Half-Way Covenant: Church Membership in Puritan New England.* Princeton, N. J.: Princeton University Press, 1969.

Porter, Larry C. "A Study of the Origins of the Church of Jesus Christ of Latter-day Saints in the States of New York and Pennsylvania, 1816–1831." Ph.D. dissertation. Brigham Young University, 1971.

Rendina, Claudio. *The Popes: Histories and Secrets.* Translated by Paul D. McClusker. Santa Ana, Calif.: Seven Locks Press, 2002.

Reynolds, Noel B. *Early Christians in Disarray.* Provo: Brigham Young University Press, 2005.

Roberts, B. H. *A Comprehensive History of The Church of Jesus Christ of Latter-day Saints.* 6 vols. Salt Lake City: Deseret News Press, 1930.

Roberts, Alexander, and James Donaldson, eds. *The Ante-Nicene Fathers.* 10 vols. 1885.

Reprint, Peabody, Mass.: Hendrickson Publishers, 1999.

———. *The Post-Nicene Fathers.* Series 1. 14 vols. 1885. Reprint, Peabody, Mass.: Hendrickson Publishers, 1999.

———. *The Post Nicene Fathers,* Series 2. 14 vols. 1885. Reprint, Peabody, Mass.: Hendrickson Publishers, 1999.

Robinson, James M., ed. *The Nag Hammadi Library in English.* Leiden: E. J. Brill, 1988.

Robinson, Stephen E. *The Testament of Adam.* SBL Dissertation Series 52. Chico, Calif.: Scholars Press, 1982.

Rusch, William G., ed. and trans. *The Trinitarian Controversy.* Philadelphia: Fortress Press, 1980.

Rust, E. C. "Interpreting the Resurrection." In *Journal of Bible and Religion* 29 (1961).

Rudolph, Kurt. *Gnosis: The Nature and History of Gnosticism.* San Francisco: HarperSanFrancisco, 1987.

Schneemelcher, Wilhelm, ed. *New Testament Apocrypha.* 2 vols. Louisville, Ky.: Westminster/ John Knox Press, 1991.

Schuer, Emil. *A History of the Jewish People in the Time of Christ.* 6 vols. Peabody, Mass.: Hendrickson Publishers, 2003.

Schwartz, Jeffrey M., and Sharon Begley. *The Mind and the Brain: Neuroplasticity and the Power of Mental Force.* New York: Harper Collins, Regan Books, 2002).

Shanks, Hershel, ed. *Understanding the Dead Sea Scrolls.* New York: Random House, 1992.

Simpson, Cuthbert A. *The Book of Genesis: Introduction and Exegesis, in the Interpreter's Bible.* 12 vols. New York: Abingdon Press, 1952–57.

Smith, John. *Works, 1608–1631.* Edited by Edward Arber. 2 vols. Westminster, 1895.

Smith, Joseph. *History of The Church of Jesus Christ of Latter-day Saints.* Edited by B. H. Roberts. 2d ed. rev. 7 vols. Salt Lake City: The Church of Jesus Christ of Latter-day Saints, 1932–51.

———. "Joseph Smith–History." In *The Pearl of Great Price.* Salt Lake City: The Church of Jesus Christ of Latter-day Saints, 1981.

Smith, Lucy Mack. *The History of Joseph Smith by His Mother.* Edited by Scot Facer Proctor and Maurine Jensen Proctor. Salt Lake City: Bookcraft, 1996.

Smith, Lucy. *Biographical Sketches of Joseph Smith, the Prophet, and His Progenitors for Many Generations.* London and Liverpool: S. W. Richards, 1853. Reprint, New York: Arno Press and the New York Times, 1969.

Smith, George A. "Memoirs: Sketch of the Autobiography of George Albert Smith." *Deseret News,* August 11, 1858.

Smith, William. *Smith's Dictionary of the Bible.* Boston: Houghton, Mifflin, 1896.

Spinka, Matthew. *John Hus and the Council of Constance.* New York: Columbia University Press, 1965.

Spitz, Lewis W., ed. *The Protestant Reformation.* St. Louis, Mo.: Concordia Publishing House, 1997.

Stephen, Leslie, and Sidney Lee, ed. *The Dictionary of National Biography.* 22 vols. London, 1917.

Stifler, James Madison. *The Religion of Benjamin Franklin.* New York: D. Appleton, 1925.

Strickland, W. P., ed. *Autobiography of Rev. James B. Finley; Or, Pioneer Life in the West.* Cincinnati: Methodist Book Concern, 1854.

———. *Autobiography of Peter Cartwright.* New York: Carlton and Porter, 1857.

Strong, James. *The Strongest Strong's Exhaustive Concordance of the Bible.* Edited by John R. Kohlenberger III and James A. Swanson. Grand Rapids, Mich.: Zondervan, 2001.

Swanson, R. N. *Religion and Devotion in Europe.* Cambridge: Cambridge University Press, 1995.

Talmage, James E. *Jesus the Christ.* Salt Lake City: Deseret Book, 1976.

Tenny, Merrill C., and J. D. Douglas, eds. *Bible Dictionary.* 4 vols. Grand Rapids, Mich.: Zondervan Press, 1987.

Tierney, Brian, and Sidney Painter. *Western Europe in the Middle Ages, 300–1475.* New York: Alfred A. Knopf, 1970).

Tocqueville, Alexis de. *Democracy in America.* Translated by Henry Reeve. 2 vols. Cambridge, 1864.

Torchia, N., and O. P. Joseph. *Creatio ex Nihilo and the Theology of St. Augustine.* New York: Peter Lang, 1999.

Torrey, C. C. *The Apocryphal Literature.* New Haven, Conn.: Yale University Press, 1945.

Tucker, Pomeroy. *Origin, Rise, and Progress of Mormonism.* New York: D. Appleton, 1867.

Tvednes, John. "Baptism for the Dead in Early Christianity." In *The Temple in Time and Eternity.* Edited by Donald W. Parry and Stephen D. Ricks. Provo, Utah: Foundation for Ancient Research and Mormon Studies (FARMS), 1999.

———. "Glowing Stones in Ancient and Medieval Lore." In *The Book of Mormon and Other Hidden Books: Out of Darkness unto Light.* Provo, Utah: Foundation for Ancient Research and Mormon Studies (FARMS), 2000.

Twigg, Joseph W. *Origen.* New York: Routledge Press, 1998.

Van Dam, Cornelius. *The Urim and Thummim: A Means of Revelation in Ancient Israel.* Rev. ed. Winona Lake, Ind.: Eisenbrauns, 1997.

van Unnik, Willem C. *Newly Discovered Gnostic Writing.* Naperville, Ill: Allenson, 1960.

Weber, Alfred, and Ralph Barton Perry. *History of Philosophy.* New York: Charles Scribners Sons, 1925.

Webster, William. *The Matthew 16 Controversy.* Battle Ground, Wash.: Christian Resources, 1996.

Weisberger, Bernard A. *They Gathered at the River.* Boston: Little, Brown, 1958.

Weiss, Hans-Friedrich. *Untersuchungen zur Kosmologie des hellenistischen und palastinischen Judentums.* Berlin: Akadamie-Verlag, 1966.

Welch, John, ed. *Reexploring the Book of Mormon.* Salt Lake City: Deseret Book, 1992.

Wellnitz, Marcus von. "The Catholic Liturgy and the Mormon Temple." *BYU Studies* 21, no. 1 (1981).

Wesley, John. *Collected Works.* 7 vols. Grand Rapids, Mich.: Baker Book House, 2002.

———. *The Journal of the Rev. John Wesley.* 4 vols. London: J. M. Dent, n.d.

Westbrook, Perry D. *William Bradford.* Boston: Twayne Publishers, 1978.

Whitmer, David. *An Address to All Believers in Christ.* Richmond, Mo., 1887.

Williams, Colin W. *John Wesley's Theology Today.* New York: Abingdon Press, 1960.

Wilson, Marvin R. *Our Father Abraham: Jewish Roots of the Christian Faith.* Grand Rapids, Mich.: William B. Eerdmans, 1989.

Winthrop, John. *History of New England.* Edited by James Kendall Hosmer. 2 vols. New York: Barnes and Noble, 1946.

Wolfson, Harry Austryn. *Philo: Foundations of Religious Philosophy in Judaism, Christianity, and Islam.* 2 vols. Cambridge: Harvard University Press, 1948.

Woodbridge, John D., and David F. Wright. *The Birth of the Church.* Grand Rapids, Mich.: Baker Books, 2004.

INDEX

Aaron, 55, 59, 269, 355

Aaronic Priesthood: in place of Melchizedek Priesthood, 35, 51; no longer sufficient, 59, 61; washing and anointing as part of, 101; restoration of, to Joseph Smith and Oliver Cowdery, 322–24

Abel, 18, 19

Abraham: dispensation of, 18, 32–34; chosen by God, 313

Act of Supremacy, 255

Acts of Andrew, 116

Adam: God's covenant with, 17, 21, 39–40, 71; dispensation of, 18–19; transgression of, 22, 26–29, 222; learns of Christ's atonement and ministry, 23–24; death of, 97; eternal marriage of, 104; in premortal existence, 108; fallacies concerning, 222

Adams, John, 299

Address to the Greeks, 9

Adoptionism, 156–57

African Church, North, 151, 200. *See also* Cyprian of Carthage

Against All Heresies, 9

Against Celsus, 156

Against Heresies, 9, 125, 147–48

Against Praxeas, 157

Against the Heresy of One Noetus, 9

Age of Reason, 271, 298–304

Agency: to choose or reject God's will, 4, 18, 96, 296n42, 303; taught by God to prophets, 24–25; apocryphal writings on, 41n21, 213–15; as part of premortal existence, 87, 89; apostasy, result of, 115; as part of foreordination, 162–64; countered with military force, 199–202; applies to salvation, 260, 332–33; religious suppression of, 281, 287; debate over, fuels Great Awakenings, 291, 293–94, 298; Methodist belief in, 303. *See also* Two Ways, doctrine of

Agrippina, 114

Ahaz, 40n4, 77n2

Albigenses (Carthari), 201

Alden, John, 284

Alexander of Alexandria, 157

Alexander the coppersmith, 74

Alexander III (pope), 239

Alexander V (pope), 232

Alexander VI (pope), 221, 238, 243, 267

Alexandrian (Egypt) School of Theology, 9, 38, 149–50, 184

Alexis, Saint, 239

Allerton, Isaac, 284

Allerton, John, 284

Ambrose of Milan, 28, 103, 186, 218

America: as promised land, 275, 277, 294, 310; colonizing of, 281–86, 290, 306

American Revolution, 294, 307

Ammonius Saccas, 150

Amos, 71, 72

Anabaptist movement: beginning of, 249;

lems within, bring about the Reformation, 238; Martin Luther breaks from, 246–50; Church of England breaks from, 254–56; Counter-Reformation of, 256–58; in colonial America, 289; nineteenth century teachings of, 298. *See also* Universal Church

Catholic League, 257

Cavendish, Thomas, 278

Celibacy, 49, 222, 225–28

Celsus, 150

Cephas, 141n204

Chadwick, Henry: on Didache, 13n14; on choosing church leaders, 127; on Clement of Alexandria, 149; on doctrine of early church, 196n128, 196n130

Chalcedon: Fourth Ecumenical Council at, 165, 218, 222, 229, 297

Charles I (king), 280, 285, 289

Charles II (king), 289

Charles V (king), 254, 256

Charles (king), 220

Charles, R. H., 11–12

Charlesworth, James H., 7, 11, 13n5

Chauncy, Charles, 301

Cheetam, Nicolas: on Nero, 115; on Constantius, 153; on simony, 203; on papal authority, 218; on Rome as center of Church, 229, 230; on Pope Pius IV, 257

Child, Jacob T., 361

Children, innocence of, 26–29

Chillingworth, 179

Chilton, James, 284

Christian Association of Washington, 304

Christianity: in first and second centuries, 6–7, 190; in third and fourth centuries, 6, 144, 213

Christian-Jews, 75, 111

Christian Scientists, 315

Christological debates, 153–59, 164–66, 197–98

Chrysostom, John, 113, 186

Church of England: establishment of, 254–56; persecutes Puritans, 280–81; disestablishment of, in America, 294; in Colonial America, 290, 294, 297, 306–7

Church of Jesus Christ, 109–10, 208–9. *See also* Church, primitive

Church of Jesus Christ of Latter-day Saints, The: formal organization of, 325–26; Apostles of, are chosen, 326–28

Church of the Middle Ages. *See* Universal Church

Church, primitive: on preaching original sin, 27–28; in framework of kingdom of God, 46, 51–52; offices and organization of, 53–54, 208–9; keys preserved within, 56–59; properly ordained priesthood within, 59–63; revelation for, received by prophets, 63–66; apostate beliefs and traitors within, 75–77, 114; salvation doctrines of, 93–95, 261–65; salvation for dead taught to, 95–96, 332; baptism for the dead taught in, 96–97; eternal reward and punishment taught to, 97–99; washing and anointing as part of, 99–103; prayer circle of, 103–4; eternal marriage within, 104–6; Second Coming beliefs of, 106–7; persecution of, 110, 113–15, 152; problem solving of, 111–13; members of, 118–20; deterioration of, 120–26, 144–46, 152; creation beliefs of, 215–18

Circuit preachers, 308–9

Circumcision, 48, 111–13

City of God, The, 211–12

Clark, Richard, 284

Clement of Alexandria: as Polemecist, 9, 149–50; on Shepherd of Hermas, 11; knows of book of Enoch, 11; on innocence of children, 27; on ancient

ABOUT THE AUTHOR

In 1997, entrepreneur Scott R. Petersen and his former business partner sold their first company, freeing Scott to fulfill a lifelong dream: conduct an intense study of Christian history. For the next five years, often fourteen to sixteen hours a day, Scott explored early Christian roots, beginning with Adam and Eve and then turning to the patriarchs and prophets who followed. His research led him to a detailed examination of each significant religious period in the history of Judeo-Christian theology and development.

Though Scott is intimately conversant on the most critical historical-theological texts and exegetes, with all their academic trappings, he has written this volume from a layman's perspective, hoping to share in simple and understandable terms valuable insights into the early Christian church—its doctrine, development, and destiny.

Scott continues to research early Christian history, but he has returned to his entrepreneurial roots. Currently, he is the CEO of another successful business venture. He also serves on several business and philanthropic boards and is actively involved in developing collegiate entrepreneurs.

Scott and his wife, Marilyn, are the parents of five children.